PLAYS AND PLAYWRIGHTS

2005

edited and with an introduction by

Martin Denton

Published by The New York Theatre Experience, Inc.
P.O. Box 1606, Murray Hill Station, New York, NY 10156
www.nytheatre.com
email: info@newyorktheatreexperience.org

ISBN 09670234-6-7
ISSN 1546-1319

Plays and Playwrights 2005 is made possible, in part, with public funds from the New York State Council on the Arts, a state agency.

Plays and Playwrights 2005 is also made possible, in part, with public funds from the New York City Department of Cultural Affairs.

Plays and Playwrights 2005 is also made possible, in part, by support from the Peg Santvoord Foundation.

Book designed by Nita Congress
Cover designed by Steven Waxman

PERMISSIONS

TABLE OF CONTENTS

FOREWORD

The most corrosive aspect of any writer's life is isolation. We often say that we lose our good dramatists to TV, but I'm convinced we lose scads more to disillusionment. Many gifted young playwrights simply give up when they believe there's no audience out there for them. Martin Denton has provided in this anthology, first and foremost, a sense of belonging for tyro authors—an *appreciation*—and, in turn, maybe given them a wider audience. The worth of this gesture cannot be overprized: At a time when playwrights can't diminish their expectations any further, being published in an anthology like *Plays and Playwrights* can be tantamount to life support.

Paula Vogel once told me that playwriting is less a career than it is a hazing process. She's right. We endure readings and workshops where audience members actively rewrite our plays during "talkbacks." We watch chuckleheaded comedies being produced while challenging drama doesn't even blip on the radar screen. We get promises of productions from suddenly bold artistic directors who mysteriously lose our phone numbers only days later. Sure, it was ever thus, but it was easier to endure these slings and arrows years ago—even only ten years ago, in the Clintonian '90s, when the New American Play still seemed important, necessary...if underfunded. In this current cultural malaise (and if ever that word was apt, it is *now*) playwrights wonder whether what they do is worth anything at all, because plays first have to be collected, read, *passed around*...before they can cause audiences to gasp, or hiss, or cry, or argue, or applaud.

If you are reading these words, then, you are already one of the few who understand that what Martin and NYTE have been doing since 1999 is noble. It's a big word, but there it is: noble. This book is a noble act. Collections like these tell playwrights that they still matter. Now all you have to do, dear reader, is *appreciate* these damned good, important new plays. And then, maybe, pass 'em on. Enjoy!

Steven Drukman
December 2004

PREFACE

For the sixth year in a row, I feel proud and privileged to present some of the most exciting new plays from the off-off-Broadway theatre to readers all over the world. The goal of this enterprise is to call attention to worthy new work and to the remarkable artists who create it. Since we started the *Plays and Playwrights* series in 2000, we've published sixty-seven plays by seventy-eight playwrights. I hope this year's authors will join the ranks of some of our most successful alumni, such as Kirk Wood Bromley (who won the Berilla Kerr Award and the Best Playwright Award at the New York International Fringe Festival), C.J. Hopkins (whose *Horse Country* went on to the Edinburgh Fringe Festival and an international tour and has since been published as a stand-alone volume by Methuen), Robert Simonson (who wrote a popular book about theatre this year called *On Broadway, Men Still Wear Hats*), Julia Lee Barclay (who has become a teaching fellow at Northampton University in the U.K.), Trav S.D. (who is working on a history of vaudeville to be published this year), Jeff Hylton and Tim Werenko (who are collaborating on a new musical with composer Georgia Stitt), Joe Godfrey (whose play, *A Queer Carol*, was chosen by the New York Gay & Lesbian Center for its 2004 benefit in a reading that starred Malcolm Gets and Max Von Essen), Edward Musto (who was nominated for an Edgar Award this year), David Pumo (whose *Auntie Mayhem* was nominated for a GLAAD theatre award), Richard Day and Brian Sloan (whose plays *Straight-Jacket* and *WTC View* were both filmed this year), and Jon Schumacher (who won the FringeNYC Best Director Award).

On the back of our first volume, *Plays and Playwrights for the New Millennium*, I wrote, "These writers, and their work, are boldly pushing contemporary theatre into the 21st century, helping to shape and define the themes and structures of the next wave of American drama." Every day, the achievements of these talented individuals prove me right.

And so, here is *Plays and Playwrights 2005*, with a dozen more plays that I hope will thrill, enervate, challenge, and entertain those who read them; and twenty more playwrights, at least some of whose names will, I am sure, become very well-known. Every year, I firmly believe that this year's book is the best one yet, and 2005 is no exception. Enjoy it!

Creation of a volume such as this is only possible because of the enthusiastic and dedicated efforts of a great many people. I would like to acknowledge their invaluable contributions now. To begin, I want to thank the authors of these twelve plays for entrusting their work to me: Qui Nguyen and Robert Ross Parker, Neal Utterback, Josh Chambers, Kevin Augustine, Stephen Svoboda, Tom O'Brien, Margie Stokley, Alberto Bonilla, Katie Bull and Hillary Rollins, Hamilton Clancy, Brian Dykstra, Andrea Moon, Scott Baker, Stephen Bittrich, Joanna Cherensky, Allison Moore, Don Carter, Paul Knox, and Eric Michael Kochmer.

I also want to express sincere appreciation to the people who led me to these plays—the press agents, producers, actors, and other artists who steered me to these particular works during the past year: Elena K. Holy and Shelley Burch of the New York International Fringe Festival, Kimo DeSean and Erez Ziv of Horse Trade Theatre Group, Tim Cusack, Robin Reed, Joe LaRue, Tim Fannon, Jocelyn Szabo, Ethan Duff, Joe Trentacosta, Joshua Briggs, Jessica Davis-Irons, Adam Klasfeld, Ruth and Eric Nightengale of 78th Street Theatre Lab, Beck Lee, Geeta Citygirl, Sam Rudy, Bob Lasko, and Brian Snapp of Feed the Herd Theatre Company.

Dozens of talented people participated in the publicity events for *Plays and Playwrights 2004*. Thanks to all of them, especially: Tom Ridgely at the Peoples Improv Theater, Rob Reese, Jason Evans, Kelly McAllister, Stan Richardson, David Pumo, Brian Sloan, Michael Stock, John Jahnke, Allen Hubby of Drama Book Shop, Frank Cwiklik, Steven Gridley, Jon Schumacher, Christy Meyer, Judith Jarosz and David Fuller of Theater Ten Ten, Tim Errickson, Jeff Hylton and Tim Werenko, Tom X. Chao, Matt Freeman, and Carolyn Hughes at the Astor Place Barnes & Noble.

Nita Congress copy edits and designs our books every year—her contributions are limitless and her dedication is unrivaled. Steven Waxman once again has designed our book cover. Rochelle Denton, NYTE's Managing Director, does all the behind-the-scenes planning and operations stuff, and, without her, there would be no books ever. To all three go my heartfelt thanks.

Finally, I want to mention four people who are inordinately responsible—more than they know, I think—for this book. Mark Lonergan, Jonathan Bank, Sandra Nordgren, and Tim Cusack were the very first theatre artists to become friends and supporters of my work; each in his or her own way introduced me to the off-off-Broadway theatre community that has now become my professional home. Without their encouragement, there probably would not have been an nytheatre.com website and, consequently, a *Plays and Playwrights* anthology series. Their fellowship helped lead me to the most rewarding vocation I can imagine and literally changed my life. This volume is dedicated to them.

Martin Denton
New York City
December 2004

INTRODUCTION

Martin Denton

We live in an era of instant messaging, iPODs, satellite radio, cell phones that take pictures, and digital video technology that can make anyone a movie director. Yet live theatre remains compelling and irreplaceable: it morphs, transforms itself, adapts; steals and borrows from new media, and teaches itself new tricks. A "play" in 2005 is not necessarily a familiar-looking structure with acts and scenes and dialogue and stage directions; not even, always, a text in any traditional sense. Today's playwrights are breaking new ground and breaking down barriers, pushing American drama into the technological age and redefining it as a collaborative composition that is created jointly by artists of all kinds and the audience. *Plays and Playwrights 2005* is at once a demonstration of this new Alive Theatre and a celebration of it.

In this book, you will discover a play in which modern martial arts fight choreography is an integral element (*Vampire Cowboy Trilogy*) and a docudrama that is "interrupted" by a dozen original thirty-second videotaped "commercials" (*Walking to America*). One play (*Odysseus Died from AIDS*) takes place entirely inside the dying brain of a sick young man; another (*second.*) tells three simultaneous stories on a single set at the same time. The seven one-acts comprising *HONOR* force audiences to witness a man burning an American flag and the death of an American GI; the four-part play cycle *The 29 Questions Project* is intended to be staged environmentally in a nontraditional space and includes pre- and post-show components that make the piece as much a "happening" as a drama. *Elephant* defies traditional time and space linearities, challenging its auditors to piece together the story at its core; while *Platonov! Platonov! Platonov!* uses hip-hop sampling techniques and Internet Google searches to deconstruct and reconstruct the work of Anton Chekhov. One of the plays in this book (*Animal*) is written to be performed by humans and puppet creatures, while another (*Bull Spears*) contains almost no dialogue at all. Even the two most "conventional" works in this volume involve their audiences in other-than-conventional ways: in *Kalighat*, we are swept into the chaotic atmosphere of Mother Teresa's first home for the dying and destitute in a crowded Calcutta neighborhood, while *Maggie May*'s original director Jocelyn Szabo placed the audience in a balcony looking down on the action as they watched this romantic comedy.

The twelve new theatre works included in *Plays and Playwrights 2005* thus represent a dazzling array of styles, forms, subjects, and attitudes. Similarly, the twenty writers responsible for them are a diverse lot: men, women, immigrants from Honduras and Canada (plus a son of immigrants from Vietnam). About half of the authors in this book are in their twenties, but several are much older than that; one never wrote a play before the one we're publishing here, while others have produced dozens of works. The playwrights in this volume are also actors, directors, composers, producers, filmmakers, screenwriters for movies and TV, teachers, students, and bloggers; there's a jazz singer, a fight choreographer, and a painter among their number as well. This is the world of theatre in the twenty-first century, where artists sample disciplines and improvise and experiment to find meaningful ways to communicate compelling content to an audience that's ever more savvy and ever more tempted to resist the active and seemingly exotic challenge of attending and participating in live performance.

These playwrights are heroes; their voices are part of the burgeoning movement of new theatre that's changing the nature of American drama. *Plays and Playwrights 2005* is intended to provide a tantalizing introduction to them and the very exciting, very individual work that they're producing. I hope you will seek out further examples; I expect that some, if not all, will become "stars" of the next generation of theatre artists.

⇥ ⇤

This volume begins with *Vampire Cowboy Trilogy*, which was created by Qui Nguyen and Robert Ross Parker when they were both in the master's degree program at Ohio University's theatre department. Its New York debut was in March 2004 at a small black box space in the Theatre District, and it went on to become one of the most popular shows at the New York International Fringe Festival the following summer.

VC3, as its authors like to abbreviate it, is a live-action stage cartoon replete with chop-socky fight sequences; it's a paean to classic comic book/pulp forms as well as to more contemporary realizations like the recent TV series *Xena*. It is, above all else, a great deal of fun—it asks its actors to be proficient in a variety of esoteric skills, but it asks its audiences only to have a great time and immerse themselves in the pop culture iconography of their youths. One of the best things about *VC3* is that whatever your age, you're almost certain to find references that resonate: whether you grew up reading Action Comics in the Cold War era or learning inane canned dialogues in French class or wondering whether this or that superhero might be gay, there's something here for you.

Fight choreography is tightly integrated into the play and is extremely important to it—the Vampire Cowboy ethos is that theatre should first and foremost be a hoot, and Nguyen and Parker have built a script here that pretty much guarantees one to actors and audiences alike. A light touch, a broad sense of the absurd, and fearlessness in the face of ridiculousness are the other prerequisites for successfully mounting a work that asks its actors to speak wonderfully hokey, tongue-in-cheek dialogue like this:

> LIBERTY LADY: Oh no, Cap, he still has the detonator!
>
> CAPTAIN JUSTICE: Menace, don't do anything rash.
>
> HOODED MENACE: The only way the citizens of this crappy capitalistic continent will ever be safe is once I rule it and turn it into…a Communist nation.
>
> CAPTAIN JUSTICE: Menace, you know as well as I do, not even I, Captain Justice, have the power to give you that.
>
> HOODED MENACE: Well, how about just Alaska and Hawaii?
>
> CAPTAIN JUSTICE: Not even those.

An exciting aspect of *VC3*'s combat sequences is that they are pitched heavily toward females: women are involved in virtually every fight scene in the play (and in the original production, the three fight interludes that connect the parts of the trilogy were performed by women as well, even though they're written for cow*boys*).

Horse Trade Theatre Group, which operates three fine, intimate houses in the East Village, has been one of the most reliable incubators of new talent in the New York City theatre community. Neal Utterback, author of *second.*, joins Frank Cwiklik, Tom X. Chao, Joseph Langham, and Marc Morales on the list of Horse Trade resident company playwrights whose works have been included in this series.

second. premiered in April 2004 at Under St. Marks in a splendid production directed by Joe LaRue. On a single unchanging set, *second.* tells three stories at the same time; it's only near the end of the play that we start to recognize the inextricable links among the plotlines. All three involve a Mystery Man who—seemingly miraculously—saved the life of a woman who had been run down by a car on a busy Manhattan Street. Witnesses saw this young, anonymous stranger simply reach down and touch the battered body and apparently restore it to life. Now some people believe—or at least want to believe—that the Mystery Man is the second coming of Christ. In the middle of an apocalyptic snowstorm on Christmas Eve, a pair of kidnappers, a lesbian doctor and her TV journalist longtime companion, and a prostitute and her john all find their destinies wrapped up with that of the Mystery Man, who has disappeared.

So *second.* is a sort of mystery play, one with two layers: the characters on stage engage in one kind of search for answers, while the members of the audience have to decide for themselves what they will finally believe or disbelieve about Utterback's central enigmatic hero. Watching it is like being on a roller coaster, with the three narratives building up emotional steam until, in the play's stunning climax, they converge in a nearly cathartic collision.

I hasten to add that each of three stories that unfolds within *second.* is told with enormous humanity and humor—Utterback is a writer of genuine compassion, as we see from passages like this one:

> VICK: *(Looking out the window.)* It's this blizzard. It's like *The Shining.*
>
> LAUREN: I hope for hope.
>
> VICK: This storm is like this malignant, carnivorous animal.
>
> LAUREN: Hope, hope, hope.
>
> VICK: You can feel it trying to creep through the windows/ driving everyone to spontaneous insanity.
>
> LAUREN: /It's one of those words that make you giddier the more you say it. I hope for a greater capacity for hope.
>
> VICK: But what is that? That doesn't do anything. That doesn't *change* anything.
>
> LAUREN: If I can *hope* more, then I will *believe* in more, which will lead to *trusting* more, which is the foundation of love. *I* will become the change.

It's always thrilling to discover something entirely new in the theatre. That's what happened to me when I saw *Bull Spears* last August at Clemente Solo Velez Cultural Center on the Lower East Side: this artful blend of music, movies, combat and dance choreography, live action, songs, and Microsoft PowerPoint slides affected me powerfully and viscerally. No mere gimmicky multimedia playground, the compositional landscape of this remarkable work uses an array of technologies and media available to its creator, the prodigiously talented Josh Chambers, to take on the iconography of the mythological American West, at once deconstructing and re-imagining the meaning of its symbolism in provocative and thought-provoking ways.

Chambers is, with actor Timothy Fannon, the co-founder and co-artistic director of Fovea Floods, a smart and adventurous young theatre company whose work I have been following for several years. Fovea Floods is a group of Skidmore College graduates, all now in their late twenties, whose passion for creating meaningful, relevant theatre has led them to look beyond the boundaries of traditional theatre and to incorporate an impressively varied stock of visual and aural presentation styles in their work. *Bull Spears*, their first full-length original work in New York, reveals the fruits of their audacious (but not arrogant!) vision, and portends even more remarkable work to come.

Chambers describes *Bull Spears* as a "silent film for the stage." Its three acts, each one crafted in an arrestingly different style from the others, tell the story of a reluctant cowboy named One Pump who rescues the beautiful barmaid Milky Hills from the clutches of villainous bad guy Horse Dick. He rides off into the mountains with her, where they encounter a ghostly woman called The Bonnet and uncover the tragic secret of a long-ago inferno. In the final act, One Pump arrives in corrupt Knife City, which is run by a trio of decadent sadists who have enslaved the population. *Bull Spears*, which is named for the fictitious town in Nevada where it begins, reaches its climax with a duel between the salacious leader called The Roué and our embattled hero.

All of the foregoing plays out with barely a single spoken word of dialogue; Chambers communicates to the audience with dance, movement, titles, film sequences, and a gorgeous continuous synchronized original score (his own composition, which you cannot hear in the book, alas; there's information at the end of this introduction and in the section on *Bull Spears* about how you *can* hear it). Chambers's distinctive style as musician, director, and scenarist is matched by his skill as a poet. Here's the refrain of One Pump's number, sung just before his first fight with the wicked Horse Dick:

Take me out to Derelict Mount
Kick out all my teeth
My gun gets excited
My horses retreat
And I can't be a cowboy tonight
I can't be a cowboy tonight

Just as *Bull Spears* represents a departure for the *Plays & Playwrights* series in its lack of traditional dialogue, so too is *Animal* something different for this series. For, except for one young man named Jeff, all of the characters in this powerful work by Kevin Augustine are nonhuman creatures; most of them are meant to be played by puppets. In the original production, Augustine and three associates animated these figures, a dazzling collection of remarkably lifelike creatures created by Augustine himself.

I've been a fan of Kevin Augustine's puppet theatre since I first saw him at the 1998 New York International Fringe Festival in *Big Top Machine*. Augustine's artistry as an actor-puppeteer is without parallel in my experience; as he explains in his note to *Animal*, he doesn't even attempt anything like ventriloquism; he animates his puppets in a more fundamental way, imbuing them with something that feels like a soul. Anyone who's seen his work will come away with a new conception of what puppetry in the theatre can be. I hope that the presentation of *Animal* on this pages will encourage many readers to seek out Augustine's work and experience it for themselves.

Of course, *Animal* wouldn't be in this book if Augustine weren't also a terrific writer. He is—a resoundingly talented and smart one, with no little self-awareness, as demonstrated in this exchange between Eugene, the principal puppet character in the play, and a green felt frog hand puppet that is his only toy:

FROG: I don't feel anything either.

EUGENE: Oh, that's because you don't have any feelings. You don't even have a soul.

FROG: Who took away my soul? Where did it go??

EUGENE: Well, you never had one—you're empty. You are not even really alive.

FROG: I am too alive, see?

(EUGENE animates FROG in a sing-songy way, bouncing him around inside the cage.)

FROG: Because I can do this, and this, and doo-dee-doo-dee-doo!

> EUGENE: *(Halts FROG's demonstration, taking him in both hands.)* Oh, that's not really alive, just because you can walk and talk and eat and sleep and breathe. *(He brings him close to his face.)* No. You're... you're dead.

In a way, *Animal* is entirely about what it means to be alive; or rather, what it means to be not alive, even though you can walk and talk and eat and sleep and breathe. Its story is of a depressed young man (Jeff) who takes a class in shamanism in a futile effort to overcome his depression. In his shamanic vision, he encounters Eugene, a five-eighths-human genetically altered test subject, who becomes his animal guide. The history of their relationship and their quest for comfort and meaning fills out this deeply moving play about discovering our capacity for being human.

≈§ §≈

Elliot Hayes, the thirty-year-old protagonist of Stephen Svoboda's *Odysseus Died from AIDS*, has been sick for ten years. The play takes place in a hospital where Elliot, in the final stages of his disease, has come to die. But it really happens inside Elliot's very vivid imagination, where, in the confusion of his disintegrating mind, he has become the great legendary hero Odysseus, making his eventful journey home after the conquest of Troy. Other patients on the AIDS ward become the goddess Athena or the monster Cyclops; the doctor attending him is mighty Poseidon:

> ELLIOT: And Poseidon saw Odysseus.
>
> DOROTHY [THE NURSE]: Code Blue! Code Blue!
>
> *(The alarms start to ring, and a blue light flashes in waves across the stage. The screens begin to move in a chaotic pattern around the bed. DOCTOR and DOROTHY begin attaching tubes to the bed.)*
>
> DOCTOR: This patient is crashing.
>
> ELLIOT: Poseidon gathered the clouds, and, gripping his trident, he stirred the sea.
>
> DOROTHY: I have no pulse.
>
> ELLIOT: The winds blew hard from every direction, and lightning-charged Boreas rolled in a big wave. Poseidon gave him potassium through an intravenous line.

Svoboda creates a strange, wonderfully vivid language for Elliot, who is gradually losing the ability to string words together in normal sentences, just as he creates a poetic, surreal world for Elliot to occupy in this majestic play. But *Odysseus* is not just a study of a dying brilliant mind: Elliot is damaged, not only by AIDS, which he got during his one and only, very brief, love affair, with a handsome swimmer at college; but perhaps even more tragically by the fear of love that this sad and senseless affair engendered in him. Elliot retreated to his mother's house and his books since his diagnosis when he was twenty. Now, in the final days of his life, he has come to understand that he needs to reach out to other human beings before he can go to his final rest—before the Odysseus inside him can go "home."

Svoboda fleshes out this mighty idea in his beautifully wrought script, which despite the complexity of its structure and its relatively large number of characters (ten) is simplicity itself to produce, as he demonstrated in his staging of the play at the 2004 New York International Fringe Festival (where the production received, deservedly, an award for outstanding ensemble). Elliot and his "crew"—his fellow patients on the AIDS ward—are heroic and wise, and they deserve renewed life in productions of *Odysseus Died from AIDS* for years to come.

❧ ❦

A romantic comedy of the screwball variety, *Maggie May* by Tom O'Brien also looks at a young man going after a second chance at life and love, albeit in much lighter, happier circumstances. Set on an island in the Bahamas, *Maggie May* is the story of Donny, a sweet, shy young man who has always backed away from the things he wants, and consequently is single and alone. He hatches a scheme to bring an old girlfriend (the title character) on vacation in the Caribbean, where he hopes he will somehow manage to woo and win her. Of course, complications interfere with his plans, in the form of another old friend, Mark, who happens to work on the island as a tour boat fisherman for a wealthy ex-businessman. Mark moves in on Maggie May, naturally, leaving poor Donny out in the cold. Will he be able to assert himself and go after the woman of his dreams?

You'll have to read the play to find out. You'll have a grand time doing so, I think; *Maggie May* is a delightfully crafted comedy, reminiscent of the daffy romances of Preston Sturges or Kaufman and Hart, but with a warmth and contemporary zing that are uniquely O'Brien's. It's a very funny play; here's Donny in the very first scene, trying to call down to the hotel's front desk:

> DONNY: Hi, this is Donald O'Connor in room... Yes, like the dancer. We just checked in... No, I'm not the dancer. He's dead... I'm sorry too. I loved his work. Anyway, we just... Yes, that's right. They were very different, I think. He wasn't as well known as Fred Astaire but in terms of... My mom was a big fan of his, yes...

And it's also gently wise, as in these remarks by Mark's boss, self-described "pleasure-seeker" Charlie:

> CHARLIE: Most of the time we're too afraid to live. We say, "I couldn't do that. I couldn't be with her. I don't want to be happy." We talk ourselves out of living. But it's still out there. It's waiting for you. It's happening whether you choose it or not. It's just a question of whether you're gonna go for the ride or sit on the sidelines hopin' and dreamin'. All you have to do is step into it. *(Beat.)* A life unlived is not a life at all.

Maggie May scans as a fairly traditional four-character comedy, but its exotic setting and its modern sensibility render it anything but. Director Jocelyn Szabo recognized this is in her staging of the piece at the Belt Theatre. She placed all of the scenic elements on stage and moved her actors through them, while the audience—seated in the balcony—looked down on the action like proverbial flies on the wall. An inventive and elegant approach to the material!

Margie Stokley (pronounced with a hard "g," by the way), the young actor-turned-playwright whose first play *Elephant* is, told me that she was surprised and glad that I called her work a comedy in the short description on the back cover of this volume. Its subject, after all, is a serious one: a close-knit family working through their grief and sense of loss following the sudden accidental death of the oldest son, Jay. But *Elephant* is nevertheless and very appropriately a comedy, both in the classical sense and in the more familiar sense of being warmly human and humorous.

It is, too, a wise play, mature beyond the playwright's years in many ways (Stokley is in her twenties); but then, the experience of losing a sibling, which actually happened to her seven years ago, makes a person grow up pretty quickly.

Stokley has shaped her play without regard for the "rules"—it takes place in two different automobiles and an art studio, plus a variety of other locales within the memories of the various inhabitants of these spaces. All were seen on stage side by side in Jessica Irons-Davis's spare and very effective staging at the Ontological Theatre in August 2004. This is the sort of play that engages its audience's imagination wholeheartedly throughout; from our seats, we fill in all the blanks deliberately left by the author and the canny director and actors who interpret this work.

Stokley bends time as well in *Elephant*, moving backward and forward from scene to scene, gradually building a portrait of this singularly loving family and their journey away from tragedy. None of the survivors—mother, father, sister, girlfriend—knows exactly how to go about managing their recovery; each stakes out territory on his or her own to work through the sadness, yet their support for one another remains palpable—that's the key to *Elephant*'s potency. All the characters are fully three dimensional and written with love and authenticity. Look, for example, at this scene between Jay's mother Kathleen and his pregnant girlfriend Ellen:

> KATHLEEN: …You said "No"?
>
> ELLEN: I knew he was going to be my life. I didn't have to admit it. I wanted to wait, get pregnant, and then take him for granted. I'm a child. How can I be having one? I can't do this on my own.
>
> KATHLEEN: You have us. We are your family with or without a certificate.
>
> ELLEN: I don't want you. I want Jay.
>
> KATHLEEN: I don't want you. I want Jay.

Actors will, I think, clamor to bring these vivid individuals to life.

Theoretically, the cutoff date for *Plays and Playwrights 2005* was August 31, 2004. However, when I saw Alberto Bonilla's *Walking to America* at 78th Street Theatre Lab just two days later, I felt no compunction in bending the rules and including it in this collection. The message of this play is so important that I didn't want to wait a year to share it with readers. And so there are twelve plays in this collection, more than we've ever published in any previous volume.

Bonilla based his play on the true story of a homeless, orphaned Honduran boy who decides to escape the poverty and violence of his life on the streets by walking to the land of his dreams—the USA. "He didn't hitchhike, he didn't take a bus, he didn't hitch rides on rail cars," Bonilla tells us in his notes to the play, "he walked. From his street corner in Honduras, Oscar walked for twenty-four months across four countries and over twenty-four hundred miles to the American border." And once he got here, he was arrested as an illegal immigrant and sent back to Tegucigalpa.

This is a story that hasn't been told enough, about a boy (and thousands just like him) about whom most people never give a thought. This fact alone merits a place for *Walking to America* in this book, but Bonilla doesn't stop there. For interspersed in the straightforward docudrama that Bonilla crafted around this story are a series of pre-recorded satirical "commercials," advertisements for the life that the play's young protagonist thinks he desires that are also jibes at the values and attitudes of the residents of the world's most affluent—and, increasingly, most isolated and intolerant—nation.

Bonilla's attacks are not at all subtle. After scenes depicting the Honduran boy starving and begging for food, he shows us spots for "Shugga Crax Cereal" (which begins with a kid whining, "Breakfast just isn't fun anymore, Mom") and a TV show of the *Fear Factor* variety:

> VOICEOVER: On the next "Last Man Standing"…
>
> HOST: Whoever eats the most worms…
>
> VOICEOVER: The contestants face their greatest challenge yet, the Madagascar worm. But one of them will take it too far! A shocking secret is revealed.
>
> HOST: I'm sorry but you're not the last man standing.

Walking to America is a very necessary wakeup call, reminding us that our fellow humans all around the planet need our attention every day of the year, not just when catastrophe strikes.

❦ ❧

The events of September 11, 2001, remain indelibly etched in our consciousnesses, and continue to inspire playwrights and other artists to try to understand the causes and effects of the events of that momentous day. *The 29 Questions Project*, written by Katie Bull and Hillary Rollins, approaches this enormous task with probity and conscience. At the center of this four-play cycle is Rollins's *29 Questions*, in which two longtime friends, one of whom has just moved from New York to Los Angeles, play one of those time-wasting email games in which you answer random, trivial questions about yourself and then forward the responses to colleagues. The twist here is that the East Coast friend has just been killed in the World Trade Center attack. Rollins captures one of the fundamental lessons of that terrible day—that nothing in human relations is ever trivial.

Surrounding this powerful but brief two-person drama are three response pieces penned by Bull, each of which considers, in a different way, some dimension of the complex array of social and political issues that made 9/11 possible. Fearlessly and idealistically, Bull takes on topics such as prejudice, religious intolerance, the war in Iraq, and the culture of fear that has become all-pervasive during the past several years. There is material in *The 29 Questions Project* that may inflame or even alarm, but I strongly hope that it will serve, in its small way, as a beacon for understanding and compassion.

The project's production history reflects its origins in a unique way: it was staged at Yaffa's T Room, a restaurant located in downtown

Manhattan, just a few blocks from Ground Zero, one of many local businesses that provided support and comfort to the men and women who worked on the search-and-rescue teams in the aftermath of 9/11. In notes to the play, Bull provides guidance to readers about the ways she and her collaborators transformed their four scripts into a positive, healing event in the style of a '60s-era "happening," and encourages future presenters of this work (who will be, I hope, numerous) to do the same.

The beauty of Bull and Rollins's writing, finally, is that it transcends any particulars of time and place:

> ACTRESS 2: The glass is twice as big as it needs to be… isn't that great?! No, it's half full. I *know* that's the truth. I just can't always get there.
>
> ACTRESS 1: So she wasn't a saint. Just an angel. *(To ACTRESS 2.)* Is the glass half full or half empty? Half empty, of course. Everyone knows that, don't they?
>
> ACTRESS 2: Unless it's filled with good red wine! No, it's half full. I *know* that's the truth.
>
> ACTRESS 1: *(To audience.)* I just can't always get there.

TheDrillingCompaNY has been creating evenings of theatre around a single unifying theme for five years now. Under the leadership of producing artistic director Hamilton Clancy, the company commissions a number of playwrights to write short original pieces about a particular subject or idea, and then selects some of these to form a compelling program which is performed at their home base at 78th Street Theatre Lab. In 2004, the very politically minded Clancy selected "honor" as the topic, and the resultant collection, also called *HONOR*, proved to be as resonant as it is varied.

HONOR contains seven short plays, ten to thirty minutes long, that riff on the various meanings of the word in exciting ways. Joanna Cherensky (in *'Til Death Do Us Part*) and Andrea Moon (in *A Friday Night Trans Am Ride*) explore the personal connotations, the former looking comically at a wedding ceremony that goes awry, while the latter depicts the vagaries of pride among three very different couples who come together on visiting day at the prison where the men are all incarcerated. Scott Baker's *For the Benefit of Alfred Beamer* is a light-hearted piece about a fellow who throws himself a party because, apparently, no one else will. Taking a somewhat broader perspective are Allison Moore, who in the monologue *CUTRS!* presents us with a woman who fancies herself a patriot because she's following the president's bidding and going shopping; Stephen Bittrich, whose *Duty Honor Country* takes us to the frontlines of the war in Iraq; and Brian Dykstra, who in *Mick Just Shrugs* audaciously gives us a high school student trying to burn an American flag as part of an art project. Dykstra's play, which had a surprising and undeniably visceral impact in performance, includes a scathing and memorable monologue—later repeated in somewhat altered form in his solo show *Brian Dykstra: Cornered & Alone*—that constitutes a compendium of catastrophic choices future American generations may need to grapple with:

> MICK: In the name of fighting terrorism, civil rights are being denied citizens of this country every single day. And most of the time, we don't even know it.
>
> We eat shit.
>
> Intelligent people are marginalized by being branded "the Cultural Elite" while the government is reacting to polling that gets taken in Darwin's waiting room.
>
> I haven't even really gotten started on Iraq.
>
> Half the people can't afford a hospital stay.
>
> SUVs get shitty gas mileage. And nobody cares..

Don Carter's gorgeous, abstract, Wilderesque piece, *Coming to the Table*, offers a summing up of *HONOR*'s themes with touching simplicity. Singularly and as a group, these seven plays, representing the work of some very talented and prolific authors, are deserving of more attention.

꙳ ꙳

Paul Knox chooses as an epigram for his play *Kalighat* the famous words of John Donne: "No man is an island... any man's death diminishes me, because I am involved in mankind." This thought is the heart and soul of Knox's remarkable play, which is an epic drama—a good two-and-a-half hours in length—about a group of European and American volunteers working at Kalighat, the first of Mother Teresa's homes for the destitute and dying in Calcutta, India.

In his script and in his staging (Knox directed *Kalighat*'s premiere in January 2004 at the Baruch Performing Arts Center's Nagelberg Theatre), the playwright immediately immerses us in the chaotic, brutal world of the poorest of the poor—a world, we are loathe to admit, that is daily existence for most of the people on this planet. Knox doesn't flinch: he shows us the ugliness, the disease, the prejudice and intolerance and poverty; he depicts the valiant efforts of Mother Teresa's nuns and the hard-working volunteers, and the ultimate futility of all that they do in the face of too few resources and too many people who need their help.

In the midst of it all, he introduces us to Peter, a young gay New Yorker whose journey to Kalighat is at least part intended to appease some lingering guilt, and to a group of other conflicted Westerners, including a young Canadian woman trying to decide whether she should devote her life to the church and a young English man who is struggling with his sexuality. Theirs and others' stories are rendered with compassion and humor; they can't help but do some growing up in a setting this remote from their former lives:

> PATIENT 23: *(To PETER.)* Brother, *pani.*
>
> BRIGID: That's water. See if he has a cup under his bed.
>
> (PETER fills his cup just as two OTHERS ask for water.)
>
> PETER: Here you go. *Pani*, huh? I'll be speaking Bengali in no time.
>
> *(Several other PATIENTS ask for* pani.*)*
>
> PETER: Okay, okay, brother *pani*, brother *pani*!
>
> PATIENT 37: Brother, *jhol.*
>
> BRIGID: That's water too. He's a Hindu.
>
> PETER: Different water?
>
> BRIGID: Same water, different word.

Kalighat, like *Walking to America*, is important as a wakeup call: it makes us confront truths we'd rather not think about, but need to take to heart because, as Donne says, we are involved in mankind.

☙ ❧

For sheer gutsy, edgy, envelope-pushing vitality, few NYC theatre companies can match Feed the Herd, a collective of rowdy cross-discipline, barrier-breaking young artists led by Brian Snapp who, in just a few years, have built a small following among audience members in search of visceral adventure in the theatre. My first encounter with them was in 2001 with *Seven Seconds*, an eerie multimedia work about the last moments inside the brain of a murdered man. In January 2004, they presented the third annual Stampede Festival, a month-long showcase of new theatre and music by emerging artists that proved to be one of the highlights of my year.

One of the hits of Stampede 2004 was Eric Michael Kochmer's *Platonov! Platonov! Platonov!, or the case of a very Angry Duck*, which is the final play of this volume. If you know the work of Anton Chekhov, then you will probably have already guessed that this is based somehow on the great playwright's early comedy *Platonov*.

Kochmer says in his note to the play that he intended to create the stupidest possible version of Chekhov. And in a way, *Platonov! Platonov! Platonov!*—with its characters running around videotaping one another while they prattle endlessly about their myopic concerns, its eponymous protagonist protesting that he is in fact a duck, not to mention the very silly surname Yagorovnachorgaforgagorgaforgaborgachobia assigned to one of the characters or the preponderance of allusions to rubber chickens—is exactly that:

> ANNA: Enough, you fool! Go hunt some more rubber chickens and bring them to me... I'll take them... I'll take your rubber chickens as any good widow would... only promise me this: Don't touch Platonov! Platonov! Platonov! Do you hear me? Do you want to end up in prison? Or worse, in a monastery? There there don't cry. What are you, a child? Enough, I'm going home. Don't you dare touch him...
>
> OSIP: I will kill him, your ladyship. Once a rubber chicken, always a rubber chicken.

But look beneath the surface and you'll see there's much more going on here than mere sophomoric shenanigans. Kochmer, with his close collaborator/director Ross Peabody, deconstructs Chekhov using the devices of post-modernism and, more tellingly, hip-hop-style sampling; and then reconstructs him to both comment on and explicate the enduring appeal of his work. The play explodes with the antic giddiness and excess of its young creators, but their intelligence and their formidable talents are evident everywhere in it.

⤙ ⤚

What's presented on the pages that follow are only the texts of these twelve plays, along with some notes and background material that, it is hoped, will provide some context for them. These are the blueprints that will enable readers to make vivid, at least in their mind's eye, these remarkable new works; and that will entice actors, directors, designers, and producers to bring these pieces to life in new stagings in the months and years to come.

To help the process along, however, *Plays and Playwrights 2005* is providing readers with a companion website. Visit www.newyork theatreexperience.org/pp05web to access supplementary multimedia content that will augment and enhance your experiences with these plays. Here's some of what you'll find here:

- Discussion guides for each of the twelve plays
- Production photos
- Set/costume design sketches, staging diagrams, and other illustrative materials

- Audio clips from the score of *Bull Spears*

The *Plays and Playwrights 2005* website is intended to offer an active play-reading experience analogous to the participatory style of theatre-going that's inherent in all of the works included here. This book and the website are guides to a new movement that's transforming the nature of American drama—a theatre that challenges and engages its audiences using new paradigms of presentation and new forms that meld disciplines and emerging technologies.

This work makes my job, as theatre reviewer and editor of these volumes, as refreshing as it is rewarding. I can only hope your experience with these new plays will be as exciting, entertaining, and fun as mine. Enjoy!

VAMPIRE COWBOY TRILOGY

Qui Nguyen and Robert Ross Parker

QUI NGUYEN, co-founder and co-artistic director of Vampire Cowboys Theatre Company, is originally from southern Arkansas. His plays have been produced at Center Stage and Common Basis Theatre in New York City, the Wing & Groove Theatre of Chicago, Noho Studios of Los Angeles, the Midtown International Theatre Festival, and the New York International Fringe Festival. His scripts have also been part of staged reading series at the Goodman Theatre, Pan Asian Rep, New Dramatists, DueEast Theatre of Chicago, Ma-Yi Theater, and Queens Theatre in the Park. He has received the Ohio University Scott McPherson Playwriting Award, the New Dramatists' Gilman Award, and a commission from Ma-Yi Theater and the Jerome Foundation. His short film, *Take Back*, directed by John Eung Soo Kim and Henry Ko, was part of the 2004 Asian American International Film Festival. Qui holds an MFA in playwriting from the Ohio University School of Theatre. He is a recognized advanced actor/combatant with the Society of American Fight Directors.

ROBERT ROSS PARKER, co-founder and co-artistic director of Vampire Cowboys Theatre Company, is from Canada. Most recently, Robert played the title role in the Flying Machine's production of *Frankenstein* at Soho Rep. He was the associate director of *Silent Laughter* at the Lamb's Theatre and the assistant director for *Roulette* at Ensemble Studio Theatre, where he is currently a young director in residence. He has toured extensively with his solo works *Confession of an Undead Actor* and *Chasing Napoleon*, and his two-person commedia dell'arte–based creation, *Dunghill, Dunghill, Dunghill*. Robert has also worked extensively with created/adapted work, directing such productions as *A Midsummer Night's Dream Project*, *Pseudolus* (Toronto

Fringe Festival), and *The System of Dr. Tarr & Prof. Fether* (Centaur Theatre). Most recent directing credits include *F*cking Love* (Wej Productions) and *Stained Glass Ugly* by Qui Nguyen (Midtown International Theatre Festival). Robert holds an MFA in directing from Ohio University's School of Theatre.

Vampire Cowboy Trilogy was originally workshopped at Ohio University in May 2000. The cast included Dan Deming, Rich Davis, Courtney Decoskey, Melissa Paladino, Lauren Smith, Genevieve Cox, and Heidi Slone. The stage manager was Stephanie Dean; lighting design was by Isaac Castille.

Vampire Cowboy Trilogy was presented by Vampire Cowboys Theatre Company on March 5, 2004, at Common Basis Theatre, with the following cast and credits:

Jake Misco, Hooded Menace, Inachus .... Dan Deming
Molly, Gabbi .... Caitlin Dick
Vampire Cowboy, Ninja, Zombie Cheerleader,
    M. Linstructeur .... Margie Freeswick
Vampire Cowboy, Ninja, Zombie Cheerleader,
    Justo the Justice Dog .... Megan Ketch
Kooky Flight Attendant, Liberty Lady, Tina .... Melissa Paladino
Stranger, The Spectator, Missy .... Andrea Marie Smith
Janitor Jim, Captain Justice, Brad .... Temar Underwood

Directed by: Robert Ross Parker and Qui Nguyen
Assistant Directors: S. Caden Hethorn and Nathan Lemoine
Scene/Lighting Designer: Nick Francone
Costume Designer: Christopher M. Domanski
Sound Designer: Matthew Given
Fight Choreographer: Qui Nguyen
Fight Captain/Composer: Dan Deming
Dance Choreographer: Sarah Maxfield
Dance Captain: Margie Freeswick
Stage Manager: Jennifer B. Havey
Production Manager: Abby Marcus
Fundraising Coordinator: Jaclyn Gleisinger
Publicity/Press Rep: Adam Klasfeld, Klasfeld Publicity

Vampire Cowboy Trilogy was subsequently produced at the 2004 New York International Fringe Festival (Elena K. Holy, Producing Artistic Director), with the same cast and credits except that Emily Edwards replaced Megan Ketch.

The music for the songs contained in *Vampire Cowboy Trilogy* may be obtained by contacting Qui Nguyen at info@vampirecowboys.com.

PRODUCTION NOTE

We first wrote and produced *Vampire Cowboy Trilogy* while graduate students at Ohio University. We had a quarter without a major project, we'd enjoyed working together on a one-act earlier in the year, and we had a common interest in comic books. Most of all, however, we created *VC3* out of frustration. Frustration with dusty theatre productions that we felt didn't speak to us or our fellow students, and frustration over poorly written formulaic Hollywood pap that magically could move us in ways that theatre couldn't. We saw *VC3* as a scornful reaction against, and a loving celebration of, both vacuous film and deadly theatre. So we formulated a script, assembled a team, and, with little more than bottomless enthusiasm, put it up. It was a modest hit amongst the students. The majority of the faculty (with some notable exceptions) were perplexed, to say the least, and it was carefully explained to us that this was definitely not a direction that we should be exploring. This was not the "theatre" that they were teaching us. Our reaction is what you would expect: elation. Clearly, we felt we were on to something.

Four years later, we found ourselves in New York with a burning desire to bring the *Vampire Cowboy* experience to a larger audience, coupled with a burning desire to be doing something more than just waiting tables. So we founded a theatre company. Our first major project: Bring *VC3* to NYC. In the end, the reaction was what we hoped: Huge praise from those who got it and huge question marks from those who didn't. To us, it was an undeniable success.

On the surface, *VC3* is a goofy, weird, and sometimes incidentally insightful comedy. Beneath that colorful top layer, though, is the spirit of two artists who just want to do theatre their way. As a show, it has given us an infinite amount of laughs and smiles, as well as a few bruises. We hope that you enjoy reading *VC3* as much as we enjoyed creating it. It is our fondest wish that *VC3* will receive countless productions at universities and schools around the country where it will, once again, be deemed "inappropriate material for an academic setting." Nothing would make us prouder.

Warmly,

Qui Nguyen & Robert Ross Parker
(The Vampire Cowboys)

WARNINGS

A FLIGHT ATTENDANT enters and helps us to understand the following. THE CAPTAIN speaks over a loud speaker.

THE CAPTAIN: Good evening, ladies and gentlemen, and welcome aboard! I'd like to take a few moments prior to take-off to review some of the safety features of this production. Please ensure that your seatbacks are in their full upright position, and that all your personal belongings are neatly stowed underneath your seat. We ask that you refrain from using the over-head bin, as it does not exist. Also, we remind you to turn off any unapproved electronic devices that may beep, tweet, or chirp. Our playing time today will be approximately ninety minutes with no intermission, so we should be touching down at approximately 21:30 local time. 9:30 local time.

WARNING! Should we need to evacuate this theatre for any reason, please exit the theatre through the door you came in by. Exits backstage do not exist. In the event of an emergency over water, your seat will sink like a rock.

WARNING! A cigarette will be smoked.

WARNING! A second cigarette will be smoked.

WARNING! Adult language will be used. Including fuck, fucked, fucking, fucker, fuck off, shit, shitty, shitless, and shit-tastic.

WARNING! The following warning is in Croatian.

(Spoken in Croatian.) WARNING! Croatian will be spoken during the show. If you do not understand Croatian, you will not understand the Croatian section. The Croatian section will be exclusively in Croatian, and will not offer translation or explanation for non-Croatian speakers. If you wish to fully experience the humor of this production, we strongly urge you to learn Croatian immediately.

(In English.) WARNING! That was the end of the Croatian section.

WARNING! This is the end of the warnings.

Thank you for choosing *Vampire Cowboy Trilogy.*

THEME SONG

A VOICE: At the close of the day, when the sun goes down
 And the hours of the evening grow later
 They ride through your lawn with their six-shooters drawn
 On their way to the local theater.
 Your blood runs cold when they enter the room
 And you scream as their fangs draw nearer
 But they're at their greatest power when you're in the shower
 For you can't see them in the mirror.
 And they sing oh-o-o-yah!
 And they sing oh-o-o-yah!

VAMPIRE COWBOY SEQUENCE #1

Two COWBOYS face each other in a classic showdown. Slowly and dangerously, they advance toward one another. They stare each other down, ready to draw their guns at any moment. Suddenly, one of the COWBOYS bares his fangs and sinks them deep into the neck of the other.

NON-VAMPIRE COWBOY: Ohgodno!

(Blackout.)

#1
JAKE MISCO, OUTER BOROUGH PARANORMAL INVESTIGATOR, IN THE CASE OF THE UNRELENTING UNDEAD SPOUSE

At rise: The stage is dark. A cigarette is slowly lit onstage as lights come up on JAKE. MOLLY works in the background.

JAKE: It's another one of those nights in the dark city. The kind of night that brings sober men to the bottle and virtuous women to bars. Calling tonight a bad night would be an understatement. Trouble is in the air as it usually is in the hustle and bustle of Williamsburg, Brooklyn... Nowhere else will you find a more wretched hive of scum and villainy.

MOLLY: Jake, will you please stop talking to yourself?

JAKE: This dame here is Molly. She's been working for me for a year now. Cute, feisty, and possesses an acute ear to dimensions not our own. She's a mind reader. A psychic. And...my French secretary. Oui, oui, oui.

MOLLY: I'm not French.

JAKE: See? She heard my thoughts.

MOLLY: Jake, I'm trying to work.

JAKE: Molly, it's late. Why don't you take off those spectacles of yours, let your hair down, and let's have a little rendezvous?

MOLLY: I'm working.

JAKE: Molly can be quite a sexy little broad when she wants to. Sadly, she spends most of her time with her nose in books.

MOLLY: Well, if I didn't, you'd be in jail by now.

JAKE: A modern woman through and through. You're cute, Molly, why don't you just go find yourself some independently wealthy detective and live it up some?

MOLLY: Uh... no.

JAKE: Your loss, ma petite croissant. My name is Jake. Jake Misco, Outer Borough Paranormal Detective. I run a small private agency for the investigation and the removal of those pesky insects we call ghosts. And this is just another one of my nights.

(JANITOR JIM enters.)

JANITOR JIM: Oh damn it, I'm late. I hate this job.

JAKE: The stinky guy with the mop is the janitor to this old building. He's poorer than dirt, but dependable. Lives down in Jersey City, a small backwoods community of drunks, cheap whores, and lumberjacks. His name is Jim Smiley. Kind of an ironic name since he doesn't smile too often. He's a worthless little gnat, but I find ways to stand him.

MOLLY: Jake, that's not very nice.

JAKE: What's the rush, Jim? If I were you, I wouldn't be too excited about going back to the slums.

JANITOR JIM: Well, I have plans with a hot broad tonight if you need to know.

JAKE: No need to get angry, Jim. I'm just making friendly conversation.

JANITOR JIM: I'm not angry, Jake. Just anxious.

JAKE: Fine. For such a bum, he sure has a way with the ladies. Personally, I can't see how they can stand the odor. Then again, I'm sure this hot dame he's talking about is just some street hooker.

MOLLY: Jake, he can hear you. Stop it.

JAKE: No, he can't, ma cherie. You're just reading my mind again.

MOLLY: I'm not a mind reader, Jake.

JANITOR JIM: I'll see you guys later.

MOLLY: Bye, Jim. Sorry he's such a idiot.

JANITOR JIM: I'm used to it by now, Miss Molly. One day, Jake will get his. Oh yes, Jake will get his. *(Exits.)*

MOLLY: I think what you do to him is very inappropriate.

JAKE: As I planned, Molly and I finally get to be alone.

MOLLY: Will you please shut up and listen to me?

JAKE: I got you a gift. It's for our first year anniversary.

(JAKE gives her a stacking set of pots and pans.)

MOLLY: Jake, I will not sleep with you.

JAKE: I just want you to feel at home. Here, just take them.

(JAKE gives MOLLY a pan.)

JAKE: Now you can make French toast.

MOLLY: Gee, thanks.

JAKE: Bon voyage! That means "you're welcome."

MOLLY: Lovely…

JAKE: What Molly doesn't know is that I have many secret affections for her.

MOLLY: Yes, I do know.

JAKE: No, she doesn't. I long to have her approval. Waiting for the day she tells me that I did a great job. I long to hear those words from her. Actually, I guess I just long for her. It's tough being a loner.

MOLLY: Look, Jake, I know you like me, but that doesn't excuse the way you treat poor Jim.

(SOMEONE knocks.)

JAKE: And then, there's a knock at my door.

MOLLY: Will you answer that?

JAKE: "Who could be coming to my office at this hour?," I ask myself as I hear the tap tap tapping at my office door. It could be anyone. A drunk looking for a bit of change, a soliciting pro, maybe even an enemy looking to exact his revenge?

(Another knock.)

MOLLY: Jake!

JAKE: Maybe I'm just hearing things. This very building has much paranormal activity. It could be the Bedford spirits rising from their graves. This hour is quite late. It's one of those nights you don't forget very easily. There's a constant chill about it.

(Another knock.)

MOLLY: Jake!

JAKE: What is it, Molly?

MOLLY: Answer the friggin' door.

JAKE: I don't have a good feeling about this. Maybe I should just ignore it until whomever it is leaves. I sense the individual on the other side is up to no good.

(Another knock.)

MOLLY: Right. Fine. I'll do it.

JAKE: Be careful, Molly. It could be anyone.

MOLLY: I'll be fine. *(Answers the door.)* May I help you?

STRANGER: Hello, I'm looking for an outer borough paranormal investigator.

MOLLY: Well, you've come to the right place.

JAKE: A mysterious, yet lovely stranger is at my door looking for my services.

STRANGER: Is he in?

MOLLY: Unfortunately, yes.

JAKE: This intriguing young lady is quite…intriguing. I can tell she can sense my strong sexual prowess even from this distance.

MOLLY: He's the idiot mumbling to himself.

STRANGER: Are you Jake Misco?

JAKE: That's what's on my business card.

STRANGER: You're cute. I didn't expect you to be so cute.

JAKE: You ain't seen nothing yet. I have a picture of Humphrey Bogart tattooed across my chest.

STRANGER: Life-sized?

JAKE: Oh, yeah.

STRANGER: I'm in need of your help.

JAKE: Everyone is in the need of some sort of help, lady. The weak, the lost, the disease-ridden. There're all sorts of folks who take care of that. How do you know I'm the right guy you should be asking for?

STRANGER: Someone told me that you'd be the right dick for me. I have a job I think you'd be very interested in.

JAKE: Really?

STRANGER: An apparition seems to be haunting my bedroom.

JAKE: An invisible man, sleeping in your bed? Who ya gonna call?

STRANGER: Well, I called you.

JAKE: Right.

STRANGER: I need you to go over there tonight and show it who's boss.

JAKE: A ghost, huh?

STRANGER: Yes, of my deceased husband. Would you like to come over and search my premises?

JAKE: Hmmm.

STRANGER: What does "hmmm" mean?

JAKE: Hmmm means hmmm, sweetcakes.

STRANGER: So, are you interested?

JAKE: Let me think this over. I see this woman is in trouble. She's desperate. Probably fearing for her life. I must help her. This is my job. My calling. Besides, solving this case may finally win Molly. And if not Molly, maybe a night with this beautiful stranger wouldn't be so bad either.

STRANGER: Well?

JAKE: Alright, lady, spill the beans! What's your name? Who's your husband? Why do you think he's come back from the dead to haunt you?

STRANGER: Well, I'm not sure where to begin.

JAKE: At the beginning, toots… if that's really your name.

STRANGER: That's the problem… this may be hard to believe, but I don't remember.

JAKE: What?

STRANGER: I've lost all recollection of it. My husband must have erased it from my memory.

JAKE: A woman being haunted and suffering from amnesia too.

STRANGER: I'm desperate, Jake. It's horrible not feeling safe in your own home. Especially when you're all alone dressed in your favorite see-through negligees.

JAKE: Maybe I can do something.

STRANGER: I'll do anything. Anything to get rid of him.

JAKE: So, you have no idea what your name possibly could be?

STRANGER: No. This ghost is ruining my life. You must help me.

MOLLY: Jake?

JAKE: Yes, Molly?

MOLLY: Could I have a word in private?

JAKE: What is it?

MOLLY: I don't like this woman. She seems a bit sketchy. And kinda…slutty.

JAKE: Nonsense, Molly, the broad is just scared.

MOLLY: Yeah, she seems right scared. The way she keeps puckering her lips and grinding her ass on that chair is a sure sign of horrid fear. Look at the way she's dressed. She's not troubled, Jake. She's horny.

JAKE: Molly, is this jealousy I'm sensing from you?

MOLLY: Jealousy? Is that what you think this is? I'm just looking out for you.

JAKE: I'm sorry, ma petite freedom fry, if this line of work bothers you, but you knew who I was before you got into this.

MOLLY: Into what?

JAKE: Never mind.

MOLLY: I don't think she's telling the truth.

JAKE: Molly, don't worry about this. I may not be a psychic, but I do know a thing or two about people.

STRANGER: So, have you come to a decision?

JAKE: Yeah, sweetcakes, I'll do it.

MOLLY: Jake.

JAKE: But it's going to cost you a chunk of change.

STRANGER: That's not a problem. I'm filthy rich. Can you really exorcise my poltergeist?

JAKE: Of course I can. Now, what was your husband's name?

STRANGER: I don't know. I have amnesia.

JAKE: Crap, I forgot. I hope it's not catching. Well, ma'am, this does complicate matters. I can't exorcise a spirit without knowing its name.

STRANGER: I'm sure we have something back at my place. Maybe by the bed somewhere.

JAKE: I have an idea. My psychic French secretary will just scan your mind and reveal all the information we are searching for. Molly?

MOLLY: I'm not a psychic, Jake.

JAKE: Molly, I just need a name. Can you picture a name in your mind?

MOLLY: How about Asshole?

JAKE: Think harder and deeper. You are a mind reader. Read her mind.

MOLLY: No, Jake. I don't know it. I won't know it. And there's nothing I could possibly do to figure it out. I'm not a psychic.

JAKE: You've lost your confidence, Molly. Just believe and it will happen.

MOLLY: No, Jake. I'll file papers, bail you out of jail when needed, and finish up your insurance forms. But I'm not going to pretend to know this lady's late husband's name.

STRANGER: What's wrong?

JAKE: Sit down.

STRANGER: Why?

JAKE: I'm just going to have to do this myself. I'm not the psychic my French secretary is, but I will figure out your husband's name.

STRANGER: You can do that?

JAKE: I will have to make him materialize from the netherworld.

STRANGER: Do you think it would help if we were closer to the actual haunting site? Like perhaps in my hot tub?

JAKE: Apparently, this ghost has attached itself to you. It doesn't matter how close or far we are to your home. It's freeing him from your psyche that we need to worry about.

(STRANGER sits down in a chair.)

JAKE: Close your eyes. I will make your husband appear in front of you.

STRANGER: You will?

JAKE: Yes. Now just relax. Close your eyes and picture his face.

This is quite a long shot. But when you're in the field I'm in, sometimes long shots is all you got. She doesn't even remember her name. But if this ghost is haunting her as badly as she claims, his face will be imprinted in her memory.

Are you picturing his face?

STRANGER: Sure?

JAKE: That's very good. Keep breathing. Sustain his face in your mind.

As I figured. The trauma of this situation has, at least, cemented one memory in her mind. You know, from here, I can see down her shirt. Nice.

STRANGER: Thank you.

JAKE: Damn mind readers.

Now just keep breathing. Call out to him.

Then I realize, how can she call out to him when she doesn't even know his name?

STRANGER: Hey you, come here.

JAKE: That'll work, I guess.

STRANGER: Come here.

JAKE: I sense him.

STRANGER: You do?

JAKE: He's here.

STRANGER: Where?

JAKE: Open your eyes.

STRANGER: Where is he?

JAKE: He's right over there.

STRANGER: What?

JAKE: Hi there? I would like to talk to you, Mister Apparition. I need you to leave this world and go into the light. Go into the light. Go-go! Go into the light!

(STRANGER throws herself onto JAKE and begins to kiss him.)

JAKE: What are you doing?

STRANGER: You're my hero, Jake. Have I ever told you? I have a thing for dicks.

JAKE: Hello.

(The TWO begin sucking face and rolling around on the floor.)

MOLLY: Could you not do that on the floor? There's a perfectly good motel down the street.

STRANGER: I think I love you, Jake. I've never felt such intense passion so quickly for anyone before.

JAKE: I have feelings for you too, Mysterious Stranger Lady.

Or at least that's what I tell her as I gaze into her beautiful eyes knowing that—

STRANGER: Shut up.

JAKE: Okay.

MOLLY: Really. I don't want to see this. Jake!

(JAKE stops suddenly.)

JAKE: The ghost! We can't leave him unattended. He hasn't gone into the light yet. Molly. He's heading for Molly.

MOLLY: No, he's not.

STRANGER: Jake, no, come here.

JAKE: Oh no, he's probably already got her.

MOLLY: Nobody has me.

JAKE: Stop, Ghost. I command thee by the authority of the King's County Paranormal Detectives' Association—

MOLLY: There's no need to scream.

JAKE: Molly? Is that really you, Molly?

MOLLY: Yes, it is.

JAKE: How can I know for sure?

MOLLY: Jake, it's me. I'm tired of watching you play fucking *Ghostbusters*. I'm going home.

JAKE: The real Molly can read my mind. What am I thinking right now? Well? Answer me.

MOLLY: I don't know.

JAKE: See!

MOLLY: That doesn't prove a thing. I never could read your mind, Jake.

JAKE: No, you can't, Mister Ghost. But my Molly can.

MOLLY: I'm going home, Jake, and giving you and your new girlfriend some private time in the office.

JAKE: No, Ghost, you're not going anywhere. You think I would be foolish enough to just let you walk out? Never! You will leave this vessel and go into the light.

MOLLY: Get out of my way.

JAKE: Come here, Ghosty!

MOLLY: Look, Jake, the reason I can't tell you what you're thinking is because you're not talking to yourself. Wait, you aren't talking to yourself—Jake, why are you so quiet?

JAKE: I'm not quiet. I'm angry because you're possessed.

MOLLY: Really?

JAKE: Yes, Really. No, no, Molly, he has possessed me.

MOLLY: What was that?

JAKE: Oh, nothing, I'm just talking to myself, I guess. He's lying, Molly, don't listen to him. Shut up! You have no say in this matter. This is my body! I command thee to leave! Oh, shut up, already.

MOLLY: So I'm right! You are possessed.

JAKE: Fine, you got me. I'm possessed. No, Molly, stop him. I'm running this show NOW!!! So, if you ladies don't mind, I'll be leaving.

STRANGER: Wait.

JAKE: And what do you want?

STRANGER: Take me home with you.

JAKE: Sure. Come on, sweetcakes.

MOLLY: You're not going anywhere.

JAKE: And how you going to stop me?

MOLLY: French toast.

(MOLLY takes a swing at JAKE's head with a frying pan. He blocks it, and they get into a struggle. JAKE has MOLLY in a head-lock.)

JAKE: So you want to take a swing at me, huh? How does this feel?

MOLLY: Stop it, Jake!

JAKE: There is no Jake here.

MOLLY: Hey, stranger lady, help!

(STRANGER shrugs.)

MOLLY: You're bloody worthless.

(MOLLY gets out of the headlock, and the TWO begin fighting again. An elaborate pot-and-pan fight erupts. Finally, STRANGER pulls out a very small pan from her purse and points it at JAKE and MOLLY.)

STRANGER: Everybody freeze!

(JAKE and MOLLY stop fighting. HUS-BAND enters.)

HUSBAND: You were taking too long.

STRANGER: I was trying my best.

JAKE: It's the ghost.

MOLLY: He was the guy that was in you?

JAKE: I guess.

HUSBAND: Now, we're just going to have to do this here. Go get his wallet.

MOLLY: Jake, that doesn't really sound like dread and fear she's emoting at the sight of him.

JAKE: Leave her alone.

HUSBAND: What are you going to do to stop me?

JAKE: I command thee by the power of—

HUSBAND: How about the power of a .44? *(Pulls out a gun.)*

MOLLY: That's a very good rebuttal.

HUSBAND: Get the wallet.

STRANGER: Alright. You heard him. Hand it over.

JAKE: You don't have to do this. He's just a ghost. He can't hurt you.

MOLLY: Um, Jake, I don't think he's a ghost.

STRANGER: I know I don't have to. Oh come on, Jake. You really can't be as dumb as you look.

JAKE: Why do you want my wallet? I have no money.

STRANGER: It has to look like a robbery, sweetcakes.

MOLLY: What do you mean, it has to look like a robbery?

HUSBAND: I'm sorry you had to get involved, but it was the detective that I wanted.

MOLLY: Jake, these guys have come here with planned murder in mind.

STRANGER: That's my favorite kind. And as long as the cops think crooks did it, we get to be long gone before they suspect it was anyone Jake actually knew.

JAKE: Look, you'll never get away with this.

HUSBAND: Either way, you're still dead.

MOLLY: Please, leave us alone.

HUSBAND: This is taking too long. Just get out of the way, I'll shoot him, and we'll just get the wallet from his dead carcass.

JAKE: You said you loved me.

STRANGER: I lied.

JAKE: But the way you kissed me.

STRANGER: It was just an act.

JAKE: Come on, sugah, I know what a lady means when she kisses. You meant it.

MOLLY: Jake, maybe this isn't the best time to discuss the downfall of your short-lived fake romance.

HUSBAND: Hurry up.

STRANGER: You have no idea what you're talking about.

JAKE: Come on, people don't kiss that way unless they mean it.

HUSBAND: How did you kiss him?

JAKE: French. Isn't that right, Molly? French.

(JAKE give a big wink at MOLLY. MOLLY, realizing what JAKE is hinting, picks up the frying pan.)

MOLLY: Oh, yeah. Your girlfriend really did seem pretty committed. I think she likes him quite a bit.

JAKE: And the way you were petting me.

HUSBAND: What petting?

STRANGER: My hands were nowhere near his—

JAKE: It's okay. It's not like he can kill me twice. Just tell him.

HUSBAND: Tell me what?

JAKE: Molly, in France, how do you show someone how you feel for them?

MOLLY: Like this.

(Slow-motion movement sequence as MOLLY uses the frying pan to knock the gun out of HUSBAND's hand.)

ALL: Noooooooooooooooooooooooooo.

JAKE: *(As he retrieves gun.)* You can't trust anyone French, can ya?

STRANGER: Jake, you saved me.

JAKE: Can it.

MOLLY: Now, let's see who our ghost really is.

(JAKE pulls a fake mustache off HUSBAND.)

ALL: Janitor Jim!

MOLLY: What? Why?

JAKE: I'll tell you why. He's from Jersey. Poor. Jealous of my money and my lifestyle. He watches enviously as I work in this prestigious field and he's stuck sweeping my floors. Isn't that right?

JANITOR JIM: No. You're just freaking annoying. You pissed me off. How many more days do you think I could take listening to you blab to yourself about how rancid you think I am? You think that doesn't bother me? I could care less about money. I've just been wanting to close your yapping mouth forever.

JAKE: Well, I may have been talking too much, Jim, but you apparently weren't talking enough. If only you would have just told me how this made you feel, we could have prevented this whole ordeal.

JANITOR JIM: I did! You just wouldn't listen. My mama always told me—

JAKE: Well, it's too late now.

MOLLY: And let's see who this really is…

(MOLLY takes the fake mustache that was once on JANITOR JIM and places it on STRANGER.)

ALL: OLD MAN CALHOUN!

MOLLY: The cranky riverboat captain!

OLD MAN CALHOUN: And I would have gotten away with it too, if it weren't for you and that stupid psychic French secretary!

MOLLY: Jake.

JAKE: Call the police, Molly. We have two non-paranormals to put away.

MOLLY: Great job, Jake.

JAKE: Thanks.

MOLLY: Wait just a minute, I have a question. If neither one of those two were ghosts, why'd you hit me?

JAKE: That is an intriguing question. But it's one that will just have to be left unexplained.

MOLLY: Jake, don't ignore me.

JAKE: Like the sounds you hear upstairs while the lights are out…

MOLLY: Jake Misco, you put me in a headlock.

JAKE: …or those moments when you feel someone breathing on your neck as you lie on an empty bed.

MOLLY: You tried to squash me with a frying pan.

JAKE: This is just another one of those nights for a paranormal detective simply named—

MOLLY: Jake Misco!

JAKE: That's me.

(Blackout.)

THEME SONG

A VOICE: They'll put on a show in the
    dead of night
  And if you don't find them amusin'
  They'll kick you in the crotch and force
    you to watch
  Reruns of *Suddenly Susan*
  They aren't afraid when you show
    them a cross
  And garlic is out of the question
  For they'll stand straight and tall and
    swallow it all
  Sayin' garlic's good for the digestion
  And they sing oh-o-o-yah!
  And they sing oh-o-o-yah!

VAMPIRE COWBOY SEQUENCE #2

Two COWBOYS face each other in a classic showdown. Slowly and dangerously, they advance toward one another. They stare each other down, ready to draw their guns at any moment. Suddenly, they both fall back into complex kung fu positions. They attack each other with impressive martial arts skill. Though the fight is fast and violent, it finally ends when one of the cowboys bares his fangs and sinks them deep into the neck of the other.

NON-VAMPIRE COWBOY: Ohgodno!

#2
THE ADVENTURES OF CAPTAIN JUSTICE AND LIBERTY LADY

Scene 1

ANNOUNCER: Last we saw our heroes, they were face to face with Cap's sworn enemy—the Hooded Menace.

HOODED MENACE: Justice, this time I have the world in my clutches. One more step my way and I will use this remote detonating device to activate fifty nuclear missiles aimed at major cities across North America.

LIBERTY LADY: Golly, Cap, that would kill millions and millions of innocent lives.

CAPTAIN JUSTICE: Hooded Menace, what do you want?

HOODED MENACE: What does any Supervillain want?

CAPTAIN JUSTICE: Obviously, you want to destroy democracy forever!

HOODED MENACE: I say, Justice, if I didn't know you were such a goody goody I'd swear you've been reading my diary.

LIBERTY LADY: You keep a diary?

HOODED MENACE: No. Not only do I want to take complete and utter control of this country, I also want something else.

LIBERTY LADY: Something else?

HOODED MENACE: I also want to finally annihilate its superheroic champions forever.

CAPTAIN JUSTICE: You'll never be rid of us, we're like a bad smell that won't go away. And that smell, Menace, that smell is America!

LIBERTY LADY: You tell 'em, Cap.

HOODED MENACE: That's what you think! Take this!

(HOODED MENACE produces a second evil electronic device and activates it. CAPTAIN JUSTICE and LIBERTY LADY put their hands over their ears and writhe in pain. MENACE laughs with glee.)

LIBERTY LADY: Cap, my ears. They hurt.

CAPTAIN JUSTICE: Mine too, Lady. The pain is unbearable.

LIBERTY LADY: Menace must be using some kind of supersonic tone to scramble our superhearing.

HOODED MENACE: Hope you enjoy my little surprise, I designed it specially for you.

CAPTAIN JUSTICE: Can't focus. Sense of justice weakening.

LIBERTY LADY: Superstrength less super.

HOODED MENACE: (Deactivates the evil device.) Now that I've softened you up, I've invited a few more friends to finish the job. (Calling.) Krogstad, Elvsted, Rosmersholm!

(MENACE speaks into his evil communicator. CAP and LADY are suddenly surrounded by a team of...)

LIBERTY LADY: Oh no, Cap, Menace's team of Norwegian Ninjas are surrounding us.

CAPTAIN JUSTICE: You have to be kidding me, Menace. Even with busted eardrums, we can still show these guys a true American welcome.

(CAP and LADY fight the NINJAS. The NORWEGIAN NINJAS are not particularly crafty and the fight is hardly fair. After *toying with their ill-equipped ADVERSAR-IES for a while, CAP and LADY easily dispose of them.)*

HOODED MENACE: Impressive. However, though you may have defeated my Norwegian Ninjas, I still hold all North America hostage.

LIBERTY LADY: Oh no, Cap, he still has the detonator!

CAPTAIN JUSTICE: Menace, don't do anything rash.

HOODED MENACE: The only way the citizens of this crappy capitalistic continent will ever be safe is once I rule it and turn it into…a Communist nation.

CAPTAIN JUSTICE: Menace, you know as well as I do, not even I, Captain Justice, have the power to give you that.

HOODED MENACE: Well, how about just Alaska and Hawaii?

CAPTAIN JUSTICE: Not even those.

HOODED MENACE: Well then, Justice, it seems to me your favorite nation is about to get quite a drastic makeover.

CAPTAIN JUSTICE: Never!

LIBERTY LADY: I think he's serious, Cap. What should we do?

CAPTAIN JUSTICE: I have a plan. You distract him, while I knock that remote out of his hand with a Disk of Democracy.

LIBERTY LADY: You got it, Cap.

HOODED MENACE: What are you two saying? No whispering!

CAPTAIN JUSTICE: Well, Liberty Lady, I think the Hooded Menace has finally got us beat. I guess I'll just go and get the contracts from the president and hand

over North America to Communism and Tyranny.

LIBERTY LADY: You're right, Cap. I guess it's time for me to remove this snazzy jumpsuit of justice, and trade it in for a shapeless sack of Communism, where everybody is the same, and no one is special.

CAPTAIN JUSTICE: We should look at the silver lining, Lady, at least we found a way to end this Cold War.

LIBERTY LADY: I'll miss fighting crime with you, Cap.

CAPTAIN JUSTICE: As will I, Lady. *(CAP pretends to leave.)*

HOODED MENACE: Finally! I win. I win. I win!

LIBERTY LADY: Well, Menace, I guess you won.

HOODED MENACE: Of course I would. Ha Ha Ha!

LIBERTY LADY: So, you want all of North America? Even Canada and Mexico too?

HOODED MENACE: Actually, I didn't even think of those.

LIBERTY LADY: Don't worry. No one else does either. That's quite a bit of land you're acquiring there. Do you think you could spare a piece for a retiring Superhero's faithful sidekick?

HOODED MENACE: Well, don't tell anyone but…I've always had a thing for the Liberty Lady.

LIBERTY LADY: Really?

HOODED MENACE: Oh yes, every little boy does.

LIBERTY LADY: What are you implying, Menace?

HOODED MENACE: I do need someone to rule beside me. You're cute, I'm the leader of an underground organized crime ring. I think we would make quite a lovely couple. Interested?

LIBERTY LADY: Sure.

HOODED MENACE: Well, what shall we rename our country, Lady?

LIBERTY LADY: How about… AMERICA! Now, Captain Justice!

(CAP throws a frisbee at MENACE and knocks the remote out of his hands.)

HOODED MENACE: No!

CAPTAIN JUSTICE: Well, Menace, I guess you once again underestimated the power of Truth, Justice, and the American Way.

HOODED MENACE: I was so close!

LIBERTY LADY: You were never close, Menace. There's no way we would have let you turn America to Godless Communism.

HOODED MENACE: I'll get my revenge, Justice. Just wait and see. I will crush you and take over this stinking country!

CAPTAIN JUSTICE: Menace, the only place you will be taking over will be behind the walls of a maximum security prison.

LIBERTY LADY: You tell him, Cap!

CAPTAIN JUSTICE: Lady, it looks like our job here is done. Let's go spread—

LIBERTY LADY: Liberty—

CAPTAIN JUSTICE: And Justice—

CAPTAIN and LADY: For all!!!

ANNOUNCER: In a time where Communism threatens to destroy the fabric of our blessed United States, only two people stand in the way of total Democratic Annihilation. Two Americans, genetically enhanced by a team of Government Scientists, now possess superhuman abilities. With their heightened strength, speed, and intelligence, they have dedicated their lives to the preservation of a free country. They are our secret weapon against all Communism. They are Captain Justice and Liberty Lady. So, sit back, Cap fans, and welcome to another exciting installment of everyone's favorite fighting duo. At the Condo of Justice, we find Liberty Lady and Captain Justice spending a quiet crime-free afternoon.

SCENE 2

CAPTAIN JUSTICE: What's wrong, Lady? You seem bothered.

LIBERTY LADY: I'm bored. Ever since we finally nabbed Menace, everything has become so quiet.

CAPTAIN JUSTICE: You should view that as a good thing.

LIBERTY LADY: And there's nothing on television, Cap. I know we're Superheroes, but I'm sure getting cable won't impede any of our work.

CAPTAIN JUSTICE: That's a silly notion, Liberty Lady.

LIBERTY LADY: Why?

CAPTAIN JUSTICE: Lady, you're not looking at the big picture. Don't you know that Communistic Propaganda is subliminally spread through liberal television programming? There's nothing but sex, violence, and pro wrestling on cable. It undermines everything we hold dear as law-abiding and morally conscious superhuman beings. Now, do you want to end up becoming a Commie couch potato?

LIBERTY LADY: No. Of course not. Golly, Cap, I never looked at it that way.

CAPTAIN JUSTICE: That's why I'm the Captain and you're just a simple lady.

LIBERTY LADY: So very simple.

SCENE 3

ANNOUNCER: Meanwhile, in a nearby alleyway, two suspicious characters are found lurking.

HOODED MENACE: Hey, what gives? Who are you? How'd you get me out?

SPECTATOR: I'm in the need of your services.

HOODED MENACE: You a Supervillain?

SPECTATOR: We seem to have a common foe that needs handling. And I will need your help to get him.

HOODED MENACE: Who are you?

SPECTATOR: They call me "The Spectator."

HOODED MENACE: The Spectator, huh? What's your superpower? Let me guess, you watch people really intensely.

SPECTATOR: No. I see across planes.

HOODED MENACE: Like Kansas?

SPECTATOR: No. Other worlds. Dimensions not our own.

HOODED MENACE: Seeing is your superpower. What could possibly be your weakness? Foggy days? Rainy nights? Really dirty sunglasses?

SPECTATOR: Mock if you wish, but sometimes being able to see is the greatest weapon against your adversary.

HOODED MENACE: Can you at least blast laser beams out of your eyes also?

SPECTATOR: No.

HOODED MENACE: How about strength? Do you at least have super-strength?

SPECTATOR: It's not needed. What I possess is the key to finally demolishing—

HOODED MENACE: You're nuts. Thanks for bailing me out, but I have some plans of my own.

SPECTATOR: I need your help to capture Captain Justice and Liberty Lady.

HOODED MENACE: Look, Spectator, it takes a lot more than "seeing" to stop the Amazing Americans. I had atomic weapons and they foiled me. What could really good eyesight do?

SPECTATOR: You don't understand the full nature of my powers.

HOODED MENACE: Being annoying isn't a superpower. I'll see you around.

SPECTATOR: Don't you want to finally get revenge on Captain Justice and destroy him forever? Maybe you're not much of a menace at all.

HOODED MENACE: What did you just say?

SPECTATOR: You heard me, hooded pussy.

HOODED MENACE: Are you calling me a cat!?

SPECTATOR: No I'm calling you a pussy. You know, pussy!

HOODED MENACE: Oh…Oh! How exactly can you help me?

SPECTATOR: Along with the ability to "see really well," I can also alter and manipulate reality.

HOODED MENACE: If your powers are so great, why don't you just do this on your own?

SPECTATOR: Getting one person out of jail is easy. But the only way to fully use my powers is if I'm in clear view of my opponent. I need you to get him in the same room as myself.

HOODED MENACE: That shouldn't be a problem. But why do you want to get rid of Justice?

SPECTATOR: He just makes me feel bad inside, I guess. So, do we have an understanding?

HOODED MENACE: Sure.

SCENE 4

ANNOUNCER: Oh no, it seems Menace is back on the scene. And who is this mysterious Spectator? With these two in the sack, Cap's work has just doubled. Back at the Condo of Justice, Captain and Lady get an unexpected call.

(The phone rings.)

LIBERTY LADY: Is that what I think it is?

CAPTAIN JUSTICE: The Phone of Justice! Quick, Lady, the world might be in danger once again.

LIBERTY LADY: (Answering the phone.) Hello?… Sergeant Pistof? What seems to be the problem?… The Hooded Menace, you say?… He's escaped?… Do we have any leads, Pistof?… That is interesting. We're right on it, sir!

CAPTAIN JUSTICE: Who was that?

LIBERTY LADY: Pistof.

CAPTAIN JUSTICE: How was he?

LIBERTY LADY: Kind of upset.

CAPTAIN JUSTICE: Well, what's wrong?

LIBERTY LADY: It seems we'll have to cut this vacation short after all. Our Arch-nemesis has escaped New City Prison again.

CAPTAIN JUSTICE: I guess there's never rest when the defense of true American values is concerned. What did Pistof find?

LIBERTY LADY: Well he just spoke to the prison guards at New City and, apparently, Menace was just standing there breaking rocks one minute and the next, he was gone.

CAPTAIN JUSTICE: How very strange! We have to locate Menace before he gets his hands on another dozen nuclear warheads. I wish there was some way to just stop him for good.

LIBERTY LADY: Well, there is one way, Cap.

CAPTAIN JUSTICE: What are you saying, Lady?

LIBERTY LADY: He is a threat to all that is Constitutional. I mean, how many times has he endangered the lives of millions and millions of innocents? Would he really be missed?

CAPTAIN JUSTICE: No, Lady. We have been given a very special honor. We are the Superheroes of this great country of ours. We uphold good American Virtues. If we started acting like that, we would be no better than the heartless criminals that we battle.

LIBERTY LADY: Golly, Cap. I wasn't thinking.

(Enter JUSTO.)

JUSTO, THE JUSTICE DOG: Ruff, ruff, grrr.

CAPTAIN JUSTICE: What's wrong with Justo, the Justice Dog?

LIBERTY LADY: It looks like he has something in his mouth.

CAPTAIN JUSTICE: It's a small brown envelope. I'm deducing it could be a clue.

LIBERTY LADY: Good Work, Justo!

JUSTO, THE JUSTICE DOG: Ruff, ruff!

CAPTAIN JUSTICE: What does it say?

LIBERTY LADY: "You're about to see, signed, The Spectator."

CAPTAIN JUSTICE: The Spectator, huh? So, we know the person we're up against has eyes.

LIBERTY LADY: I guess that rules out The Dreaded Batboy, The Mole, and The Cataract.

CAPTAIN JUSTICE: Run all matches on the Justice Computer and find me some suspects with eyes.

LIBERTY LADY: Yes, sir!

CAPTAIN JUSTICE: Hooded Menace, where could you be?

SCENE 5

ANNOUNCER: Meanwhile, the Hooded Menace returns to his lair.

HOODED MENACE: And this is my lair.

SPECTATOR: Nice. Very nice. And you say that you can bait both Captain Justice and Liberty Lady here?

HOODED MENACE: Look, we aren't archenemies for nothing. Captain Justice eventually always finds his way to my secret hiding places without any problem. That's what makes him so fucking annoying.

SPECTATOR: What did you just say, Menace?

HOODED MENACE: Fucking.

SPECTATOR: What language you have! You are a very corrupted baddie, aren't you?

HOODED MENACE: Yes, and soon, Justice will be fucked! HA HA HA!!!

SPECTATOR: Do we have the trap set?

HOODED MENACE: Oh yes. Instead of getting Norwegian Ninjas, I did as you asked and just got a couple of normal Japanese ones that actually knew martial arts.

SPECTATOR: Good.

HOODED MENACE: But their names are so boring. Kawasaki and Toyota. It just doesn't carry that ring that "Norwegian Ninjas" has.

SPECTATOR: Trust me, Menace. Real Ninjas are far more dangerous to our adversary than frightening names.

HOODED MENACE: They do eat raw fish. That's very frightening in itself.

SPECTATOR: So, Menace, what clues have you given Justice to find your whereabouts?

HOODED MENACE: Not to worry, my reality-bending friend. I've left clues that he's sure to be able to deduce. Soon, Spectator, with Captain Justice out of the way, I will rule all of North America. The U.S. will be mine. HA HA HA!

SPECTATOR: No, Menace, you have that all wrong. It already is yours.

HOODED MENACE: Spectator, you're my kinda gal

SPECTATOR: Don't touch me.

HOODED MENACE: My bad.

SCENE 6

ANNOUNCER: At the Justice Lab, we find our heroes in a mound of research.

CAPTAIN JUSTICE: This is so frustrating. Why can't we find Menace? It's like he's just disappeared off the map.

LIBERTY LADY: We'll find him soon, Cap. Don't worry.

CAPTAIN JUSTICE: I just hate being so emotional.

LIBERTY LADY: It's like you say all the time. It's better to be emotional than a passionless Commie, right?

CAPTAIN JUSTICE: You're right. I guess I'm just getting carried away.

LIBERTY LADY: Look, Cap, a message is being sent here through the Justice Computer. It's from Menace. It says "We are at Communist Island. Neener, neener, neener. Catch me if you can, you a-hole."

CAPTAIN JUSTICE: Of course! He must have returned there. A criminal always goes back to the scene of the crime.

LIBERTY LADY: What does "a-hole" mean?

CAPTAIN JUSTICE: American hole, perhaps.

LIBERTY LADY: Now let's go spread some Liberty—

CAPTAIN JUSTICE: And Justice—

CAPTAIN JUSTICE and LADY: For ALL!

CAPTAIN JUSTICE: Quick! To the Justice Mobile.

SCENE 7

ANNOUNCER: At Menace's secret lair, the Hooded Menace waits patiently to execute his plan.

HOODED MENACE: Soon, Spectator, the whole planet is going to be mine. This is going to be the shizzy.

SPECTATOR: This is so easy, I feel like he actually deserves what's coming to him.

HOODED MENACE: Between you and me, Spectator, I have to admit, I will hate no longer seeing Liberty Lady, though. She's definitely one nice piece of ass.

SPECTATOR: I'll ignore that you just said that.

(An alarm sounds!)

HOODED MENACE: The Commie Cam has caught them on tape. They're coming this way. Go make yourself scarce. I'll handle greeting our guests from here. I'm going to layeth the smacketh down on their candyasses. If ya smell what the Hood is cooking...

(CAP and LADY enter.)

CAPTAIN JUSTICE: Hello, Menace.

HOODED MENACE: Oh no, it's Captain Jerk Off and the Limp Dick Lady.

LIBERTY LADY: What did he just say?

CAPTAIN JUSTICE: Well, it seems you're breaking parole again, Menace. You're not allowed to come home for lunch in prison.

HOODED MENACE: Well, it looks like I'm busted. Guess you'll just have to take me back in, Captain.

CAPTAIN JUSTICE: That's good, Menace. I'm glad you're making this easy on yourself.

HOODED MENACE: Fuck easy, motherfucker. Just bring it.

(MENACE and CAP begin fighting. CAP is easily winning this battle. MENACE is being beaten to a pulp. Suddenly, MENACE grabs one of CAP's Disks of Democracy and nails him in the head, knocking him to *the floor. MENACE gets into a position to smash CAP's head in, when, suddenly, LIBERTY LADY gets involved and knocks MENACE away from CAP.)*

HOODED MENACE: You're such a bitch. You know, this is definitely not a fair fight. Let's even this match up, shall we? Non-Norwegian Ninjas, attack!

(Two NINJAS appear.)

CAPTAIN JUSTICE and LIBERTY LADY: Ninja, please!

(LIBERTY LADY begins to fight the NINJAS, but they are clearly better fighters than she. CAP tries to help, but gets beaten down for his help.)

LIBERTY LADY: These aren't regular Norwegian Ninjas, Cap!

CAPTAIN JUSTICE: No, they're not. There's only one way to stop these guys.

LIBERTY LADY: The Disks of Democracy!

(CAP and LADY free themselves from the fight and nail the two NINJAS with their frisbees, knocking them unconscious.)

HOODED MENACE: No!!! Damn it to fuck! You know how much money I lose every time you guys use those things?

CAPTAIN JUSTICE: Will you ever learn, Menace?

LIBERTY LADY: I guess not even Pinko Commie Ninjas can stop Justice.

ANNOUNCER: It seems the Hooded Menace's plan has been foiled once again by America's favorite fighting duo—

HOODED MENACE: Guess again, American-Hole! Now, Spectator.

(The lights come up with an ominous sound revealing the audience, the ANNOUNCER, and everything.)

LIBERTY LADY: What's all this?

HOODED MENACE: My world, bitch.

CAPTAIN JUSTICE: Well, your world ends now. You're coming with us.

(CAPTAIN JUSTICE throws a disk and hits MENACE in the chest with it. It just bounces off.)

LIBERTY LADY: The Disk of Democracy!

HOODED MENACE: You mean this frisbee?

LIBERTY LADY: Cap, the Disk just bounced off of him. What has he done?

CAPTAIN JUSTICE: I'm not sure. That's never happened before.

HOODED MENACE: That's 'cause this "Disk of Democracy" of yours is just a cheap piece of plastic. Welcome to the real world, Captain Dumbass, where stupid American Idealism doesn't mean jack diddly.

LIBERTY LADY: Who are all these people?

AUDIENCE PLANT #1: Hey, baby. Nice ass!

CAPTAIN JUSTICE: Are they Americans?

AUDIENCE PLANT #2: Hey, Cap, nice codpiece!

HOODED MENACE: This is the real America, Justice. Not a campy old television program.

CAPTAIN JUSTICE: What? Hello, do you believe in the American Way? Truth, Justice, Freedom for all?

AUDIENCE PLANT #3: I believe you can kiss my ass. Someone kill somebody already!

LIBERTY LADY: How did we get here, Captain?

SPECTATOR: I am how.

LIBERTY LADY: Who are you?

SPECTATOR: I am The Spectator.

LIBERTY LADY: Why are you doing this?

SPECTATOR: I represent all these people who watch you, Lady. The couch potatoes, the TV Landers, the late-night skin-o-maxers.

CAPTAIN JUSTICE: What do you want, Spectator? The U.S.? North America? The world? What?

SPECTATOR: I cross planes, Captain Justice, in search of obsolete Superheroes. And unfortunately for you—America isn't so damn cheesy. We've gotten over the Cold War. We want something you can't give us anymore.

LIBERTY LADY: This can't be true.

HOODED MENACE: Yep, Lady. It seems that the motto these days is good guys finish last. And guess what? Americans don't believe in Truth, Justice, and the American Way like they used to. Americans believe in Money, Power, and Self-Satisfying Gluttony. Wait, I guess that makes me their champion now, not you. Tough titty, huh?

SPECTATOR: I'm here to put you in a museum, or storage. You're a bad reminder of what we used to be, Captain.

CAPTAIN JUSTICE: What?

LIBERTY LADY: No.

SPECTATOR: Come on, don't fight me on this.

LIBERTY LADY: No. Take this and this.

(LADY tries to fight SPECTATOR, but her punches have no force in them. She then throws a frisbee at her. SPECTATOR catches it.)

SPECTATOR: Please, stop throwing the fucking frisbee. They get annoying.

(SPECTATOR throws it back at LADY and hits her with it. LADY screams in dreaded pain for several seconds and then suddenly stops, realizing that she is okay.)

HOODED MENACE: HA HA HA! It seems I get the last laugh after all. How does it feel, Cap? You're just a has-been who can't deliver anymore.

CAPTAIN JUSTICE: Stop.

LIBERTY LADY: Let go of me!

SPECTATOR: Stop struggling.

HOODED MENACE: If you want to see me kick this son-of-a-bitch's ass, give me a "Hell yeah."

AUDIENCE PLANTS: Hell yeah!

HOODED MENACE: Any last words, Captain Jerk Off?

CAPTAIN JUSTICE: I am not obsolete.

SPECTATOR: I'm here to give you guys your retirement check, Cap.

CAPTAIN JUSTICE: No.

HOODED MENACE: What the fuck are you going to do about it?

(CAP puts a hand around MENACE's neck.)

HOODED MENACE: Hey, what are you doing?

SPECTATOR: It's no use, Captain. Throwing Menace in jail isn't going to help you.

CAPTAIN JUSTICE: Let Liberty Lady go.

SPECTATOR: Your world is over, Captain.

CAPTAIN JUSTICE: No, it's not.

HOODED MENACE: Just admit it, your America is dead.

SPECTATOR: Justice, what are you doing?

CAPTAIN JUSTICE: Becoming a modern-day hero.

SPECTATOR: What?

HOODED MENACE: Will someone get him off of—

(CAP breaks MENACE's neck. MENACE falls to the ground dead.)

CAPTAIN JUSTICE: I refuse to be a museum piece, Spectator. Now, let Liberty Lady go.

SPECTATOR: Oh my God.

LIBERTY LADY: Cap, what have you done?

CAPTAIN JUSTICE: Are you all right?

LIBERTY LADY: Yes.

SPECTATOR: Captain Justice, why did you do that?

CAPTAIN JUSTICE: It's what you wanted to see, wasn't it?

SPECTATOR: I guess it was.

CAPTAIN JUSTICE: Send us home, Spectator. We're not the guys you're looking for.

SPECTATOR: As you wish.

(The lights shift.)

LIBERTY LADY: You okay, Cap?

CAPTAIN JUSTICE: Do you think Captain England ever has problems like these?

LIBERTY LADY: Nah. Those guys can't

even handle Good Oral Hygiene, much less an evil Supervillain.

CAPTAIN JUSTICE: Let's go home.

LIBERTY LADY: You killed someone today, Cap.

CAPTAIN JUSTICE: I know.

LIBERTY LADY: Why?

CAPTAIN JUSTICE: To please the crowd.

(Blackout.)

THEME SONG

A VOICE: It seems like you're in some horrible dream
From which you'll never wake up
With their hot fetid breath and their faces pale as death
My friend, that ain't stage makeup
Don't ever get caught in a showdown with them
For you'll be sorry you tried
As if prearranged, they'll quickly change
Into bats with wings of rawhide
And they sing oh-o-o-yah!
And they sing oh-o-o-yah!

VAMPIRE COWBOY SEQUENCE #3

Two COWBOYS face each other in a classic showdown. Slowly and dangerously, they advance toward one another. They stare each other down, ready to draw their guns at any moment. Suddenly, both of them pull out samurai swords. They run toward each other and begin fighting an elaborate sword spectacle. But even though the blades are sharp and their skills are impressive, the fight ends when one of the cowboys bares his fangs and sinks them deep into the neck of the other.

NON-VAMPIRE COWBOY: Ohgodno!

#3
TINA: TEENAGE WARRIOR PRINCESS

SCENE 1

A school bell rings.

GABBI: Come on, Tina, that was the bell! We're gonna get in trouble! We shouldn't be in the hallway.

TINA: Gabbi, stop freaking out. I just need to find my homework. No problem.

GABBI: See, that's a problem. Every time you say there isn't going to be a problem, poof! There's a problem. You're like a problem magnet.

TINA: Well, if I don't have it, I'm going to have quite a problem with…what's the class with all the test tubes, beakers, and burner thingies?

GABBI: Chemistry?

TINA: Chemistry.

GABBI: You don't even know what class we're supposed to be in!

TINA: It doesn't matter.

GABBI: You can copy my homework. Let's just get out of—

TINA: Nope, I'm done with that, Gabbi. I'm a changed woman. A changed woman I am. I'm a homeworkaholic. Crap, did I leave it at home?

GABBI: Seriously, Tina, this doesn't feel particularly safe.

TINA: What could possibly go wrong? We're in a normal average All American High School, we're two normal average All American High School kids, I'm a warrior princess, you're my dorky, yet faithful sidekick, and I have this big frickin' Chinese broadsword. What could possibly go wrong?

(Suddenly a gang of ZOMBIE CHEER-LEADERS jumps out.)

GABBI: Well, for example, we could be attacked by a gang of Undead Zombie Cheerleaders…

TINA: Dammit. And I was rooting for the other team.

(TINA screams a brutal war cry, and attacks. She easily disposes of the ZOMBIE CHEERLEADERS.)

TINA: Oops, I guess I scared the life out of them.

GABBi: That's bad.

TINA: Hey. My fight. My wordplay.

(Blackout.)

SCENE 2

TINA and GABBI in the cafeteria having lunch.

GABBI: I knew we shouldn't have been out in the hallway without a pass.

TINA: Take it easy, Gabbi.

GABBI: What would have happened if you weren't there? I could've gotten hurt or maimed or worse… I could have been turned into an Undead Zombie Cheerleader.

TINA: Gabbi, that would never happen.

GABBI: Would you still like me if I became a Cheerleader?

TINA: Gabbi, calm down.

GABBI: Would you?

TINA: Gabbi, I would never let that happen.

GABBI: You're the best.

(Enter MISSY, the most popular girl at Hellenic High.)

MISSY: Tina. I thought I might find you here.

TINA: Missy!

MISSY: Did you make it to class on time?

TINA: I should have known.

MISSY: By the way, nice outfit. Very 326 A.D.

TINA: Cut the crap. You sent those Zombie Cheerleaders, didn't you.

MISSY: Who, little ol' me?

TINA: You are evil and rotten to your very core, and I will do everything in my power to stop you and your dastardly plan.

GABBI: Actually, she hasn't mentioned a plan yet.

TINA: Gabbi, please.

MISSY: That doesn't sound like the old Tina I knew so well.

GABBI: What?

TINA: That Tina is dead. And no matter how hard you dig, you'll never find her body.

MISSY: Oh really?

TINA: Yes. Even if you get down on your little hands and knees and dig through the polluted earth, you'll never find her rotting, stinking remains because her bones have been sucked clean by the maggots of guilt and remorse.

MISSY: Ew. That's totally gross!

GABBI: She's right, that was a little gross—

TINA: Gabbi!

GABBI: Sorry.

MISSY: I need that old Tina back, for one final job. The cheerleading squad is going to the state finals, and we need you to choreograph the winning number.

GABBI: What's she talking about, Tina?

TINA: I'd rather choke slowly on the vomit of the Lernaean Hydra.

MISSY: Again with the gross stuff.

TINA: I've left that life behind me. I only use my powers for good now, to help the poor and weak who cannot defend themselves.

MISSY: Hanging with the poor and weak is definitely not cool.

TINA: Now leave this place!

MISSY: Not so fast, princess, perhaps this will help convince you.

BRAD: *(Voiceover.)* Tina…help me.

TINA: Brad?

BRAD: *(Voiceover.)* Please Tina, only you can save me.

TINA: Brad!

GABBI: Who's Brad?

MISSY: Oh, nobody special. Just Tina's loser BOYFRIEND!

GABBI: What? What boyfriend?

BRAD: *(Voiceover.)* Tina, I can't move … help… the smell is so bad here… I can't fight the smell… It's like poo!

TINA: I'll find you, Brad. You fiend. How can you sleep with yourself?

MISSY: I don't have to. That's what the football team is for. I expect the new cheerleading number by final period today, or you can say goodbye to Brad forever. Forever, Tina. Forever. Ha ha ha. *(She disappears.)*

GABBI: Holy crap, Tina! She disappeared.

TINA: She has grown more powerful since our last meeting.

GABBI: What are you talking about? How do you know Missy McGuire, the most popular girl in the school? And what did she mean the old Tina? And who is Brad?

TINA: All in good time, Gabbi. But for the moment we're no longer safe in the caf. Come on!

GABBI: And when did you get a boyfriend?

Scene 3

BRAD and MISSY are in the gym equipment room. BRAD has sweat socks tied to his head.

BRAD: Missy, please, the smell.

MISSY: Stop your whining, you pathetic excuse for an athlete. Not even Tina can save you now. Oh she'll try, but she'll fail and when she does she'll have no choice but to choreograph the number. And after she does I'll use the Sweat Socks of Hephaestus on her. Once she's under my power, I'll claim credit for the winning routine. I won't just be the most popular girl in the school, I'll be the most popular girl in the town, in the state, no, why should I stop there? I'll be the most popular girl in the whole freaking world, and there will be no one to stop us this time! Ha, ha, ha.

BRAD: Tinaaaaaaaaaaaaaaaaaaaaaaaaaa!

Scene 4

TINA and GABBI are in French class passing notes. M. LINSTRUCTEUR is teaching.

M. LINSTRUCTEUR: Maintenant mes étudiants, écoutez-moi s'il vous plaît, maintenant le verbe avoir. Avoir quelque chose. Avoir un ananas. J'ai un ananas.

Avoir aucune idée. Je n'ai aucune idée. Avoir une bicyclette orange. J'ai une bicyclette orange. Et aussi un ananas. Regardez-vous.

GABBI: Tina, I'm so confused. Why would Missy make up those terrible stories about you?

TINA: I'm afraid she wasn't making them up.

M. LINSTRUCTEUR: Où est mon ananas? Il est là. A côté de la bicyclette orange.

TINA: You see, long before you transferred to Hellenic High, I had a different life. I was a different person.

GABBI: But a cheerleader?

TINA: Yes, the vilest of the vile. Before Missy McGuire, I was the most popular girl in the school, and an evil award-winning cheer choreographer.

GABBI: But then how did you become a warrior princess?

M. LINSTRUCTEUR: J'ai un ananas et j'ai une bicyclette orange. Est-ce que j'ai un poisson? Non, c'est le poisson de mon oncle.

TINA: There was a young boy who was trying out for the football team. He was lame, and a bit blind in one eye. His hearing wasn't very good either. And he had some really bad asthma, but you didn't really notice the wheezing because of this weird nervous tic. Anyways, all the kids would tease him mercilessly which only made his nosebleeds worse.

M. LINSTRUCTEUR: Où est le poisson? Je ne sais pas. C'est le poisson de mon oncle. J'ai aucune idée. J'ai un ananas.

TINA: I remember it like it was yesterday.

(We flash back. BRAD is on the ground, TINA and MISSY are standing over him.)

BRAD: Please don't tease me anymore, please.

TINA: Why? Are you gonna cry? Are you gonna cry, you big baby?

MISSY: Yeah, you big baby, are you gonna cry?

BRAD: Leave me alone, my nose is starting to bleed.

TINA: Oh, does it smart, poor baby?

MISSY: Yeah, does it smart?

TINA: Or maybe it dumbs?

BRAD: Stop it, you mean girls.

TINA: Does it dumb?

MISSY: Yeah, does it dumb?

BRAD: IT DOESN'T DUMB!

TINA: Yes it does, it dumbs.

MISSY: Yeah, it dumbs.

BRAD: You don't have to do this! Look inside yourselves.

TINA: What?

MISSY: Yeah, what?

BRAD: How would you like it if somebody teased you?

(We are back in the French class.)

BRAD: *(Voiceover, echoing.)* How would you like it if somebody teased you?

TINA: How would you like it if somebody teased you?

M. LINSTRUCTEUR: J'ai mangé le poisson.

TINA: His words echoed in my head.

BRAD: *(Voiceover, one more echo.)* How would you like it if somebody teased you?

GABBI: It's like I can hear them!

M. LINSTRUCTEUR: Le poisson de mon oncle. Où est mon oncle? Il est sur la bicyclette orange.

TINA: Later that night, after we'd finished beating him up, I couldn't stop thinking about what that boy had said. And so I decided to leave Missy McGuire and put my evil cheerleading ways behind me.

GABBI: No wonder Missy hates you so much!

TINA: From that day forward, I dedicated my life to helping others, the meek, the poor, the pathetic, the destitute, and the deranged. The hideously mutilated and the absolutely filthy. The smelly, the foolish, and the badly dressed. The horrendous, the heartbreakingly hopeless, and the helpless hacks whose horrendous hair hangs half-heartedly from their horrid heads. And that's how I met you, Gabbi.

M. LINSTRUCTEUR: Je ne peux pas voir mon oncle. Il s'est caché derrière l'ananas, parce qu'il a volé ma bicyclette orange. Je ne veux pas lécher le poisson. Il n'est pas orange.

TINA: I decided to become a warrior princess, and I went and apologized to the boy. And that boy, that boy's name was Brad.

GABBI: SO, HE WASN'T YOUR BOYFRIEND!

M. LINSTRUCTEUR: Ecoutez, s'il vous plaît!

GABBI: I mean… he wasn't your boyfriend?

TINA: Of course not.

GABBI: I just knew it wasn't all true. Whatever you did in the past doesn't matter, Tina, you're my best friend now. And best friends lick together.

TINA: Stick.

GABBI: What?

TINA: Stick together. Uh, you just said lick.

GABBI: No I didn't.

TINA: Whatever. It's time to go save Brad. Can I go to the bathroom?

M. LINSTRUCTEUR: Est-ce que je peux aller aux toilettes? Est-ce que je peux? Non, vous n'avez pas un ananas. Un ananas.

TINA: Thanks. And Gabbi's coming with me.

GABBI: Sweet.

SCENE 5

GABBI and TINA are on the football field.

GABBI: I don't understand, Tina, what are we doing here on the football field?

TINA: Brad said the smell was terrible.

GABBI: So?

TINA: I suspect Missy is keeping Brad prisoner by using the Sweat Socks of Hephaestus.

GABBI: But the Sweat Socks will over-power anyone who smells them.

TINA: That's why we're here. There is only one object that can help us to defeat the socks. The Insoles of Inachus.

GABBI: The Insoles of Inachus? But they're kept high on the goalpost of the field.

TINA: I know, and the goalpost is said to be guarded. You wait here.

GABBI: But I want to help you.

TINA: I've already been responsible for too much pain and suffering. I would never forgive myself if anything happened to you. Gabbi…

GABBI: Tina…

(Moment of awkward sexual tension.)

TINA: Stay here no matter what happens.

GABBI: I'll wait for you.

TINA: I know you will. I come for the Insoles of Inachus!

MISSY: *(Voiceover.)* Tina, give up your futile quest. The insoles are guarded; you will only perish if you attempt to win them. Choreograph the routine and I will release Brad from the sweat socks.

TINA: Never. I come for the Insoles of Inachus.

MISSY: *(Voiceover.)* You stubborn fool!

TINA: I will never bow to your will.

MISSY: *(Voiceover.)* Then I leave you to your foolish death!

TINA: I come for the insoles!

(Two HIPPIE STONERS appear. They attack TINA.)

GABBI: Look out, Tina! Stoner Hippies!

TINA: Hey guys, Jerry Garcia called …He wants his band back.

(An elaborate fight. Eventually, TINA defeats the STONERS.)

TINA: And that's what I call the Grateful Dead.

GABBI: Still bad.

TINA: Kiss off. I claim the Insoles of Inachus!

(A great rumbling. Lights flicker. Jimi Hendrix is played in the background. And

magically, an old, strangely Roman HIPPIE appears.)

INACHUS: I am Inachus. I see you have bested my powerful potheads. How may I reward you?

TINA: I need your insoles.

INACHUS: Are you sure you want them, dude?

TINA: It's a matter of life and death.

INACHUS: Okay.

(He removes his sandals, and gives her the insoles.)

GABBI: Right on, Tina! Shitastic!

(MISSY appears and with her pom-poms puts a spell on GABBI.)

TINA: Gabbi!

MISSY: You may have the insoles, Tina. But I have your little friend. Choreograph the routine or she dies. Ha, ha, ha.

(They disappear.)

TINA: Noooooooooooooooo!

SCENE 6

TINA is searching for GABBI and BRAD.

TINA: I must find where Missy is holding Gabbi and Brad before it is too late! I refuse to have the death of one more innocent on my hands. Even if I have to choreograph the cheer, I'll do whatever it takes to save them. Wait a minute, what's that smell? It's coming from the gym. It's like the normal gym smell, but worse: stronger somehow. Wait a minute, that is no mortal stench, only the Sweat Socks of Hephaestus could be so malevolently malodorous. Wait a minute, they must be close by. But where? Oh mighty gods all powerful, all knowing, all seeing, and all

smelling, help me in my time of need. Assist me to know the right path so that I can save my friends. Please. Will you say nothing? Will you sit silent and watch from atop Olympus as innocents are slaughtered? I charge you speak!

PRINCIPAL: *(Voiceover.)* Attention students, at the end of the day there are just a few announcements.

TINA: I hear you; show me the way.

PRINCIPAL: *(Voiceover.)* A reminder that the Geometry Club will be holding their annual mixer this Thursday night. Both members and nonmembers are welcome.

TINA: I don't understand, all-powerful ones.

PRINCIPAL: *(Voiceover.)* Also could Vincent Cardinal please report to the Main Office, your mother is here with your retainer.

TINA: You mock me with riddles. Where are they?

PRINCIPAL: *(Voiceover.)* The equipment locker...

TINA: What.

PRINCIPAL: *(Voiceover.)* The gymnasium equipment locker...

TINA: Is that where I should look?

PRINCIPAL: *(Voiceover.)* Yes, the equipment locker is where you should look for all your equipment needs. But as always at this time of year, it is in need of a good cleaning!

TINA: Yes!

PRINCIPAL: *(Voiceover.)* And we are looking for a few brave volunteers to answer the call.

TINA: I am your servant! *(TINA departs.)*

PRINCIPAL: *(Voiceover.)* Those who are interested can see Ms. Maureen Wagner in the Gym Office. Thank you for your attention and good afternoon. Holy fuck, Vicki, please tell me it's Friday. I need a couple of days away from these psycho little... What? The mike is still what... oh no...

SCENE 7

The gym equipment locker.

TINA: All right Missy, show yourself. I know you're here. I can smell the Sweat Socks of Hephaestus. I bring the Insoles of Inachus!

MISSY: *(Voiceover.)* Too late you, feudal fashion faux pas! The insoles are useless now! I have your friends to help me.

(BRAD and GABBI enter; they have been transformed into ZOMBIE CHEERLEAD-ERS. They are terrifyingly upbeat and happy.)

BRAD and GABBI: Missy, Missy, she's the one!
    She's the chick who gets the job done!
    She rocks to the left,
    She rocks to the right,
    She'll rock that Tina right outta sight!

TINA: Nooooo!

BRAD and GABBI: Now heeeeeeeeeeere's Missy!

(MISSY enters.)

MISSY: You see, warrior wimp, your friends are now on my squad. They are Zombie Cheerleaders under my power. Observe.

BRAD: Does my bum look fat in this?

GABBI: Oh God, does mine?

TINA: Poor Gabbi. I'm sorry I failed you.

MISSY: You have no choice but to choreograph the routine. Do it now and I will

release them. If not, they will be mine forever!

BRAD and GABBI: Yeeeaaaa forever!

TINA: I'll see you in hell first!

(TINA attacks MISSY; they fight.)

BRAD and GABBI: Missy, Missy, she's got the plan.
    If she can't do it, no one can!

MISSY: It's futile, Princess Poseur, I'm too powerful for you.

BRAD and GABBI: Give us an M, give us an I, give us an S, how about another S, now where's that Y? What d'you got? MISSY! Goooooooo MISSY!

(TINA starts to weaken.)

TINA: Your overconfidence is your weakness.

MISSY: Your faith in your friends is yours.

BRAD and GABBI: Go Missy, Go Missy, Go Missy, Go Missy, Go Missy, Goooooooo Missy, Missy GO!

TINA: Cheers...too...strong...can't keep fighting.

BRAD and GABBI: Missy is so good,
    Missy is so great,
    She is my best friend,
    I could eat her on a plate!
    YUM!

MISSY: Feel yourself weakening, Tina the Tired. The positive energy of the cheers is too much. I totally have that psychological advantage thing. Give up before you are destroyed.

BRAD and GABBI: Give it up bitch,
    Give it up bitch, bitch!

TINA: Never, not while there is a breath of air in my body. While there is a hair on my head and a nail on my finger, I will fight evil everywhere I see it, and smell it.

(With the last of her strength, she throws MISSY down and runs over to the CHEER- LEADERS.)

TINA: Come on girls, new cheer! Okay crew, to the left.

BRAD and GABBI: To the left.

TINA: That's right, now to the right.

MISSY: Stay away from them!

TINA: Two up high!

BRAD and GABBI: UP HIGH!

TINA: Oh my!

BRAD and GABBI: Oh my!

TINA: You know it now, crew, take it!!

(Music comes up as they break into an elaborate dance routine. MISSY crumbles in pain. TINA steps away from the dance number as the music swells. MISSY attacks. TINA fights her.)

TINA: Ahhhhhhhhhhhhhhhh!

(TINA throws MISSY to the ground.)

BRAD and GABBI: That's Tina!

TINA: Missy, your evil reign is over. Never again will you terrorize the poor, defenseless, and half-witted students of Hellenic High.

GABBI: Yeah, Tina! FINISH HER!

(TINA raises her sword to slay MISSY, but stops...)

TINA: No. This is wrong.

GABBI: What? Of all people, Tina, I would never expect you to come to have mercy on one who had so misused you.

TINA: Gabbi, today I have learnt a powerful lesson. It is wrong to hate someone just because he, she, or it is different from you. Missy hated me because I was no longer a cheerleader. Must I hate her because she is? It is true that she has been evil, and has tried to destroy me and everything that I hold dear. To ruin my life and leave me a shallow husk of my former self. But I must forgive her, because we all know that... *(Singing.)* Killing is wrong, killing is bad
It serves no one, but it hurts your fellow man

(INACHUS appears with a guitar.)

BRAD and GABBI: Killing is wrong, killing is bad
It serves no one, but it hurts your fellow man

TINA: Though she tried to kidnap you and hurt all of my friends

GABBI: Destroy the whole world, bring it to an end

BRAD: Yes she might be evil, she may want to rain death from above
But even one so cruel could use a little love

TINA, GABBI, and BRAD: Killing is wrong, killing is bad
It serves no one, but it hurts your fellow man
Oh, killing is wrong, killing is bad
It serves no one, but it hurts your fellow man

MISSY: You thought you could find justice by breaking someone's neck
But as we all learned today, killing just brings ya heck

INACHUS: Destroying a life could probably please the masses
But you'd end up in jail where you'd

have to lick a lot of asses
Everybody now...

THE CAST: Killing is wrong, killing is bad
    It serves no one, but it hurts your fel-
      low man
    Oh, killing is wrong, killing is bad
    It serves no one, but it hurts your fel-
      low man

BRAD: God bless us everyone.

(TINA and GABBI begin furiously kissing.)

(Blackout.)

THEME SONG

A VOICE: It's a bitter battle to the death

Full of heartache, woe, and sorrow.
But if you're not satisfied with the vio-
    lence they provide
They'll do it all again tomorrow.
I just got bit by a vampire cowboy
And my symptoms are beginning to
    worsen
Since I began this hymn, I've become
    one of them
From now on, I'll sing in first person
And we sing oh-o-o-yah!
And we sing oh-o-o-yah!
Vampire cowboy-oy-oy-yah!
Vampire cowboy-oy-oy-yah!

(END OF PLAY... for now.)

SECOND.

Neal Utterback

NEAL UTTERBACK was born on June 6, 1971, in Monticello, Indiana. After being stationed in Baumholder, Germany, with the U.S. Army, he graduated with a bachelor's in theatre from Coastal Carolina University (under Sandi Shackleford). An MFA in acting led him to the University of Florida (Mikell Pinkney, David Shelton, Ralf Remshardt). His first play, *The Liar's Poem*, was produced at One Arm Red in DUMBO, Brooklyn. Utterback is currently the Playwright-in-Residence for Tobacco Bar Theatre Company. He resides in Brooklyn with his partner, Tim.

second. was first presented by Horse Trade Theater Group (Kimo DeSean, Producing Artistic Director; Erez Ziv, Managing Director) in a Tobacco Bar Theatre Company production (Joe LaRue, Artistic Director) on April 22, 2004, at Under St. Marks, New York City, with the following cast and credits:

Lauren	Lisa Kay Powers
Vick	Eve Eaton
Jake	Joel Nagle
Davey	Mike Doyle
John	Tim Altmeyer
T	Sadie Jones
Man	Mark Stanton

Director: Joe LaRue
Technical Director: Mark Sanders
Costume Design: Steven White
Sound Design and Original Music: Paul Gill
Prop Construction: John T. Sheets and Robert LaRue
Marketing Assistant: Christin Seidel
Supplemental Marketing and PR: Raymie Moynagh, QPR+Events
Tobacco Bar Theatre Company: Joe LaRue, Leslie Meisel, Michael Mangione, Dana Panepinto, Donna Robinson, Jaki Silver, Neal Utterback

Visit www.tobaccobar.com.

CHARACTERS

LAUREN: Female, mid- to late thirties. She is a successful New York surgeon and Vick's partner. She is upbeat and hopeful even when what she is saying may appear dark or cynical.

VICK: Female, mid- to late thirties. A tough, no-nonsense reporter who is finding her career somewhat challenged. Though she is outwardly selfish, she deeply loves Lauren.

JAKE: Male, early forties. This job is his last best chance for his and his son's future.

DAVEY: Male, late twenties. He is a self-educated street kid who looks to Jake as a kind of big brother figure.

JOHN: Male, looks mid-thirties. He is handsome if a bit odd.

T: Female, mid-twenties, but looks younger. Beautiful and earthy, she, like all the characters, has an inner positive energy that shows through the hard exterior.

MAN: Male, late twenties or early thirties. An everyman.

PRODUCTION SUPPLEMENTAL

Our production team faced numerous challenges while working on *second.* We believed that ultimately this is a play about hope and the power of possibility, but we also wanted to keep it light and fun. The answer seems to lie in the tone in which the story is told—one that draws a fine line between the ache and longing of these characters and a conspicuous, playful "bounce."

The following are provided as helpful hints that we discovered in production. My hope is that you will find your own challenges and have as much enjoyment solving them as we did.

• Actors and directors should strive to play positive, buoyant actions. This will help "lift" the play and the characters.

• I tried to create a cleanliness and precision about the text. We found that the play works best when the acting style mimics the writing—i.e., emotional and intellectual economy.

• This economy applies to cues as well. Keep them tight and think on the lines, not between them. The only exception is where punctuation indicates a "moment" (a pause, beat, silence, or ellipsis). Another important note: slashes (/) are interruptions. One character's slash will match up with the slash in the next character's line.

- There are essentially three simultaneous scenarios (Lauren/Vick, T/John, and Jake/Davey/Man) going on in the play. The play is broken up into three "scenes," with a prologue, main play, and epilogue. It's best if one thinks of the bulk of the play as one continuous scene with breaks only occurring after the prologue and before the epilogue. As one pair of characters replaces another, there should be a seamlessness with the exchange. This way the energy of the play is never dropped.

That said, enjoy *second*.

Two pillars and a crossbeam create three doorways, each with a different molding. They indicate the three different locations of this story. Stage left is VICK and LAUREN's apartment, the center is MAN's, and stage right is a hotel room for JOHN and T. Downstage left is a common "window" for all three rooms that looks out on the audience. It has no frame. As the play opens, the stage is bare except for the doorways. Two blocks and a chair sit to the side behind the structure.

Darkness. Swelling, cacophonous sound. Like something massive approaching. Sound peaks and abruptly stops. Lights come up to reveal LAUREN crouching by MAN who lies motionless on the floor. T and VICK stand over them. The remaining ACTORS 1, 2, and 3 stand in various spots on the stage, addressing the audience. NOTE: Song lyrics in the prologue and epilogue are spoken rather than sung.

ACTOR 1 (JAKE): It came upon a midnight clear.

LAUREN: *(Wincing in pain and exhilaration.)* Oh…God.

VICK: Lauren?

ACTOR 2 (JOHN): That glorious song of old, from angels bending near the earth/ to touch their harps of gold—

ACTOR 3 (DAVEY): /Come they told me, pa rum pum pum pum—

ACTOR 1 (JAKE, AS REPORTER): —Four teens gunned down today in a vicious tragedy—

ACTORS 3 (DAVEY): —pa rum pum pum pum—

LAUREN: Something's not… I think something's—

VICK: What is it? Are you sick?

T: Doctor, do you need a doctor?

ACTOR 2 (JOHN, AS REPORTER): —Miracle Man still at large this holiday—

ACTOR 3 (DAVEY): Peace on earth, goodwill to men from heaven's/all gracious king!

ACTOR 1 (JAKE): /Said the night wind/ to the little lamb—

ACTOR 2 (JOHN): /The hunt for the terrorist leader/

LAUREN: /I don't believe this.

VICK: Believe what?

ACTOR 3 (DAVEY): Do you hear/what I hear?

LAUREN: *(She contracts.)* /Oh, God.

T: Help!

ACTOR 1 (JAKE): The world in solemn stillness lay—

ACTOR 2 (JOHN): To hear the angels sing.

LAUREN: I think I'm having a/

ACTOR 3 (DAVEY): /Wait a/

ACTOR 2 (JOHN): /Wait a/

ACTOR 1 (JAKE): /Wait a second!

(ACTORS 4, 5, and 6 stand and address the audience.)

ACTOR 4 (T): Go back.

ACTOR 3 (DAVEY): Déjà vu.

ACTOR 2 (JOHN): Christmas Eve.

ACTOR 6 (LAUREN): New York City.

ACTOR 5 (VICK): The worst blizzard in recorded history.

ACTOR 4 (T): The edge of oblivion.

(Blackout. Sounds of the snowstorm begin to build. In darkness, the ACTORS move the blocks and chair into position: one long block down right, one cube up left, and the chair centered beneath the middle arch. Lights come up to reveal JAKE and DAVEY. JAKE is cleaning his handgun. MAN is gagged and bound to the chair, bleeding from the forehead. A newspaper sits on the up left block. It remains onstage throughout. An enthusiastic DAVEY is in the middle of a very good story.)

DAVEY: And. In the, like 1500s—or maybe it was the fifteenth century—I can't remember—but these people were getting trashed, right? On like, mead, or nog, or whatever, and the alcohol was mixing with the lead in the— *(DAVEY makes a shape like a cup with his hands.)*

JAKE: Bucket?

DAVEY: No.

JAKE: Urn?

DAVEY: That they drank out of?

JAKE: A glass?

DAVEY: No, like a—

JAKE: A chalice?

DAVEY: Isn't that a chair?

JAKE: No, Davey, it's not a chair.

DAVEY: I think it's a chair. A goblet. A lead goblet.

JAKE: Are you going to be like this all night? 'Cause I'll shoot you right now.

DAVEY: You wouldn't shoot me.

JAKE: Just finish your stupid story.

DAVEY: Where was I?

JAKE: They're drinking out of goblets.

DAVEY: And they're all passing out 'cause the alcohol is mixing with the lead so they look like they're dead and they buried them. Alive.

JAKE: Uh huh.

DAVEY: *Alive.*

JAKE: Yeah, I heard you.

DAVEY: And they didn't have enough coffins or whatever, so they dug these people back up and found scratch marks on the inside.

JAKE: Uh huh.

DAVEY: They were buried alive.

JAKE: Yes, I know.

DAVEY: So, they started attaching strings to people's fingers when they buried them and the strings were attached to a bell, which is where we get/

JAKE and DAVEY: /Dead ringer.

JAKE: You're a wealth.

DAVEY: You know this?

JAKE: Everyone knows this.

DAVEY: I didn't know this.

JAKE: Everyone except you.

DAVEY: But I still don't know why "dead ringer" means something that looks just like something else. Buried alive, can you imagine? Scary, huh?

JAKE: What's *scary* is that the bulk of your knowledge comes from forwarded emails.

DAVEY: *(To MAN.)* You were scared, weren't you?

(MAN doesn't move.)

DAVEY: Did you know that some of the most famous deaths are fakes?

JAKE: What are you talking about?

DAVEY: Like JFK, the president. There's actually a group of people who believe JFK wasn't shot at all. It was his dippledonger and that the real/

JAKE: /Doppelgänger.

DAVEY: What?

JAKE: His doppelgänger.

DAVEY: What's that?

JAKE: What you're trying to say.

DAVEY: Dippledonger.

JAKE: No, doppelgänger.

DAVEY: I don't think that's right.

JAKE: His double?

DAVEY: Like his evil twin but maybe not evil.

JAKE: The word is doppelgänger.

DAVEY: Whatever, I'm not going to argue over Semitism.

JAKE: Semantics.

DAVEY: Why you gotta correct everything I say?

JAKE: Because everything you say is wrong.

DAVEY: Death freaks me out.

JAKE: Everybody dies.

DAVEY: Yeah, exactly. But you don't know how or when but you know it's gonna happen. Buried alive. I can't imagine a worse way to die.

JAKE: Would you just shut the hell up, *please?*

DAVEY: What? Are we just gonna sit here in silence?

JAKE: Yeah.

(Silence.)

DAVEY: A rusty nail driven through your skull.

JAKE: What?

DAVEY: That's worse.

JAKE: Well, yeah, I guess so.

DAVEY: You sure you got a good signal?

JAKE: What?

DAVEY: On your phone?

JAKE: Yeah.

DAVEY: The storm may be interfering.

JAKE: I got a good signal.

DAVEY: Do you think he's gonna call?

JAKE: Yes.

DAVEY: I don't think I've ever been up in this neighborhood before.

JAKE: I had a girlfriend lived up here once.

DAVEY: Nice?

JAKE: Yeah, it's a nice neighborhood.

DAVEY: No, your girlfriend.

JAKE: What?

DAVEY: Was she nice?

JAKE: No, she was a bitch.

DAVEY: Oh.

(Silence.)

DAVEY: Yeah, relationships are tough. *(Goes to the window.)* It's nice up here. I could live up here. Shitty apartment, though. You got a shitty apartment, dude. Man, look at the snow.

JAKE: Get away from the window.

DAVEY: It's really snowing.

JAKE: It's winter. That happens.

DAVEY: They're saying it's going to be the worst snowstorm ever.

JAKE: Well, they're idiots.

DAVEY: *(Singing.)* "Oh, come all ye faithful, joyful/"

JAKE: /Don't do that.

DAVEY: It's Christmas.

JAKE: *(Looks at his watch.)* Not yet.

DAVEY: *(Looking out the window.)* Man, it is really coming down.

JAKE: *(Being very clear.)* Get away from the window.

DAVEY: What if we get snowed in here for weeks with this guy? Dude, we'd have to eat each other.

JAKE: Why would we have to eat each other?

DAVEY: I bet this guy doesn't have any food in this place. *(To MAN.)* You don't

have anything to eat, do you? *(Goes to the kitchen.)* Dude, this creepy silent bastard doesn't have... Pop Tarts, he has Pop Tarts. And he's got—

JAKE: Why don't you go get something and bring it back?

DAVEY: I'm not goin' out there again.

JAKE: Then shut up.

DAVEY: ...Would you eat me?

JAKE: Excuse me?

DAVEY: If we got snowed in here forever, would you eat me?

JAKE: I'm sure the neighbors have food.

DAVEY: Hypothetically, sayin' they don't. Would you eat me?

JAKE: Davey.

DAVEY: Yeah?

JAKE: I think I can say without reservation that I would never eat you.

DAVEY: That would be a pretty horrible way to die, huh?

JAKE: Sure.

DAVEY: ...I'd eat *you.*

JAKE: Fine.

DAVEY: 'Cause I sure the hell ain't gonna starve to death. That'd really suck.

(JAKE picks up his cell phone. He dials.)

DAVEY: Whataya doin', Jake?

JAKE: Checkin' messages. And don't use my name.

DAVEY: You called me Davey.

JAKE: No, I didn't.

DAVEY: Yeah, you did.

JAKE: No. I didn't.

DAVEY: *(To MAN.)* He did, didn't he?

JAKE: Oh God, I'm in hell.

DAVEY: Did he call?

JAKE: ...No.

DAVEY: I'm serious. It is really coming down. Come look.

(JAKE doesn't.)

DAVEY: Damn, I hate the winter. I hate the cold. When I was living in Florida, man... You ever been to Miami? It is paradise. Hotties walking around sh-boom titties all sh-bang. I had bitches smokin' my bong every night, man. It was the goddamn Garden of Eden.

JAKE: So, why'd you come to New York?

DAVEY: Dude, Miami's expensive.

(Silence.)

DAVEY: ...You hungry? You look hungry.

JAKE: No.

DAVEY: You want a Pop Tart? *(To MAN.)* Dude, can we have a Pop Tart?

JAKE: We're not eating his food.

DAVEY: We could order something.

JAKE: Are you nuts?

DAVEY: I dunno.

JAKE: ...I look hungry?

DAVEY: Yeah, you know?

JAKE: What does that mean?

DAVEY: It means you look hungry. What do you mean what does it mean?

JAKE: Am I not being clear?

DAVEY: I'm just asking.

JAKE: Because I want to be clear.

DAVEY: I know that.

JAKE: Do you?

DAVEY: Of course.

JAKE: Do you *know* that?

DAVEY: I know that.

JAKE: Good.

DAVEY: Of course, I know that.

JAKE: Because all I want from life—you hear me?—All I ever want, when they bury me, lay me dead in the ground, and tie a stupid string to *my* finger—you know what I want my grave to say?

DAVEY: I don't think they still tie string/

JAKE: /"He was clear." No bullshit, no confusion. Clear.

DAVEY: Yeah, dude, you're totally clear.

JAKE: That's all I want.

DAVEY: I can see through you, you're so clear.

JAKE: That's all I want.

(Silence.)

DAVEY: It's hard to know though, isn't it?

JAKE: What is?

DAVEY: Who we are or what we truly want.

JAKE: No, it's not. You just choose.

DAVEY: Do you ever wish you had a dippledonger?

JAKE: Doppelgänger.

DAVEY: Like...the one of you that's really you...the *you*-you...and the other one, the one who takes all of the risks, makes the mistakes.

JAKE: The you-*who*.

DAVEY: The one that makes all of the mistakes.

JAKE: What?

DAVEY: That's who.

JAKE: Who what?

DAVEY: The other you.

JAKE: Yeah, the you-*who*.

DAVEY: The one that makes all of the …did we just go into some parallel Abbott and Costello/

JAKE: /You said the *you*-you and I said the you-*who*, who is the other you…the you *who* could make…

DAVEY and JAKE: All the mistakes.

JAKE: Get it?

DAVEY: Got it. The you-you…

JAKE: Yeah.

DAVEY: And the—

LAUREN: —Yoo-hoo, I'm home.

(LAUREN enters her apartment through the stage left arch with a travel bag, having just arrived from the airport. Christmas lights, hung with obligation, illuminate. LAUREN stops and listens for a response. JAKE and DAVEY exit. LAUREN briefly goes out and returns sans bag, now with a glass and a bottle of red wine. She pours. LAUREN puts a hand to her stomach. Something is odd or curious. She toasts.)

LAUREN: Merry fucking Christmas.

(She drinks. She stares out the window. After a moment, VICK enters in a huff.)

VICK: This assignment. My God. The crap they will send me on. Have you been following this? I am an award-winning journalist, for Chrissake. So, this guy— have you been watching the news? Some bum, some homeless guy—or maybe he's not, no one knows—this guy, claims to be the Second Coming of…well, no, he's not claiming it. Everyone *else* is claiming it. *(She briefly exits to remove her jacket.) He's* not saying anything. No one can even find him. You didn't hear about this? It all started like two weeks ago. *(She returns.)* This old lady is walking down Eighth Avenue. Meanwhile, this cop car is giving chase to some criminal…a car chase—in Manhattan—in December. The cars whip onto Eighth, the lady is walking cautiously because of the ice, the first car hits the ice, careens out of control, SMACK, right into grandma. She goes flying like ten feet onto the pavement. Head cracked wide open, blood everywhere. *(Clearly still too warm or too cold or…something, she goes back to change, talking all the while.)* The driver regains control. The cops race after the other car. A group of people converge around the victim, they call 911, they're frantic, "Oh my God, what do we do, blah blah blah." And from out of the crowd comes this youngish looking, attractive or maybe not, white, African American or Hispanic, male with dark hair or wearing a ski cap who may or may not have a beard depending on who you ask—but he's clearly down on his luck, ratty clothes, a bum. *(She returns wearing a colorful robe.)* This guy comes out of the crowd, kneels down by the woman, lays his hand on her head, and— *(She snaps her fingers.)* —she's fine, a little dazed but fine. Then the Miracle Man vanishes somehow—evangelical evanescence—in a crowd of New Yorkers—not a word from him, no one stops him. *And.* Although, we live in an age of palm-sized video recorders, of reality TV home movie bloopers, of cell phone cameras, for the love of God—does anyone get a picture of our hero? NO. They all, all twenty-two of them that stuck around, gave a vaguely similar description, which gave us this. *(She holds a copy of a* New York Times *front-page story—which remains on stage for the entire play—of the "Miracle Man" with an artist's rendering of a nondescript man.)* Who is this? This could be anyone. This could be my accountant brother in Connecticut. But they all claim they have seen a miracle. Maybe, maybe even, the Messiah. Amazing, you say? No. It's ridiculous. I mean, if you ask me, the real miracle is getting twenty-two New Yorkers to believe such a preposterous thing. And he can't be found. No one is coming forward—or rather everyone is coming forward saying they are sure their neighbor is "the Miracle Man," or "Saint Nicholas," or "Captain Christmas" if you work for the *Post.* But you know what it is? It's Prescott, that prick. He's afraid of me. He's afraid and he's determined to sabotage my career and my credibility and take me out of the running for his job, which I am in. So, on some level I have to respect that fat, sweaty troll bastard. But that smarmy creep has a second thing coming, believe you me. I will get his job and run him out of the business and the tri-state area. *(She goes to get a glass and returns.)* And then there's this Armageddon blizzard. You're lucky your plane even made it in. Another hour and no way, baby. Henry is calling for it to be the worst storm in *recorded history.* Of course, Henry doesn't know the first thing about the weather. They only keep him on because he's older than Moses. Prescott, as God is my witness, he's actually moist. His skin has this… it's like his parents hawked up a loogie and christened it. *(She pours a glass of wine.)* Oh, *and,* of the twenty-two people who stuck around and gave their names, half of them are hookers, drug addicts, or criminals themselves. These are

my sources? They're no help. I tried interviewing one guy, who I tracked, I swear to God, into an abandoned warehouse. He couldn't get through an entire sentence without having some kind of *(VICK begins jerking in spasms.)* fit. Oh, which reminds me. *(She goes back to the bedroom to get her phone.)*

LAUREN: The funeral was great, thanks for asking.

VICK: *(To LAUREN from the bedroom.)* What's that? *(Coming back into the room talking on her phone.)* Hey, it's Vicky; call me. *(She hangs up.)* I'm sorry, honey.

(She kisses LAUREN.)

VICK: How was the funeral?

LAUREN: Wonderful. There were clowns and pony rides.

VICK: Did you have cotton candy?

LAUREN: And elephant ears, I won't eat for a week.

VICK: I'm a shit, I'm sorry.

LAUREN: Yes, you are.

VICK: You must be exhausted.

LAUREN: I feel like I've been on a plane all year.

VICK: Well, you have been, pretty much. Why don't you take some time off from the hospital? Don't they owe you some bereavement, for God's sake?

LAUREN: I have to go in tonight.

VICK: It's Christmas Eve.

LAUREN: I told Sarah I'd cover for her. Her daughter's in some Christmas pageant, playing an ox or…

VICK: Lauren, you're exhausted.

LAUREN: I know. I haven't had my period for—I don't even remember how long.

VICK: You're stressed out, honey. Flying back and forth for eight months—

LAUREN: Nine.

VICK: *Nine* months, dealing with your mother, keeping your patient load, it's bound to catch up with you.

LAUREN: Mom didn't even know who we were those last days.

VICK: Who?

LAUREN: What?

VICK: We who?

LAUREN: We who what?

VICK: You said your mother didn't know who "we" were.

LAUREN: Did I? Huh.

VICK: I would have come, Lauren. I'm just not good—

LAUREN and VICK: —with death.

LAUREN: Because I'm great with it. The hours of sobbing—the salt from the tears is a natural exfoliate giving your skin that red, puffy look that's in all the magazines.

(VICK's phone rings.)

VICK: Lover, I'm sorry. *(VICK answers the phone.)* Hey, Maggie, you old dyke. *(To LAUREN.)* It's Maggie. *(Into the phone.)* Well, thank you, Merry Christmas to you. Lauren says Merry— Uh huh…uh huh…oh no…oh no! *(To LAUREN.)* Little Joey got food poisoning at Maggie's mother's house and the next day threw up on Santa at Macy's. *(Into the phone.)* I tell you, Margaret, I do not know why you raise a child in this city. It's unsanitary.

LAUREN: The city or the child?

VICK: Yeah, she just got home. She's a trooper. Of course, I'll tell her. Listen, let me go. I'll call you about New Year's. Yeah, okay, hotstuff, you have a good one. We love you. Give Joey a kiss…after you wipe him down. Uh huh, bye-bye. *(To LAUREN.)* The phone calls, my God. You'd think it was Christmas. Maggie sends her condolences. What were you saying?

LAUREN: I needed you there.

VICK: Where?

LAUREN: Mom's funeral.

VICK: Lauren, God knows I'm sorry about your mother, but I have been extremely busy. And not like "I was washing my hair" busy, I mean— *(Can't find the word.)* Aarg! You've been gone for eight months and/

LAUREN: /Nine.

VICK: Nine, whatever, a long time. You knew it was coming. And you weren't even close to the woman.

LAUREN: Still.

VICK: I can't handle that much… emotion. Besides, most of the time your mother hated me, so my absence was hardly a loss to her. And, sweetie, she didn't much care for you either. And I hate being put in the position where I am supposed to feel or act a certain way and then feel guilty if I don't. *And* I can't look at dead people.

LAUREN: She was cremated.

VICK: …Well… she *was* good at saving space. I'm glad you're back.

LAUREN: Me too.

VICK: Merry Christmas.

LAUREN: Merry Christmas.

VICK: This snow, my God, can you believe it?

LAUREN: What's to believe?

VICK: What happened to global warming?

LAUREN: We'll have to work harder to destroy the planet.

VICK: Oh, speaking of phone calls.

LAUREN: Thought we were talking about snow.

VICK: Who calls me yesterday?

LAUREN: The Pope.

VICK: Barbara fucking Walters.

LAUREN: I was close.

VICK: Wishes me happy holidays and congrats on the orphanage scoop, which Prescott said was human interest fluff.

LAUREN: That actually...I need to tell you some/

VICK: /I'm sorry but this whole thing is just eating me up. This is the second bogus assignment I've had in as many months. Prescott is trying to crucify me, I swear to God.

LAUREN: What if it's true?

VICK: The Miracle Man? Are you kidding? It's not even worth my abilities. The-enlightened-but-crazy-bum-turned-savior-thing is so overdone. What's worse is, I can't win. I look like the bad guy, or worse, the idiot, regardless of how I approach the story. If I discredit him at Christmas time, I look like some typical loud-mouthed atheist cynic, which I am, but still—not a good career move. And if I allude to the possibility that it could be true, then it will look like I believe him,

like I support this nut, and what intelligent person would believe a story like that? I know, I know, why not just be impartial? But come on, that's just not realistic. The whole city is crazy about this. I'm sorry, I don't mean crazy like—

LAUREN: The last thing Mom said to me was that I should have a child.

VICK: ...I take it back, I do mean "crazy."

LAUREN: She was quoting Revelations and speaking in Latin.

VICK: Judith spoke Latin?

LAUREN: No. I mean, yes she *was* speaking Latin but she couldn't before. The cancer spread, it developed into lesions on her temporal lobe.

VICK: Is that bad?

LAUREN: Well...she's dead. She was having hallucinations. She would talk to God.

VICK: Did God talk back?

LAUREN: They had tea together everyday. Apparently, God is a terrible bore. He goes on and on about the Coming.

VICK: Is that a euphemism?

LAUREN: And God talks about His guilt and regret regarding His children.

VICK: So, God is a he?

LAUREN: Well, actually, no, God is an androgynous, iridescent Jell-O mold.

VICK: I knew it.

LAUREN: Mom wouldn't take her medication so when she would have these seizures—she was blissfully happy. I mean, Vicky, you can't imagine her conviction, it was impressive and...enviable. I've never believed anything that much.

VICK: I wonder if all religious zealots really are crazy.

LAUREN: She wasn't… well, okay, she was crazy.

VICK: If you take every religious fanatic—would they all test positive for some neurological or chemical imbalance?

LAUREN: Is true faith only possible—can you only believe in the ethereal when the physical fails?

VICK: Maybe this Miracle Man is reducible to a few synaptic misfires. Ooh, maybe that's my angle.

LAUREN: But is it totally impossible for it to be true? I mean, maybe Mom's visions—the, the lesions gave her sight—that she could see things to which we have become blind.

VICK: Honey, your mother was obviously expressing guilt over her own misguided parenting.

LAUREN: And you said this Miracle Man isn't even the one claiming this event is true.

VICK: No, it's the rest of the city; he's not saying anything.

LAUREN: But isn't that faith? What does it take to believe in something beyond your understanding?

VICK: Apparently, a swift whack to the temples does the trick.

LAUREN: Sometimes, I want so desperately to have religion, to believe in… anything. Part of me was so jealous of my mother. Just to know the sheer bliss of belief—even in a Jell-O mold.

VICK: I think we still have a little fruit cup in the fridge. You wanna…

LAUREN: She spoke Latin.

VICK: How do you know it was Latin?

LAUREN: It was Latin.

VICK: Maybe it wasn't your mother *speaking* Latin but you *hearing* Latin.

LAUREN: That's my point. What if the lesions weren't a manifestation of the cancer spreading but a result of a genetic vulnerability? What if I have a predestined, preprogrammed genetic proclivity to either cancer or, specifically, temporal lobe damage? How would I know if I was hallucinating if I believe what I see to be true? And maybe that doesn't matter. I'd lose my job, my social standing; I'd be an outcast—

VICK: —But happy?

LAUREN: But blissfully happy.

VICK: I'll visit you in the asylum.

LAUREN: Maybe you do have to lose everything before you find yourself.

VICK: If you keep thinking about it, you'll make it happen. Power of suggestion.

LAUREN: Mother would talk about a sensation in her stomach, like riding a roller coaster and that would spread into a warm, tingly feeling over her entire body. Then she would have these spontaneous, intense surges of joy and sadness, confusing and wonderful. And that's how she knew *It* was around.

VICK: God?

LAUREN: God.

VICK: The Jell-O mold?

LAUREN: And she would hear music.

VICK: Like a choir of angels? Harps and eunuchs?

LAUREN: James Brown.

VICK: James Brown?

LAUREN and VICK: The Godfather of Soul.

VICK: A method to her madness.

LAUREN: And that's what scares me, Vick, because lately—lately, I hear music.

(JOHN enters through stage right doorway and crosses to the window.)

VICK: James Brown?

LAUREN: Christmas carols.

VICK: Okay, Lauren, it's Christmas.

LAUREN: No, in my head, I hear Christmas carols, I hear—

(A hotel room. That same night. T, a beautiful young woman wearing headphones, enters. LAUREN and VICK exit.)

T: *(Singing.)* "Santa baby, hurry down the—" *(Removing her headphones.)* Oh, Hi. I hate Christmas but I love Christmas music, is that weird? I'm T.

JOHN: T?

T: T.

JOHN: Like "a cup of"?

T: Like the letter.

JOHN: Does it stand for anything?

T: No. What do you stand for…?

JOHN: John.

T: Right, *John*. Can't beat a classic.

JOHN: How do you mean?

T: You're a "John"…

JOHN: Yes…?

T: Never mind.

JOHN: You look just like your picture in the/

T: /Money before funny.

JOHN: Aren't you afraid I might be a cop?

T: Are you a cop, *John*?

JOHN: No.

T: Didn't think so. It's three hundred for just showing up. Three-fifty if you touch me, four hundred if I touch you.

JOHN: You have beautiful hair.

T: It's fake. Four-fifty if you perform oral on me, five hundred if I perform on you.

JOHN: You have sort of, uh, a bedside manner/issue, or—

T: /Five-fifty if you screw me, six hundred if I screw you and an even thousand for anything involving bodily fluids.

JOHN: I don't usually/

T: /Sure/

JOHN: /Do this. In fact/

T: /It's your first time?

JOHN: You don't believe me?

T: Hey, I'll believe anything you want for the next hour.

JOHN: Is that really an option? You screwing me?

T: It's a surprisingly popular choice. *(Starts to take off her top.)*

JOHN: What if I just want to talk?

T: You're kidding.

JOHN: No, I'm not actually.

T: Dirty?

JOHN: No, just…regular.

T: I don't get it—are you gonna whack off while we talk? Or…

JOHN: No, there's nothing, um… I just want to talk.

T: Is this some Julia Roberts-*Pretty Woman* fetish?

JOHN: No.

T: So, you're not going to buy me things, sweep me off my feet?

JOHN: No.

T: Oh. Then I guess…three hundred. Don't try anything.

JOHN: I won't.

T: I'm serious. I know seven ways to kill you and I won't break a sweat.

JOHN: No one's going to die. How do you know seven ways—what's one of them?

(T nonchalantly pulls out a knife from her backpack.)

JOHN: Oh.

T: *(Takes out an apple from her backpack.)* I was in the Army. Is this what you wanted to talk about, 'cause the meter's runnin'.

JOHN: Yes, no. So… I appreciate you coming…Christmas Eve…in the storm and all.

T: It's my job.

JOHN: Did you take the train or… you were in the Army? I guess not many people ask you to—

T: More often than I'd like. Mind if I sit? *(She does. She pulls another apple out of her backpack.)* Want an apple?

JOHN: No, thank you.

T: It'll make you smart.

JOHN: Said the serpent.

T: Apple a day, keeps the doctor away.

JOHN: I'm not worried about the doctor.

T: Oh, just take the goddamn apple.

JOHN: I, uh, thank you. *(Takes the apple.)* Why don't you like Christmas?

T: *(Carves and eats her apple.)* I'm allergic to tinsel.

JOHN: That's a joke, right?

T: Well, I thought so, but… No, I don't like Christmas.

JOHN: But it's a time of hope and forgiveness, isn't it?

T: Oh, don't get me wrong, it's a brilliant gag. Man has managed to make a buck on everything, what…sacred? Death, religion, sex. Did you know that you can actually hire someone over the Internet to pray for you? Brilliant.

JOHN: I didn't know that.

T: Stick with me, kid, I'll learn ya. I do love the winters, though. The way the cold burns like a lover that's a little rough. I read that somewhere. The snow wipes everything clean and then it melts and you can start all over, be someone new.

JOHN: I wish that were true.

T: It is. Or, it is if you *want* it to be. You just choose. If you choose to believe that a virgin magically gave birth in some stable in the middle of the desert then, hey, why not.

JOHN: There are things I tried very hard to believe didn't happen—but they did.

T: You're not trying hard enough.

JOH-N: What do you believe?

T: I believe that children are our future. Teach them well and let them lead the way.

JOHN: Really?

T: No, man, it's a song. *(Singing.)* "I believe that children are our future. Teach them well and let them hm hm hm…" Hi, where have you been for the last, like, century?

JOHN: Funny you should ask.

T: Did you have your sense of humor surgically removed?

JOHN: It's hard to find things to laugh about.

T: You need to ask Santa for some jokes.

JOHN: You still didn't say why you hate Christmas.

T: I'm actually glad you called.

JOHN: Don't you have family to spend the holidays with?

T: Don't you?

JOHN: No, I don't. Well, not really.

T: Why are you asking so many questions?

JOHN: I think I should get to know you before I spill my guts.

T: Like my mama always said, "Don't spill nothin' you can't wipe up." I think she said that. But I make up memories all the time so…

JOHN: And what does your mother think of your career?

T: I was abandoned by my mother, crack whore slut, and left, literally, on the doorstep of a clinic. Only she was stoned and she didn't realize, or who knows, maybe she did, that she had left me at a veterinarian clinic. It's why I'm such an animal. Growl.

JOHN: My God, is that true?

T: Do you want it to be true?

JOHN: Is it?

T: No, my mother's a librarian on Long Island. I'm a compulsive liar. And you are gullible. How old are you?

JOHN: Older.

T: Than what?

JOHN: Than you would think.

T: I don't know, I think a lot.

JOHN: You, now, you're smarter than—

T: You would think?

JOHN: Sorry.

T: I'm a hooker, not an idiot.

JOHN: So, how old are you?

T: You don't want to know.

JOHN: Would I go to jail?

T: You're hiring a prostitute. Either way…

JOHN: I see your point.

T: Why are you hiring a prostitute to talk to?

JOHN: Why am I hiring a prostitute to talk to?

T: You have an embarrassingly small penis?

JOHN: I do have an embarrassingly small penis.

T: I was kidding.

JOHN: No, it's okay, I do. But that's not why.

T: That's not why?

JOHN: I believe my immortal soul is in peril.

T: …And you *don't* want a blowjob?

JOHN: And I think you were there.

T: I was where?

JOHN: So, really...how old?

T: Seventeen.

JOHN: Seventeen?

T: I'm kidding. I'm twenty-two.

JOHN: It's just that the truth is important to me.

T: Well, how old are you?

JOHN: Older.

T: Lie.

JOHN: I don't want to lie.

T: I told you I'd believe anything you wanted.

JOHN: But you won't tell me anything I can believe?

T: ...I'm twenty-six...going on thirty. The clothes and everything—the hair—makes me look younger.

JOHN: Yes.

T: People will believe pretty much anything you tell them.

(LAUREN and VICK enter.)

JOHN: Will they?

T: And I can charge more if they think I'm younger.

JOHN: Does that mean I get a rebate?

T: Ha.

(She tosses JOHN her backpack.)

T: You kill me.

(T exits, and JOHN follows her, compelled.)

LAUREN: I wanted to kill Mom. I wanted to kill her for being such a bitch all of those years, for being in so much pain, for knowing such joy.

VICK: I want to kill Prescott, that sanctimonious, homophobic...homophobe.

LAUREN: I mean, the level of hate required to kill someone—you've got to *hate* someone to imagine killing them. So, maybe, to have aroused that much hate, passion, to have made that kind of impact...you know? Maybe that could be seen as a *good* thing.

VICK: How long have you been drinking?

LAUREN: Have you ever wanted to kill me?

VICK: No, of course not.

LAUREN: I want to kill you. All the time.

VICK: Welcome home.

(VICK kisses LAUREN.)

LAUREN: Thank you.

VICK: I worked out with the hottest chick at the gym today.

LAUREN: And that's why I want to kill you.

VICK: She's an underwear model or something.

LAUREN: How wonderful for you.

VICK: And *she* approached *me*.

LAUREN: You can die now.

VICK: And she didn't know who I was.

LAUREN: Honey, you're a TV news reporter, not Madonna.

VICK: Oh, now...don't...go...

LAUREN: What?

VICK: All...like...

LAUREN: Yeah, okay, you're going to have to use full sentences.

VICK: You're upset.

LAUREN: I'm not upset.

VICK: Why is it wrong for me to feel good/to feel attractive if a really hot woman comes up to me and asks me to work out?

LAUREN: /It's not "wrong." I just find it interesting that you place so much importance on it.

VICK: It's not like you've never thought about other people. *(She looks out the window.)*

LAUREN: ...Listen/

VICK: /God, look at... there's something in the air, *something*... You're lucky your plane made it in. It's the end of the world out there.

LAUREN: Are you listening?

VICK: Hank called.

LAUREN: ...Hank who?

VICK: Your Hank.

LAUREN: My Hank?

VICK: Yes, you remember, your ex-husband, *Hank*.

LAUREN: When did he call?

VICK: I don't know. Yesterday.

LAUREN: Here?

VICK: Where else would— *Yeah*, here.

LAUREN: What did he want?

VICK: Didn't say.

LAUREN: He didn't say?

VICK: He didn't say.

LAUREN: Did you talk to him?

VICK: He left a message. I don't know.

LAUREN: Did you save it?

VICK: No.

LAUREN: Vicky.

VICK: *Lauren.*

LAUREN: Why do you do things like this?

VICK: Why don't you just call him back? Didn't you see him when you were home?

LAUREN: No. *(Pours herself more wine.)* This wine is horrible. Did you get this? What is this crap? *(Looks at the bottle.)* Australia? They don't make wine in Australia.

VICK: Clearly they do.

LAUREN: Well, not very well.

(LAUREN takes the paper and sits on the "sofa" down right. Silence. VICK playfully slinks over to LAUREN and waits.)

LAUREN: What?

VICK: What?

LAUREN: What?

VICK: *What?*

LAUREN: I'm reading.

VICK: I want to play.

LAUREN: And I want to read.

(LAUREN sees VICK's reaction.)

VICK: I haven't seen you for eight months.

LAUREN: Nine. And it's not like I didn't come home every other week.

VICK: I was going through some old boxes.

LAUREN: Oh?

VICK: Spring cleaning.

LAUREN: It's Christmas.

VICK: And do you know what I found?

LAUREN: I couldn't possibly guess.

VICK: Try.

LAUREN: I don't want to try.

VICK: Come on, guess.

LAUREN: The Ark of the Covenant.

VICK: The first poem you ever wrote me.

LAUREN: I wrote you a poem?

VICK: When we first met.

LAUREN: Huh.

VICK: Listen:
I wash your feet and I believe in hope
Faith in you is my sanctuary from an un-
   certain tomorrow
Your sweat and tears baptize me and I am
   reborn.

LAUREN: …Is that it?

VICK: Isn't it beautiful?

LAUREN: If by "beautiful" you mean "ridiculous," then…

VICK: You wrote this for me when we first met.

LAUREN: Vicky, I was in medical school. I was so high on amphetamines I probably thought I was Gertrude Stein.

VICK: Where did that woman go?

LAUREN: Gertrude Stein? She's dead.

VICK: Who are you?

LAUREN: Can I read please?

(Silence.)

VICK: 'Cause, it's just that we used to have sex all the time and this last year…twice. TWICE. And the second time wasn't even really sex; it was like *(She wiggles.)* and nakedness. And I know you've had your mother and everything but I have needs too.

LAUREN: My mother was on her deathbed. I'm off my cycle. I'm exhausted. I'm—

VICK: But in *addition* to everything else.

LAUREN: What everything else?

VICK: Not wanting to join the gym with me when you said you would.

LAUREN: *Might.*

VICK: Not wanting the dog you said we were going to get.

LAUREN: I don't want a dog.

VICK: You said.

LAUREN: When did I say this, Vicky?

VICK: When we moved in together. You said.

LAUREN: No, Victoria, I never said.

VICK: She said, she said.

LAUREN: Things change, things evolve.

VICK: Who are you? You are like, Lauren's evil twin sent to sabotage our relationship. And you look heavy.

LAUREN: Fine, we'll have sex— I look heavy?

VICK: You've put on weight; you have and don't placate me.

LAUREN: I'm not.

VICK: You are.

LAUREN: I want you. Oh, baby, oh, baby.

VICK: …I could *kill* you for this, you know?

(LAUREN contracts slightly. A sensation.)

VICK: What's wrong?

LAUREN: Nothing.

(*Silence. T and JOHN, with backpack, enter.*)

LAUREN: I did see Hank.

VICK: You did? How often?

LAUREN: Often.

VICK: You lied to me?

LAUREN: I lied to you.

VICK: Why?

LAUREN: Because I had to.

VICK: You had no choice?

LAUREN: Because I chose to.

VICK: Are you screwing around on me?

LAUREN: Vicky.

VICK: Who are you?

T: Why? Do I look like a rookie?

(*LAUREN and VICK exit.*)

JOHN: No. I mean, tonight. Am I your first?

T: Do you want to be my first?

JOHN: I'm just asking. (*Sets down the bag.*)

T: No.

JOHN: How many?

T: You're my second.

JOHN: Was he nice to you?

T: *She* was very nice. Ugly as sin, but nice. So, I lie a little more, tell her she's hot. It's Christmas.

JOHN: Don't you find it hard to lie so much?

T: Well, I'm pathological. I lie so well even I believe half the shit I say is true. Hell, you could be a lie. You might not even exist and I'm really home in bed. But when I fuck someone—and I mean that in the best sense of the word—it is truth, incomparable and pure. All parties want the same thing. This accordance makes lies and pretense unnecessary. Sex is the perfect religion. It's tangible and true.

JOHN: Is there ever love?

T: Come on.

JOHN: What?

T: Come on.

JOHN: *What?*

T: What is love?

JOHN: Love is patient... Love is kind...

T: Love is a battlefield.

JOHN: That's so sad and cynical and *cliché.*

T: You've hired a hooker to "talk to." Cliché, hi? A fuck is a fuck. Call it anything else and you pollute it with the demons of human frailty—ego, expectation, jealousy. Who needs *that?*

JOHN: Still.

T: In a world of deceit and a city of make-believe where everyone tries to be something they're not, it's uncommonly honest.

JOHN: This from a pathological liar?

T: I connect intensely with everyone I meet on an immediate, animal level.

(*JAKE and DAVEY enter.*)

JOHN: Primal.

T: *Primary.* Sex is always first and foremost. It is the impulse that leads to all others.

JOHN: Nevertheless, here *we* are. Two strangers who would otherwise probably never have met, in this moment, in this place. Vulnerable. Connecting. *Not* having sex. Just *talking.*

(T and JOHN exit.)

DAVEY: Why doesn't this guy *talk? (To MAN as if he were deaf.)* Why don't you talk?

JAKE: I dunno, maybe 'cause he's gagged.

DAVEY: But he's not even trying. Wonder what his neighbors think of this guy. You just never know who you're living next to in this city.

JAKE: Lotta weirdos in this city.

(Silence. DAVEY picks up the paper and reads.)

DAVEY: Ommagod. A fourteen-year-old girl didn't know she was pregnant when she gave birth to a baby boy. Claiming she is still a virgin, she got scared and tried to flush, FLUSH, the underdeveloped baby down the toilet.

JAKE: The holidays suck.

DAVEY: And if she was still a virgin… I mean this could have been a patheno-, *patheno-?*—

JAKE: What are you saying? *(To the heavens.)* Why do you hate me? What did I do?

DAVEY: —Partigenisis? Partheno-? Parthenogenesis? *(To MAN.)* Do you have a dictionary? *(To JAKE.)* Parthenogenesis. Virgin birth. Like what's her name, Mary.

JAKE: That's ridiculous.

DAVEY: It's like spontaneous combustion. You don't know anyone that it's happened to but there isn't enough scientific evidence to say it doesn't.

JAKE: You can't give birth spontaneously.

DAVEY: Some insects do. Not spontaneously but… and some frogs or something even change sex to do it.

JAKE: It's frightening. You know just enough information to be a danger and a burden to society.

DAVEY: Hey, what are you going to do with your share of the money?

JAKE: Don't worry about what I'm gonna do with my money.

DAVEY: Is it for your son?

JAKE: Do you not hear well?

DAVEY: Mine's for my mother. She's pretty bad off. Did I tell you? Yeah, and the house smells like ass on account she can't do anything for herself. But I'd like to have a kid someday. What time is it? What do we do if he doesn't call?

JAKE: Why wouldn't he call?

DAVEY: I don't know, maybe something happened. Maybe he changed his mind.

JAKE: He'll call.

DAVEY: Yeah, okay, but what if he doesn't, is all I'm sayin'. What do we do with him?

JAKE: I don't know. *(Beat.)* Kill him, I guess.

DAVEY: *(To MAN.)* Hey… *(To JAKE.)* I'm gonna take his thing off.

JAKE: No.

DAVEY: Come on.

JAKE: No.

DAVEY: If he makes a noise, I'll put it back.

JAKE: Am I not being clear?

DAVEY: *(Like a child.)* Please.

(JAKE relents.)

DAVEY: *(To MAN.)* You'll be good, right? Now…

(DAVEY takes out MAN's gag.)

DAVEY: Don't make any noise. Here's what I'm thinkin'. Being as you are coming from a unique perspective and all… if you had your choice…how would you want to die?

JAKE: He doesn't get a choice.

DAVEY: I'm saying *if* he got his choice, how would he want to go.

JAKE: Why did I agree to take you along on this?

DAVEY: *(Singing.)* "O, holy night, the stars are brightly/"

JAKE: /Davey.

DAVEY: C'mon, man, 'tis the season and shit. Whatchya doin' for Christmas? You and your— what's your son's name?

JAKE: …Abel.

DAVEY: Abel, right. Yeah. Kind of ironic, huh?

JAKE: Ironic?

DAVEY: Yeah, you know?

JAKE: How is it ironic?

DAVEY: Well, his name's Abel but he's not, you know, *able*… 'cause he can't… I mean, he's got…

JAKE: What's he got, Davey? Is it some kind of joke?

DAVEY: No, man, no. I wasn't trying to be funny or nothin'.

JAKE: See that you don't.

DAVEY: It's just— everybody's got something. It's like the whole human race is falling apart, you know? Like one day we'll be like, "Hi, I'm Davey, I'm a Gemini, I'm five-nine, and I have the following shit wrong with me."

JAKE: You don't even know what you're talking about.

DAVEY: *(To MAN.)* What about you? If you were to die by disease, which one would you choose?

JAKE: …See. He thinks you're as stupid as I do.

DAVEY: Don't you even wanna know why we're doing this?

JAKE: He probably knows why we're doing this.

DAVEY: Do you? Maybe we're doing this because we just don't like your stinkin' ass.

JAKE: Why did your mama drop you?

DAVEY: Or maybe we're on, like, a mission from God, man.

(MAN inhales audibly.)

DAVEY: SHUT UP you cocksucking stupid…! *(Raises his fist to MAN.)* One more sound out of you and I will cut off your nuts with a butter knife and stuff 'em down your fuck-stupid mouth.

JAKE: Put the gag back on.

DAVEY: Sorry, dude, but you brought this on yourself.

(He puts the gag back on MAN.)

DAVEY: Give 'em an inch…

(Silence.)

DAVEY: You think when you die you go to heaven?

JAKE: No.

DAVEY: What about reincarnation?

JAKE: No.

DAVEY: Me neither. Why do people always think they were somebody important in a past life? Me? I was probably a shoe salesman.

JAKE: Well, that would be an improvement.

DAVEY: You know what I think?

JAKE: I couldn't possibly imagine.

DAVEY: That it's all just infinite memories, like a huge, what's it called, database.

JAKE: What is?

DAVEY: Past lives.

JAKE: You just said you don't believe in reincarnation.

DAVEY: No, I don't.

JAKE: Don't say you don't if you really do.

DAVEY: I don't.

JAKE: We define ourselves by the choices we make. Be clear.

DAVEY: *(Very clear.)* I don't. But this collective database— you are born, see, with your parents' memories already programmed into your subconscious and subsequently your parents' parents' memories.

JAKE: Then why don't we remember them?

DAVEY: See, that's just it, dude. Maybe we do.

JAKE: We don't.

DAVEY: But *maybe* we do.

JAKE: But we don't.

DAVEY: Maybe that's what we call instinct…or past lives. Or like…when a

child seems to have an uncanny talent… maybe it's not so much that he's a progeny, but somewhere along his/

JAKE: /He might not be a *prodigy*.

DAVEY: That's what I'm saying.

JAKE: No, you said he might not be a *progeny*.

DAVEY: Yeah.

JAKE: Of course he's a progeny. He has to be a progeny. You mean a *prodigy*.

DAVEY: That's what I said.

JAKE: Progeny and prodigy are not the same word, cock-drip.

DAVEY: Like your son, maybe Abel has inherited knowledge or skills or whatever from you or from someone in your family that has reoccurred in the child's brain/

JAKE: /I've got a headache/

DAVEY: /which means that born talent is really just second-hand skill.

JAKE: Shut the shut shut, shitlick. Dead is dead. No second chance. No collective nothin'. You're just dead. That's what makes it such a bitch. *(To MAN.)* Ain't that right, Chatty? *(To DAVEY.)* Besides, even if you were right, which you're not, it would only be a copy of someone else's memory or skill. And a copy is never as good as the original so, either way, it's a completely unreliable source; ergo, it's a limp-dick sucky idea so, I win, you lose and everything once again is copacetic in the universe. And, you bring up my son one more time and I will gut you where you stand. Now, shut up shut up shut up.

(Silence.)

DAVEY: He's not gonna call.

JAKE: He'll call.

DAVEY: Damn, look at that snow. What floor are we on?

JAKE: Fourteen. Get away from/

DAVEY: /Fourteen stories? *(Looks out again.)* That'd kill a guy, huh? If he fell?

JAKE: The fall alone might kill you.

DAVEY: You mean before you hit?

JAKE: The shock.

DAVEY: But if the fall didn't kill you, do you think that there would be, like, a split second where you would feel your body hit?

JAKE: Your bones would probably shatter so fast/

DAVEY: /Yeah, but like the muscle and the fat… the snow…it might be enough to cushion the fall for a second, huh? One second of immaculate agony.

JAKE: I don't know, man.

DAVEY: *(To MAN.)* You must be scared shitless, huh? *(To JAKE.)* Seriously, what do you think he did?

JAKE: That's between him and his maker.

(Silently, tears begin to fall from MAN's eyes.)

DAVEY: Look, he's crying. Why you crying, you little bitch?

JAKE: Just ignore him.

DAVEY: I can't.

JAKE: I was talking to *him*.

(LAUREN and VICK enter.)

DAVEY: Maybe he's already in shock.

JAKE: Maybe.

DAVEY: *(Quietly, intently, scrutinizes his specimen.)* Do you even know who you are?

VICK: I am the woman who loves you, Lauren.

(JAKE and DAVEY exit.)

LAUREN: Really?

VICK: There are only two people in this world that I love.

LAUREN: Yourself—

VICK: And you.

LAUREN: But a distant second.

VICK: I wouldn't say "distant."

LAUREN: Oh, thank you, then what would you say?

VICK: Look, I know second, okay? In my life, I was always second. As a lesbian you feel like a second-class citizen. I was the second child, *vice* president in student council—

LAUREN: You were my first woman.

VICK: But your second spouse. And that's fine, it's fine. I learned long ago to put *myself* first.

LAUREN: I hate that. If you build a partnership, a true partnership, you have to put the other person's needs before your own. And ideally they are putting yours before theirs. And you lean, you support each other. It's a—

VICK: Co-dependency.

LAUREN: Funny, we used to call *that* "love." *(LAUREN experiences a spasm in her belly. She grimaces in confusion, wonderment, and concern.)* Oh.

VICK: What's wrong with you?

LAUREN: I don't know. Nothing.

(Silence.)

VICK: My cameraman committed suicide.

LAUREN: My God, Chris?

VICK: Yeah, he was way too perky. It was bound to catch up with him sooner or later.

LAUREN: What did—*my God*—I'm so sorry, did he leave a note?

VICK: It said, "I have seen too much." Which is poetic and pathetic. He watched it all through his lens for years and it was just too much in the end.

LAUREN: That's horrible.

VICK: I worked with him for, what, almost four years. He commits suicide and I am disturbingly indifferent about it.

LAUREN: You're probably still in shock.

VICK: But it's Christmas time, peace on Earth, goodwill toward men. After 9/11, remember how helpful and kind everyone was to each other? Where did that go? We're right back where we were. Maybe even farther back. There's all this tension. All this withdrawing. It's the end of the world.

LAUREN: Well… and this isn't so much of a judgment, per say…

VICK: Just say it.

LAUREN: You're a TV news reporter.

VICK: I'm a journalist.

LAUREN: You're a *TV news reporter*.

VICK: Your point?

LAUREN: Aren't you really somewhat responsible for all of this?

VICK: I tell the stories that are out there, Lauren. Look around. We are surrounded by death and destruction and human misery, violence and infidelity.

LAUREN: It's sensational. The *news*. It capitalizes on our propensity for fear and guilt.

VICK: Do you think that it's what I *want* to do, the stories I *want* to tell? This country is caught up in this sweeping insanity.

LAUREN: And you sell it like it was a commodity. Our children are damned, our future bleak. The news, the commercials, buy, sell.

VICK: The people tune in. You can look at the numbers. It's what they want.

LAUREN: What do *you* want?

VICK: …I started in journalism to tell the truth, to record in a *journal* the world and its experiences in black and white fact. There was a time when truth was simple.

LAUREN: What happened to that passion?

VICK: It went out the window three promotions ago.

LAUREN: Had to make room for all that ambition.

VICK: You think I've sold out?

LAUREN: I think you're scared.

VICK: Of course, I'm scared.

(JOHN and T enter.)

VICK: Scared I'll lose my job. Scared a bomb will go off in the subway or the plane will crash. Scared you'll leave me. Yes, Lauren, I'm scared.

LAUREN: I'm scared, too.

VICK: …Why can't I make you happy?

LAUREN: I have to tell you something.

VICK: Okay.

LAUREN: And I don't want to fight about it.

T: I love to fight.

LAUREN: I'm pregnant.

T: That's not true. I don't love to fight. But given my life, the military seemed the perfect place to go straight, as it were.

JOHN: I can't believe you were in the Army.

T: Because I'm a woman?

JOHN: I haven't had a very good experience with the military.

T: I loved it. I would have stayed longer. It was during the whole "Don't ask, Don't tell" thing. They forgot to say, "Don't do."

JOHN: Which you did, of course?

T: Of course.

JOHN: And they caught you?

T: Surprise inspection. Which totally sucked. They kept trying to get me to say I was a dyke and I was like, "Hey, I'm not gay," and they're all, "Yeah, but we caught you having sex with a woman," and I'm like, "Yeah, so?" Do you like uniforms?

JOHN: I don't know, maybe.

T: And everyone was doing it.

JOHN: Really?

T: You're in this violent, very male, world. You're being trained to kill; you're all working and sweating together, living together. And there comes a point you've got to either fuck 'em or kill 'em.

JOHN: I never thought of it like that.

T: Let me unravel the secrets of the universe for you.

JOHN: Please, I'm dying to know.

T: Everyone in your life—you either want to fuck them or kill them, am I right?

JOHN: Sometimes both.

T: Yeah. Okay… truth. I did get caught with a woman but… I hate Christmas because while I was in the military I met a man, fell in love, got pregnant. He decided at seven months that he didn't want a kid and on Christmas morning…beat me. To a pulp. I lost the baby and, for a while, my mind. Why am I telling you this?

JOHN: Is that…true?

T: That's the beauty of being a compulsive liar. No one ever really knows if you're telling the truth. What do you believe? Yes. It's true.

JOHN: I'm sorry.

T: (Clutching her stomach.) Ugh. Telling the truth gives me gas. You didn't really just get me here to talk, did you?

JOHN: I need a confessor.

T: For what?

JOHN: My sins.

T: So, it's a Catholic-guilt-freaky-nun-fantasy-thing? It's cool, I've done that.

JOHN: No, it's not… well, maybe *some* of that.

T: Okay, why me?

JOHN: We are both… we've both sold what is most precious of ourselves to people who will never fully understand or appreciate it… we're both whores.

T: But of all the whores in this city…*why me?*

JOHN: You were there.

T: So you said. And where was this?

JOHN: Can I tell you a story?

T: I love stories.

JOHN: I don't think you'll like me much afterward.

T: Who says I like you now?

JOHN: I did something awful.

T: Oh, God, here it comes. Who d'ya kill?

JOHN: No one, although perhaps what I did was worse.

T: What did you do?

JOHN: I abandoned something.

T: ...Like a puppy?

JOHN: Like a child.

T: Your child?

JOHN: I suppose. In a way.

T: It either was or it wasn't.

JOHN: I created it.

T: How romantic. So, you brought this child into the world and then ditched it? You're right, I don't like you.

JOHN: I thought that I was protecting it—*him*, saving him from the world.

T: When did you abandon him—how old was he?

JOHN: Seven. I left him at a shelter.

T: Jesus Christ.

JOHN: Yes.

T: Goddamn, that pisses me off. After what I just told you. It took you seven years to decide, "Gee, I guess I don't want a kid"?

JOHN: It wasn't that simple.

T: No, it is that simple. You made a choice. This is a horrible, scary world. It will either fuck you or kill you.

JOHN: Sometimes both.

T: And you send this helpless child—old enough to realize what is happening to him—into the woods, into the desert—did you visit him? What was his name?

JOHN: Jay—his name was Jay. No, I never visited him.

T: What happened to him?

JOHN: I don't know. Or didn't know.

T: Oh, you know now?

JOHN: I think so.

T: And where was the mother in all of this?

JOHN: She died during childbirth.

T: And you weren't man enough to raise your son?

JOHN: He wasn't exactly *my* son.

T: Well, then what exactly was he?

JOHN: A clone.

VICK: Alright, start from the beginning.

JOHN: In 1970, a team of scientists was brought together by the United States Defense Department. Their goal was the cloning of a human being.

LAUREN: I've decided I'm going to have a baby.

VICK and T: Say what?

JOHN: A clone.

LAUREN: A baby.

VICK: That's funny because I thought you said that you've decided to have a baby.

LAUREN: That's what I said.

JOHN: The government gave these scientists everything they could possibly desire... money, equipment, everything... they were treated like gods. One of the embryologists, Dr. Clarke, decided this clone was his ticket to historical immortality.

VICK: I'm no doctor but I think there's more to it than just *deciding* to have a baby.

JOHN: When you are given freedom from the very law you are working for—federal exemption from moral mandates—I assure you, anything is possible.

T: Why would the government want a clone?

JOHN: Combined with stem cell technology, cloning could provide an end to many diseases, starvation, and, let's face it, there would be countless other economic assets. With their goal clearly laid out before them—their hubris, the force of discovery—Clarke and the others marked a course for conception.

VICK: It's not an act of will. "Oh, I'll have a baby." Poof! A baby.

LAUREN: I'm *going* to have baby.

VICK: I-I-I-I'm, I'm, I'm—

LAUREN: Breathe.

VICK: I'm in shock.

LAUREN: It was my mother's dying wish.

VICK: Your mother prayed to Jell-O.

LAUREN: I've thought this all through.

VICK: No child is going to save us.

LAUREN: "Save us"?

VICK: Lauren, I'm too young to… I could have a brilliant career.

LAUREN: Chasing Miracle Men that don't exist?

VICK: I want to be free to travel. Bangkok. I've never been to Bangkok. I mean, how would/

T: /you clone a human?

LAUREN: The usual way, I guess.

VICK: I'm a little confused.

JOHN: In reproductive cloning, one uses a process called somatic cell nuclear transfer.

LAUREN: Sperm cells surround an egg in the fallopian tube.

T: Yeah, baby.

JOHN: One takes a donor egg and removes the nucleus from it.

T: Yeah, dude, take it.

LAUREN: The sperm releases enzymes that break down the outer membrane.

JOHN: Thus creating an enucleated egg, which is then electrically fused/together—

T: /Fuse it, yeah, that's it.

JOHN: —with DNA from the subject to be cloned.

LAUREN: Once fertilized, the zygote begins the process of cellular division.

T: I am so hot right now.

LAUREN: This blastocyst finds its way to the uterine wall.

VICK: Fine, stop, I get it. Even talking about it makes me queasy.

JOHN: Once the embryo reaches a sustainable stage of development, it is inserted into the host uterus. The first attempt at impregnation was a failure but the second…the second took. When one considers that today, thirty years later, cloning a sheep took two hundred and seventy-six attempts, the fact that this team had a viable fetus after just the second was…miraculous.

VICK: How can you want a child when only a month ago I wanted a dog?

LAUREN: I don't want a dog.

VICK: Good, because a baby would be so much easier to raise.

LAUREN: I'd quit my job.

VICK: Are you drunk?

LAUREN: On hope.

VICK: Is that from a play?! What is that? Lauren, I don't want a child.

LAUREN: I'm having this child with or without you.

JOHN: The success of this child would bring people together, cure disease, end pain. This clone, this child would be the harbinger of—

JOHN and LAUREN: Hope.

VICK: *(Looking out the window.)* It's this blizzard. It's like *The Shining*.

LAUREN: I hope for hope.

VICK: This storm is like this malignant, carnivorous animal.

LAUREN: Hope, hope, hope.

VICK: You can feel it trying to creep through the windows/driving everyone to spontaneous insanity.

LAUREN: /It's one of those words that make you giddier the more you say it. I hope for a greater capacity for hope.

VICK: But what is that? That doesn't do anything. That doesn't *change* anything.

LAUREN: If I can *hope* more, then I will *believe* in more, which will lead to *trusting* more, which is the foundation of love. *I* will become the change.

(VICK shakes her head.)

LAUREN: Make fun if you want.

VICK: You weren't going to tell me about this?

LAUREN: I was going to tell you about this.

VICK: When?

LAUREN: …Now. I want to be a good person.

VICK: You are.

LAUREN: I want to be better.

VICK: Breeding does not make one better.

LAUREN: I want to make a *contribution*.

VICK: I knew you looked heavy.

T: Even in theory, if this is true—

JOHN: It is.

T: What happened to this technology? Why isn't it being done today?

JOHN: There was a…fire…in the lab.

T: Well, of course there was. But why would these scientists agree to do this when every scientific advancement in history has been used as a weapon— you said they *knew!*

JOHN: /But you hope: this time—this time it will be different.

LAUREN: I just feel this urge. The need to settle. To nest.

VICK: What are we? What is this? We *nest.*

LAUREN: It's a calling… like I was meant to do more, *be* more with my life.

VICK: You are a brilliant surgeon.

LAUREN: I'm an astronomically priced tailor to the well-to-do.

VICK: Who are you? *(Inspecting her.)* You've been dealing with your mother's funky *lobe* thing and you've created this psychosomatic—*you're crazy.*

LAUREN: Maybe I am crazy. I have no right to make the money I make, providing health care. *Health care.* Goodwill toward men, my ass. It's extortion.

VICK: It's capitalism.

LAUREN: Capitalizing on human frailty and misery.

VICK: Oh, for the love of God, Lauren, now you sound like *my* mother. And if you are pregnant, why are you drinking so much? Not that I…*care* or…

LAUREN: *(Silence.)* I don't think I'm pregnant.

VICK: What?

LAUREN: I'm not pregnant. But I am trying.

VICK: You're not pregnant?

LAUREN: I needed to see how you would react.

VICK: Oh, thank God. This isn't like you …I can barely breathe…

LAUREN: It wasn't mature, but it was necessary.

VICK: I hate the holidays, I really, really do.

LAUREN: *(Pause.)* I want to hope for the beautiful and the seemingly impossible. Did you know I started playing the lottery? Me. I need to believe that improbable things can happen. So, I play the lottery, building faith. And what is faith really but a commitment to hope. It's hope without the logical affliction of worry. One simply has to let go and say, "I choose to believe—between hope and worry—I choose hope." And if you can do that—that's faith. Or love, which is really the same thing, faith and love. In fact, love, in and of itself, doesn't exist. What we know, or think we know of love, is an amalgam of trust, or faith, and lust. To say "I love you" has little or no impact. To say, "I trust you," which is to say, "I have faith in you," is a far greater proclamation. If you asked anyone on the street, "Whom do you love?"—they could probably rattle off a dozen names. Ask him, "Whom do you *trust*?"—most people are lucky if they could name one. Lust is easy. *You* lust for virtually every other woman you see in the city. But trust? Faith?

VICK: *(Trying to understand.)* …Yeah… Okay, honey, I didn't really get much of that.

LAUREN: Well, how can/I make this any clearer?

VICK: /No, it's, it's totally cool. Hey, it's cool.

LAUREN: I have this—sensation, or—I have to believe that good things can happen with the same dramatic abruptness as violence.

VICK: I've never seen it happen.

LAUREN: But that doesn't mean they don't happen.

(JAKE and DAVEY enter.)

(Silence.)

VICK: So… if you're trying to get pregnant—

LAUREN: Yes?

VICK: Where exactly would you get the, the— *(Makes a swirling motion around her pelvis.)*

LAUREN: —Semen?

VICK: Yes, that. *(Beat, figuring it out.)* Oh…*often.*

LAUREN: What's that?

VICK: You were seeing Hank *often*, you said.

LAUREN: I don't want to fight about this.

VICK: Have you been…? Oh, my God.

DAVEY: *(Reading the newspaper.)* "Two juggernaut black holes," he actually uses the word "juggernaut…"

VICK: Your mother wanted you to have a baby because a Jell-O mold told her you should.

LAUREN: Yes.

DAVEY: "Two juggernaut black holes have been found in the same galaxy and are on a collision course with one another."

VICK: And you think you're going crazy because you hear Christmas carols.

LAUREN: Yes.

DAVEY: "The impact will be so violent that devastating radioactive and gravitational energy will explode in powerful waves from the galaxy's center."

VICK: So, you decided to have a baby you weren't going to tell me about.

LAUREN: Yes.

VICK: And you've been going back and forth, dealing with your mother for eight months—

LAUREN: Nine.

VICK: —But also to fuck your ex-husband.

LAUREN: Yes.

VICK: You're a liar and an adulteress.

LAUREN: Yes.

VICK: You're not crazy; you're a cunt.

LAUREN: I know.

VICK: How am I supposed to feel about this?

(VICK's phone rings.)

LAUREN: Please don't answer that.

VICK: It's work, I have to.

LAUREN: I'm asking you, please don't, not now.

(VICK answers the phone.)

JAKE: Why do you read that crap?

DAVEY: It's amazing.

JAKE: It's a hole. How can it move?

DAVEY: Armageddon is upon us, dude. And this freak blizzard. If these aren't signs then… did you hear about that asteroid that almost hit the Earth?

JAKE: Must have missed that one.

DAVEY: They didn't even see the damn thing until it passed us.

JAKE: Whataya know?

DAVEY: How can you miss a big-ass rock flying through space right at you?

JAKE: You look too far ahead.

VICK: Yes. I'm running out now. Okay. Okay. Yeah, kiss my ass. *(VICK hangs up. She darts back to the bedroom to grab her coat and sweater.)* Goddamn it, this is horrible. The Angel Gabriel, naked except for the C4 strapped to his chest, is holding St. Patrick's hostage demanding that the Miracle Man show himself. *(She stops and looks at LAUREN.)* You demonize me, make me feel like the villain and the whole time… I don't believe… I don't think you should be here when I get… I don't believe…

JAKE: You don't see what's right in front of you.

(VICK is out the door.)

LAUREN: Merry fucking Christmas. *(LAUREN exits.)*

JOHN: Clarke and the scientists—overwhelmed by arrogance and a certain purposeful desire to do good—could not see their folly. The clone, born deaf and dumb, was the poetic offspring of parents who were utterly blind.

T: *(Realizing.)* It was never about the *cloning—*

JOHN: It was about the clone.

T: Who did they clone?

JOHN: Jesus.

T: Jesus?

JOHN: Jesus.

T: Jesus who?

JOHN: Jesus Christ.

T: Like, of Nazareth?

JOHN: Yes.

T: Okay. Okay, I'm not into cults but it's all-good. I don't care if you're a Moonie, a Raelian, or a Republican—just give me the pamphlet and let me/

JOHN: /T, you have to believe me. You must.

T: The United States of America cloned Jesus Christ?

JOHN: Yes.

T: Did JC leave a sample at the sperm bank or…?

JOHN: The scientists discovered that the genetic material they had been working with was taken from blood found on the Shroud of Turin.

T: The shouting turban?

JOHN: The Shroud of Turin.

T: Ah, the Shroud of Turin

JOHN: The cloth used to bury Christ after his crucifixion.

T: The Michelangelo painting thing.

JOHN: Da Vinci, actually. How did you—?

T: History Channel.

JOHN: Right. No, it's real. Well, the one they have now is a fraud but the *original* one—

T: And *why* would they do this?

JOHN: Because if it worked, the clone could be used to discredit every Eastern, non-Christian faith, crippling nations around the world, and the United States would finally, ultimately become "one nation under God." The perfect weapon.

T: What were they going to do? Fire Christ out of a cannon?

JOHN: I know how it sounds.

T: What if it worked and/

JOHN: /It did work/

T: /And he turned out to be just… some…*guy?*

JOHN: They didn't assume it would fail.

T: Christian arrogance. And where is this Messiah clown—

JOHN: Clone.

T: I know what I said—where he is now?

JOHN: Realizing what he had done, Dr. Clarke stole the child from the lab, destroying the research and hid the child, left him at a shelter. Between foster homes, adoption, and running away, Clarke lost track of the clone, of Jay.

T: *(Cautious.)* And what does this have to do with you?

JOHN: T, it is vital that you believe me. To truly forgive me you must believe me.

T: Oh, we're tight, baby.

JOHN: I am that scientist.

T: You are that scientist?

JOHN: I am Dr. John Clarke.

T: Is this some kind of game?

JOHN: Not at all.

T: I tell you about my child—I give you that part of me because—and you dump this load of of/

JOHN: /I would never do that. I've already caused too much pain.

T: Okay, well, this part doesn't take a rocket scientist. If you were this scientist in 1970—whatever—?

JOHN: Yes.

T: That would make you fifty or sixty years old, at least.

JOHN: I'm sixty-seven.

(T laughs hysterically and then, grimly, realizes JOHN doesn't seem to be joking.)

JOHN: I can't explain it. It's beyond comprehension. But it's true. I haven't aged, I don't get sick. It is my punishment, my purgatory for what I've done. Life everlasting. I am immortal.

T: Well, thank you, this has been very entertaining. Why do I get all the freaks? You look great for your age, by the way.

JOHN: I know it sounds incredible.

T: I mean, I've told some great lies in my time, but *you*—

JOHN: I know it's hard to believe.

T: It's pretty easy *not* to believe.

JOHN: You have to. I need you to forgive me.

T: What about the…clone…Jesus, Junior?

JOHN: Jay. J2…actually.

T: If he's your son, your creation, shouldn't *J2* forgive you? I mean, if he's Jesus' twin, he's the guy to do it, right? *(To herself.)* Why am I still here? Why am I having this— If there was a clone of Christ running around, wouldn't somebody know about it?

JOHN: I believe you already do.

T: What do you mean?

JOHN: You were there.

T: *Where?!*

JOHN: I believe this is J2. *(JOHN holds up a picture of the* New York Times *article with the "Miracle Man" sketch.)*

T: Holy—

DAVEY: —Shit.

(DAVEY takes the paper from JOHN.)

JAKE: What?

DAVEY: *(DAVEY looks at MAN and then back to the paper.)* Holy shit.

JAKE: *What?*

DAVEY: "Miracle Man Still At Large."

JAKE: So?

DAVEY: Look at him. He's the Miracle Man.

JAKE: It looks like everyone, Davey.

DAVEY: No, dude, look.

(DAVEY hands JAKE the paper. JAKE reads, looks at MAN, and then back to the paper.)

JAKE: It just *looks* like him.

DAVEY: He's a dead ringer. Dead ringer? Déjà vu. *(To MAN.)* Is this you?

JAKE: So, what if it is the same guy? He's clearly not making any miracles happen tonight.

DAVEY: How do you know?

JAKE: Because he's still tied to a chair, for one.

DAVEY: Maybe he needs his hands free. Or maybe he's so powerful he doesn't need to— maybe he's reading our thoughts— Oh, my God.

JAKE: This is ridiculous.

DAVEY: *(Pointing to the phone.)* But this guy—our guy—the guy who hired us— he must think he's who he says he is.

JAKE: He *who* says who is he?

DAVEY: He, him, who… wait.

JAKE: Never mind, I get it.

DAVEY: Good, 'cause I'm not sure I do.

JAKE: But. If that is the reason. If our guy wanted this guy because he thought he was who he said he was—

DAVEY: Jesus?

JAKE: Then maybe we can ask for more. Hell, we could be famous.

DAVEY: What do you mean?

JAKE: I'm just saying. If our guy… *(Sotto voce.)* If our guy is willing to pay seven for this crackpot, whether he is or he isn't who he says he is, maybe he or someone else is willing to pay more.

DAVEY: Who is he, Jake?

JAKE: Who is who?

DAVEY: The guy, our guy.

JAKE: What did I tell you?

DAVEY: Please, Jake.

JAKE: I was perfectly clear about this.

DAVEY: I gotta know.

JAKE: I told you if you were gonna be part of this you couldn't ask about "the guy."

DAVEY: You have to tell me now.

JAKE: I don't have to do anything.

DAVEY: I'm scared now.

JAKE: If I told you it was the goddamn Roman Catholic Church or the President of the United States, would it make a difference?

DAVEY: Is that who it is?

JAKE: He's a guy who doesn't like a lot of questions, which is fine by me.

DAVEY: But what if this guy is…?

JAKE: Is what?

DAVEY: You know… *(Sotto voce.)* the Second Coming.

JAKE: You're not hearing me. It doesn't matter.

DAVEY: How can it not matter?

JAKE: He hasn't said he is.

DAVEY: It says right here. *(He indicates the paper.)*

JAKE: *He* hasn't said anything to us.

DAVEY: He hasn't said *anything*!

JAKE: Exactly.

DAVEY: Maybe he thinks we have all the evidence we need to make the right decision.

JAKE: And maybe he's a lunatic with delusions of grandeur who's gonna make us very rich. Think, Davey, think. Who gets broken into, tied up, and doesn't say a goddamn word?

DAVEY: He's sorry; he didn't mean to say "goddamn."

JAKE: Davey!

DAVEY: Wait a second.

JAKE: What?

DAVEY: Wait a second. Oh my God.

JAKE: What?

DAVEY: How much was he sold out for?

JAKE: Who?

DAVEY: Jesus, in the Bible, how much?

JAKE: I don't remember.

DAVEY: Wasn't it like thirty silver pieces or something?

JAKE: What's your point?

DAVEY: How much are we being paid?

JAKE: A little more.

DAVEY: Yeah, okay, but with inflation and the exchange rate—

JAKE: Don't lose your shit on me.

DAVEY: Then Judas exploded and his insides fell out.

JAKE: Fine. Leave.

DAVEY: I don't want my insides to fall out.

JAKE: Then go. I'll take the whole roll. What would your mother do then?

DAVEY: Don't do that to me, Jake.

JAKE: Did you believe this Miracle Man crap before today?

T: No, I don't believe it. I'm sorry, I didn't see what everyone else saw that night. The old lady *wasn't* hit that hard, there *wasn't* blood everywhere, and no one performed any miracles. And that is the truth. Is this what all of this is about? How did you find me?

JOHN: You were in the paper. I saw your picture and then I saw your ad in the— I read the interview.

T: Wow, I'm sorry, bud, but it ain't true.

JOHN: But the *interview*, you said—

T: That stupid reporter only used about half of what I said and edited it to look like I agreed with everyone else. Which I totally respect because I do that every day.

JOHN: Why, why would he do that?

T: Because people are desperate. No one wants to *not* believe it.

JOHN: But there's me.

T: Just to play along, assuming all of this was true—

JOHN: It is.

T: Your cells repair, reproduce or whatever, faster. So does cancer.

JOHN: It's not a cancer.

T: You're a scientist.

JOHN: Yes.

T: Have you researched every possible explanation? Or did you just *want* to believe this?

JOHN: What about faith? Some things require/

T: /Did you exhaust every other/

JOHN: /No, probably not.

T: Besides…assuming this clone is the real deal, you know what the world will do with it?

JOHN: What?

T: Fuck it or kill it.

JOHN: But what if he can save the world? *What if?*

T: If they believe it, they'll fuck it. If they don't…

JOHN: Or sometimes both.

T: Or sometimes both.

JOHN: God, what have I done?

T: You're sweet. You're crazy but you're sweet.

JOHN: You think I'm crazy?

T: I think… *(Looks at her watch.)* I think your time's up.

JOHN: You don't believe me?

T: You're cute. We should have fucked.

JOHN: I need you to believe me.

T: You know, that picture, the Miracle Man, it kinda looks like you, too, you know?

(JOHN and T exit.)

JAKE: It looks like everyone, that's why it's such a scam.

DAVEY: Think, think, think.

JAKE: Why would God choose New York to stage his comeback? And, if he is Christ, why would he hide? Why would he live *here*? And why *him*? Just look at him.

(They do.)

DAVEY: I don't know. I just feel… *(Feels the air around him.)*

JAKE: It's just a job.

DAVEY: What if he has a family? Jesus had a brother, didn't he?

JAKE: Where are the pictures? No pictures, no letters…no phone—the son of a bitch doesn't even have a phone.

DAVEY: *(Growing desperate.)* Where's your phone, dude?

JAKE: He doesn't have a phone. And do you know why he doesn't have a phone?

DAVEY: Why?

JAKE: Because he's a wing nut!

DAVEY: But how did people in the Bible know? They had to make a choice, right? How would we know now?

JAKE: You're making a leap of faith. And do you know what happens to people who make leaps of faith?

DAVEY: What?

JAKE: They end up living in deserts, Davey. Do you want to live in a desert?

DAVEY: No.

JAKE: Jesus was just a great con man with a few sleight-of-hand tricks, some major ballsy boasts, and, *and*, here's the really important part, an ability to capitalize on man's fear of the unknown. Fear and guilt are always stronger than faith and hope. But let's assume all of it was true. What has *our* guy done? Nothing.

DAVEY: Well, let's give him a chance. *(To MAN.)* I'm gonna get you… hold on. *(Goes to the kitchen.)* Dude, you really don't have to shit in here.

JAKE: *(To MAN.)* Do you see what you're doing? The trouble you're causing?

DAVEY: *(Coming back in with a glass of water, a half loaf of moldy bread, and frozen fish sticks.)* Okay, God, your choice.

JAKE: What is that?

DAVEY: You know.

JAKE: What?

DAVEY: Water to wine…the bread…fish.

JAKE: Those are fish sticks, Davey.

DAVEY: Yeah.

JAKE: What is he supposed to do with fish sticks?

DAVEY: Make more, I guess.

JAKE: Case in point, Davey, why does our King of Kings have fish sticks?

DAVEY: The guy's gotta eat.

JAKE: *(To MAN.)* Well? Let's see your stuff.

(Silence. They watch MAN, who does nothing.)

DAVEY: Maybe he needs his hands free.

JAKE: Oh, for the love of… fine.

(DAVEY unties MAN.)

DAVEY: Don't let me down, please.

(They wait. MAN sits perfectly motionless.)

JAKE: Satisfied?

DAVEY: Well, he's not a clown, Jake. God doesn't have to do tricks.

JAKE: Yeah, he does, Davey. After all he's done or let be done to this world, he better pull rabbits out of his ass.

DAVEY: It still could be true. That's what faith is, right? What time is it?

(Silence.)

DAVEY: Come on, Jake, what time? He was supposed to call at eleven, right? It's gotta be after midnight.

JAKE: *(Checks his watch.)* Yeah, so?

DAVEY: It's Christmas. Oh Jesus… It's his birthday!

JAKE: Just relax.

DAVEY: This is a total cosmic mind fuck.

JAKE: Breathe, Davey.

DAVEY: Man, my head's all full and tight. Like my brain is getting a boner.

JAKE: I'm about to starve.

DAVEY: Crucifixion.

JAKE: What?

DAVEY: That would be the worst. Spikes being hammered into your hands and feet—hearing the sound of bones cracking. You'd probably have to hold onto the spikes just to hold yourself up on the cross. *(To MAN.)* Did you? Did you have to hold yourself up?

JAKE: HE WASN'T THERE! …Go down to the Bodega at the corner and get me something to eat.

DAVEY: It's a blizzard.

JAKE: They're plowing the streets.

DAVEY: *(Going to the window.)* You can't see anything, it's completely white.

JAKE: Just go, Davey.

DAVEY: It's Christmas, nothing's open.

JAKE: They had a sign, they're open.

DAVEY: Why don't you go down?

JAKE: Davey, I have passed hungry and gone to stark raving famished. I'm getting a little dizzy and it's making me crazy. Now before I flip out, go and get me a sandwich.

DAVEY: Why don't we just eat his fish sticks or Pop Tarts?

JAKE: Davey.

DAVEY: What about Jesus?

JAKE: Stop calling him that.

DAVEY: Well, what about him?

JAKE: We'll be fine.

DAVEY: What if he calls?

JAKE: I won't do anything until you get back.

DAVEY: Promise?

JAKE: Trust me.

DAVEY: Alright. Jesus, you want anything?

JAKE: GO!

(DAVEY grabs his coat and leaves.)

JAKE: Jesus Christ. Jesus Christ. I don't mind telling you I think you're full of shit. Come on, con to con; tell me I'm right. I mean, even if you are the Second Coming, you're full of shit, so either way, I don't care. *(JAKE takes the food back to the kitchen. He returns.)* I want to show you something. *(Takes out his wallet and shows MAN the pictures in it.)* Take a look. That's my son, Abel. This was taken last year on his seventh birthday. We went to Coney Island. Cute, huh. He's got his mother's eyes… that bitch. And do you know what that is?

(JAKE points to the photo. MAN looks at JAKE. MAN's eyes are soft.)

JAKE: Oh, I don't want your pity, you creepy silent faggot, I want the money your ass is gonna bring. Because that money is my son's second chance—the chance that you or God or Buddha—took from him. So, you can understand if I'm a little peeved with the landlord upstairs. And not you or Allah or that *(Points out to the door from which DAVEY left.)* jackass cheerleader you've got is going to SCREW THIS UP! 'Cause I've been screwed by God all of my life.

(Silence.)

JAKE: God, I'm hungry.

(Silence.)

JAKE: You know… *(Laughs.)* Maybe—maybe I should screw you. Would you like that? Maybe I should screw God the way you've screwed me all my life. I bet you'd like that. I'll fuck you and then kill you.

(JAKE lunges for MAN and grabs him violently off the chair.)

JAKE: Why don't you say anything?!

(DAVEY returns.)

DAVEY: Hey, HEY, Jake, what the hell're you doing?

JAKE: Where's my food, Davey?

DAVEY: The elevator's broke.

JAKE: It was working when we came up.

DAVEY: Well, it's broke now.

JAKE: Then take the stairs.

DAVEY: What are you doing, Jake?

JAKE: Get me my food, Davey.

DAVEY: I'm not taking the stairs.

JAKE: Take the stairs, Davey.

DAVEY: It's fourteen floors.

JAKE: TAKE THE STAIRS AND GET ME MY—

(The cell phone rings. No one moves for a moment. Finally, both JAKE and DAVEY dive for the phone. DAVEY gets it but does not answer it.)

JAKE: Give me the phone, Davey.

DAVEY: What we're doing, it's not right.

JAKE: Give me the phone or so help me I'll shoot you both.

DAVEY: You'd shoot me, Jake?

JAKE: GIVE ME THE GODDAMN PHONE!

(Another ring. DAVEY gives JAKE the phone. He answers it.)

JAKE: Yeah? Yes, sir. Uh, huh. No, no sir he hasn't… no, he hasn't said a word. *(Silence.)* I see. No… no, sir, we don't have a problem with that. What should, uh… what should the note say? *(He scurries for a pen and paper.)* Just a… *(He finds pen and paper.)* Okay. *(In silence, he writes.)* Yeah, yeah I got it. Should he write it? No, I guess it wouldn't matter. Now uh… right, I understand… but the thing is, see…the thing is, we were talking and we were thinking we should get, uh, get more. Well, on account that we saw the article… in the paper… it's not? I see. Well, it's just that… yes, sir. Yes, sir. Yes, sir. *(Hangs up.)*

(Silence.)

DAVEY: Well? What did he say?

JAKE: Now listen to me very carefully.

DAVEY: Yeah?

JAKE: I want to be very clear on this.

DAVEY: Okay.

JAKE: I'm going to tell you what we're going to do—

DAVEY: Okay.

JAKE: And there's not going to be a discussion—

DAVEY: Okay.

JAKE: And then we're going to do it.

DAVEY: …Okay.

JAKE: Okay?

DAVEY: Okay. So, what what what does he want us to do?

JAKE: Like we said, like we thought.

DAVEY: That he's Jesus and we should let him go?

JAKE: No, Davey, no. He's not Jesus. He's just a guy.

DAVEY: But he might be.

JAKE: No, Davey, our guy says he's not.

DAVEY: How does he know?

JAKE: If we want the money we have to do this.

DAVEY: What…what…what?

JAKE: We forge this suicide note/

DAVEY: /Oh, God/

JAKE: /We forge this suicide note and throw him out the window.

DAVEY: I can't, I can't, Jake.

JAKE: Davey.

DAVEY: I can't, Jake, you do it. You take the money.

JAKE: Davey, if you don't do this… Davey, you have to do this.

DAVEY: I'm too scared, I can't.

JAKE: If you don't I'll have to kill you, too.

(Silence.)

JAKE: And then what would your mother do?

DAVEY: You'd do that?

JAKE: You're either part of the solution or part of the problem.

(JOHN and T enter.)

DAVEY: You'd kill me?

JAKE: I don't have a choice.

DAVEY: Of course you do.

JOHN: I can prove it.

T: Prove what?

JAKE: We do this now, Davey.

DAVEY: Maybe there's another way.

JOHN: I can prove what I've said. (Quickly rummages through T's backpack.)

T: You've said a lot, which part? What the hell are you doing?

JAKE: I was clear on this, Davey, there is no discussion.

DAVEY: Please God tell me what to do.

JOHN: (Pulls out the knife from T's backpack.) This part.

T: Oh, God, I hate Christmas.

JAKE: Are you in or out?

DAVEY: I'm just conflicted—

JOHN: Stab me.

T: Whatever this is, I'm not into it.

JAKE: In or out?

DAVEY: —'Cause this could be a really—

JOHN: Take it.

T: This is a lie, it's not happening.

JOHN: Do it.

T: You need help.

(T makes a move for the door. JOHN stops her.)

T: Get out of my way.

JOHN: You won't hurt me.

T: If you don't get out of my way, I will hurt you.

JAKE: In or out?

DAVEY: —I mean, we're talking about the most significant—

JAKE: (Points his gun at DAVEY.) IN OR OUT? I won't ask again.

DAVEY: Wait a second, I just have to figure it out.

JAKE: Grab his feet.

JOHN: Do it.

T: No.

JAKE: Davey, grab his feet or I swear to God I'll kill you.

JOHN: Do it.

T: Please stop, you're scaring me.

JOHN: Grab the knife.

JAKE: Grab his feet.

T: No, please, HELP!

JOHN: Do it. Do it. DO IT!

DAVEY: No, I can't, I won't, I won't do it. That's my choice.

JAKE: Fine.

JOHN: NOW!

(Simultaneously, JOHN grabs T's hand, pulls it to the knife, and plunges it into his side as JAKE shoots DAVEY. DAVEY dies. T screams and runs out the door. JOHN falls to his knees, reaching for T. JAKE grabs MAN by the shirt and drags him into the bedroom. There is the sound of a window opening, followed by the sound of impact of MAN's fallen body on the snowy ground below. Finally, JAKE re-emerges from the bedroom. Lights fade to black. The furniture and props are quickly cleared. Lights up to reveal MAN, lying akimbo and silent in the snow, and ACTORS 1, 2, and 3 on the periphery.)

ACTOR 2 (JOHN): Christmas morning.

ACTOR 1 (JAKE): New York City.

ACTOR 3 (DAVEY): A city gone insane.

ACTOR 1 (JAKE): The worst blizzard in recorded history.

ACTOR 2 (JOHN): A man lies shivering and injured on the ground.

(T, frantic and freezing, comes upon MAN.)

T: HELP! Sir?

ACTOR 3 (DAVEY): A nearby hospital.

(VICK and LAUREN enter.)

VICK: What the hell is going on here?

LAUREN: *(With a flashlight.)* We've lost main power. The generators are barely working. The phones are down.

VICK: They're rioting; the whole city has lost its mind.

LAUREN: Yeah, and they're all coming here. Why are you here?

VICK: I want to kill you.

LAUREN: I'm a little busy. How about next week?

VICK: So, you're a comedian and a whore?

LAUREN: Don't worry, I won't be coming home.

VICK: That's not what I want.

LAUREN: It's the story of a lifetime out there. Shouldn't you be covering it?

VICK: Not anymore.

LAUREN: Your angel blow himself up?

VICK: I didn't go.

LAUREN: *(To a NURSE offstage.)* Where are you going with them? You can't— *(To VICK.)* Look, I know we need to talk but I can't— *(Her belly cramps. She tries to hide it.)* You're going to have to— *(It cramps again.)*

VICK: Lauren?

T: *(To MAN.)* Sir?

VICK: Are you okay?

T: Oh my God, you're— What happened to you?

LAUREN: Just leave me alone.

T: What the hell is going on tonight? Let me help you.

(MAN, semiconscious, recoils from T.)

LAUREN: I don't need anyone's help.

T and VICK: Trust me.

T: I'll call an ambulance. *(T takes out her cell phone.)* God, I hate Christmas.

LAUREN: I didn't think you wanted to see me again.

VICK: I don't *want* to.

T: Damn. The storm's interfering… Come on, we'll take my car.

(*T lifts MAN into her arms, which causes him great pain.*)

T: Sorry. I'm sorry.

(*MAN gathers himself, and they leave.*)

VICK: We have to deal with this.

LAUREN: Vicky, it's a madhouse. I can't deal with/

VICK: /No no no. No.

LAUREN: Why aren't you covering this? The world's falling apart.

VICK: We're falling apart.

LAUREN: We're hardly newsworthy.

VICK: You're not getting away from me.

LAUREN: You're only chasing because I'm running away.

VICK: Then stop running.

LAUREN: We want different things.

VICK: All of this is about a baby?

LAUREN: Yes. No. Yes and no.

VICK: You cheated on me. All your talk of trust and faith. I've never screwed around on you. Ever. So, why do I feel like the bad guy?

LAUREN: There are no good guys or bad guys. Miracles don't happen anymore. You proved that to me. Look at it. The world is shit. It's just real people making real mistakes and trying to find a little peace and hope. That's what I wanted this Christmas, Vick, and, God love you, you can't give that to me.

VICK: Oh, get off the cross.

LAUREN: Excuse me?

VICK: People stone martyrs, Lauren. It's not a productive occupation. I'm doing my best. I'm invested in this. And I'm certainly not going to lose you to some man. A *man*, Lauren. And your ex-husband to boot.

LAUREN: This isn't about men or women or who screws who.

VICK: You want hope, you want a miracle? *We* are a miracle. The fact that two people can find each other in this world *is* a miracle. Yes, we have problems, everyone has problems, everybody's screwed up. But I love you. I want to grow old with you. The thought of not having your arm around me as I sleep or never again waking up to the smell of you in the morning terrifies me. What would I do without the sound of your keys at my door?

LAUREN: Our door.

VICK: *Our* door.

LAUREN: What about Hank?

VICK: I'm still considering killing you.

LAUREN: This would be the place to do it.

VICK: I'm not condoning this in any way but—my mother cheated on my father and they got through it. Your father cheated on your mother—and I'm not sure you can blame the guy—but they worked through it. People make mistakes. I forgive you. What could be more divine than forgiveness?

LAUREN: What am I supposed to do with that?

VICK: You're supposed to beg me for a second chance.

LAUREN: A second chance?

VICK: And then I'll be pissed off and you'll bring me flowers and I'll look into your eyes and know that, even though we're both selfish bitches, I never want to spend a day without you.

LAUREN: And what about a baby?

(T enters dragging an unconscious MAN behind her.)

T: Help, I need help!

LAUREN: *(To T.)* Put him down. *(To VICK.)* Vicky, you're going to have to leave.

VICK: I'm not leaving without you.

T: I think he's dead.

VICK: Okay, I'm leaving.

LAUREN: Put him down.

T: On the ground?

LAUREN: We don't have a bed. Or power.

T: You don't have power?

LAUREN: Put him down.

(T does. LAUREN crouches next to MAN.)

LAUREN: What's his name?

T: I don't know, Miracle Man, I guess.

LAUREN: What? *(To MAN.)* Sir? SIR!?

VICK: *(Beginning to recognize MAN.)* Oh, my God.

LAUREN: *(To T.)* What happened?

T: I don't know, I just found him. And I think I killed someone, or not, maybe I made up the whole thing, he said he was immortal and he made me do it.

VICK: *(To MAN.)* Oh, my God.

T: I know, but he made me. *And* he didn't pay me!

LAUREN: Did you call an ambulance? The police?

T: I don't know, I don't know, I didn't know what to do—

VICK: *(To MAN.)* What happened to you?

T: *(Frantic.)* —I couldn't, the storm, I drove.

LAUREN: You shouldn't be driving in this storm.

T: It's just snow! For God's sake, he needs a doctor.

LAUREN: Just calm down.

VICK: *(To MAN.)* Did someone do this to you? *(To T.)* Why isn't he talking?

LAUREN: Vicky leave.

VICK: *(To T.)* Are you sure this is the Miracle Man?

T: *(To VICK.)* NO, for God's sake, I'm not sure of anything!

VICK: *(To MAN.)* Hey, will you give me an exclusive?

LAUREN: *(To offstage.)* I need some help here.

VICK: *(To T.)* Why won't he say anything?

T: He needs a doctor!

LAUREN: I am a doctor. Stop yelling.

T: Okay!

LAUREN: He's not breathing. I can't find a pulse. Where the hell is— I need some help over here!

(Suddenly, MAN's eyes open, he stiffens and sits up part-way. LAUREN inhales with a

mixture of ecstasy and trepidation. With tre-
mendous effort, MAN speaks. It is barely
audible.)

MAN: There…is…hope.

(LAUREN exhales. MAN dies. Moment of
silence.)

VICK: There is ho?

T: What did he say?

VICK: I think he said, "There is ho."

LAUREN: (Quietly.) Help. Someone?

T: Was he calling me a ho?

VICK: There is ho?

T: Is he dead? 'Cause if not I'll kill him.

LAUREN: He said, "There is ho—"
(Spasm.) —Oh.

VICK: Lauren? Honey, are you—

LAUREN: (Wincing in pain. Or is it surprise? Or joy?) Oh…God.

VICK: Lauren?

ACTOR 1 (JAKE): It came upon a midnight clear.

ACTOR 2 (JOHN): Yet with the woes of
sin and strife the world has suffered long—

LAUREN: Something's not… I think
something's—

VICK: What is it? Are you sick?

T: Doctor, do you need a doctor?

ACTOR 1 (JAKE): Beneath the angel-strain
have rolled two thousand years of wrong.

ACTOR 3 (DAVEY): Pa rum pum pum
pum.

LAUREN: I don't believe this.

VICK: Believe what?

LAUREN: (Wincing.) Oh, God.

T: Help!

ACTOR 1 (JAKE): And man at war/with
man, hears not—

ACTOR 2 (JOHN): /Said the king to the
people ev'rywhere—

ACTOR 3 (DAVEY): The love song,
which they bring—

ACTOR 2 (JOHN): —Pray for peace,
people ev'rywhere—

ACTOR 3 (DAVEY): O, hush the noise,
ye men of strife—

LAUREN: I think I'm having a—

VICK: Having a?

T: Having a?

LAUREN: Having a—

ACTORS 1, 2, 3: And hear the angels
sing.

LAUREN: Jesus Christ, I'm having a
baby!

(Lights out except for a spot on DAVEY.)

ACTOR 3 (DAVEY): Pa rum pum pum
pum.

(Blackout.)

(END OF PLAY.)

BULL SPEARS

Josh Chambers

JOSH CHAMBERS, co-artistic director of Fovea Floods Theater, is a director, composer, playwright, and actor. During the past eight years, he has directed twenty productions with the company, including *Edmond, The Bitter Tears of Petra Von Kant, Jungle of Cities*, and *Dollbody* (Atlantic Theatre Studio, New York City); *Goose/Goose, A Party for Boris, Tunnel*, and *Baal* (Proctors' Too, Schenectady, New York); *Paul Pry* (Saratoga Stages, Saratoga Springs, New York); *Mount Weather* (DC Arts Center, Washington, D.C.); and *The Resistible Rise of Arturo Ui* (Ontological-Hysteric Theatre, New York City). In 1999, Chambers co-wrote and directed *A Sleep of Reason Creates Monsters* with Scott Feldsher for the first Chekhov Now Festival in New York. His composing credits include *US Highway Love Slaves Pt. III – South of Heaven* with Sledgehammer Theatre in San Diego; *The Butterfly's Evil Spell, The Madwoman of Chaillot*, and *Vinegar Tom*, all directed by Alma Becker for Skidmore College; and the world premieres of Erik Ehn's *Imp of Simplicity* and *Book of Tink*. Other composing credits include *Mary/Mary*, a feature film now in festivals across the United States; Amanda Maddock's *Timepiece, Thursday's Child*, and *Your Birthday Slumber Party*; Noel Allain's *Wolfbrow*; and *The Body Snatcher*, co-written with Peter Maradudin and Scott Feldsher. Chambers holds a BS in theatre from Skidmore, where he was a Filene Music Scholar in classical guitar. He splits his time between New York City and Los Angeles.

Bull Spears was first presented in its entirety by Fovea Floods Theater (Josh Chambers and Timothy Fannon, Co-Artistic Directors) on August 7, 2004, at the La Tea Theater in the Clemente Solo Velez Cultural Center, New York City, with the following cast and credits:

Acting Ensemble: Noel Allain, Linsey Bostwick, Timothy Fannon, Justin Fayne, Richard Hawk, Sue Kessler, Rebecca Marzalek-Kelly, Cate Owren, Jane Pickett, Will Schmerge

Directed and Composed by: Josh Chambers
Assistant Director/Stage Manager: Ramona Fantino
Lighting and Video Design: Jared Klein
Sound Design and Technical Direction: Jay Maury
Scenic Design: Sue Kessler
Costume Design: Leah Piehl
Choreography: Fovea Floods

Special thanks to: Janet Simone for appearing in our workshop presentation of Act I in August 2003, Anna Owren for her cameo appearance in our video sequences, and all Fovea Floods' supporters and friends.

Original music is integral to this production and may be obtained by contacting the playwright at evilbbc@yahoo.com.

Some of the material in Act III is based on the writings of the Marquis De Sade.

I'd like to thank Fovea Floods more than anything—for being my reason to persevere in life and theatre.

> *Peer into this handsome corpse*
> *And see the scars between*
> *His left ear and his spleen*
> *His mighty mighty heart*
> *Connect them all*
> *And find a line*
> *That weaves itself inside*
>
> *Entangles him in our memory*
> *We chose this man to fight*
> *Peer into his handsome corpse*
> *And see into his eyes*
> *Ride into the night*
> *Prepare this child to fight!*

> —Robert Pollard, Guided By Voices

AUTHOR'S NOTE

Bull Spears is an exploration of the Western as the mythological center of American culture. It is the fourth in a series of "silent films for the stage" that I have created with my company, Fovea Floods, over a period of seven years.

There are no rules to this text. I encourage potential directors and producers of this work to avail themselves of all means of communication and theatrics to get the play across in the most vivid and anarchic terms possible. I advocate blasphemy, sabotage, and critique in both the reading and the staging of this play.

EDITOR'S NOTE

Bull Spears, as you will discover, contains practically no dialogue; it's a composition incorporating meticulous movement performed by live actors, a continuous original score, songs, titles (in the manner of a silent film), videos, and diverse other multimedia elements. We've tried to create a coherent text here to convey the piece as clearly and directly as possible. But it occurs to me that readers may want to know a little more about how *Bull Spears* actually looked, sounded, and felt in the theatre.

The short answer is that it felt different from anything I've ever experienced in several decades of theatre-going. Each of the three acts was staged in a different style; reference to three film directors will provide, I think, a kind of shorthand to the tone and pacing of each. Act I, set in the Saddle Wound Saloon, felt like a burlesque (in the parodic sense) of Sam Peckinpah; Act II, on Stab Mountain, conjured an ethereal/surreal landscape à la Terry Gilliam; and the third act, in debauched Knife City, channeled late Pasolini.

The music, all composed by Chambers, never stopped; movement and choreography were meticulously and painstakingly synchronized to it. The videos, all black and white, looked like old-fashioned 10mm films. The stage sets and costumes, on the other hand were explosively rich in color and detail. All of the live action was stylized (no real blood, no nudity, etc.).

Hopefully, this will help fix some of what you are about to read more precisely in your mind's eye.

Then let your imagination run wild.

VIDEO #1
Pre-Show

This video plays as the audience enters the space. It is a silent black-and-white film about fifteen minutes in length, with spare piano scoring. A single long shot of a small wooden schoolhouse situated in the middle of a huge country field is used throughout with various images cut into it.

Small CHILDREN are seen walking through the field to the schoolhouse. They come in groups: first two little GIRLS are seen skipping through the field, jump ropes and books in hand. Second, a lone shy-looking BOY makes his way through the field, "mowing" the long grass with his book belt. Third, a group of three ROUGH BOYS are pushing each other and wrestling. They overtake the SHY BOY and knock his books out of his hands. Fourth, two SISTERS, hand in hand, approach the schoolhouse. The littlest SISTER stops halfway to inspect a birdhouse in the middle of the field, and they continue on.

Lastly, a WOMAN wearing a long dress and large bonnet enters the frame. She turns and looks directly into the camera for several moments and then continues through the field toward the school.

The first image that is cut into the film is an image of the two SISTERS walking past an ominous-looking barn. After they pass, a well-tailored ARM appears from within the shadows of the barn and gestures flamboyantly with a handkerchief.

The second image is of one of the rough boys sitting on the front porch of the schoolhouse wearing a dunce cap.

The third image is of the three ROUGH BOYS staring out to the horizon. They put on cowboy hats in unison.

NOTES: These three images should be cut in at five-minute intervals. Also, in terms of casting, costume, and video direction, it is important to understand that, in the video sequences, the CHILDREN represent actual characters introduced later in the play. The purpose of the video is to show the history and tragedy of the town of Bull Spears in a folkloric, "cause-and-effect" context. Therefore, the oldest sister grows up to be MILKY HILLS, the shy boy is ONE PUMP, the three rough boys are HORSE DICK, PONY COCK, and HOG ROD, the teacher with the bonnet is THE BONNET, and the well-tailored arm with the handkerchief is THE ROUÉ. Great care should be taken to make sure these identities remain clear and consistent throughout.

ACT I
Saloon

NOTE: At the beginning of each act, there is a series of video "mug shots" that introduce iconic images of each character. These images are accompanied by a VOICEOVER that provides information about the character's function/history. Also, all scene titles and voiceover text are projected on video monitors in PowerPoint format. This text (shown in this font*) is usually triggered by the action of the TELEGRAPH OPERATOR operating the telegraph. Any additional text from the script can also be included in the PowerPoint if it is needed to clarify or intensify the action.*

DRAMATIS PERSONAE:

<u>CUD BREATH</u>—Telegraph Operator. Keeps the Story in Motion. Fond of Hats.

<u>MILKY HILLS</u>—Voluptuous Barmaid. Owner of the Saloon and Baroness of the Bughouse. Tits out to Here.

CLOVER TWAT—The Spiritual Center of Bull Spears. Sells Flowers, Prays, and Attempts Difficult Yoga. Invented the "Four-Dicked Pilgrim" as a Religious Sacrament.

COYOTE COOCH—Knife-Throwing Hellcat. Once a Circus Performer, She Now Specializes in Knife Throwing, Pickpocketing, and Bar Tricks. Wears Brass Knuckles.

CHAW BRAIN—Sheriff of Bull Spears. Shifty-Ass Drunk Motherfucker. Falls Down a Lot. Loses Things. Also Plays Piano.

HORSE DICK—145 Pounds of Horsemeat. Sick as Fuck. Born to Die.

PONY COCK—Tough as Nails but a Little Young. His Laugh Is the Laugh of a Child Burning Ants With a Magnifying Glass. Drowning Kittens in the River. Fucking Chickens in the Barn. Also Known as "Psycho."

HOG ROD—Big Hoss. Fuck Fist. Illiterate.

SPUR TITS—The Jewel of the Prairie. Stolen, Beaten, Destroyed. A Fallen Angel.

ONE PUMP—The Reluctant Hero. Wants to Be Heroic, but Is Plagued by an Erratic Heatseeker. The Gun Jumper. Pop Goes the Weasel.

SCENE 1: THE TELEGRAPH

In the Saddle Wound Saloon. Evening.

A MAN staggers onto the stage, gasping, as if trying to speak. He coughs, blood spills from his mouth, and he turns and collapses against the bar. A knife is lodged in his back on which is impaled a poster, which reads: "WANTED FOR RAPE, LARCENY, AND MURDER—HORSE DICK," accompanied by an image of the grizzled visage of the outlaw. Music begins.

Lights up on CUD BREATH, isolated at a table in the far corner of the saloon. He begins telegraphing the text, which appears on video monitors throughout the playing space.

A voiceover begins as COYOTE COOCH and CLOVER TWAT, the two barmaids, enter to remove the body.

VOICEOVER: Bull Spears, NV. A town where the tumbleweeds don't dare to drift. A town where the crab lice will crawl right out of your long johns and head toward the Smoky Mountains just to get away from the shadows. The Dick Town. Piss and Shit Village. Who Gives a Fucksville. And in this town of Bull Spears, NV, just west of Knife City and south of Stab Mountain, there lies a little saloon. This story begins in that saloon.

(COYOTE COOCH re-enters and begins slowly mopping up the blood. CLOVER TWAT enters with a cocktail tray. Furtive glances.)

VOICEOVER: For this saloon is being frequented, as of late, by a gang of cutthroats and marauders. A nexus of evil that finds its apex and its full expression in the character of one man. Horse Dick.

(The saloon doors are thrown open, and HORSE DICK, PONY COCK, and HOG ROD enter. COYOTE COOCH hides behind the bar. CLOVER TWAT freezes with her back to the door in an effort to become invisible. Dead silence. Slowly, HOG ROD sidles up to CLOVER TWAT, as PONY COCK saunters to the bar in search of booze. Dead silence. With fingers twitching, HOG ROD grabs CLOVER TWAT and lifts her into the air. Music explodes. Simultaneously, COYOTE COOCH shoots out from under the bar between PONY COCK's legs with a knife in her hand ready for an ambush. Struggle ensues on both sides. HORSE DICK stands alone in the center of the room heating two branding irons to a glowing red. Impulsively, CLOVER TWAT smacks HOG ROD across the face with her cocktail tray. All action stops. Dead silence.)

VOICEOVER: Horse Dick and his side-kick, Pony Cock, have chosen this saloon as their point of liberation. They exude the muscular musk of propriety. They've even gone so far as to brand the barmaids.

(HORSE DICK throws the MEN the branding irons. The two MEN force the WOMEN into position. A press and a yelp. The MEN exit. The WOMEN lift their skirts to reveal "HD" branded on their backsides.)

VOICEOVER: But one woman resists all brands. Her capacity for revenge cannot be quantified, and she's raw as a whip. Her name is Milky Hills.

(MILKY HILLS enters, reaches into her bra and pulls out two shot glasses, which she slams onto the bar. She spits a flammable liquid into the glasses and lights them on fire. A customer, CHAW BRAIN, is thrown through the saloon doors by HORSE DICK and his MEN. He picks himself up and staggers to the bar, where he lights a smoke on the flaming shot.)

VOICEOVER: Tonight Milky Hills is preparing a special libation in honor of the tenth anniversary of the annexation of her saloon by Horse Dick and his men. Three parts straight Kentucky bourbon, one part rare desert mushroom that Clover Twat found growing out of rattlesnake shit at midnight under a full moon on X-mas Eve.

(The ritual begins. MILKY HILLS begins pouring booze into a clear tumbler, as CLOVER TWAT and COYOTE COOCH violently chop the desert mushroom into pieces. The WOMEN pass the pieces of mushroom to each other using their mouths—"kissing" the mushroom to MILKY HILLS, who spits it into the tumbler. The liquid turns from clear to bright blue.)

VOICEOVER: It's called a "Four-Dicked Pilgrim," and it is said to have turned boys to men, men to heroes, and heroes to gods. What she needs tonight is a man, any man, who's willing to be immortal for a moment. A vessel for her wrath. A surrogate. A mark. A savior.

(The doors swing open and we see the long shadow of a lone gunman cast across the stage. ONE PUMP enters.)

SCENE 2: PERHAPS I'LL WET MY WHISTLE

ONE PUMP sits and surveys his surroundings. He calls for a drink. Furtive glances. MILKY HILLS serves him the Four-Dicked Pilgrim. It is blue in color and boiling hot. ONE PUMP inspects this bizarre cocktail for a moment, and suddenly guzzles the whole concoction. As ONE PUMP slams down his glass, the music explodes. Two and a half minutes of frenetic celebration ensues. All action happens simultaneously in a vertiginous montage of boozing and carousing. CLOVER TWAT backflips across the bar and downs forty shots of whiskey in fifteen seconds. CHAW BRAIN gets drunk and picks a fight with CUD BREATH, who responds by cracking a bottle over his head and subsequently dancing with his inert body. COYOTE COOCH throws knives into the wall in a pattern that spells out the phrase "VICTORY IS OURS." MILKY HILLS strips. ONE PUMP sits quietly in the midst of it all. Brazenly, MILKY HILLS reaches into ONE PUMP's pants to reward his valiance, but instead touches his gun, which discharges, shooting off the TELEGRAPH OPERATOR's hat.

SCENE 3: SKIN THAT SMOKE WAGON AND SEE WHAT HAPPENS

Stunned silence. ONE PUMP and the REST of the saloon face each other in a pal-

pable tension. Finally, ONE PUMP lays his gun down on a table and courteously exits to retrieve the TELEGRAPH OPERATOR's hat. As soon as he's offstage, the saloon doors swing open, and HORSE DICK enters. The PATRONS and STAFF of the saloon duck and cover. MILKY HILLS slips beside the saloon doors and raises a large flowerpot over her head in anticipation of attack.

HORSE DICK is pulling a battered and bloodied WOMAN through the doors by her hair. When he crosses the threshold, he throws her into the saloon. She is SPUR TITS. As he throws SPUR TITS to the floor, MILKY HILLS goes in for the kill, bringing the flowerpot down on HORSE DICK's head. In a flash, the pot is shot out of her hands. PONY COCK enters from the other side of the saloon and holsters his gun.

When HORSE DICK forces MILKY HILLS back to the bar for a drink, SPUR TITS makes a break for it. She is intercepted by PONY COCK, who aggressively dances with her for a while, and then lets her run. As HORSE DICK slams his empty whiskey glass down, PONY COCK shoots SPUR TITS in the back.

HORSE DICK reaches under the bar and pulls CHAW BRAIN out from hiding by the scruff of his neck. He forces him to drink a bottle of whiskey, then throws him to the ground and kicks him in the stomach while PONY COCK, who fancies himself a poet, forces CUD BREATH at gunpoint to telegraph some of his lewdest and crudest verses onto the video monitors. (NOTE: The verses used in the original production were: "Roses Iz Redd/Violenz Iz Blu/Fuck A Duk, Fred/Cuz I Fukked Her Too" and "Biches Iz Cheep/An So Iz My Sock/I'll Smash In Yor Teef/Wid The Tip Of My Cock.")

HORSE DICK discovers CLOVER TWAT in hiding across the room and hurls her against the bar. MILKY HILLS tries to es-

cape, only to encounter HOG ROD's gun barrel poking through the saloon doors. COYOTE COOCH attempts an ambush of HORSE DICK, but is caught by PONY COCK. MILKY HILLS is forced to take HOG ROD's gun barrel down her throat as CLOVER TWAT and COYOTE COOCH are forced to deep kiss at gunpoint.

ONE PUMP re-enters with the TELEGRAPH OPERATOR's hat. Unnoticed by the VILLAINS, ONE PUMP drops to his hands and knees and crawls across the stage in an attempt to retrieve his gun. He reaches for the gun on the table where he left it, but as soon as he makes contact with it, it discharges, shooting a painting off the wall. Furtive glances. Awkward pause. All action stops. Again, ONE PUMP reaches for the gun and again it discharges. On the third try, he manages to grasp the weapon. He holsters the gun and tries to nonchalantly exit the premises as if nothing has happened. PONY COCK catches him at the door and presses a silver-plated six-shooter against his skull. HOG ROD raises his rifle. HORSE DICK pushes ONE PUMP against a table and grabs his balls in a death grip.

SCENE 4: MY GUN, MY CURSE

Precisely at this moment, with his balls in the viselike grip of HORSE DICK's fist, ONE PUMP opens his mouth and begins to sing the story of his life as a failed gunslinger in a high falsetto. Stillness ensues.

ONE PUMP: *(In voiceover, sings.)*
The willow is wild
The cacti is sharp
My heart is a farm
That grows fireless sparks

My head is a spoon
That shovels out blanks
My pistol's so hot
That it's drooling

Take me out to Derelict Mount
Kick out all my teeth
My gun gets excited
My horses retreat
And I can't be a cowboy tonight
I can't be a cowboy tonight

Pick up the scraps
That I've shit down my back
Put me in line
With the retards

My prick don't stand up
When I piss in a cup
I divine only wine
From my tear ducts

Take me out to Derelict Mount
Kick out all my teeth
My gun gets excited
My horses retreat
And I can't be a cowboy tonight
I can't be a cowboy tonight

This gun will bring me down
This gun will bring me down
Light a small fire in the center of town
This gun will bring me down
This gun won't bring me around

I'm sorry to all
My skin is so thin
My armor's made of
Bed sheets

I'll cry out at night
To bring us the light
But for now we fight
In the darkness

Take me out to Derelict Mount
Kick out all my teeth
My gun gets excited
My horses retreat
And I can't be a cowboy tonight
I can't be a cowboy tonight

SCENE 5: ESCAPE FROM BULL SPEARS

On the last note of the song, ONE PUMP has removed his gun from its holster in a gesture of subordination. As he passes it to HORSE DICK, it discharges, killing HOG ROD dead. Awkward pause. HORSE DICK looks at HOG ROD's body for a moment. Stillness, then HORSE DICK pistol-whips ONE PUMP across the face. Music explodes.

Inspired by ONE PUMP's heartfelt verse, the ENTIRE SALOON goes into full attack mode against the VILLAINS. ONE PUMP's gun is continually misfiring, and, in the midst of the battle, he runs around trying to fix the damage.

ONE PUMP is experiencing what is known as "dumb luck," and he is unconsciously swaying the battle in MILKY HILLS's favor. When he gets a broom to clean up some bottles that he shot, he manages to knock PONY COCK temporarily unconscious. Whilst straightening a painting that has fallen awry, he deflects several of HORSE DICK's bullets. At the apex of battle, he comes downstage to clean some blood off the floor with a rag and bottle of rotgut. He notices the skull and crossbones and the word "FLAMMABLE" on the bottle and hastily puts it away.

As he turns back to the saloon from the bar area, he is surprised by HORSE DICK and PONY COCK, who catch him in their cross hairs and demand his pistol. As ONE PUMP is removing his gun from its holster, MILKY HILLS asserts a brilliant bit of strategy by whistling for ONE PUMP's attention, and flashing him her breasts. Immediately, and of its own accord, the pistol discharges, killing PONY COCK. Unfortunately, the pistol continues to discharge, ejaculating a torrent of bullets that ricochet through the saloon, shattering bottles, punc-

turing whiskey casks, and knocking paintings off the walls. In the spectacular blur of fusillade, CUD BREATH, CHAW BRAIN, COYOTE COOCH, and CLOVER TWAT all sustain fatal injuries. When the smoke clears, ONE PUMP is sprawled on the saloon floor with HORSE DICK standing malevolently over him. HORSE DICK raises his gun as MILKY HILLS miraculously appears from behind the bar, cocktail tray in hand. In a single sweep, she smashes the tray down on HORSE DICK's head, rendering him unconscious.

CUD BREATH crawls to the telegraph table, pulls himself up with his hands and types out his final words:

I'm Hit…

He dies.

ONE PUMP looks at his pistol mournfully, and then slowly walks across the saloon to the wall, where he hangs the gun on an empty hook. Still pause. His gun has been retired. He turns to leave. Suddenly, MILKY HILLS whistles. She steps out from behind the bar, takes off her apron, and hangs her corkscrew on the wall next to ONE PUMP's gun. They look at each other.

After a moment, ONE PUMP offers MILKY HILLS his hand. They walk toward the exit.

At the exit, they pause. ONE PUMP lights a cigarette. MILKY HILLS deliberates, then takes the still-burning match and throws it back into the tavern.

An earthshaking explosion as the saloon is blown to smithereens. The explosion is long, slow, and balletic—the sound of the flames is slowly overtaken by the sound and projected image of a huge flock of birds taking flight. Human hands reach through the flames and find nothing. MILKY HILLS and ONE PUMP stand at the exit, locked in a passionate kiss amidst the smoking BODIES of the saloon. The birds begin to sing.

End of Act I.

VIDEO #2
CIRCUS OF KNIVES

This video begins with a closeup of the SHY BOY's feet walking along a dirt road, his books dragging on the ground behind him. He stops at a tree on the path which has a knife sunk into it, attached to a colorful circus poster. The poster is garishly decorated in an exaggerated manner and reads: KNIFE CITY—NO RULES! NO BEDTIMES! CURSING ENCOURAGED!!!" The BOY looks at the poster briefly and continues on. Next we see the three ROUGH BOYS carousing on the road. Last, we see the two SISTERS walking down the road, holding hands. The OLDEST SISTER picks a large orange flower from the tall grass by the side of the road. As they pass the tree with the flyer, the point of view changes to a handheld shot from behind the tree. It is from THE ROUÉ's perspective. He begins to follow the CHILDREN from a distance. Occasionally, we see the CHILDREN fearfully glance over their shoulders.

Next, we see a closeup of the façade of the schoolhouse. Prominent in the shot is a handmade wooden sign that reads "The Whippoorwill School for Country Youths." As the camera pans back, we see the two SISTERS and the SHY BOY on the porch playing an elaborate game of pattycake. Two other little GIRLS are nearby learning hand gestures for a song that they are singing. (See Scene 7: A Bonnet of Whippoorwills.) The rest of the CHILDREN are engaged in a vigorous round of jump rope. (See Scene 8: To Stab Mountain.) The three ROUGH BOYS are making it their mission to disrupt the OTHERS by stealing their books, shoving, and general mischief.

Intercut with the recreational scenes are closeups of the ominous-looking barn from Video #1. Disturbing images of THE ROUÉ emanate from this abysmal lair. A HAND with a handkerchief gestures extravagantly, a jug of alcohol is raised, a string of knives grows like weeds in a dark corner. We never see THE ROUÉ's face during any of these shots, but we do occasionally see the CHILDREN walking past the barn on the dirt road.

Finally, THE BONNET approaches the schoolyard and rustles the CHILDREN into the building. At the door of the schoolhouse, she again looks into the camera. The point of view changes to THE ROUÉ's perspective from a distance across the field. He is moving toward the schoolhouse.

Whiteout.

ACT II
STAB MOUNTAIN

STAB MOUNTAIN—North of Bull Spears and Northwest of Knife City. Nothing Echoes in the Desert and Nothing Grows. A Mountain of Scars. Bruised Geology. The Dead Peer out From Beneath the Rocks.

DRAMATIS PERSONAE:

THE BONNET—Faceless, Nameless. Hovers on the Perimeter of Stab Mountain Like a Wrinkled Ghost. A Photo Negative With Cut-Out Eyes.

THE HARVESTERS—Barren. Desiccated. Violence Is Breaking out. Reports of Madness and of Devils in Pursuit.

MIASMAS—Echoes of School Bells. Memory Rattles. Bird Musk.

THE CYSTICS—Savage Revolutionaries in Exile. They Are in Training to Complete Their Prime Objective: Destroy Knife City.

CYSTIC RIVER—The Cystic General. The General Surgeon. The Scalpel.

SCENE 6: MUEZZIN

The morning sun is creeping brilliantly over the parched desert landscape. The plaintive singing of a solitary bird echoes through the canyon. A deep orange is bleeding into every crevice and rock.

The birdsong swings abruptly into counterpoint as the sun finally cracks over the horizon, and we hear the staccato prayer calls of THE HARVESTERS. Backlit by the sun, THE HARVESTERS enter. Two of THE HARVESTERS fall into the playing space at the same time, exhausted. A MAN carries a WOMAN on his back across the space as if he were a yoked ox. A third MAN throws his pickaxe onto the stage, and then stumbles across the space, collapsing on top of it.

The FOREMAN flaccidly calls THE CREW to attention, and they begin to sluggishly stab the earth with shovels and picks. There is a sense of vengeance in this act, as if they are trying to bruise and beat the world, but are too spent to be effective.

After several minutes of this activity, two of the WOMEN collapse from exhaustion. All work ceases. Two of the MEN stagger to where the WOMEN lie. Using their pickaxes, the MEN lift the WOMEN's skirts into the air. The WOMEN involuntarily spread their legs. The MEN reach in between the WOMEN's legs, searching. When they withdraw their hands, they blow across their open palms, sending a cloud of dust into the air.

Defeated, all HARVESTERS collapse and fan themselves in unison with their hats. ONE PUMP and MILKY HILLS enter over the horizon, having just escaped from Bull Spears, NV. They move through the desert with the grace and cadence of blown grass.

A MAN falls to the ground in the grips of a seizure. ONE PUMP and MILKY HILLS rush to his aid. ONE PUMP gives him a stick to hold in his teeth. The other HARVESTERS don't seem to notice.

Silence.

A WOMAN, screaming profanities, smashes a MAN in the back of the head with a shovel, hits him again on the back, and raises the shovel over her head as he cowers in fear beneath her.

A long tense pause as MILKY HILLS delicately makes her way to the WOMAN, and gently pries the shovel from her grip. THE WOMAN immediately and tightly embraces MILKY HILLS.

More (and longer) silence.

Just as the tension subsides, another WOMAN viciously attacks a MAN who has knelt to catch his breath. She subdues him with her pickaxe and mounts him crudely, engaging in a grotesque mockery of male sexual technique. The MAN, clearly humiliated and in pain, struggles to break free from her assault, as a SECOND MAN approaches the WOMAN from behind and lodges the handle of his shovel into her mouth. Using both hands to lift her up, yoke-style, he gets her into a standing crucifix position with the shovel handle still in her teeth and her stomach exposed.

The FIRST MAN cocks his fist, but then hesitates. He is still for a moment and then he lunges forward and rips the shovel from the WOMAN's mouth. With both hands on the shovel, he strikes the SECOND MAN with an uppercut to the chin. The WOMAN falls and cradles her stomach.

As the FIRST MAN stands over the SECOND MAN, shovel still at shoulder height, ONE PUMP approaches him from behind

and calmly puts his hands on the shovel. ONE PUMP turns the MAN forward, and the MAN falls to his knees with his hands still gripping the shovel above him as if he were in the stocks.

Slowly and smoothly, THE BONNET enters from behind them.

Scene 7: A Bonnet of Whippoorwills

THE BONNET is a tall willow of a woman, who glides through space with the lubricity of an apparition. She wears a Sunday dress that has been burnt to tatters, and her bonnet has been pulled over her backward like a mask, with holes cut out for her eyes. It looks as if the bonnet has been melted to her face.

As THE BONNET sings, she performs the kind of representational hand gestures that one would associate with children's songs. Her sign language is compact and contained, but often fractured by the spasms of her seemingly damaged body.

THE BONNET: *(In voiceover, sings.)*
Where are the little ones?
For whom the rain never came
My little birds.
Who had to fly away.
When the weather changed.
They left the open range
And flew
Flew
Flew
Flew
Into the graveyards
Of Stab Mountain.

There was a time
When this country was in bloom.
Flowers and babies
Coming up under the moon
Now, all the little birds

Have flown away too soon
Into the graveyards
Of Stab Mountain.

I told the little birds
That the scarecrows wouldn't sting
The sun was a branding iron
Melting off our wings
There's dust in the autumn
And there's stillbirth in the spring
From out of the graveyards
Of Stab Mountain.

Leave no tear unspeared
In Stab Mountain

Pull the cold over your ear
In Stab Mountain

There's a scar that surrounds
In Stab Mountain

Put it back in the ground
At Stab Mountain

Flew
Flew
Flew
Flew

(Blackout.)

(NOTE: The following video accompanies
this song and tells the back-story of the Whippoorwill School for Country Youths. The song
that THE BONNET is teaching the children in this video is the same song she performs live, and it is accompanied by the same
hand gestures.)

VIDEO #3
THE WHIPPOORWILL SCHOOL FOR
COUNTRY YOUTHS

The CHILDREN are filing into the rustic
one-room schoolhouse. In the back, the three
BOYS are wrestling. A lone GIRL is staring
at a glass case that holds snakeskins and bird
nests. She traces their outline against the glass

with her finger. The two SISTERS make
their way to the front of the class, where they
carefully place the large orange flower on
THE BONNET's desk.

THE BONNET enters and the CHIL-
DREN take their seats. She picks up the
flower, puts it to her nose, and places it in a
small vase on her desk. She then picks up a
piece of chalk and begins a science lesson on
the subject of ornithology. She draws skeletal
diagrams of birds on the blackboard, connecting the various organs with lines and
labels.

The CHILDREN are instructed to copy the
diagram on the slates at their desks. We see
them working diligently for a while, but then
the camera moves to the back of the room
where one of the rough boys (PONY) is creating quite a sensation with his drawing.
THE BONNET calls the class to attention,
and we see the STUDENTS each flip up
their slates in a round, one at a time, to reveal their diagrams. PONY's is last, and, as
the camera closes in on the drawing, we see
a picture of complete carnage—a flock of
birds impaled by knives. PONY's face is steely
and defiant.

THE BONNET calls PONY to the front of
the classroom and places a dunce cap on his
head. She points the way to the exit. As
PONY exits, she orders the other two boys,
HORSE and HOG, to put their heads down
on their desks. PONY walks through the
classroom door and sits down on the front
porch.

THE BONNET begins a music lesson. All
CHILDREN are learning a song with sign
language/hand gestures. We see different shots
of them performing it from their seats, from
the head of the class, and so on. Intercut with
these shots is a tracking shot of THE ROUÉ's
ARM. He is moving through the field, carrying a large jug of alcohol with a handker-

chief wrapped around its handle. Occasionally, he drinks. We cannot see his face.

As THE ROUÉ gets closer to the school, we see PONY's reaction to his approach. It is one of fear and awe. THE ROUÉ removes a Knife City flyer from his coat and throws it on the porch it front of PONY. He then removes a knife from his coat and hurls it into the note. The knife wobbles in the wood of the schoolhouse porch. Cut back to music lesson.

Cut to: PONY watches as THE ROUÉ walks away around the building. He pulls the knife from the wood and examines the note.

Cut to interior: The CHILDREN are startled from their lesson by the sound of liquid hitting the windows of the schoolhouse. They turn to the windows and see a splash of clear liquid. THE BONNET is panicked and calls them to the center of the classroom away from the windows. Pandemonium ensues, as the entire schoolhouse is soaked in a terrifying act of baptism. HORSE and HOG rise up out of their seats, enthralled. MILKY and her SISTER manage to break free from the riot and make their way to the door. At the door, they pause. THE BONNET reaches out to them. They exit.

More splashes and screams from the CHILDREN. HOG and HORSE, in the back of the classroom, rise defiantly and slowly exit. Through the window, a HAND is holding a flaming silk handkerchief. The HAND moves in closer. Closeup of THE BONNET.

Cut to exterior: We see MILKY and her SISTER run past PONY on the porch out into the field. HOG and HORSE step out behind them. Over the BOYS' shoulders, we see the GIRLS run away. PONY passes HORSE the knife. HORSE raises his arm and throws. From the field, we see MILKY's SISTER get hit by the knife and fall. MILKY looks back toward the flaming schoolhouse.

In closeup, the three BOYS slowly put on cowboy hats in unison.

MILKY slowly turns her head to look out across the field as the schoolhouse silently burns.

Whiteout.

SCENE 8: TO STAB MOUNTAIN

Stab Mountain at twilight. The sound of crickets and faint music is heard. The light is blue-green, and there is lushness to the cap of the mountain that did not exist at the base. A small cemetery is seen where green grass grows thickly and gray moss hangs limply from the trees. Small grave markers make concentric rings around the top of the mountain, and a stone mausoleum cuts an imposing figure to the south.

The site of the schoolhouse fire, Stab Mountain is a repository of uneasy souls. The gravesite itself continues to suck the life from the surrounding lands like a verdant sponge. While the area beneath the mountain is dry and devoid of flora and fauna, the graveyard produces both on a nightly basis. All the parasitic energy seems to fuel a single host—a large and beautiful orange flower that grows out of the mausoleum and radiates in the pale twilight. THE BONNET believes that this flower could restore life to the land.

A FIGURE materializes over one of the gravestones. It begins to undulate rapidly, its hands stabbing the air. More FIGURES appear. They are wearing tattered school uniforms and appear to have small scissors in their hands. The stone door of the mausoleum falls open to reveal four more FIGURES inside. They are MIASMAS.

The MIASMAS begin a ritual while seated on the gravestones. They lift and pin back their dresses, as if they were about to have a medical exam, and then they begin spasti-

cally cutting away at their laps, their hands frantic and rhythmical.

As the stabbing continues, the MIASMAS begin to pull pieces of a dripping black cord from between their legs. Thick fleshy cables and black liquids are discharged in the process. Two of the MIASMAS take this cabling into their hands and begin to whip the earth, bringing it down over their heads in a crude evocation of a jump rope game.

ONE PUMP and MILKY HILLS enter from over the ridge of the mountain. They see the orange flower growing from the top of the mausoleum. As soon as this information can register, they are surrounded by the MIASMAS, who are spinning and whipping their cables in an attempt to corral the couple.

Once they have positioned themselves between two MIASMAS, MILKY HILLS jumps through the outstretched cord and arrives at the base of the central mausoleum. ONE PUMP attempts to follow, but is immediately blocked by a long sinew of black rope that has been shot/thrown between the MIASMAS. As ONE PUMP reaches forward, he is blocked by an intestinal web. The MIASMAS keep him at bay by engaging him in a lethal game of double-dutch jump rope.

As ONE PUMP is tied up and subdued by the MIASMAS, MILKY HILLS climbs to the summit of the mausoleum, where she encounters a single MIASMA guarding the huge orange flower. She wrestles with the MIASMA, eventually managing to cut the flower with the MIASMA's scissors.

The music dilates to a low moan as all MIASMAS go limp.

Scene 9: Birdstorm

THE BONNET appears and begins to glide through the graveyard toward MILKY HILLS. Four MIASMAS start to shake and

shudder, arms flapping. They pull two additional cables from within their bodies, taking an end each, and crossing them tautly in front of THE BONNET, framing her in an X. The REGIMENT moves forward toward the mausoleum.

Over the X created by the crossed cables, THE BONNET reaches out to MILKY HILLS. As MILKY HILLS releases the flower, the MIASMAS savagely pin her to the mausoleum with the cables. THE BONNET presses the flower under MILKY HILLS's skirt and between her legs. The MIASMAS are crawling out of their skin. As THE BONNET removes the flower, the MIASMAS split apart one by one as flocks of white birds emerge from within their chests and fly into the air. THE BONNET begins to glide away. The MIASMAS try to follow THE BONNET but fall limp. MILKY HILLS collapses, unconscious.

Crickets.

Blackout.

Scene 10: Lullaby

Still twilight. ONE PUMP is lying stock still at a makeshift camp. MILKY HILLS is crouched over him, undulating slightly in a style similar to the MIASMAS'. It is hard to discern whether she is crying or having a physical attack. Finally, she stands and turns, revealing a baby that she has been cradling and rocking. With the crickets and whippoorwills in the background, she hums the CHILD a soft and spare lullaby (it is the melody from "A Bonnet of Whippoorwills"). ONE PUMP puts his hat over his face and goes to sleep. MILKY HILLS removes her shawl. Night falls and the scythe moon rises brightly behind them.

After several minutes, a twig cracks. The crickets abruptly stop. MILKY HILLS's song trails off, and she stares out into the wild.

Silence.

The crickets resume. Slowly, MILKY HILLS begins to sing again.

A twig cracks loudly. Again, the crickets and MILKY HILLS are silent.

After a moment, MILKY HILLS gasps loudly.

Blackout.

SCENE 11: OUT OF THE STAB AND ONTO THE KNIFE

In the predawn light, ONE PUMP suddenly stirs from sleep. The world is silent. He looks around for MILKY HILLS, but she is nowhere to be found. He notices her shawl on the ground beside him. A loud rustling in the bushes.

More rustling. ONE PUMP crouches into a ready stance, but suddenly trips. As he falls to his hands, he realizes that he is being hoisted into the air by a rope that has been tied to his ankles. When he is completely off the ground, four FIGURES appear from the shadows.

They are THE CYSTICS, a cult of dissenters exiled from Knife City, who have heard the revelation that a child has been born on Stab Mountain. They are eager to find the mother and child to prevent the infant from falling into the hands of THE ROUÉ—the sadistic libertine overlord of Knife City. Since the schoolhouse fire, THE ROUÉ has been working to rid growth, stop production, and create a clean slate on which he will build a new order of civilization. To hear that a child has been born on Stab Mountain—that life exists outside his gates—is a great threat to his colossal plan.

THE CYSTICS introduce themselves by way of an impressive veneer of intimidation. They

salute, throw gang signs, and march in a manic but supremely disciplined fashion. Each MEMBER carries two knives, and each makes a point of showing his or her proficiency with this form of weapon. CYSTIC RIVER, the gang leader, cuts the wrist of one of her subordinates and smears the blood crudely on her face like war paint. She then tears open ONE PUMP's shirt and uses the blood to tattoo the image of a knife on his chest.

Believing ONE PUMP to be one of THE ROUÉ's henchmen, they begin their interrogation by pushing his suspended body back and forth amongst the assembled. He is spun, under-dogged, and whirled at extreme velocity until CYSTIC RIVER calls the company to a halt. THE CYSTICS raise the body of ONE PUMP slowly over their heads, as CYSTIC RIVER removes her longest knife from its sheath.

As CYSTIC RIVER advances for the kill, we hear snatches of a familiar lullaby. Slowly, the shadow image of MILKY HILLS cradling a BABY appears in the scythe moon.

As realization sinks in, THE CYSTICS drop ONE PUMP and lower him to the ground. There is now a sense of care and delicacy in how they handle him. They know his identity and have heard the mythology that surrounds him: He is the gunslinger who single-handedly defeated Bull Spears's three most notorious outlaws.

Still entranced by the image of MILKY HILLS, CYSTIC RIVER produces a long shiny knife and passes it into ONE PUMP's palm.

They are Knife City-bound.

Blackout.

End of Act II.

VIDEO #4
PURE

This video is essentially a horror film, meant to deepen the associations between the props, imagery, and character of THE ROUÉ and the plotlines of the previous two acts. By Act III, we should have a clear sense of the history of Bull Spears—that the seminal event in the creation of the town's myth and tragedy was the burning of a schoolhouse by THE ROUÉ. Also, the idea of an alternative government/culture has been introduced in the flyers and imagery of Knife City. THE ROUÉ's recruitment of HORSE DICK, PONY COCK, and HOG ROD should be reemphasized in this section, as their deaths at ONE PUMP's hands will give added urgency to THE ROUÉ's need to kill ONE PUMP, as well as his need to capture and enslave MILKY HILLS and her immaculately conceived CHILD.

This film can be approached as a collage film—previously used footage can be utilized, juxtaposed, effected, and reordered to give the imagery new fangs. Cut from the closeups of the liquid splashing on the windows to the more bucolic pictures of the CHILDREN playing, singing, etc. It should suggest ejaculation—THE ROUÉ's semen staining the pristine faces of the innocent.

INTERLUDE
AN INJECTION OF MILK

This section is reminiscent of a magic show or vaudeville act. Two red curtains are parted at either side of the stage. One side reveals MILKY HILLS, strapped to an examining table, struggling against the belts that bind her. On the opposite side, we see CISCO SCRATCH, also tied down, with a belt cinched to his arm to facilitate an injection. Three FIGURES hover over him, but their backs remain turned to us. They are THE ROUÉ, COMMODORE NUTT, and THE WASP.

In THE ROUÉ's hands is a piece of fabric, similar to the kind of handkerchief used in a magic trick. On this handkerchief is drawn a sketch of MILKY HILLS.

THE WASP prepares a needle with a milky solution. She advances and plunges the needle into CISCO SCRATCH's skin. The handkerchief disappears from THE ROUÉ's hands in a puff of smoke.

MILKY HILLS evaporates into thin air as she is injected into CISCO SCRATCH's arm. CISCO passes out.

Curtains.

ACT III
KNIFE CITY

KNIFE CITY—No Guns, No Laws, No Limits. An Experimental Society Advocating New Avenues of Medicine and Recreation. The Tracks to Which Milky Hills Is Tied. The Tomb Where She Withers. No Guns, No Laws, No Limits.

DRAMATIS PERSONAE:

THE ROUÉ—Mayor of Knife City. Aka the Great Cackler. Aka the Chaos Goose.

COMMODORE NUTT—Administrative Assistant to the Roué. A Death Clown in Soiled Pants. Shit Cakes. The Babysitter.

THE WASP—Entertainment Coordinator for Knife City. Likes Music, Drama, and Public Execution. Licks Chicken. Flicks Piss.

THE SPATIAL LOBOTOMIES—Inmates at the Auditorium. Dissenters, Deviants, and Sexual Desirables. Almost Fully "Corrected."

CISCO SCRATCH—Morphine Addict, Orphan, Cipher. Resists Rehabilitation. Makes Pictures.

"THEY have infiltrated the system for so long that every word, intonation, tone, meter, rhythm, melody, & numeric measure has its own subterranean meaning & symbolism. Correspondingly, every operatic confluence of symbols, whether in a parade, play, movie, sporting event, political convention, anything televised, radio-waved or printed, commands a complex array of perverse forces of sex and death to concentrate power to the masters and weakness to the slaves."

—James Shelby Downard

Scene 12: Knife City

CYSTIC RIVER has led ONE PUMP to the front door of the walled compound of Knife City. The outside walls are covered in leaflets, wanted posters, and pro-knife propaganda of all kinds. The wanted posters feature ONE PUMP's face, and accuse him of being a "savage" with a "mania for guns" on account of the massive slaying in the town of Bull Spears. ONE PUMP knocks on the door. His knock echoes throughout the city. Silence. Finally, CYSTIC RIVER steps forward and picks the lock with her knife. They slip through the door unnoticed.

As soon as they make it over the threshold, the entire front wall of the compound comes crashing down, and the whole of the city is revealed. Knife City is an industrial prison-like compound made entirely of sharp silver knives. Bursts of visual and sonic static echo off of these surfaces and provide a maddening counterpoint to the violence of the city's design.

Knife City is ostensibly a progressive city— for instance, THE ROUÉ has banned guns of any kind from entering the perimeter of the compound. This is part of his "Grand Outline" for the rehabilitation of man.

In the cerebellum of Knife City exists a correctional facility for the criminally insane, where inmates are cured through geometrical movement and kinesthetic response meth-

ods. It is THE ROUÉ's aim to "rehabilitate" the prisoners (mainly dissenters or sexual desirables) by teaching them structure, grid work, and Pavlovian response. This institute is known as "the Auditorium."

As ONE PUMP steps into Knife City, he witnesses an onslaught of activity. Music explodes from gigantic speakers. THE SPATIAL LOBOTOMIES are in the midst of a ferocious therapy session. They respond to his entrance like fish in a school. One of the inmates, CISCO SCRATCH, is within the grid, but abstains from the session. He is hanging from the wall on the southwest side of the grid, furiously sketching in a notebook. His line drawing animations are projected above the heads of the other INMATES, and are accompanied by voiceover in the voices of the PRISONERS.

Simultaneously, ONE PUMP notices a whirl of shadow, as effigies and vestiges of MILKY HILLS appear spinning throughout the room. Different parts of her body are projected, seen, puppeteered, etc., across the wide expanse of windows, walls, and doorways at a blistering rate. As soon as he can take one in and start toward it, a new one appears. The opera builds and builds.

CISCO SCRATCH draws first sketch in his notebook.

VOICEOVER: Two of the inmates are planning an escape. A third hears about it and tattletales to the authorities. The punishments are doled out accordingly, and the third is led to the arena expecting a reward. Upon seeing her, the men hold her down, give her fifty lashes each, and cut off her arm.

"It's not fair!" she protests.

"Were it fair," he says, wiping his razor, "it would surely fail to give us an erection."

(CISCO SCRATCH draws second sketch in his notebook.)

VOICEOVER: A group of inmates complain of thirst. They are led into a dark chamber where their captors await them, costumed as nurses. They are fed unlimited champagne, and then strapped to medical tables where they are sewn shut. An orchestra is brought in to play as their bodies explode.

(CISCO SCRATCH draws third sketch in his notebook.)

VOICEOVER: The Roué is bound hand and foot, as if he were a wild beast, and he is draped in a tiger's skin. When this is done, he is aroused, irritated, whipped, and beaten. Opposite him is a plump young inmate, naked and tied by his feet to the floor in such a way that he cannot move. When The Roué is in a sweat, his captors free him; he leaps upon the boy, bites him everywhere, and removes the boy's eye with his teeth.

(CISCO SCRATCH draws fourth sketch in his notebook.)

VOICEOVER: One of the inmates is overheard complaining of a toothache. When she is brought before the authorities, they are all costumed as dentists. They extract all her teeth, replacing each one with a red-hot nail, which they secure in place with a hammer.

(As this activity and narration reaches a level of unbearable intensity, ONE PUMP instinctively reaches for the knife that he obtained from THE CYSTICS. He advances to where he sees the effigies of MILKY HILLS and begins to tear away the walls that he saw her image on. He is like a dog barking at a picture of a dog on a television set.)

(Three FIGURES appear on the parapet above the Auditorium. The therapy session suddenly freezes.)

SCENE 13: PRO-KNIFE

COMMODORE NUTT and THE WASP appear to the left and right of THE ROUÉ on the high platform. Music plays, and the three MEN begin a welcoming ceremony eerily reminiscent of "We Welcome You to Munchkinland," but containing a cryptocracy of coded violence, bizarre sexual innuendo, and voodoo hexes. There is a military quality to the choreography that implies a violent rehearsal process.

THE ROUÉ: *(Lip-synchs with voiceover.)*
    Who's got the Vizard Mask?
    I do. I do.
    Who's got the Vizard Mask?
    Me. Me.
    Who's got the Vizard Mask?
    I wear it on my tiny eye!
    Who's got the Vizard Mask?
    I do.

    Where is my tiny eye?
    Where? Where?
    Where is my tiny eye?
    Where?
    Where is my tiny eye?
    Look! My eyes are normal size!
    Where is my tiny eye—where?

(As the chorus of the song commences, COMMODORE NUTT and THE WASP release all of the INMATES, with the exception of CISCO SCRATCH, onto the floor where they begin their chores. CISCO SCRATCH shoots up and nods off in the corner of the Auditorium.)

THE ROUÉ, COMMODORE NUTT, and THE WASP: *(Lip-synch with voiceover.)*
    Pro knife
    Saving life
    All the slices take a bite
    I cut the tongue from the belle
    'Cause I'm slitty

    I breathe death
    Stay abreast

Let's ingest and get undressed
'Cause the nest where I rest is Knife
City

(The song builds and courses to a sweeping finale, whereupon at the final chord, ONE PUMP and CYSTIC RIVER are savagely beaten and firmly restrained.)

SCENE 14: DINE!

All of the INMATES, with the exception of CISCO, stand in front of a large banquet table, sharpening knives. THE ROUÉ, THE WASP, and COMMODORE NUTT eye them warily. The INMATES stop sharpening and plunge the knives into the banquet table. The VILLAINS continue to stare. Long pause. Abruptly, the VILLAINS slide into their seats. The INMATES respond like a school of fish and exit the premises.

A lone INMATE returns carrying a large birdcage filled with eggs. The INMATE stops in front of each VILLAIN as they point to the egg of their choice. COMMODORE NUTT has a great deal of difficulty deciding, and, after several awkward moments, begins to reach for one of the knives lodged in the table. The INMATE exits.

Three INMATES enter carrying three silver platters with covers. They are placed in front of each of the VILLAINS. The INMATES wait attentively as the three VILLAINS stare holes through their souls. Grand pause. Strategically, the three VILLAINS whip the covers off their platters in unison, sending the INMATES kinesthetically sprawling back to the kitchen. On the plates are three large, dead, inert birds. There is much confusion as to what to do next.

All eyes are on THE WASP, as she lifts the bird from its plate and makes it dance. This forces the other VILLAINS to reconsider their plans of attack. COMMODORE NUTT

finger fucks his bird, as THE ROUÉ slides his knife beneath his bird and repeatedly urges it to be silent. All three VILLAINS are suddenly overtaken by the urge to place tiny kisses on the necks of the animals. Intimacy ensues, then disgust. They slam the covers back on the platters and open their mouths like baby birds waiting to be fed.

Their plates are cleared, and a lone INMATE re-enters. He stands on the table, and walks down the line urinating into each of the VILLAINS' open mouths. The VILLAINS are momentarily satisfied, until the thought slowly dawns on them that "this piss is not up to par with the piss we had yesterday." Mild frustration ensues.

Three INMATES return with three ceramic bowls. They place the bowls in front of the VILLAINS, climb onto the table, and squat over the bowls, defecating in canon. Upon completion, they wait at attention as COMMODORE NUTT wafts the delicate bouquet of the bowls to his nose. The three VILLAINS dig in, and dessert is going smashingly for a moment, until all three notice a faint "oaky" quality to the flavor of the feces, which quickly overtakes the dominant citrus and smoke flavors they had been savoring, and causes them to end the course abruptly. It is clear from the look on THE ROUÉ's face that this shit is clearly "off," and may even be "corked."

With a nod of his head, THE ROUÉ summons the INMATES to where the VILLAINS are sitting. The INMATES kneel and purse their lips into a kiss. The VILLAINS grab the side of the INMATES' heads and vigorously wipe their mouths against the lips of the INMATES, effectively removing any traces of the offending meal. This is followed by another round of "piss sorbet," at which point it is time for the evening's entertainment.

THE ROUÉ slowly climbs the table, arches his back and purses his lips. He begins to whistle, all the while bobbing his head and strutting like a rooster. He continues his birdsong through the following scene.

SCENE 15: IN THE AUDITORIUM

When ONE PUMP awakes, he and CYSTIC RIVER are in the bowels of the Auditorium. Nearby is CISCO SCRATCH, who, as usual, is furiously drawing imagery into his notebook. His drawings are once again animated and projected above the stage. However, there is something different about these animations from the images ONE PUMP saw previously. They are softer, sweeter, and somewhat familiar to him. ONE PUMP begins to take interest.

DRAWING #1: A stick figure cowboy in a bar. He is waiting for a drink. A stick figure lady comes nervously forward and serves him a bluish cocktail. He tips his hat to her.

DRAWING #2: A stick figure cowboy is singing a song, while another stick figure cowboy holds his crotch. Some words to the song are projected coming out of his mouth.

DRAWING #3: A stick figure cowboy hangs up his gun. A buxom stick figure lady hangs up a corkscrew. The cowboy cries. The woman wipes his tears.

DRAWING #4: A stick figure cowboy takes a shovel out of a violent man's hands. A stick figure woman embraces a violent woman.

DRAWING #5: A stick figure man gets roped by child demons, as a stick figure woman cuts a flower in a cemetery.

DRAWING #6: A stick figure woman is gently singing a lullaby to a bundle in her arms as a stick figure cowboy sleeps. The woman and baby fly to the moon and continue singing down at the man. He wakes, and they disappear.

Enraged at seeing his personal memories on display, ONE PUMP viciously grabs CISCO SCRATCH's writing arm and knocks the pencil away.

Meanwhile, in the dining room, THE ROUÉ's whistling is hitting a climax. An INMATE has brought in a nest of eggs for him to fertilize, and, rubbing hand lotion furiously into his hands, he ejaculates onto the nest and passes out.

SCENE 16: TIED TO THE TRACKS/ PRISON RIOT

All attention is suddenly on the Auditorium as ONE PUMP pulls CISCO SCRATCH up by his wrist and reveals a strange marking on his arm:

DRAWING #7: Connecting the track marks of CISCO's junk-addled skin is a clear image of a railroad track. As ONE PUMP stares, an image appears—MILKY HILLS is tied to the track. In the distance, we see the smoke of an oncoming train.

The stick figure MILKY HILLS cries out, "HELP ME," in a speech bubble.

Immediately, THE ROUÉ sounds a frightful alarm as the INMATES in the Auditorium wreak havoc. The grid is lost, and we are in the midst of a full-on riot. Water hoses are employed, dogs are unleashed, but nothing will quell the onslaught of chaos.

As ONE PUMP and CYSTIC RIVER struggle with CISCO SCRATCH, who is now desperately trying to shed his skin, THE WASP sneaks into the Auditorium, knife in hand. COMMODORE NUTT enters from the opposite side of the compound, pushing a baby carriage. They observe.

In the midst of the commotion, a WOMAN INMATE approaches ONE PUMP. He recognizes her immediately as SPUR TITS from

Act I. She thrusts a charred fabric bundle into his hands. ONE PUMP unwraps it.

It is his gun.

THE ROUÉ appears on the floor, suckling a BABY to his breast.

SCENE 17: SHOWDOWN

THE WASP throws ONE PUMP onto the floor of the arena, where THE ROUÉ is waiting with the BABY. He places the BABY back into the carriage and instructs COMMODORE NUTT to set it high atop the parapet. They now stand alone amidst a gallery of silent INMATES and COMMANDANTS.

Knowing Knife City's strict gun policy, ONE PUMP assumes that everyone is unarmed, and feels that he is at a clear advantage. He drills THE WASP with lead, turns back to THE ROUÉ and fancily spins his pistol in the air. THE ROUÉ smiles slightly, and quickly pulls a revolver from his garter and guns down COMMODORE NUTT. This irreverence for the life of one of his own men inspires a fit of maniacal giggles in THE ROUÉ, and sets the stage for the showdown.

The two MEN slowly back into opposite corners of the stage—as far apart as space will allow. The tension mounts as small gestures and tics of the fingers give voice to the turmoil that is brewing within. The first draw is pulled by THE ROUÉ, in a move so staggeringly fast that ONE PUMP can't even get his hand to his holster. THE ROUÉ has drawn a hand fan, which he uses to fan his face. Throughout the rest of the showdown, THE ROUÉ mercilessly mocks ONE PUMP by pulling an assortment of silk handkerchiefs, hand lotion, combs, and other accoutrements from his garter and belts, before ONE PUMP can react.

At the height of THE ROUÉ's audacity and arrogance, he summons the SPATIAL

LOBOTOMIES to his side of the showdown to serve as stylists/makeup artists. They do his hair, manicure his nails, powder his face, and even give him oral sex. At the end of the sequence, they show him a mirror. He is horribly offended by his appearance and smashes the mirror against the floor.

By this point, ONE PUMP appears to have slightly disengaged from the showdown. He turns his back and begins the slow internal psych-up for his revenge.

THE ROUÉ then pulls a long strand of pearls from his anus, and motions for the INMATES to do the same. Eventually, four long strands of pearls are spread out and spinning behind him like plumage circling a sadistic rooster. As he strains to move himself forward and dislocate more of the beads, he begins spinning four silk handkerchiefs in manic figure eights. In a grand finale, he whips all handkerchiefs into the air and smiles in satisfaction. A single bead of sweat drops from THE ROUÉ's forehead to the ground. He pulls out a fifth handkerchief and mops his brow. Immediately realizing he's made a grave mistake, he freezes. Both MEN go for their guns. Both shoot.

Silence.

THE ROUÉ falls to the ground.

Silence.

CISCO SCRATCH falls forward from the Auditorium platform.

Seeing CISCO fall, ONE PUMP rushes to his prone body. He examines CISCO at length, holding the tracks of his arm to his chest.

Silence.

CISCO SCRATCH, in the death throes, draws an image of MILKY HILLS.

DRAWING #8: MILKY HILLS is standing alone in a country field next to a small wooden schoolhouse. The field is full of scare-crows. One by one, birds fly into the field and perch on the scarecrows. Eventually, the field is covered with flocks of birds. They lift the scarecrows off of their stakes and into the air. MILKY HILLS waves goodbye from the drawing and walks into the schoolhouse. The wood from the schoolhouse disintegrates and crumbles to the earth, where it is turned back into seeds, which grow up through the ground into trees. Nests can be seen in the treetops. Eggs are laid and baby birds hatch. The birds sing.

Pause.

CYSTIC RIVER appears, holding MILKY HILLS's BABY in her hands. She hands the CHILD to ONE PUMP. ONE PUMP cradles the CHILD in his arms. CYSTIC RIVER walks to where the body of THE ROUÉ lies, bends down, and pulls two knives from THE ROUÉ's coat. She physically salutes the empty space with the knives.

Silence.

Slowly, the SPATIAL LOBOTOMIES line up behind CYSTIC RIVER. In unison, they roughly imitate CYSTIC RIVER's salute with their hands. She turns to face them. They begin to shed elements of their uni-forms. CYSTIC RIVER shouts for attention and begins leading the newly liberated IN-MATES through a series of drills and sa-lutes. She is preparing her new army.

ONE PUMP slowly walks to the far exit of the compound with CHILD in hand. He becomes a silhouette in the distance. His mouth opens and from his mouth, we hear a chorus of birds singing a familiar lullaby.

Fade to black.

End of play.

ANIMAL

Kevin Augustine

KEVIN AUGUSTINE was born in Philadelphia, and began playing with puppets at a young age. Not until graduating from the University of the Arts in Philadelphia and embarking upon the path of a solo theatre artist did he revisit his partnership with puppets. As a result, his company, Lone Wolf Tribe, was formed in 1997. Lone Wolf Tribe productions—written and directed by Augustine, and performed with puppets made and animated by Augustine (as well as other puppeteers at times)—have been performed in New York at HERE, P.S. 122, the Present Company, and at the New York International Fringe Festival; and at the San Francisco Fringe Festival, the Independent Eye in Philadelphia, and numerous colleges. Past productions include *Once Vaudeville*, *Big Top Machine* (winner of the FringeNYC Overall Excellence award) and *10* (winner of the San Francisco *Examiner's* Critic's Choice award). Augustine traveled to Zimbabwe in 2004 with *Once Vaudeville*, as part of the Harare International Festival of the Arts. A two-time McDowell Colony fellow, Augustine has received grants and fellowships from both the Pennsylvania and New York State Councils on the Arts, and the Jim Henson Foundation. He has created puppets for several New York theatre companies and was a lead puppeteer in Basil Twist's tour of *Petruska* which premiered at Lincoln Center. He is a teaching artist at the New Victory Theater in New York and offers classes and workshops in puppet making, technique, and solo performance. He is currently working on Lone Wolf Tribe's fifth full-length production, *The Bride*. He resides in Brooklyn.

Animal was commissioned and produced by the Dream Music Puppetry Program at HERE Arts Center and workshopped through its HERE Artist Residency Program in New York City. Funded in part through grants by the Jim Henson Foundation, the Axe Houghton Foundation, and the New York State Council on the Arts and the Field's sponsored artist program, *Animal* was developed over three years with Lone Wolf Tribe's Genesis Ensemble—an artist collective working collaboratively to explore concepts, character, and story. *Animal* had a work-in-progress showing at the Philadelphia Live Arts Festival in September 2003 and debuted in New York at HERE Arts Center on October 24, 2003, running for three weeks. *Animal* had a return engagement at HERE in October 2004 with support from the Henson International Festival of Puppet Theatre.

The cast and credits for the New York City premiere were as follows:

Jeff .... Kevin Augustine
Puppeteers .... Lindsay Abromaitis-Smith, David Michael Friend,
                                                                         Jessica Scott

Set Design: David Evans Morris
Lighting Design: Andrew Hill
Costume Design: Michael Oberle
Sound Design: Sean McFaul
Dramaturg: Rachel Schroeder
Production Stage Manager: Emily Durning/Amber Hall

Select set pieces, devices, and apparatus designed and built by David Michael Friend.

Visit www.lonewolftribe.com.

A WORD ABOUT THE PUPPETS

In *Animal*, the parts of Jeff and the Technicians were played by human performers, while all other characters were represented by life-sized foam rubber puppets created by Kevin Augustine. The puppets were designed to allow Augustine, when operating solo, to use his feet as well as his hands. This was intended to physicalize the close, symbiotic bond between the Shaman and his animal guide.

All performers animate the puppets.

Depending on a scene's technical requirements, one to three puppeteers would work a single puppet, while two pairs would often facilitate two puppets interacting. Two of the puppeteers play the Technicians. The fourth puppeteer in the cast was "unseen"—dressed and masked entirely in black, and mostly paired with Jeff to bring Eugene to life.

The puppets are operated in a *Bunraku* style (a form of puppetry from Japan), and, to a lesser extent, in the Czech black light technique—where it is desirous for the puppeteer to become "invisible" on stage. This was not a stringent guideline, but used occasionally for moments like "floating the ball."

Various noises were made by the performers on stage including barks, growls, whimpers, and screams. All puppet dialogue was spoken by Kevin Augustine. No attempt was made on his part to conceal his obviously moving lips—if the puppet is sufficiently and believably (magically) brought to life through committed acting and technique, the audience will be captivated not with the puppeteer's lips, but with the puppet speaking the lines.

Animal is part of Lone WolfTribe's touring repertory and is available for booking. Any parties interested in presenting *Animal* in its original production format may inquire at www.lonewolftribe.com.

A WORD ABOUT SHAMANISM

Shaman (pronounced SHAH-mann) is a word from the language of the Tungus people of Siberia, and has been adopted widely by anthropologists to refer to persons in a great variety of non-Western cultures who were previously known by such terms as "witch," "witch-doctor," "medicine man," "sorcerer," "wizard," "magic man," "magician," and "seer." A shaman is a man or woman who enters an altered state of consciousness—at will—to contact and utilize an ordinarily hidden reality in order to acquire knowledge, power, and to help other persons.

—*The Way of the Shaman*
Michael Harner

The stage is set with a series of black metal poles rising from floor to ceiling throughout the space; on these poles at various heights and configurations are empty picture frames painted varying shades of gray. The frames perhaps are smaller at the back, creating a distanced perspective. These are the many cages of Ward B.

Upstage right is a very large scrimmed frame, behind which is a tattered rocking armchair. This is the HOME where all the TV scenes take place.

Downstage right, on the proscenium wall, is a large, empty gold frame. The painting auctions will appear here.

As much of the puppetry happens at ground level, a playing platform may be needed if audience sight-line issues dictate it. In the original production, a platform fourteen inches high, six inches wide, and twelve inches long was used.

DESCENDING VISION

Darkness. A heart beats. Shallow breathing is heard...

Dim light rises slowly on the APPARATUS: a corroded metal contraption whose purpose could never be genial. Strapped inside, in a forced bent stance, is a naked, five-inch-tall puppet CREATURE. Its hands and feet are shackled to the frame, its head compelled to jut forward into a harness clamping open its mouth. A cloudy intravenous bag hangs with a tube trailing down to a vein. A urine bag, full and heavy, dangles near the CREATURE's crotch amid various electrical wires. The CREATURE slowly breathes. This is EUGENE.

The sound of a beating heart continues...

EAGLE FEATHER: (Voiceover.) Continue to breath—

(Slowly, lights rise on the opposite side of the stage from the APPARATUS, revealing a MAN with eyes closed; he too slowly breathes. This is JEFF.)

EAGLE FEATHER: (Voiceover.) Inhale and exhale...let your mind relax as you descend into the lower world of consciousness...

(Out of the darkness beside the APPARATUS emerges an ominous FIGURE. Except for its long black rubber gloves which hold a clipboard, it is dressed and masked entirely in white—an eerie cross between a doctor and a wraith. With efficiently minimal movements, it looks over EUGENE and begins to notate. This is a TECHNICIAN.)

EAGLE FEATHER: (Voiceover.) In this place, you will meet your spiritual guide— your POWER ANIMAL—who will lead your quest for self-healing...

(TECHNICIAN, taking hold of a lever on the APPARATUS, forces EUGENE's head further forward. On his scalp, skin flaps are pulled and pinned back via a large incision to reveal his exposed brain; EUGENE winces as TECHNICIAN inspects his frontal lobe with a ballpoint pen. JEFF, with eyes closed, winces at this vision...)

EAGLE FEATHER: (Voiceover.) Don't question your shamanic visions, simply go with them—

(TECHNICIAN notates. JEFF shifts his head, then peeks open one eye and then the other. He addresses EAGLE FEATHER.)

JEFF: (Whispering.) Uh, how do we know when this is over?

(The lights fade on the APPARATUS. We hear the repeated percussive rhythm of shamanic drumming.)

EAGLE FEATHER: *(Voiceover.)* Let the drumming carry you through your journey—until you hear—

(The drumming changes into a "signal call"—quick, successive, syncopated beats—then returns to the former rhythm.)

EAGLE FEATHER: *(Voiceover.)*—Then you must return to the world's reality and share your healing discoveries with the group…

(The voice and drums fade away, as if a great distance were put between them and the listener…)

JEFF MEETS HIS ANIMAL GUIDE

Sounds of machines replace the drums: ominous cranks and pistons grate and hiss. In the distance, BABIES can be heard crying. Lights rise to reveal the foreign gray landscape of cages and poles that is JEFF's vision. JEFF is cautious not to venture too far into it.

JEFF: Uh, hello? *(He looks around.)* Hello…? *(Pause. He puts his hand to his head, sighing at the amount of effort this venture might seemingly take. Not sure who he's talking to.)* I'm…in my vision… *(He cautiously moves toward a column of frames/cages, recoiling at the foul-smelling substance left on his fingers where they touched the cage. He tries to wipe it off. A bit louder now.)* Um, I'm taking a workshop… *(To himself.)* I don't know why I signed up for this. This is the last thing I'm going to try. This is great. *(Again he tries to get someone's attention within his own vision.)* I'm taking a workshop on shamanism and I'm supposed to meet my animal guide? I'm waiting for my animal guide, hello??

(A white-shrouded and -masked TECHNICIAN enters with outstretched hands, covered in elbow-length industrial black rubber gloves. In its grip is a small squirming

puppet BABY—a grotesque but tender hybrid animal.)*

JEFF: *(To TECHNICIAN.)* Uh, hi. Is that…my animal guide?

(JEFF crosses to TECHNICIAN.)

JEFF: Uh, I thought I might see an eagle or a bear—not a little squishy…guy.

(TECHNICIAN puts BABY into JEFF's uncertain hands.)

JEFF: *(To BABY.)* Um, okay. Hi. Hi there. *(To TECHNICIAN.)* Uh, thanks—what am I supposed to do with—?

(TECHNICIAN recedes into the shadows, continuing to watch the interaction between JEFF and his GUIDE. Suddenly a MECHANICAL VOICE interrupts the blended soundscape of machinery and BABIES.)

MACHINE VOICE: Six hundred thirty-four!

(A loud electrical scan machine noise is heard, followed by a screaming BABY. JEFF's BABY is extremely frightened by this.)

JEFF: It's okay, it's alright. I'm not going to hurt you. I'm not going to hurt you, because you have to help me. I don't know, you're pretty small, and I need a lot of help.

(Trying to pacify BABY in his arms, JEFF nervously looks around while walking across the stage.)

JEFF: What's your name, hmm? My name is Jeff, but I'm also a shaman. Well, in training. And we're going to go on a journey together.

MACHINE VOICE: Six hundred thirty-three!

(The machine scan noise erupts again, with the ensuing screams of a BABY. JEFF's

BABY's face contorts in fear, and begins to cry.)

JEFF: Oh—it's okay. Don't be scared— it's just my vision. Just the way I see things. Lovely right? Oh you're shaking—Here...

(He steps up onto the platform, sits down, and puts BABY up on his knee.)

JEFF: It's okay, little guy. Little guy with little toes.

(He touches BABY's toes. BABY then reaches down and touches the toes JEFF touched.)

JEFF: You know what you look like, hmm? You look like a "Eugene." Hello Eugene. Hello.

(EUGENE reaches out and playfully touches JEFF's nose—then he touches his own nose.)

JEFF: Yes, that's a nose. That's what that is. Ha, ha.

(TECHNICIAN, observing from the shadows, has never seen this kind of interaction before. It now steps forward, removing a black rubber glove, only to reveal a white glove beneath it. It reaches out to touch EUGENE's nose, but EUGENE shifts away. TECHNICIAN tries to hold EUGENE's little hand in his, but EUGENE nervously clutches onto JEFF's face. TECHNICIAN steps back, cocks its head slightly, then materializes a RED BALL in the palm of its white-gloved hand. TECHNICIAN floats BALL a few inches into the air and then back into its hand. It does this once again as EUGENE watches transfixed. Music that will become the ball theme begins to play. This time BALL floats up out of its palm, then slowly descends to the platform, coming to rest a short distance in front of JEFF and EUGENE. EUGENE whimpers with delight, then looks to JEFF.)

JEFF: That's a ball. You like that huh? You want to play with the ball?

(BABY EUGENE squeals. JEFF cautiously looks at nearby TECHNICIAN.)

JEFF: Okay, let's play with the ball. Up we go...

(JEFF lifts EUGENE up into the air and then gently lowers him down to stand on his own little feet. EUGENE slowly, painstakingly, begins to walk to BALL. He looks to the audience, opening his mouth to let out a squeal of delight at his progress. One more step and he reaches BALL, only to have it lift up into the air and out of his grasp! Under TECHNICIAN's spell, BALL temptingly lowers again within reach, but then floats up even higher. BABY EUGENE reaches valiantly for it, but when BALL hovers unobtainably above him, he begins to cry. JEFF looks at TECHNICIAN, who then lowers BALL (with the subtle gesture of a finger or some other appropriate measure.) into EUGENE's welcoming arms. He is extremely happy as he plops down to play with his treasure. He looks up at JEFF.)

JEFF: You like that huh? That's a ball.

(EUGENE laughs.)

MACHINE VOICE: Two hundred fifty-one!

(TECHNICIAN suddenly reaches down and snatches BALL away from EUGENE. Simultaneously, another TECHNICIAN enters, pushing in a large corroded piece of equipment with many wires. The first TECHNICIAN quickly lifts EUGENE up, securing him into the machine.)

JEFF: Hey—what are you doing—Be careful! That's my animal guide—

(EUGENE squirms and cries as a grimy headpiece is locked down onto his skull. JEFF crosses to a TECHNICIAN, trying to intervene.)

JEFF: Hey that's Eugene!

(JEFF is pushed back with a determined arm. A TECHNICIAN throws a switch, and a red light flashes inside the headpiece. A searing electrical current crackles! [This should be a louder version of the previous scan machine noises.] EUGENE's face contorts in pain, as the TECHNICIANS casually look over to an upstage frame. Briefly illuminated, the frame reveals a reddish picture of a brain scan. EUGENE cries in pain, and JEFF does not know what to do.)

JEFF: It's okay—Shhhh! It's okay!

(As the scan image fades, one TECHNICIAN exits with the machine, while the OTHER deposits EUGENE into a downstage cage, where he writhes and wails, clutching his head. Laughter is heard. Lights fade first on JEFF, helplessly watching, and then on the injured EUGENE.)

WELCOME TO THE TV

A flickering, bluish glow rises behind the large scrimmed frame upstage. This is the home. In profile, dressed in a shirt and sweater and old plaid pants is a puppet FIGURE. Seated in the tattered armchair, he holds a remote control in his hand. The laughter continues until he changes the channel—

TV: Is your baby really happy? Give them what they really want! No-leak diapers that won't sag or bunch—

(Change channel.)

TV: *(A soap opera.)* But Olivia, you know it's not yours—I don't care, Bradley I'm going to love and raise that child as if it were—and one day, he'll inherit the—

(Change channel.)

TV: *(A reality game show.)* Well, what it really comes down to, John, is survival of the fittest in this exciting contest—Which

lucky contestants will advance to the next round and who will be sacrificed?

(Change channel.)

TV: *(A peculiar-sounding voice.)* Are you sad? Are you feeling lost and alone?

(He quickly changes the channel. The sound of cowboys and Indians fighting is heard. Suddenly, a RED BALL floats into FIGURE's room and passes by his armchair. He turns, looks down, and watches it slowly float away…The TV changes channels on its own:)

TV: Monday.

(Change channel.)

TV: Tuesday.

(Change channel.)

TV: Wednesday…

(FIGURE sinks into the chair, looking blankly ahead toward the flickering screen. Time ticking is heard…)

PUPPY LOVE

Over the sound of passing time, we begin to hear the sound of a countless number of PUPPIES barking. As the home scene fades out, a light rises on an elevated frame/cage upstage; it contains a solitary BEAGLE puppy (a puppet). It whimpers, scratching the walls of its cage. Slowly, RED BALL rolls in from out of the darkness, coming to rest beneath the cage. DOG looks down, pawing and whimpering, but it cannot reach BALL… Time ticking is heard…

MACHINE VOICE: September, October, November—

HAPPY BIRTHDAY

Lights cross fade onto JEFF slowly entering downstage. His steps are heavy as he carries a small gift box. He pauses, looks back, and sighs. He peers into the now-empty cage that once held BABY EUGENE. He sits on the platform beneath it. Looking at his watch, he is somewhat unsettled to discover it has ceased to work.

JEFF: *(To himself.)* It's not working. *(Looking around.)* I'm not sure this is working…

(A TECHNICIAN enters, carrying a small puppet CREATURE in its arms. The CREATURE wears a black neck collar and has a bloody bandage on his head. He is probably five years old. He is placed in the empty cage that held BABY EUGENE. TECHNICIAN crosses to exit.)

JEFF: *(To TECHNICIAN.)* How are you?

(With its back already to JEFF, TECHNICIAN momentarily stops and cocks its head, but offers no acknowledgment and exits. JEFF steals a glance at the CREATURE lying prostrate in the cage. Then, like a parent who must feign a mood for the sake of his child, he takes a deep breath and puts on a smile.)

JEFF: *(To CREATURE.)* Hey Eugene, how are you?

(EUGENE begins to slowly pick himself up to sit in his cage.)

JEFF: Hey, you're looking good! How did the test go? *(Whispering.)* I heard it went well, so I got you a present. Because you know what today is? *(He reaches for the box.)* Today is Happy Birthday! Look what I've got for you! Someone to say—

(He opens the gift box and pulls out a green-felt hand puppet in the form of a FROG.)

JEFF: *(Animating FROG.)* Hey Eugene! Happy birthday to you! Happy birthday to you! Happy birthday dear—

(EUGENE turns away and delicately touches the bandage on his head.)

EUGENE: *(To JEFF.)* Why?

JEFF: *(He lowers FROG PUPPET.)* Why? *(Pauses.)* Why. Because I'm sad.

EUGENE: I sad too.

JEFF: I know. I know it hurts.

(He takes EUGENE's little hand in his.)

JEFF: I do, because I have something called…depression. *(As FROG PUPPET.)* And that means you're sad all the time! *(As himself.)* And you want to be happy, right?

(EUGENE nods.)

JEFF: Yeah, me too. But I don't know how to find it anymore. I forget how to get there. *(To FROG.)* So he has a very important job—

FROG: Really?

JEFF: Yes. He's like my, my…seeing eye dog. *(To EUGENE.)* Because you're going to be the one to lead the way, and go out and find the happiness for us. Because you're my animal guide!

EUGENE: *(Looks out past the fourth wall at the other INMATES' cages and points to one of them.)* Big Toes?

JEFF: Who? In that cage, 311 is Big Toes?

(EUGENE nods.)

JEFF: No, Big Toes is not my animal guide—only you are! Just you and me. Slap me five!

(He does. JEFF uses FROG PUPPET to boost EUGENE's spirits.)

FROG: And not him either—who's he in that cage?

EUGENE: Big Ears.

JEFF: Nineteen is Big Ears? *(Looking closer.)* Yeah, he does have big ears.

FROG: What's Big Ears doing?

EUGENE: Rocking.

FROG: Oh, you're smart. And who's in that one down there—

JEFF: Oh—that one is empty—

EUGENE: *(Reaches out and takes hold of FROG. Whispering.)* Shhh!

MACHINE VOICE: Five hundred six!

(Across the stage, a TECHNICIAN enters and reaches into a seemingly empty frame/cage...)

EUGENE: *(To FROG PUPPET.)* That was Freddie's!

(A high-pitched scream pierces the room as TECHNICIAN forcibly extricates 506 from his cage. We see glimpses of its puppet HEAD AND ARMS struggling against TECHNICIAN's grasp. They exit. EUGENE grimaces, drops FROG, and covers his ears with his hands and automatically begins to violently rock and bang inside his cage.)

JEFF: *(Nervously trying to pacify.)* It's okay—shhh! Hey come, on, it's okay—Hey—

(He awkwardly animates FROG for distraction, but the screaming is taking a toll on his nerves as well.)

FROG: Hey! Happy birthday Eugene! Happy, happy—

(EUGENE falls to the floor shaking. A TECHNICIAN enters and is about to exit upstage when JEFF hurriedly beckons—)

JEFF: Excuse me! Hello! Hello?? Do you have the paintbrush? Do you have the paintbrush yet?? I've been waiting for it—

(TECHNICIAN stares for a moment at JEFF, despite there being no eyeholes in its

mask, then produces a small paintbrush. The screaming has finally died down, but EUGENE is still shaking. JEFF takes the brush.)

JEFF: Okay Eugene—look!.

(TECHNICIAN exits.)

JEFF: *(To EUGENE.)* Hey Eugene, look! Look what we've got. See? It finally came in—the last piece! Because we had our paper—*(He reveals an easel with white paper and a jar of red paint sitting on the platform.)* —and our paint, now we have our brush. See? It's okay, it's alright... *(He is trying to convince himself as well.)* Okay, here we go—

(He reaches into the cage and gently takes EUGENE out, cradling him in his arms. EUGENE weakly looks up at JEFF, then rests his head on his shoulder.)

JEFF: So now we can paint pictures. 'Cause I think it would be good to get some of these feelings out while you still can. Because, you know,

(EUGENE looks at him.)

JEFF: —a lot of these other kids in cages, they're just smearing their poop around.

EUGENE: It stinky.

JEFF: I know—

(He lowers EUGENE down to stand, while kneeling beside him.)

JEFF: —but now you're going to be able to express yourself, and paint your feelings, *(Whispering.)* because you're going to be better than all the rest of them. You have to be.

(A pause.)

JEFF: So what you do, you take your brush and load it up with the paint and then you can just...paint how you feel.

(JEFF hesitates, then demonstrates by pressing the brush hard against the paper, making smeary red splotches in the middle of it. However, he soon becomes self-conscious of the effort, smiles feebly, and offers the brush to EUGENE.)

JEFF: But I want you to do it. You to do it. So what you do is, you take your brush—and you hold it tight now. Got it?

(EUGENE takes hold of the brush in his hand.)

JEFF: Okay. Now you just…paint what's inside.

(JEFF recedes from the scene. EUGENE looks curiously at the brush, then at the paper. He takes a step or two toward the easel, then begins to add to JEFF's contribution. After a few strokes, he looks at his work, sensing something inherent in it. He continues, painstakingly creating a red, smeary circle. One last dab of paint and a memory unfolds. He reaches to touch the red ball on the paper… The ball theme music begins to play… EUGENE looks out, as if expecting to see his long-ago toy. Lights fade. The sound of medium-sized DOGS barking is heard—)

A TRANSGENIC'S BEST FRIEND

Lights rise on the Puppy Love scene—The PUPPY has grown into a medium-sized beagle (its cage, however, has not gotten any bigger). It whimpers, still looking down at the unattainable RED BALL. The sound of a door opening… Five-year-old EUGENE slowly walks into the room and goes excitedly to his BALL. He gently takes it up, holds it, caresses it to his face, and begins to depart—but the whimpering of the BEAGLE stops him. He shows his treasure to DOG.

EUGENE: *(To DOG.)* Ball.

(DOG continues to whimper—EUGENE takes a few steps closer. He bounces BALL, catches it, then proudly says again his favorite word.)

EUGENE: Ball!

(He thinks for a moment, considering what he has and what DOG does not; so he lifts his arms to share his only possession—but he is not tall enough to reach DOG. Spying a small block on the floor, he puts down BALL, positions the block, then takes up BALL again, stepping now to gain height, and gives it to DOG, who happily plays with it in its cramped cage. EUGENE stretches to pet his newfound friend.)

EUGENE: Dog!

(Suddenly, a TECHNICIAN emerges from the darkness and clasps a heavy chain to the back of EUGENE's collar. The sound of all the DOGS barking erupts! The chain is yanked, and EUGENE is dragged backwards, struggling against it while reaching for DOG. TECHNICIAN then snatches EUGENE up from the platform and pulls him into the darkness. DOG is left alone with BALL, barking after his friend… Lights fade.)

(The sound of an AUCTIONEER's voice in the blackness—)

AUCTIONEER: *(Voiceover.)* This next work is an early piece entitled "Home." We will start the bidding at:

(We hear thousands of dollars being bid, in ascending order. A light rises on the gold frame on the wall. It contains the picture of EUGENE's ball painting. The auction numbers steadily rise, but are overtaken by the sound of a soaring jumbo jet, which blends into the sound of a cracking whip as a mechanized version of the song "Ten Little Indians" begins playing. Cross fade.)

CARRY THE WEIGHT

Lights fade on the painting and rise on EUGENE pushing a heavy gray block across the platform. He struggles and strains against its weight. A TECHNICIAN enters, crossing downstage with a bullwhip, while ANOTHER sits on a gray block monitoring EUGENE's progress. EUGENE is panting and his effort slipping; JEFF attempts to assist… The seated TECHNICIAN twists its head at this infraction, and the other TECHNICIAN immediately wheels around—ready to crack the weapon. JEFF quickly removes his hand from the block, sheepishly bowing his head, and whispers to EUGENE to resume his task. But there is no strength left in him, and he soon collapses exhausted. TECHNICIAN tosses the length of the whip across the floor, ready to strike—)

JEFF: Okay—time out! Time out! Uh…alright, uh…just a second…

(He pats EUGENE, slowly rises, and begins to cautiously cross to the two TECHNICIANS.)

JEFF: Um…I don't want to tell you how to do your job or anything…but don't you think it's just a little bit overkill with the bullwhip? I mean, it's like twelve feet long—he's three feet high—

(The seated TECHNICIAN rises, lifts its block, and crosses to stack it on top of EUGENE's. EUGENE looks up at this and drops his head, sighing. JEFF feels helpless. During JEFF's monologue, TECHNICIANS move about him: countering and stealthily blocking him like dangerous chess-pieces planning their kill.)

JEFF: Right. Um, I'm taking a workshop, up there— *(He points to the ceiling.)* —on "How to Be a Shaman"—how to find your healing, you know? And he's supposed to help me with that.

(EUGENE peeks around the blocks.)

JEFF: But I'm not sure how far we're going to get if you just completely exhaust him.

(TECHNICIANS look over at EUGENE, who quickly retreats behind the blocks.)

JEFF: *(Whispering.)* I mean, I think I see where you're trying to go with all this: depression equals lethargy, lack of motivation…but, um, I paid a lot of money for this workshop and I just don't want to wind up at the end of it empty-handed and wake up with nothing because he was too tired to find me anything!

(The lack of response from TECHNICIANS is frustrating JEFF.)

JEFF: No response. Okay. This is the silent type, tough love approach, right? Great. Okay, well I don't know what to say, because if this is the way you do things down here, then why don't we just, just add another block? Hmmm? Yeah, let's add another block and then we can speed things up a little quicker and get to my cure that much faster! Huh? Does that make sense? That makes sense to me! Whattaya think??

(He approaches EUGENE and starts to pound on the blocks.)

JEFF: Okay Eugene, you know what we have to do? We have to push. We have to push harder! Come on. Let's go. Because what's his name? Big Ears! Big Ears was pushing— *(To TECHNICIANS.)* —how many? Right! *(To EUGENE.)* He was pushing ten blocks as soon as he was out of surgery! *(To TECHNICIANS.)* See? Work on his competitive insecurities! *(To EUGENE.)* Come on Eugene! You want to be the winner don't you? Don't want to be a loser all your life?? You're never going to amount to anything!

(EUGENE is valiantly trying. JEFF is getting carried away trying to prove his point to TECHNICIANS; he pushes the blocks out of the way, causing EUGENE to fall to the ground.)

JEFF: See! Look how easy it is! You know what we need to do?

(He picks EUGENE up to stand on his feet.)

JEFF: We need to pretend it's Sunday! It's "running in place" day! Come on—

(JEFF takes EUGENE and forces him to run in place.)

JEFF: Lift those legs! Faster!

(He glances over at the stoic TECHNICIANS.)

JEFF: Come on now, this is the way we do things—we can't question the system!

(EUGENE begins to pant and lose his balance.)

JEFF: Come on! You want to help me don't you? Come on, left, right, left, right, left, right, left, right, left, right! Left—

(EUGENE stumbles and drops exhausted. He lies on the floor breathing heavily... JEFF rests a guilty hand gently on EUGENE.)

JEFF: *(To TECHNICIANS.)* Maybe something like that? Hmm? Because this is about him and me. That's what it said in the brochure. You, I don't even know what you're supposed to be! You're just obstacles in the vision. That's what you are. You're monsters in the dream. And when you have a monster in your dream, it doesn't exist.

(JEFF relies on the fragile confidence of this new realization as he approaches the standing TECHNICIANS.)

JEFF: Do you dream? Ever have one? Because you don't have to be afraid. All you have to do, is go up to the monster and say, "Hey Monster—"

(He raises a hand up to the blank white face of a TECHNICIAN...)

JEFF: "—you don't exist!"

(From behind, the SECOND TECHNICIAN quickly gets JEFF in a choke-hold with a black baton. The FIRST TECHNICIAN rams a fist deep into his exposed stomach. JEFF drops down to the ground in a heap. TECHNICIAN raises the baton for a second strike, but the OTHER prevents it with a sharp look. They both exit. JEFF and EUGENE lie in identical breathing humps. Laughter is heard... Lights cross fade.)

1:23 P.M.

Lights rise on the home; the laughter continues. FIGURE is still sitting in his chair, bathed in the flickering blue light of the TV. Channel switch.

TV: Jon, these contestants have got to have stamina and endurance and the will to survive to win this ultimate contest!—

(Switch.)

TV: The death toll continues to rise from today's horrific bombing—

(Switch. FIGURE looks down where RED BALL had once floated past; he reaches down, feeling for it, but there is no ball.)

TV: After a long day's work, you're tired and deserve to relax—what you want now is a nice cold—

(Switch.)

TV: —regain your confidence again with Hair Weave 2000—

(Switch. FIGURE sits back in his chair, staring blankly ahead.)

TV: This station is conducting a test, this is only a test:

(A emergency broadcast tone blares, getting louder. As the home scene quickly fades out, the shaman workshop light—the same as the first time JEFF was seen—snaps on. JEFF opens his eyes, blinking, startled out of his vision/trance. The emergency tone stops. JEFF awakes (momentarily). Looking out across the darkened workshop, JEFF tries to get SOMEONE's attention.)

JEFF: Uh—Eagle Feather? Shhh—

(He becomes aware of a PARTICIPANT in the workshop—no doubt trying to concentrate on her own vision.)

JEFF: Eagle Feather? Hi, um, sorry—but I'm not sure this is working—Um…I'm getting hurt in my vision—

(Again, he is disturbing a PARTICIPANT.)

JEFF: Sorry, shhh. *(Whispering to EAGLE FEATHER.)* Everyone else is probably being led by eagles and bears—I've got a genetically altered test subject!

EAGLE FEATHER: *(Voiceover.)* Your vision is your gift.

JEFF: But—he's not even all animal—he's five-eighths human—

EAGLE FEATHER: *(Voiceover.)* Trust what you are given.

JEFF: But he's getting hurt too—

EAGLE FEATHER: *(Voiceover.)* Awareness will come…return to your vision…inhale, exhale…

(JEFF reluctantly closes his eyes once more and exhales… The lab world sound resumes as the shaman light fades.)

DOLLHOUSE

A light rises on a gray dollhouse. Five-year-old EUGENE cautiously steps from behind it and looks around. He no longer has a head bandage. A TECHNICIAN enters, crosses to him, and motions to the dollhouse. EUGENE obediently goes behind the dollhouse and then emerges with (one at a time) three stuffed animals: a rabbit, a cat, and a dog. Placing the first two down on the platform, he plays only with the dog, rocking while petting it. TECHNICIAN points to the other toys. EUGENE shakes his head and pushes them away, resuming his petting. TECHNICIAN reaches down and extends from the stuffed dog's head a long silver antenna. EUGENE continues to pet the dog with a now-protruding antenna. TECHNICIAN depresses a button on a hand-held device, and a sharp electrical current is heard—EUGENE drops his toy in pain. TECHNICIAN gestures to the dog. EUGENE tries again to touch it, but is zapped a second, then third, time. He looks at his pained hand, then moves away from the dog. TECHNICIAN reaches for it—but EUGENE puts out a hand, shaking his head, to protect TECHNICIAN. TECHNICIAN takes the dog and begins to pet it, then holds the toy out to EUGENE. Hesitantly, he takes it in his arms again, moves away from TECHNICIAN, and rocks with his toy once more. TECHNICIAN zaps him one long last time. EUGENE drops the dog in pain, nervously pushes it away, and huddles against the dollhouse.

THE LAZY ANIMAL

Another TECHNICIAN enters, carrying a large black book and sits down on a gray block. The FIRST TECHNICIAN scoops up EUGENE and places him on the seated TECHNICIAN's lap. The book is opened and both EUGENE and TECHNICIAN look down at its pages. *A MECHANICAL VOICE is heard. EUGENE follows the words being read.*

MACHINE VOICE: "The quick brown fox jumped over the lazy dog."

EUGENE: *(Looking up at TECHNICIAN.)* "Dog."

MACHINE VOICE: "The lazy dog has fleas."

(TECHNICIAN turns a page.)

MACHINE VOICE: "The lazy dog doesn't like—"

(TECHNICIAN taps a gloved finger on the book.)

EUGENE: "Me."

MACHINE VOICE: "No one likes—"

(TECHNICIAN taps again.)

EUGENE: "Me. I have no friends."

(TECHNICIAN turns a page.)

MACHINE VOICE: "There is nothing special about—"

EUGENE: *(Anticipating the next word.)* "Me!" *(Looking at the next page.)* "I am wor-"? *(EUGENE looks up at TECHNICIAN, then tries again.)* "I am wor- wor-"?

(EUGENE wrinkles his brow as he has trouble pronouncing the word. JEFF, having been in the shadows behind EUGENE, now peeks over his shoulder. TECHNICIAN sharply tilts its head at him; JEFF sheepishly smiles.)

JEFF: *(Reading.)* "Worthless." "T-h." Worth-less. "I am…worthless." *(JEFF recedes again.)*

EUGENE: "I am worthless."

(TECHNICIAN closes the book as SECOND TECHNICIAN steps from behind and gently—at first—takes hold of EUGENE's head. He whimpers as the skin flaps on his scalp are separated, revealing his brain. A long probe with wires is inserted directly into his frontal lobe. EUGENE yelps and squirms in its grip. The brain scan noise is heard. TECHNICIANS casually glance over at the noticeably darker brain image—Cross fade.)

SUICIDE PENMANSHIP

In the darkness, we hear: "I am worthless, I am worthless…" Lights rise on BIG EUGENE (the puppet from the Descending Vision scene), wearing a black neck collar, sitting in a cramped desk with large textbooks stacked on its bottom rack. He has a test before him, large pencil in hand.

EUGENE: *(Reading.)* "Do you feel severely worthless, moderately worthless, or minimal- *(He has trouble pronouncing the word.)* minima- minimally worthless?" Hmmm.

(He bites on the pencil's eraser as a TECHNICIAN appears beside him.)

EUGENE: *(To TECHNICIAN.)* Ummm…B? Moderately? Moderately! *(He marks "B" on his test. To TECHNICIAN.)* Is that right?

(Offering no help, TECHNICIAN exits.)

EUGENE: *(Calling after.)* Is that right?

(JEFF appears from behind EUGENE. Throughout the scene, he ducks and whispers, cautious of any TECHNICIAN overhearing him.)

JEFF: Psst.

EUGENE: Oh, hi! How are you?

JEFF: Uh, I'm fine. Yeah, but I don't think that one's right.

EUGENE: It's not?

JEFF: No, I think it should be "A."

EUGENE: "A, I feel severely worthless"?

JEFF: I think so...

EUGENE: Are you sure? How do you know?

JEFF: Uh, just a hunch. See, because if the healing we want to find—

EUGENE: Your cure.

JEFF: Right. My cure. Well, if it's strong enough to work on "severely," then that's going to be better than if it just fixes "moderately." Because, see, we want to find the strongest cure, so, I think it's "A."

EUGENE: Oh. Well, that makes sense. Okay. Eraser time! Eraser time! *(EUGENE vigorously uses his eraser.)*

JEFF: Okay. Not so hard—

EUGENE: Eraser time!

(JEFF stops him, while trying to keep his voice down.)

JEFF: Not so hard! You're going to rip the checklist! And they'll take points off for that. So, um, can I do it?

(He takes the pencil from EUGENE.)

EUGENE: Oh. Okay...

JEFF: See, because you got this one wrong too—

EUGENE: Oh, I'm sorry.

JEFF: It's okay. It's alright. I just know this checklist pretty well— *(JEFF discreetly erases the mistake on the test.)*

EUGENE: *(After a pause.)* Jeff?

JEFF: *(Filling in answers.)* Yeah?

EUGENE: Did you see all those rabbits without any eyes—in that little room down the hall?

JEFF: Yeah, I saw them.

EUGENE: Do you think they feel severely worthless too?

JEFF: I don't know— *(He goes back to the test.)*

EUGENE: Or that cigar-smoking monkey? Why does he smoke so much?

JEFF: I don't know Eugene. Let's just focus on the test, okay?

EUGENE: Oh, okay. *(EUGENE sways his legs back and forth in the desk while thinking about the monkey.)* You know, he's orange. I like orange!

JEFF: *(Becoming a bit frustrated, but trying not to show it, he puts the pencil down.)* Eugene? How many are left in your group?

EUGENE: On Ward B?

JEFF: Yeah.

EUGENE: Uh, *(A mnemonic singsong.)* One little two little, three little—six!

JEFF: Six. That means there's still five others you have to compete against. And you know—

EUGENE: I know, I have to be the best.

JEFF: You're going to be the best right?

EUGENE: *(With self-doubt.)* Yes.

JEFF: Okay. So I really need you to concentrate—

EUGENE: Okay. Jeff, I'll concentrate.

JEFF: *(Back to the test.)* Okay.

EUGENE: *(Looks down at the test, with a slight double take.)* But you just changed that one there to "has difficulty concentrating." Right?

JEFF: *(Perplexed, looking at the test.)* Right—

EUGENE: Well, that doesn't make any sense, Jeffrey. How can I concentrate if I "have difficulty concentrating"? Doesn't makah no sense. No sir!

JEFF: *(Hanging his head.)* You're right. None of this makes any sense.

EUGENE: What's the matter?

JEFF: Nothing.

EUGENE: Oh, it's me again isn't it? Oh, I'm an idiot aren't I? I can't do this. *(EUGENE bangs the desk in frustration.)*

JEFF: Yes you can—

EUGENE: No, I'm a dummy! I'm never going to be the best!

JEFF: Yes you will—because I'm helping you, okay? Even though you're the one supposed to be helping me!

EUGENE: Oh, I know, I know—I'll do better—I'm sorry—I will. But— *(Looking around, whispering.)* —why are there so many tests?

JEFF: Because you're a test subject, dummy.

(EUGENE is hurt.)

JEFF: I'm sorry. Hey, it was just a joke. "These are the jokes folks!" Remember? Okay, hey, come on now, number eight. Let's do number eight. Oh, this is an easy one! *(Reading.)* "Do things that once gave you pleasure no longer provide satisfaction?" Now what do you think the answer to that one is?

EUGENE: Satisfaction? What's that?

JEFF: Oh. It means, make you happy.

EUGENE: Oh. *(Closing his eyes, thinking.)* Ummmm…oh! Like the ball?

JEFF: What ball?

EUGENE: Oh, you remember. *(He gestures.)* The ball and the dog! Oh, they made me happy.

JEFF: *(Having forgotten.)* The ball. Right. Well, um, the ball can't make you happy.

EUGENE: It can't?

JEFF: No.

EUGENE: Well, why not?

JEFF: Well, because it's just a ball—it doesn't mean anything.

EUGENE: It doesn't?

JEFF: No, so you have to forget about the ball.

EUGENE: Forget about the ball?

JEFF: Yes.

EUGENE: Will that make you happy, if I forget about it?

JEFF: Look, that's not the point. And the bell is going to ring soon—see the little hand? *(He points to an imaginary clock.)* So here, take the pencil—I don't want to do everything for you—you have to learn how to do this. So just put, "Yes" it doesn't give me pleasure…

EUGENE: *(He hesitates.)* But…I think maybe it still might…

JEFF: Look, Eugene, I know this may be hard to understand, but to find the cure—

EUGENE: Yeah.

JEFF: You first have to feel the way I do.

EUGENE: Okay. How do you feel?

JEFF: *(He struggles to explain.)* I…I don't have any feelings, really. I feel very empty inside…and I don't care about anything anymore. Do you understand?

EUGENE: I understand, but, but I think maybe I still do—

JEFF: *(Pointing.)* You know 419?? He got an "A" on his test!!

EUGENE: Rocks Alot? He did?

JEFF: Who?!

EUGENE: Rocks Alot—419, he's "Rocks Alot," remember? He rocks a lot, so he's "Rocks Alot."

JEFF: Well, maybe I should have "Rocks Alot" as my animal guide instead of you!

(EUGENE looks dejected. A loud buzzer sounds.)

JEFF: See?? Just fill in the "scale of one to ten" questions. Ten is the worst, just put "ten, ten, ten, ten"!

(JEFF quickly disappears behind the desk when a TECHNICIAN appears beside EUGENE, taking away his pencil and test. JEFF slowly peeks around EUGENE's shoulder.)

JEFF: Okay now, we don't want to be late for your next class—

(Lights fade out.)

THE SONIC HALLWAY

MECHANICAL VOICE: *(In darkness.)* Sublevel Twelve. East Corridor. Tuesday.

(A tight shuttered light rises, creating the look of a long stark hallway. EUGENE stands at the top of the hall; in his hand he holds the FROG PUPPET.)

EUGENE: Tuesday. Not my favorite day.

(EUGENE begins walking in place "down the hall." An eerie soundscape of noises is heard. Two TECHNICIANS pass by him on either side, holding long rectangular frames denoting doors in the hallway; EUGENE continues to walk in place as they pass by him, creating the illusion that he is moving down the length of the corridor. From behind the doors TECHNICIANS hold, we hear various caged and extremely unhappy ANIMALS. The closer the doors get to EUGENE, the louder the noises become.)

(First door: screaming CHIMPS. Second door: a room full of highly agitated CATS. EUGENE winces and passes by these quickly. The sound of DOGS barking is getting closer…)

(EUGENE stops at the DOG door; the TECHNICIAN also stops. EUGENE looks both ways, then cautiously takes hold of the frame; we hear squeaky hinges as he opens the door, hoping to see his old friend. He peeks inside…)

EUGENE: Hello…?

(The sound of a door slamming shut is heard as TECHNICIAN suddenly pivots the frame back into its grasp.)

EUGENE: *(Startled.)* Oh! Sorry. Just forget about the ball.

(He quickly "walks" away from the door, TECHNICIAN exiting up the hall.)

EUGENE: I forgot. I forgot to knock. *(To his FROG.)* Knock, knock?

FROG: Who's there?

EUGENE: Eugene.

FROG: Eugene who?

EUGENE: *(Now walks the actual distance it takes to get to the edge of the stage, and looks through a picture/window frame suddenly held up by a TECHNICIAN at the end of the hallway. Looking out at the audience.)* Eugene from Sublevel Twelve! Who do you think? (Pausing for the timing.)

These are the jokes folks! *(If the audience does not laugh, EUGENE sometimes will add:)* Well, I thought it was funny.

(He turns right, and a perpendicular hallway light rises to denote a new hallway. The first hallway light fades out.)

EUGENE: *(To himself, walking.)* Last door on the right.

(A TECHNICIAN walks toward him holding another door frame. A squeaky door is heard as EUGENE pushes it open. He "walks" past it, and nervously looks behind him upon its ominous closing sound. Another sound draws EUGENE's attention: Coming toward him is a TECHNICIAN, pushing in a strange-looking chair with torn upholstery, riddled with electrodes and restraining straps; at the ends of its armrests are two large spring-loaded buttons connected to trailing wires. EUGENE attempts a struggle as he is forced into the chair, but the raising of a TECHNICIAN's gloved finger quickly subdues him. EUGENE's FROG PUPPET is taken away while his arms are strapped into the chair.)

EUGENE: *(To one TECHNICIAN.)* That's my frog… *(To OTHER.)* How are you?

(While TECHNICIAN kneels to strap in his feet, EUGENE decides to ask a question.)

EUGENE: Um…is it true, the rumor circulating, that…loincloths will be distributed? Is that true?

(A corroded metal box with various knobs and wires descends from the ceiling above the chair; TECHNICIANS secure it to EUGENE's head, leaving only his mouth visible beneath the box.)

EUGENE: Uh, it's a little snug, a little snug there—not complaining mind you…

THE AUDIO TRIP

A TECHNICIAN activates the audio loop by pressing a button on the box. Both TECHNICIANS exit. The VOICE has the attempted comforting quality of any ubiquitous automated response system.

VOICE: Hello. How are you feeling? Are you exhausted by the daily grind? Are you questioning what it's all about? Do you long for escape? If yes, press one, if no, press two.

(EUGENE looks at both button choices, then presses the one at the end of the left armrest.)

VOICE: First let's decide where you would like to go. Press one for a big city adventure, press two for a tropical paradise.

(EUGENE presses the button on the right.)

VOICE: All aboard! Your paradise awaits you as you stand on deck of an elegant steamship. Dressed in your custom-made suit, fellow passengers consider you an individual of sophistication and taste.

(EUGENE's posture straightens at this welcome compliment. The steamship's horn lets out a pleasant toot.)

VOICE: Press one to enjoy the view, press two for a tour of the ship—

(EUGENE is about to press one.)

VOICE: —press three for a musical medley by our cruiseline band, "The Voyagers"!

(EUGENE's masked head looks around for a third button.)

EUGENE: Three? There is no three! Trick question! One!

(EUGENE presses one. He is able to "see"' all of the sights the VOICE depicts for him, and he reacts with pleasure at each one.)

VOICE: A breathtaking panorama unfolds before your eyes. Brilliant blue sky, sparkling green waters. On the horizon, your island paradise is just coming into view, and you are filled with gratitude to simply be alive. Press one for more sights, press two for some sounds—

(He presses two. The sound of ocean waves, sea gulls, and a peaceful "new age" music soundtrack begins playing. EUGENE enjoys this, swaying to the windchimes in his strapped chair. Suddenly, the tranquil sounds are overtaken by the ship's massive motor malfunctioning. We hear sirens and alarms! EUGENE is startled out of his moment.)

VOICE: This is your captain speaking. Please quickly make your way to the lifeboats.

(Sirens!)

VOICE: PRESS ONE NOW! PRESS ONE NOW!

(EUGENE quickly presses one.)

VOICE: The lifeboats are all filled. Press one to go down with the ship, press two to jump overboard.

EUGENE: But I can't swim!

VOICE: That is an invalid option. You plunge headlong into the surprisingly frigid waters, and are desperately struggling to stay afloat.

EUGENE: Because I can't swim!!! *(EUGENE struggles in his chair, his arms and legs pulling against their straps.)*

VOICE: Your thrashing begins to attract large menacing shapes beneath the water's surface. Press one to stop thrashing, press two—

(EUGENE hurriedly presses one.)

VOICE: If you stop thrashing, you will drown. The predatory shapes begin to encircle you.

EUGENE: What do I do? What do I do??

VOICE: Suddenly a massive shape erupts from below, blocking your island paradise view. Press one to fight this shape, press two to scream helplessly.

EUGENE: These are not good choices!

VOICE: You must respond within five seconds.

EUGENE: Okay. One! One! I'll fight it!

VOICE: You swing, and its teeth sink deep into your arm, severing it just below the tibia.

EUGENE: Tibia?! That's in my leg!!

VOICE: Press one to continue fighting, two to submit.

EUGENE: This is not fair!!

VOICE: Suddenly a second predator breaks through the churning water. Press one to confront this new foe, press two to continue your initial fight.

EUGENE: Help! Stop! I can't win! *(Becoming very agitated, EUGENE presses buttons erratically and randomly.)*

VOICE: That is not a valid option. That is an incorrect choice.

EUGENE: Nothing I do works! Help! They're tearing me apart!! I quit! I quit! *(He is panicking, thrashing against the restraints.)*

VOICE: That is not a—Press one to engage—Press one to—that is not a valid—Press two to—

EUGENE: I give up!!

VOICE: Hello. How are you feeling?

(EUGENE hangs his head, breathing heavily.)

VOICE: Are you exhausted by the daily grind? Are you questioning what it's all about? Would you like to get away from it all and feel good again? If yes, press one; if no, press two.

(The VOICE and lights fade out.)

2:13 A.M.

In darkness, the sound of falling rain and rolling thunder. Slowly, a light rises, softly illuminating the dollhouse; on its second level, a solitary window flickers from within with a blue light. A blue flickering light rises slowly on the home: FIGURE sits rocking in his chair, half-heartedly watching the TV.

TV: *(Seductive female voice.)* Are you lonely? Need a friend? We're lonely too— call us—

(Change channel.)

TV: *(Evangelist preacher.)* Are you saved? If not, my friend, you are jeopardizing your eternal happiness! Call us now—

(Change channel.)

TV: Is your pet happy and healthy?

(The sound of lightning crashing extinguishes all lights on stage save for an electric flash that briefly illuminates the dog cage. Inside it, just for a moment, we see BEAGLE, now fully grown, whimpering and cramped. RED BALL is still in the cage with him. Lights fade on DOG and come up again on the home: this time FIGURE is nowhere to be seen, replaced instead by JEFF sitting in the chair, slowly rocking. JEFF, as if waking from a dream, looks around his unfamiliar surroundings, unsure how he got here.)

TV: It's a close race now Jon, only three contestants left competing for the "ultimate challenge"! We'll find out who's going to be sacrificed next, after this word from our sponsor—

(Change channel.)

TV: *(We hear the same peculiar-sounding voice we heard on the commercial from the Welcome to the TV scene.)* Are you sad? Feeling lost and alone? Want to feel like your old self again? It may be time for you to take the next step. Vibratech 8000!

(Recognizing the voice, JEFF looks up at the TV.)

TV: Take it from me, Eugene! If it worked for me, it will work for you.

(Amazed, JEFF points to the TV and laughs. Lights fade to black. In the darkness, the sound of the cavalry still battling the Indians is heard.)

MACHINE VOICE: Monday, Tuesday, Wednesday…

TO FROG WITH LOVE

Lights rise on EUGENE kneeling on the platform, hunched inside a cage. This cage is positioned beneath the floating one that once held the two younger versions of EUGENE. He wears a bandage on his head, dried blood showing through. In his hand is his FROG PUPPET.

EUGENE: *(To himself.)* On a scale of one to ten, how do you feel? A? B? C? D? X: I don't feel anything.

(He looks down at his FROG, lifts it up, and begins to animate it.)

FROG: I don't feel anything either.

EUGENE: Oh, that's because you don't have any feelings. You don't even have a soul.

FROG: Who took away my soul? Where did it go??

EUGENE: Well, you never had one—you're empty. You are not even really alive.

FROG: I am too alive, see?

(EUGENE animates FROG in a sing-songy way, bouncing him around inside the cage.)

FROG: Because I can do this, and this, and doo-dee-doo-dee-doo!

EUGENE: *(Halts FROG's demonstration, taking him in both hands.)* Oh, that's not really alive, just because you can walk and talk and eat and sleep and breathe. *(He brings him close to his face.)* No. You're... you're dead.

FROG: No, I am alive!

EUGENE: *(Handling FROG with increasing violence.)* No, you're only alive when I make you live! When I stick my hand up into your hole, and out your silly little frog face to make you go where needs to be gone, and— *(Using FROG's voice.)* —say what needs to be said...

FROG: *(Taunting EUGENE.)* There are still four left, and you'll never be the best!!

EUGENE: Wrong!

(EUGENE slams FROG down, banging its head against the floor. The little FROG PUPPET cries in pain.)

EUGENE: Oh, stop it—you can't feel anything! You can't feel this—

(Slam!)

EUGENE: —or this!

(Slam!)

FROG: *(Weakly.)* Yes I can.

EUGENE: No, those are not real screams—

FROG: Yes they are...

EUGENE: No—you're just squeaking like a rusty hinge! *(EUGENE, breathing heavily, rocks back and forth, pressing FROG into the ground while looking from side to side with a wide-eyed stare.)* You're wrong, because I will be the best! I will be...the best...

(Blackout.)

SHAMAN COAXES

Lights rise on EUGENE lying in his cage with his back to the audience. We see him slowly breathing. JEFF sits beside him holding a dented, rusty food bowl in his lap. He eats the food pellet contents.

JEFF: *(To EUGENE.)* You know, I haven't been hungry in so long. No appetite really. Too busy to make food. But these aren't so bad actually. Junk food. Just been eating a lot of junk food lately. *(He stops eating, grimacing.)* These have a funny aftertaste though, don't they? You want one?

(No response from EUGENE.)

JEFF: Not hungry right? You just want to sleep all the time now, am I right? How did I know? I know what you're thinking. *(JEFF stares out ahead.)* You're thinking, "What's the point of getting up out of bed again today, with all the work it's going to take to just get through another twenty-four hours?" Right? Another twenty-four hours where nothing goes right, nothing feels right, you just can't fit in, and it all starts to seem very, very pointless. So you start to think, maybe it would be better if I just...never woke up again. *(He looks over at EUGENE.)* Well, I'm telling you, that's a good thing to think! Because it means we're so close now! Because you're going to be the best! Because I saw you on TV! That's what I've been trying to tell you—

I had a vision in my vision and you were on the commercial, in a blue suit—looking very sharp—and you said it's all going to change! Said "If it worked for me—it will work for you." See? So we'll be celebrating soon! Hey, are you listening to me? Sit up. Come, on, this is important. Eugene? Sit up.

EUGENE: I don't want to.

(JEFF helps an uncooperative EUGENE to sit up.)

JEFF: Hey, come on, help me here, you weigh a thousand pounds! Did you hear what I just said?

EUGENE: *(Sits crouched, his head in his knees.)* I heard you, but I don't believe you.

JEFF: What do you mean, you don't believe me, I saw it on the TV! It's in the future—

EUGENE: You said when you're really depressed, you can't even think about the future—so how could you see it?

JEFF: Because… *(Searching for an answer.)* Because I'm a shaman, and "shaman" means "seer." See? So I saw it. I got a glimpse!

EUGENE: But you're not a real shaman. You're just taking a forty-eight-dollar class.

JEFF: Hey, it's an eighty-four-dollar seminar, okay? And besides, Eagle Feather said to everybody, we're all shamans…we all have the potential…to be healers.

EUGENE: So then why don't you heal yourself?

JEFF: Because I don't know how! I need you to find it for me.

EUGENE: But what if I don't want to anymore?

JEFF: But Eugene, what am I supposed to do? I've tried everything else. I've tried every depression support group there is, every double-blind experimental medication study they have. It works for a while, then they need to up the dosage, then it doesn't work, so they up it, then I can't afford it. So I tried books on tape and magnets and crystals and meditation, but there are too many car alarms all the time—so I took a workshop to get in touch with my inner fetus and then a past life regression seminar—you know what I was in my past life? I was an Egyptian slave! That's what I saw, okay?! So none of that works. I can't go into the past anymore—I've already been there. I need the future. Something undiscovered and cutting edge! That's where you come in. So enough about me, okay?

EUGENE: Yes, enough about you. It's all about you.

JEFF: What is that supposed to mean?

EUGENE: Everything is about you! What about me?

JEFF: Eugene, if there was any another way, don't you think I would? But you're the test subject.

EUGENE: I thought I was a power animal, or an animal guide, something fancy, now I'm just a test subject?

JEFF: You are. But, it's just the way my vision is.

EUGENE: Your vision! You, you, you! All about you!

JEFF: Would you stop saying that! It's not just about me! Okay? Because there are a lot of other people out there who feel bad. And you're going to help heal all them too!

EUGENE: Why don't they heal them-selves?!

JEFF: You know, you sound really selfish right now. Really selfish! Care about no-body but Mr. Eugene!

EUGENE: Oh, I'm selfish.

JEFF: Yes you are! And it's not very be-coming for a national TV spokesperson. *(Whispering.)* Because you know, there's still two others left on the ward. So maybe 312 or what's-his-name, "Has No Skin," should get the job.

EUGENE: You said I was the one.

JEFF: Yeah, well, then maybe you had better practice your speech.

EUGENE: Fine! Then let me practice.

JEFF: Then go ahead and practice!

EUGENE: Then leave me alone!!

(JEFF recedes, leaving EUGENE frustrated and alone in his cage. He leans against the bars and practices his memorized speech.)

EUGENE: *(Looking to the audience.)* Are you sad? Feeling lost and alone? I can help. Take it from me, Eugene. If it worked for me, it will work for you.

(The "Ten Little Indians" song plays again, counting down how many little Indians are remaining. On top of this, the MACHINE VOICE counts down the competition.)

MACHINE VOICE: Three twelve.

(INMATE 312's screams are heard as it is removed somewhere from its cage.)

MACHINE VOICE: Nineteen.

(NUMBER 19's screams join with 312's. EUGENE closes his eyes, slowly putting his hands to his ears, and begins rocking in his cage. The lights fade to black.)

A FRIENDLY GIFT

Lights rise on EUGENE, prostrate in his cage. Softly, the first notes of the ball theme lift out of the darkness. From the shadows, BEAGLE emerges with RED BALL in its mouth. Parts of DOG's fur and skin have been removed, exposing raw, pink flesh. He walks slowly to EUGENE's cage and gently places BALL inside. EUGENE opens his eyes, weakly touching BALL. He then sees DOG (its tail vigorously wagging) and with effort rises to his knees. EUGENE pets and hugs his friend, and DOG excitedly licks his face and hands.

EUGENE: Oh, hello! Hello doggie! I thought I'd never see you again! Oh, how are you?

(EUGENE unintentionally pets DOG on an exposed part of its skin. DOG recoils, whimpering.)

EUGENE: Oh! I'm sorry. Did I hurt you?

(He reaches to DOG through the bars, but it backs away.)

EUGENE: It's alright. See, I hurt too. See? This is where I hurt— *(He touches his head.)* —in my, uh, chapter three. My hip-pocampus! See, it's alright.

(DOG lets EUGENE pet him again.)

EUGENE: Because I'm going to make it all better. I'm going to heal everybody! Because I'm going to be on TV and wear blue clothes. Because I'm going to be the best! Ha, ha! I just have to get all the way to number ten on the checklist… *(He puts a hand up, covering his eyes to remember properly.)* "Subject has recurrent thoughts of suici—sum-i-mi-icides—" *(He can't pronounce the word. Frustrated.)* Oh, I can never say that word!

(DOG looks down at BALL and barks.)

EUGENE: Shhh! Not so loud. Don't want to get into trouble. *(EUGENE touches BALL, the memories coming back to him.)* You remember this?

(He rolls BALL to DOG. DOG rolls it back to EUGENE.)

EUGENE: Ball. B-a-l-l. Can you say ball? Oh, that's easy. That's review material, that is.

(He rolls BALL to DOG, who sits down, resting its head on top of it, its paws beside it. EUGENE sighs heavily.)

EUGENE: Doggie?

(DOG looks up.)

EUGENE: Why does it have to be so hard?

(EUGENE rests his head on top of DOG's; his tail gently wagging.)

EUGENE: Why does it have to be so hard?

(Lights fade to black.)

DOG AUCTION

Lights rise on the gold frame containing a heavy black-lined painting depicting EU-GENE offering RED BALL to DOG. They are both smiling. It is being auctioned.

AUCTIONEER: *(Voiceover.)* Next lot up, an extremely valuable piece—Number 427. We'll start the bidding at:

(Numbers rise in the hundreds of thousands. Lights cross fade back to the cage.)

JEFF SPEAKS

JEFF sits beside the now-empty cage. He holds FROG PUPPET in his hand, limply animating him.

JEFF: It's not just about me. It's not. *(He gestures to the painting before its light fades out.)* See? The proceeds to all his paintings are going to help fund the research for everybody else. Nineteen million! That's the figure. It's nineteen million people now in this country alone that feel bad. And that's seven percent more than last year. And next year it'll be seven percent more than this year. That's what the government says. It's getting out of control. They don't know why. But every year it's more, more, more. So, see it's not just about me.

FROG: Then why do you feel so alone?

JEFF: *(He pauses, then slowly crushes the FROG's face in his hands.)* You ask dumb questions. Because I'm not going to be. It's all going to change as soon as he gets out. *(He animates FROG, almost unconsciously.)*

FROG: Of isolation.

(JEFF takes his hand out of FROG and puts it over PUPPET's mouth.)

JEFF: Yeah, shhh. It's almost over. *(He speaks as FROG without animating it.)*

FROG: Four more months.

JEFF: Yes but then it'll be finished. It will all be over. And he'll be cured. Because they're going to install it— *(He gestures to his temple.)* —and it will regulate everything. And it will work for him! And then they'll give it to me, and it will work for me! And then we can give it to everybody who needs it and we'll go everywhere and share the good news, like Las Vegas—

(The sound of a plane soaring overhead.)

AIRPORT VOICE: Now arriving in Las Vegas—

JEFF: —Or South Dakota, North Dakota—

(A puppet LECTURER dressed in a crisp blue suit, standing behind a lectern is wheeled onto stage into a blue light. Flanked by TECHNICIANS, LECTURER moves his lips in silence and gestures in slow motion, giving an unheard speech. Both he and JEFF's gestures are synchronized at times.)

JEFF: And we'll say to everyone—"Don't you want to feel happy again? Aren't you tired of being dissatisfied with your life?" *(He waves FROG PUPPET in the air.)* Well I am! Well, no more, because we found the way! We found the cutting-edge path into the future! Because the future is here today and it is time to stop the pain! *(To FROG.)* That's the slogan—"IT IS TIME TO STOP THE PAIN!' *(JEFF begins walking off the stage while still chanting.)* IT IS TIME TO STOP THE PAIN! IT IS TIME TO STOP—

(As JEFF exits behind LECTURER, his blue light changes to bright white, and we realize the lecturer is EUGENE. The end of the slogan is finished by EUGENE's voice:)

EUGENE: —THE PAIN! Take it from me, Eugene—IF IT WORKED FOR ME, IT WILL WORK FOR YOU!

(Applause is heard.)

EUGENE: Thank you! Thank you, you're beautiful!

(EUGENE waves to the crowds as he is wheeled offstage by TECHNICIANS; revealed is BEAGLE framed behind a ground-level picture frame, holding RED BALL in his mouth. He breathes slowly, valiantly standing on three legs—one having been surgically removed. The applause is fading out as MACHINE VOICE becomes audible—)

DOG JOURNEY

MACHINE VOICE: *(Slower pace.)* Monday…Tuesday…Wednesday… *(Begins skipping—)* Wednesday, Wednesday, Wednesday…Merry Christmas!

(The ball theme begins to play—it is altered, slower, or fractured. DOG looks out to the audience, blinking, then exhales and begins to hobble toward the isolation cage: a small, squat, dirty gray box with air holes and a grimy food slot near the bottom. DOG places BALL beside the cage and begins to whimper. EUGENE's hand slowly emerges from the food slot. DOG nudges BALL to EUGENE, and he begins to wag his tail. EUGENE's hand slowly nudges it back to DOG… Suddenly, a TECHNICIAN enters and locks a chain onto DOG's collar, dragging it, yelping, offstage. The sound of many DOGS barking is heard as EUGENE is left to reach for the unattainable RED BALL… Lights fade to black.)

KILLER BALL

The cavalry battle is heard once more, but there are only two or three Indian voices left yelling amidst the military onslaught. A volley of gunshots resounds, artillery explodes, and then the voice of the Indians is heard no more; replaced by the beeping of a life support monitor. A light rises on the brain scan. It is a deep, dark purple. Simultaneously, a line from the "Ten Little Indians" song begins repeating:)

SONG: One little Indian boy, one little Indian boy, one little Indian boy… *(Fades out.)*

(Lights rise on EUGENE sitting slumped in a chair. TECHNICIAN kneels beside him.)

TV VOICES: It all pays off with this moment Jon—The sole survivor of the contest! That's right John—He has made it to the ultimate challenge—the last test! Let's hear if he has any final words before he crosses the finish line.

(Another TECHNICIAN enters with a sleek, black rectangular box. EUGENE slowly breathes, but does not react.)

TV VOICES: No final words Jon. Boy Jon, you could cut this tension with a knife…

(TECHNICIAN opens the box; nestled in its red velvet lining is a long, sharp, silver knife. The knife is gently placed in EUGENE's hand. Clenching it, he extends his other arm and slowly, compulsorily places the blade against his wrist. TECHNICIAN places its white-gloved hand over EUGENE's vein, halting his action; then, producing RED BALL, puts it in EUGENE's extended hand. The life support beeping continues. EUGENE looks up at both TECHNI-CIANS. He hesitates. A faint light rises on the dog cage—inside BEAGLE lies, faintly breathing. One of the TECHNICIANS nods to EUGENE… He closes his eyes, exhales deeply, and slowly plunges the knife into BALL. The beeping is interrupted by a flatline tone. DOG draws his last breath and dies. Applause!)

THE DEMONSTRATION

Applause! Lecturer EUGENE is wheeled in behind his podium flanked by JEFF. They cross from one side of the stage to the other, as if crossing the country.

EUGENE: Thank you Alabama! Thank you Detroit, Arizona—New Mexico—California!

(They "arrive" in California; TECHNI-CIAN enters, flanking the podium to facilitate the animation of EUGENE.)

EUGENE: How do you feel? Do You Want To Feel Happy Again? Are You Tired Of Being Dissatisfied With Your Life? Maybe It's Time To Take The Next Step—Vibratech 8000! The Future's Weapon For Pain Relief Today! You tried everything else, right Jeff?

JEFF: That's right—nothing else worked for me!

EUGENE: Nothing Else Compares With Vibratech's Cutting-Edge Technology! The Most Advanced Scientific Break-through Ever Developed!

OLD MAN IN AUDIENCE: *(Voiceover.)* What about all the suffering?

JEFF: What about it? That's why we're here—to put an end to the suffering.

EUGENE: That's right. I have suffered so you no longer have to—

JEFF: Tell him about the offer.

EUGENE: If you sign up today, sir, you'll get your first three-month supply of Vibratech at half price—

JEFF: And the tote bag—

EUGENE: Yes—Plus a complimentary tote bag!

JEFF: For free!

EUGENE: Complimentary, they're synonyms—it's redundant, Jeff.

JEFF: Oh. Sorry.

EUGENE: It's alright.

AUDIENCE MEMBER: *(Voiceover.)* Eugene, how do you feel about all the test subjects who were sacrificed to find this cure? How do you think they felt?

JEFF: Oh, now—

EUGENE: No, I know how they felt— they were proud of their commitment for humanity's survival—as am I, being five-eighths human—How else can we find the cure for Today's Pain?

ACTIVIST: EUGENE!!

EUGENE: Thank You! You're Beautiful!

(EUGENE and JEFF move back to the other side of the stage/country.)

EUGENE: Thank you Oregon, Washington, Chicago, Cincinnati! *(Arriving.)* Do You Want To Feel Happy Again? Well, Maybe It's Time To Take The Next Step! If It Worked For Me—It Will Work For You!

(A bluish light envelops EUGENE as JEFF breaks away from animating EUGENE, letting TECHNICIANS take over, implementing the earlier slow-motion stylistic gesticulations. JEFF stands in a separate light.)

JEFF: *(Talking to himself.)* If it worked for me, it will work for you. I didn't think it was going to work—I had my doubts, but he did it—he led the way and here I am and I feel great. That is my animal guide— thank you very much! I'm ready to go back and spread the news—Eagle Feather— *(Looking up.)* —hit me back with the signal drums!

(Still in slow motion, EUGENE falters at his podium. A TECHNICIAN passes a strange black device with red glowing lights over EUGENE's head. JEFF looks over.)

JEFF: Wait—it's just one maintenance application.

EUGENE: Not anymore.

JEFF: Since when?

EUGENE: Since Texas.

(Applause! EUGENE's blue light turns bright white as he again crosses the country on his lecture tour.)

EUGENE: Thank you! We have to go now to New York City—to the kindergarten class!

(During the following exchange, the home light rises, revealing FIGURE watching the proceedings from his armchair.)

EUGENE: Hey kids! Do you want to feel happy again? Are you tired of being dissatisfied with your life? Well I know what you need—oh, a question—yes?

KID: *(Voiceover.)* Do you go out on Halloween?

EUGENE: Oh, I wish I could, but I'm too busy spreading the good news—

KID: *(Voiceover.)* Because your face is scary!

(EUGENE is hurt by the comment. JEFF has moved back to EUGENE's side.)

JEFF: They're so cute at this age, aren't they?

KID: *(Voiceover.)* Eugene, did you poop in your cage? Did you go poopin' in your cage?

(EUGENE is slightly disoriented by the line of questions.)

JEFF: *(To EUGENE.)* You're sweating— Are you alright?

EUGENE: I'm fine. I'm fine.

(JEFF pats down EUGENE's sweating brow. EUGENE tries to concentrate on his duties and pushes away his hand.)

ACTIVIST: *(Voiceover.)* Does Vibratech have any long-term side effects that will show up in the future?

EUGENE: This is the future! It's May, June, July! *(EUGENE pounds the podium for emphasis, but then misses it, causing him to fall forward.)*

JEFF: *(Helping EUGENE.)* That's right—this is Mr. Future right here. And I think it's time for him to take a break—

EUGENE: No, the little girl there—

JEFF: No, I think you had enough for today—

EUGENE: No, I'm fine! *(To the GIRL.)* Yes? Speak directly into the microphone.

GIRL: *(Voiceover.)* Eugene?

EUGENE: *(Having difficulty concentrating on the question, breathing with some labor now.)* Yes, I'm Eugene.

GIRL: *(Voiceover.)* What happened to—

EUGENE: What happened to what?

GIRL: *(Voiceover.)* What happened to your dog? Wasn't he your friend?

(Taken by surprise and unsettled, EUGENE fumbles with his papers.)

EUGENE: Uh…that's not…written here…uh, no comment.

ACTIVIST: *(Voiceover.)* Eugene!

EUGENE: Thank You! You're Beautiful. Uh, we have to move on now—have to go to…Atlanta!

(EUGENE pushes his podium out of the light—home FIGURE is looking on.)

EUGENE: Thank You Atlanta! You're Beautiful. Like in New Jersey! *(He pushes the podium to a new locale.)* It's not "Old" Jersey, it's "New" Jersey! *(Pushes the podium again.)* Now where. Where do we go next?

JEFF: Why don't you sit down?

EUGENE: I'm fine—Where do we go to next?

HOME FIGURE: *(Leaning in his chair, speaking to EUGENE.)* Delaware.

EUGENE: *(To JEFF.)* Where?

(Lights rise brighter on the home space, revealing FIGURE's resemblance to an older EUGENE.)

HOME FIGURE: Delaware.

(EUGENE and JEFF glance back to FIGURE in the home.)

JEFF: *(To EUGENE.)* No—you're not scheduled for Delaware—take a rest.

EUGENE: No, there's so many people to save, I'd like to read a, a test-i-monial now—

(EUGENE slips from the podium, falling backwards to the platform. The workshop drums are suddenly heard… JEFF pushes past TECHNICIANS to the fallen EUGENE.)

JEFF: Are you okay? You okay??

EUGENE Just a little dizzy…

(The drums continue to beat out the signal rhythm. EUGENE looks up, listening, his breathing labored.)

EUGENE: You hear the drums? That means you have to go back, Jeff. And I have to go to someplace called Delaware…

JEFF: No, shhh—

EUGENE: No, I can see the future now too. I can see it—I'm in a chair, in a room…in a house. Or a home. *(He looks to JEFF.)* What's the difference?

(JEFF holds EUGENE, stealing glances at his future self upstage in the home.)

EUGENE: And I can see myself watching myself on the television. On the commercial. But that's the end of the vision for me.

JEFF: No, that's not the end—

EUGENE: I'm sorry I didn't do better.

JEFF: Well, we'll just have to try harder—

EUGENE: I'm sorry. I tried my best.

(The drumming intensifies, pulsing into a much faster beat. TECHNICIANS disrupt the embrace, lifting EUGENE up by the arms.)

JEFF: Wait, what are you doing?

(TECHNICIANS begin walking EUGENE offstage. JEFF runs after them, trying to halt their departure.)

JEFF: Wait, what are you doing? Where are you taking him? Wait! He needs to read a testimonial—he can't leave, that would just leave me back at the beginning!! Wait!

(He chases them to the edge of the stage, as one final, reverberating drumbeat resounds, bringing JEFF back into the real-world workshop, with its light snapping on.)

JEFF: *(His eyes blinking.)* Wait! Um…can you play the drums a little longer, I have to go back into my vision. That can't be the end because I don't—I wouldn't have any healing to share with the group… *(He looks out into the audience/workshop participants. He points—)*

JEFF: Did you, you had an eagle? Did your eagle fly away? Did anyone have a bear who just dropped off and hibernated? Because my animal guide was just dragged off to a nursing home in Delaware. So I have nothing to share because I didn't get any healing.

EAGLE FEATHER: *(Voiceover.)* Your animal gave you nothing?

JEFF: Didn't you just hear what I—No! I didn't get anything! I don't believe this. I said this was the last thing I was going to try. I paid a lot of—I don't know. I don't know if it's me—maybe it's me. Or if it's this workshop, but I'm feeling a bit worse than when I started. *(He looks around helplessly.)* So I guess you all just share amongst yourself about your bears and porcupines…and…great. Thanks.

(The sound of TV. Static is heard as the lights fade to black.)

DARKEST BEFORE THE DAWN

Lights rise on the home where JEFF, seated in the armchair, stares blankly ahead, the TV light glowing over him as the static continues. After a few beats, he shakes his head in resigned disbelief and searches for the remote. He finds it, but keeps his eyes on something else while he turns off the TV. He lifts from the chair RED BALL.

PUPPY LOVE

JEFF looks around.

JEFF: Eugene? *(He rises from his chair.)* Eugene? *(JEFF walks into a downstage pool of light. He holds BALL, but doesn't quite know what to do with it. He sits down on the platform edge, looking out at the audience.)*

JEFF: I got a ball? A little red ball. What am I supposed to do with this, Eugene?

(After a pause, a whimper is heard and from behind JEFF a small BEAGLE PUPPY emerges beside him.)

JEFF: Where did you come from?

(PUPPY puts its two front paws up onto JEFF's leg and eagerly reaches its snout up to his face. PUPPY then looks down at BALL still in JEFF's hand. JEFF, hesitantly petting DOG, looks down at BALL.)

JEFF: *(Softly.)* Hey, look what I got. Look what…someone gave to me…

(He takes PUPPY in his hands, their noses touching as he pets his new friend. A soft light rises on the painting of EUGENE sharing BALL with DOG—both smiling. The lights fade first on JEFF and PUPPY, leaving the painting lit for a brief moment before it too fades to black.)

(THE END.)

ODYSSEUS DIED FROM AIDS

Stephen Svoboda

STEPHEN SVOBODA was born in New Rochelle, New York, in 1976. He is currently a professor in the Theatre Arts Department at the University of Miami where he teaches directing and playwriting, and serves as the producer for the University of Miami's Studio Theatre Series. He is also the director of the university's Summer Theatre Academy. Svoboda holds a BA in biology and theatre from SUNY Plattsburgh. He received his MFA in dramatic writing from Ohio University School of Theater, where he studied under Vincent J. Cardinal and received the Scott McPherson Award for Excellence in Playwriting. Both his full-length plays *Fore* and *Sleep Walker* were produced at Ohio University. Svoboda's play, *So Anyway...*, was produced by the Proud Hearts Players as a touring production at more than twenty universities in the Northeast. The Proud Hearts Players also produced the Chasing a Dream Benefit, a three-day AIDS Awareness fundraiser for northeastern New York, of which Svoboda's play *Chasing a Dream* was the centerpiece. For the daytime drama *Guiding Light*, he worked in production and in writing. His new play, *Reconstructing Mama*, was featured at the Play by Play New Play Festival in Michigan. Svoboda is currently working on a docudrama project that explores the impact of the AIDS crisis in Africa and the position of the American public on the global AIDS epidemic.

Odysseus Died from AIDS was first produced as a workshop production by Fresco Productions (Stephen Svoboda, Artistic Director; Elizabeth Naranjo, Artistic Associate) and the University of Miami Department of Theatre Arts (Vincent J. Cardinal, Department Chair) in June 2004, with the following cast and credits:

Elliot Hayes .... John Bixler
Margaret Hayes .... Ariana Shore
Resean Williams .... Randall Pollard
Nurse Dorothy McCarthy .... Kat Lower
Nick Dondero .... Brett Friedmann
Adam Collins .... Adam Perabo
Maha Swenson .... Maha McCain
Mrs. Collins .... Lindsey Erdahl
Doctor Roberts .... Christian Mansfield
The Swimmer Ethan .... Matthew Harrell

Director: Stephen Svoboda
Sets and Costumes: Michiko Kitayama
Lighting: Micheal Foster
Sound Design: Christian Mansfield
Stage Managers: Thomas Recktenwald and Lindsay Levine
Dramaturg: Eli Sands

Odysseus Died from AIDS was subsequently produced by Fresco Productions, the University of Miami Department of Theatre Arts, and the Present Company as part of the New York International Fringe Festival (Elena K. Holy, Producing Artistic Director), on August 13, 2004, at the Schaeberle Studio Theatre at Pace University, New York City, with the same cast and credits.

THE CHARACTERS

ELLIOT HAYES, a very young thirty and a great lover of books. He has been HIV positive for ten years.

MARGARET HAYES, Elliot's overprotective mother.

RESEAN WILLIAMS, thirty-something, a patient on the AIDS ward. Resean is a pre-op transsexual.

NICK DONDERO, late twenties and a patient on the AIDS ward. Nick, a bully, is in denial about his condition.

MAHA SWENSON, nineteen, a recovering junkie and a patient on the AIDS ward.

NURSE DOROTHY McCARTHY, the head nurse on the AIDS ward.

ADAM COLLINS, early twenties, a club kid. Estranged from his family over his sexuality. He is the newest patient on the ward.

MRS. COLLINS, Adam's mother, the picture of Westchester society.

DOCTOR ROBERTS, thirty, the young doctor who runs the AIDS ward.

THE SWIMMER ETHAN, the vision of Elliot's idealized former lover.

NOTES ON STAGING

It is important to keep in mind that this play is a record of events as perceived by Elliot Hayes during his final days on the AIDS ward of Moriah Memorial Hospital. As such, the patients should not wear any makeup to make them seem sick, and medical procedures should not be staged realistically. Whenever Adam is speaking directly to the audience, he should appear lit from behind his screen, while the other characters in the scene react as if Adam was in his hospital bed. All that is required to stage this production is a hospital bed and three screens.

Lights up on MRS. HAYES. She is alone onstage. She is sitting holding ELLIOT's journal. She opens it and reads to us. As she reads, the PATIENTS appear behind their screens.

MRS. HAYES: Sing to me of the man, Muse, of the clever hero blown time and again off course, once he had sacked the famous city of Troy.

(Lights up on Moriah Memorial Hospital AIDS ward. 2004. There are three blue hospital screens that can move around the space. ELLIOT crosses and sits next to MRS. HAYES. DOROTHY, a nurse making her rounds, enters and tends to ELLIOT.)

DOROTHY: What are you reading?

ELLIOT: Favorite.

MRS. HAYES: Pay attention to the nurse, Elliot.

DOROTHY: Graphomania?

MRS. HAYES: Well, he's writing everything down.

DOROTHY: *(Holding up a book.)* Homer?

ELLIOT: Don't touch.

MRS. HAYES: Elliot's very protective of his books.

DOROTHY: Sorry.

ELLIOT: *Odyssey.*

DOROTHY: Intelligent favorite.

MRS. HAYES: Elliot studied English at Columbia.

(Lights shift to fantasy. We hear crashing waves and tinkling chimes.)

ELLIOT: Of all the nations he saw, the minds he grasped.

MRS. HAYES: Elliot—

ELLIOT: The suffering deep in his heart, as he struggled to bring his men safely home.

(Lights shift.)

MRS. HAYES: Elliot, don't you go escaping into your book.

(As DOROTHY enters a PATIENT's room, she rotates the screen to reveal each PATIENT: RESEAN, MAHA, and NICK. They are each sitting on chairs in their areas. The PATIENTS wear no makeup. They look perfectly normal.)

RESEAN: *(Singing.)* "I'm forever blowing bubbles, pretty bubbles in the air."

DOROTHY: *(Taking RESEAN's chart.)* Good morning, Resean.

ELLIOT: I, Odysseus, would arrive today in an uncharted land.

DOROTHY: How are you feeling this morning?

RESEAN: *(To DOROTHY.)* Divine, darling.

MAHA: Then give me one of his/hers/its painkillers too.

ELLIOT: In this new land we would live, separated by only thin blue curtains.

RESEAN: I'm divine.

MRS. HAYES: You are always reading or writing something.

NICK: I need to piss.

DOROTHY: Hold it.

ELLIOT: With only the illusion of privacy.

MAHA: Give me my drugs now.

DOROTHY: *(To RESEAN.)* Did you sleep?

RESEAN: Sleeping Beauty.

NICK: I'll piss right here.

DOROTHY: Go ahead.

ELLIOT: My crew and I would keep no secrets from each other.

MAHA: If you don't give me my drugs, I'm going to grab that fucking clipboard and shove it so far up your ass that you'll be shitting in triplicate for weeks.

DOROTHY: Maha, you had your medication this morning.

NICK: I'm pissing.

DOROTHY: Catheters from now on.

MAHA: I'm in pain.

RESEAN: Put that puny thing away.

ELLIOT: I, Odysseus, would spend my first night away from home in ten years.

NICK: *(To RESEAN.)* I'm going to water the Trannie.

MAHA: Please, give it to me. Please.

NICK: My piss will make his titties grow.

DOROTHY: No.

NICK: Grow little titties. Grow.

RESEAN: Piss off.

ELLIOT: In every other hospital, I was always confident that my men and I would escape.

MAHA: I said please.

DOROTHY: Your mother teach you to act like that?

MAHA: My mother would kick your ass.

ELLIOT: This is the first land where fear was stronger than hope.

DOROTHY: I hope you like the smell of piss.

NICK: *(To ELLIOT.)* Want a taste?

(Lights break abruptly.)

ELLIOT: Who? Me?

DOROTHY: You'll be smelling it for the rest of the day.

NICK: *(To ELLIOT.)* You want a lick?

ELLIOT: I…no…I…thanks.

NICK: The idiot wants a lick.

MRS. HAYES: Leave him alone.

NICK: Does Mama want a taste too? There's plenty to go around.

MRS. HAYES: Nurse. Help. Please.

DOROTHY: Nick, put it away. Back to your room before your medication is blocked.

NICK: Maybe later. *(NICK exits.)*

MRS. HAYES: *(To ELLIOT.)* Didn't I teach you not to talk to strangers?

ELLIOT: Sorry.

(DOROTHY crosses to ELLIOT and MRS. HAYES. ELLIOT begins writing down everything they say.)

DOROTHY: Name?

ELLIOT: *(Struggling.)* Elliot.

MRS. HAYES: Elliot Hayes. I'm Margaret, the doting mother.

ELLIOT: Mom.

DOROTHY: Nurse Dorothy McCarthy. The patients call me Dot.

ELLIOT: Dot?

DOROTHY: It's my nickname.

MRS. HAYES: *(To ELLIOT.)* Where did you get that pen?

ELLIOT: Found it.

MRS. HAYES: No, don't touch anything here. *(Taking a pen from her purse.)* Use this one from home. We'll be in and out and home for dinner.

DOROTHY: We'll work as fast as we can.

MRS. HAYES: The nurse downstairs promised me.

ELLIOT: Slower.

MRS. HAYES: In and out and home for dinner. Do you want a drink?

ELLIOT: No.

MRS. HAYES: I'm going to get you a drink. *(To DOROTHY.)* Nurse, I think my son is thirsty. Well he won't admit to being thirsty, but I'm his mother and I can tell when he's thirsty. Could you possibly, if it's not too much of a hassle, get us something to drink?

DOROTHY: As soon as I'm finished—

MRS. HAYES: Water. If you have it.

DOROTHY: One second.

MRS. HAYES: Thank you. You are a darling.

(DOROTHY exits to get water.)

MRS. HAYES: They tell you horror stories about hospitals. Horror stories. The first hospital we went to, Elliot, the nurse, she appeared to be a nice, black lady, well she went to take your blood and she didn't put on gloves. Can you imagine that? No gloves. Well, I don't need to tell you how dangerous that is.

ELLIOT: I there…remember.

MRS. HAYES: The nerve of that woman, touching my beautiful son without gloves. I let her have it. I said, "What do you think you're doing?" She smiled at me. She thought I was trying to protect her. "I don't know where your hands have been and if we leave here with some strange fungus, some streptococci thingy, it will be your fault." She put on gloves after that, I'll tell you. What are you writing? I didn't say that.

ELLIOT: Sorry.

MRS. HAYES: Shhhh. Honey, don't upset yourself.

(DOROTHY hands MRS. HAYES a cup of water.)

DOROTHY: Here you go.

MRS. HAYES: Has this been sterilized?

DOROTHY: New out of the package.

MRS. HAYES: The water?

DOROTHY: Bottled.

MRS. HAYES: Thank you. *(To ELLIOT.)* Drink, honey.

ELLIOT: No.

MRS. HAYES: Just a sip.

ELLIOT: Fine.

MRS. HAYES: Good. Have another.

ELLIOT: Not camel.

MRS. HAYES: It's time to take your pills anyway.

ELLIOT: *(To DOROTHY.)* Help!

MRS. HAYES: Go ahead, bat your brown eyes, but it won't change the fact that water is good for you and it's time to take your pills.

DOROTHY: While Elliot's here, I'll be helping to take care of him.

MRS. HAYES: Shouldn't you be wearing gloves?

DOROTHY: Right now I only need to get some information.

MRS. HAYES: I keep a box of gloves in every room. One by the sofa, one in the dish cupboard, one in the glove compartment. You can never be too careful. Just in case.

DOROTHY: I need to get a history.

MRS. HAYES: Well Elliot was born here in Ithaca. He went to Columbia, for a while. He's a writer. Novels, mostly. Have you heard of him?

DOROTHY: A medical history.

ELLIOT: Likes brag.

MRS. HAYES: There is nothing wrong with being proud of your son.

(Lights up on RESEAN.)

RESEAN: Odysseus came out to his mother in high school.

MRS. HAYES: Shouldn't I tell that kind of information to the doctor?

DOROTHY: Everything you tell me is confidential.

MAHA: His mother cried at first. Then she hugged him to her chest and whispered that she would always love him.

MRS. HAYES: A doctor is going to look at him today?

NICK: She bought him a gay porn magazine to show him how "cool" she was with it all.

DOROTHY: As soon as we finish up the preliminary evaluation.

MAHA: In college she would mail him a box of condoms each month with her award-winning oatmeal raisin cookies.

MRS. HAYES: Elliot was diagnosed with HIV ten years ago.

NICK: Kept the cookies, chucked the condoms.

MRS. HAYES: What is this information used for?

DOROTHY: It is a standard patient information form. Name, age?

MRS. HAYES: Elliot Hayes. Thirty years old.

ELLIOT: I would bring my crew home.

(Lights change. The PATIENTS begin chanting. ELLIOT struggles to write it all down.)

ELLIOT: My ship's crew roster.

RESEAN: Resean Williams. Twenty-nine years old. Female.

MAHA: Maha Swenson. Nineteen.

NICK: Nicholas Dondero. Nick. Twenty-six.

DOROTHY: Last CD4 count?

ELLIOT: Two-fifty.

MRS. HAYES: About two weeks ago. It was two hundred and fifty.

RESEAN: One hundred.

MAHA: Sixty.

NICK: Less than fifty.

DOROTHY: Opportunistic infections?

MRS. HAYES: One case of pneumonia two months ago. Otherwise relatively clean.

RESEAN: Pneumocystis carinii Pneumonia. Third prolonged incident.

MAHA: Histoplasmosis, neurosyphilis, CMV colitis.

NICK: CMV retinitis. CMV esophagitis. Oh yeah, herpes.

(ELLIOT reads from his journal.)

ELLIOT: The recklessness of their own ways destroyed them all.

DOROTHY: Medications?

MRS. HAYES: Combavir. Amoxicillin. Vicodin for the pain.

RESEAN: Bactrim, Spectra, 3TC, AZT, Sustiva, Noravir.

MAHA: Cidofovir, ganciclovir, foscarnet.

NICK: Benzathine, penicillin.

MAHA: Amphotericin, itraconazole.

NICK: Ceftriaxone, doxycycline.

ELLIOT: And blind fools, they devoured the cattle of the Sun and the Sun God blotted out the day of their return.

DOROTHY: Diagnosis?

RESEAN: Treatable. For now. Hopefully?

NICK: Blindness. Followed by breakdown of the digestive system. Eventual death.

MAHA: Well, terminal.

ELLIOT: Launch out on his story, Muse, daughter of Zeus, start from where you will sing for our time too.

MRS. HAYES: Elliot. ELLIOT!

(The illusion is broken. The PATIENTS return to their seats. The lights shift back to reality.)

ELLIOT: Sorry.

MRS. HAYES: Did I raise you to be this rude? Really. Now put your journal away. The nurse is talking to you.

DOROTHY: Elliot, have you ever had an extended hospital stay?

ELLIOT: No.

MRS. HAYES: Never. We are very careful. Extremely. He only leaves the house for doctor's appointments or to go to the library. I disinfect everything. I'm not really sure how this, whatever this is, happened.

DOROTHY: When did the symptoms start?

RESEAN: Odysseus fell in love hard at eighteen. Ethan: Pretty boy, swimmer's build, eight inches, you know.

MRS. HAYES: Last week. I noticed he started stumbling with words.

RESEAN: And Mr. Swimmer seemed to fancy him some Elliot.

MRS. HAYES: Did I mention that Elliot was a— is a writer. He is wonderful with words.

ELLIOT: Ink!

MRS. HAYES: Honey, please.

ELLIOT: Pen!

MRS. HAYES: At first it was only a little odd. Wrong word, same word twice in a row, those sort of things. This morning he woke up and he could only speak in short phrases, words.

DOROTHY: And what about the writing?

ELLIOT: Kleos.

DOROTHY: Your notebook?

ELLIOT: Glory.

MRS. HAYES: Glory. Kleos. That's all I hear about. He won't stop writing. I tell him, "Your life isn't so fascinating. It's okay if we miss something."

ELLIOT: Must record.

MRS. HAYES: He just keeps writing.

DOROTHY: Elliot, I'll need you to stop writing in order to get some blood.

ELLIOT: Can't.

DOROTHY: It'll only take a few seconds.

ELLIOT: No.

MRS. HAYES: Elliot, let's make a deal, you stop writing for one minute and Nurse Dotty here won't say anything, or do anything, worth writing down.

DOROTHY: But—

MRS. HAYES: Hush, dear. It shouldn't be very difficult for you to be unremarkable.

DOROTHY: Excuse me.

MRS. HAYES: And if by some miracle something does happen, some Kleos, then when Dot is done I'll help you remember. Deal?

ELLIOT: Deal.

MRS. HAYES: Nurse Dot?

DOROTHY: Thank you.

MRS. HAYES: Crisis averted.

(DOCTOR enters. ADAM walks in behind him and sits in a chair.)

DOCTOR: Adam Collins. Twenty years old. Advanced AIDS. Pneumonia and complications from Kaposi's sarcoma.

DOROTHY: Curtain three.

ELLIOT: Who?

MRS. HAYES: Elliot, don't look at that. Give them some privacy.

DOCTOR: Nurse, start an IV.

DOROTHY: Right away, Doctor.

ELLIOT: What…happening?

MRS. HAYES: It's rude to stare.

DOCTOR: Mr. Collins, can you hear me?

ADAM: Yes.

RESEAN: Adam was a twink.

DOCTOR: Do you know where you are?

ADAM: The hospital.

MAHA: He had highlighted hair and was wearing a tight Superman T-shirt.

DOROTHY: Breath sounds are weak.

NICK: He was such a fag.

ADAM: I'm having trouble breathing.

ELLIOT: Help…okay?

MRS. HAYES: The doctor is doing everything he can.

ELLIOT: We help.

MRS. HAYES: Read your book.

ELLIOT: No.

DOROTHY: Mrs. Hayes, perhaps you should take Elliot outside.

(The CHARACTERS begin coming forward one at a time until they form a line at the front of the stage.)

MAHA: Adam had a rash of purple splotches up and down his arms.

DOCTOR: Nurse, where's that IV?

DOROTHY: Coming.

RESEAN: But that boy sported his spots like he was wrapped in some rainbow flag…riding on top of some float…in a Pride parade.

ELLIOT: He's beautiful.

MRS. HAYES: Oh Elliot, really.

NICK: He was crying, pussy.

ADAM: It hurts.

DOCTOR: Mr. Collins, is there anyone with you?

ALL: I'm alone.

ADAM: I'm alone.

ELLIOT: *(Shouting.)* Not alone.

DOCTOR: Remove that patient, Dorothy.

ELLIOT: Not alone. Crew.

DOROTHY: Mrs. Hayes, please.

MRS. HAYES: Elliot, let's go to the book shop. I'll buy you a new book. Or a crossword puzzle.

ELLIOT: Help!

DOROTHY: His vitals are dropping.

DOCTOR: Get this patient a bed.

(DOCTOR and DOROTHY move ADAM behind his screen at the foot of his bed. They begin attaching medical tubing to the bed poles.)

DOROTHY: Thank you, Doctor.

ELLIOT: Help him!

DOCTOR: Shut that patient up, Nurse.

(Lights change. ELLIOT watches from on top of his chair.)

ELLIOT: And Poseidon saw Odysseus.

DOROTHY: Code Blue! Code Blue!

(The alarms start to ring, and a blue light flashes in waves across the stage. The screens begin to move in a chaotic pattern around the bed. DOCTOR and DOROTHY begin attaching tubes to the bed.)

DOCTOR: This patient is crashing.

ELLIOT: Poseidon gathered the clouds, and, gripping his trident, he stirred the sea.

DOROTHY: I have no pulse.

ELLIOT: The winds blew hard from every direction, and lightning-charged Boreas rolled in a big wave. Poseidon gave him potassium through an intravenous line.

MAHA: They stuck his arms and legs with needles.

RESEAN: They started a blood transfusion.

NICK: He shocked him. Bam. Like you see on TV.

RESEAN: Poseidon believed he could bring him back from death.

ELLIOT: Here, in this land, this doctor is God.

(The blue lights turn off.)

MAHA: Now Adam looked like he'd be better off dead.

NICK: A crime scene photo from a gay bashing.

RESEAN: Sometimes "helping" someone don't mean keeping them alive. Sugar, they put a tube through his nostril and down into his windpipe.

NICK: Now Adam pees through a catheter stuck into his cock. Fucking rude, man.

MAHA: They needed to insert a chest tube to help Adam to breathe easier.

ELLIOT: The doctor asked Adam if there was anyone he would like them to call. Adam said:

(ADAM is "caught" in a small pool of downlight behind his screen.)

ADAM: My mom.

MAHA: Adam's body was so swollen, it resembled a balloon from the Macy's Thanksgiving Day Parade.

RESEAN: They didn't help him.

NICK: They ruined him.

(Lights change.)

ELLIOT: He okay?

MRS. HAYES: If you can call that okay. Such a shame.

ELLIOT: What?

MRS. HAYES: He used to be so beautiful.

ELLIOT: Still is.

(Scene shift. ADAM's bed rotates upstage. MRS. HAYES is holding ELLIOT's journal. She is now transcribing. ELLIOT is organizing his books on the floor around his chair. He takes off his shoes and starts making himself comfortable. DOROTHY crosses to them.)

MRS. HAYES: Don't ask me where he gets it from. I never read to him as a child. I'd rather watch *Murder, She Wrote*, but Elliot lives through those books.

DOROTHY: This place looks like a library, not a hospital room.

ELLIOT: My books.

DOROTHY: The doctor will be here in a minute.

NICK: The day Odysseus found out he was sick, he ran home to his mommy.

ELLIOT: Write Mom.

DOROTHY: I see Elliot's found himself a new recorder.

MRS. HAYES: I warned him I have bad handwriting, but he insisted.

MAHA: He dropped out of college.

(DOCTOR enters.)

DOCTOR: Mrs. Hayes, Elliot.

ELLIOT: What's up…Doc?

MRS. HAYES: Barrel of laughs.

ELLIOT: Write.

RESEAN: Odysseus never returned any of the Swimmer's phone calls.

DOCTOR: I'm Doctor Roberts.

MRS. HAYES: Aren't you a little young to be a doctor?

DOCTOR: I get that a lot.

DOROTHY: Doctor Roberts is one of the best.

DOCTOR: This is my last residency rotation.

MRS. HAYES: But you are a doctor?

DOCTOR: Technically. This is my first placement job.

DOROTHY: Undergraduate from Columbia. Medical degree from Yale.

DOCTOR: Almost.

ELLIOT: Impressive.

MRS. HAYES: But do you have experience with these sorts of things?

DOCTOR: I've been working with AIDS patients for the last two years.

NICK: His mom wanted Odysseus to be a doctor.

DOROTHY: Doctor Roberts has had over five articles on AIDS complications published in prestigious medical journals.

MRS. HAYES: Your mother must be so proud. How old are you?

DOCTOR: Thirty next month.

MRS. HAYES: You and Elliot would've been in the same class at school.

DOROTHY: I assure you, Mrs. Hayes, your son is in good hands.

ELLIOT: Zeus-like.

DOCTOR: Thank you. Now that's a compliment I haven't heard before. Your cat scan reveals that you are suffering from swelling in the Broca area of the brain.

ELLIOT: Slower.

MRS. HAYES: Listen to the doctor, Elliot.

DOCTOR: As the swelling increases, your ability to communicate will decrease.

MRS. HAYES: Ability to communicate will decrease.

DOCTOR: Elliot will need to spend the night for testing.

MRS. HAYES: Oh no.

ELLIOT: Go home.

DOCTOR: We could be looking at a long-term stay.

MRS. HAYES: Elliot will need to come home with me.

DOCTOR: Mrs. Hayes, the swelling in his brain indicates the possibility of infection, a possible tumor, there are any number of possibilities.

MRS. HAYES: We'll be going.

DOCTOR: We need to take precautions to make sure this doesn't progress and become life threatening.

MRS. HAYES: He has AIDS, Doctor. Everything is life threatening.

ELLIOT: Don't...stay...here.

MRS. HAYES: Elliot, pack up your things.

DOROTHY: Mrs. Hayes, I don't recommend—

MRS. HAYES: Elliot has never spent the night away from me since he became ill.

RESEAN: Honey, Odysseus cut himself off from the world.

ELLIOT: Scared here.

RESEAN: Darling the only other "gays" this boy has seen were in magazines.

MAHA: And forget about seein' blacks.

DOCTOR: I assure you, Elliot will get the best care here.

ELLIOT: Other patients.

NICK: He was shit-ass scared of us.

MRS. HAYES: Elliot will come home with *me*.

DOROTHY: You are risking your son's life.

MRS. HAYES: We will get a second opinion.

ELLIOT: Can...me...you...save?

DOCTOR: I believe so, Elliot, but I need you to agree to at least spend the night.

ELLIOT: Can Mom stay?

DOCTOR: She can stay in the visitors' area.

ELLIOT: Not me?

DOCTOR: No. I'm afraid not.

DOROTHY: It's against hospital policy.

MRS. HAYES: Hospital policy. I think you need some new hospital policies. Elliot, where's your shoe?

ELLIOT: And Zeus turned and said:

(Lights shift to fantasy.)

DOCTOR: You've been our messenger before. Go tell that ringleted nymph it is my will to have that patient man Odysseus stay here.

DOROTHY: What about the mother?

DOCTOR: I can't waste any more time here. (DOCTOR exits.)

ELLIOT: When she finally arrived at the distant island, the nurse stepped from the violet-tinctured sea onto dry land and proceeded to the cavern where Calypso lived.

DOROTHY: Odysseus, I need you to agree to stay the night for testing.

ELLIOT: I'm not sure.

DOROTHY: I can stay with you until you fall asleep.

(Lights shift back to reality.)

MRS. HAYES: Nurse, I appreciate your concern, but your input is not needed at this time.

ELLIOT: Stop.

MRS. HAYES: I'm sure there are other patients you need to look in on. The one moaning over there perhaps.

ELLIOT: Mom.

(Lights change back into fantasy.)

DOROTHY: The man's not fated to rot at home far from his friends.

MRS. HAYES: You gods think you are so wise. So infallible.

DOROTHY: It is his destiny to see his dear ones again.

MRS. HAYES: Look around you. You are in the halls of the dying. This is no place for my son.

DOROTHY: You can't keep him in a bubble.

MRS. HAYES: Odysseus, tie your shoes.

DOROTHY: The AIDS will get to him.

MRS. HAYES: I loved him.

DOROTHY: It has gotten to him.

MRS. HAYES: I told him I'd make him immortal and ageless all of his days.

DOROTHY: Stay here and you will become a hero. You will be Odysseus.

(Lights break to reality.)

ELLIOT: I stay.

MRS. HAYES: Elliot?

ELLIOT: I need to stay.

MRS. HAYES: But—

ELLIOT: Nurse papers.

DOROTHY: You need to sign here, here, and here.

MRS. HAYES: That'll be all, Nurse.

ELLIOT: *(To DOROTHY.)* Thank you.

DOROTHY: Nothing will happen to him. I promise. *(DOROTHY exits.)*

MRS. HAYES: Well, you've done it this time.

ELLIOT: Sorry.

MRS. HAYES: If you wanted a vacation, there are easier ways.

(Lights change to fantasy.)

ELLIOT: Goddess and mistress Calypso, don't be angry with me.

MRS. HAYES: If you had any idea all the pain you are destined to suffer before getting home, you'd stay with me, deathless—

ELLIOT: If some god hits me hard as I sail the deep purple, I'll weather it like the sea-bitten veteran I am. God knows I've suffered and had my share of sorrow. I can take more if I have to.

(Lights change back to reality.)

MRS. HAYES: How, I don't know. But I'll help you. I'll do everything I can to get you back safely to my heart. Elliot, my strong little boy. I'll be here first thing tomorrow. When you open your eyes. I'll be here. Holding pancakes and eggs.

ELLIOT: With turkey bacon.

MRS. HAYES: And don't go wandering off, talking to strangers. Stay here. In this room. Where you're safe. You know the phone number, right? I'll leave the phone by my bed—

ELLIOT: Shhhhhhh. Love you.

MRS. HAYES: I love you too.

(MRS. HAYES exits. Lights up on NICK and MAHA. He is doing crunches. She is holding his feet.)

MAHA: I followed the plan like you told me.

NICK: One. HIV is not in me. Two. HIV is not in me.

MAHA: I held it under my tongue for six hours.

NICK: Three. HIV is not in me.

(ELLIOT enters and watches them. He is recording what they are saying.)

MAHA: Then she caught me spitting the fucker out.

NICK: Four. HIV is not in me.

MAHA: Confiscated my shit.

NICK: I'll get us some more.

MAHA: How? They ain't going to give us shit out of the supply closet 'cause we ask.

NICK: *(Seeing ELLIOT.)* What you want?

ELLIOT: Nothing.

MAHA: Hey Bubble Boy.

ELLIOT: *(Offering his hand.)* Elliot.

MAHA: Charmed.

NICK: What you writing?

ELLIOT: Nothing.

NICK: Let us see.

ELLIOT: Mine.

NICK: Give it to me.

ELLIOT: No.

(ELLIOT goes to leave. MAHA stops him.)

MAHA: You runnin' home, Bubble Boy.

ELLIOT: Leave…me…alone…

NICK: Do you hear that shit? "Leave… me…alone…"

MAHA: Uht, Home School.

NICK: *(Acting like a dog.)* Ruff, ruff, ruff, ruff.

(NICK grabs the journal from ELLIOT.)

NICK: What's it say?

ELLIOT: Read it.

NICK: *(Handing the book to MAHA.)* Maha, what's it say?

MAHA: He's been writin' down everything we say.

ELLIOT: Record.

NICK: You a spy?

ELLIOT: No.

MAHA: He's a spy.

NICK: *(Taking the book from MAHA.)* This is evidence.

MAHA: Do you know what we do to spies here?

(DOROTHY enters. She is carrying a specimen cup.)

DOROTHY: What's going on in here?

NICK: Nothing.

DOROTHY: Give Elliot back his book.

NICK: I was just looking at it.

DOROTHY: You can't read.

NICK: I can so read.

DOROTHY: You can't even see an exit sign, how are you going to read a book?

NICK: *(Throwing the book at ELLIOT.)* My vision's just fine.

ELLIOT: *(To DOROTHY.)* Thanks.

DOROTHY: I see you've ventured out from your room.

ELLIOT: Say hi.

DOROTHY: Watch yourself around these two.

ELLIOT: Check.

MAHA: *(Dancing.)* "Go Maha, it's your birthday, get busy, get your meds on."

DOROTHY: You've been blocked. No more night-time meds.

MAHA: What's blocked?

DOROTHY: No meds on. *(To NICK.)* Leave him alone, Nick.

MAHA: Why you got to play like that?

DOROTHY: Not playing.

MAHA: What I ever do to you?

DOROTHY: Doctor's orders.

MAHA: We'll see about that. *(MAHA exits.)*

DOROTHY: Pee in the cup, Nick.

NICK: *(Doing sit-ups.)* Five. HIV is not in me.

ELLIOT: Not...time...good.

NICK: Six. HIV is not in me.

DOROTHY: There's never a good time with Nick here.

NICK: Fuck off.

DOROTHY: Pee in the cup, Nick.

ELLIOT: He busy.

DOROTHY: Pee Nick.

NICK: I don't have AIDS.

DOROTHY: Pee and I'll get your drugs, Nick.

NICK: Give me the cup.

(NICK takes the cup and turns around to pee in it.)

NICK: *(To ELLIOT.)* Want to watch?

ELLIOT: No.

DOROTHY: Nick, make sure you get it in the cup this time.

ELLIOT: Bad aim?

DOROTHY: Among other things, Nick is going blind.

NICK: No I'm not.

DOROTHY: Denial.

NICK: Fuck off. *(NICK finishes and starts doing one-armed push-ups.)*

DOROTHY: Urine sample?

NICK: Where are my fucking drugs?

DOROTHY: Give me the sample and I'll go get them.

NICK: How dumb do you think I am?

ELLIOT: Dumb.

NICK: What'd you say?

ELLIOT: Nothing.

NICK: *(To ELLIOT.)* You want to see my dick, don't you?

DOROTHY: He doesn't want to see your dick, Nick. Give me the sample so we can run your tests.

NICK: I don't need any tests.

DOROTHY: Nick, you are very sick.

NICK: Lying bitch.

DOROTHY: Most of your major organs are in some form of deterioration.

NICK: 'Cept the only organ that counts.

ELLIOT: Hurt pee.

NICK: What's "Rain Man" saying?

ELLIOT: *(Demonstrating.)* You...pee... owwww...problem.

NICK: You want me to kick your ass?

DOROTHY: He's saying your kidneys are failing.

NICK: Give me my Demerol and every-thing will be all right.

DOROTHY: We need to cut back on your painkillers.

NICK: No fucking way. *(NICK jumps on his chair.)*

DOROTHY: Elliot, go back to your room.

ELLIOT: I help.

DOROTHY: Elliot.

ELLIOT: *(To NICK.)* You sick.

NICK: Give me my fucking pills.

ELLIOT: Me AIDS.

NICK: I DON'T HAVE AIDS.

DOROTHY: Nick, calm down.

ELLIOT: You AIDS.

NICK: I told you bitches. I don't have it.

(NICK throws the specimen cup at ELLIOT. The lights change.)

DOROTHY: Jesus Christ!

RESEAN: The cup hit Elliot.

MAHA: Urine splashed all over him.

RESEAN: Infected urine.

NICK: I don't have AIDS.

DOROTHY: Don't move, Elliot.

(Lights change to fantasy.)

ELLIOT: Every wind in the world is howl-ing around me.

MAHA: Odysseus just stood there.

ELLIOT: As it is, I am doomed to a wretched death at sea.

MAHA: The rudder flew from his hands.

RESEAN: The mast cracked in two.

ELLIOT: I was under a long time, unable to surface from the heaving swell of the monstrous wave.

RESEAN: At last he came up, spitting out saltwater.

MAHA: Sea-brine gurgling from his nos-trils and mouth.

RESEAN: The nurse wiped the urine from his face.

ELLIOT: Calypso was right on target when she said I would have my fill of sor-row.

MAHA: For all his distress, he remem-bered his raft.

(Lights change back to reality.)

ELLIOT: Mom. Need Mom.

DOROTHY: I'll call her.

ELLIOT: *(To NICK.)* Shit...face.

NICK: Now you're talking.

DOROTHY: Blocked, Nick. Do you hear me? You're blocked.

NICK: Only the doctor can—

DOROTHY: You'd be surprised.

NICK: I told the bitch I didn't have it.

(DOROTHY closes NICK's curtain.)

RESEAN: Odysseus lunged through the waves, caught hold of his raft, and huddled down in its center shrinking from death.

DOROTHY: Your mom will be here soon.

ELLIOT: I go home.

(DOROTHY closes ELLIOT's curtain. MRS. HAYES enters. Her hair is in curlers.)

MRS. HAYES: Where is he? Elliot? Elliot?

DOROTHY: Mrs. Hayes, the other patients are sleeping.

MRS. HAYES: I don't care. You call me in the middle of the night. You say there's been some sort of incident. How there can be incidents in a hospital is beyond my understanding.

DOROTHY: Elliot had an altercation with another patient.

MRS. HAYES: My son has never been in a fight in his entire life. He doesn't even know how to make a fist.

DOROTHY: Another patient attacked him.

MRS. HAYES: Elliot? Elliot?

DOROTHY: Mrs. Hayes—

MRS. HAYES: We're leaving.

(DOROTHY pulls back the curtain to reveal ELLIOT. He is sitting with his bookbag

on his lap. His books have all been packed. He is ready to go.)

ELLIOT: Time to go?

MRS. HAYES: Yes.

DOROTHY: I don't advise taking Elliot out of the hospital.

ELLIOT: Home.

DOROTHY: If Elliot leaves, it will be against medical advice.

ELLIOT: Not safe here.

MRS. HAYES: Where's the doctor?

DOROTHY: It's the middle of night.

MRS. HAYES: So the doctor's not here?

DOROTHY: He's on call.

MRS. HAYES: Well then, it's basically like home, except here Elliot gets attacked by patients, and at home he gets to fall asleep in his bed.

ELLIOT: Going.

DOROTHY: Mrs. Hayes. I'll need you to sign a few papers saying you took Elliot against medical advice.

MRS. HAYES: Fine. Stay right here, Elliot. Don't move. Don't talk to anyone.

ELLIOT: Check.

(MRS. HAYES and DOROTHY exit. ELLIOT sits onstage, alone.)

RESEAN: *(Singing.)* "I'm forever blowing bubbles, pretty bubbles in the air."

ELLIOT: Hello?

RESEAN: *(Pulls open her curtain. Singing.)* "They fly so high, nearly reach the sky…"

ELLIOT: Who…you?

RESEAN: Twenty-eight, forever, alcoholic, recovering, transsexual, lesbian.

ELLIOT: Nice…you…hi.

RESEAN: I see you got a "word" difficulty thing going on.

ELLIOT: The AIDS.

RESEAN: The troubles, I respect that. Me, I got PCP, pneumonia not the drug, I wish.

ELLIOT: Dying?

RESEAN: Third time's the charm they say. You either beat it or it beats you. Now, I know a thing or two about gettin' beat, and I got odds on this girl here to take it.

ELLIOT: You…win.

RESEAN: Sugar, from the looks of it, you're gettin' out of town.

ELLIOT: Going.

RESEAN: You all fixed up?

ELLIOT: Better.

RESEAN: Now, why you got to start blowin' smoke up my ass when I was just starting to like you. I know you got a hot shower tonight from "Nick the Prick." And I know that you runnin' to Mama 'cause you scared.

ELLIOT: Nice to…meet…you.

RESEAN: Ohh, sugar, you got some attitude on you. Not that I blame you. Get while the gettin' is good they always say. I hope it's not too long for me. They don't give me my pills in here.

ELLIOT: Bad…drugs.

RESEAN: Bad drugs? Listen to you, sugar, I'm talking about my hormones.

ELLIOT: Sorry.

RESEAN: I've given up the junk entirely since I went on them and I haven't tried to kill myself. Not even once. Not even Erica was enough to do that.

ELLIOT: Erica?

RESEAN: My daughter, Erica Kane. I named her after my personal hero.

ELLIOT: Who her mother?

RESEAN: She died of the troubles. Now I'm mama and papa all rolled into one. She's my little miracle. Born with the troubles and now trouble free.

ELLIOT: A miracle.

RESEAN: She's in foster care. They took her away from me when I ended up in here. What about you? You write someone's name, with little hearts, in that diary of yours?

ELLIOT: Nope.

RESEAN: Shame. Cute boy like you. You should have a conga line at your back door.

ELLIOT: No one.

RESEAN: Someone in the grocery store you saw buying orange juice? Someone at the video store?

ELLIOT: Not out much.

RESEAN: I know, maybe you could meet someone here. Another patient, or a doctor. Medical love. It could be all *General Hospital.*

ELLIOT: Who?

RESEAN: Well, we'll never know 'cause you're leavin'.

ELLIOT: You difficult.

RESEAN: Heart-breaking, heart-wrenching, and heart-stopping all in one. I can't be too hard on you though, sugar. If I had a family to run to, I'd sling my six-inch heels over my shoulder and sashay all the way back to Chattanooga.

ELLIOT: Where your mother?

RESEAN: No one will admit to being my mother.

ELLIOT: I'll…try…visit.

RESEAN: Why not stay?

ELLIOT: Home.

RESEAN: Home is where you lay your tiara.

ELLIOT: Why you…me stay?

RESEAN: First off I hate to see "Nick the Prick" win, second it seems like your little speech thingy might need more work than Mama's home cookin', and I like you. And I don't like white boys very often.

ELLIOT: Athena.

RESEAN: A-who-a?

ELLIOT: Goddess.

RESEAN: Why thank you.

ELLIOT: I Odysseus.

RESEAN: Is this a white people's game?

(Lights change into fantasy.)

ELLIOT: I am Odysseus, known for my cunning throughout the world and my fame reaches even to heaven.

RESEAN: Not even you recognized Athena, I who stand by you in all your troubles.

ELLIOT: It would be hard for the most discerning man alive to see through all your disguises, Goddess.

RESEAN: I wanted to be the first to welcome you home to your native land.

ELLIOT: This is not my home.

RESEAN: Don't you recognize it here? *(Pointing to NICK.)* There are the fights you didn't fight. *(Pointing to MAHA.)* There are the parties you missed. *(Pointing to ADAM.)* And over there under this cavern's roof, the sacrifices you did not make and the love from a nymph that went unnurtured.

ELLIOT: I never thought I would see these things again.

RESEAN: Welcome home, Odysseus.

ELLIOT: But these very walls are plagued.

RESEAN: And what of your crew? Shall they remain between these walls?

ELLIOT: But I am sick.

RESEAN: No. You are Odysseus. Here we are, the two shrewdest minds in the universe. You far away the best man on Earth in plotting strategies and I famed among the gods for my clever schemes. Who else can save them?

ELLIOT: I will try and weather this storm and if I escape the day of my doom, I will always be your friend.

RESEAN: Divine, darling.

(Lights break to reality.)

RESEAN: Divine. While you're here. We'll talk romance, play story time, and watch my soaps. You do watch soaps?

ELLIOT: Books.

RESEAN: They still make those?

ELLIOT: Read?

RESEAN: Give me a *Soap Opera Digest* any day.

ELLIOT: I tell you.

RESEAN: That might take a while.

ELLIOT: Poseidon…Doctor…Kleos…I have while.

RESEAN: We'll be goddess and hero.

ELLIOT: Athena Odysseus.

RESEAN: Them.

ELLIOT: Temporary.

RESEAN: Everyone in this place is temporary.

ELLIOT: Day…two…most.

RESEAN: I bet I'll be gone before you.

ELLIOT: Thanks…Athena.

RESEAN: My girlfriends call me Resean. *(Spelling it for ELLIOT.)* R-E-S-E-A-N.

ELLIOT: Resean.

RESEAN: Now don't you be spreading that around.

(RESEAN crosses back to her area. MRS. HAYES and DOCTOR enter. MRS. HAYES crosses to ELLIOT. DOCTOR and RESEAN remain watching them.)

ELLIOT: Mom.

MRS. HAYES: Elliot, I need to—

ELLIOT: Can't.

MRS. HAYES: Shhh, honey, don't talk. I know there must be so many words going through your head, so many things you want to say, but right now, this second, I need you to listen to me. Can you do that? Listen?

ELLIOT: Can't…home.

MRS. HAYES: I know, sweetie. I know you want to go home, but right now I need you to listen. So listen to the doctor.

ELLIOT: What?

DOCTOR: Your test results from this—

MRS. HAYES: The doctor and Nurse McCarthy showed me some of your test results from this afternoon.

ELLIOT: Swollen brain.

MRS. HAYES: You have something called progressive multifocal leuk— *(She looks to DOCTOR for help.)*

DOCTOR: Progressive multifocal leukoencephalopathy.

ELLIOT: Confused.

MRS. HAYES: See honey, there are these lesions, sores really, and they are on your brain, and they are what is stopping you from speaking.

ELLIOT: Slower.

DOCTOR: It is caused by the JC virus which infects oligodendrocytes, brain cells.

ELLIOT: Slower.

MRS. HAYES: I know you want to go home.

ELLIOT: No.

MRS. HAYES: Elliot, listen. Right now you need to stay here.

ELLIOT: How bad?

MRS. HAYES: These lesions are on other parts of your brain as well.

ELLIOT: Dying?

MRS. HAYES: Dying? Hello, Mr. Jump to Conclusions. There will be no dying while I'm still around.

ELLIOT: *(To DOCTOR.)* Dying?

DOCTOR: There is no treatment for PML.

ELLIOT: *(To MRS. HAYES.)* See.

DOCTOR: At best the medicine will prolong your life for a few months, maybe years.

MRS. HAYES: Medical science can be wrong. Ten years ago they told us two years. Well, it's been ten. New drugs come out every week. Ten years. What if we had given up then? Think of all the things you would have missed—

ELLIOT: Have missed.

MRS. HAYES: So now you regret coming home to your mother. What were you going to do? Play house with that boy who did this to you?

ELLIOT: Maybe.

MRS. HAYES: Maybe. He says, "maybe." Look how brave you suddenly are with a few brain lesions.

ELLIOT: Not funny.

MRS. HAYES: We will beat these lesions, just like we have beaten everything else. Together. Promise me you'll fight.

ELLIOT: Promise.

MRS. HAYES: And we've never broken a promise.

ELLIOT: I'm staying.

MRS. HAYES: I'm visiting.

ELLIOT: Good.

(Lights change. MRS. HAYES exits.)

ELLIOT: I am Odysseus, great Laertes' son, known for my cunning throughout the world and my fame reaches even to heaven. Nothing is sweeter than your own country and your own mother, but every man must embark on his own journey. Let me tell you of mine. Here is my journey home that Zeus sent me on when I sailed from Troy.

(MRS. COLLINS enters. The sound of her high heels can be heard echoing through the halls. She crosses to DOROTHY.)

MRS. COLLINS: *(To DOROTHY.)* I have been waiting for someone for almost an hour.

DOROTHY: My name is Nurse—

MRS. COLLINS: I'm here to see my son.

ELLIOT: Nine days of bad winds blew us across the teeming seas.

MRS. COLLINS: His name is Adam, Adam Collins.

ELLIOT: On the tenth day we came to the land of the Lotus Eaters.

(DOROTHY crosses to ADAM's area. She pulls back the curtains to reveal ADAM and his bed. The bed still has medical tubing hanging from the bed poles. ADAM remains behind his screen at the back of his bed, looking out at the audience.)

MRS. COLLINS: Dear God.

DOROTHY: It's not as bad as it looks.

MRS. COLLINS: His eyes are open? Can he understand us?

DOROTHY: Yes.

MRS. COLLINS: *(To ADAM.)* Your father and I warned you this would happen.

ADAM: I hadn't heard my mother's voice in five years.

MRS. COLLINS: What are his chances?

DOROTHY: The doctor is doing everything—

MRS. COLLINS: I am not a stupid woman, Nurse— *(Reading from name tag.)* McCarthy. I don't gush over babies and I don't gasp at the dying.

DOROTHY: Adam's condition is critical.

ADAM: She sounded like the love I'd been looking for.

DOROTHY: Does your son have a DNR?

MRS. COLLINS: I don't know what that is.

DOROTHY: Do not resuscitate. If his heart stops beating or— It limits the lengths we will go to to keep him alive.

MRS. COLLINS: My family does not believe in suicide.

DOROTHY: It's not— It's meant to limit any unnecessary pain or suffering.

MRS. COLLINS: Can he speak?

DOROTHY: His cognitive abilities aren't impaired, but his chest tube prevents him from—

MRS. COLLINS: Remove it.

DOROTHY: The chest tube is helping him to breathe.

MRS. COLLINS: I said remove it.

DOROTHY: Only the doctor can—

MRS. COLLINS: Then get him.

(DOROTHY exits.)

MRS. COLLINS: Mommy's here now.

RESEAN: Adam worked on the conservative golf courses of Scarsdale.

MRS. COLLINS: There's nothing to be scared of.

MAHA: Where he was his mother's golden boy.

MRS. COLLINS: You are going to beat this for Mommy.

NICK: Until Mommy caught Adam schtupping the golf pro.

(DOROTHY and DOCTOR enter. They pull the screens in front of ADAM's bed.)

DOCTOR: Mrs. Collins, my name is Doctor Roberts. I understand you've—

MRS. COLLINS: I wish to speak to my son.

DOCTOR: I assure you he can hear you.

MRS. COLLINS: I wish for my son to speak to me.

DOROTHY: I've already explained to Mrs. Collins that the chest tube is helping Adam to breathe.

MRS. COLLINS: Will he die if you take it out?

DOCTOR: It's precautionary, but—

MRS. COLLINS: Then do it.

DOCTOR: I don't recommend—

MRS. COLLINS: This may be the last chance I have to engage in a conversation with my son before he dies. A son whose last words to his mother were "I hate you."

DOCTOR: Nurse McCarthy and I will need to be present in case of an emergency.

DOROTHY: But Doctor—

MRS. COLLINS: Thank you, Doctor Roberts. It is nice to see that my son is in good hands.

(DOCTOR crosses behind the screens.)

ELLIOT: I sent Adam out to scout and sound out the locals. He headed out and made contact with the Lotus Eaters.

(DOROTHY pulls back the screens to reveal ADAM in bed, wearing hospital garb.)

ADAM: Mom, glad you could make it.

MRS. COLLINS: Your father's out of town so—

ADAM: I'm sorry I had to bother you.

MRS. COLLINS: I'm your mother.

ELLIOT: Who meant no harm but did give Adam some lotus to eat.

ADAM: There was no one else I could call.

MRS. COLLINS: Monkey, of course you should have called me.

ADAM: I've been sick for so long, Mom.

MRS. COLLINS: That's what you get for running away like that. You listen to Mommy and no one's going to hurt you again.

ELLIOT: Whoever ate that sweet fruit lost the will to report back, preferring instead to stay there, munching lotus, oblivious to loss, or pain, or suffering.

DOROTHY: Mr. Collins?

ADAM: Yes.

DOROTHY: We need to discuss your wishes regarding a DNR.

MRS. COLLINS: Is this really necessary?

DOCTOR: In the event that your son needs to be intubated again, this might be our only chance to discuss his wishes.

MRS. COLLINS: It sounds like you are giving up on my son because he is a deviant.

DOCTOR: I assure you that we will continue to work diligently to provide the—

MRS. COLLINS: Do you see that? Look in his eyes. His eyes are twinkling. Adam is happy to have his mother here now.

DOROTHY: Adam, are you in pain?

ADAM: Mom, stay with me.

MRS. COLLINS: Adam, shoulders back, chin up. You are going to face this like a Collins. You are going to beat this for me. Something's wrong. What's wrong with him?

DOROTHY: Code Blue. Code Blue.

(The blue alarm starts going off. The screens again circle the bed in a chaotic pattern. DOCTOR and DOROTHY attach more cords to the bed.)

DOCTOR: He's in cardiac arrest.

ELLIOT: When the doctor had finished Adam was caught in the tangled vines of the Lotus Flower. He was connected to monitors, IV poles, urine bags, suction devices. And at the center of it all, smiling down on him, was the Lotus Flower herself, his mother.

(DOCTOR comes out from behind the screens. The alarms turn off. By this point, there are ten tubes attached to ADAM's bed.)

DOCTOR: He's back.

MRS. COLLINS: I've read about lots of people with AIDS who come back from death's door. How long has Magic Johnson been sick? Twelve years? Fifteen? Give my son whatever he's taking and then we can talk about how there is nothing medical science can do. They're doing it for a basketball star. Do it for my son.

DOCTOR: Mrs. Collins—

MRS. COLLINS: If my son dies, my husband will have both of your jobs.

DOROTHY: Let's go get a cup of coffee.

MRS. COLLINS: You will never work in a hospital again.

DOCTOR: Prep him for another chest tube.

DOROTHY: Isn't that excessive?

DOCTOR: Our job is to keep him alive as long as possible. Unless Mrs. Collins decides to sign a DNR, or the son is able to speak, that's what we'll do.

DOROTHY: A chest tube.

DOCTOR: No questions asked.

DOROTHY: Right away, Doctor.

(ADAM is once again "caught" in his light.)

MRS. COLLINS: Thank you.

ELLIOT: The sparkle in Adam's eye was back.

(Lights change.)

ELLIOT: We sailed on, our morale sinking, and we came to the land of the Cyclopses. I wanted to find out what those men were like. Wild savages with no sense of right or wrong or hospitable folk who fear the gods.

(Lights up on NICK. He is doing push-ups.)

NICK: Forty-eight. HIV is not in me. Forty-nine. HIV is not in me.

(ELLIOT crosses to him.)

ELLIOT: Hi.

NICK: Thought I scared you away.

ELLIOT: Nope.

NICK: Pretty tough for a retard.

ELLIOT: Thanks.

NICK: What do you want?

ELLIOT: We are Greeks, blown off course by every wind. Now we are here, suppliants at your knee, hoping you will be generous with us and give us the gifts that are due to strangers.

NICK: Friends? You've got to be kidding me.

ELLIOT: Nope.

(DOROTHY enters.)

DOROTHY: *(To ELLIOT.)* Sure you should be in here?

ELLIOT: Okay.

NICK: We're cool.

DOROTHY: Hall meeting in twenty minutes.

NICK: No fucking way.

DOROTHY: I thought you might like to come.

NICK: Fifty. HIV is not in me.

DOROTHY: You, Elliot?

ELLIOT: Be there.

NICK: Fifty-one.

DOROTHY: Nick?

NICK: I'll check my date book.

DOROTHY: We're planning a birthday party for Maha. *(DOROTHY exits.)*

NICK: Fucking bitches think we're in summer camp or something. *(Yelling after DOROTHY.)* Birthday party my ass.

(Lights change to fantasy.)

ELLIOT: Respect the gods, sir. We are her patients, and Dorothy smites disrespectful patients.

NICK: You're dumb, stranger, or from far away, if you ask me to fear her. Cyclopses don't care about Zeus or his gods, since we are much stronger.

ELLIOT: Nurse's hot.

(Lights back to reality.)

NICK: Hot. Shit yeah, I'd fuck her.

ELLIOT: Me too.

NICK: I figured you for a fudge packer.

ELLIOT: Me? Fuck…girls…yeah.

NICK: Always nice to have another brother on the block.

ELLIOT: Nice tits.

NICK: Ripe and firm just like I like them. Spot me.

(ELLIOT goes over and holds NICK's feet while he does sit-ups. He has difficulty holding his feet and writing at the same time.)

NICK: Fifty-two. HIV is not in me.

ELLIOT: Sorry.

NICK: Why you write everything down?

ELLIOT: Record.

NICK: That's cool. Like a history of what happens here. Make sure you describe me as hot.

ELLIOT: Hot. Check.

NICK: Sorry about the pee thing. I didn't mean to—

ELLIOT: No problem.

NICK: Tell me your name.

(Lights to fantasy.)

ELLIOT: Noman is my name. They call me Noman— My mother, my father, and all my friends, too.

NICK: Nick.

(Lights to reality.)

NICK: You know, you're the one with power in here. I've got to stay in shape to stop those bastards from fucking with me. But you, you're like a fucking superhero.

ELLIOT: Really?

NICK: Yeah. I mean you're fucking poison. You've got death running through your veins.

ELLIOT: Gross.

NICK: You ever see how fast they all run if you just cut open your hand.

ELLIOT: Ouch.

NICK: All that blood. All that death. See if they fuck with you after that. Just put out your bloody hands and go crazy. *(Demonstrating.)* Ruff, ruff, ruff, ruff. You try.

(ELLIOT puts out his hands and barks anemically.)

ELLIOT: Good?

NICK: The barks not your thing. Put your arms out and yell "AIDS!"

ELLIOT: Sure?

NICK: Yeah. Give it a go.

ELLIOT: *(Demonstrating badly.)* AIDS.

NICK: They'll run. I promise.

(DOROTHY enters with a tray of pills.)

ELLIOT: Medicine?

DOROTHY: Here you go, Elliot.

NICK: Where's mine?

DOROTHY: You're blocked, remember?

NICK: We're friends now. See. Forgiven. Pills, please?

DOROTHY: I'll have to check with the doctor.

NICK: "You" the boss, Dorothy, or "he" the boss?

DOROTHY: He's the boss.

(MRS. COLLINS comes storming into the room.)

MRS. COLLINS: There's something wrong with Adam.

DOROTHY: Mrs. Collins, someone at the nurses' station—

MRS. COLLINS: I don't care if you're treating the Queen of Sheba.

NICK: Who you calling a queen, lady?

MRS. COLLINS: I'm not talking to you.

DOROTHY: Mrs. Collins, my job is not to cater to your—

MRS. COLLINS: If my son dies, you'll have the biggest lawsuit.

NICK: *(Barking at MRS. COLLINS.)* Ruff, ruff, ruff, ruff!

(NICK chases MRS. COLLINS off.)

DOROTHY: Thank you.

NICK: See what I mean.

ELLIOT: Yeah.

DOROTHY: Don't forget the meeting. *(DOROTHY exits.)*

NICK: *(Yelling after her.)* Don't forget my pills.

ELLIOT: Us friends?

NICK: Don't go that far. We're buds. Amigos.

ELLIOT: Okay.

NICK: We got to get to know each other better before we're friends.

ELLIOT: *(Offering his pills.)* Want mine?

NICK: You sicko, you palmed them.

ELLIOT: You want?

NICK: Fuck yeah.

(Lights shift to fantasy.)

ELLIOT: Cyclops, have some wine now that you have eaten your human flesh.

NICK: Noman, I will eat last after his crew. Crew first, you last. That's my gift to you.

(NICK takes the pills and downs them. Lights break back.)

ELLIOT: Welcome.

NICK: Don't tell that bitch Dorothy or I'll kill you.

ELLIOT: Friends.

(Lights change. We are at the hall meeting. PATIENTS enter, each bringing a chair as they arrive. ADAM remains at his bed. MAHA, RESEAN, and DOROTHY are at group when ELLIOT arrives.)

DOROTHY: How about the circus?

MAHA: I told you where I want to go.

DOROTHY: Are you sure, Maha?

RESEAN: We could go to the zoo or a movie just as easily.

MAHA: You aren't hearing me.

(ELLIOT crosses over to them with his chair and journal.)

ELLIOT: Ladies?

MAHA: She's retarded.

DOROTHY: I think that there are better things to do for your birthday than go to McDonald's.

MAHA: Shows what you know.

NICK: Maha's mother threw her a McDonald's birthday party when she was four.

DOROTHY: How about the beach?

ELLIOT: February.

RESEAN: Sugar, not helping.

MAHA: I like McDonald's.

NICK: It was the only birthday party her mother ever threw for her.

DOROTHY: Is there something special you want to buy?

MAHA: Food.

DOROTHY: Well, I could pick it up for you if you like.

RESEAN: Then we could choose something a little more decadent to do.

MAHA: I don't want her doing me any favors.

RESEAN: It's just so— There are better places to have a birthday party.

MAHA: *(Singing.)* "Big Mac, Filet O' Fish, Quarter Pounder, French Fries, icy Coke, thick shakes, sundaes and apple pies." *(Normal.)* There's Ronald, the Hamburglar, and Grimace. I want to have my picture taken with Grimace.

(NICK joins the hall meeting.)

NICK: Who the fuck is Grimace?

MAHA: The big purple guy.

NICK: Barney?

MAHA: No! Ronald's best friend.

DOROTHY: There are too many people who would be put in danger.

MAHA: From what?

DOROTHY: You might be exposed to any number of—

MAHA: *(To RESEAN.)* She just accused me of wanting to infect Ronald McDonald.

RESEAN: We all have compromised immune systems.

MAHA: *(To DOROTHY.)* My mother raised me better than that.

DOROTHY: Maha, I'm not concerned with you infecting anyone. I'm concerned about you getting sicker. Going into such a public place can expose you to any number of health risks.

MAHA: There can't be anything worse than what's floating around here.

RESEAN: *(To DOROTHY.)* How you think we are going to go to the circus?

DOROTHY: The circus was merely a suggestion.

ELLIOT: Stars.

RESEAN: You mean soap stars? My dream is to have Miss Susan Lucci blow out my candles.

ELLIOT: Sky stars.

MAHA: What's "Forrest Gump" yapping about?

DOROTHY: Elliot, what about the stars?

ELLIOT: Go see.

MAHA: Look out your window. We're going to McDonald's.

ELLIOT: Planet—

DOROTHY: Planetarium. You want to go to the planetarium?

ELLIOT: Yes.

MAHA: No.

RESEAN: I don't know, it might be fun spending the night looking up at the stars. Romantic. Can we bring a picnic?

MAHA: Boring.

NICK: Listen, sweetheart, there might be a lot of cute pussy at the planetarium. I'm gonna get me a piece of Natalie Wood.

RESEAN: It's like some bad horror movie. Poor innocent girl looking up at the stars, Nick jumps out of the bushes screaming, and murder ensues.

NICK: You just want me to jump out of the bushes at you.

RESEAN: I may have tits, but I could still kick your Helen Keller ass.

MAHA: Okay, well, my vote is for McDonald's.

DOROTHY: Are you getting all of this down, Elliot?

ELLIOT: Yes.

DOROTHY: We can talk slower.

MAHA: I'll talk as fast as I want to.

RESEAN: Dorothy, do you think it's right to stalk girls at the planetarium?

DOROTHY: I can't imagine it.

NICK: I'll show you.

DOROTHY: And I don't want to.

ELLIOT: Stars are map.

MAHA: Maybe McDonald's will have a map.

ELLIOT: Elliot find home.

NICK: *(Being E.T.)* Elliot, phone home.

MAHA: This is home now, Elliot. You're stuck here, just like the rest of us.

ELLIOT: No "home." Death.

(Silence.)

DOROTHY: Valentine's Day is coming up and I thought—

NICK: Oooooowwwww.

DOROTHY: You okay, Nick?

NICK: My stomach.

RESEAN: Hello? Someone? He needs medical attention.

NICK: My fucking stomach feels like it's going to explode.

MAHA: Don't you go all *Aliens* on me.

ELLIOT: That's how we twirled the fiery-pointed stake into the Cyclops's eye.

DOROTHY: Describe the pain.

NICK: I feel like someone stabbed me in my fucking stomach.

ELLIOT: The boiling blood bubbled all over.

DOROTHY: What did you eat today?

NICK: Nothing. Jell-O.

ELLIOT: The roots of his eye sputtered in the fire.

NICK: Fuck me!

ELLIOT: He screamed and the rock walls rang with his voice.

DOROTHY: Did you take anything?

NICK: No.

DOROTHY: This is serious. I need to know if you took anything.

NICK: Just some shit Elliot gave me.

RESEAN: You dealing drugs now, girlfriend?

ELLIOT: Not bad.

(Lights change to fantasy.)

NICK: Noman is killing me by some kind of trick.

ELLIOT: If no man is killing you, then your sickness comes from Zeus and can't be helped.

DOROTHY: Elliot, did you give him your pills?

(Lights snap back to reality.)

ELLIOT: Don't know.

DOROTHY: Elliot, if you gave him your pills, I need to know. You won't be in trouble.

NICK: I'm gonna fuckin' kill you.

RESEAN: You won't be in trouble, sweetie.

ELLIOT: Yes.

DOROTHY: *(Breaks out laughing.)* Go to the bathroom, Nick.

NICK: But my stomach?

DOROTHY: He gave you his laxative.

MAHA: He played you.

NICK: I'm blind.

MAHA: Nick got played by Home School. Ouch.

NICK: Shut the fuck up.

(Change to fantasy.)

ELLIOT: So Cyclops, you got yours in the end, didn't you? You had the gall to eat your guests in your own house, and Zeus made you pay for it.

(The blue alarm starts sounding. DOCTOR enters and crosses to ADAM's bed. He begins connecting more tubes to the bed. The web has started to overtake the bed.)

RESEAN: It's Adam.

ELLIOT: Help him.

DOROTHY: The doctor has it under control.

MAHA: Why don't they just let the sucker go?

DOROTHY: His mother wants us to keep him alive.

NICK: I'm not ending up like that fucking monster.

RESEAN: Honey, you are a monster.

NICK: I'll blow my brains out first.

ELLIOT: *(To DOROTHY.)* Adam pain?

DOROTHY: We give him morphine.

MAHA: Lucky fuck.

DOROTHY: His nerve endings are numb from the medication.

RESEAN: I don't care what you say about medicine. That boy is hurting.

DOROTHY: Adam's brain can't register any physical pain.

ELLIOT: Mind pain?

RESEAN: Girlfriend, his mind is hurting so bad his body had to blow itself up to keep it all inside.

ELLIOT: *(To DOROTHY.)* Help him.

DOROTHY: I can't. Adam's happy to be with his mother.

(The blue alarms stop. DOCTOR exits.)

DOROTHY: So the planetarium it is.

MAHA: But it's my birthday and I want to go to—

DOROTHY: Back to your rooms.

(The PATIENTS return to their beds, except for ELLIOT. He watches MRS. COLLINS and ADAM.)

MRS. COLLINS: *(Reading.)* "Man over board!" the sailors cried as they threw him a lifebelt. George caught it and held on. At last he was safe on board. The man in the yellow hat looked at George and said "You silly monkey. Look at what you've done."

(ELLIOT crosses to them.)

ELLIOT: Hello.

MRS. COLLINS: Who are you?

ELLIOT: Friend Adam.

ADAM: Buttoned-down shirt, khaki pants, glasses. He definitely wasn't going to the club in that gear.

MRS. COLLINS: Can I help you?

ELLIOT: What reading?

MRS. COLLINS: *Curious George*. It's Adam's favorite. His nickname's monkey.

ELLIOT: *(Handing MRS. COLLINS a book.)* Here.

MRS. COLLINS: Mark Twain? What do you want me to—?

ELLIOT: Essays Adam.

ADAM: He was such a dork he was cool.

MRS. COLLINS: I used to read *Curious George* to my son when he was a baby.

ELLIOT: Not baby now.

ADAM: I'd fuck him.

MRS. COLLINS: He always hated it.

ELLIOT: Try this.

MRS. COLLINS: Is everyone in this place insane?

ELLIOT: Yes. Goodbye. *(ELLIOT crosses back to his room and watches.)*

MRS. COLLINS: *(Reading.)* "Life was not a valuable gift, but death was. Life was a fever-dream made up of joys embittered by sorrows, pleasure poisoned by pain…"

(MRS. COLLINS continues to read to herself as ELLIOT takes over.)

ELLIOT: "The heaviest curse devisable by divine ingenuity; but death was sweet, death was gentle, death was kind; death healed the bruised spirit and the broken heart, and gave them rest and forgetfulness; death was man's best friend; when man could endure life no longer, death came and set him free."

MRS. COLLINS: *(To ADAM.)* That boy's morbid. The nurse should give him some Valium.

(Lights change. MAHA comes storming in.)

MAHA: I'm gonna kick your little white booty.

ELLIOT: Okay.

MAHA: The god damn stars.

ELLIOT: Sorry.

MAHA: Do you know how long I've been in this joint? Six months. Six months trapped in the fuckin' halls of death and all I want to do is go to McDonald's. And your white-ass has to say the god damn stars. Come here boy.

(MAHA puts ELLIOT in a headlock.)

ELLIOT: Wait.

MAHA: I'm gonna give you a noogie until your head bleeds.

ELLIOT: Stop! Ouch!!!

(MRS. HAYES enters, carrying a stack of books.)

MRS. HAYES: Just what is going on here?

(MAHA releases ELLIOT.)

MAHA: Nothin'.

MRS. HAYES: It doesn't look like nothing, young lady.

MAHA: We were just playing. Right, Elliot?

ELLIOT: Right.

MRS. HAYES: These are some friends you've made here, Elliot. One throws pee in your face, the other I find beating you up. I'm going to ask the nurse to give us a nice private room on a different floor.

ELLIOT: No.

MRS. HAYES: I think these lesions are affecting more than your speech. I'm going to ask that nice doctor if there is a region of the brain that causes stubbornness, because if there is, you have a great big lesion there. *(To MAHA.)* What's your name?

MAHA: Maha. Maha Swenson, Miss.

MRS. HAYES: Call me Margaret. So you're the one.

ELLIOT: Bring it?

MRS. HAYES: Of course I brought it. Although I'd like to know why. You call me up in the middle of the night. Make me think something terrible has happened. And let me tell you, you are hard enough to understand when I'm awake. "Mom." "Kleos." "Bring." "Maha." "Birthday." "McDonald's." Well, I didn't know what you might want so I brought you the menu.

ELLIOT: Thanks. *(To MAHA.)* Here.

MRS. HAYES: What's so special about McDonald's?

MAHA: You brought me a menu?

ELLIOT: Sorry…stars.

MRS. HAYES: I thought you might like to see what they have there.

MAHA: I've eaten at McDonald's before.

MRS. HAYES: *(To ELLIOT.)* You sure about this? She seems rather difficult.

ELLIOT: Yes.

MRS. HAYES: *(To MAHA.)* I thought maybe you might like to plan your party. Make a guest list, pick out the goody bags.

MAHA: My mom never planned a party before.

MRS. HAYES: When I first start planning a party, I have to come up with a theme.

MAHA: Theme?

MRS. HAYES: Like the Olympics, or superheroes, or…

ELLIOT: Odyssey.

MRS. HAYES: Or the Odyssey.

MAHA: I'll do my party my mother's way.

MRS. HAYES: Suit yourself. *(To ELLIOT.)* Well, honey, I tried. Some people just don't know how to be helped.

(Lights shift to fantasy.)

ELLIOT: We sailed on and came to the island that is home to Circe. I sent Maha out to scout for food. When she didn't return I went in search of her.

(DOROTHY enters.)

RESEAN: Circe flung open the blue curtains and invited Odysseus in.

(Lights switch back.)

DOROTHY: Mrs. Hayes, Elliot. Maha, what are you doing in here?

ELLIOT: Visiting.

DOROTHY: Maha needs rest. She should be in her room.

MRS. HAYES: Let them visit.

DOROTHY: Maha. To your room.

MAHA: I ain't going nowhere.

ELLIOT: She nowhere.

DOROTHY: It's time for your pain medi-cation.

RESEAN: She brewed up a potion of Vicodin, Demerol, Valium, with pale honey stirred in. An insidious drug that would make them forget who they were and what they wanted.

ELLIOT: Maha stay.

DOROTHY: Say thank you to Elliot and Mrs. Hayes for spending time with you.

MAHA: Thank you, Elliot. Thank you, Margaret.

ELLIOT: Maha McDonald's.

MRS. HAYES: We're planning to take Maha to McDonald's for her birthday.

ELLIOT: Yeah.

MAHA: Yeah.

DOROTHY: Maha's not allowed to leave the hospital without proper supervision.

ELLIOT: *(To DOROTHY.)* You mean.

DOROTHY: I'm just following the rules.

ELLIOT: Bend rules.

MRS. HAYES: Yes, in this case, for her birthday, we will of course need to bend the rules.

DOROTHY: We don't bend the rules here.

ELLIOT: She dying.

DOROTHY: We have the patient's safety to consider.

MRS. HAYES: The only thing she wants to do is go to McDonald's.

DOROTHY: Maha needs to remain where it is safe. Here in her bed.

ELLIOT: Picture Grimace.

DOROTHY: Elliot, I'm not a miracle worker. Maha, back to your room and I'll give you the rest of your medication.

RESEAN: And Circe threw Maha Oxycontin and Xanax.

DOROTHY: Maha doesn't really want to go, anyway. Tell them Maha.

MAHA: I don't really need to go.

ELLIOT: You going.

DOROTHY: Maha says she doesn't want to go. Tell them, Maha.

MAHA: I don't really want to go.

MRS. HAYES: You're making her say that.

DOROTHY: Back to bed, Maha, or you'll be blocked.

RESEAN: Circe struck Maha with her wand and herded Maha back to her sty.

DOROTHY: Off to the sty with the rest of your friends.

MAHA: I'm going. *(MAHA exits.)*

MRS. HAYES: Do you really think all of this is necessary?

DOROTHY: Maha's immune system is nonexistent. We sterilize everything here. We coordinate the patients' diet. There is the chance of bacterial infection from the animal fat in the grease. There are all the children with runny noses and a host of other possible infections in the play place. If she leaves the hospital, she could very well catch something and die. I don't think a trip to McDonald's is worth that risk.

MRS. HAYES: Point taken.

DOROTHY: Elliot, I want you to understand. I'm not inhuman. I understand how your heart goes out to her, but you can't go around interfering in everyone else's lives. Focus on getting better. On trying to go home for a little while before the end.

ELLIOT: Kleos.

DOROTHY: Glory like that only happens in your books. *(DOROTHY exits.)*

MRS. HAYES: She is only doing her job, Elliot. I'll stop by McDonald's and pick something up for Maha.

ELLIOT: No.

MRS. HAYES: I'll get one of everything on the menu.

ELLIOT: Wants…picture…Grimace. Need plan.

(Lights change. MRS. HAYES exits. RESEAN crosses to ELLIOT.)

RESEAN: Where are you off to now, Odysseus, alone and in rough, uncharted terrain?

ELLIOT: To find my missing crew.

RESEAN: Your crew are up in Circe's house, penned like pigs into crowded little sties.

ELLIOT: I have come to save them.

RESEAN: I don't think so. You'll never rescue them and you'll have to stay there too.

ELLIOT: I must do whatever it takes to rescue my crew from this horrible fate.

RESEAN: The first, you lost to the power of the Lotus Flower.

(Lights up ADAM.)

ADAM: Every day, every hour, another one of my organs stopped working.

(Lights up on NICK. He is lifting his chair over his head like it is a set of weights.)

RESEAN: You defeated the Cyclops, but he still rages against you.

NICK: Two hundred and one. HIV is not in me.

(Lights up on MAHA.)

RESEAN: While the other one wallows in mud, longing for the intoxicating drink of Circe.

MAHA: I know you can hear me. Where are my damn pills?

ELLIOT: Stop. Do not show me my failures. I have a plan to rescue my crew.

RESEAN: There you go again. Always the hero. Won't you yield even to the immortals?

ELLIOT: I will not yield until all of my crew have found peace.

RESEAN: AIDS is an immortal evil, Dread, dire, ferocious, unfightable. There is no defense. It's flight, not fight.

ELLIOT: I will fight.

RESEAN: Be careful, my brave Odysseus.

(MRS. HAYES enters.)

MRS. HAYES: So how are the valentines coming?

(Lights break back to reality. They are making construction paper valentines. ELLIOT holds up a valentine.)

ELLIOT: Adam.

MRS. HAYES: Let me see. "Dear Adam, happy Valentine's Day. I've spent hours trying to come up with the right words that would make you understand how I feel. I've searched my books to find some poem or passage that would express how beautiful I think you are—"

RESEAN: Enough, enough. It's trash, sugar, trash.

ELLIOT: Good, right?

RESEAN: It's supposed to say "Be mine." That's it.

MRS. HAYES: It's not a bad start, just needs some editing.

RESEAN: Construction paper valentines. Are we from the AIDS ghetto?

MRS. HAYES: Mr. Adam will love it.

RESEAN: That boy's a vegetable. We can't give him that.

(ELLIOT rips up ADAM's valentine.)

MRS. HAYES: Honey, don't.

ELLIOT: Tacky.

MRS. HAYES: What kind of talk is that? Did I raise you to give up like that? I don't think so.

ELLIOT: Sorry.

MRS. HAYES: Princess, dear, why don't you go back to your room?

RESEAN: Don't you two watch soaps?

ELLIOT: Nope.

RESEAN: This is supposed to be our catfight. I say something bitchy to you, you retort, we slap each other, pull each other's hair, and fall in the pool.

MRS. HAYES: Resean, I don't understand. You were excited about making the Valentine's cards.

RESEAN: Tell me you're not mad sugar. Give Resean some love.

ELLIOT: *(Giving her a valentine.)* Love.

RESEAN: You should be giving a valentine to Adam.

ELLIOT: Too soon.

RESEAN: Too soon. Listen to him. Too soon.

MRS. HAYES: Don't pressure him.

RESEAN: There ain't soon enough in this place.

MRS. HAYES: He's been out of the dating pool for ten years. And look how his last date turned out.

ELLIOT: Don't.

RESEAN: Sugar, you're afraid of love.

ELLIOT: No not.

MRS. HAYES: He always has been. Maybe I didn't hug him enough as a child. Who knows? But Elliot runs whenever a boy looks at him. And if they talk to him? Forget it. He is so mean, they run away with their tails between their legs.

ELLIOT: Why catfight?

RESEAN: I just found out I've got to hire me a lawyer.

MRS. HAYES: Are you in trouble with the cops, Resean?

RESEAN: I'm in trouble with Social Services. If I want to get Erica Kane back, it's gonna cost me five thousand dollars.

MRS. HAYES: Isn't that that soap opera character you love?

ELLIOT: Daughter.

RESEAN: I'm a father.

MRS. HAYES: Oh. Well, that's...oh.

RESEAN: You aren't the only one who's speechless now, hunh?

ELLIOT: Good job.

RESEAN: It's either pay for my surgery or get back my daughter. I guess I won't be a woman before I go. You should go visit him.

ELLIOT: Who?

RESEAN: Adam, sugar. Lord knows he can't come to you.

MRS. HAYES: Elliot, you don't have to do anything you don't want to.

RESEAN: Yes, he does.

MRS. HAYES: No, you don't.

ELLIOT: Scary.

RESEAN: Dying is scary, falling in love is fun.

ELLIOT: No.

RESEAN: Then turn on the TV. Your mom and I are gonna watch us some "All My Kids."

ELLIOT: Ethan.

MRS. HAYES: Elliot, we don't have to talk about this. Thank you, Resean, but Elliot and I are going to finish making valentines. What color paper do you want? Purple? Can we make purple hearts?

RESEAN: Honey breathe. Who's Ethan?

ELLIOT: The one.

RESEAN: Ohhh, the one.

ELLIOT: Swimmer.

RESEAN: Keep talking.

ELLIOT: First time.

MRS. HAYES: Really?

RESEAN: Shhh. It's getting good.

ELLIOT: I fell him.

RESEAN: The first fall is always the hardest.

ELLIOT: He many.

RESEAN: Swimmers always do.

MRS. HAYES: He was a cruel man. He hurt you, Elliot. We don't need to talk about it.

ELLIOT: I special.

MRS. HAYES: You don't know that. You just said he had many boyfriends.

ELLIOT: No. Many sex. One boyfriend. Me.

MRS. HAYES: You never told me that.

ELLIOT: Not ask.

RESEAN: What happened to him?

ELLIOT: Don't know.

RESEAN: That settles it. You are marching into Adam's room and starting up a conversation.

MRS. HAYES: They both can't speak.

RESEAN: Then use gesture.

ELLIOT: Dorothy. Rules.

MRS. HAYES: Rules are meant to be broken.

ELLIOT: You trouble.

RESEAN: *(Singing.)* "I'm forever blowing bubbles."

ELLIOT: Don't ignore.

RESEAN and MRS. HAYES: *(Singing.)* "Pretty bubbles in the air."

ELLIOT: Fine.

(Lights change.)

ELLIOT: And on I went, brooding darkly on many things.

(ELLIOT crosses to DOROTHY. She is in ADAM's room.)

DOROTHY: You're not supposed to be in here, Elliot.

ELLIOT: Visiting.

DOROTHY: Go back to your room and I'll bring you your medicine.

ELLIOT: No.

DOROTHY: I don't make the rules, I just have to enforce them.

ELLIOT: Staying to see Adam.

DOROTHY: If Mrs. Collins finds you in here, she'll—

ELLIOT: Not afraid her.

DOROTHY: Put gloves on at least.

ELLIOT: Record.

(ELLIOT gives DOROTHY his book.)

ELLIOT: You kids?

DOROTHY: That's really none of your business.

ELLIOT: Sorry. What if Adam son?

DOROTHY: My job doesn't allow me to consider that, Elliot.

ELLIOT: But if your kid?

DOROTHY: He's a patient. I have to finish in here.

ELLIOT: Should let Adam die.

DOROTHY: When I first started here, I wore my bleeding heart on my sleeve too. Trust me, you don't help anyone that way.

ELLIOT: Still try.

DOROTHY: Last month I tried to comfort Nick. He spit in my face. Right in my eye.

ELLIOT: You okay?

DOROTHY: Yes. Elliot, I'm pregnant, three months. I can't do anything that would put me or my baby at risk.

ELLIOT: Why stay here?

DOROTHY: My husband asks me that every morning. I'm not going to abandon them, I'm going to do my job and not put myself in any extra danger.

ELLIOT: Easier you.

(Lights shift to fantasy.)

DOROTHY: Who are you, and where do you come from? No one else has ever defied me once my potion has passed their lips.

ELLIOT: I am wily Odysseus.

DOROTHY: You should be in bed, resting. Getting better so you can go home. Not running around here playing hero to people who will never appreciate it.

ELLIOT: If you really want me to eat and drink, set my men free and let me see them.

DOROTHY: Stay if you want, but don't let Mrs. Collins catch you in here. She went to get coffee. You have at most twenty minutes.

(ELLIOT takes his pills. DOROTHY gives him back his notebook and exits.)

ELLIOT: Hi Adam. Can hear?

ADAM: I nodded my head "yes."

ELLIOT: Okay I visit?

ADAM: Again "yes."

ELLIOT: How doing?

(Lights change to fantasy. ADAM crosses out from behind his screen.)

ADAM: Been better.

ELLIOT: You're an amazing fighter.

ADAM: No I'm not.

ELLIOT: My name's Elliot.

ADAM: I know. I watch you sometimes. Is that weird?

ELLIOT: I don't think so. I watch everybody. Is that weird?

ADAM: You're a writer. It's your job to watch people.

ELLIOT: I don't get out much.

ADAM: I go out all the time.

ELLIOT: I go to the library.

ADAM: Clubbing, dancing on plywood boxes, parties at rich people's mansions, making porn, and living soap operas.

(ADAM sits with ELLIOT on the front of the bed.)

ELLIOT: I read a lot.

ADAM: I read comic books.

ELLIOT: I used to hope I'd bump into a boy like you at the library.

ADAM: I've never been to a library.

ELLIOT: I've always wanted to live your life. Parties, drugs...boys.

ADAM: Funny. I've always wanted your life.

ELLIOT: It's kind of boring.

ADAM: It's sophisticated.

ELLIOT: You think?

ADAM: Weird, how we had to end up here to meet each other, hunh?

ELLIOT: If Odysseus had never lost his way, he wouldn't have become a hero.

ADAM: Yeah, don't know it.

ELLIOT: I'll read it to you.

ADAM: In bed?

ELLIOT: 'kay.

ADAM: Naked?

ELLIOT: I guess.

ADAM: Eating M&M's?

ELLIOT: I'm allergic to chocolate.

ADAM: Then whatever you like.

ELLIOT: You're kind of slutty.

ADAM: Sorry.

ELLIOT: No, I like it.

ADAM: Really?

ELLIOT: Really. Can I touch you?

ADAM: Touch me? But I'm ugly.

ELLIOT: You're beautiful.

ADAM: You can touch my hand.

ELLIOT: Sure.

ADAM: Without gloves.

ELLIOT: Okay.

(ELLIOT takes off his gloves and touches ADAM's hand.)

ADAM: You are the first person to really touch me since I got here.

ELLIOT: How long have you been sick?

ADAM: Three years. You?

ELLIOT: Ten.

ADAM: Wow. How did you make it so long?

ELLIOT: My mom took care of me.

ADAM: Lucky. I like talking to you.

ELLIOT: I like you.

ADAM: I like you too.

ELLIOT: Are you in pain?

ADAM: Not really.

ELLIOT: We're friends now. Friends tell the truth.

ADAM: It hurts to breathe.

ELLIOT: Are you afraid to die?

ADAM: Not really.

ELLIOT: Then why are you still fighting?

ADAM: My mom loves me now. She says my eyes twinkle when she's here. I like that.

ELLIOT: Your mom loves you always.

ADAM: Not my mom.

(The sound of high heels can be heard coming down the hallway. ADAM gets up and goes behind the screen.)

ADAM: She won't like you being in here.

ELLIOT: I'm not afraid of her.

ADAM: Be careful around my mom.

(MRS. COLLINS enters.)

MRS. COLLINS: What are you doing in here?

ADAM: She's here.

(Lights break back to reality.)

ELLIOT: I visiting.

MRS. COLLINS: Nurse! Nurse!

ELLIOT: Relax.

MRS. COLLINS: Get out of here. Go. Get.

ELLIOT: Not leaving.

MRS. COLLINS: I'll get the nurse in here and bar you from ever seeing my son again.

ELLIOT: Crazy.

MRS. COLLINS: He asked me to take care of him.

ELLIOT: You want...stop gay.

MRS. COLLINS: If he would, he could come home to his family.

(ADAM talks from behind his screen.)

ADAM: I can't.

MRS. COLLINS: It doesn't seem like much for someone to do in exchange for a whole family.

ELLIOT: Won't better.

MRS. COLLINS: Most of us live by the rules.

ADAM: I tried.

MRS. COLLINS: He didn't even try.

ADAM: I fucked Suzi Shaw in Dad's pickup truck.

ELLIOT: Sex not simple.

ADAM: I tore off her panties with my teeth.

ELLIOT: Adam wants love.

MRS. COLLINS: His father thinks I'm at Niagara Falls.

ADAM: She laughed at me when I couldn't cum.

MRS. COLLINS: What he thinks I am doing at Niagara Falls alone, I have no idea. He says Adam's not our son as long as Adam chooses to be a homosexual.

ELLIOT: Love him.

MRS. COLLINS: I am here. I am loving my son. I am making sure he gets the best medical treatment.

ELLIOT: Say.

ADAM: I did it for you, Mom.

MRS. COLLINS: I will call my husband. He will have you removed from this hospital.

ELLIOT: Say I love you.

(DOROTHY enters.)

DOROTHY: What's going on in here?

MRS. COLLINS: This patient is trespassing.

ELLIOT: Adam friend.

MRS. COLLINS: I want him barred from my son's room.

DOROTHY: Do you really think that's necessary?

MRS. COLLINS: He could be carrying all sorts of filthy diseases. If my son gets sicker it will be his fault.

DOROTHY: Elliot won't bother you or Adam again.

MRS. COLLINS: *(To ELLIOT.)* You come near my son again, and my husband will sue you for everything your parents own. Their house, their savings, their silverware. You understand me?

ELLIOT: Me not understand.

(Lights change. ELLIOT returns to his room. DOCTOR enters and crosses to him.)

DOCTOR: Mr. Hayes? Mr. Hayes? Morning, Mr. Hayes.

ELLIOT: Elliot.

DOCTOR: Elliot.

ELLIOT: Got news?

DOCTOR: Yes. The level of virus in your brain cells—

ELLIOT: Wait. Okay.

DOCTOR: Has increased significantly. The medication—

ELLIOT: Wait. Okay.

DOCTOR: Elliot, I need you to stop writing.

ELLIOT: Wait. Okay.

DOCTOR: The medication isn't working. You have only a few days until your brain hemorrhages.

ELLIOT: Three days?

DOCTOR: Forty-eight hours.

ELLIOT: *(Stops writing.)* How I die?

DOCTOR: The lesions on your brain will start affecting your nervous system. Your brain will start sending false electrical impulses to your body. Eventually, one will reach your heart and tell it to stop beating.

ELLIOT: Not what. I low.

DOCTOR: Let me call your mother.

ELLIOT: You give something me do.

DOCTOR: How would I know?

ELLIOT: You see die all time.

DOCTOR: That's different.

ELLIOT: What they do?

DOCTOR: To be honest, Elliot, I'm always too busy trying to save them. I don't notice what they're doing.

ELLIOT: *(Picking up notebook.)* Okay. Well. Thanks.

DOCTOR: I don't think I helped.

ELLIOT: Nope. Bye.

DOCTOR: I think Elliot, that maybe, like when you write your stories, somehow you just know what's supposed to happen.

ELLIOT: Write it?

DOCTOR: When death comes, you will know what to do.

ELLIOT: Write for me.

DOCTOR: I'm not a writer, Elliot.

ELLIOT: I'll help.

DOCTOR: *(Writing in the notebook.)* It's like you're packing for a journey.

ELLIOT: Where to?

DOCTOR: On a journey across the sea. You'll board Death's ship and unfurl the sail.

ELLIOT: Write that.

DOCTOR: You will find your way by the map of the stars.

ELLIOT: And my crew?

DOCTOR: Then you will rouse your men and order the crew onto the deck and cast off.

ELLIOT: Who crew?

DOCTOR: What do you want him to look like?

ELLIOT: I him eye twinkle.

DOCTOR: Then his eyes will twinkle.

ELLIOT: Now what?

DOCTOR: The wind picks up, and as the sail bellies out, the ship will fly though the deep blue water taking you "home."

ELLIOT: *(Taking back notebook.)* Thank you.

DOCTOR: I'll have Nurse McCarthy bring you some more pain medication.

ELLIOT: No thanks.

DOCTOR: If that's what you want, Elliot.

ELLIOT: Don't Mom.

DOCTOR: She can help you deal with some of the issues.

ELLIOT: Don't want worry.

DOCTOR: I understand. Thank you, Elliot. *(DOCTOR exits.)*

ELLIOT: This broke my spirit. I sat on the bed and wept. I had no will to live, nor did I care if I ever saw the sunlight again. And Circe said:

(Lights up on DOROTHY.)

DOROTHY: My wily Odysseus—there is another journey you must make first—to the house of Hades and the dread Swimmer Ethan. He will tell you the route and how long it will take for you to reach home over the teeming deep.

(Lights out on DOROTHY. The screens form a wall behind Elliot. We can see the silhouettes of the PATIENTS through the screens.)

ELLIOT: The souls of the dead congregated, the ghosts of brides and bachelors, old men worn out from their toil, soft young men with hearts new to sorrow, and brave men who had been killed in battle.

They came from every quarter with a strange cry, and pale fear seized me.

(The SWIMMER ETHAN enters through the center.)

ELLIOT: And then came the ghost of the Swimmer Ethan. He *knew* me and said:

ETHAN: It's been a long time, Mr. Man.

ELLIOT: Too long.

ETHAN: Some might argue not long enough.

ELLIOT: I had hoped you'd still be alive.

ETHAN: Waiting for the day to gather up the courage to see me? Too late.

ELLIOT: I'm sorry.

ETHAN: Don't. Don't do that. I'm the one that should be saying I'm sorry to you.

ELLIOT: I have come to find the route home.

ETHAN: And I will give it to you. For a price.

ELLIOT: What more could I possibly give you?

ETHAN: Forgiveness.

ELLIOT: I don't have that to give. You were my home.

ETHAN: Why did you run?

ELLIOT: I was afraid you'd be gone, either to death, or to someone else, and I'd have to do it all alone. Mom was so safe, so warm, so comforting.

ETHAN: We all do it alone in the end.

ELLIOT: I have to believe I can be remembered. You achieved Kleos.

ETHAN: No, I'm here in Hades aren't I?

ELLIOT: But I have remembered you.

ETHAN: Not in glory, but in shame and regret. I can't go home until you forgive me.

ELLIOT: In this new land, I have seen so much pain. I've watched a son trying so hard to stay alive to please his mother. To make her forgive him. To try and forgive her.

ETHAN: But there's something about him?

ELLIOT: I am just like him. I've spent the last ten years of my life hiding from you, from love, from life. From forgiving you.

ETHAN: If you forgive me, you can move on from me.

ELLIOT: I forgive you.

ETHAN: Oh, look. Look at the stars.

ELLIOT: I don't see them.

ETHAN: It's a map of the way home. You'll see it soon enough.

ELLIOT: Goodbye, Ethan.

ETHAN: Go, Mr. Man. Save Adam. He is a lucky boy. Goodbye, Elliot.

(Lights change ETHAN exits. The other PATIENTS have set up for group. ELLIOT takes a moment, then joins them.)

MAHA: Where's Nurse Party Pooper?

ELLIOT: Not coming.

MAHA: Then why I am here?

ELLIOT: I call meeting.

RESEAN: You a doctor now, sweetie?

ELLIOT: Need favor.

RESEAN: I love you girlfriend, but I'm missing my soap for this.

MAHA: We're sick of your ideas, Home School.

RESEAN: Let's hear him out.

(NICK enters.)

NICK: What the fuck am I doing here?

ELLIOT: Show for Adam.

MAHA: Show? Like a play? Uht, don't act.

ELLIOT: Please.

RESEAN: Sugar, I want to help you, but a show?

ELLIOT: Nick?

NICK: Fuck no. I haven't forgotten what you did to my stomach.

ELLIOT: Girlfriend. Here. *(ELLIOT holds out a* Soap Opera Digest.*)*

RESEAN: Do I look like I'm for sale?

ELLIOT: Lucci pictures.

RESEAN: *(Taking the magazine.)* I'm in.

ELLIOT: Maha?

MAHA: I want to help, but I get stage fright.

ELLIOT: Still McDonald's.

MAHA: Dorothy won't let us.

ELLIOT: I plan. Big Mac tomorrow.

MAHA: I'm in.

ELLIOT: Nick?

NICK: You talking to me?

RESEAN: Come on Nick, honey, we're all going to do it.

NICK: Since when am I part of your we?

MAHA: Stop playing hard to get.

NICK: You all got something for helping. What do I get?

ELLIOT: No drugs.

NICK: You think I'm dumb enough to take something you give me?

MAHA: Yes.

RESEAN: What, Nick, could you possibly want? A machine gun?

MAHA: A switchblade?

ELLIOT: A date?

NICK: A kite.

ELLIOT: Kite?

RESEAN: What kind of drug is kite?

NICK: When I was a kid I liked kites. Watching a kite, you know you're alive. A kite is always moving forward. If it stops moving, it dies.

ELLIOT: Bring kite, you help?

NICK: I'll do it.

RESEAN: So what's this play about?

ELLIOT: You'll see.

MAHA: Can I make the costumes?

ELLIOT: Sure.

RESEAN: If there's any singing, that's my department.

NICK: Does it matter that I can't see?

ELLIOT: Nope. Here's plan.

(Lights change. The other PATIENTS exit behind ADAM's curtain. ELLIOT steps forward.)

ELLIOT: Meanwhile, our boat was approaching the Sirens' island, when suddenly the wind died down and we were stilled. There was not a breath of wind.

(*ELLIOT pulls back the curtain to ADAM's room to reveal ADAM's bed. The PATIENTS are dressed in sheet-togas that they have created. ADAM is behind his screen.*)

NICK: Where am I?

MAHA: Over here. Shhh.

ADAM: What's happening?

ELLIOT: Present.

ADAM: For me?

ELLIOT: Me. You. Valentine.

ADAM: You don't have to.

ELLIOT: Listen. Crew.

MAHA: That's us?

RESEAN: Yes, sugar.

NICK: I'm not playing no fairy.

RESEAN: It's a temptress.

NICK: No one can be tempted by me. I've got herpes on my forehead.

MAHA: I'm wearing a diaper.

RESEAN: Elliot will make us beautiful.

ELLIOT: I want you Adam to see love. To be seduced by its song. We are surging ahead, when the Sirens see our ship. Their song pierces the air.

(*Soft music begins to play under the scene. As ADAM comes out from behind his screen, ELLIOT and ADAM progress toward each other.*)

RESEAN: The moon sets over western mountains as the sun rises from the red water.

MAHA: Rising and setting, time's dividers portend the rise and fall of our lovers' fortunes.

NICK: They call on Zeus, Poseidon, Aphrodite.

RESEAN: They call on Athena.

MAHA: They call on love to bless this union.

NICK: They bow to the stars, to the dynasty of ancestors, to the honor of devotion.

RESEAN: They declare pure love.

ELLIOT: I only loved once before and it has brought me pain, sickness, and regret.

ADAM: Do you bring me pain? Do you bring me sickness? Do you bring me regret?

ELLIOT: My love will bring you home.

ADAM: But my mother gave me life.

ELLIOT: Love will bring you peace.

(*ADAM and ELLIOT kneel together at the front of the stage. RESEAN, MAHA, and NICK move toward them and stand like priestesses overseeing the wedding.*)

RESEAN: Love is blown from dark sea to dark sea at a fearful rate, but its first blush never loses its happy youth, a truth that no opinion can vulgarize. We stand witness to your blessed vows. We stand witness to your sacred union. We stand witness to the sanctity of this marriage.

(*ADAM and ELLIOT kiss. MAHA and NICK begin to blow bubbles. MRS. COLLINS storms in. The illusion is broken. ADAM moves back behind his screen and is once again caught in the light.*)

MRS. COLLINS: I will have my lawyers on the phone in three seconds.

RESEAN: Run!

NICK: Where?

MRS. COLLINS: This hospital will have to close down in order to pay the damages.

(The screens are moved in front of ADAM's bed. DOCTOR and DOROTHY enter. DOROTHY crosses back and forth behind the screens tending to ADAM.)

DOCTOR: That won't be necessary, Mrs. Collins. We will handle this. *(To ELLIOT.)* What were you thinking?

ELLIOT: Present Adam.

DOROTHY: His vitals are good.

ELLIOT: We not hurt.

DOCTOR: You could've killed him.

RESEAN: Elliot was only trying to make Adam happy.

MRS. COLLINS: Adam is happy because I'm here with him. He doesn't need this, this spectacle, to be happy.

MAHA: He seemed happy.

MRS. COLLINS: Did anyone ask you?

DOCTOR: All of you go back to your rooms. There will be no trip to the planetarium. There will be no more hall activities.

NICK: We're not in prison.

DOCTOR: That's right. You are in a hospital. A place where people are dying.

RESEAN: Oh, no, we're living. We may be living in the halls of death, but we're living.

NICK: Living terminal.

DOCTOR: To your rooms.

(MAHA, RESEAN, and NICK start to exit.)

NICK: *(To ELLIOT.)* So I still get my kite?

ELLIOT: Yes.

DOCTOR: Go.

(The PATIENTS exit.)

DOROTHY: Doctor, Adam's trying to speak. He's going to choke on his tube unless I remove it.

DOCTOR: His vitals are good. Take it out.

(DOCTOR pushes open the screens to reveal ADAM in bed.)

ADAM: Elliot. Mom.

DOROTHY: Easy, Adam. Don't talk. Take deep breaths.

MRS. COLLINS: What about him?

DOCTOR: Elliot, I am going to speak to your mother about providing you with home care.

ELLIOT: But—

DOCTOR: You are too much of a disruption to the rest of the ward.

ELLIOT: He better.

DOCTOR: You will be going home tomorrow.

ELLIOT: Can't.

DOCTOR: You have no choice. *(To MRS. COLLINS.)* Is this satisfactory?

MRS. COLLINS: Yes. Completely.

DOCTOR: Let Elliot say goodbye and then escort him to his room. *(DOCTOR exits.)*

ELLIOT: Adam.

ADAM: Don't, Elliot.

ELLIOT: Wish.

ADAM: Don't leave me here.

MRS. COLLINS: He's speaking gibberish.

ELLIOT: No choice.

ADAM: It's too much.

ELLIOT: Love you.

ADAM: Take me home.

ELLIOT: Try.

DOROTHY: That's enough, Elliot, back to your room.

MRS. COLLINS: Now you both can get some rest.

ELLIOT: *(To DOROTHY.)* I'm sorry.

DOROTHY: I don't want to hear it.

(Lights change. ELLIOT returns to his room. MRS. HAYES enters carrying a duffel bag.)

MRS. HAYES: I got here as soon as I could.

ELLIOT: Thank you.

MRS. HAYES: Maybe if I explain to the other mother she might understand.

ELLIOT: Evil.

MRS. HAYES: Well, don't exaggerate, Elliot. She's just worried about her son.

(RESEAN and MAHA enter.)

RESEAN: She's evil, girlfriend.

MAHA: That bitch is crazy.

ELLIOT: Where Nick?

MAHA: Dorothy's in with him.

RESEAN: He took a turn for the worse last night.

MRS. HAYES: Will he be okay?

RESEAN: He's boarding the ship.

MRS. HAYES: Terrible.

MAHA: At least we'll know someone when we get there.

RESEAN: Even if it is Nick the Prick.

ELLIOT: Where kite?

MRS. HAYES: Well, see, Elliot I was so busy getting your things together, clothes, bags, books, that I didn't really have—

ELLIOT: Forgot.

MRS. HAYES: I forgot.

ELLIOT: Nick need kite.

MRS. HAYES: I know honey, but Resean just said he—

ELLIOT: Need kite live.

RESEAN: Sugar, he needs a gift from God, not some toy.

ELLIOT: He need kite.

RESEAN: Rin Tin Tin don't need any help from us.

ELLIOT: I promise.

RESEAN: Don't worry, sugar, you leave this in Resean's hands. She'll get a kite to where it's going.

ELLIOT: Goddess and hero.

RESEAN: Hero. You take care of yourself.

ELLIOT: You too.

(RESEAN exits.)

ELLIOT: Ready?

MAHA: As I'll ever be.

MRS. HAYES: I remembered the clothes like you asked. Are you sure we want to do this? It sounds awfully risky.

ELLIOT: Only chance.

MAHA: I'm supposed to wear these.

ELLIOT: Go change.

MRS. HAYES: Hurry, honey. This whole thing depends on timing.

(MAHA exits behind her curtain with the duffel bag of clothes.)

ELLIOT: Thanks, Mom.

MRS. HAYES: You're turning me into a fugitive. You sure you don't just want to come home?

ELLIOT: I am home.

MRS. HAYES: I know.

(DOROTHY enters with a wheelchair.)

DOROTHY: Time to go, Elliot.

MRS. HAYES: I'll handle it from here.

DOROTHY: It's hospital policy that a nurse escorts the patient off the ward.

MRS. HAYES: My son is upset enough at having to leave. You are sending a sick boy away from his friends and the doctors and telling him to go home and die. I will not have you make it worse by forcing him to have you push him out of here in that thing.

DOROTHY: Mrs. Hayes—

MRS. HAYES: Don't push me. You think that mother in with Elliot's friend is bad? You haven't seen nothing, lady.

DOROTHY: Go ahead.

(DOROTHY exits. MRS. HAYES follows and watches till she leaves.)

MRS. HAYES: She's gone.

ELLIOT: Maha.

(MAHA enters dressed in ELLIOT's clothes. She is wearing a hoodie sweatshirt with the hood pulled up to hide her face.)

MAHA: I feel white.

ELLIOT: Good.

MRS. HAYES: Get in the wheelchair and don't say a word.

ELLIOT: Got hurry.

MRS. HAYES: Elliot, sweetie, be careful.

ELLIOT: Nurse catch us.

MRS. HAYES: I'll see you soon.

ELLIOT: To McDonald's.

MAHA: To McDonald's.

MRS. HAYES: To McDonald's.

(MRS. HAYES pushes MAHA offstage. RESEAN enters NICK's room with a make-shift kite. ELLIOT watches from his chair.)

NICK: Who's there?

RESEAN: It's Resean, sugar.

NICK: I'm not really sick, I'm just fucking tired.

RESEAN: Too much exercise today?

NICK: Yeah. Too much exercise.

RESEAN: Elliot got himself into some trouble and—

NICK: He promised.

RESEAN: So I had to make one for you.

NICK: What the fuck kind of kite is this?

RESEAN: I gave up a few of my most prized possessions to make that for you.

NICK: I can't see it—

RESEAN: Part of my robe.

NICK: But I can feel it.

RESEAN: The underwire from my favorite bra.

NICK: This shit won't fly.

RESEAN: Say thank you.

NICK: Thank you.

RESEAN: Tell me you're sorry.

NICK: I'm sorry.

RESEAN: Tell me I'm beautiful.

NICK: No fucking way.

RESEAN: I might be able to make a pillow out of it.

NICK: You're beautiful. You're a fucking super model.

RESEAN: Here you go, sweetie. Play with your kite. I think you're beautiful too.

(Lights change. ELLIOT crosses to ADAM's room and watches ADAM and MRS. COLLINS. ADAM is lying in bed, the web of ropes still holding him there. MRS. COLLINS is reading to ADAM.)

MRS. COLLINS: "A soap bubble is the most beautiful thing and the most exquisite in nature; it is a human life." A soap bubble?

ADAM: Mother, read.

ELLIOT: "We are blown upon this world; we float buoyantly upon this summer air a little while, complacently showing off our grace of form and our dainty iridescent colors."

ADAM: I like that. Dainty, iridescent colors.

MRS. COLLINS: Very amusing.

ELLIOT: "Then we vanish with a little puff, leaving nothing behind but a memory."

MRS. COLLINS: We are not that fragile.

ADAM: I think it's beautiful.

MRS. COLLINS: Who wrote it?

ELLIOT: Mark Twain.

(ELLIOT enters ADAM's room.)

MRS. COLLINS: Oh, this useless ritual again.

ELLIOT: Here save Adam.

ADAM: Hi, Elliot.

MRS. COLLINS: I thought you were shipped out this morning.

ADAM: Mom, please.

MRS. COLLINS: Should I call the nurse, or will you leave on your own?

ADAM: Mother.

MRS. COLLINS: What?

ADAM: Elliot is my guest. Treat him as such.

MRS. COLLINS: Adam, monkey, don't tell me that you actually want this, well this deviant, to visit.

ADAM: Yes, Mother. I do. *(To ELLIOT.)* Thank you for the play and the book.

ELLIOT: It's time.

ADAM: I know.

MRS. COLLINS: Dare I ask?

ELLIOT: Say goodbye.

MRS. COLLINS. Don't forget your book.

ELLIOT: Goodbye you.

ADAM: It was wrong of me to ask you to come.

MRS. COLLINS: I only wanted to make sure you had the best care.

ADAM: Did you miss me all those years?

MRS. COLLINS: Of course. How can you ask that?

ELLIOT: Mother wants here you.

ADAM: You never wrote.

ELLIOT: She wants alive for her.

MRS. COLLINS: What would have been the point? You wouldn't change. Your father wouldn't change.

ELLIOT: Adam, Mother never gave up.

ADAM: Do you love me?

MRS. COLLINS: I love you.

ELLIOT: Know before die.

ADAM: I love you too.

ELLIOT: Good.

ADAM: I'm all worn out, Mom. It's time to go.

MRS. COLLINS: Who will make sure you get the care you deserve?

ADAM: No more needles or tubes.

MRS. COLLINS: Collinses don't give up.

ADAM: It's time for me to go.

MRS. COLLINS: We fight. You'll get well. We can go home.

ADAM: Don't make promises you can't keep, Mother.

MRS. COLLINS: I'll tell your father.

ADAM: Thank you for coming. You've made it easier to say goodbye.

MRS. COLLINS: Shh, monkey, rest.

ELLIOT: Love you Adam.

ADAM: I love you too, Elliot.

DOROTHY: Code Blue! Code Blue!

(The blue lights begin to flash. DOROTHY and DOCTOR come running in. They begin tying big long cords of medical tubing from all over the stage. The web begins to overtake the playing area.)

DOCTOR: He's in V-tac.

DOROTHY: What happened?

MRS. COLLINS: He was talking and then—

DOROTHY: Breath sounds are weak.

DOCTOR: Prepare to intubate.

ELLIOT: No.

DOROTHY: Elliot, go back to your room.

ELLIOT: Adam said no.

DOCTOR: Nurse.

DOROTHY: Elliot, did Adam ask to be DNR?

ELLIOT: Yes.

DOROTHY: Mrs. Collins?

DOCTOR: We need to intubate now.

DOROTHY: Mrs. Collins, did Adam ask to be DNR?

MRS. COLLINS: No.

ELLIOT: Liar.

DOROTHY: Doctor, we need to intubate.

DOCTOR: Hold his head.

ELLIOT: Stop. Don't. He not want.

DOCTOR: Elliot, get out of the way.

ELLIOT: He not want. *(ELLIOT stabs his hand with his pen.)* AIDS!!!

DOROTHY: Elliot.

ELLIOT: I bleed you.

MRS. COLLINS: What?

ELLIOT: Come closer I bleed you.

DOCTOR: Dorothy, call security.

DOROTHY: Elliot, you don't have to do this. Let me help you.

ELLIOT: AIDS!!!

(*ELLIOT and the PATIENTS come forward, each with a bloody hand and form a line at the front of the stage. DOCTOR, DOROTHY, and MRS. COLLINS join them.*)

ALL: AIDS! AIDS! AIDS!

(*Lights change to fantasy.*)

ELLIOT: We sailed up the narrow channel, Scylla on one side, Charybdis on the other. Scylla seized six of my men from our ship. Adam, do you want me to help you go? I need you to tell me.

ADAM: Please let me go.

PATIENTS: Please let me go.

(*DOCTOR, DOROTHY, and MRS. COLLINS exit.*)

ELLIOT: We waited until the sun set on the island of the Lotus Eaters, when all was quiet on the hall. Come on men, this isn't the first time we've run into trouble. One day we will look back on this.

(*ELLIOT and the PATIENTS begin removing the tubing from the bed. The wedding music plays softly under the scene.*)

NICK: Odysseus began to whack at the vines that held Adam to his bed. Slowly at first and then faster and faster.

MAHA: He removed the IV bags, the transfusion needles, the heart monitor.

RESEAN: Elliot helped Adam to make his escape.

(*ELLIOT removes the final piece of tubing. ADAM gets out of the bed, removing his hospital garb, and revealing his original outfit.*)

ADAM: Kleos.

ELLIOT: I'll be home soon.

ADAM: I'll be waiting.

NICK: Odysseus held Adam's hand for a long time, watching the life escaping from his body.

RESEAN: The life swirling together to make a strong wind.

ELLIOT: A wind that would fill Adam's sail and take him home.

(*ADAM exits. NICK and RESEAN push the hospital bed offstage. MRS. HAYES enters, pushing MAHA in the wheelchair. MAHA has a bunch of McDonald's bags on her lap.*)

MRS. HAYES: (*Singing the end of the song.*) "Happy birthday to Maha. Happy birthday to you."

MAHA: Yeah!!!

MRS. HAYES: I hope everyone's hungry.

MAHA: I guess we did get a little carried away.

MRS. HAYES: This is going to be the best birthday party ever.

(*DOROTHY crosses to them.*)

DOROTHY: Mrs. Hayes. Maha.

MRS. HAYES: Before you start yelling at us, we know we broke—

DOROTHY: Adam's dead.

MAHA: Shit.

MRS. HAYES: Poor Elliot.

DOROTHY: Someone unplugged Adam's life support.

MAHA: Damn.

MRS. HAYES: Not my Elliot.

DOROTHY: They're investigating.

MRS. HAYES: My baby could never.

DOROTHY: Elliot could be charged with Adam's murder.

(MRS. HAYES crosses to ELLIOT.)

DOROTHY: I'm confiscating all of this food.

MAHA: I brought it back to have a party with my friends.

DOROTHY: The patients are on a strict diet. No fast food.

MAHA: Don't touch my stuff.

DOROTHY: Adam is dead.

MAHA: Bitch, you never helped any of us.

DOROTHY: Who brings you your meds? Who changes your diapers?

MAHA: That's your job.

DOROTHY: I'm not your mother, Maha.

MAHA: So stop acting like her. It's bad enough that we have to wear diapers, you don't have to treat us like babies.

DOROTHY: I'm sorry. You better get to your room.

MAHA: I'm not feeling so good.

DOROTHY: I'll be there in a minute with your medication.

(MAHA exits. DOROTHY takes MAHA's bags and follows her. Lights up on MRS. HAYES and ELLIOT. She is cleaning the blood off of ELLIOT's hand.)

MRS. HAYES: Honey, Elliot, baby, what have you—? I shouldn't have left you here. I should have taken you—

ELLIOT: Stop.

MRS. HAYES: It's those lesions on your brain. Brains are scary things. They just do things and we have no control.

ELLIOT: Not ashamed.

MRS. HAYES: Adam's dead, sweetie.

ELLIOT: He wanted go.

MRS. HAYES: His mother claims—

ELLIOT: Mother lie.

MRS. HAYES: Honey, I want to believe you, but I—

ELLIOT: I never lie you.

(DOCTOR and DOROTHY enter pushing the bed. During the following monologue, they help ELLIOT into the bed.)

MRS. HAYES: I know. I know. Even when you used to wet the bed. You'd wake me up in the middle of the night, tears pouring down your face, your pajamas soaked through. "I did it again, Mama." That's what you'd say. "I did it again." You never tried to hide the sheets or cover it up, but this is much bigger than wetting the bed.

ELLIOT: Swear Adam ask.

MRS. HAYES: I know, honey. I know. I believe you.

(RESEAN enters with her bags.)

RESEAN: I've been given my walking papers.

ELLIOT: Congrat—lations.

MRS. HAYES: Out into the real world again.

RESEAN: Going to make things right with my Erica Kane.

MRS. HAYES: And Maha?

RESEAN: I've seen the doctor in there with her all night.

ELLIOT: What wrong?

RESEAN: The nurses say she's crashing. Caught something on her trip to McDonald's. I say she's lost the spark to fight.

MRS. HAYES: This is all so much for me. I wish Elliot had just stayed home with me. No one would have been hurt. No one would have suffered.

RESEAN: No one would've lived. These were the best few weeks of most of our lives, Mrs. Hayes. And we have your son to thank for that.

ELLIOT: Nick kite?

RESEAN: I gave it to him honey, but he can't see well enough to scratch his butt. That boy ain't going to be flying no kites.

ELLIOT: Must help.

MRS. HAYES: Elliot, you can't leave your room.

ELLIOT: Promised.

MRS. HAYES: Haven't you gotten in enough trouble today? Resean will help him.

RESEAN: Don't look at me.

MRS. HAYES: Won't you, Resean?

RESEAN: I've done my charity event for the year. I'm done.

ELLIOT: Mom go.

MRS. HAYES: I'm not leaving you. What if— Well we won't say what if. I am staying right here, next to you, where I can watch you take every single breath.

RESEAN: I'll babysit.

MRS. HAYES: Don't you two look at me like that.

ELLIOT: Last wish.

MRS. HAYES: Last wish? Do you hear him? Last wish? I should spank you for saying that. Last wish? How can I say no to that?

ELLIOT: Thank you.

(Lights change. Lights come up on MAHA and DOROTHY. MAHA is sitting in her chair. ELLIOT and RESEAN watch the following sequences.)

MAHA: I'm in pain.

DOROTHY: I've given you some morphine. It'll kick in any second.

MAHA: Can I have more?

DOROTHY: I'll check with the doctor.

MAHA: Thanks, Dorothy.

DOROTHY: I found this in one of the McDonald's bags.

MAHA: My picture with Grimace.

DOROTHY: I thought you might want to keep it.

MAHA: No thanks.

DOROTHY: A souvenir? Your mother seems important to you. This whole trip to McDonald's— Would you like me to call her?

MAHA: No.

DOROTHY: But you could have some closure.

MAHA: McDonald's is the only thing I have that reminds me of my mother. Going to McDonald's was the best way to say goodbye. (MAHA begins to rip up her picture.) This is for keeping cocaine in the house.

NICK: Maha cut her mother's throat, lashed into her, and carved out her thigh joints.

MAHA: This is for telling me I was ugly.

NICK: She was a fucking wildcat tearing at her picture. Her mother's blood spurting all over the place.

MAHA: This is for throwing me out of the house.

NICK: And she scattered the ashes of her mother to the wind.

MAHA: Goodbye.

NICK: Circe took Maha's hand and led her to the shore.

(Lights fade on MAHA and come up on MRS. HAYES and NICK.)

MRS. HAYES: Hello?

NICK: Get out.

MRS. HAYES: Not up for company today? What a shame. I'll tell Elliot you were too busy to see me.

NICK: Elliot sent you?

MRS. HAYES: He asked me to fly a kite with you.

NICK: I'm blind.

MRS. HAYES: They mentioned you might be difficult. I'm the definition of the word. My son is down the hall dying, and instead of being there, holding his hand, having a moment, I am here. Being barked by a Neanderthal, expected to fly a kite. Why don't we work together? What do you say?

NICK: Where are we going to fly it?

MRS. HAYES: How about out the window?

NICK: Is it windy?

MRS. HAYES: A blustery February night.

NICK: Are there stars?

MRS. HAYES: I can see the Big Dipper and Orion.

NICK: I hope Elliot gets to see his stars.

MRS. HAYES: Give me your kite.

NICK: Careful with it.

MRS. HAYES: I'll get it going.

NICK: My friend made it for me.

MRS. HAYES: I'll take good care of it. Trust me.

NICK: What's happening?

(MRS. HAYES stands behind NICK. She does not actually do any of the following things.)

MRS. HAYES: Okay. I'm opening the window. I'm going to toss the kite out the window now. Hold on tight to the string.

NICK: I got it.

MRS. HAYES: One, two, three. There it goes.

NICK: It's flying!

MRS. HAYES: It's catching the wind. There. There it goes.

(MRS. HAYES is pulling on the kite to simulate its flight.)

NICK: It's tugging.

MRS. HAYES: It's soaring. Floating out there among the stars. A big white bed sheet on your mom's clothesline catching the wind. It's a full sail on a fair night. You want to grab onto it. Hold on... sail away home.

NICK: Can I tell you a secret?

MRS. HAYES: Of course. Go ahead.

NICK: I got it. I don't want anyone to know. But I got it.

MRS. HAYES: My lips are sealed.

NICK: I can see it.

MRS. HAYES: I know you can. I know.

(Lights fade on NICK and MRS. HAYES and come up on ELLIOT and RESEAN.)

ELLIOT: I was tossed and turned by the sea until dawn when I reached Scylla's cliff and dread Charybdis.

(MRS. HAYES enters. ELLIOT is delirious.)

MRS. HAYES: How is he?

RESEAN: In and out of— Sometimes he makes sense—

ELLIOT: I tightened my grip and held on.

RESEAN: Other times he doesn't.

ELLIOT: It seemed like forever.

MRS. HAYES: We have a present for you.

RESEAN: You shouldn't have. What is it?

MRS. HAYES: Our, my, phone number.

RESEAN: Are you cruising me, Mrs. Hayes?

MRS. HAYES: Don't make me blush. I want you to call if you are ever in trouble or need any help with Erica.

ELLIOT: I floated on for nine days.

RESEAN: Thank you, Mrs. Hayes.

MRS. HAYES: Margaret.

(DOROTHY enters.)

DOROTHY: How's Elliot?

MRS. HAYES: He seems to be lost in one of his fantasies.

DOROTHY: I hope it is someplace better than here.

ELLIOT: On the last day, the gods brought me to Calypso, the mother who took care of me.

RESEAN: He's on his way home.

MRS. HAYES: And Maha?

DOROTHY: She passed away.

RESEAN: Why didn't you get me? I didn't want her to be alone.

DOROTHY: She wasn't alone. I held her hand.

ELLIOT: Mom.

MRS. HAYES: Look who's come back to their senses. We've missed you. Your girlfriend came by to say goodbye.

ELLIOT: You good?

RESEAN: I'm fierce.

ELLIOT: Check. I'm going.

RESEAN: I know, sugar, I know.

ELLIOT: Take care Mom me.

RESEAN: We'll take care of each other.

ELLIOT: Good.

RESEAN: I'll be seeing you soon.

ELLIOT: Hope not.

RESEAN: Oh I will. It comes for us all eventually. I'm thinking maybe May sweeps.

MRS. HAYES: Thank you, Resean.

(RESEAN takes her bags and exits singing.)

RESEAN: *(Singing.)* "I'm forever blowing bubbles. Pretty bubbles in the air. They fly so high, they nearly touch the sky, then, like my dreams, they fade and die."

(The screens close in front of ELLIOT's bed. ELLIOT crosses to the front of the stage.)

ELLIOT: I found myself here. In the halls of death, but I have told you that tale only today, here, to you and your friends, and I wouldn't trouble you by telling it again.

MRS. HAYES: I'm going to need to get you another journal, this one's almost full.

ELLIOT: Flip to end.

MRS. HAYES: What's this?

ELLIOT: How I go.

MRS. HAYES: Elliot, please. Stay with me. I'll take care of you. I won't let anything hurt you.

ELLIOT: I love you.

MRS. HAYES: I love you too, sweetie.

ELLIOT: Thank you.

MRS. HAYES: Oh please. I'm your mother. It's my job.

ELLIOT: Read.

MRS. HAYES: Elliot?

ELLIOT: Read.

MRS. HAYES: Odysseus, gripped by an evil disease, was melting away, but through his Kleos, he was released from suffering in a spasm of joy. Free to finish the great adventure that would bring him home.

(The screens part to reveal ADAM's bed. The bed has been transformed into a mock sailboat with an IV pole as a mast and a long sheet as a sail. The sky is blue and full of stars.)

ADAM: Hi, Elliot.

ELLIOT: Adam.

ADAM: I was wondering if you'd ever get here.

ELLIOT: Sorry. I have a story to finish.

MRS. HAYES: Sing to me of the man, Muse.

ELLIOT: Of the clever hero blown time and again off course, once he had sacked the famous city of Troy.

(NICK enters.)

ELLIOT: Of all the nations he saw, the minds he grasped.

(MAHA enters.)

ELLIOT: The suffering deep in his heart, as he struggled to bring his men safely home.

(RESEAN enters.)

ELLIOT: But do what he might, he could not save them from disaster—the rashness of their ways doomed them all.

(NICK and MAHA board the boat.)

ELLIOT: They exhausted themselves in pleasures, and Zeus denied them their homecoming. *(To MRS. HAYES.)* Launch out on his story, Muse, daughter of Zeus, start from where you will sing from our time too.

(ELLIOT hugs his MOTHER. ELLIOT and ADAM climb on board. DOROTHY, DOCTOR, and MRS. COLLINS enter and push the screens in front of the boat.)

MRS. HAYES: And Athena, her eyes smiling, blew them a strong wind that sped their ship across the dark sea, taking them home.

(The lights dim as we see the boat sailing away.)

MRS. HAYES: Kleos.

(Blackout.)

MAGGIE MAY

Tom O'Brien

TOM O'BRIEN is a writer and actor who lives in New York City.
Tom started writing about eight years ago with the support and encouragement of All Seasons Theater Group and its artistic director,
John McCormack. His first play, *Lonnie*, was read at Naked Angels
and later produced at the Access Theater. Tom's play *The Group*, a
comedy about group therapy, was produced by All Seasons at Ensemble Studio Theater. His one-act play *Stage Left* was part of the
inaugural series at the Zipper Theater on 37th Street. *The Casanova*,
a one-act romantic comedy about a young writer in Venice, was produced downtown at New York Performance Works in Tribeca and
later in Los Angeles as part of the Ensemble Studio Theater-LA Project's
Winterfest. *Danny Ho*, a full-length drama based on a school shooting in Massachusetts, was part of a reading series at the Flea Theater.
Tom has been a finalist at both First Stage in Los Angeles and for the
Heideman Award at the Actors Theatre of Louisville.

Maggie May was first presented by Wildfire Productions (Jocelyn Szabo, Artistic Director), in association with All Seasons Theater Group (John McCormack, Artistic Director), on February 9, 2004, at the Belt Theatre, New York City, with the following cast and credits:

Donny .... Ean Sheehy
Maggie .... Christiane Szabo
Mark .... Ethan James Duff
Charlie .... Stephen Bradbury

Directed by: Jocelyn Szabo
Sets: Christina Aprea
Lights: Dimitri Lopes
Costumes: Lauren Cordes
Stage Manager: Tara Greico

Tom began his writing career after meeting several very influential people who went on to become his mentors—Jane Hoffman, Maureen McDuffie, and Christopher Gorman.

Theatre artists need a place to work and learn and fall on their face and to figure out what works onstage and what doesn't. John McCormack and the All Seasons Theater Group have provided that.

> *"Ask yourself in the most silent hour of your night: must I write?*
> *Dig into yourself for a deep answer. And if this answer rings out*
> *in assent, if you meet this solemn question with a strong, simple*
> *'I must,' then build your life in accordance with this necessity."*
> —Rilke

CHARACTERS

DONNY: A hopeless romantic.

MAGGIE: Beautiful in a down-to-earth kind of way. The perfect girlfriend.

MARK: A rugged, handsome fisherman.

CHARLIE: Ex-NFL owner. A self-proclaimed "pleasure seeker."

SETTING

TIME: The present.

PLACE: An island in the Bahamas.

The action takes place in Donny and Maggie's hotel room and the docks where Charlie's boat is anchored.

AUTHOR'S NOTE

It is best if the actors can move easily from one area to the other without having to wait for set changes.

The pay-per-view movie in Scene 2 can be changed to whatever might be on pay-per-view at the time of the production. It should be something that you would only watch on pay-per-view during a thunderstorm.

SCENE 1

Lights up. A hotel room. MAGGIE and DONNY are heard offstage.

MAGGIE: Other way! It goes the other way!

DONNY: Will you stop pushing! I got it.

MAGGIE: *(Laughing.)* You want me to do it?

DONNY: I think I can handle it, Mag. There we go.

(MAGGIE runs onstage, followed by DONNY.)

MAGGIE: Wow. Cool.

DONNY: Just took a little touch. That's all.

MAGGIE: It's so funky.

DONNY: That's what the guidebook said. "Funky cool."

MAGGIE: I love it.

DONNY: I knew you would.

MAGGIE: This is gonna be so much fun.

(She jumps in his arms and hugs him.)

DONNY: Whoa.

MAGGIE: What should we do first?

DONNY: Well, we could settle in. Maybe unpack a little.

MAGGIE: Let's go to the beach!

DONNY: Or we could go to the beach.

(DONNY sits down to look at the guide-book. MAGGIE sits on the bed and checks it out.)

DONNY: So, it says here that they have snorkeling trips that leave from the beach right in front of this hotel.

MAGGIE: Cool.

DONNY: How's the bed? Soft?

MAGGIE: Yeah, it's great. I mean—

DONNY: What?

MAGGIE: There's only one of them, but…

DONNY: Oh, yeah. Shit.

MAGGIE: It's okay.

DONNY: No, 'cause when I filled out the thing, they said, will you be needing twin beds? And I definitely said…

MAGGIE: Don't worry about it.

DONNY: No, I distinctly remember…

MAGGIE: Donny, I think we can manage.

DONNY: Maybe they have another room with two beds.

MAGGIE: No, I love this room.

DONNY: Are you sure?

MAGGIE: Yeah, totally.

DONNY: I can always sleep on the floor.

MAGGIE: Shut up.

DONNY: Or we could do like the head-to-toe thing.

MAGGIE: I'd rather not do the head-to-toe thing.

DONNY: Yeah, me neither.

MAGGIE: I'm gonna check out the bath-room. *(She exits to the bathroom.)*

DONNY: Cool. *(Goes back to the guide-book.)*

MAGGIE: *(Calls from the bathroom.)* Wow!

DONNY: What?

MAGGIE: *(From bathroom.)* A heart-shaped Jacuzzi.

DONNY: No!

(MAGGIE comes out of the bathroom.)

MAGGIE: Donny, I think this is the hon-eymoon suite.

DONNY: That's crazy. I told them… Lemme call the front desk.

MAGGIE: I don't mind.

DONNY: Yeah, but they may have mixed us up with another… 'cause I think the sweepstakes had several winners, so maybe… I should just check it out.

(DONNY dials the front desk. MAGGIE unpacks some things.)

DONNY: Hi, this is Donald O'Connor in room… Yes, like the dancer. We just checked in… No, I'm not the dancer. He's dead… I'm sorry too. I loved his work. Anyway, we just… Yes, that's right. They were very different, I think. He wasn't as well known as Fred Astaire but in terms of… My mom was a big fan of his, yes… Well, thank you, I will tell her that. Any-way, the reason I was calling was that I think we got the honeymoon suite and we were… Yes, we were the sweepstakes winners and we may have been confused with another couple… No, we're just friends… Yeah, no, not a couple, right, so it would be a little…you see what I'm say-ing? Do you have another room that might have twin beds?… Uh huh. I see.

MAGGIE: Donny, forget it. It's fine.

DONNY: You know what? It's fine... Yes, I'm sure... Okay, you too. Bye now... No, I think that was Gene Kelly... The more masculine one, yes. Okay, bye now. Thank you, Juanita. *(He hangs up.)* Oh my God.

MAGGIE: She was chatty.

DONNY: Nobody understands the whole platonic friendship thing these days.

MAGGIE: Well, they just see two people together and they assume...

DONNY: I know. But why?

MAGGIE: It's just what they're used to seeing, I guess.

DONNY: I know, but it just bothers me. It's like you have to fit into these little categories that society deems normal or else... I mean, God forbid...

MAGGIE: Donny...

DONNY: It's like when you get to a certain age, if you're not married there must be something wrong with you.

MAGGIE: C'mon, don't get philosophical. We're in the Bahamas!

DONNY: You're right. You're right. I'm sorry.

MAGGIE: Have I thanked you, by the way?

DONNY: I think so. It was sort of implied.

(She hugs him.)

MAGGIE: You're the best. Okay. I'm gonna change, and then we'll go down to the beach.

DONNY: Sounds like a plan.

MAGGIE: Okay.

DONNY: Okay?

MAGGIE: What?

DONNY: "Sounds like a plan." You always hated when people said that.

MAGGIE: Oh my God. I forgot that I hated that.

DONNY: Oh, Maggie, Maggie May. It hasn't been that long, has it?

MAGGIE: It's been a while.

DONNY: I guess it has been a while.

MAGGIE: How long has it been since...

DONNY: Since we...

MAGGIE: Yeah, whatever.

DONNY: I don't know. It feels like forever.

MAGGIE: It does.

DONNY: Does anyone else call you "Maggie May"?

MAGGIE: You're kidding, right?

DONNY: No.

MAGGIE: I think every guy I've ever dated has sung that song to me.

DONNY: *(Singing.)* "Wake up, Maggie, I think I got something to say to you."

MAGGIE: Ah, yes. Lovely.

DONNY: *(Singing.)* "It's late September and I really should be back at school."

MAGGIE: C'mon, c'mon, we're missing the PTH.

DONNY: The what?

MAGGIE: Prime tanning hours?

DONNY: I hope you're kidding.

MAGGIE: Let's go.

DONNY: Look who you're talking to. I'm not exactly a sun god here.

MAGGIE: You get color.

DONNY: I wear pants on the beach.

MAGGIE: Shut up.

DONNY: The big sun hat. I carry the parasol. You don't remember going to the beach with me, do you?

MAGGIE: Have we ever been to the beach together?

DONNY: You're kidding, right?

MAGGIE: No.

DONNY: This is really insulting.

MAGGIE: Have we? I'm sorry.

DONNY: No, it's fine. Obviously our relationship was not that memorable for you.

MAGGIE: Yes it was. Oh wait! The Hamptons!

DONNY: Cape Cod, the Hamptons, they're similar. There's lots of sand and water...

MAGGIE: Oh my God! That's right. Your aunt's house in Yarmouthport.

DONNY: Now it's all coming back.

MAGGIE: You got so sunburned.

DONNY: Exactly.

MAGGIE: That was awful. You could barely move.

DONNY: You see what I'm saying.

MAGGIE: I'm sorry.

DONNY: Hey, I...

MAGGIE: I have sun block.

DONNY: I hope it's SPF 45, because if it's anything less I may as well stay inside.

MAGGIE: You'll be fine. All right, I'm gonna...

DONNY: Hey.

MAGGIE: What?

DONNY: It's good to see you, Maggie.

MAGGIE: It's good to see you too, Donny. Are we gonna have a little touching moment here?

DONNY: Shut up, will you please?

MAGGIE: All right, I'm gonna change. *(She exits to the bathroom.)*

DONNY: Don't ever change, baby. *(Beat.)* Just kidding.

MAGGIE: *(From bathroom.)* Have you gotten less funny since I've seen you?

DONNY: Oh, that hurts.

MAGGIE: *(From bathroom.)* So, is everything paid for?

DONNY: It's everything. It's all inclusive.

MAGGIE: *(From bathroom.)* But who... I mean...

DONNY: The sweepstakes people. I don't know.

MAGGIE: *(From bathroom.)* Do they have like a person?

DONNY: A sweepstakes person?

MAGGIE: *(From bathroom.)* Yeah.

DONNY: No.

MAGGIE: *(From bathroom.)* Well, who... I don't understand.

DONNY: Don't understand it. Just enjoy it.

MAGGIE: *(From bathroom.)* Okay. Okay.

DONNY: *(Goes to the window; after a moment.)* Do you think I'm a loser?

MAGGIE: *(From bathroom.)* What are you talking about?

DONNY: Because I didn't have anybody better to take?

MAGGIE: *(From bathroom.)* Oh, thanks a lot.

DONNY: No, I mean, I haven't seen you in…I don't know how long and I call you out of the blue and say, "Hey, let's go to the Bahamas."

MAGGIE: *(From bathroom.)* I mean, I was surprised.

DONNY: And you thought I was a loser?

MAGGIE: *(From bathroom.)* No.

DONNY: A little bit of a loser?

MAGGIE: *(From bathroom.)* A little bit of a loser, but I wasn't gonna pass up a free trip to the Bahamas.

DONNY: You're funny. I can still call somebody else, you know.

(She comes out of the bathroom.)

MAGGIE: No, you can't. You're stuck with me.

DONNY: Just think of it as the trip I never took you on when we were dating.

MAGGIE: Did we date?

DONNY: Whatever you want to call it.

MAGGIE: Dude, are we gonna spend this whole vacation in the hotel room?

DONNY: I had other options, you know.

MAGGIE: Oh my God.

DONNY: No, it's just… I don't want you to think like I don't have any friends and…

MAGGIE: I didn't think that.

DONNY: Okay. Good.

MAGGIE: Ready?

DONNY: Let's go to the beach, kid.

(As they exit, their conversation continues.)

MAGGIE: I really don't think it's me.

DONNY: What?

MAGGIE: You just don't seem as funny.

DONNY: You better shut up right now.

MAGGIE: You shut up.

SCENE 2

The lights stay up on the hotel room for a moment. Crash of thunder. Lightning. The rain pours outside. After a moment, DONNY and MAGGIE come running in, soaked and laughing.

MAGGIE: Oh my God. I can't believe it!

DONNY: It's fucking pouring.

MAGGIE: I think it's a sign.

DONNY: It's just a passing storm.

MAGGIE: No, it's probably a hurricane.

DONNY: Oh, that's the attitude.

MAGGIE: No wonder they gave you a free trip. It's hurricane season.

DONNY: Okay, Miss Negative. *(Goes to the window.)* Oh, yeah, I think it's letting up.

(Another crash of thunder and lightning.)

DONNY: This sucks.

MAGGIE: C'mon, let's make the best of it. What's in the ol' mini-bar? *(Goes to the mini-bar and opens it.)*

DONNY: I didn't even know we had a mini-bar.

MAGGIE: Let's see, what do we have here?

DONNY: *(Hops on the bed and picks up the remote control.)* Oh, dude. We have pay-per-view.

MAGGIE: And we have rum!

DONNY: We have rum in the mini-bar? That's fantastic.

MAGGIE: This is the Bahamas. They have rum everywhere. I'm gonna make rum punch.

DONNY: Yes, we'll get drunk and watch… *Tuck Everlasting.*

(DONNY watches TV as MAGGIE looks around the room.)

MAGGIE: Hey, is there sugar anywhere?

DONNY: Where?

MAGGIE: I don't know. Have you seen any?

DONNY: Have I seen any sugar in the room? I don't know. Where would that be?

MAGGIE: I don't know.

DONNY: *(Beat.)* Are you dating anyone right now?

MAGGIE: What?

DONNY: I don't know. I just thought… I don't know. Are you?

MAGGIE: Umm… I don't know, sort of.

DONNY: "Sort of"? I'm glad I'm not that guy.

MAGGIE: No, it's nothing serious.

DONNY: Yeah, from your end, but that poor bastard. What's his name?

MAGGIE: Why?

DONNY: Just wondering. I'm sorry. I didn't mean to…

MAGGIE: No, I just… what made you think of that?

DONNY: Do you like him?

MAGGIE: No, I hate him.

DONNY: I mean, do you like him as much as you liked me?

MAGGIE: Will you stop?

DONNY: What? We're just a couple of friends talking.

MAGGIE: What about you?

DONNY: No, I just sit at home looking at a picture of you.

MAGGIE: Shut up. Who are you dating?

DONNY: Never mind that. What's his name?

MAGGIE: It's not… I'm not telling you.

DONNY: It's Bob, isn't it?

MAGGIE: No.

DONNY: Greg?

MAGGIE: What's your girlfriend's name?

DONNY: Maggie.

MAGGIE: Shut up. What's her name?

DONNY: None of your business.

MAGGIE: Good, I'm not telling you what my boyfriend's name is.

DONNY: Oh my God. What are you, six?

MAGGIE: You started it.

DONNY: Do you think if I had a girlfriend you'd be here right now?

MAGGIE: Well, I don't know. Maybe you'll meet someone down here.

DONNY: That's true. We should work out a system. Like sock on the door means don't come in.

MAGGIE: What is this, a frat house?

DONNY: Well, you might meet someone too.

MAGGIE: I'm not gonna take them back to the room.

DONNY: Okay, Miss Prude.

MAGGIE: I'm not a prude.

DONNY: That's true. You're not.

MAGGIE: Hey.

DONNY: What? I'm just agreeing with you.

MAGGIE: Just behave.

DONNY: Jeez, I can't win.

(MAGGIE starts to go.)

DONNY: Where are you going?

MAGGIE: I need juice for this punch.

DONNY: It's pouring out.

MAGGIE: I'm just going down to the lobby.

DONNY: Want me to come?

MAGGIE: I think I'll be fine.

DONNY: Okay.

(MAGGIE exits just as MARK enters. The next scene begins as if the conversation has been going on for a while.)

SCENE 3

MARK: …Paula Catalano. Holy shit, she was hot.

DONNY: You know who she ended up marryin'?

MARK: Who?

DONNY: Dave Delflorio.

MARK: Get the fuck outta here?

DONNY: I shit you not.

MARK: Dave Delflorio? The kid that was in the drama club?

DONNY: That's the one.

MARK: He was as queer as a three-dollar bill.

DONNY: Apparently not.

MARK: C'mon, Delflorio?

DONNY: Yeah, I mean, he's like a completely different person now.

MARK: Really?

DONNY: Yeah, he's this hotshot entrepreneur now. He made a bundle during the whole dot com thing and he's also gotten a lot more masculine as he's gotten older.

MARK: Good for him.

DONNY: I know.

MARK: Fucking Donny boy!

DONNY: I can't believe I just bumped into you, man. It's so funny.

MARK: I know, right?

DONNY: I thought you were in Mexico.

MARK: I was for a while and then we sailed over here.

DONNY: Wow, that's great.

MARK: Yeah, it's a good time.

DONNY: It's good to see you.

MARK: Yeah, same here, buddy. Hey, why don't you come out on the boat tomorrow?

DONNY: Oh, you're still doing the fishing thing?

MARK: Yeah, man.

DONNY: That sounds good.

MARK: I don't see anybody anymore.

DONNY: I don't think anybody knows how to get in touch with you down here.

MARK: Yeah, I sort of like it that way.

DONNY: So, you're still liking it, doing the whole… you know, what type of fishing is it?

MARK: Sport fishing.

DONNY: Oh, sports fishing, right.

MARK: Basically I work for this rich guy. He used to own half of the old Houston Oilers back when Earl Johnson used to play and shit. Now he's retired. He has this big beautiful boat and he loves to fish. But he can't do it to save his life. So he basically hires me to do everything. Then when I hook a fish, I hand him the rod and let him reel it in. Then we go crazy and pretend like he actually hooked it.

DONNY: That sounds cool.

MARK: It beats working in an office.

DONNY: I'm sure.

MARK: You still working in an office?

DONNY: Naaaw, I stopped that months ago.

MARK: That's good. Those fucking office jobs'll strangle your soul, dude.

DONNY: Tell me about it.

MARK: Where you working now?

DONNY: Well, it's a marketing firm, but it's not an office position. It's more of a field position. I'm out on the open road a lot, top down, just driving… you know, to the branch offices of the marketing firm. I'm looking into some other options right now.

MARK: Yeah, man. You got to.

DONNY: Totally. You do.

MARK: All of a sudden you wake up and your life has passed you by.

DONNY: Yeah, I hear you.

MARK: How the ladies treatin' you?

DONNY: Ahh, fair. They treat me okay.

MARK: The chicks that come down here are unbelievable, man.

DONNY: Yeah?

MARK: And they just want to have a good time, you know? And then they're outta here, back to their lives.

DONNY: It sounds like you got the life, my friend.

MARK: Hey, there's a cruise ship docking at six tomorrow night.

DONNY: Oh, yeah.

MARK: Those are always the big nights on the island. The talent…

DONNY: Oh, yeah?

MARK: The talent is top notch, my friend.

DONNY: Nice.

MARK: It's a beautiful thing, buddy.

DONNY: I bet.

MARK: I usually come in about then and head over to Carlos and Charlie's, that little bar by the docks. But you might have your hands full already with what's-her-name.

DONNY: Who, Maggie? No, we're just friends.

MARK: Is she hot?

DONNY: I think so, yeah.

MARK: You gonna lay it down?

DONNY: Huh?

MARK: You working that shit?

DONNY: Oh, no, no. It's totally… we're just… you know, we used to date years ago. But, ahh…

MARK: Once you throw it in, you always throw it in.

DONNY: No, we're much better as friends.

MARK: All right, okay. That's cool. Well, that frees you up for Carlos and Charlie's and all the cruise ship babes.

DONNY: Cool. That sounds cool.

(MAGGIE enters.)

MAGGIE: Guess who just won three hundred dollars at the casino?!

DONNY: You did?

MAGGIE: Yup.

MARK: Nice.

DONNY: Wow. That's great, Mag. Maggie, this is a friend of mine from way back. This is Mark.

MAGGIE: Hi, Mark

MARK: Hey.

DONNY: This is Maggie.

MARK: You a gambler, Maggie?

MAGGIE: I am today.

DONNY: I haven't seen Mark in ages. A friend of his is staying in this hotel.

MAGGIE: That's great. Did you guys grow up together?

DONNY: Yeah. Lewis Avenue.

MARK: It was a few lifetimes ago.

DONNY: We dominated in street hockey.

MARK: That's right. What were we called again?

DONNY: The Lewis Avenue…Streeters.

MAGGIE: "Streeters"?

MARK: Terrible name.

DONNY: Good team though.

MARK: Great team.

MAGGIE: And you live here now?

DONNY: Yeah, he lives here.

MAGGIE: That must be great.

DONNY: He's a fisherman.

MAGGIE: Really? Wow.

MARK: I was telling Donny here that you guys should come out on the boat tomorrow.

MAGGIE: Cool. I'd love to do that.

DONNY: Well, I told him we'd see 'cause I know you wanted to do that thing that you said you wanted to do.

MAGGIE: I got nothing to do. Let's go out on the boat. I've never been fishing.

MARK: You got to be up early. The boat leaves at six.

DONNY: We'll try and be there.

MAGGIE: We'll get up. Don't you worry.

DONNY: Yeah, I mean, we'll see how it goes. The good thing is that, like Mark says, there's no plans on the island. You just go with it. You don't make…

MARK: Boat leaves at six. You show, you go.

MAGGIE: Oh, we'll show. *(Gets the punch from the fridge.)*

MARK: Good. It'll be a pleasure to have you aboard.

(MARK shoots DONNY a look. "She's all right.")

MAGGIE: Did you guys try the punch yet?

DONNY: No, we been going with the beers.

MAGGIE: Beers are for the mainland. This is an island drink. *(Pours the punch.)*

MARK: How do you guys like the island so far?

(DONNIE and MAGGIE speak simultaneously.)

DONNY: We haven't really seen it yet.

MAGGIE: We love it.

DONNY: I mean, what we've seen.

MARK: You guys should see the sights.

DONNY: Definitely.

MARK: Lotta history here. I mean, if you're into that kind of thing.

MAGGIE: I was a history major.

DONNY: Well, art history.

MAGGIE: No, it was European history.

MARK: I'm kind of a history buff myself.

DONNY: European? Because I always thought…

MAGGIE: I mean, I ended up in art history, but originally…

MARK: We have a great art museum here too.

MAGGIE: Well, if it keeps raining.

DONNY: Never would have took you for the museum type, Mark.

MARK: I like 'em in small doses. I get tired quick.

MAGGIE: Me too. But if you're going for a specific show…

MARK: That's the only way to do it.

DONNY: But the real question is, where can we go parasailing?

MARK: Oh, you can do that anywhere.

MAGGIE: Yeah, we might as well get a little culture while we're here.

DONNY: Culture schmulture.

MARK: If you like De Kooning, there's…

MAGGIE: I love De Kooning.

MARK: Do you really? There's a De Kooning show there right now.

MAGGIE: Donny, remember the Met?

DONNY: Yeah.

MAGGIE: That was one of our first dates.

MARK: Really.

DONNY: Was it?

MAGGIE: Yeah, don't you remember?

MARK: Smooth move, Donny.

MAGGIE: It was my idea, actually. It was when Donny first came up to Columbia and…

MARK: You went to Columbia?

MAGGIE: Yeah.

MARK: That's great.

MAGGIE: Yeah, I liked it. So, Donny comes to visit and of course he wanted to do all these cheesy tourist things.

DONNY: Oh, yeah. Like the Met's not a tourist trap.

MAGGIE: Well, but he wanted to like go to the Empire State Building and the Statue of Liberty.

MARK: Oh, God.

DONNY: I had never seen them before.

MAGGIE: And he wanted to ride in one of those horse-drawn carriages.

MARK: That's terrible.

DONNY: Sue me. I was being romantic.

MAGGIE: Those things are awful. I feel so bad for those poor horses.

MARK: I know. It's so cruel. I used to always have this dream of going around late at night and freeing them.

MAGGIE: I know. I always wanted to do that too.

DONNY: When were you in New York, Mark?

MARK: My sister lives there. I go all the time.

MAGGIE: It would be so great to just see them all escape and run free.

MARK: It'd be amazing.

DONNY: They probably wouldn't even go anywhere.

MAGGIE: What?

DONNY: I'm saying if you freed them. They'd probably just stand there. 'Cause they don't know anything else.

MAGGIE: Oh, so that makes it right to chain them up.

DONNY: No, I'm just saying.

MARK: Donny, the realist.

DONNY: Hey, I like horses as much as the next guy. I'm just saying those things are bred to pull carriages.

MAGGIE: The point being that we ended up going to the Met. And the first painting I saw, I loved, and when I looked at the title, it was Willem De Kooning. I didn't even know who he was at the time. And then we were walking through another section of the museum, and I was drawn to another painting and it was his. Something kept drawing me to him.

MARK: Totally. He's got such emotion. I mean, other artists are more technically skilled...

MAGGIE: Right.

MARK: But he's got this beautiful mix of abstractness and realism. It's...

DONNY: Expressionism.

MARK: What?

DONNY: He was part of the Expressionist movement.

MARK: That's right.

DONNY: A fisherman who appreciates art. How 'bout that, Mag?

MARK: Donny always thought I was just a dumb jock.

MAGGIE: Ohhhh.

DONNY: No, I didn't.

MARK: I knew you college boys looked down on me.

DONNY: That's not true. We were all jealous. We were studying for exams and you were out sailing the islands.

MAGGIE: I think you made the right choice, Mark.

MARK: Well, you guys'll get a little taste of it tomorrow.

MAGGIE: Yeah, we will.

DONNY: Maybe, yeah.

MARK: All right. I got to hit it. Thanks for the drink.

DONNY: Already?

MARK: Yeah. *(He gets up.)*

MAGGIE: It was nice meeting you.

MARK: Likewise. Good to see you, Donny.

DONNY: You too, buddy. And if we don't make it in the morning, there's always the thing at Carlos and Charlie's.

MARK: Have a good night, guys.

MAGGIE: Good night.

(MARK exits.)

MAGGIE: So… he seems nice.

DONNY: Who, Mark? Yeah, he's a great guy.

MAGGIE: Yeah, he's really interesting.

(DONNY laughs.)

MAGGIE: What?

DONNY: "Really interesting"?

MAGGIE: Yeah, he seems like an…

DONNY: Okay.

MAGGIE: What?

DONNY: No, I just didn't want to make any definite plans 'cause we might not feel like getting up.

MAGGIE: Oh, we'll get up.

DONNY: All right.

MAGGIE: What is the matter with you?

DONNY: Nothing. I just thought you laid it on a little thick with the whole art bit.

MAGGIE: Shut up. That was true.

DONNY: "I love De Kooning."

MAGGIE: I do.

DONNY: I know you do. It's just… you were a little obvious.

MAGGIE: What are you talking about?

DONNY: C'mon, Mag. You were so "into" him.

MAGGIE: I wasn't into him. I was having a conversation.

DONNY: Okay.

MAGGIE: I mean, he's definitely cute.

DONNY: Definitely.

MAGGIE: Donny, you are not seriously mad 'cause I found your friend attractive?

DONNY: No.

MAGGIE: You are?

DONNY: I could care less if you find him attractive. I just don't know if I feel like getting up at six in the morning, that's all.

MAGGIE: We don't have to go.

DONNY: No, we'll go if it means that much to you.

MAGGIE: Donny, will you stop?

DONNY: What?

MAGGIE: You might be the first person to ever be mad in the Bahamas.

DONNY: "I've always wanted to do that too, Mark."

MAGGIE: Shut up.

DONNY: "Free the horses!"

(She pushes him.)

MAGGIE: Shut up, man.

(He pushes her onto the bed.)

DONNY: Now you're dead!

MAGGIE: Owww! No! Help!

(He tickles her.)

SCENE 4

Music transition to the docks. Lights up. MARK, MAGGIE, and CHARLIE sit on the docks drinking beers. DONNY sits behind them looking sick. It's sunset.

DONNY: No, I'm fine.

CHARLIE: Got to get your sea legs, that's all.

MAGGIE: Are you sure you're all right?

DONNY: No, yeah... I mean, it was amazing, as soon as I stepped off the boat I felt fine.

MARK: That's what always happens.

CHARLIE: Yankees, water gets a little choppy and they're done.

(They laugh.)

DONNY: This never happens to me.

MARK: Not this one, though. She was right up on deck hooking 'em, reeling 'em in.

MAGGIE: Oh, stop.

CHARLIE: She was impressive, that's for sure.

MAGGIE: C'mon.

DONNY: I've never been seasick in my life.

CHARLIE: You were. Don't be humble. That was a blue marlin you reeled in. You know how rare that is? I got to tell you, when I saw that thing jumpin' out of the water, I was a little jealous.

MAGGIE: Mark hooked it though. I just...

MARK: I didn't do anything. We drove right through that school of marlin. I just handed you the rod.

DONNY: That's great, Mag.

MAGGIE: It was so fun. It was like... it just felt great to reel it in. I'm glad we let him go, though.

MARK: What are you gonna do, stuff it and hang it over your bed? It's a sport.

CHARLIE: You got a natural ability, kid.

DONNY: I'm feeling like I'm back in the game now.

MARK: She looks good on the boat too.

MAGGIE: Shut up.

CHARLIE: I got a charter this weekend. I could use another hand to help Mark out.

MAGGIE: No.

MARK: She is good. It'd help me out a lot.

MAGGIE: You guys are just being nice. I'm not a fisherman.

DONNY: You guys ever do any night fishing?

CHARLIE: Water's not any calmer at night, Sally.

(They all laugh. DONNY forces a laugh to play along.)

DONNY: That's funny. No, seriously. Do you ever fish at night?

MARK: We're not supposed to.

CHARLIE: We're not supposed to do a lot of things.

DONNY: *(Gets up.)* I'm up for it. Maggie?

MARK: I don't know, man.

MAGGIE: Tonight?

DONNY: Why not?

MAGGIE: We've been fishing all day.

CHARLIE: Some of us worked today.

DONNY: Oh, what? You're tired, tough guy?

CHARLIE: Well, that and the cabin still smells like puke.

DONNY: So what? That wouldn't have stopped... The old man in the sea. C'mon, let's go night fishing.

MAGGIE: Donny, sit down.

MARK: Yeah, lemme get you another bitters and soda.

DONNY: No, I'll have a beer please.

(MARK goes to the cooler.)

MAGGIE: Maybe we could go another day. If it's all right with Charlie.

CHARLIE: Sure. There's always another day.

DONNY: I been on boats my whole life.

CHARLIE: Where? On the lake?

(They laugh.)

DONNY: No. The ocean. On the "Great Atlantic," my friend.

CHARLIE: Okay.

DONNY: What? You don't believe me?

MAGGIE: We believe you, Donny.

CHARLIE: Sure we do.

(CHARLIE laughs. MARK hands out the beers.)

DONNY: You know what? The Houston Oilers sucked.

CHARLIE: Whoa, easy there, big fella.

MAGGIE: Donny, we're just kidding.

DONNY: No they did. They fucking sucked.

MAGGIE: Donny.

CHARLIE: C'mon, kid. We don't get mad on this island. It's all in good fun.

DONNY: I'm just saying. Bum Phillips? Did you make that decision?

MARK: It was a little choppy out there. I was feelin' it a bit myself.

CHARLIE: It could have happened to anyone.

DONNY: Yeah.

MARK: We do have a little tradition down here though.

CHARLIE: Oh, that's right.

MAGGIE: Tradition?

MARK: Yeah, for your first marlin catch.

DONNY: What is it?

(CHARLIE stands and takes MAGGIE's beer from her.)

CHARLIE: Can I just hold this for a second?

MAGGIE: Wait, what's going on?

DONNY: What are you guys doing?

(MARK picks up MAGGIE over his shoulder.)

MAGGIE: Ahhhh! What are you doing?!

MARK: It's initiation!

DONNY: Easy there.

CHARLIE: It's tradition.

MAGGIE: Help! Put me down!

DONNY: Maybe you should put her down.

CHARLIE: Welcome to the Bahamas!

MAGGIE: AAAAAhhhh!

(They run downstage to where the water would be. CHARLIE follows them, leaving DONNY alone onstage.)

DONNY: Oh, careful! It's slippery there! Oh, no, don't! Not with her clothes on! Oh, you guys.

(They can be heard throwing her into the water. Splashing and laughing.)

DONNY: Oh my God! There you go! Now you're all soaked! That's funny… you guys are… You guys all right? Okay. Come on outta there now.

(DONNY stands alone watching them, forcibly smiling. Music comes up, and, after a moment, DONNY decides to join them.)

DONNY: Hey! You guys! Geroni-moooooooo! *(Runs and jumps into the water.)*

SCENE 5

Transition. Later on. DONNY and CHARLIE sit on the docks drinking beers.

CHARLIE: Three wives yeah. Now I'm happy as I ever been. Free. No ties. Fish all day, drink all night. I'm living the life Jimmy Buffett sings about.

DONNY: Is that satisfying?

CHARLIE: Who gives a shit?

DONNY: So you're happy?

CHARLIE: Blissfully.

DONNY: I don't know. Sometimes when I'm on vacation, I just feel like I should get home.

CHARLIE: That's fucking stupid.

DONNY: Oh, thank you.

CHARLIE: I did all that shit, kid. The career-oriented bullshit. I was obsessed with my business. Making it the best. I made a lot of money, no doubt about it. And I was good at what I did, that's for sure. But… you want another beer? *(Moves to the cooler and continues.)*

DONNY: Ummm…

CHARLIE: Sure you do. It's all nothing really. You realize that when you get older. All that stuff you were dying to get, to achieve, a status or whatever. It's all bullshit. When you finally get it, it isn't what you thought it would be anyway. And then you're like, okay. I spent my whole life trying to get this thing and this isn't even it. That's when I realized fun is all there is. I sold my business. Bought the football team. Bought the boat. I seek pleasure. I am a pleasure seeker.

DONNY: But doesn't it wear off?

CHARLIE: Doesn't it wear off? I live on a tropical island. I eat at the nicest restaurants. I fuck the hottest young girls. Yeah, it wears off and then you just start it up all over again. All happiness is, kid, is a whole lotta pleasure strung together.

DONNY: They been gone for a while now.

CHARLIE: That Mark is a smooth character.

DONNY: What do you mean by that?

CHARLIE: She's not your girlfriend, is she?

DONNY: No.

CHARLIE: That's good.

DONNY: Why?

CHARLIE: I'm just saying.

DONNY: Oh. *(Beat.)* Saying what?

CHARLIE: He does all right with the ladies.

DONNY: Oh, she's not... Maggie's not really looking...

CHARLIE: They never are.

DONNY: No, she's not like that.

CHARLIE: Not like what?

DONNY: She's just not here to hook up.

CHARLIE: Oh, and you know this how?

DONNY: Just by... she's a friend of mine, and I know her really well.

CHARLIE: Oh, okay. Why did she go for the walk then?

DONNY: She just wanted to go for a walk.

CHARLIE: You guys are down here together?

DONNY: Yeah.

CHARLIE: But she's not your girlfriend?

DONNY: No.

CHARLIE: Would you like her to be your girlfriend?

DONNY: No, we're just friends.

CHARLIE: Uh huh.

DONNY: We are. I mean, she and I have known each other for a long time.

CHARLIE: And?

DONNY: And... I mean, at one time we did date. But... I don't know. It's hard to explain our relationship really. It's complicated.

CHARLIE: Complicated, huh?

DONNY: Yeah, I mean, we ahh... we really care about each other and there is a deep love and understanding on so many levels in a totally nonspecific type of way. We're not able to be together right now because we're both sort of going through things, finding ourselves in terms of...

CHARLIE: Do you want to fuck her?

DONNY: What?

CHARLIE: Are you sexually attracted to her?

DONNY: Yes. No, but, I mean, I was. But not anymore.

CHARLIE: That's horseshit.

DONNY: No it isn't.

CHARLIE: Yes it is.

DONNY: It's not horseshit, Charlie.

CHARLIE: "Not anymore," gimme a break.

DONNY: Why is it so hard to understand? We used to date and now we're friends.

CHARLIE: You're lying to yourself!

DONNY: Whoa, easy there.

CHARLIE: I mean, come on. You make up this whole sweepstakes thing just to...

DONNY: What?

CHARLIE: She told me about this sweepstakes thing on the boat while you were...indisposed.

DONNY: I didn't make that up. It's a real…

CHARLIE: Hey, Samson, you think I'm an idiot? I know the owner of that hotel, Joey Fatts, he don't give away nothing, all right? So don't bullshit me.

DONNY: I'm not. It wasn't through the hotel. It was through the airlines.

CHARLIE: The airlines, huh?

DONNY: Yeah.

CHARLIE: Look me in the eye and tell me…

DONNY: I'm not gonna look you in the eye. What do you care anyway?

CHARLIE: I'm just saying. You're going all around it. Be direct.

DONNY: About what? There's nothing to be direct about. I'm just down here with a friend of mine having a good time.

CHARLIE: I been there, kid. You don't want any regrets in life.

DONNY: Thanks. I'll remember that.

CHARLIE: Do. Do remember that. Before it's too late.

SCENE 6

The lights shift to MARK and MAGGIE on the other side of the stage. They are on their walk.

MAGGIE: Owww.

MARK: You okay?

MAGGIE: Yeah, yeah.

MARK: Here, let's sit here for a sec.

(MAGGIE sits on the sea wall. MARK rubs her calf.)

MAGGIE: Okay.

MARK: Is that it?

MAGGIE: Yeah, right there. Oww.

MARK: It's just a cramp.

MAGGIE: That never happens to me.

MARK: You want to rest?

MAGGIE: Maybe just for a second. I'm usually not this much of a wimp.

MARK: Don't worry about it.

(Beat. MARK looks out at the water.)

MAGGIE: It's such a great night.

MARK: Never get tired of these nights.

MAGGIE: How could you?

MARK: I don't know. So?

MAGGIE: So?

MARK: You and Donny seem cool together.

MAGGIE: Yeah, he's great.

MARK: I could never be like that with one of my exes.

MAGGIE: Really?

MARK: No, cut it clean and don't look back. That's the way I do it.

MAGGIE: Really? I'm friends with all my exes.

MARK: Every guy you ever went out with?

MAGGIE: The major ones. I mean, I haven't really gone out with that many guys.

MARK: Come on. I don't believe that for a second.

MAGGIE: I haven't.

MARK: That's crazy.

MAGGIE: I didn't even really date till college.

MARK: Why?

MAGGIE: I don't know. I was really shy and I was into school, my grades and stuff.

MARK: Oh, you were a good girl.

MAGGIE: Boring right?

MARK: No, good girls are cool.

MAGGIE: As long as they have a wild side.

MARK: Exactly. But you and Donny dated for a while, right?

MAGGIE: Umm, yeah. It was sort of off and on. So it was never really clear when we were dating and when we were...

MARK: Oh, one of those, huh?

MAGGIE: Yeah.

MARK: So, you guys met at Brown?

MAGGIE: No, I went to Columbia.

MARK: That's right.

MAGGIE: But Donny did a semester at Columbia and we had an art course together.

MARK: Nice.

MAGGIE: "Watercolors in the Twentieth Century."

MARK: Donny took a watercolor class?

MAGGIE: I know, right?

MARK: He was probably just trying to meet girls.

MAGGIE: Probably.

MARK: Well, it worked.

MAGGIE: I know. It did.

MARK: That guy cracks me up. I can picture him being all into the watercolor class.

MAGGIE: He was.

(They laugh.)

MARK: I'm sure he planned it all out in advance too.

MAGGIE: What do you mean?

MARK: He's so funny with girls. He always has these intricate plans devised.

MAGGIE: Really?

MARK: Yeah. (Laughs.)

MAGGIE: What?

MARK: No, I was just thinking of this girl in junior high that Donny...

MAGGIE: What?

MARK: Ahh, I shouldn't be telling tales out of school.

MAGGIE: C'mon.

MARK: No, no, he wouldn't...

MAGGIE: C'mon, you can't start a story and then stop like that.

MARK: Oh, man...

MAGGIE: Pleeeeeeaaase!

MARK: All right, all right. When we were growing up, there was this girl, Kelly Seabury, and she was so cute. She was...

MAGGIE: How old were you guys?

MARK: We were in seventh grade and she was in eighth. I mean, she's a pig now but in eighth grade she was amazing.

MAGGIE: Oh, that's nice.

MARK: I'm kidding, but you know what I mean. The girls that were hot in the eighth grade usually don't...travel well. If you know what I'm sayin'.

MAGGIE: That's true, actually, now that I think about it.

MARK: Right? But in eighth grade, Kelly Seabury was a knockout. And Donny had a huge crush on her. He actually went to the freshman semi-formal with her best friend just so he could ride in the limo with her.

MAGGIE: Oh my God.

MARK: I know.

MAGGIE: I'm surprised he never told me about her.

MARK: It's probably a bad memory.

MAGGIE: Why?

MARK: Well after the semi, he actually became friends with her and was slowly making his move. I mean, we were well into sophomore year at this point. He said he had a four-year plan for asking her out.

(MAGGIE laughs.)

MARK: I know, right? And so one day, we were on the overpass hanging out and…

MAGGIE: The overpass?

MARK: Yeah. You know the… you didn't have overpasses between the buildings?

MAGGIE: No.

MARK: Well, we did. And so we were hanging out one day and it had become known that Donny was obsessed with her. I think everybody knew except Kelly… actually, she probably knew too. But anyway, Donny was talking to her, and Paul Vargas was standing behind Kelly making faces. And Donny was trying so hard not to laugh. Then all of a sudden, Paul contorted his face into like this monkey-man thing. I don't know how he did it,

but Donny lost it and…literally pissed his pants laughing.

MAGGIE: No.

MARK: I'm not joking. There was a puddle.

MAGGIE: Oh my God. That's horrible.

MARK: I know. It's legendary back home. Donny still hasn't lived it down.

MAGGIE: Really?

MARK: Yeah.

MAGGIE: That's so sad.

MARK: Very sad. That's why Donny transferred to prep school.

MAGGIE: Poor Donny.

MARK: Yeah, he's never been exactly smooth with the ladies. I mean, he's stopped pissing himself. Which is good. He's great though. You gotta love him.

MAGGIE: You do.

MARK: So, how come it didn't work out with you guys? You seem like you'd be a scorching couple.

MAGGIE: I don't know. Timing I guess. I wasn't ready. I kinda freaked out when things got too serious.

MARK: You sound like a guy.

MAGGIE: I'm always the guy in relationships. Isn't that sad?

MARK: Relationships are tough.

MAGGIE: Yeah? What about you? You ever gonna give up the philandering fisherman thing?

MARK: Hey, if it ain't broke… I don't know. I always pictured myself having the family and the whole bit but… ahhh, what else you gonna picture when you're a kid. You know?

MAGGIE: Yeah.

MARK: *(Beat.)* You ready there, cripple?

MAGGIE: *(She gets up.)* Yeah.

MARK: Let's get that liquor.

SCENE 7

Lights shift back to DONNY and CHARLIE on the docks.

DONNY: Jesus, I think I'm a little drunk. Where the hell are they anyway?

CHARLIE: You watch them when they come back. You can always tell when two people have hooked up.

DONNY: How do you tell that?

CHARLIE: You see it in their eyes. It's a glassy look. It's sort of like a crackhead's eyes, but slightly different. And you'll see little looks between them. Quick little glances that they think other people don't notice. And little touches. Like when she gets up to go to the cooler she'll put her hands on his shoulders or touch his waist as she walks behind him. If they have hooked up, you'll just sense a different energy about them. It's a release of the sexual flirtation.

DONNY: What are you talking about? I didn't notice any sexual flirtation.

CHARLIE: That's because you're not perceptive.

DONNY: Yes I am.

CHARLIE: No, you're not. Everybody thinks they're perceptive but you thinking you're perceptive proves that you're not perceptive.

DONNY: How?

CHARLIE: Because you're not perceptive.

DONNY: How do you know?

CHARLIE: It was my business for twenty years.

DONNY: Perception?

CHARLIE: I was a private investigator.

DONNY: I thought you were a venture capitalist?

CHARLIE: That was my cover.

DONNY: Oh, this gets better and better. Where the hell are they? How long does it take to get a bottle of tequila? Did they go to Mexico, for chrissakes?

CHARLIE: Relax, kid. Everything happens slower on the island.

DONNY: I guess I should have read the handbook before I came.

CHARLIE: You a gambling man, Tony?

DONNY: Donny.

CHARLIE: Can I call you Tony?

DONNY: No.

CHARLIE: What do you say you and I make a little wager on whether they hooked up or not?

DONNY: Don't be ridiculous.

CHARLIE: It's an easy bet for you, right? You said she's not here to hook up.

DONNY: She's not.

CHARLIE: All right then. What do you got to lose?

DONNY: Nothing. I don't have anything to lose and I don't have anything to gain and I'm not... besides, how would we tell?

CHARLIE: I told you, from the little subtleties.

DONNY: Oh, right. From your private eye days.

CHARLIE: C'mon, let's just bet for fun.

DONNY: I'm not gonna bet.

CHARLIE: C'mon, pussy willow.

DONNY: She's a friend of mine, for godssakes. She's not a racehorse.

CHARLIE: Gambling just makes life more interesting. It ups the stakes.

DONNY: No.

CHARLIE: Gentlemen's bet just for the fun of it.

DONNY: No, those are stupid. If you're gonna bet, you might as well... a hundred bucks they didn't even kiss.

CHARLIE: Oh, I like your style, Tony.

DONNY: Donny!

CHARLIE: Right. You're on. Let's smoke on it.

DONNY: What?

CHARLIE: What do you say we smoke some fine Jamaican herb to seal the deal? *(Pulls out a pipe and a bag of weed.)*

DONNY: Oh, this is beautiful. A pot-smoking private eye.

CHARLIE: C'mon, you need to take the edge off.

DONNY: I'm not edgy.

CHARLIE: Yeah.

DONNY: I mean, I'll smoke with you. But I'm not edgy.

CHARLIE: *(Packs the bowl.)* I got this from my Jamaican friends. I gave them a free charter and they supplied me with a trash bag full of this stuff.

(He takes a hit and passes it to DONNY.)

CHARLIE: Careful, it's strong.

DONNY: Oh, that tastes nice.

CHARLIE: It's the finest you can get.

DONNY: Holy shit, that's good.

CHARLIE: That's what I'm saying, kid, huh?

DONNY: Yeah.

CHARLIE: That's what I'm saying.

DONNY: Uh huh, yup.

CHARLIE: That don't get old.

DONNY: No, oh that's nice. *(He is in a bit of a stoned haze.)*

CHARLIE: I mean, you're drinking Budweisers and smoking some cheap-ass-back-of-the-school-bus weed. It gets old. But if you drink the finest imported wines, have steak that melts in your mouth, scotch, cigars, this beautiful Jamaican herb. It is happiness. This is it. They don't want to tell you that. But here it is, my friend. Happiness. They don't know. The people writing the self-help books? The "happiness comes from within" bullshit. They don't got access to this stuff. How would they know happiness when they don't even know what the world has to offer? Do I look unhappy? Do I look like I'm searching for meaning in life? Like I'm looking for a soul mate to spend my golden years with? Fuck off! They're all golden years. I'm living a golden life. I beat the fucking system, kid.

(DONNY is lost in his haze.)

CHARLIE: And then my grandpappy made love to me in an outhouse.

DONNY: What?

CHARLIE: Just seeing if you're still listening.

DONNY: Sorry.

CHARLIE: Thinking about your girl?

DONNY: No.

CHARLIE: Yeah you are.

DONNY: Charlie, I'm not. I'm telling you.

CHARLIE: I been there, kid. I know what you're going through. Don't make decisions based on fear. That's death.

DONNY: I'm not. I…

CHARLIE: Listen to me. Here's the deal, okay. There's all these lives out there just floating around waiting for you to live them. You have all these choices to make. Every choice you make splits things off into another parallel universe that's happening simultaneously to your own pathetic reality.

DONNY: What?

CHARLIE: There's two lives in front of you right this second. A fork in the road, shall we say. Two roads diverged in the yellow wood. Which one you gonna take, bubba, huh?

DONNY: I don't know. Wait, what the fuck are you talking about?

CHARLIE: Think about it. Most of the time we're too afraid to live. We say, "I couldn't do that. I couldn't be with her. I don't want to be happy." We talk ourselves out of living. But it's still out there. It's waiting for you. It's happening whether you choose it or not. It's just a question of whether you're gonna go for the ride or sit on the sidelines hopin' and dreamin'. All you have to do is step into it. *(Beat.)* A life unlived is not a life at all.

DONNY: The Tao of Charlie.

CHARLIE: You joke now. But someday you'll realize I was right. Hopin' and dreamin', kid, is no way to go through life.

DONNY: Look, Charlie, that's all very interesting. But here's the thing. In my life from my… whatever. I don't know about the roads and the paths and all that. But I do know that I love her. I love her. I know she'll always be in my life. I want her to be happy. But I'm not in love with her.

CHARLIE: Do you beat off to her?

DONNY: Charlie, Charlie…

CHARLIE: What?

DONNY: Charlie, Charlie Brown! I love you, baby. But I ain't near stoned enough to talk about my masturbation habits with you.

CHARLIE: Don't be bashful.

DONNY: It's not that. It's just that…

CHARLIE: The sign of a truly confident man is a man who can admit to his own masturbation.

DONNY: I mean, I'm not saying I haven't tried it.

CHARLIE: You'll know if you're in love with the woman. The supreme test is the beat-off test. And believe you me, my dick has fooled me many times into thinking that absolute cunts were beautiful, well-rounded people. But I wasn't in love with the person. I was creating a person that lived inside this fucking fabulous body. You know, the supple breasts, tight stomach, skin so soft you don't want to stop caressing it. That shit blinds you into thinking that she's a cool woman. I don't particularly think that about Maggie. I mean, she's a beautiful woman, but in a down-to-earth well-rounded type of way.

DONNY: She's a great woman. She's gonna make some guy really happy someday. It's not gonna be me, but…

CHARLIE: Why not?

DONNY: Because what I've been…

CHARLIE: You can be that guy.

DONNY: But I'm not. I…

CHARLIE: Be that guy, Donny.

DONNY: I'm…

CHARLIE: Ah, ahhhhh, be that guy, Donny.

DONNY: Okay.

CHARLIE: You're the guy.

DONNY: Okay. I'm the guy. But the thing is…

CHARLIE: Stop it right now. And decide to be the man you've always secretly wanted to be.

(DONNY is silent. CHARLIE gets up for a beer.)

CHARLIE: Did you know that Earl Johnson was a chronic masturbator?

DONNY: No I didn't.

CHARLIE: I mean constantly. Before games. After games. He used to do it in front of the other players. That always seemed a little strange to me. I mean, here's the other guys getting ready for the game and the best running back in the NFL is walking around the locker room with a hard-on.

DONNY: Charlie.

CHARLIE: Smaller than you might think too.

DONNY: Oh my God.

CHARLIE: Because he was a large black man.

DONNY: Yes he was.

CHARLIE: His thighs were immense.

DONNY: I can imagine.

CHARLIE: And here he was proudly walking around with this little pencil dick sticking out of these gigantic black thighs. It was a striking image.

DONNY: I bet.

(MARK and MAGGIE are heard offstage.)

DONNY: Oh, thank God they're back.

CHARLIE: Don't forget now. Watch for the subtleties.

DONNY: Right.

CHARLIE: I'm gonna teach you to be perceptive.

DONNY: I just hope they have the tequila.

(They come on laughing.)

MAGGIE: Oh my God.

DONNY: Hey.

MAGGIE: Oh my God. We were… look at his shoes!

(MARK is wearing black loafers. MAGGIE continues laughing.)

DONNY: Where did you get those?

MAGGIE: We were on our way to get the bottle and… it was hilarious. *(She can't contain her laughter.)*

MARK: We stopped by the disco.

MAGGIE: But there's a dress code, right?

DONNY: You stopped by the disco?

MARK: But I was wearing my flip flops.

DONNY: 'Cause we were wondering where you were.

MARK: But you can't wear open-toed shoes in the disco.

DONNY: That is funny.

MAGGIE: That's not the funny part. So they wouldn't let us in, right? So Mark walks out into the middle of the street and flags down this carload of Spanish guys.

MARK: Sometimes you really want to go to the disco.

DONNY: Right.

MAGGIE: So…

CHARLIE: This is a man who knows what he wants.

MAGGIE: So the car…

CHARLIE: That's why I hired him. He stops at nothing.

MARK: Sometimes you really feel like dancing.

CHARLIE: You sure do, buddy.

DONNY: So what happened?

MAGGIE: So this car-full of Spanish guys pulls over, yelling in Spanish. I mean, I was scared at first but they were all drunk and happy.

CHARLIE: There are no angry drunks on this island.

MARK: Amen!

MAGGIE: So they're all laughing and yelling at Mark. And by this time there are cars behind them. So there's this whole traffic jam, horns honking…

MARK: I didn't even hear the horns.

MAGGIE: I can't believe you didn't hear them. They were so loud. But again it wasn't like they were mad car horns. The whole line of traffic was sort of beeping in a fun way.

DONNY: Yes. They have happy horns on this island.

CHARLIE: Lowest crime rate of any island in the Bahamas.

MARK: That is true.

CHARLIE: There's just no need for crime when you're this happy.

MARK: Truer words were never spoke!

DONNY: Okay we've established that. So what happened?

MAGGIE: So, Mark tries to buy the guy's shoes. I mean, the driver, he's like miming that he wants his shoes. And they're all getting a big kick out of it. They're laughing their asses off.

MARK: At this point I was getting desperate because of the long line of traffic.

DONNY: I thought you didn't hear the horns?

MARK: What?

DONNY: You said you didn't hear the…

MARK: I was so into it that I didn't hear anything. And I'm yelling at them as if they'll understand English if I say it really loudly, you know?

(MAGGIE touches MARK's shoulders. CHARLIE coughs and shoots DONNY a look.)

MAGGIE: No, but you're forgetting the best part. All the guys in the car were repeating everything in English, everything Mark was saying.

MARK: Oh, that's right. That was so funny. And the louder and more intense I got, the louder they would repeat everything.

MAGGIE: So, he takes out money and starts waving it around and pointing to their shoes. And I mean, he literally took the driver's shoes off of his feet and gave him the money.

MARK: I gave him my flip flops too. It was a trade.

DONNY: God that is funny.

MAGGIE: Wait, that's not even the funniest part!

DONNY: There's more?

MAGGIE: The rest of the guys in the car started giving him their shoes too. And Mark's trying to say, "No, I only need one pair." But they're laughing and throwing shoes out the window and then they peel out.

DONNY: They just left without their shoes?

MAGGIE: Yes!

CHARLIE: That's hilarious!

MAGGIE: Then every car that passed by would throw shoes out the window. I mean, it was so funny, for like ten minutes people were throwing shoes at us.

DONNY: You stood there for ten minutes?

MAGGIE: Well, it seemed like ten minutes.

MARK: So there's shoes all over the road and by this time there's a crowd watching and the bouncers at the nightclub are laughing their asses off.

MAGGIE: So, Mark puts on the first pair of shoes and we go in and the whole crowd gives us a standing ovation and the bouncers bought us drinks. It was unbelievable.

CHARLIE: That is a great story.

DONNY: That is unbelievable.

CHARLIE: This guy, huh? Never takes no for an answer. That's why we love him.

MARK: Sometimes you just feel like dancing.

DONNY: Absolutely.

MAGGIE: The most amazing part about the whole thing was everybody's attitude. I mean, if this happened in New York, the cops would have been there and people would have been bitching about the shoes in the road. But here, it was like everybody just turned it into a carnival or something.

CHARLIE: That's because everybody's happy here.

MARK: Damn straight!

MAGGIE: It's so true. I mean, where else could that happen?

MARK: Nowhere.

CHARLIE: The happiness is contagious.

DONNY: Well, Bermuda maybe.

MARK: What?

DONNY: I'm just saying that maybe this sort of thing might happen in Bermuda.

CHARLIE: Naawww!

MARK: Bermuda?! That's like the last place.

MAGGIE: Have you ever been there, Donny?

MARK: That place is so uptight.

DONNY: I've never been there, I'm just saying.

CHARLIE: That story they just told could never happen in Bermuda.

DONNY: Okay. I didn't mean, Bermuda per se, I just meant like it could happen on another island... I mean, people are happy on most islands, probably.

MAGGIE: What are you trying to say?

DONNY: Nothing. I'm just...

CHARLIE: Did all of them really throw their shoes!?

MARK: Yeah, all of them.

(EVERYBODY except DONNY starts laughing again.)

MAGGIE: It was just like shoes everywhere!

CHARLIE: I think that's the funniest story I ever heard.

DONNY: It is.

MAGGIE: Oh my God. I need a beer. I'm exhausted from laughing so hard.

(She crosses behind MARK, touching his waist. CHARLIE shoots DONNY another look.)

MAGGIE: You want one, Mark?

MARK: Yeah, that'd be great.

DONNY: I'm all set.

MAGGIE: Oh, you want one? It looks like you got a full one there.

DONNY: Not for long. *(Downs his beer.)*

MARK: Yeah, Donny.

MAGGIE: Wow, okay. *(Goes to the cooler.)*

MARK: Donny's picking it up a notch.

DONNY: Yeah, man. Let's fire it up!

MARK: Yeah!

DONNY: I mean, this is the Bahamas, right!

CHARLIE: Marky, you want a little weed?

MARK: Yes I do.

(He takes the pipe from CHARLIE.)

DONNY: We're on the island of happiness. Let's get fucking happy!

(MAGGIE comes back with the beers. MARK touches her back softly. DONNY notices.)

MAGGIE: Here we go, boys.

MARK: *(Sings.)* "Oh, Maggie, I think I got something to say to you."

DONNY: Never heard that one before, huh, Mag?

MARK: I know. All your boyfriends probably sing that song to you.

MAGGIE: Well, but not like that.

DONNY: Yes, that was a beautiful rendition.

MAGGIE: Yes it was.

DONNY: Here's to Mark's beautiful rendition of "Maggie May"! Yeah! Whoo!

MAGGIE: Are you all right, Donny?

DONNY: What are you talking about? I'm fucking great.

MAGGIE: Okay.

MARK: Have a little of this weed, Maggie May.

DONNY: She doesn't smoke.

MAGGIE: Once in a while I do.

DONNY: You do?

CHARLIE: Well, this is once in a while.

MAGGIE: I'll take a little.

(MARK holds the pipe. MAGGIE takes a hit and starts to cough.)

MARK: Hold it down, you coughing bastard.

CHARLIE: You cough, you get off.

DONNY: Careful. It's strong stuff.

MARK: Oh, yeah.

DONNY: I'll take another hit.

(DONNY takes the pipe. He tries to smoke it, but it's out. MARK and MAGGIE laugh.)

DONNY: This is out. Who's got the light?

MARK: It took you long enough to realize it was out.

MAGGIE: It was out the whole time.

DONNY: That's funny. Where's the light?

(MARK gives it to him.)

CHARLIE: That shoe story kills me! I just keep picturing the shoes all over the road.

(They start laughing again.)

MAGGIE: I wish I had a camera. It was amazing.

MARK: It really was.

DONNY: It's not that amazing, okay. So some guys threw some shoes out the window. Oh, that's fucking hilarious.

MAGGIE: Donny.

DONNY: Where's the bottle, by the way?

MAGGIE: Oh my God!

MARK: Holy shit! We forgot the bottle.

(They laugh.)

DONNY: Now that's funny. No bottle. Wow, well at least you got the shoe story.

MARK: It was worth it.

MAGGIE: Totally.

DONNY: Oh, yeah. We'll be sober as a judge, but at least we'll laugh about the shoe story all night.

CHARLIE: I got a bottle on the boat.

MARK: Charlie saves the day!

(CHARLIE goes to DONNY. DONNY has his back to MARK and MAGGIE.)

CHARLIE: You can owe me.

DONNY: What?

(DONNY turns and notices the look between MARK and MAGGIE.)

CHARLIE: Like I says, you can owe me. *(Goes to the boat.)*

MARK: How 'bout some tunes too, Charlie!

CHARLIE: You leave it to the DJ.

MARK: Charlie has the best tunes.

DONNY: Charlie has the best everything.

(DONNY watches as MARK and MAGGIE have a little private moment. MAGGIE sees him noticing and stops the moment.)

MAGGIE: So, Donny.

DONNY: So, Maggie.

MAGGIE: What have you guys been doing while we were gone?

DONNY: Fun, fun, fun, I mean, you think you had a good time?

MAGGIE: Oh, yeah?

DONNY: Oh, yeah.

MARK: Charlie's a good hang, isn't he?

DONNY: Charlie's a great hang.

MAGGIE: What did you guys do?

DONNY: Well, it would be hard to top the shoe story, but we had our own fun here at the homestead.

MAGGIE: What happened?

DONNY: Did you know Earl Johnson has a small dick?

MARK: What?

MAGGIE: Who's Earl Johnson?

DONNY: And he beats off like a champion.

MARK: Are you serious?

DONNY: Why would I lie about that?

MAGGIE: Who's Earl Johnson?

DONNY: Charlie! Charlie!? Earl Johnson, does he or does he not have the smallest dick in professional sports!?

(A kick-ass dance tune comes blaring on.)

MAGGIE: Oh my God! I love this song!

MARK: Jam master Charlie!

(MAGGIE starts to seductively dance for the BOYS. After a moment, MARK joins in. DONNY then tries awkwardly to join in the dancing, but after a moment, he starts to feel like a third wheel in the dance, so he casually sits back down. CHARLIE enters, wielding a bottle of tequila. The music slowly fades down, but plays softly under the rest of the scene.)

CHARLIE: We have tequila!

MARK: We love you, Charlie!

CHARLIE: Did I come through or did I come through?

DONNY: Charlie, tell these guys about Earl Johnson's dick. C'mon, tell 'em.

CHARLIE: Like I says, kid. You can owe me.

DONNY: Huh?

(DONNY turns to notice MARK and MAGGIE close dancing. CHARLIE goes back to the boat. After a moment of the dancing, MAGGIE stops.)

MAGGIE: I have to use the ahhh… facilities. *(Exits to the boat.)*

(MARK sits with DONNY.)

MARK: This place is great, huh?

DONNY: The best.

MARK: How you doin', man?

DONNY: Me? Good. I'm great.

MARK: Maggie's a cool chick.

DONNY: Yeah.

MARK: Great body on her.

DONNY: She's a pretty girl, yeah.

MARK: Very pretty, yeah. Yup.

DONNY: Charlie's a very… nice man.

MARK: He is a nice man.

DONNY: Lotta stories.

MARK: They get old pretty quick.

DONNY: I bet.

MARK: So, I don't want to step on anybody's toes. So what's the deal with you and Maggie?

DONNY: Me and Maggie?

MARK: Yeah.

DONNY: I told you we're friends.

MARK: But are you into her? Because I don't want to…

DONNY: No.

MARK: All right. Good. I mean, that's what I thought 'cause I'm kinda getting a vibe from her.

DONNY: You're getting a vibe from her?

MARK: A little bit, yeah.

DONNY: I think you might be misreading that.

MARK: Donny boy, I think I know when I'm getting a vibe.

DONNY: I'm sure you do, but it's…

MARK: What? She's got a boyfriend back home? They all do, buddy.

DONNY: No, it's just… she's not that kind of girl.

MARK: What kind of girl?

DONNY: Just don't.

MARK: What are you, her dad?

DONNY: No, I'm saying just don't dick her over. That's all.

MARK: I'm not gonna dick her over. I really like her.

DONNY: You really like her? You've known her for a day.

MARK: Yeah, but she's different than most of the girls that come down here. She's funny. She's smart. She's the kinda girl I could see myself with.

DONNY: What?

MARK: I'm serious, man.

DONNY: And what is she gonna do, move down here and fish with you?

MARK: I'm not gonna do this for the rest of my life. I got to settle down someday.

DONNY: Settle down? You just met the girl.

MARK: What are you getting excited about?

DONNY: I'm not. I just… whatever. I hope you guys are very happy together.

MARK: Why are you getting bent out of shape?

DONNY: I'm not.

MARK: All right. All right, cool. 'Cause I don't want a girl to come between us.

DONNY: Never.

MARK: I mean, we're still blood brothers right?

DONNY: Totally. Wait, blood brothers?

MARK: Yeah, man. You don't remember? Eighth grade? You me and Harold MacGilvrey. We became blood brothers at Barry Park.

DONNY: No, that wasn't me.

MARK: What are you talking about? Yeah, it was.

DONNY: No, that was you, Harold, and Chip Caswell.

MARK: It was?

DONNY: Yeah.

MARK: Oh. *(Beat.)* What's old Chip Caswell up to these days?

DONNY: I don't know, I haven't seen him.

(MAGGIE and CHARLIE come on carrying shot glasses.)

CHARLIE: Time for some of Charlie's special shots!

MAGGIE: Charlie used to be a bartender!

DONNY: Of course he was.

MARK: Oh, get ready. These things are killer.

CHARLIE: *(Raises a glass.)* "We worked hard all day. We're exhausted and hot. We should probably rest, but hell, let's have a shot!"

(They all drink.)

MAGGIE: Oh my God. That was awesome.

MARK: Right to the heart.

MAGGIE: I love that, when you do a shot and you get that warm feeling in your heart.

MARK: Yeah.

CHARLIE: Nothing like it.

DONNY: What was in that?

MARK: Charlie's secret recipe.

CHARLIE: All natural ingredients.

(CHARLIE and MARK laugh.)

DONNY: What?

MARK: Don't worry about it.

CHARLIE: It's happy juice!

MARK: Charlie!

CHARLIE: Marko!

MARK: Polo!

(MARK picks up the joint. He and CHARLIE sit on the edge of the dock. DONNY notices that MAGGIE looks a little woozy. He goes to her. MARK and CHARLIE remain on stage and talk quietly throughout the scene with DONNY and MAGGIE.)

DONNY: You okay, Mag?

MAGGIE: Yeah, yeah, I'm just... *(She sits.)*

DONNY: Are you all right?

MAGGIE: Yeah, I just think that shot really hit me.

DONNY: Do you want to go back to the hotel?

MAGGIE: No, I'm having fun.

DONNY: You are?

MAGGIE: Yeah, aren't you?

DONNY: I guess.

MAGGIE: Donny.

DONNY: Maggie.

MAGGIE: What's up with you tonight?

DONNY: Nothing.

MAGGIE: You seem like you're mad at me or something.

DONNY: I'm not mad at you.

MAGGIE: Are you sure?

DONNY: Yeah, why?

MAGGIE: I don't know. You seem a little distant right now.

DONNY: I do?

MAGGIE: Yeah.

DONNY: Well, I'm not.

MAGGIE: No?

DONNY: Nope.

MAGGIE: Donny.

DONNY: What?

MAGGIE: C'mon, we're in the Bahamas and you're not even having fun.

DONNY: I'm having fun. Loads.

MAGGIE: You don't seem it.

DONNY: What do you want me to do? Backflips? I'm having a great time.

MAGGIE: *(Beat.)* Nothing happened.

DONNY: What?

MAGGIE: With me and Mark on the walk. I mean, if that's…

DONNY: I don't care.

MAGGIE: Oh, okay good, I just…

(MARK and CHARLIE's conversation gets loud for a moment.)

MARK: Coolooocoocoo!

CHARLIE: Donny's nuts! Grab 'em!

(They laugh.)

DONNY: Sounds like they're having a good time over there.

MAGGIE: Yeah. *(Laughs.)*

DONNY: Oh, are you doing that thing where we pretend to be having a better time than them? Okay. *(Laughs loudly.)* Oh yeah! Whooo hooo!

MAGGIE: No, stop. I wasn't doing that.

DONNY: You weren't doing the laughing thing?

MAGGIE: No.

DONNY: What's so funny then?

MAGGIE: How come you never told me about Kelly Seabury?

DONNY: What?

MAGGIE: Kelly Seabury?

DONNY: What did he say?

MAGGIE: Nothing, he just… *(She laughs.)*

DONNY: Real funny. *(To MARK.)* Dick!

MARK: What?

DONNY: Want to hear some stories about Mark?

MARK: What are you talking about?

DONNY: Kelly Seabury, huh?

MARK: Maggie!

DONNY: I'm sorry. It's just such a great story.

CHARLIE: Kelly Seabury!? The piss puddle girl?!

DONNY: I guess you told the whole fucking island?

MARK: C'mon, Donny. We can laugh about it now.

CHARLIE: That's a classic.

DONNY: Yeah, sure we can laugh about it. You know what else we can laugh about?

MARK: Donny boy!

DONNY: You know what else we can laugh about?

MAGGIE: It's okay. Donny, you were a kid.

MARK: Happens to the best of 'em.

DONNY: Just ask Mark about Chloe Benjamin.

MAGGIE: Chloe Benjamin!

MARK: Hey, seriously now, that's wrong. You know Chloe Benjamin is off limits.

DONNY: Oh, but Kelly Seabury is fine.

MARK: Donny, don't fuck around.

MAGGIE: This sounds good.

DONNY: It was prom night and Mark…

MARK: Donny.

DONNY: Mark was dating Chloe Benjamin.

MAGGIE: Okay.

CHARLIE: If I was Chloe Benjamin, I would caress myself.

DONNY: She broke up with Mark the day before the prom and…

MAGGIE: That's awful.

DONNY: And Chloe told all her friends that she broke up with Mark because he never tried anything with her.

MARK: You want to play games?

DONNY: So, she thought Mark was gay.

MAGGIE: Ooohhhhh.

DONNY: So she told the whole school…

MARK: All right, sweepstakes!

DONNY: (Looks shocked.) Mark.

MARK: What? It was through the airlines, right?

MAGGIE: What?

MARK: You told her it was a joke, right?

MAGGIE: What's a joke?

DONNY: That's enough.

MARK: What? You wanted to play around.

DONNY: Yeah, you win.

(Silence.)

MAGGIE: Are you guys all right?

DONNY: Yeah. You know what, it's late. Maggie, I'll see you back at the hotel.

MARK: Oh, come on. I was kidding.

DONNY: I know. I know you were kidding. I was going anyway. I'm exhausted.

MARK: You're not leaving. C'mon, Charlie, mix up another batch of shots. Turn the tunes up!

DONNY: Have a good night.

MAGGIE: Donny.

MARK: I'm sorry. I thought we were joking around.

DONNY: It's not 'cause of that. I'm tired. I'll see you guys tomorrow.

MAGGIE: Well, I'll go with you.

DONNY: No, stay here. Have a good time. Don't worry, I'll be fine.

MARK: This is crazy.

DONNY: Good night, all.

MARK: Are you pissed?

DONNY: No, don't worry about it. It was a great day. Great day.

MARK: All right. Later, man.

DONNY: Good night, Chuck.

CHARLIE: Calling it a night?

DONNY: Yeah, I got an early day tomorrow. (He leaves.)

MARK: Shit.

MAGGIE: What just happened?

MARK: I just… I should shut up.

MAGGIE: Everybody was having such a good time and then all of a sudden it turned.

MARK: Yeah, I know. Well… let's have some drinks.

MAGGIE: I should probably go talk to him. He seemed kind of upset.

MARK: Look, he probably just needs to walk it off.

MAGGIE: Yeah?

MARK: I think he needs to be alone right now.

MAGGIE: Well, it is late.

MARK: You got to finish your drink at least.

MAGGIE: No, thanks.

MARK: I don't want you to go.

CHARLIE: Oh, Jesus.

MARK: C'mon, have a heart. Don't leave me alone with Charlie.

MAGGIE: I'll talk to you tomorrow.

MARK: Come're.

MAGGIE: What?

MARK: I got to tell you something.

MAGGIE: What?

MARK: It's a secret.

(She goes to him. He leans in to kiss her. She kisses him for a moment and then stops.)

MAGGIE: Good night.

MARK: Sweet dreams.

(She starts to go.)

MAGGIE: Good night, Charlie.

CHARLIE: Good night, kid.

(She exits. CHARLIE stares at MARK.)

CHARLIE: Please tell me you didn't just use the "I have to tell you a secret" line?

MARK: Shut up, all right?

CHARLIE: Say it isn't so. "Come're I have to tell you a secret."

MARK: Fuck off. It worked didn't it?

CHARLIE: Ahhh… No.

MARK: She'll be back. This was a setup night. I was just setting it up.

CHARLIE: Yes, perhaps next time you could use the old yawn and stretch your arm around her.

MARK: Fuck off.

(MARK exits. CHARLIE laughs and is left alone onstage. His laughter recedes to a deep sadness. He stares out to sea. Lights come up on the hotel room as DONNY packs a bag. MAGGIE sits on the bed watching him. There is a moment of both sides of the stage being lit. After a moment CHARLIE exits and the lights go down on the docks.)

SCENE 8

MAGGIE: You have to leave right now?

DONNY: Yeah.

MAGGIE: I thought we were on the same flight?

DONNY: I changed it.

MAGGIE: It's three in the morning.

DONNY: It's the red eye.

MAGGIE: Donny, at least wait till the morning.

DONNY: No, this is better. This way I can sleep on the flight. It'll be great.

MAGGIE: This is crazy.

DONNY: I know. I'm sorry.

MAGGIE: I just don't understand what's going on right now.

DONNY: I'm just a little vacationed out, that's all.

MAGGIE: What did I do?

DONNY: Nothing. You didn't do anything.

MAGGIE: Then why are you leaving?

DONNY: I got a lot to do back home.

MAGGIE: Like what?

DONNY: Work. It suddenly got crazy and they need me. I just feel like. There's just a lot going on. It's a little overwhelming. *(Beat.)* I'm sorry about the whole sweepstakes thing...

MAGGIE: Look, I don't care about that. I'm flattered that... I just feel like we're not... I mean, I'm gonna pay you.

DONNY: No you're not.

MAGGIE: Donny.

DONNY: Seriously, Maggie. I got such a ridiculous Christmas bonus and...

MAGGIE: Donny, I'm paying for my half.

DONNY: No, you're not. I needed someone to go with anyway.

MAGGIE: Why me?

DONNY: Ummm... you were the first person that came to mind.

MAGGIE: Seriously, Donny.

DONNY: Seriously, I have no idea. I mean, I don't have a lot of friends. I hadn't seen you in a while. I thought it would be a nice way to catch up or...whatever. But I felt weird about just asking you straight up. I thought you'd be more apt to come if it was a free trip. But I didn't want you to think that... I don't know. I don't know what the fuck I'm doing. Hey, stay here, enjoy yourself. You know you can call the boys. I think Mark really likes you.

MAGGIE: Donny.

DONNY: You never know where things might lead. You have to make choices in life. There are always two roads to go down and... one is yellow and...wooded. It was great seeing you again.

MAGGIE: I can't believe you're leaving right now.

DONNY: So long, kid.

MAGGIE: Donny.

(They hug.)

DONNY: All right. *(He leaves.)*

MAGGIE: Bye.

(MAGGIE sits on the bed. She flicks on the TV, then shuts it off. She goes to the door and then back to the bed. She lays back and starts to fall asleep. After a moment, there is a knock at the door. She excitedly jumps up and runs to get it. It's MARK. He comes in carrying a six-pack.)

MARK: Hey.

MAGGIE: Hi.

MARK: I just wanted to apologize for...

MAGGIE: You didn't have to do that.

MARK: No, no. It's not how I usually do things.

MAGGIE: It's okay.

MARK: I'm pretty wasted and I shouldn't have... where's Donny?

MAGGIE: He left.

MARK: He left?

MAGGIE: Yeah.

MARK: Like left the island?

MAGGIE: Yup. He's gone.

MARK: What are you talking about?

MAGGIE: He changed his flight and he just left.

MARK: When?

MAGGIE: Just like ten minutes ago.

MARK: It's three in the morning.

MAGGIE: He's taking the red eye.

MARK: Red eye?! No, no. What's his cell? *(Pulls out his phone to call him.)*

MAGGIE: He doesn't have one.

MARK: He doesn't have a cell phone?

MAGGIE: He says they're a fad.

MARK: *(Laughs.)* Fucking Donny boy. I can't believe he's just gonna leave without saying anything. I mean, I hope it's not 'cause of what happened?

MAGGIE: I don't think it was.

(DONNY calls from beneath the balcony.)

DONNY: Maggie!

MAGGIE: Donny!

(She runs to the balcony and looks down. MARK follows her.)

DONNY: Maggie! I think I'm stuck. Can you give me a hand?

MAGGIE: What are you doing?

DONNY: What do you mean, "What am I doing"? I was trying to climb this thing, but there's nowhere to climb now and I can't see behind me to climb down.

MAGGIE: What do you want me to do?

DONNY: Can you reach down here and give me a hand?

MAGGIE: *(She tries.)* I can't reach.

DONNY: Do you have a long stick or something?

MAGGIE: A what?

DONNY: A stick!

(She turns to MARK.)

MAGGIE: Are there any sticks in the room?

MARK: What kind of sticks?

MAGGIE: I don't know.

DONNY: My grip is slipping!

MAGGIE: What kind of stick!?

DONNY: Who gives a shit! Throw me anything! A sheet!

(MAGGIE is panicking. MARK hands her the sheet off the bed, and she immediately throws the entire sheet over the railing.)

MAGGIE: Here, Donny! *(She realizes she was supposed to hang onto the other side of the sheet.)* Oh, shit!

DONNY: Great! Now I can't see.

(MARK goes over the balcony.)

DONNY: Help!!!!! Please help me!!!

MARK: Hang on there, buddy!

MAGGIE: Be careful!

(MARK pulls himself back over the railing and tumbles into the room with DONNY clinging to his back like a papoose. DONNY still has the sheet over his head. He quickly scrambles to his feet.)

MAGGIE: Are you okay?

DONNY: Yeah, I'm fine. Thank you.

MARK: What the hell were you doing over there?

DONNY: I was climbing.

MAGGIE: Why were you climbing the balcony?

MARK: Yeah.

DONNY: Huh? Can I just catch my breath here for a second?

MAGGIE: Yeah, yeah.

MARK: I'll get you some water. *(Exits to the bathroom.)*

DONNY: What's he doing here?

MAGGIE: Nothing. He just came over after you left.

DONNY: Am I interrupting something, or…

MAGGIE: No.

DONNY: Maybe I should just…

(DONNY starts back toward the balcony. MARK cuts him off with a glass of water.)

MARK: Here you go, pal.

DONNY: Thanks, man.

(DONNY slowly downs the entire glass. MARK and MAGGIE stare at him.)

MARK: Worked up a thirst out there, huh?

DONNY: Yeah.

(Awkward moment.)

DONNY: Well, here we all are.

MARK: Yeah.

DONNY: Yeah.

MAGGIE: So…

MARK: So what's up?

MAGGIE: Mark, I think maybe…

DONNY: Oh, there it is. *(Goes to the bedside table and picks up some lotion.)*

MAGGIE: What's that?

DONNY: It's that coconut lotion I loved so much. That's why I came back and I had already turned my key in and so I figured it would be easier to just hop over the balcony and grab it. But now I have it, so I can ahhhh… good seeing you guys again.

MARK: Come on, man. Don't leave. We got a great party on the boat later. Charlie's buddies from the Oilers are coming down.

DONNY: No, I'm a little partied out.

MARK: Look I'm sorry about before. I didn't mean to be a dick.

DONNY: You weren't a dick.

MAGGIE: Mark do you think Donny and I could have a little…

MARK: Oh, yeah, yeah. You don't have to hit me over the head.

MAGGIE: Thanks, I appreciate that.

MARK: Sure, take as much time as you need.

(MAGGIE thinks MARK is going to leave. Instead, he picks up the remote and sits on the bed to watch TV.)

MAGGIE: Oh. *(She turns to DONNY.)* What are you doing?

DONNY: What do you mean?

MAGGIE: Why did you come back?

DONNY: To get my lotion.

MAGGIE: Shut up.

DONNY: Look, Mag. I'm obviously intruding here.

MAGGIE: No, you're not. I told you nothing happened.

DONNY: I guess I had an impulse that maybe…

MAGGIE: What?

DONNY: I don't know. That maybe there was a chance that… I don't know.

MAGGIE: Donny, will you just tell me what's going on with you.

DONNY: I…

(MARK laughs loudly at the TV. They turn to him.)

MARK: Sorry.

DONNY: Maybe I'm just making it all up in my head, you know how I do that… but I'd be lying to you if I said I didn't think about you. I mean, not all the time, not like a stalker or something… I should go.

MAGGIE: Don't go.

DONNY: I feel really uncomfortable and…

MAGGIE: I want you to stay.

DONNY: No, you don't.

MAGGIE: Donny, will you listen to me?

MARK: *(Laughs again.)* Did you guys ever see this *Honeymooners* episode? It's a classic! You got to see this. *(Notices they are in an intense conversation.)* Oh my God. I'm being so rude. I'm sorry. *(He turns the TV off and gets up.)* I'm gonna leave you guys alone.

DONNY: That's all right. Because I have to go anyway.

MAGGIE: What?

MARK: I'm the one who has to go.

DONNY: No, man. Stay. I really have to…

MAGGIE: Don't fight about it.

MARK: This is ridiculous. I'm outta here. You guys stay and talk and you know… whatever you kids do these days… have a little breakfast, and I expect to see you both on the boat later. It's gonna rock. You haven't partied till you party with the Oilers. What do you say, Donny? Are we cool?

DONNY: Yeah, we're cool.

MARK: All right good. Later, kids.

MAGGIE: Bye.

MARK: Rock and roll.

(MARK exits. DONNY and MAGGIE look at each other.)

DONNY: So… umm…

MAGGIE: Yeah?

DONNY: H-how are you?

MAGGIE: I'm good, how are you?

DONNY: I'm good. I'm good. Pretty good.

MAGGIE: So…

DONNY: So that was quite a romantic entrance I made.

MAGGIE: It was cute.

DONNY: I had a rose in my teeth, but I dropped it when I was screaming for help.

MAGGIE: Yeah?

DONNY: Yup.

MAGGIE: Are you gonna kiss me right now or…

DONNY: Do you want me to or…

MAGGIE: Oh my God…

DONNY: Okay, okay, just don't put so much pressure on me.

MAGGIE: You don't have to.

DONNY: No, I want to. All right, here we go. *(He starts forward and then stops.)* I just hate that he got to be Bogey. 'Cause I'm always Bogey. And he got such a great exit line. "Rock and roll." I mean, I'm never this guy, I...

(She kisses him. A beautiful sweet kiss. Big band music comes up.)

(The End.)

ELEPHANT

Margie Stokley

MARGIE STOKLEY was born in Boston and grew up in various states before settling in New York City. She's a graduate of the New York University Tisch School of the Arts, and studied playwriting at NYU's School for Continuing Education with Christopher Shinn. In the theatre, she has worked mostly as an actor, appearing regionally at the McCarter Theater, Williamstown Theatre Festival, and Theatre Under the Stars; and in New York with Andhow! Theater Company, Playwrights Horizons, New Georges Theatre, Joint Stock Theatre Alliance, Musicals Tonight!, and the adobe theater company. She is currently writing a new play called "Wonder Dam" and continuing her career as an actress. When not performing or writing, Stokley freelances as an artist, painting murals, furniture, and rooms. *Elephant* is her first play.

Elephant was first presented by Andhow! Theater Company (Jessica Davis-Irons, Artistic Director; Andrew Irons, Producing Director) on August 24, 2004, at the Ontological Theater, New York City, with the following cast and credits:

Michelle/Tollbooth Gal .... Jessica Dickey
Ellen/Daisy .... Amy Brienes
Jay.. Arthur Aulisi
Henry .... Stan Lachow
Kathleen/Barbara .... Maria Cellario

Directed by: Jessica Davis-Irons
Scenic Design: Neal Wilkinson
Lighting Design: Joshua Briggs
Costume Design: Anastasia Williams
Sound Design: Jill BC DuBoff
Properties: Sarah Kranin
Assistant Director: Hannah Lilly
Stage Manager: Jim MacEachron
Assistant Stage Manager: Kate Farrington
Production Assistant: Sophia Haas
Sound Board Operator: Daniel Burson
Technical Director: Mark Constable
Master Carpenter: Anthony Cerratto
Associate Producer: Danya Haber

The author wishes to thank Jessica Davis-Irons for her unwavering enthusiasm and seamless direction, the cast for their heart and humor, and all of Andhow!'s loyal contributors for making this production possible. Thank you to Josh Briggs for granting us a space to grow, Andrew Irons for his insight, Fred Stokley for editing, and Norellen Stokley for... well, existing.

Thank you to the Andhow!'s usual suspects: Clayton Dowty, Owen Hughes, Brian PJ Cronin, Kristin Pratt, Danya Haber, and Michael Haber.

She would also like to thank Donna DeStefano, Norman Twain, and Dulcina Eisen and Associates for all their enthusiasm and creative support.

Prior to production there were many readings of *Elephant* at the Blue Heron Arts Center in New York City, so thank you to everyone whose voices and ideas helped develop the play: Erin Quinn Purcell, Nicole Ortho-Pallovacinni, Alan Coates, Jacqueline Knapp, Christy Meyer, and Tom Bloom; and a special thanks to Jessica Dickey and Arthur Aulisi for being in it for the long haul.

AUTHOR'S NOTE

The play captures the elemental moral expressed by the poet Philip Larkin: "The elephant in our room shows us we should be careful of each other, we should be kind while there is still time."

When someone dies, you miss hearing their name but also the trivial details about their day, their loves, their life. My brother Jonathan was killed at the young age of twenty-five. It is a great gift to hear someone say, "Jon would have loved that movie," or "Do you remember when Jon…" I wrote my first full-length play because I wanted to talk to my brother. I wanted everyone to talk about him. The play is fictional, but the family history was inspired by what I know. My Mom, Dad, and sister are why I get up in the morning. They are my constant source of amusement, emotion, and stories. Everyone grieves differently, but what we all share is the shock that follows after someone you love has been ripped from your everyday. This play starts six months after the family's tragedy, so what you witness is them rediscovering their relationships to one another by exposing what hurts with humor and heart.

I dedicate this play to my family—Fred, Norellen, Siobhan, Jonathan, and Fredrick—and to the families of Peter Dillehay, Douglas Caramagna, and Renee Berger.

CHARACTERS

MICHELLE: Seventeen years old, intelligent and direct.

ELLEN: Early twenties, an artist.

JAY: A U.S. Marine in his mid-twenties.

HENRY: Early sixties, Kathleen's husband.

BLAISE: A German shepherd, heard onstage but not seen.

KATHLEEN: Early fifties, Henry's wife.

TOLLBOOTH GAL: Played by actor who plays Michelle.

DAISY: Waitress on the road, played by actor who plays Ellen.

BARBARA: Dog breeder in Tucson, Arizona, played by actor who plays Kathleen.

FANG: Age seven, appears only in Prologue.

PLACE

MICHELLE is in a car traveling to Soundview Institute in Tarrytown, New York.

HENRY and JAY are together in a car driving cross-country.

ELLEN is in her art studio in New Jersey.

KATHLEEN is at her home in Montclair, New Jersey.

TIME

August 1998 with periodic flashbacks from the past year.

NOTE: Except for Kathleen and Fang, once the characters have entered the world of the play, they remain onstage in their respective worlds for the length of the show. Ellen's progress with her painting parallels the emotional landscape of the play, and her canvas should be visible to the audience at all times. The two cars and the art studio are the only permanent set pieces; to allow the scenes to flow seamlessly, all other locations should never be fully realized.

PROLOGUE

As the audience enters the theatre, with the house lights up, onstage we see a small child wearing a T-shirt inscribed FANG, dancing to "Burn" by Usher. She dances with abandon, all over the stage, as if it is her living room. It is possible that this could be done on a very large screen as a home movie, but a child performing live would be preferred. Blackout. In the blackout, we hear a dog barking ferociously.

GOODBYE

Lights up. MICHELLE begins speaking immediately. She is alone center facing the audience. JAY and HENRY are in their car stage left.

MICHELLE: I hate you. I hate you. I hope I never grow up to be like you. You have no idea what I am going through. It is all about you.

Mom don't do this to me. Don't. Don't make me go. Daddy? Don't.

What are you going to tell people? I don't know why I did it. I am just sad and I don't know how to…

Forget it. Fuck you. *(A pause.)* Shotgun.

(MICHELLE gets into the passenger's seat of another car stage right and returns there after every scene. ELLEN enters her studio and sits staring at her canvas.)

BLAISE

Lights up on HENRY, a man in his mid-sixties, who is driving with his German shepherd, BLAISE. JAY, a young man in his twenties, is in the passenger's seat. They are driving cross-country. JAY is not confined to the car. He moves freely around the stage. HENRY is unaffected by his movement and remains in his seat.

HENRY: I have to call my wife every few hours. She hates highways with their trucks and buses. I want to stop at the Grand Canyon. Then make my way down to Tucson. I think if we drive fourteen hours a day, we can get to Arizona on time. I don't know where you want to get off. I can't remember when I told Barbara I would be arriving. I think I said around four p.m. on Thursday. I have to fly back on Friday morning. Blaise likes you. I am surprised! Are you hungry? There should be snacks in the backseat. I'll take a Twizzler.

(We hear BLAISE's howl and whine. JAY begins to imitate and provoke him to continue.)

HENRY: I think if we keep him in the car, he'll be okay. I can't wait to tell Kathleen, Blaise likes you. I don't really want to be doing this... He's too kind to be a police dog and too ferocious to give away to another family. He only bit one person, but a police report was filed and you know... I don't know. I am going to miss him. Kathleen is convinced he'll bite anyone who crosses his path. So here we are. She'll be relieved that I have a copilot. In her heart she wanted to come with me, but she's impossible to drive with. I am used to it after all these years, but this is a long journey and she hates the road. There are too many eighteen-wheelers and buses. She just...

JAY: My wife gets spooked easily, too.

PROPOSAL

Flashback. ELLEN is in her studio, but blocked from JAY's sight by her canvas. She is screaming her lines to JAY, as if he is in another room. Both have been drinking, but JAY is not as obviously drunk.

ELLEN: Jay! Jay! Come on. I'm ready! Jay. God dammit...why do shirts have buttons? I HATE BUTTONS! Where are you? I told you I have something to show you... come here.

JAY: I'm here... it's blank? I thought you wanted to show me your work?

ELLEN: Who cares... *(She reveals herself to him and strikes a pose; most of her shirt is off.)* ...ME! I wanted to show you me! *(She throws her shirt to the ground.)* What do you think?

JAY: *(Amused.)* Oh boy.

ELLEN: *(Looking at her canvas.)* You're right. It's white. Weird. Why white? White why? White why, why white why...

(JAY gets down on one knee, then both knees, and then he puts one up. ELLEN is baffled by how he is positioning himself. He takes her hands. She goes to join him on her knees.)

JAY: No. Don't come down here... wait.

ELLEN: But... *(She almost falls as she tries to stand.)*

JAY: You stand. Okay. I am going to kneel.

ELLEN: You are kneeling, okay. I'll stand. Here we go.

JAY: I love you. You make me...

ELLEN: Ohhhh monkey!

JAY: Wait. You are really going to want to listen. *(A pause.)* I love you. You make me a better person, more alive, more thoughtful but most of all more interested...in everything! I laugh more, I feel more, and I definitely talk more. Hell, I write "Thank you" cards now because of being with you. I want to thank you for all the time you've shared with me and ask you to share every day that follows with me as well. Ellen, you are charming, strong, beautiful, and now half-naked... I need you in my life. Will you marry me?

ELLEN: Jay...you love me?

JAY: I love you. Will you marry me?

ELLEN: You've only known me for two weeks.

JAY: I know but… I feel… How do you feel?

ELLEN: *(In shock.)* I love you. I do. Oh my god! Holy shit!

(ELLEN begins to jump up and down and spin in ecstasy. After a moment, JAY begins jumping with her.)

JAY: Marry me?

ELLEN: *(Ecstatic.)* You've got to be kidding me… I can't believe it… I am in love! I didn't even realize it… and you…you just knew. Amazing!

(She pulls him close and kisses him.)

ELLEN: I love you. I love you. I love you.

JAY: Will you marry me?

ELLEN: I don't know… don't kill this moment. I am so excited that I feel it. Come here, my love.

(She caresses his face.)

ELLEN: My love, I like that.

(JAY returns to the car. ELLEN stays in her studio and begins to paint.)

FOREST

Soundview Institute, Tarrytown, New York. MICHELLE is in a group therapy session. She treats the audience as her group. She applies lipstick as she speaks. She speaks in a manner that is challenging, but with ease.

MICHELLE: Hi. My name is Michelle. *(She does a crazy gesture and noise that somehow mocks suicide.)* Just kidding. No, really—thrilled to be here. What do you want to know? What do you want me to say…

(Silence.)

MICHELLE: Oh wait, that's right. This is not a conversation—it's a session. This is my time to share, with *complete strangers*, how I feel… Well, I feel like talking about trees. How do you feel about them? Wait. Please, don't speak… let me. My fascination *stems* from this one tree. *(She silently mouths "stems" again to emphasize the irony.)* Rough crowd. *(A pause.)* Well, it's gigantic and right outside my bedroom window. Some nights I feel like it wants in. Wants in to my perfect pink-and-white-striped room. My room is perfect, not because it's everything I want. It's just perfectly planned, the pillows, the balloon shades, the pictures, the bed, the window seat, my stuffed animals. I have even more animals under my bed. I have guilt about suffocating them… I feel… it doesn't matter. They don't match. *(A pause.)* They really don't. Well, it can't fall now because I just predicted it. What you think is going to happen—never does. It's a relief. You can't know it all. I just feel like in *my movie* that's what will happen. There'll be a huge thunderstorm with lightning, my tree will explode, and I'll be crushed. I can see myself split in half. I don't want to be surrounded by all those people who would need to be there if I got crushed. I am over groups. No offense. *(MICHELLE returns to the car.)*

RIDE ON

JAY and HENRY are driving.

JAY: There's this spot in Arizona where the cacti begin to grow. The landscape is totally blank, and then after a curve the first one appears. It looks like a man saying hello or goodbye… depending on which way you're traveling. I can't remember the actual name… it's round and tall. Why do they grow in that one spot and not five feet from it?

HENRY: Mystical almost.

JAY: I want to pay the tolls or at least for the gas. I have money. I'm just hitchhiking because my Jeep broke down.

HENRY: No. Save your money. I like the company.

THE GIFT

A flashback. JAY, MICHELLE, and ELLEN are playing their own version of Balderdash and cracking up.

MICHELLE: What's the title? Tell me the title.

JAY: I will, chill out.

(MICHELLE looks over his shoulder.)

MICHELLE: The movie title is *The Gift*. Easy.

ELLEN: So, what do I do?

JAY: You have to make up a story.

MICHELLE: *(Rapid speed.)* No, you make up the premise. You create the film's synopsis. Then he'll read the real one alongside the fake ones. Then we all guess which one we think is the real one. We get points if you guess ours but since Jay knows the real one, he'll have to try to make us believe that the real one is fake.

ELLEN: Okay. How long do we have?

MICHELLE: It's not an essay.

JAY: Easy killer.

MICHELLE: *(To ELLEN.)* It's a sentence.

JAY: Take as long as you need. Okay, are we all clear?

MICHELLE: I am.

ELLEN: Yes.

(JAY passes out paper. They write.)

JAY: Ellen, are you ready?

MICHELLE: Do you understand?

ELLEN: I just have to get the phrasing right.

MICHELLE: I don't mind explaining it again.

(MICHELLE tries to wait patiently but can't take the silence.)

MICHELLE: Don't worry, it's hard playing with only three people.

JAY: Hey, I'll write a fake one too. Then whoever reads them aloud can get double points. We'll rotate.

ELLEN: I have no idea what you are talking about, but just keep going and I'll catch up.

(She hands JAY her paper.)

ELLEN: Now do I read this?

JAY and MICHELLE: No!

JAY: *(Simultaneous with MICHELLE.)* I do.

MICHELLE: *(Simultaneous with JAY.)* No! Jay does because he already knows the true pitch line.

ELLEN: Okay. Just take it. Mine is so obviously mine.

MICHELLE: Now he will read them all in the same tone and announce the title before each one.

JAY: Why, thank you, Michelle, here we go! *The Gift*—A coming-of-age story about a young man and his dog as they journey through the Sahara. *The Gift*— An old-fashioned drama about the cruel sinking of what was called a... Come on, who wrote this one?

MICHELLE: Shut up. You're not allowed to talk while you read. You'll give it away. Start over.

JAY: I don't have to start over.

(ELLEN touches JAY.)

JAY: Okay, I'll start over. *(He reads them again very fast.) The Gift*—A coming-of-age story about a young man and his dog as they journey through the Sahara. *The Gift*—An old-fashioned drama about the cruel sinking of what was called an un-sinkable ship. *(He slows down.) The Gift*— A fifty-five-year-old bank worker decides to take an early retirement after a night with an expensive hooker. *The Gift*—A documentary short about a man with... *(He breaks into hysterical laughter and can't complete the sentence.)* A documentary short about... I can't.

MICHELLE: Come on finish it. Finish the sentence. JAY!

ELLEN: What is it? I want to know.

(ELLEN grabs it from him.)

ELLEN: Oh my god... *(To MICHELLE.)* is this yours? *(To JAY.)* You know I didn't write that. *(ELLEN tries to read it out loud and can't stop laughing.)*

MICHELLE: You guys don't know how to play. Forget it.

JAY: Michelle, come on, I didn't want to laugh. I'll read it. *The Gift*—A documentary short about a man with two...

(He starts to laugh again. MICHELLE grabs it.)

MICHELLE: *The Gift*—A documentary short about a man with two penises. *(She is unamused.)* I didn't write that.

JAY: I know. I did.

MICHELLE: Then why are you laughing?

JAY: I don't know. It just hit me as funny. You be quiet. You didn't take this round seriously either, you wrote the synopsis of *Titanic*.

ELLEN: *(Still laughing.)* No. She didn't. I did. I thought it would be funny. Sorry.

MICHELLE: Do you guys even want to play?

(ELLEN and JAY cuddle and kiss.)

MICHELLE: It's lucky you have one another because no one else thinks it's funny.

ELLEN: Okay. Let's play for real. Jay and I will be good.

JAY: Sorry, Lil'shit, let's do a word now, not a movie. Movies are hard to bluff.

MICHELLE: Ellen, which one did you think was the real premise, the banker or the boy going through the Sahara?

(JAY tries to indicate to her which one was MICHELLE's.)

ELLEN: The banker, I mean the boy and his dog.

MICHELLE: See, I am good. That was mine.

JAY: Okay—you get a point. Now let's do a word. Michelle, you be the reader. Pick a word from the dictionary.

MICHELLE: I don't need a dictionary. The word is pyrosis. P-Y-R-O-S-I-S.

(She hands out paper, and they all begin writing.)

MICHELLE: Okay—here we go.

JAY: I am done.

ELLEN: So am I.

MICHELLE: Pyrosis—A skin disease usually caused by old age. Pyrosis—Heart-burn. Pyrosis—An affliction that is usually caused by indigestion. Pyrosis—To ig-nite one's sister. *(She doesn't laugh.)*

ELLEN: What did you just say?

MICHELLE: *(To JAY.)* That was mean. Merry Christmas!

JAY: I was kidding. I knew the word. It means heartburn. Michelle, have a sense of humor.

ELLEN: Come on. Stay. He'll stop. Jay.

(MICHELLE exits and goes back to the car.)

ELLEN: "Pyrosis—To ignite one's sister?" Nice—well, that was fun. Now your family loves me and hates you.

(They kiss and then return to their respective worlds.)

BITE

KATHLEEN enters using very grandiose hand gestures and, despite the subject matter, is very upbeat.

KATHLEEN: "Nein! Nein! Nein!," we were screaming, but the puppy was having none of it. He was trained in German. I thought of every phrase possible to get him to stop—to no avail. He only bit Kyle once. Then his tail fell between his legs and he ran back into the garage. German shepherds are known for being able to anticipate. That's why they're working dogs. They herd sheep. Lead the blind. We should've given him a job, but now it's too late. The damage was done, but it could have been worse. His teeth are filed sharper than most knives. He was bred in Arizona, and all they have there is volcanic rock. He carries this one rock in his mouth wherever he goes. It wasn't his fault. Kyle is my nephew, He is only ten. He himself was an accident. My sister didn't mean to have another. Kyle is ten years younger than her eldest son. I am telling you this because he requires a lot of attention. I make up all these activities for him. Give him little rewards. Try to keep him active. I bet the sugar was to blame. It

made him become raucous. It was the Fourth of July... our first family function since the funeral. All of us were trying to put on a happy face. *(Abrupt shift.)* When can I speak to Michelle? Well, I'd like to speak to my daughter. No. Mr.... I'm sorry, I forgot your name. Well, Tad, I know you are her counselor but I am her mother. I taught her how to speak and have been speaking with her every day... Fine. Explain your verbal deprivation method to me again! One more time. *(A pause.)* Tad, I have lost two sons... losing Michelle over the last few months is killing me. I am not trying to be difficult. I am trying to be a mother. *(A pause.)* Henry and I were distracted with cooking and entertaining our guests. It's hard to babysit when you're hosting. All the adults were gathered on the porch, and I guess Kyle, being out of our sight, took to jabbing Blaise with a stick through the gate. I believe Kyle liked hearing him bark. He talks. He makes these noises. *(KATHLEEN demonstrates BLAISE howl.)* I don't know why Michelle opened the door and let Blaise out. My sister called the cops and the rest you know. The weeks that followed were miserable. As if life wasn't already rough enough, now my own daughter won't look me in the eye or talk to me in complete sentences. She shut down... I feared she would... she may have even tried. *(A pause.)* She was screaming "Nein," too. If that makes a difference. She let Blaise out, but she was devastated when she saw what was happening. We were all screaming, "Nein, Nein, Sitz, Nein, Sitz!"

BLAISE TOO

HENRY and JAY are in the car, stopped at a tollbooth.

TOLLBOOTH GAL: Well, that's a beautiful dog!

(We hear ferocious barking.)

JAY: Oh my god!

HENRY: Nein! Nein! It'll be fine. *(To TOLLBOOTH GAL.)* Nein. Sorry about that, he's very protective. Have a nice night.

JAY: Holy shit. That was insane. I've never seen anything like that.

HENRY: He's very protective of his family.

JAY: I guess so. Cool.

HENRY: He's just a pup. He has a loud bark but he does it out of fear.

JAY: That lady was so freaked. "Beautiful dog" is right! That was amazing! Now look at him, tongue hanging out. Totally calm.

HENRY: Are you stationed in Arizona? I noticed your bag.

JAY: No. I used to be. Now I live in Jersey with my wife. I am going to Arizona to finish getting my pilot's license. When you start something like that somewhere, you want to finish it there. You can drop me off in Prescott. We'll pass it on our way to Tucson, I think. It doesn't matter. Anywhere in Arizona is close enough.

HENRY: So, are you Army or Marine?

JAY: Marine, of course.

HENRY: "Semper Fi." My son was a Marine. He always said there was a big distinction, but I was never in the military... so...

JAY: Army means—Aren't Ready for Marines Yet.

HENRY: Spoken like a true Marine. Were you at Parris Island?

JAY: Yes sir.

HENRY: I took the tour. What a challenge.

JAY: We couldn't call out, but we got letters. My mother wrote every day.

HENRY: My wife sent my son with a stack of envelopes already stamped and self-addressed to her.

JAY: What's his rank?

HENRY: He was a lance corporal.

FRIENDLY VOICE

HENRY's cell phone rings. KATHLEEN enters. She is talking on her cordless phone.

HENRY: Hello.

KATHLEEN: It's me.

HENRY: I know. Hi, honey.

KATHLEEN: I spoke to Michelle's therapist. *(A beat.)* Hi. He was awfully quiet. He said I was only allowed to speak to Michelle if he was listening in. But she got my letter. Can they do that? I know we brought her to them, but she is still my daughter... Henry, are you there?

HENRY: *(To JAY.)* It'll just be a minute. On second thought, I don't think I should tell her about you. She won't respond well to me picking up a hitchhiker. *(Into the phone.)* I'm sorry, honey, I'm driving so I can't really talk.

KATHLEEN: Okay... but you can listen. So, I went to the dentist again. Today. All by myself. Of course, I couldn't stop crying. It was so embarrassing. It wasn't about my fear of the dentist anymore, but I couldn't explain to him that I was crying because Michelle wasn't there to hold my hand. They just thought I was being childish...

HENRY: I am sure they didn't think that.

KATHLEEN: Well, they gave me a teddy bear to hold... seems pretty childish to me.

HENRY: What did you do?

KATHLEEN: I took it. They wanted to call you... but I told them you were out of the country.

HENRY: Why did you tell them that?

KATHLEEN: Well, it feels like you are. I don't know. You can't tell me what to say now. I've been humiliated enough today.

HENRY: Humiliated? Come on, honey.

KATHLEEN: Well, I'm sure you have no idea what that feels like... *(A pause.)* I didn't want you to know. That's why they didn't call you.

HENRY: Well, I couldn't do anything from the road.

KATHLEEN: I know that. That's why I told them you were busy.

HENRY: Busy... out of the country?

KATHLEEN: Henry, stop it! Be nice. You know I had a hard day. How are you doing?

HENRY: We are doing well...making great time.

KATHLEEN: Are you still coming back on Friday? Are you lonely? Are you sleeping?

HENRY: I sleep. *(A pause.)* Did you say you spoke with Michelle?

KATHLEEN: He wouldn't let me.

HENRY: We'll see her on Friday.

KATHLEEN: I know. Look... call me when you stop. I don't want to distract you while you drive.

HENRY: Alright. I'm proud of you.

KATHLEEN: I know. Thank you.

(KATHLEEN exits.)

MASCARA

Flashback. MICHELLE gets in the driver's seat.

MICHELLE: Get in.

(ELLEN sits in the passenger's seat. MICHELLE does a silent scream. ELLEN is in freeze frame.)

ELLEN: Are you sure you can drive?

MICHELLE: I am sure you can't. You're pregnant.

ELLEN: Only two months... I can still drive. You didn't answer my question.

MICHELLE: Yes. I can drive. *(Goes to put on the radio.)*

ELLEN: Hey, no radio. Focus... in silence.

MICHELLE: It was your idea. You be silent. I need to fill my head with something besides chitter chatter. If one more person says: You're in our prayers, he's in a better place, or take care of your parents, I AM GOING TO DIE!

ELLEN: Michelle. It's a wake.

MICHELLE: *(Snaps.)* I know. Sorry. We don't have to listen to anything. Ignore me.

(Silence.)

MICHELLE: Where are we going? What did you tell them we were doing?

ELLEN: I said I needed to go to the drug store...for mascara.

MICHELLE: Mascara? You're kidding, right?

ELLEN: No. That's what I said.

MICHELLE: Why the hell do you need mascara? *(A pause.)* Ellen.

ELLEN: I couldn't think. It just came out. I don't know. This morning your mom and I were putting on makeup and crying, so I suggested we get waterproof mascara… it just stayed with me.

MICHELLE: Well, we need to pull out of the driveway.

ELLEN: Well, then pull out. I don't care where we go. Just go. Go anywhere.

MICHELLE: Should we go get mascara?

(Silence. MICHELLE begins to sniff her shirt and then her armpit.)

MICHELLE: I smell. I thought it was everyone else, but now I know… it's clearly me. I could use some deodorant. We should go to the drug store.

(They both are unamused and silent.)

MICHELLE: I know… we can go to the duck pond. It's around the corner.

(They pull out of the driveway. ELLEN turns on the radio. It's in the middle of the country song "I Never Promised You a Rose Garden." They listen for as long as dramatically possible. The music shifts from the GIRLS' car to JAY and HENRY's car.)

HOME

HENRY and JAY driving. "I Never Promised You a Rose Garden" continues playing in their car.

HENRY: So, what does your wife do?

JAY: She paints. She's an artist.

HENRY: Mine too. Well, she was before we had kids. I'd like her to paint more but time keeps us busy.

JAY: She can't paint in front of me. She does it whenever I leave. She says I always…

JAY and HENRY: …want to know what it is.

HENRY: Funny.

JAY: I just want to know what she's thinking. She says she's not… that's the trick.

HENRY: Women go on impulse. Men chart. It took me a month to plan this trip. Kathleen wanted me to leave the day Blaise bit our nephew.

JAY: Is he all right?

HENRY: Kyle, oh he's fine. Blaise barely broke the skin. But the act sent shock waves through our neighborhood. It's a shame. We had to put him in a kennel. My daughter started crying and didn't speak to me for days. It's all such a shame. *(HENRY turns off the radio.)*

JAY: How long have you had him?

HENRY: We got him after…my son trained him in German to be a guard dog. He wanted to make sure no one could make him attack in English. I thought it was a good idea at the time.

JAY: He must be very…

HENRY: He's dead… my son. He died… was killed in a car accident. Six months ago. Blaise hasn't been himself since. I took him in, hoping we could help him adapt, make him feel at home without…

JAY: There's no way to tell a dog… that his…

HENRY: You're right. He doesn't know what happened or what's happening… I wish this wasn't happening.

JAY: I'm sure. He's a beautiful dog.

GAME OVER

MICHELLE is in another group therapy session.

MICHELLE: He died twenty minutes from our house… don't bother leaning in, Tad, that's about all you're gonna get. Stay tuned. I know this girl… Danielle… her best friend Cheryl was killed last year. They weren't family. They chose to spend the years together, and that's cool. I didn't know Cheryl well. We weren't really friendly. She sat in front of me in Social Studies. But after she died, Danielle looked different. I looked at her differently… everyone did. Kinda like the way you are all looking at me now. You feel sorry for me. You can't help it. I get it. But when Danielle came to my brother's wake—I was excited—for real excited! Excited that finally there was someone in the fucking room who had been broken too. And it gave me hope. *(Exaggerated.)* HOPE. Hope that someday I'll walk into a room and the sign on my forehead reading lost, broken, and angry will be gone. The good news is he can't die twice. Once you're dead… you're dead! Game over. You go to rest knowing you'll never be sad again. You'll never be told "no." You'll never have someone you know die. You'll never be sent to an institution and forced to take someone named Tad seriously. Sounds like heaven to me. Sign me up! Now let's recap—My brother's dead. My family can't start over. I'm here. My life sucks. Next.

(MICHELLE returns to the car.)

ELEPHANT

Flashback. ELLEN is painting and singing to music. The elephant she has been painting is full figured, and she is taking her time detailing it. JAY startles her when he enters.

JAY: Well…

(ELLEN screams.)

JAY: I am going. Sorry to interrupt you and your zoo. I just checked on the puppy. He seems restful. Be aware he's here.

ELLEN: I know. I am.

JAY: I didn't mean it like you wouldn't… you know what I meant. I have to be at the base by Friday 0600. *(A pause.)* Six a.m.

ELLEN: I know. Why are you leaving tonight?

JAY: The weather might act up. I should get an early start.

(JAY exits. JAY re-enters. She screams.)

ELLEN: You have got to be kidding me. What? I know. Go.

JAY: Do you want me to stay? I thought you painted better when I was out?

ELLEN: My work is not about you being out. I have my supplies and music.

(He smiles.)

ELLEN: I am not talking about when I sing.

JAY: Would you rather I leave in the morning?

ELLEN: Wouldn't you rather leave tonight?

JAY: Ellen.

ELLEN: Jay.

JAY: Ellen…

ELLEN: Go.

JAY: I love you. Please smile. *(A pause.)* I'm gonna go. *(He leaves.)*

ELLEN: Bye. *(To herself.)* Bye.

(He calls to ELLEN from outside the room, but is still visible to the audience.)

JAY: Ellen. I'm not going.

ELLEN: Yes, you are! Come in here.

JAY: You hate me.

(Long silence.)

JAY: You hate me?

ELLEN: You're a romantic.

JAY: You hate me because I'm a romantic?

ELLEN: No. Yes! You buy me CDs, get me flowers, and a dog. A dog you now doubt I will remember? Even though he is living and breathing in the same house with me?

JAY: I didn't mean it like that.

ELLEN: Jay. You said, "Be aware he is here." *(A pause.)* You said…

JAY: I know.

ELLEN: I am carrying… you can't even trust me with a dog. How can you trust with a child? *(A pause.)* Jay, Look at me… I'm a mom. Do you see a mom?! Because I am not like your mom. She is a mom! I am fat, emotional, selfish, and, for the past few weeks, mean. I can't smile. It's really hard for me to smile. I thought love would fuel me… not suck me dry. I am perpetually in shock. Ever since—you entered my studio… you… you! Soft, sweet, smiling you… and every time you leave… I think, good! Go! I could use some time alone. But then you go… and you are just gone and I wish you were here.

(He hugs her.)

ELLEN: I'm pregnant and we live in Jersey.

JAY: I know.

ELLEN: I was nicer when we lived in Arizona.

JAY: No. No, you weren't.

ELLEN: Jay, stop it. Don't make me laugh. Nothing is funny.

JAY: Okay. *(JAY begins jumping up and down.)* Marry me.

ELLEN: I'm pregnant and we aren't even married… don't say it… I know what you are gonna say…

JAY: …you wanted to wait.

ELLEN: Well, congrats! You win. I lose. I'd only known you for two weeks… two weeks! I didn't want to ruin it.

JAY: Let's ruin it and get married now. Marry me.

ELLEN: No. *(A beat.)* Of course. I'm having a child and my life is over… over! We met and you have been great ever since. You are great! Your whole family is great. I am not great. I don't know what I am. I suck.

JAY: I suck.

ELLEN: No. I suck.

JAY: No. I suck.

ELLEN: Stop it, Jay. *(A pause.)* I suck.

JAY: No, honey, I really suck.

ELLEN: Okay. Game over. I love you. I know nothing.

JAY: I know.

ELLEN: You're fired. Now go. You can go.

(JAY pulls ELLEN close.)

ELLEN: If you are worried about the weather, you…

(JAY kisses her and then hands her a brush. She takes it and goes back to work.)

JAY: I'll take my chances.

ELLEN: Good.

(ELLEN continues painting. JAY returns to the car.)

ROCKY ROAD

JAY and HENRY are still driving.

JAY: How long have you been married?

HENRY: Twenty-seven years.

JAY: Wow. Do you ever get annoyed with your wife? I don't mean I do. I just think I annoy her.

HENRY: *(Amused.)* I don't think about it that way. She is just my Kathleen.

JAY: How did you know?

HENRY: Know what?

JAY: Know she was your Kathleen.

HENRY: It hit me when I picked her up. She was walking to work. She was a hitch-hiker too. Well, not really, she was just walking from the bus stop. She and I worked in the same building. She recognized me when I pulled up, so she got in. I liked the way she walked. Women have that way, or she does, of whooshing from side to side. She still walks like that. She was beautiful. Younger than me by a few years and very innocent. But none of that's why I married her. She was chatting away in the car and all of a sudden this feeling rushed over me. It wasn't about her looks or what she said, it was how she made me feel. I wanted to keep feeling it. So, I asked her to marry me.

JAY: How?

HENRY: I said, "I love you. Will you marry me?"

JAY: What did she say?

HENRY: She said, "Yes."

JAY: Well, my wife says she saw me first. I like that she believes that but I asked her out first... or I tried to. She said, no... she didn't mean to. I misunderstood her

response and left. She was too flustered to speak up. So I just watched her from afar for a few months. Then the week before I graduated, she came up and asked me out for coffee... so we went and got tea.

(Silence. They drive for a bit.)

HENRY: Do you have any sisters? They usually help.

JAY: Yeah, one. She's younger and a little intense. She's vegan.

THE POOL

Flashback. MICHELLE and JAY are poolside at a resort.

MICHELLE: I'm gonna go. What are you doing?

JAY: Where are you going?

MICHELLE: Mom and Dad are out... so Jib is alone. I'm gonna go back to the condo. Do you wanna stay?

JAY: Let him sleep.

MICHELLE: I don't want to leave him alone for too long. I wish they'd allow dogs by the pool.

JAY: We should bring him anyway.

MICHELLE: Yeah, I'll go get him and say, "Excuse me, I don't care about your rules, my dog is dying. In fact, he could be dead right now." Oh wait... that wouldn't work. They wouldn't want the responsibility. *(A pause.)* Do you want me to stay?

JAY: Why? We could sue if he dies here.

MICHELLE: Are you hungry? I could go see Jib and get some food for us. Should I go? Are you gonna stay?

JAY: How's the water? Is it heated? I hate when pools are heated. We should have gone to the shore. Dogs are allowed on the beach.

MICHELLE: But they have a spa here.

JAY: Yeah, but so… what does Jib get… no air… and stairs! Our condo is three stories?! He's almost blind and now he has to walk up stairs!

MICHELLE: I know. It's awful. *(A pause.)* He wasn't blind yesterday. Can I have a smoke?

JAY: I thought you said Mom and Dad are coming back?

MICHELLE: They are but… so? I can see the parking lot. I don't care… they know. How can they not know? I can't believe you started smoking.

(JAY defensively overlaps MICHELLE's lines as she accuses him.)

MICHELLE: Does Ellen know you smoke?

JAY: I don't really smoke.

MICHELLE: So, she doesn't know.

JAY: I don't smoke.

(He hands her a smoke. MICHELLE holds it, but doesn't light it.)

JAY: I can quit. When I was at Parris Island… that's when I started. You buy cigarettes to trade with… I need them when I play poker and shit.

MICHELLE: You had money at boot camp?

JAY: They pay us, you know? Marines get paid.

MICHELLE: I knew that. I mean, I guess I knew that. You should quit. Hell, our dog is dying of cancer… we should both quit… for Jib!

JAY: Maybe he died from your second-hand smoke. *(A pause.)* You smoke when you walk him. Maybe you killed him.

MICHELLE: Shut up. He's not dead… so don't say that. Are you going with them tomorrow? I can't.

JAY: I can't. No way. I'd shoot the doctor for killing my dog.

MICHELLE: Have you ever shot any-one… you know… as a Marine?

JAY: Yeah, totally, I killed a private in my platoon for… No, what, are you retarded? We haven't been sent out. I don't know… I don't know if I could. If they make me a sniper, I'll have to.

(MICHELLE pulls out her journal.)

JAY: What are you doing? Writing about me killing a fellow Marine?

MICHELLE: No, it's a poem…do you want to hear it?

(He nods.)

MICHELLE: It's about Jib. "A dog is a dream made of love you can hold.
My family's first loss, first illness, first death.
Little is left and even less to show.
Oh please, I can't let Jib go!
He is so simple and true. He won't let him-self die.
I won't make him stay. I can't hear him cry."
(She looks to JAY for approval.)

MICHELLE: I know it's cheesy. I just wrote it fast. It's true though… it's cheesy, I guess.

JAY: It's okay.

MICHELLE: Thanks.

(The sound of a car pulling into the parking lot is heard. MICHELLE panics and shoves

the unlit cigarette into her pocket. They both realize it's not their PARENTS. JAY laughs at MICHELLE's paranoia.)

JAY: Are you gonna smoke that?

MICHELLE: No. *(She smiles.)* So, where's your lady?

JAY: She's at her parents'. *(A pause.)* You want to know a secret?

MICHELLE: *(Ecstatic.)* Yes! *(Coolly.)* I mean, yeah.

JAY: I got her a gift.

MICHELLE: Oh my god… I fucking knew it. I knew it. You are too young. You can't marry her. I like her but, jesus, Jay… Mom is going to flip. Does she even like me? That should matter… if I am going to spend the rest of my life in a family with her… if she's going to be my sister, she needs to like me. I matter.

JAY: You are insane and even knowing that she likes you. But we are not getting married… not yet. That's not the surprise. I already asked her but she put me on hold… so who knows.

MICHELLE: On hold? What is that supposed to mean?

JAY: Michelle, don't worry about it. She loves me, she just…

MICHELLE: …is smarter than you. You've only been together…

JAY: Dad proposed to Mom after one date.

MICHELLE: So, that was totally different… they were older. Weren't they? Plus, Dad is older than Mom by a… like a… a lot!

JAY: Michelle, I love Ellen. I am going to marry her. I am going to get old with her… that's not my secret. What I was trying to tell you is I got her a puppy.

MICHELLE: A what?

JAY: A German shepherd puppy.

MICHELLE: *(She is ecstatic.)* A puppy? Oh my god! A puppy! I am so jealous. Can I borrow him… what are you going to name him?

JAY: Blaise.

MICHELLE: Blaise? Blaise. Okay. *(Gushing at the idea.)* Blaise!

(They separate and return to their cars.)

FANG

JAY and HENRY on the road.

JAY: That's such a great name. Blaise. I always tease my wife and say I am going to name our kids Cougar, Sergeant, Wolf, and Fang. However, if we have girls… well, that would be unfortunate for them. She doesn't get my sense of humor. She used to, but we've had some obstacles over the past few months… she's pregnant. I feel bad that I left… but I think she needed a break.

HENRY: Did you need a break?

JAY: I had already planned this trip… I love her. I love that we're having a baby but she doesn't like surprises.

HENRY: Well, my wife doesn't like kidding.

JAY: What does that mean?

HENRY: People do it all the time. They sort of insult or tease you and follow it by saying "Just kidding." She believes if you say it, you mean it.

JAY: Whoa.

HENRY: I know.

JAY: She's right.

HENRY: I know.

JAY: That's true. *(He laughs.)* She's right.

HENRY: Don't tell her I said this but…
she's always right… women's intuition, I
think.

TIME

*Soundview Institute, Tarrytown, New York.
MICHELLE is in another group therapy session. She is holding a letter.*

MICHELLE: *(She waves the letter.)* I am
not going to read this… I was doing well
without her. *(She opens the letter and stares
at it.)* Fine. "Dear Michelle. The life span
of a butterfly is two weeks after it cocoons.
We lost our first son, Henry, at six weeks.
We were newlyweds, and I was just in the
other room when he stopped breathing.
We had been married only a year. Your
father… just kept trying to breathe… into
him. The police arrived first. We got in
the back seat and Henry kept trying to
put breath… into him. We were so helpless. I felt pain drowning the house, the
last year, his face, even the trees." *(A pause.)*
I don't understand why you are making
me read this in group? *(Long pause.)* Whatever, I don't care. I already know the story.
It's not about me. *(She begins to read the
letter.)* "We were so helpless. I felt pain
drowning the house, the last year, his face,
even the trees. Everything went into watercolor. I couldn't make out the faces or
voices of family and friends. I was beneath
it all, washing myself of the half-hour. The
half-hour I left him to nap in the nursery.
The nursery we painted like a magical forest. I left it to chat, to vacuum, to cook, to
plant, to answer the phone… I don't know
where I went. I was out of his room and
then his life in a half-hour. He was gone.
I have loved your father for twenty-seven
years, but I can't even remember how we

found one another after that day but we
drifted together. I don't mean we held on,
but we rode the water side by side to having two other beautiful children. You are
what carried us. Jay gave us activity. You
gave us heart. You are why I got up for
fifty-three years. You are why I said yes to
marrying a man I barely knew on our first
date. Right now, you are too young to have
faith. Faith that someday, all those lonely
days will be building blocks for a few great
ones. You can hate me. I don't care. I hate
myself for so many things but I don't feel
sorry for you. I am not mad at you. I am
glad you are confused. Once you find your
way through this, it will be yours. Your
fight, your memory, your life. Today may
feel like just another stupid day, but for
me it is a triumph. My funny, sweet, and
courageous daughter is here, breathing,
wearing too much makeup, looking me
in the eye. You may be wishing I were
dead, and one day I will be, but not today. Today is about you. What do you
want to do?"

*(MICHELLE is standing motionless hold-
ing the letter. She is silent for a few moments.)*

MICHELLE: I miss… I miss my brother…

*(MICHELLE goes back to the passenger's
seat of her car stage right.)*

DAISY

*HENRY and JAY are stopped at a drive-
thru window. DAISY is an aggressive waitress who talks in a very loud Southern accent, and who happens to be seven months'
pregnant.*

JAY: I'm sorry. I ordered a chicken sandwich, not a burger. She's not listening.

DAISY: Can I help you?

HENRY: Yes. He ordered a chicken filet,
not a hamburger.

DAISY: I just order what I hear. *(To HENRY.)* Sir, would you like cream for your coffee?

HENRY: No. Thank you.

DAISY: Here you go. *(A pause.)* Can I get you anything else?

JAY: I'm sorry...

HENRY: Yes.

JAY: I ordered a chicken cutlet and you gave me a burger, I think.

DAISY: What would you like?

JAY: Well. I'd like a chicken sandwich.

HENRY: A chicken sandwich.

DAISY: Would you like that with cheese?

JAY: Yes.

HENRY: Thank you.

DAISY: How would you like that cooked?

JAY: What do you mean? It's chicken. I am ordering the chicken sandwich, not the...

HENRY: I think she's teasing you.

DAISY: Spicy or traditional?

HENRY: It doesn't matter.

DAISY: I think it might. Spicy or traditional?

JAY: *(Defeated.)* Traditional.

HENRY: Traditional will work.

DAISY: That'll be two-fify.

HENRY: Right-o.

DAISY: What?

JAY: In addition. Forget it.

HENRY: Forget it. We're really very happy with the burger. Thank you.

(They drive off.)

JAY: My god! Am I crazy or was her voice ear piercing?

HENRY: She was having a hard night.

JAY: No kidding. So was I.

HENRY: Did you get what you wanted?

JAY: I think so. Why was she talking so loud? I was so in shock I actually forgot what I ordered. I am not even hungry now.

HENRY: You meet a lot of interesting people on the road.

JAY: I've noticed. *(A pause.)* I'm not used to being in the passenger's seat. The last time I was driven around... I was a kid. Every Sunday my mother would suggest we take a drive. She would preface it by saying there was this restaurant she read about, that we should go and check it out. Food was always the reward for our endless travel. I just wished the radio could have been my reward.

HENRY: Do you want me to turn the radio on?

JAY: No, it wasn't a hint. *(A pause.)* My favorite trips were to the City. My sister and Mom would go shopping. Dad and I would go to the *Intrepid*. Then we'd all meet up in the Village for Mexican food. It was a reward to have Mexican because in Jersey, well, there is none... anywhere. It's odd. My sister was obsessed with fried ice cream. I like that other dessert...

(He struggles for a moment to remember, and then turns to HENRY.)

HENRY: Flan?

JAY: Flan! Yeah, I love flan. *(A pause.)* I remember this one day... I can't believe I did this... I was young... never mind.

(ELLEN re-enters and begins to cover her painting with white paint. She is seven months' pregnant.)

HENRY: I won't tell on you. I was young once too.

JAY: No, I know. But I've kept it to myself for so long… I forgot I did it. If I say it out loud, it'll become real.

HENRY: I am intrigued.

JAY: I got lost.

HENRY: Oh well… I know how hard that can be for a man to admit.

JAY: No, that's not why it's hard to admit. I lost myself. I let them keep walking. I started walking slower. I wanted to see if they'd noticed. I can't believe I did this… I was looking in a window of a store… a liquor store. I saw their reflection crossing the street… and I let them go… without me. My Dad grabbed my Mom's arm, and she immediately panicked and started screaming my name. I stood still. Frozen. I had begun something I didn't know how to get out of… I froze… and then hid in the liquor store. I fucking hid and watched them through the glass. I saw my Dad pass the store and I started to cry. I was being erased. I was scared to walk out and have them see me… what would be my excuse? But my exit was prompted by a store clerk who knew I was too young to buy anything. As I crossed the street, I screamed, "Mom!" I just kept yelling "Mom. Mom! Mom!" It was now their fault. They had disappeared… and let me go. How could they. I was pissed. Crazy, right? My folks felt bad but my sister… my sister knew I was lying. I hated her that day for seeing through me… but today I hate myself for disappearing.

(Silence.)

HENRY: I am gonna pull off at the next exit.

MOMMY TOO

KATHLEEN enters ELLEN's studio. ELLEN is still in the process of painting over the elephant.

KATHLEEN: I'm sorry. I know, I'm early.

ELLEN: No. It's okay.

KATHLEEN: Are you okay?

ELLEN: Yes. I'm fine. How are you?

KATHLEEN: Good.

ELLEN: Good. *(A pause.)* How's Henry?

KATHLEEN: Oh, he's doing fine… making good time. To my surprise, the puppy hasn't bit anyone.

ELLEN: If I had kept Blaise here, he never would have…

KATHLEEN: He was a lot to handle… even for three of us. Ellen, we don't have to do this… be cordial… ever again. I'm not good and look at you… you are seven months' pregnant, you obviously can't paint, and your husband's dead.

(ELLEN continues covering the painting in white all throughout the following dialogue.)

ELLEN: *(Softly.)* He wasn't my husband.

KATHLEEN: Yes, he was.

ELLEN: No. He wasn't. We acted like we were married, but we never got to have the shotgun wedding of our dreams.

KATHLEEN: I thought you didn't want one?

ELLEN: I am being sarcastic.

KATHLEEN: I thought you were waiting so the baby could be there?

ELLEN: I wanted the baby to think we had a choice. We were waiting for me. *(A pause.)* It's true. Now look at us. Alone. No choice.

KATHLEEN: You have a choice.

ELLEN: Then I choose Jay.

KATHLEEN: Ellen, what's going on?

ELLEN: I don't want to go to the doctor with you. I don't want to name my baby Fang but I am going to. I don't want to be here. I want to get drunk. I want my boyfriend to ask me to marry him, after only knowing me for two weeks, and this time I want to say, "Yes!" I want to say it immediately.

KATHLEEN: Two weeks?

ELLEN: Yes.

KATHLEEN: Good for him. You said "No"?

ELLEN: I knew he was going to be my life. I didn't have to admit it. I wanted to wait, get pregnant, and then take him for granted. I'm a child. How can I be having one? I can't do this on my own.

KATHLEEN: You have us. We are your family with or without a certificate.

ELLEN: I don't want you. I want Jay.

KATHLEEN: I don't want you. I want Jay. *(A pause.)* Are you ready? We should get going. Ellen? Do you hear me?

(ELLEN stops painting.)

ELLEN: I knew there would be an exchange rate on happiness. *(A pause.)* Maybe I knew... knew he was going to die, so I pushed him away. He would be safe right now... if we hadn't fought that night. If I had walked the dog that morning... if I had carried his bag... if I had

called his name while he was pulling out of the driveway... if I drank coffee instead of tea... He would be here.

KATHLEEN: He loved you.

ELLEN: What did I do? What did I do to lose him? My love... my sweet guy... all by himself... what was he thinking? Did he know... was he scared... did it hurt? I can't stand it! I hear him calling my name. I close my eyes and hear him but when I open them all I see is the crash. I know he was thinking of me. Thinking I better not die or she'll be pissed. And I am...I am pissed. I hate him. I hate him for being everything. I hate myself for not knowing but I hate him more...more because he was the good part. I have nothing to share. He was my only good part.

(Silence.)

ELLEN: Kathleen, I am not going to the doctor today. I am unable...

KATHLEEN: Yes. Yes, you are. Would you like to hear a funny story?

ELLEN: No.

(A pause.)

KATHLEEN: Well, it's about Michelle.

ELLEN: Have I heard it before?

KATHLEEN: No.

ELLEN: How is she?

KATHLEEN: They're letting her come home on Friday. I don't know how she is... I am not allowed to call. She and her therapist call me once a week. I feel like we are putting on a show. I guess...I am the one putting on the show. We'll just have to wait and see. I was driving Michelle to school one morning, and I was so upset. I had cracked my tooth and I didn't want anyone to know. I was trying to keep the humiliation and fear to myself… I didn't even tell Henry. But it was Michelle who made me calm down. I can't tell you how hard it was to let my seventeen-year-old daughter take my hand because I was scared. But I did. I did and now look at me. I have a beautiful smile and my daughter hates me. So, cheer up and let's go.

ELLEN: Kathleen, you are only one of the reasons she's in there.

(They both smile.)

KATHLEEN: I can see why he fell in love with you.

ELLEN: He was obviously looking for a mother figure. *(A pause.)* I'm kidding.

KATHLEEN: Get in the car.

(ELLEN exits.)

MOM'S TRIP

Flashback. KATHLEEN remains onstage calling to MICHELLE, who is already seated in the car.

KATHLEEN: Michelle! Michelle? I can't be late.

(KATHLEEN gets in the car and is surprised to see MICHELLE waiting for her.)

KATHLEEN: Why can't you get up when your father wakes you?

MICHELLE: I do.

KATHLEEN: Maybe he needs to wake you earlier.

MICHELLE: Mom. No. It is seven-thirty a.m. School is eight o'clock and we're half a block away. Chill.

KATHLEEN: What?

MICHELLE: Calm down.

KATHLEEN: I'm fine.

MICHELLE: Whatever.

KATHLEEN: Now, what does that mean?

MICHELLE: Nothing, Mom, just watch the road.

(They drive for a bit in silence. MICHELLE leans down to get her bag and finds some ripped-out sheets from the yellow pages.)

MICHELLE: What are these?

KATHLEEN: I don't know. Michelle, don't distract me! You may not be late but I am going to be.

MICHELLE: Hey look, someone went to town on the D's.

KATHLEEN: Michelle, we're here. Put those down and get out of the car.

MICHELLE: What is your problem? These aren't sacred. They are the yellow pages.

KATHLEEN: I know Michelle, please…

MICHELLE: Well, I hope no one needs a dentist…

KATHLEEN: Me too. Now go.

MICHELLE: Mom, do you need a dentist?

KATHLEEN: I don't know! No! Leave those pages alone. Please go to school.

MICHELLE: If you need a dentist, call Dad.

KATHLEEN: Don't you dare tell you father.

MICHELLE: Mom… what are you doing? What's wrong with you?

KATHLEEN: Nothing. I'm fine. *(Breaking down.)* My tooth is cracked, that's all.

MICHELLE: Okay.

KATHLEEN: It's cracked. I don't know what to do. I look so awful and old.

MICHELLE: Why are you crying? No, you don't. You can't even tell. Smile.

(KATHLEEN tries to smile, but her hand is covering half her face.)

KATHLEEN: No, Michelle, I will not smile.

MICHELLE: *(Laughing.)* Why aren't you telling Dad again? And more importantly, why did you rip out the D section of the phone book?

KATHLEEN: I wanted to do it on my own. Your father has been nagging me for years about going to the dentist. And everything was fine until today. I just don't want to tell him. He'll just say, "I told you so."

MICHELLE: You're having a meltdown. I'm sorry, but you have to… turn the car around. We're going home. I'll call Dad at the office and we'll work it out. I'll say… who cares. Turn the car around.

KATHLEEN: No.

MICHELLE: Yes.

KATHLEEN: No.

MICHELLE: Yes.

KATHLEEN: Okay. *(A pause.)* What about school?

MICHELLE: What about it? Let me go with you. I'll call Dad and find out about the insurance… Mom, let me help, please. Look at yourself.

KATHLEEN: I am just scared. I don't know why. I hate dentists. Please don't ever marry one.

MICHELLE: I won't. You'll be fine.

KATHLEEN: Don't tell anyone, please.

MICHELLE: *(Laughing.)* MOM, who would I tell? No one likes the dentist, but few make it into a covert operation. You will survive.

KATHLEEN: I love you.

(She goes to hug MICHELLE.)

MICHELLE: Stop it, Mom. Don't. Just drive.

CANYON

JAY and HENRY are at the Grand Canyon. The sun has set.

HENRY: We made it.

JAY: The Grand Canyon.

HENRY: Amazing.

JAY: Amazing is right.

HENRY: It really is a sight to see… when you can see it.

JAY: I know.

HENRY: We tried.

JAY: We did.

HENRY: I hoped…

JAY: I take it you've been here before?

HENRY: Once, with my son on a family trip. They aren't all bad. You'll want to take them when you're a father. He'd scare the hell out of me by walking to the tip of every ledge.

JAY: Really?

HENRY: You see that tree? He walked out beyond it. Reaching his arms out like a bird and smiled. I knew it was dangerous, but I trusted him. Jay pushed boundaries but he always calculated his risks. I envied him. He was a breath away from everything… everything he could be.

JAY: I don't know what I am doing.

HENRY: You're already doing it. You're either working your way in or out. You decide.

(ELLEN re-enters, not pregnant, and stares at her blank canvas.)

JAY: You want to go out there?

HENRY: You should go. I am too old. It's too dark.

JAY: I think you can do it. Go see how it feels. It's as safe as it will ever be.

(HENRY starts to go. JAY watches. HENRY walks to the tip of the ledge, reaching his arms out, and looks back at JAY and smiles. He remains on the ledge throughout the next scene. He returns to the car with JAY after Art Studio.)

ART STUDIO

Flashback. ELLEN begins drawing. An elephant is obvious and full figured by the end of this monologue. ELLEN is wearing headphones.

ELLEN: Oh Mister Elephant… here we go. What are you? Who are you? You are out in the blue waiting to be found. I see the texture of your heart. You have great space. So here is the space. Fill it. Feel it. You are not done. Your colors could change. You can change. Go ahead… be a dog or a butterfly. I see no limits to your growth. You can be an elephant who morphs with love into the lightest creature. Universe, I ask you to give him the gift of flight with bright colors and wings so light… he feels weightless. Go. Be free!

(JAY enters her studio, unnoticed by ELLEN.)

ELLEN: I want an elephant, a real elephant.

(She makes an elephant sound and giggles. She begins to sing "I Don't Want No Scrub" by T.L.C. She sings it badly but with abandon. While singing, she turns and sees JAY. She screams.)

ELLEN: Sorry.

JAY: No. I should've knocked.

ELLEN: There's no door.

JAY: Well… you're right.

ELLEN: So…

JAY: I'm Jay. Hi.

ELLEN: Oh! *(A pause.)* I know… I didn't know your name was Jay, but I know you. I don't know you, know you, but I know what you look like. I know your face, not your name. I've seen you before… on campus. *(She smiles.)* But never in the art department. Surprise! I am sure you've seen me… maybe you haven't. We live in the same dorm. You run by me every morning… doing drills with those guys. What I mean is… I know who you are …or what you look like… *(She takes a moment.)*

JAY: Hi. I'm Jay.

ELLEN: Nice to meet you, Jay.

JAY: We're Marines… that's why we do drills.

ELLEN: Ohhh, of course. *(A pause.)* A Marine that paints—cool!

JAY: Yeah, I don't paint.

ELLEN: Okay.

JAY: Would you like to go get some coffee… with me?

ELLEN: I don't drink coffee.

(Awkward silence. JAY, baffled, returns to the car. ELLEN, stunned, goes back to drawing.)

ELLEN: Hi. I'm Ellen. I drink tea.

DAYLIGHT

HENRY and JAY arrive at BARBARA the breeder's house. They are sitting in the car.

HENRY: Well. Here we are.

JAY: I guess so. Are you...

HENRY: Yeah. I'm fine. Thank you for coming with me. I guess this is Blaise's new home.

JAY: What if he attacks this woman... Barbara, like he did the tollbooth gal?

HENRY: Well, that's funny... it never crossed my mind. I don't know. I'm here now... so we will just have to see.

JAY: Why didn't you just fly him to Arizona?

HENRY: You can't fly pets to Arizona this time of year. It's too hot in the cargo part of the plane... they'd overheat.

JAY: I hope I didn't waste your time with all my problems.

HENRY: No. You have been... I am happy to have met you. Do you want to come in with me?

JAY: No, I think I should stay here. Take your time.

(BARBARA comes onstage. She has a very peaceful spirit and takes a moment before she crosses to the car.)

HENRY: Some of his brothers and sisters are still living here... it's possible he'll like it here.

(They sit for a moment in silence.)

BARBARA: Hey troops, you must be Henry? Barbara, nice to meet you.

HENRY: *(Gesturing to JAY.)* This is a friend of mine, who has made most of the trip with me.

BARBARA: *(Looking at JAY.)* Oh, you don't have to introduce him. I'd know him anywhere. Hey there, Blaise!

(BARBARA opens the car door. JAY bounds out of the car and stands at her side. HENRY remains seated.)

BARBARA: *(To HENRY.)* You look tired. Do you want to come in?

HENRY: No.

BARBARA: I insist. Come inside. Would you like some iced tea? I am sure Blaise wants to meet his family.

HENRY: I have a plane to catch. It's been a long drive. This is...really difficult. I can't stay. If I stay... I may not be able to leave him. I want to thank you. I'm very grateful you offered to take him in... thank you. I should go.

BARBARA: Well, I'd like to take a picture of you with Blaise.

(She gets her Polaroid camera, as HENRY slowly gets out of the car.)

HENRY: *(Quietly.)* I should not have come alone.

BARBARA: Okay, get with Blaise.

(HENRY crosses to stand with JAY. She takes the photo and hands it to him, revealing HENRY with a German shepherd.)

HENRY: I have a plane to catch. I'm picking up Michelle once I get to the... Thank you for letting him return home. You may have to retrain him. Jay spoke commands to him in German, but he's been his own boss for months now.

BARBARA: He'll be fine. Come here, Blaise.

(She hits her side. JAY goes and stands with BARBARA. HENRY can't take his eyes off him.)

BARBARA: Good boy! You have to be forceful. Act like the alpha male, that's the only way to keep control. You act like you have it.

HENRY: Good advice.

BARBARA: I'll send you pictures as time goes by. I'll let you know how he is adapting.

HENRY: Barbara, thank you again. Would it be all right...

(HENRY crosses to JAY. BARBARA backs away.)

HENRY: I have a plane to catch. I'm picking up Michelle on my way... I don't know what to say. I never did.

(He touches JAY's face.)

HENRY: Jay... I can't...

(HENRY does not acknowledge JAY's voice.)

JAY: It's hello or goodbye, depending on which way you're traveling.

(JAY and BARBARA begin to exit.)

BARBARA: Thank you for bringing Blaise home. I'll talk to you soon.

HENRY: Goodbye.

HELLO

MICHELLE and HENRY walk to the front of the stage. HENRY takes a moment and then turns to see MICHELLE looking at him.

HENRY: Michelle.

MICHELLE: Hi, Dad.

HENRY: Are you ready?

MICHELLE: What is that supposed to mean?

HENRY: Do you have your clothes and personal belongings?

MICHELLE: Yeah, you're funny.

HENRY: I am? I didn't know that.

MICHELLE: You're so direct.

HENRY: Is that good?

MICHELLE: It just is. How's the breeder lady? Does she love Blaise the way we do? Is she going to keep him?

HENRY: She was a sweet woman. Different than I expected. He has a great setup there with a big yard and... you know, some of his brothers and sisters are still living there.

(MICHELLE caves a bit emotionally. She forces herself to recuperate immediately.)

HENRY: Michelle, what's wrong? What did I say?

MICHELLE: That's great. I am happy for him.

(Silence.)

MICHELLE: Dad, I am jealous of Blaise. I am nuts.

HENRY: I was jealous too.

MICHELLE: You were? Good.

HENRY: Michelle, I couldn't have kept him in the kennel, it wasn't right.

MICHELLE: I got so mad watching Kyle taunt him with a stick. I just wanted Blaise to be free from it. I didn't think... I really didn't think he would bite him.

HENRY: Michelle, we need you. Your mother went to the dentist last week by herself.

MICHELLE: No?! You were on the road? Did she cry?

HENRY: I think so.

MICHELLE: Good for her. She can cry whenever she fucking wants too. Shit, that she gets up in the morning is a fucking miracle. She should never apologize for her tears, fuck it!

HENRY: Michelle… I know…

MICHELLE: No one should lose two sons in one lifetime.

HENRY: I know.

(He puts his arm around MICHELLE.)

HENRY: Tell me. Do they encourage that language here?

MICHELLE: It's my way of adding a youthful emphasis to my opinions. Imperfections are windows for rebirth. *(A pause.)* I hope.

HENRY: I've missed your voice.

MICHELLE: Good. Well, I think you and Mom are fucking superheroes.

HENRY: Well… fuck.

(They hug.)

(End of play.)

TIMELINE

(NOTE: Scene titles are in italics.)

JANUARY 1997
- *Art Studio:* Jay asks Ellen out.

MAY 1997
- Ellen asks Jay out. They graduate and begin dating.
- *Proposal:* Two weeks later.
- *The Pool:* Jay, Michelle, and folks go on retreat before putting Jib to sleep.
- Jay buys Ellen a German shepherd puppy, Blaise.

DECEMBER 1997
- *The Gift:* Christmas—Michelle is visiting Ellen and Jay.

JANUARY 1998
- Ellen and Jay get pregnant January 22. Baby due in October.

FEBRUARY 1998
- Ellen and Jay move from Arizona to New Jersey to be closer to his family.

MARCH 1998
- *Elephant:* March 21; Ellen is two months' pregnant.
- Jay dies on March 22.
- *Mascara:* Jay's wake is on March 24.

MAY 1998
- Ellen gives Blaise to Jay's family.
- *Mom's Trip.*

JULY 1998
- Blaise bites Kyle on July 4.

AUGUST 1998
- *Goodbye:* Michelle is sent to Soundview on August 15.
- *Forest:* Michelle addresses her group for the first time on August 18.

All cross-country scenes take place in the last week of August. They travel twenty-four hundred miles in three days.

- August 27, traveling through New Jersey, Pennsylvania, West Virginia, Ohio.
  - *Blaise.*
  - *Ride On.*
  - *Bite:* Kathleen's phone conversation with therapist.
  - *Game Over.*
  - *Blaise Too.*
- August 28, traveling through Indiana, Illinois, Missouri, Oklahoma.

WALKING TO AMERICA

Alberto Bonilla

ALBERTO BONILLA has been involved in theatre for more than fifteen years. Born in Honduras, he received his BA in acting from Arizona State University and then moved to the East Coast, where he received an MFA in acting from Rutgers University Mason Gross School of the Arts. Alberto is a director and playwright-in-residence at 78th Street Theatre Lab. Acting credits include *Boy Steals Train*, produced by 78th Street Theatre Lab at the Edinburgh Fringe Festival; and on television in *As the World Turns*, *Guiding Light*, and *All My Children*. Alberto also does fight/stunt directing for all three of these New York soaps. He currently serves as Assistant Director of Admissions at the School for Film and Television in New York City.

Walking to America was first presented by 78th Street Theatre Lab (Eric Nightengale, Artistic Director; Mark Zeller, Dana Zeller-Alexis Producing Directors; Ruth Nightengale, General Manager), New York City, in a staged reading in February 2004, with the following cast:

Palo .... Juan Martinez
Ensemble .... Joe Fellman, Gigi Jhong, Jessica Lanius, John-Andrew
                Morrison, Jessica Myhr, Paul Rolfes, Kristofer Updike

It was subsequently produced by 78th Street Theatre Lab on September 2, 2004, with the following cast and credits:

Palo .... Orlando Rios
Ensemble .... Susan Kerner, Ed Lane, Quinn Mander,
                John Andrew-Morrison, Jessica Myhr, Angela Paz

Director: Alberto Bonilla
Producer: Megan Laughton
Set Designer: Jack Hazard
Lighting Designer: Paul Hudson
Sound Designer: Dean Harper
Stage Manager: Meghan Sharer
Dialect Coach: Lisa Marie Febrega
Production Assistants: Vance Bradford, Bamba Djan Bamba
Graphic Artist: TJ Walker
Videos: Alberto Bonilla, Anne Paas, Harrison Butler, Rebecca
    Migdal, Steve Crowley, Jerry Woods

Visit www.WalkingtoAmerica.com.

AUTHOR'S NOTE

In 1998 while enrolled in my second year of the MFA Acting Program at Rutgers University, I came across a compelling National Public Radio interview while researching a role. The piece interviewed a Honduran boy named Oscar who was being held as an illegal immigrant in a Texas prison. As I listened to the interview, my heart sank. Oscar was from the same town in Honduras that I was from, only he was entirely without family or support of any kind. He was a street kid who had known no other existence than the brutally harsh street life of the capital city Tegucigalpa.

In the interview, Oscar shares how he came to the realization that his only hope for survival was to leave Honduras and journey to North America. He didn't hitchhike, he didn't take a bus, he didn't hitch rides on rail cars; he walked. From his street corner in Honduras, Oscar walked for twenty-four months across four countries and over twenty-four hundred miles to the American border.

I was so moved by Oscar's story that I tracked down the immigration lawyer who had worked on his case. When I asked him if there was a way to contact Oscar, hoping to have an opportunity to speak to him in person, he told me something that tore my heart. "Why do you want to interview Oscar? If you go down to the border, you will find hundreds of Oscars, and those are the lucky ones that actually made it to America. There are so many more that never make it that far. And the ones who do are usually sent right back to where they started. Oscar is only one of hundreds of kids."

In the years since that phone call, I have graduated and worked on many creative projects, but the story of Oscar and the thousands of children who have shared his plight has never left me. The opportunity came when I approached Eric Nightengale of 78th Street Theatre Lab with the idea of bringing Oscar's journey to the stage. Eric listened to the original interview and graciously offered me the opportunity to workshop a script—*Walking to America*.

So many people helped me in creating this play I just can't name them all, though there are a few I must. To my family for never giving up on me. To 78th Street Theatre Lab for giving me an artistic home. To Megan Laughton who walked through hell with me and always smiled. To Brad Bambo, the best writer I know, who helped me believe I could write. To Rex Reeb for always bringing me back to reality. Finally, to Jessica Myhr, my muse, my strength, and the best damn actress I have ever had the honor to work with. This play exists because of all of you. Thank you.

An estimated fifty thousand children and youth under the age of
eighteen migrate on their own each year from Central America and
Mexico to the United States. Fewer than five thousand of them actually make it to the U.S. This play is dedicated to all of them.

PRODUCTION NOTES

MULTIMEDIA. In the production of *Walking to America* at 78th
Street Theatre Lab, we used a large screen and a projector connected
to a DVD player. This can be replaced by having two large-screen
TVs downstage right and downstage left.

EDITING. All the commercials were shot on digital cameras and
edited using iMovie and Final Cut Express. They were then burned
onto DVDs using iDVD and DVD Studio Pro. Each commercial
was given a chapter on the master DVD to avoid the risk of having
one commercial run into the next and spoil a cue during the performance.

COMMERCIALS. Although the commercials may come across as a
parody in the play, they should be shot and acted as though for an
actual commercial. My note to the commercial directors was to shoot
them as though they had been hired by an advertising agency to pro-
mote the respective product.

FIREARMS. The first gunshot we hear (during the attempt on Palo's
life by Killer 2) should not be a sound effect, but a real blank fired
from a prop revolver. The second gun used in this scene (the one
aimed at Palo's head) needs to be a sliding action firearm such as a
Barretta or a .45 caliber. For safety reasons, this gun should never be
loaded with any blanks; the chamber should always be empty.

RESOURCES

AMNESTY INTERNATIONAL. Amnesty International draws
world attention to the extrajudicial executions of street children in
Honduras and advocates on behalf of children in immigration detention in the United States. Citing local nongovernmental organiza-
tions, Amnesty International estimates that more than two thousand
children and youths were killed in Honduras from 1998 to end of
2003. Amnesty says that Honduran society has greeted these killings
with "indifference and apathy." In 2003, Amnesty International USA
issued a report, *"Why Am I Here?" Children in Immigration Detention*,
which chronicled the treatment of thousands of children apprehended
and detained every year by the U.S. immigration authorities. Amnesty continues to campaign for the Unaccompanied Alien Child
Protection Act, legislation that would reform the treatment of foreign

immigrant children in U.S. custody. For more information, go to www.amnestyusa.org/refugee/index.do.

CASA ALIANZA. Casa Alianza, the Latin American arm of the New York-based Covenent House, last year provided crisis shelter, family reunification services, drug abuse programs, job training, and mother/support services to some eight thousand children of the street in Honduras, Guatemala, Nicaragua, and Mexico. If you would like more information about the work of Casa Alianza, go to www.casa-alianza.org.

SCENE 1

On stage, we see a large blank screen upstage center. The stage is bare except for some small hollow TVs the actors will use to move as boxes for various sets. On the large screen appear the words:

"INSPIRED BY A TRUE STORY"

The words fade out. The lights come up onstage. Center stage, a young Hispanic BOY looks directly into the audience. He appears to be thirteen to fifteen years of age with dark hair and dark eyes. He is tall for his age and is dressed in clothing that is too small for him. He has cut-off jeans and an old red Adidas shirt from the 1970s with white stripes. A MAN appears stage left and begins translating.

PALO: *Recuerdo... Recuerdo el dia en que decidi ir me de Honduras. Yo estuve en la Montana y... vi dos caballeros peleando por una mujer. Ambos tenian machetes. El gordo le pego al otro en la mano y grito como chanco el grito lo enfurecio mas. El flaco en su defense le respondio con otro machetaso el cual fallo y fue a dar en la cara de la mujer la cual se quebro como un mango lleno de jugo. Recuerdo que pense...*

TRANSLATOR: I remember the day I decided to leave Honduras. I was in the mountains. And I saw these two guys... Um...they were fighting over some woman. They each had machetes... and the big guy hit the other in the hand and he screamed like a pig. And got more angry. He tried to defend himself and messed up and hit the woman in the face. And her jaw burst open with juice like a mango. I remember thinking...

PALO: I can't stay here. If I stay here in the streets, I will grow up to be just like them. I don't want that. I have seen a better place. I have seen it in color. I just need to know which way is North.

(TRANSLATOR exits. Lights to half. PALO turns to watch the following commercial on the large screen as the actors set the next scene.)

VIDEO #1
FINDLOVE.COM COMMERCIAL

On the screen appear various beautiful WOMEN hitting seductive poses to the tune "American Woman" by Lenny Kravitz.

VOICEOVER: Tired of all those other dating services? With findlove.com, what you see is what you get. Log on to findlove.com. Come on, I know you want to.

SCENE 2

On the large screen appears:

"DAY 4 - TEGUCIGALPA, HONDURAS.
2,422 MILES TO AMERICA."

Store front. Lights to full. Noon. In the heat of the day, three WOMEN enter in a rush. ROSA wears a floral dress and carries a large basket with tamales. ENID is wearing a stained apron with a grocery store logo. CELIA, dressed in sweats, is carrying a backpack. They stand in front of the store window and catch the last part of an American soap opera playing on the TV in the shop window. PALO is sitting a few feet away, totally disinterested in the soap taking place.

ROSA: Hurry, we're late!

ENID: I am sorry but I had to put the vegetables out, or my boss would have had a fit.

CELIA: This is your lunch hour, *y ese Puto de Mierda* should not work you like an animal for that stupid corner store!

ENID: *¡Ay Dios!* He is going to ask her!!!

ROSA: SHHHHHH—we're missing the part—

CELIA: I missed yesterday 'cause Pepe had a diaper rash, what did I miss—

ROSA: SHHHHHHHHH!!!!!

ENID: *(In a low voice and at lightning speed.)* The blond one is Blake who just woke up from a coma of twelve years in some place called Happy Springs, Minnesota, and has come back to Pine Valley looking for Tiffany, but she has amnesia and doesn't remember that they were married—

(PALO laughs.)

ROSA: I can't hear what he's saying!

CELIA: WHAT!!! What about the other tall blond Paul the man who she is suppose to marry, and why is she a blond now I thought she had red hair two days ago???

ROSA: I can't hear!!! Ladies!

(Suddenly the TV program cuts to commercials.)

CELIA: What happened? I'm lost! Who is the new guy? Why is she blond now????

ROSA: Now look— I didn't hear what he was going to say! He was going to kiss her but stopped!

ENID: Ay, *Jesus Christo*, he is nice to look at.

(PALO rushes to the TV and sits right in front, almost knocking down one of the girls.)

ROSA: *¡Cuidado!*

PALO: *(Overly excited.)* I am sorry, this is my favorite part.

ROSA: Well, you could learn some manners.

CELIA: Watch it, he might try to pick your pocket.

PALO: Don't be like that. I want to watch the commercials! They are…

ROSA: Get out of here so we can watch our soap!

PALO: But, I want to see the commercials! Not the stupid-soap-telenovela fake stuff.

(LADIES laugh.)

ENID: You think the commercials are better than the shows??

PALO: A coma for twenty years? Please!

CELIA: Twenty! I thought it was ten! I am so lost.

ROSA: Will everyone just be quiet so I can watch the soap!

PALO: Why don't you go home and watch it in your house? Stupid telenovela fake stuff—

ROSA: Because we have been coming here to watch American satellite for over a month now. This is our spot. Find another store window.

PALO: No, no, no!!! This is my home! This is where I live. Ask anyone around here, this is my corner—

ENID: We've never seen you before. OH!!! It's starting!!!

PALO: That's 'cause I'm on my way to America, where I won't need to watch in front of a store—

CELIA, ENID, and ROSA: SHHHHH!!!!!

(PALO slowly backs away, and the three WOMEN are now fully engrossed with the soap. CARLO, an older street kid, enters and sneaks up behind PALO and smacks him playfully in the back of the head, scaring PALO.)

PALO: ¡¡¡Puneta!!! Carlo!!! ¡¡¡Me asustases!!! YOU SCARED ME FOR REAL!!!!

CARLO: I knew I would find you, *cabrón!* I just had to find a store front with American TV and I knew I would find you!

PALO: I thought you were caught by *La Imigra?*

CARLO: Those fucking cops can't even grab their dicks to take a piss. It's good to see you… *puto.* Hey, you got shoes?

PALO: Ya…

CARLO: Mani told me you were going North?

PALO: Yea, hey, where is Mani?

CARLO: In the plaza getting wallets. Lots of people there today.

PALO: *(Slightly embarrassed.)* You got any food on you?

(Pause.)

CARLO: *(Feeling very hungry too and disappointed.)* Naw, I just got some glue.

PALO: Can I have some?

CARLO: Ya man, we'll sniff our vitamins.

(CARLO takes out a Gerber baby food jar and opens the lid, offering it to PALO. PALO takes a deep breath, hands it back to CARLO, who then does the same.)

PALO: Mmmmmm mmmmmm crunchy!

(Offstage, the sound of a fast car coming to a halt and car doors opening.)

CARLO: *Loco.* You have got to stop watching that American shit, *puto,* it's going to pollute your mind and—

(Two MEN enter, wearing black hoods. KILLER 2 holds a revolver to CARLO's head. He pulls the trigger on the revolver, shooting CARLO right in the neck. CARLO falls as the three WOMEN scream and run. KILLER 2 grabs PALO by the hair and forces him down to his knees. We can hear CARLO struggling to breathe while choking on his blood. KILLER 1 puts the gun up to PALO's head. Throughout the following dialogue, KILLER 1, with the caliber gun, continually slides the action back, and it never fires. PALO begs for his life in Spanish.)

KILLER 1: Fuck! It's jammed.

KILLER 2: What.

KILLER 1: It's jammed!

KILLER 2: *(Very cold.)* It's a new gun. Pull the action.

KILLER 1: Use your gun!

KILLER 2: I had one shot left from last night. I'm out, I just used my last bullet on that trash there.

KILLER 1: Damn it!

KILLER 2: Use another clip.

KILLER 1: I left it in the car.

(KILLER 2 pushes PALO to ground, glares at KILLER 1, and KILLER 1 understands that they need to leave.)

KILLER 2: Get off our streets. Go somewhere else.

(Both KILLERS exit. We hear the sound of tires squealing away. Finally, CARLO takes one last breath and lies still. PALO is shaken, and begins to speak to CARLO.)

PALO: Carlo? Carlo?! Carlo!!! No…

(Tries to revive him by shaking him.)

PALO: I gotta go man… Gotta go… Get over it. Get over it.

(PALO slowly gets up and begins to back away. Lights to half. PALO turns to watch the following commercial on the large screen as the actors set the next scene.)

VIDEO #2
MIKIE SHOES COMMERCIAL

The following is a sports commercial for "Mikie Shoes." There are various clips of famous ATHLETES. Some clips are in black and white, others are in color. Each ATHLETE has a description in the lower left-hand corner of the screen explaining the person and his or her fame. The VOICEOVER is a strong-sounding, youthful voice. The music underscoring the commercial is "Summon the Heroes" from the Olympics.

VOICEOVER: What is American?

(New clip.)

VOICEOVER: It's saying yes, when everyone is saying no.

(New clip.)

VOICEOVER: It's giving hope when there's none left.

(New clip.)

VOICEOVER: It's not caring about your skin color, where you're from, or who you know.

(New clip.)

VOICEOVER: It's about not being afraid of anything. It's about realizing your dream.

VIDEO #3
CHILDCHOICE COMMERCIAL

On screen, we fade in on a married COUPLE; they look like the perfect parents. They look concerned, but not upset. They must not appear as salespeople or actors, but real, everyday people being interviewed. The WOMAN is about six months' pregnant.

DAD: We have two little girls—

MOM: And we love them dearly—

DAD: But we also want a boy—

MOM: You know, to balance out the family.

DAD: We tried adoption, but the paper work and the waiting…

MOM: So we contacted ChildChoice Services.

DAD: For as little as eighteen hundred dollars, you can have the peace of mind and actually choose the gender of your child.

MOM: In a completely natural way.

DAD: It's a process called preimplantation genetic diagnosis, or PGD.

MOM: Developed by the Fertility Institute of Los Angeles.

DAD: It has almost one hundred percent accuracy in selecting the sex of your baby.

MOM: We wanted "family balancing," and with ChildChoice you can feel safe about the choice you make.

DAD: And choose the family of your dreams.

VOICEOVER: Choose the family of your dreams with ChildChoice.

(A phone number appears on the screen as the PARENTS smile and look into each other's eyes.)

SCENE 3

On the large screen appears:

"DAY 72 - SANTA ANNA, EL SALVADOR"

Lights to full. PALO is seen onstage sleeping on the floor between pews of a church. The church is cold and gothic-looking with stained glass windows as its only light source. A PRIEST enters. PRIEST has white hair and small black eyeglasses, and is in a good mood. He carries a small lit candle. He walks past PALO and startles him awake.

PRIEST: I'm sorry— No, do not be afraid.

PALO: I'm sorry Father, I meant no disrespect—

PRIEST: No. You're fine. I just forgot my rosary on the altar. You can stay.

PALO: Thank you, Father.

PRIEST: Son, I don't recognize you. Where are you from?

PALO: From Tegucigalpa. Honduras. Over by the Street of Many Flowers.

PRIEST: HONDURAS???

PALO: Yes. I'm on my way to America. That's where I want to live.

PRIEST: Are you serious?

PALO: Yes, why not. I started walking a few days ago.

PRIEST: Don't lie, you're in church.

PALO: No, no Father. I would never lie. *(Looking up at the altar.)* Especially… not in front of Him.

PRIEST: *Ay Dios…* how old are you?

PALO: I don't know.

PRIEST: You don't know how old you are?

PALO: I don't need to count the days.

PRIEST: Ay ay ay… well… you've walked a long way already. Ummm…I have no money, or blanket to give you—

PALO: No Father, no, the place to sleep is more then I deserve—

PRIEST: Take the candle.

(PRIEST hands PALO the candle and lighter.)

PALO: But Father, the candle is the church's—

PRIEST: The church is made up of people. And people are made up of faith. *(Pause.)* Son, do you have faith? In God?

PALO: I don't know… I know my mom did. My mom used to bless me every night before I went to bed. She used to say *(Imitating his mom.)* "En el nombre del Padre, y del Hijo y del Espíritu Santo,* may God keep a smile on your face and your ass out of trouble." But I always got in trouble! So I think he only heard half of my mom's prayer.

PRIEST: Where is she now?

PALO: *(Pointing up.)* With Him I guess. When Hurricane Mitch hit, I guess He wanted her with Him.

PRIEST: And your father?

PALO: I never knew him. My mom used to tease me and say I smiled just like him. Like a shark.

PRIEST: Any other family? Aunts and uncles?

PALO: No… just me. But when I get to America… who knows? People are crazy about children in America. And the best part is, I get to choose the family of my dreams.

PRIEST: *(Light chuckle.)* Well it's good to have faith in something. I will pray that you will make it to America, and that God will keep you safe from harm.

PALO: Well Father, be careful now, God can be moody, He may only answer half of your prayer.

PRIEST: I'm pretty close to Him, I will see what I can do.

PALO: *Gracias Padre… (Begins to settle back down to lay on the pew.)* Oh Father… which way is North…

(PRIEST smiles at PALO and points to North.)

PALO: Ah, *buenas noches, Padre.*

PRIEST: *Buenas noches, mijo…*

(PRIEST goes to the altar, takes his rosary. PALO has now curled up next to the candle. PRIEST looks back at PALO and then walks over to the church donation box. He opens it and takes out some coins. He quietly walks over to PALO, who is now sleeping, and puts the coins next to him. PRIEST makes the sign of the cross over PALO and exits. Lights to half. PALO turns to watch the following commercial on the large screen as the actors set the next scene.)

VIDEO #4
EXTENDRA COMMERCIAL

We see several PEOPLE in a park; all are wearing bright and happy colors. The song "We Are the Champions" by Queen is playing. EVERYONE is skipping and jumping for joy as they are paired off in couples and running around in various shots.

VOICEOVER: Have you asked your doctor about Extendra? Extendra is now available in suppository form for your comfort. Now, you have a choice. Get your spring back into life with Extendra.

Warning. In some cases Extendra has been known to cause severe erectile dysfunction. If erection persists for more then three days consult your doctor. Other side effects include: bloating, paranoia, extreme fear of cats, anal leakage, sensitivity to sunlight and water. Please consult your doctor before using any medication.

Get your spring back into life with Extendra!

SCENE 4

On the large screen appears:

"DAY 184 - COLOTENGO, GUATEMALA"

Lights to full. PALO is sitting on the edge of the stage begging, when a STRANGER enters and approaches him.

PALO: Excuse me sir… can I have some change sir… or something to eat?

STRANGER: Listen… Do you want to make some money?

PALO: Yes so I can get some food…

STRANGER: Over there under the bridge… that is where all the kids make some money… or get some glue…

PALO: Please, sir… I just…

STRANGER 1: Shhhh… *(Gently, with his finger covering PALO's mouth, then touching his chin softly.)* I will see you over there…

(PALO walks center stage. He looks out into the audience and does not move. The rest of the ENSEMBLE begins to filter in from offstage, taking positions in the dark. PALO reacts to each question in improvised Spanish.)

1: It's nice to meet you—

PALO: *Gracias*—

2: Do you like it here?

PALO: *No*—

3: I like your smile.

PALO: *Dejame*—

4: Don't cry.

PALO: *No puedo*—

5: You're cute—

6: Can I play with your hair?

1 and 5: Mmmmmmmm—

3: No. I like it rough.

PALO: *Me duele*—

6: Is this ok?

PALO: *No*—

1: No like this!

PALO: YA!

(6 giggles.)

4: I have some glue.

PALO: *Si*—

5: Ya like that!

PALO: *¡¡¡NO!!!*

3: How about it?

(2 and 1 laugh.)

3 and 6: Your eyes are nice.

PALO: *(Screams low.)* *¡Dejame!*

1: STOP SCREAMING!

4: You're nice—

1 and 2: Shhhh—

1 and 5: I like—

2, 3, and 6: Your hair—

ALL: Shhhhhhhh.

1: You're very sweet.

(PALO, crying by now, takes a glass jar from his pocket filled with glue. He takes a deep breath of glue. As he inhales, the rest of the CAST disappears into the shadows. One of the strangers comes up to PALO and begins putting coins in his hand.)

STRANGER 2: Twenty-five, fifty, seventy-five. You should stop that… It's bad for you.

PALO: *(Not looking at STRANGER. Sniffing his glue.)* Which way is North?

STRANGER 2: That way I think.

(PALO does not even look at STRANGER and begins to walk. He turns to watch the following commercial on the large screen as the actors set the next scene. Lights to half.)

VIDEO #5
ANTI-DRUG COMMERCIAL

We see a very hip TEENAGER in a kitchen. She has a pan on the stove. She takes an egg and holds it up to the camera. She looks directly at the camera. The style of this should be reality TV or an MTV ad.

HIP CHICK: *(Holding up egg in one hand.)* This is your brain…

(Cracks egg open; shot of egg falling into sizzling pan.)

HIP CHICK: This is your brain on drugs…

(Shot of frying egg.)

HIP CHICK: And this is what it does to your family— *(Then she grabs the pan and begins to swing and hit everything around her, screaming the lines:)* —this is what it does to your friends! *(She is standing in the middle of a pile of messed-up and broken kitchen stuff.)* Any questions…

SCENE 5

On the large screen appears:

"DAY 200 - THE BORDER OF GUATEMALA AND MEXICO"

Lights to full. PALO is onstage as the sound of flies swarming fills the air. It is midday, and the sun is beating down on the open road. Lying on the road are two BODIES; both are in grotesque positions. As PALO tries to walk by, he begins to gag from the stench. He notices that the BODIES have shoes on. He stops and tries to see if he can peel off a pair of shoes. As he does, he finds blood and gunk on the heel. Clearly, the BODIES have decomposed. He tries to put the shoes on but they do not fit. PALO then throws the shoes in anger, goes and grabs the pair off the other BODY. He yanks them off and runs offstage. Lights to half.

SCENE 6

On the large screen appears:

"DAY 399 - ACAPULCO, MEXICO"

Lights to full. PALO moves from downstage right. He is hungry and tired. PALO hears PEOPLE singing and laughing offstage. A WEDDING PARTY enters. There is a young COUPLE, *newly married, that invites PALO to join in the celebration. The WEDDING PARTY is carrying food and wine. They all begin singing "Guantanamera." PALO looks at them and can't help but smile and begins to sing with the WEDDING PARTY. PALO is now being offered food and drink. Replenished at last, PALO is now very happy and almost drunk. The WEDDING PARTY continues to dance and celebrate as they move offstage. PALO suddenly realizes he is alone and packs up his plastic bag. He slowly finishes his tortilla alone. Lights to half. PALO turns to watch the following commercial on the large screen as the actors set the next scene.*

VIDEO #6
SHUGGA CRAX CEREAL COMMERCIAL

KID 1: Breakfast just isn't fun anymore Mom.

KID 2: Ya it's boring…

(Theme from Star Wars begins.)

MOM: Oh my look who is here!

SHUGGA CRAX MAN: *(Voiceover.)* HMMMM HMM CRUNCHY!

KID 1 and KID 2: Shugga Crax MAN!!!

(Enter SHUGGA CRAX MAN!! A guy dressed in a cape and mask here to save breakfast.)

SHUGGA CRAX MAN: Never fear!!! Shugga Crax is here!!!

(They all scream for joy.)

SHUGGA CRAX MAN: Shugga Crax cereal is bringing the fun back.

KID 1: Mom look it stays crispy and crackly, no matter WHAT!

KID 2: *(Says line like superhero.)* HMMMMM HMMMM CRUNCHY!

KID 1: You can eat them with cold milk!

MOM: I like 'em HOT! *(She is holding a lighter under the spoon like a heroin addict.)*

KID 2: They're even great straight! *(KID 2 has a row of shugga crax cubes lined up like cocaine and sucks them through a straw like an addict.)*

MOM: And they're part of this balanced breakfast!

SHUGGA CRAX MAN: MMMM MMM crunchy!! *(Runs off-camera.)*

ALL: Thanks Shugga Crax Man!

(Cut to table with cereal and toast with milk and orange juice.)

VOICEOVER: Shugga Crax is a part of this nutritional balanced breakfast. Now in new coffee flavor!

SCENE 7

On the large screen appears:

"DAY 526 - TORNIDO, MEXICO"

Lights to full. ENSEMBLE are all on stage. Each is moving in slow motion as if PALO is in a nightmare. PALO is onstage, going to each PERSON begging for food in real time.

PALO: Excuse me sir? Can I have some change please?

(PALO goes over to another PERSON onstage.)

PALO: ¿Señora, me puede dar algo de comer?

(PALO walks over to an elderly CHARAC-TER. She has no reaction to him.)

PALO: ¡Abuelita! Mire que tengo hambre… ¿me puedes dar una pesetita? ¿Algo?

(PALO, beginning to get very angry, goes to a larger CHARACTER.)

PALO: Sir, I'm hungry! Give me a quarter please?!

(PALO goes to another PERSON onstage.)

PALO: Look at me I'm hungry. Please! Why is no one listening to me why is everyone acting like I am not here. I am human too! Just like you—AND YOU AND YOU!

(PALO rushes one of the ACTORS, who is still in slow motion. She screams. EVERYONE onstage now returns to moving in real time and rushes offstage. PALO grabs her bag, hoping there is food or money. He fights her for the bag… A YOUNG MAN enters, overhearing the cry for help.)

MAN: ¡¡¡Policia!!! ¡¡Policia!!

(YOUNG MAN pulls PALO off WOMAN. PALO runs downstage. Lights change. PALO is out of breath, almost to the point of passing out. PALO rips open the bag, only to find plastic cups and plates for a child's birthday party. He rips open a present and sees a child's toy. Overwhelmed with shame and sadness, he begins to try to repair the damaged gift before he breaks down into tears. Lights to half. PALO turns to watch the following commercial on the large screen as the actors set the next scene.)

VIDEO #7
LAST MAN STANDING COMMERCIAL

This is a typical reality TV Survivor type of show. Various shots of the CONTESTANTS are shown as they participate in a challenge of eating worms. Some are disgusted, and others are obnoxious. All are dressed in drab, dirty clothing, but still look sexy.

VOICEOVER: On the next "Last Man Standing"…

HOST: Whoever eats the most worms…

VOICEOVER: The contestants face their greatest challenge yet, the Madagascar worm. But one of them will take it too far! A shocking secret is revealed.

HOST: I'm sorry but you're not the last man standing.

VOICEOVER: On the next "Last Man Standing"!

SCENE 8

On the large screen appears:

"DAY 638 - DURANGO, MEXICO"

Lights to full. PALO is standing on the corner, begging. An aristocratic Spanish WOMAN, wearing a white dress, comes strolling by PALO.

PALO: Excuse me señora, can you spare some food or change, I have not eaten in two days and I am very hungry.

SEÑORA: *Por supuesto.*

(SEÑORA gives him three pesos. PALO reacts as if he has been given five hundred dollars. He is overwhelmed.)

PALO: *¡Gracias señora!* Oh God, thank you, I swear I will not spend it on anything but food.

SEÑORA: Are you looking for work?

PALO: *(Very cautious.)* YES, YES! I can work, I am a good worker... *(Remembering the last time someone offered work.)* But I am not looking for that kind of work... *(PALO begins to back away, thinking the worst.)* Because I'm on my way to America and I can't stay here for long—

SEÑORA: *(Offended.)* No, not that work, what kind of lady do you take me for? I am not that...common. I own a factory just outside of San Luis. I am always looking for strong workers. How old are you?

PALO: I am seventeen. No eighteen, no fifteen!

SEÑORA: No... You're too tall to be that young. Which is it?

PALO: Which will get me work?

SEÑORA: Let me see your fingers.

(SEÑORA grabs PALO's hand and examines his fingers.)

SEÑORA: I am not sure... your fingers might be too large.

PALO: *No, no señora. ¡Mire!* They are tiny, lady fingers! *Mire señora*, I'm a very hard worker. I will work, and not for much.

SEÑORA: Hmmm... you might be okay.

(SEÑORA reaches in her purse and gives him a card.)

SEÑORA: Take this and show it to the bus driver on the corner of Pillar and Rosado tomorrow at seven a.m. He will be in a white and red bus and will take you to the Gato Negro Factory north of San Luis. It's only about three miles from here. Tell the driver of the bus you are a new worker for the factory. He will take you there. Now don't disappoint me. I am very picky about who I employ and I am taking a very big chance on you.

PALO: *(Very excited.)* Okay, señora! I will be there. On time. Seven a.m. Bright and early. Ready to work.

SEÑORA: Okay. If anyone asks you who you talked to, say... *(Making up name.)* Maria. *(She exits quickly.)*

PALO: *(Yelling after her.)* I will be there Maria! On time you'll see!

(A thin MAN with a goatee enters. He has a large paper bag with him.)

DEALER: Hey, *cabrón!* You looking for anything. Need anything?

PALO: *(Lying.)* I don't need anything.

DEALER: Come on. Everyone needs something. What do you need?

PALO: I don't need anything you have.

DEALER: Okay, but I will be right over there if you need anything. I am just here to help.

PALO: *¡¡Vete al carajo cabrón!!* I don't need you. I just got a job. I am better then that. I am being all I can be!

(DEALER reaches into his paper bag and pulls out a small jar of glue and puts it on the ground in front of PALO. He then backs away.)

DEALER: Okay. You go to your job. You don't need that. I'll be over on the other side of the street. Helping people who need help. I am just a helper. I just want to help. I will leave that there, in case anyone needs help. But I know you don't need it. You got a job.

PALO: *(Yelling.)* ¡Vete al carajo cabrón! ¡¡¡Largate!!! ¡¡¡Vete!!!

(DEALER exits.)

PALO: *¡Maricon!*

(PALO is alone onstage with the jar of glue. He is tempted by it and begins to get upset. Finally, he gives in and grabs the glue, unable to restrain himself. He opens the lid and inhales desperately, then collapses to the floor in tears. Lights to half.)

SCENE 9

On the large screen appears:

"DAY 645 - CIUDAD OBREGON, MEXICO"

Lights to full. Onstage we see ELENA and a couple of other PEOPLE in a circle around

the TV boxes. They are making noises and working as if they are in a factory. They are wrapping firecrackers. FLACO, a large man who supervises the FACTORY WORKERS, enters. FLACO is slow and moves like a moose. He carries a revolver in his waistband. He walks around the table, looking over the shoulders of all the WORKERS. He then exits and brings back PALO and places him in an open spot.*

FLACO: *¡Mira! ¡Trabajen!*

(PALO takes out a cigarette and places it in his mouth.)

FLACO: *¡Estupido!*

(He yanks the cigarette out of PALO's mouth and hits PALO over the head.)

FLACO: No smoking! Fireworks! Boom. *¡Mira! ¡Trabajen!*

(Enter a CALL GIRL. She is holding an open condom and is unrolling it over two fingers. She is gesturing in a seductive manner to come and play.)

CALL GIRL: Flaco!! HAHAHHAHA FLACO!!! AHAHAHA!

FLACO: *(In a sexually hungry tone.)* Mmmmmm…

(FLACO crosses to CALL GIRL and picks her up, and they both exit. Offstage, we hear them begin to have sex as "Coppa Rota" plays on a old-sounding stereo. ELENA begins to enjoy the music, as it lightens the mood. ELENA slowly begins to move as if she is wanting to have a slow dance with PALO. She then takes his hand and begins to teach him how to slow dance. PALO, caught in the romantic moment, takes his hand and brushes it on ELENA's face. She begins to panic as, unknowingly, PALO has rubbed his sulfur-covered hands over her eyes.)

ELENA: It burns!! My eyes! AHHHH!

(As ELENA is trying desperately to wipe her eyes, one of the workers grabs PALO's hand and rubs it vigorously.)

WORKER 1: *¿Que estas haciendo? ¡Tus manos!*

(Offstage music stops— Enter FLACO in a rage.)

FLACO: *¡¿Que pasa?!*

(FLACO grabs ELENA by the hair and sees she is upset because of her eyes. He begins to forcefully wipe her eyes as she screams in pain. He then forces the rest of the WORKERS back into their positions to begin working again.)

FLACO: *¡Miren! ¡A trabajar!*

(FLACO exits. PALO is now facing the audience, furious with ELENA's treatment by FLACO. The WORKERS have begun working again, and he pulls out the lighter PRIEST gave him. He then lights it and slowly lights the table on fire. EVERYONE screams and runs offstage, as FLACO re-enters and realizes the place is now ablaze.)

FLACO: *¡Ay Dios mio! ¡¡Fuego!!* Fire!!!

(FLACO runs offstage. Lights to half.)

SCENE 10

On the large screen appears:

"Day 725 - Nogales, Mexico. The Border of the United States."

Lights to full. CELENA is onstage. She's a short Hispanic woman with graying hair. CELENA's packing a candle, some tortillas, and a bottle of water into a small bag.)

ELENA: Please, I am begging you! *Ayudanos, no tenemosn a nadie mass—*

CELENA: Okay! You wait here. I'll go find Angel. He's the one that helped

Varina go across. He's expensive but he will not sell you out to La Imigra. Now you must be serious because he does not want people who will back out. He has limited space and will work with you on the price but only if you are serious.

ELENA: *Gracias Celena—*

CELENA: Now loves, you make sure to contact me when you get across. Don't make me worry about you.

PALO: We will as soon as—

CELENA: 'Cause Jesus left three weeks ago and has not contacted me—

ELENA: It's okay, we will write as soon—

CELENA: Not that he ever talked to me when he was here 'cause all he watched was football...

ELENA: I know, Celena yes—

CELENA: Him and his cousin always watching the TV while I clean the house. Because it is not like I gave birth to him or wiped his ass when he was a baby I have to deal with his...

ELENA: Celena! It's okay. We will contact you. I promise—

CELENA: Okay, 'cause if you don't, you're going to make me think things and—

ELENA: *(Hugs her sister.)* In the name of all that is holy I will contact you once we are in Arizona.

(CELENA stops talking and gives ELENA a big hug. Takes her shawl off and wraps it around ELENA's neck. Pulls back and then blesses her.)

CELENA: *En el nombre del Padre, y del Hijo y del Espíritu Santo... vaya con Dios.*

(PALO is filled with emotion. CELENA begins to exit.)

PALO: I will make sure she calls.

(CELENA stops. Looks at PALO and slowly walks over to him and begins to bless him.)

CELENA: En el nombre del Padre, y del Hijo y del Espíritu Santo… vaya con Dios. (She exits.)

PALO: You're lucky to have a sister that cares for you like that.

ELENA: She is crazy, but I love her.

(An excited COUPLE comes by, celebrating. BOTH are clearly drunk and enjoying Cinco de Mayo.)

PERSON 1: ¡Viva Mexico!

PERSON 2: ¡Viva! ¡Mexico Viva!

(The drunk COUPLE exits.)

PALO: (Excited.) ¡VIVA Mexico! ¡Viva America!

ELENA: Viva America? It's Cinco de Mayo. What is so special about America?

PALO: When I was on the road between Guatemala and Mexico, I saw this commercial. These people were singing really bad in front of some very important people. When each of them finished their song, the people behind the table made fun of the singers. Some laughed, some cried right on TV, others got very angry and screamed or yelled back. Pero esso, esso es la vida. That's the life I want.

ELENA: What? You want to sing? Join the Mariachis?

PALO: No, No! NOT SING. I don't want to sing. I want a life with a chance. Where my greatest worry is someone's opinion. Can you imagine what that must be like? To have a life so good that the thing you worry about is what someone says about you. To live in a place where you have the opportunity to make a choice. Where a nobody can get in front of important people and have a chance. It doesn't matter if you win or not. You had a chance. I don't want to become someone because I had to. I want the opportunity to become someone better.

ELENA: Who do you want to become?

PALO: I don't know. But if I stay here in the streets…

ELENA: I don't think you could ever become what you're afraid of. You are a good person.

PALO: You think so?

ELENA: Yes I do.

PALO: I am just trying to get by, you know.

ELENA: Yeah, I do know.

(Enter ANGEL, a nervous man with shifty eyes. He is eating an apple with a small pocket knife.)

ANGEL: You Elena?

PALO: Yes we are the ones trying to—

ANGEL: I didn't ask you.

ELENA: Yes I am Elena.

(Pause.)

ANGEL: One thousand American dollars.

PALO: One thousand dollars!!!!

ELENA: Shhh Palo—

PALO: This is bullshit!

ELENA: Palo, calm down.

ANGEL: Each.

PALO: Como que each? I could get forty people over for—

ELENA: PALO! Calm down.

ANGEL: Or you can work on El Ranchero.

PALO: *¿Y que es esa mierda?*

ELENA: That's where we work over there on one of their farms and they take it out of our paycheck to pay them back for the trip.

ANGEL: Yes.

PALO: Fine, let's do that.

ELENA: Okay, we'll do that.

ANGEL: Good.

(Pause.)

PALO: Did anyone ever tell you, you talk too much.

ANGEL: *(Confused.)* No.

PALO: Well you do.

ELENA: Palo.

PALO: What? I'm just saying I'm tired of all this talk—let's go. When do we get out of here?

ELENA: When can we leave?

ANGEL: Now.

PALO: Let's go— *¡Vamanos!*

ANGEL: Follow me.

(Lights to half. PALO turns to watch the following commercial as the actors set the next scene.)

VIDEO #8
AMERICAN JEANS COMMERCIAL

We hear Elvis Presley's "America" as pictures of famous landmarks appear across the screen. Scenes like the Golden Gate Bridge, Washington, D.C., New York, Seattle, Texas oil

fields, and finally the Statue of Liberty. Then across the screen we see: "PAG JEANS AMERICAN since 1982."

SCENE 11

On the large screen appears:

"DAY 730 - COYOTE WELLS, CA"

Lights to full. We see PALO lying still in the corner of a bathroom. Offstage we hear PEOPLE singing a song ("Jesus Loves Me").

MARIAN: *(Offstage.)* Honey, don't be too long!!

(HOWARD enters, a typical American father on vacation.)

HOWARD: No Marian, I am not going to take long. *(Laughing.)* No Billy, put Spike down...put... Honey, get a picture of that...

BILLY *(Offstage.)* How long till we get to Dinky Land?? DAD!! HOW LONG!!!

HOWARD: *(Sees PALO.)* Oh sorry I thought it was empty... *(Noticing.)* Oh God... Oh no... Umm...

BILLY *(Offstage.)* Dinky Land... How LONG!!!!

MARIAN *(Offstage, laughing.)* Howard... Billy is dancing with Spike... is it clean... I need to use the toilet... Howard?

HOWARD: Oh... Jesus... MARIAN!!! CALL THE POLICE NOW!!!... It's okay... Um... Oh God... I won't hurt you...

PALO: *No... No... Por favor... No...*

(Enter MARIAN, HOWARD's wife. A blond, blue-eyed, typical American woman.

MARIAN: Howard! Are you okay, honey *(Sees PALO.)* ...OH! MY God!

HOWARD: Give me the cell...

(She is in shock and does not move.)

HOWARD: Honey! The phone. Now Marian stay here, I am calling the police.

(MARIAN hands HOWARD the phone as he runs offstage. She slowly approaches PALO.)

MARIAN: It's okay… It's okay… I am just going to sit here…

PALO: *Agua, por favor, agua…*

MARIAN: Oh water oh!

(MARIAN rushes to a faucet. Turns it and nothing comes out.)

MARIAN: I am sorry there is no water… It's not working. HOWARD!!!

PALO: *Por favor… Agua…algo…agua.*

MARIAN: *(Begins to rummage through her purse.)* Oh God… wait, I have a little Diet Coke and an Atkins bar… I am on a diet so I use these. They taste better then the Slim-Fast ones… I'm trying to get my figure back…

(MARIAN helps PALO take a drink of the cola. PALO begins to cough violently.)

MARIAN: *(Getting upset.)* Howard! Call an ambulance quick!!! Howard!!!

(HOWARD enters.)

HOWARD: Help is coming…

(Howard is now leaning over PALO and holding him, trying to bring him comfort and reassure him.)

HOWARD: Help is on the way… They're almost here. They are almost here.

BILLY: *(Offstage.)* Mom, Dad what's going on? Where are you guys? When are we going to get there?

HOWARD: They're almost here…

(Lights to half. PALO turns to watch the following commercial as the actors set the next scene.)

VIDEO #9
LAW FIRM COMMERCIAL

We see two very concerned PARENTS. The WOMAN has a tissue as if she has been crying.

MAN: One day Billy comes home and is crying…

WOMAN: I asked him why he was crying and—

MAN: It seems the other kids in school were making fun of him because of his weight. They called him FAT ASS. I mean, we thought—

WOMAN: I always order the healthy stuff for him off the menu at McDougal's. He is always so happy when he eats a Double Douggie. We never knew the Happy Meal would make him so… So…

MAN: Large…

(Enter LAWYER.)

LAWYER: Hi. I'm Ira Handler. Has your son been the victim of too many Happy Meals? Has he tripled in size because you thought he was getting a healthy well-balanced meal? WELL! If you or anyone in your family has been hurt by these McDougal Happy Meals, you may be entitled to a settlement. Contact us at Ira Handler and Wine, and get the settlement you deserve. Help me help you.

(Lights to half.)

VIDEO #10
NIGHTLY NEWS

On the screen appears the nightly news. The ANCHOR is very professional, acting as if this is a CNN story.

NEWS ANCHOR 1: And now our top story. Authorities are holding an adolescent boy who escaped an abandoned U-Haul in southern California just outside of Coyote Wells. Two people at a rest stop called the police at around four-thirty p.m. after finding the young man near death from dehydration and heat exhaustion. When authorities found the truck, they discovered fifteen dead bodies inside the metal cargo cabin.

(On the TV screen flash images of the desert and a small U-Haul truck.)

NEWS ANCHOR 2: Immigration officials are saying it appears to be a human trafficking incident gone awry. The fifteen bodies have not yet been identified, but range from five to forty years of age. Authorities are speculating that the people died of heat exhaustion and suffocation, as the metal cargo container was locked from the outside with no ventilation or light. Temperatures in the area have reached record highs around one hundred twenty-two degrees, creating oven-like conditions. The boy said through an interpreter that he was in the container for three days, and that some of the people in there had died on the first day. He escaped only after prying open a small hatch at the top.

NEWS ANCHOR 3: Thank you Tiffany, thank you Chip, a sad story indeed. Is your scale sweating? Sixty-five percent of Americans are overweight, and half of all middle school kids are obese, but a new plastic surgery can shave off those pounds without the workout, for kids and adults! Wolf Stocker is here with a live report. Wolf.

(Lights to half.)

SCENE 12

On the large screen appears:

"Day 731 - Coyote Wells, CA"

PALO is lying on the bed. He is delirious and still knocked out. He flows in and out of consciousness. DR. ORLANDO is in the room finishing up a chart. NURSE bursts in as she is late.

NURSE: I am so sorry Dr. Orlando—

DR. ORLANDO: It is okay, I know there are—

NURSE: It's a goddamn circus out there with reporters— oh I didn't mean to curse— oh I am sorry— *(Whispers.)* is he sleeping—

DR. ORLANDO: Shhh… it is okay… he's resting…

(NURSE sees PALO.)

NURSE: Is that him?

DR. ORLANDO: Yes. Now listen. The patient is running a fever of a hundred and two and holding. If it goes any higher, alert Nancy at the phones. He is very badly dehydrated. His sodium is one fifty— So keep his IV at half-normal saline.

PALO: *(Stirs in bed. Half-screaming, half in dream.)* ¡Elena! ¡¡¡No machete!!!

(NURSE looks concerned and scared.)

DR. ORLANDO: It's okay… he is having nightmares and hallucinating. It is common with fevers that run that high for so long. Now Dr. Cootnick will be by shortly. So will a lawyer—Dominick Rebiles.

NURSE: I thought we were not letting anyone see him! Nancy said—

DR. ORLANDO: No, it's okay. Dominick is the state-appointed attorney in this district. He's a friend of mine. Whenever illegals come into the hospital, he is the first person I call. He is a good guy. I wanted to give him a head start with this kid.

NURSE: Okay. I'm sorry Dr. Orlando, it's just that Nancy told me that she has kicked out three reporters tying to get pictures of him. And that was just this afternoon. She even found one of them reading his preliminary chart and had to physically grab it out of his hands!

DR. ORLANDO: Did anyone get a camera in here?

NURSE: No, not a snapshot or anything. Ugh, the press, they are just disgusting.

(Enter DOMINICK, a blond-haired lawyer with a welcoming smile. He is dressed in a simple suit, probably bought at discount.)

DOMINICK: Hi Victor, *(Or Victoria, if DR. ORLANDO is played by a woman.)* how are you?

DR. ORLANDO: Hi D, how's Shannon?

DOMINICK: She's doing well. She is due in three weeks so were're on pins and needles.

DR. ORLANDO: Well, keep me informed.

(DOMINICK looks over to PALO on the bed.)

DOMINICK: So...

DR. ORLANDO: SO...

DOMINICK: So...

DR. ORLANDO: I'm sure you've heard by now.

DOMINICK: Yeah, it's all over the news.

(DR. ORLANDO pulls DOMINICK over to the side for a private conversation.)

DR. ORLANDO: This kid is in bad condition.

DOMINICK: Most are when they end up here.

DR. ORLANDO: Not like this. Aside from the dehydration and malnutrition, there was excessive residue from industrial glue around his mouth and nasal cavity. Upon examining his stool, we discovered traces of arachnid, roaches, worms, and we discovered blood.

DOMINICK: Oh God.

DR. ORLANDO: We are awaiting HIV results. This kid has been through a lot. Do you think he has a chance to stay in the country?

DOMINICK: *(Doubtful.)* Well as long as he is here in the hospital, the courts won't do anything till he's better. But—

DR. ORLANDO: Come on— he has clearly been through so much. What about— what's her name, from a couple of months ago—Maria—you got her asylum—

DOMINICK: That's 'cause she was a girl and a minor. Do we even know how old he is? Plus the laws protect female immigrants more than males, we—

(Enter BOOMER McNEIL, a hotshot Hollywood lawyer. He is dressed in a silk Armani suit.)

BOOMER: Hello Doctor, I am Boomer McNeil, defense attorney—

DR. ORLANDO: Excuse me. You cannot be in here!

BOOMER: I am going to be offering my services to your patient, if he so chooses. He is an illegal immigrant and will need a good lawyer.

DOMINICK: He already has one.

DR. ORLANDO: *(Not amused.)* Wait... I know you, you were on that OJ team, and did the Winona Ryder thing, I saw you on TV.

NURSE: Did you see him on *Late Night* promoting his book?

BOOMER: You saw me.

NURSE: Ya, you're fatter in person.

BOOMER: Please, I make more in a day than you make all year.

DR. ORLANDO: I think you should leave now.

BOOMER: Look Doctor, he is going to need a good lawyer. Now you can let some no-name state-appointed attorney screw up his chance at freedom or you can let me help him. Help me help him.

DOMINICK: Well I'm the no-name screwup, and I strongly urge you to leave this room before you get involved in a new lawsuit.

BOOMER: *(Crosses over to PALO.)* Why don't we let him decide. *Hola como estas, me llamo—*

DOMINICK: If you take one more step towards my client, I swear I'll have your license!

NURSE: Quiet! All of you. I don't care who you are but you can argue it outside. Not here. NOW!

DR. ORLANDO: Thank you Nurse. You're absolutely right. Everyone out.

BOOMER: I'll get the press in here, then we will see who he chooses. *(Exits.)*

DOMINICK: I'll get him and the press out of the parking lot and out of the hospital. Don't worry.

DR. ORLANDO: Thanks D.

(DOMINICK rushes out. DR. ORLANDO exits. After they leave, NURSE sits next to PALO. She opens up her bag and pulls out a small book and two magazines.)

NURSE: I know you probably won't understand what I'm saying. But I thought it would let you know someone was here.

PALO: *(Mumbled voice.)* Ugh... Elena... Carlo...

NURSE: Okay. I have *Popular Science*, *Highlights*, and a kids' book.

(She stops and looks at him. She reaches over with an ear thermometer and takes his temperature. She looks at it and notes the time.)

NURSE: *(In a happier mood.)* Well, you're starting to come down. I might not need to be here all night! So let's not read *Popular Science* 'cause that will make your headache worse, let's skip *Highlights* 'cause that will give me a headache and... *(Opens the children's book. She smiles.)* *The Velveteen Rabbit* or *How Toys Become Real*. There was once a Velveteen Rabbit, and in the beginning he was really splendid...

(Lights to half.)

SCENE 13

On the large screen appears:

"DAY 732 - COYOTE WELLS, CA, 1:32 A.M."

Lights remain at half for the scene. PALO is alone onstage in his hospital bed. He is having a nightmare, and the voices we hear are those in his head.

KILLER 1: Fuck it's jammed.

KILLER 2: Get off our streets.

CARLO: I knew I would find you here.

STRANGER: Want some glue?

4: Stop screaming!

PRIEST: I will pray for you.

STRANGER: Don't cry.

(ENID laughs.)

SEÑORA: Lady fingers don't let me down!

ELENA: You're cute.

CELENA: *Via Con Dios.*

KILLER 2: Get off our streets.

CARLO: Got some glue?

DEALER: I will help.

KILLER 1: It's jammed

KILLER 2: Get off our streets.

DEALER: Trying to help.

CALL GIRL: Flacito.

(ELENA screams.)

CALL GIRL: Flacito.

ELENA: You're nuts!

FLACO: Fire!!

CELENA: *Via Con Dios.*

ELENA: You're a good person.

DEALER: I just want to help. I will help.

(A gunshot is heard, and PALO bolts up in a crazed fever. He looks to stage left as two ACTORS enter with large silver machetes. PALO is trying to scream but nothing is coming out of his mouth. The two MEN with machetes slowly walk toward him, dragging the machetes on the floor. PALO quickly gets

out of bed and tears his IV out. He exits. Lights to half.)

(On the large screen appears:)

"Day 732 - Route 721, Southern CA, 2:37 a.m."

VIDEO #11
Cops Video Intro

This is a promo for a TV show similar to Cops.

SCENE 14

Offstage we hear yelling as two COPS chasing PALO run on, followed by the CAMERA MAN. The following scene is done as if the audience is watching the live taping of Cops. PALO is hallucinating. He is out of control and very violent. The COPS are having to use excessive force. The following scene appears on stage and on the TV screen via live camera from the CAMERA MAN.

COP 1: Stop now!

COP 2: Over here!

(PALO is tackled by one of the officers.)

PALO: NO!!!

COP 1: *(Out of breath.)* Ya… Whew… he gave us a run!

COP 2: Sir you need to stop moving… *¡Quedate quieto!… No te vamos a herir…*

PALO: *Dejame! Le va matar… El bebe… Le quieren matar…Tiene el Machete… El Machete…*

COP 1: What's he saying? *Esta bean carma se.*

COP 2: Something about a knife or a machete. He is hopped up on something… speed or

PALO: *No... No... me muero... (His voice trails off.)*

COP 1: Ya... We get a lot of border crashers... no IDs... they are usually hopped up on meth or glue or speed...

COP 2: Maybe all... *(To PALO.) vamos... I am going to get you up okay... Te voy a levantar... No corres okay...* Do not run...

COP 1: *Si, no correo...* I feel bad for these kids, but this suspect assaulted a clerk, stole glue, money... Clerk is being taken to County Medical...

COP 2: *¿Por que corres?* Ah? Aw damn it. I tore my shirt and cut my arm...

COP 1: 1022 we need a med unit on Route 721 near the border around mile marker 329.

COP 2: *¿Estas herido? ¿Sangrando? ¿Ingles?* He's fine, it must have been when I hit the ground damn it...

COP 1: We always treat any cuts or bruises right away. Most of these kids on drugs can have HIV... Never know... Never take chances.

COP 2: Damn... Hell of a tackle.

(BOTH laugh.)

COP 1: *Vamos al charo...*

COP 2: *Carro...* Not *charo...* the car no running... *No corras.*

(COP 2 takes PALO offstage to the car.)

COP 1: *(To an offstage camera.)* We in general have a kid like this two to three times a week. Most of the time they stop, but this guy assaulted a merchant, stole, ran... the night judge will not be lenient on him. More than likely he will go right over the border. Probably there by morning. And if Mexico doesn't want him, they will give

him a one-way ticket on a bus to wherever... After 9/11 things are different. Now it is simple. Any kind of aggravated offense— *(Whistle sound.)* kicked right out. Judge's discretion. Prisons are too crowded. It's sad but... we are just doing our job.

CAMERA MAN: *(Entering.)* And cut! Dude that was killer! Man that rocked! It will totally get on Fox!. Shit he don't speak English though? Cant get a consent signed...

(COP 2 re-enters.)

COP 2: He's in the car... Damn this hurts.

COP 1: *(Suspiciously.)* He needs to sign something?

CAMERA MAN: Naw... man we'll just fuzz out his face so no one will recognize him. We do it all the time.

(As they walk offstage, no longer on camera:)

COP 2: Did you get the cut?

CAMERA MAN: Ya man.

COP 2: Get the tackle?

CAMERA MAN: Totally man.

COP 2: Hell of a tackle... damn this hurts.

(Lights to half.)

SCENE 15

On the large screen appears:

"DAY 745 - TEGUCIGALPA, HONDURAS. 2,422 MILES TO AMERICA."

Lights to full. Onstage we see PALO once again on the ground in front of the same store front as in the beginning of the play.

His clothes are now almost devoid of any color and are covered in dirt. He has no shoes, and is clearly high on glue. Enter DANTE, the store owner. DANTE is a small, balding man with a nice smile. He is wearing all black and has a large set of shiny keys. He is just finishing locking up the store front. Enter ROSA, ENID, and CELIA. They are wearing red dresses and have been drinking on their way to the club.

DANTE: Hello ladies! Good evening!

ROSA and ENID: *(Like schoolgirls flirting.)* Good evening Dante!! *(They giggle.)*

CELIA: *(Very drunk.)* We're drinking club dance tonight…

(ROSA and ENID laugh at CELIA.)

ROSA: We're going the club near the McDonald's, over by the BMW dealership—

ENID: Why are you closing the store this late?

DANTE: I had good business today! Sold lots of TVs and radios—

CELIA: Hi Dante! We're going to Inferno for club.

(ALL laugh.)

CELIA: Did I make a funny?

ENID: Come with us!

ROSA: *Salsa y Merengue—*

ENID: You should bring and salsa!

DANTE: *(Laughing.)* You left the boys at home now didn't you?

(PALO begins to cough violently.)

ENID: *(Referring to PALO.)* He drinking too much…

DANTE: He has been here all day. Talking crazy. Saying he was in America. Look at him. I feel bad for him.

ENID: Come on! I want to go!!

ROSA: Ya let's go Dante!! Please…

DANTE: Okay! Okay! I'll go for a while!!!

(The three LADIES and DANTE exit off excitedly. DANTE has forgotten to turn off the TV in the store window. A preview for the "Movie of the Week" begins to play.)

VOICEOVER: From the producer who brought you the "OJ Files"… and "The Winona Ryder Story"… ripped from the headlines…

(PALO begins to look at the TV. Various pictures of a young, good-looking Hispanic BOY flash across the screen. We see him in a courtroom. We see a scene with him scared in the desert, walking. Then the scene changes to the BOY speaking with LAWYERS. It is clear that this is a made-for-TV movie about PALO's truck incident.)

VOICEOVER: Comes the story of pain and suffering. Three days of hell in a truck… One Boy… One Chance… One Hope for Freedom…

(PALO sits up, then walks toward the TV realizing that it's his story.)

PALO: …Ugh… that…look I am there! I'm there!!! *(Sniffs glue.)* See I told you!… I was… Look! That is me. I'm there! Look I will go again. See! I will go again. I will because I saw it! I just need to know which way is North.

VOICEOVER: *(In a gentle voice.)* This program is brought to you by Child-Choice Services. Choose the family of your dreams.

(As the preview ends, PALO is sitting alone onstage looking into the audience.)

PALO: Which way is North? Excuse me... which way is North... *permiso señor... ¿adonde esta el Norte? ¿Adonde esta El Norte? ¿Adonde esta El Norte?*

(Lights fade to black.)

THE 29 QUESTIONS PROJECT

Katie Bull and Hillary Rollins

KATIE BULL has written, directed, and performed in the following original works for the Bull Family Orchestra since 1989: *Young Lilah* (Warren Street Performance Loft), *Small Town New York City* (Gershon Resnick, producer—Summer Festival of One Acts at 29th Street Rep), *A Vegetable From the Sea* (William Redfield Theater), *Waltzing in the Wonder* (Tribeca Lab), *Caterpillar Crossing*, and *Something She Ate* (Anna Ivara, director—Greenwich Street Theatre). Since joining the Improvisational Arts Ensembles in residency at the Middle Church: *Into the Riddle, Where Are You Now?, Breaking News, Victory Hug*, and the workshop viewing of *She Has Such a Vivid Imagination*. Katie holds a BFA in acting from SUNY Purchase College Conservatory of Theatre Arts and Film. She is also a professional freelance vocal production coach for the speaking voice, and works with numerous Broadway, off-Broadway, film, and television professionals. She is currently the head of vocal production coordination at NYU's Atlantic Theater Company Acting School, a division of the Tisch School of the Arts, where she teaches Level II and Level III vocal production to sophomores, juniors, and seniors. Katie is a professional jazz singer appearing at 55BAR; her premiere CD, *Conversations With the Jokers*, was on twelve top ten College Music Jazz radio charts and is available on www.cdbaby.com. Two new CDs are soon to be released on the Corn Hill Indie label. She is married and has two children, Hannajane and Hudson.

HILLARY ROLLINS's plays have been seen in New York at Manhattan Punch Line Theater, Stage 72 Theater Workshop, Perfectly Frank Theater Workshop, the Turnip Theatre, and New Georges Theatre. They have also been produced as workshops in Los Angeles at HBO's

New Writers/New Actors Project, the Eclectic Theater Company, and
Ensemble Studio Theatre West, as well as in Arizona at the Sedona
Actor's Theater and in Florida at Miami City Theatre's Summer Shorts
Festival. Television credits include, among others, *The Mickey Mouse
Club*, the award-winning *How to Be Donna Reed*, *The Chairman's
Choice* starring Dick Van Dyke, *The National TV Comedy Test* starring
comedian Rich Hall, *Gullah Gullah Island*, *Regan Tonight*, and the
USA Network's New Year's movie marathon promotion starring Ed
Begley, Jr., and Patti Lupone. Rollins is also the author of *The Erotic
Way* and *The Empress's New Lingerie* and has contributed to two an-
thologies of essays—*An Ear to the Ground* and *In My Life: Writings on
the Beatles*. Currently, she is working on a new original musical with
Hollywood composer Howard Pearl.

Katie would like to thank the Middle Collegiate Church community
that supports the Improvisational Arts Ensembles collaborative residency: Gordon Dragt, Minister; Nora Fragosa, Church Administra-
tor; Freeman Palmer, Minister for Community Life and Outreach;
Melinda Cruz, Secretary; Jeanne Boland, Minister for Children and
Family; and Jan Fisher, Membership Coordinator. The IAE/MCC
workshops of this project were invaluable, as was the feedback of all
the workshop audiences to whom this company is indebted.

Hillary is deeply grateful to the producers, actors, directors, and designers of *The 29 Questions Project* for helping celebrate the life and
heal the loss of her friend, Laura Rockefeller. Special thanks to the
Rockefeller family, Stephen Fife, the Joelson Foundation, Jane and
Jack Rollins, and daughter Eloise.

The 29 Questions Project was first presented by the Bull Family Orchestra (Katie Bull, Artistic Director), under the nonprofit umbrella of the Improvisational Arts Ensembles, Inc., on June 7, 2004, at Yaffa's T Room, New York City, with the following cast and credits:

Message From the Driver

Woman .... Heather Oakley
Driver .... David Dartley
Doorman (Pete) .... Antonio Alvarez
Directed by: Kathryn Alexander

29 Questions

Actress 1 .... Allison Wright
Actress 2 .... Patricia Hart
Directed by: Leslie Kincaid Burby

Arm

Young College Activist .... Lillian Medville
Young American GI .... Michael Robinson
Directed by: Katie Bull

Hand

American College Tourist .... Ashley Lambert/Katey Parker
Young Palestinian Student .... Matt Sadewitz
Directed by: Katie Bull

Lighting Design: Jeff Larson
Sound Engineer: Phil Lee/Full House
Light/Sound Operator: Julie Gearheard
Production Assistant: Joy Walton
Security: Jason Elmer
Publicity: Beck Lee, Media Blitz
Yaffa's Room Manager: Yo Yo
Acceuil (Welcome Area): Joy Walton and Antonio Alvarez
Vocals: Ayelet Rose Gottlieb
Oud and Percussion: Yoel Ben Simhon
Understudies: Woman/Joy Walton, Driver and Young Palestinian Student/Antonio Alvarez, Young College Activist and American College Tourist/Katey Parker, Young American GI and Doorman/Robbie Sublett

Visit www.katiebull.com and www.improvarts.com.

THE HISTORY OF THE PROJECT
Katie Bull

In 2002, the wounds of the 9/11 disaster still felt so raw. The myriad interweavings of possible cause and effect exposed the world's disorder in ways many of us Americans had perhaps never witnessed—or chosen to notice. Like so many people, I just kept asking, *why?*

That year, Leslie Kincaid Burby, a co-founder of the Bull Family Orchestra, came to me with Hillary Rollins's play, *29 Questions*, with these words: "My friend Laura died in the South Tower and her friend Hillary wrote this short play using their verbatim email dialogue— read it…"

As an artist, I was most drawn to documentary responses to 9/11 at that time, so the notion of the questionnaire as source material caught my interest. In the wake of the disaster, the verbatim dialogue took on a haunting poetic quality. Hillary's narrative was direct and personal; the "particular" hit a universal chord. The play revealed the transformative and life-affirming impact that death can have on those left behind. Anyone who has been in proximity to death knows that the stems of broccoli take on extraordinary beauty. Nothing should be taken for granted.

I wanted to produce Hillary's play, but I found myself reacting to the notion that a response to 9/11 would *only* be about two Americans. So, I wrote *Message From the Driver* and *Hand*, and—after the U.S. entered Baghdad—added *Arm*. I wanted to place *29 Questions* within a broader perspective. I felt we needed to hear other voices asking other questions. The night needed to have a global context so that we might discover how these issues are interconnected.

The Improvisational Arts Ensembles co-produced a reading at Battery Dance, and a workshop at the Middle Collegiate Church, culminating in *The 29 Questions Project* in 2004. The works were presented at Yaffa's T Room, which was the only restaurant near Ground Zero to remain open on 9/11 and which, in the week following the disaster, fed the rescue workers and members of the downtown community who could not cook in their own homes. On 9/11, Yaffa's was also used as an EMS station and in support of Salvation Army efforts for neighborhood relief in Tribeca.

The next phase of the project is going to be Installation "Happenings" with several of the Tribeca visual artists we met while we were performing at Yaffa's. We are presently scouting raw office spaces near Ground Zero, and plan to keep the celebratory ritual alive with food, live world music, and the expanded texture of visual art made in response to 9/11 and the current world circumstance of terrorism and war.

Samir Joubran writes,

> "...the act of momentous improvisation, as well as its state, be-
> comes an act of dialogue with the other, the presence of which we
> respect and whose state of distinction we preserve."

Joubran is a Palestinian oud player. The oud is an ancient Middle
Eastern guitar, something like a lute. In ancient oud playing, improvisational dialogue is primary; as the art form evolves, the rules of the
conversation are rewritten, ...*even as we speak...*

⌒ ❧

MESSAGE FROM THE DRIVER

Katie Bull

Transition in: All the players of The 29
Questions Project *have been stationed in
and around the venue engaged in an environmental improvisation in character.
A young Pakistani TAXI DRIVER has
been sitting in the audience reading an
Arabic language newspaper. He has been
sipping a thick black Turkish coffee and
is occasionally asked to move to make room
for the arriving audience members by the
Welcome Area hosts of the evening. In these
moments, one can see him making a
mildly tense accommodation as, from time
to time, he questions the necessity of being
asked to move. He should not make a
scene; however, some resentment should be
registered.*

*Stationed beside the play space, a singing
Israeli oud player calls out a long acoustic
tone in the tradition of Pathane Khan (traditional Pakistani folk singer) as an invoca-
tion to commence the performance, and begins a gentle oud line below his canting.*

*This is the signal for DOORMAN to enter
and set a street sign on the stage that reads
HENRY HUDSON PARKWAY, and turn
a page on a preset calendar which has been
blank in plain view, so that it now reads
OCTOBER 2001. This is also the cue for
DRIVER to cross on a long diagonal toward
an imaginary taxi that is defined by three
nondescript chairs, one for the front seat, two
for the back seat. He is dressed in black jeans
and a black T-shirt, with a navy blue American brand windbreaker and American-
made sneakers.*

*Just as DRIVER is settling into his taxi and
DOORMAN is exiting, a WOMAN in her
late thirties runs boldly down a different
diagonal through the audience shouting
"TAXI," forcefully stabbing her arm into the
air, waving her hand to hail a cab. She is
holding a great many bags. She is wearing a
knee-length fall sweater with autumn colors
that accentuate her long loose hair. She has
the look now known as East Village Bohe-*

mian which she got before it was a look and which she wears unintentionally. She's clearly not a businesswoman—the WOMAN is in the arts…

Setting: New York City, borough of Manhattan, eleven p.m.

WOMAN: Taxi! *Taxi! (Makes a loud New York whistle.) Wait! Wait!*

(DRIVER sits in the front of his cab, waiting. WOMAN, bedraggled with her bags, flings herself breathlessly into his back seat. She does not look at him; she is talking as she wrestles with her stuff.)

WOMAN: God, thank God you stopped, I was thinking I wouldn't get a cab.

(Silence as she continues to untangle herself from her own things. Still not looking at him.)

WOMAN: Umm, ugh, oh, all these God Damned… alright, all…right… Okay, umm, so, up to Cabrini Boulevard, Washington Heights, around 184th Street. Is that okay?

DRIVER: Yes.

WOMAN: *(Distracted, still settling in, not looking at him.)* It's far, I know, thanks. Do you know the way or do you need me to give you directions?

DRIVER: I know. I go across on 14th, over, and up the highway to the bridge.

WOMAN: That's good. But if there's bad traffic, you can also take Riverside.

(They sit in silence, as she struggles with her bags and her seat belt. She then collapses back in her seat and gazes out the window rather absently. Sounds of distant fire truck sirens sneak into immediacy with a loud jolt.)

WOMAN: *(Following the trucks with her eyes and body, slowly at first…)* Oh my God… Oh my… *(Sits bolt upright—she's*

up against her side window, pressing on the glass, leaning toward the passing fire trucks.) What is that?! Oh my God, oh my *God*, oh my God—look at that *bank*! The smoke is billowing! It's black, pure black. There must be four, no, no five trucks… that's a five-alarm… that's…that's not a fire… no… look at the glass blown out, it's… could it be a bomb? It's a bomb. It's got to be!

DRIVER: *(Calm.)* Where?

WOMAN: Over there, over, there, behind us now, behind us! *(She's up against the back window.)*

DRIVER: Are you sure?

WOMAN: Well, it must have been, because the windows, the glass was blown out, not in. Oh, oh, listen to me… God, that's my post-9/11 thing. God. Can you imagine I'm reacting that way?!

(DRIVER laughs. WOMAN doesn't register his odd volume, she is too caught up in her own world.)

WOMAN: That's. Just this morning I was taking my kids to school, and we saw, well— *(Pause as she exhales like a tightly decompressing steam valve, her body sinking into her seat.)* I'm sure it was a bomb, in this truck. The truck was at this strange angle, and the front end of the trunk was just sort of mangled, kind of tangled and melted, and there was purple powder all around it, and the glass was everywhere too, and there was a police rope, you know, it was roped, taped off. God.

(DRIVER is silent.)

WOMAN: Nobody in the neighborhood seemed to know what it, what, it was, how, it had happened. And I have small children, I need to know "why," and "who" did that! I've got small children on my mind.

(Silence.)

WOMAN: Man, this is just the way things are now, you see things in a whole new way I guess.

(DRIVER is silent. WOMAN is becoming aware of his silence; she nearly looks at him directly—she is distracted by the traffic.)

WOMAN: Jesus Christ. Oh, we're at the highway… well, it looks alright here, but let's see how it gets uptown…

DRIVER: *(Slowly with articulation.)* Where—was—the—truck?

WOMAN: What?

DRIVER: The truck. The bomb. Where do you think the bomb was?

WOMAN: Well, the truck—was on, the truck was on Seventh Avenue, between 13th and 14th Streets. On the west side of the avenue. In front of a residential building. Why?

(Pause.)

DRIVER: I can tell you Where the bombs are.

(Silence. Silence.)

WOMAN: Oh, you can, you. Oh. *(She is looking directly at him now in the rearview mirror. She is glancing at his name plate. She decides to engage.)* How?

DRIVER: *(Slowly.)* That was not a bomb.

WOMAN: Oh.

(They are both silent. It is the first time he looks at her in his rearview mirror. They lock eyes. She is visibly scared. She redirects her focus outside of the taxi. Silence. Silence.)

WOMAN: You know, this highway traffic can be brutal it's moving now but it

could just very suddenly stop and we would be, trapped, you could, you could get off at the 71st Street exit, and maybe I could just take the A train, I mean the C train, oh, we're passing, we're we're, passing…the…

(Pause.)

DRIVER: We're okay.

(Silence.)

DRIVER: So, where were you on 9/11?

WOMAN: *(Feigned control, fast and nervous, she answers to demonstrate she is not afraid.)* I was at home, my husband took the kids to school that morning. I sat and did some work. I was writing a syllabus for my students, updating it, for the university. I didn't even know it was happening. *(WOMAN looks out the window—her rhythm shifts as her memory pulls her into imagery. She is alternately talking directly to DRIVER, then drawn back to the images of that day—looking toward the front window or the side window of the taxi, following the images. Acknowledging his presence, drifting back and forth between past and present.)* My husband called me. He just said, two planes hit the World Trade Center, they think it's terrorism. Stay where you are, I've got the kids. They were at school. But their school is on 13th Street. So they were really downtown, and the subways were shut down. God, it was so scary. *(Pause.)* We didn't know what was coming next. *(Pause.)* I went to the TV, and there it was. The first tower, black smoke billowing. And I knew it would fall right then and there. And then the doorbell rang. It was the phone guy. *(Laughs at the absurdity.)* There to fix the second jack. And I just looked at him, he had a friend with him, this woman. And we all just said, oh my God. And we all stood and watched TV. And I said, it's going to fall. And he said, no way. And I said, yes it is. And then it did. And he said, no way, again. He said, it's like a movie, and I said, God, it's not a movie. And I talked to my husband again, before the satellites went down—he was at this friend of ours' house, a mother and father of one of my daughter's classmates. The father is a former fireman. He has a construction company now. He was already going down there. He lived. He injured himself. But the satellites went down. I didn't know what was happening. But they came home later when the train lines went back up. I have never hugged like that. Never been so grateful.

(Silence. WOMAN is nearly overwhelmed by the memory. Then her focus shifts and she looks at him quite intently. Silence.)

WOMAN: *(Cautiously.)* And you? Where were you?

(Pause.)

DRIVER: Well I know something was going to happen but I never thought that. *(Smiles.)* I was in my taxi in Brooklyn listening to the radio. I just couldn't believe it.

WOMAN: *(Hiding her fear, quickly jumping in.)* Well they say that even the president knew. You know, I read that this whole thing may have been planned, or maybe part of some plan to get a war going, in Afghanistan, so we can get control of the Caspian oil… something like that… by our government, in order to get oil. That wouldn't surprise me. Because apparently when he, Bush, when he was "told," he really had already known. I read that.

(Deadlocked eye contact in the rearview mirror.)

DRIVER: Really. Where did you read that?

WOMAN: In the *Chronogram*, it's a paper upstate, serves the Hudson River Valley region. It's a really leftist paper. I don't always know what to believe. But then I read some of the same things elsewhere… in other alternative presses. And now it's coming into the mainstream. You really have to wonder. It wouldn't be the first time.

DRIVER: I am surprised they are writing about this. Maybe they are making leaks. You know, my father is in Pakistani intelligence. Do you know what that is?

WOMAN: In Pakistan? Intelligence? Yes.

DRIVER: It's like your CIA.

WOMAN: Okay. What does he say?

DRIVER: Oh you know? You know about the Pakistani CIA? *(He smiles.)*
Well.
There are so many things I could tell you. I know many things.
Let me just say.
This is so much bigger than it looks like. It has been going on for years, it has been going on for years. It is a game, so big. And your government is in this game very deeply. Remember the USS *Cole*? That was Osama, you know, bin Laden, the man they say is responsible for the Trade Center.

WOMAN: Yes I heard that.

DRIVER: And the American Embassy in Kenya. Osama.

WOMAN: Yes, they were saying that.

DRIVER: This is so huge. So huge. So far beyond you or I. So huge. You just have no idea.

WOMAN: What do you think? What do you think will happen?

DRIVER: There will be more. This is nothing.

WOMAN: What do you, do you want this? I mean, do they, do they, do you think the terrorists want a war, I mean how can we stop this? We must try and stop this!

DRIVER: No, you can't stop it. It's too late. It's too far gone. Too big.

(Silence.)

WOMAN: Well. What about ...forgiveness. I mean.
I know we have done wrong things, I didn't elect these presidents who have gone around the world and, and America has trampled with imperialism I know that, I know there has been disrespect and we have created poverty—

DRIVER: *(Interrupting/overlapping.)* There is no forgiveness. Yes. This is revenge. Do you understand the word "revenge"? It is Allah's will. We have nothing to do with this.

WOMAN: Revenge.

DRIVER: Revenge.

(Pause.)

WOMAN: Listen— *(Shifting to the edge of her seat, leaning toward him.)* if, if—if the American F-14s flew over my town and killed all of *my* family my *children, my* parents... I would, I would want *revenge* I *would*— I imagine— but, but, but... what *can WE do*?!...
Do you have children?

DRIVER: Not now, but I will someday.

WOMAN: Don't you think about their future, and the future of having the earth, the planet, here for them?

DRIVER: It is Allah's will. I don't make these decisions. And this life is only a test. This is not the real world for us, you see, this is only the test. The next life is Heaven,

and we are all going there someday. It is not in our control what happens in this life, it is in the hands of our destiny through Allah. Do you read the bible?

WOMAN: Not a lot. Some of the stories. I am not religious, although I believe in a divine force. And in prophets, the wisdom of prophets. And I go to a church, but it is very, inclusive, it's ecumenical.

DRIVER: Well we also believe in Jesus as a prophet. You see we have some things in common. *(He smiles.)* The end of the world is the beginning of *real* life. It is destiny.
Do you know the Koran?
I could give you one.

WOMAN: I, actually bought one. I want to learn more.

DRIVER: Well you should. It is really beautiful.

WOMAN: *(No judgment, just a question.)* I don't want my children to die. What if your children die? Would you want that?

DRIVER: Well, it is not my choice. And a life is determined by Allah, not me, not you. And believe me, what is coming, it is so big.
You will not know what hit you.

(Silence. Silence. Silence.)

WOMAN: Pull around to Fort Washington, and then you can go across on 181st... don't tell me anymore, I'm scared. *(She laughs in fear.)* I'm, just a singer.

DRIVER: Well,

(He laughs a very dark laugh. In the rearview mirror, their eyes meet again. Here he reveals his rage.)

DRIVER: Hah, I'm just a taxi driver.

(Silence. Silence.)

WOMAN: *(Light inquiry, masking terror.)* So, what are you doing when you're not driving a taxi, are you in school?

DRIVER: I am.

WOMAN: What are you studying?

DRIVER: Criminal justice at John Jay College of Criminal Justice.

WOMAN: Wow. Criminal justice.

DRIVER: Yes. I will defend criminals. *(He glares at her in his rearview mirror.)*

WOMAN: *(Sensing her fear is exposed.)* That's great, I always wanted to study law. Good for you. *(She looks away.)* Well, you can go up Cabrini, and yes, right here, and here we are, just, just pull up the hill, I'm that building over…right, right—here.

(Abrupt stop as she jolts forward. As she reaches for her money, it should be clear that she is trying to sneak a look at his name and medallion number on his identification plate. She is too scared to look at it directly. She can't see it.)

WOMAN: Thanks. *(Paying him.)* Keep the, keep the change— I will read my Koran and think about what you've said.

DRIVER: Yes you should.

(As she starts to exit, she sees the medallion plate but won't stop and write his number. That would be too obvious.)

WOMAN: Oh, umm, wait. May I, please, have my, receipt. It's a tax writeoff for me.

(Deadlocked eye contact. Poker face. DRIVER pauses; smiles slowly.)

DRIVER: You want your receipt?

WOMAN: Yes, please.

DRIVER: Let's see, *(Searches in his little paper cup of receipts that he collects.)* Here. *(DRIVER meticulously and deliberately folds the edge of the receipt, creasing it slowly with his nails, and tears the edge off with precision in plain view.)* Here is your receipt.

WOMAN: Thank you. It's a tax writeoff.

DRIVER: Yes, of course.

WOMAN: *(Exiting the cab.)* Good night. Let's pray for peace.

DRIVER: Right. *(He stares intently at the road and drives off.)*

(DRIVER should remain seated in his "taxi" and continue driving in silhouette, as lights rise to illuminate WOMAN as she enters her apartment building. She drags her bags inside her apartment building, and encounters the doorman, PETE.)

PETE: Hey Mrs. Prichett, how was your day?

WOMAN: Oh my God.

PETE: Are you alright?

WOMAN: Well, I was just, I was. I need to look at something right now.

(PETE helps her with her bags. With her hands trembling, she fumbles through her wallet and finds the receipt.)

WOMAN: I know what he did. I need to look… He did it.
He did it.
He tore it off.

PETE: What is it? …did you get mugged…?

WOMAN: He tore it off.
The medallion number on the receipt…
He tore it off.
He knew.
It's gone…
It's gone…
It's gone…

Transition into 29 Questions*: VOCALIST is overlapping "It's gone…" with a vocal improvisation of Middle Eastern sounds and clips of American pop culture as WOMAN begins her exit, with DOORMAN following. Simultaneously, ACTRESS 1 and ACTRESS 2 enter. Both WOMEN are in their forties. ACTRESS 1 was born and bred on the Upper West Side of Manhattan, having immigrated to LA to pursue her writing career. She has a unique mix of both coasts in her dynamic presence. ACTRESS 2 is a round, slightly overweight woman, radiating an immediate warmth and gentler openness. The rhythm of the WOMEN as they are walking should be pedestrian, not abstract, but somewhat slow so as to accentuate the spatial patterns that mirror the random and circuitous intersecting of lives. ACTRESS 1 has a notebook and pencil in hand.*

They all pass each other without seeing the other.

WOMAN and DOORMAN exit to an "offstage" location that is not concealed from the audience. During this transition, DRIVER has shifted one chair into a new position, and exited with the other "taxi" chair. DOORMAN returns at the last minute to move the third chair so that it joins into the new positioning, two chairs side by side with some distance so as to imply cyberspace.

He changes the street sign to read LAURA@AOL.COM, and tears a page off the calendar which reveals the date SEPTEMBER 2001.

29 QUESTIONS

Hillary Rollins

Setting: Hard drive memory.

ACTRESS 1 and ACTRESS 2 sit at computers on different sides of the stage. ACTRESS 2 reads an email questionnaire aloud and types in answers.

ACTRESS 2: Number 1: Living arrangement? Single, one dog, two cats. Number 2: What book are you reading now? Right now, I'm not reading, I'm typing, ha! Okay, I'm reading *The Alienist*. Number 3: What's on your mouse pad? Purple. Number 4: Favorite board game? Scrabble.

Number 5: Favorite magazine? *Vanity Fair*. 6a: Favorite smell or smells? Orange blossoms, jasmine, lily of the valley. 6b: Least favorite smell? Cigar smoke.

ACTRESS 1: *(Addresses the audience.)* Back in March of this year I received an email from my friend Laura with the subject heading "Getting to know you."

ACTRESS 2: 7a: Favorite sound? Children laughing. 7b: Least favorite sound? Motorcycles. 8: Worst feeling in the world? Despair.

ACTRESS 1: It was one of those for-warded Internet time-wasters—I'm sure you've all gotten them—twenty-nine questions designed to, quote, "teach you a lot of little-known facts about your friends."

ACTRESS 2: What is the first thing you think of when you wake up in the morn-ing? Something different every day. Usu-ally I try to remember to be grateful for the day and what's ahead. How many rings before you answer the phone? Depends on what's going on. Future child's name? Maybe Julia, maybe John Kenneth or Jake. What is the most important thing in life? Love.

ACTRESS 1: Of course, one man's spam is another man's spumoni…

ACTRESS 2: [Favorite foods? Lasagna; salads with blue cheese, pears, and wal-nuts in them; good breads, cheeses, and fruits.]* Chocolate or vanilla? Both!

ACTRESS 1: …And Laura, by her own admission, had too much time on her hands. So she filled it out and sent it on.

ACTRESS 2: Do you like to drive fast? Sometimes. Do you sleep with a stuffed animal? No, live ones. If you could meet one person dead or alive? My grandfathers. That's two, I know, so sue me. Favorite alcoholic drink? Definitely Veuve Clicquot champagne! Do you eat the stems of broc-coli? Yes, if they are tender or peeled. [If you could have any job you wanted, what would it be? Well, I'd like to revitalize the summer theatre that my parents worked at in the 1950s in the White Mountains of New Hampshire. I'd be the artistic di-rector.] Ever been in love? Yes. Is the glass half full or half empty? The glass is twice

as big as it needs to be… isn't that great?! No, it's half full. I *know* that's the truth. I just can't always get there. Favorite mov-ies? Hmm, so many… [Casablanca, *Breakfast at Tiffany's*, *The Sound of Music*, a great Irene Dunne-Cary Grant movie called *The Awful Truth*, and *What's Up, Doc?* More recently, *Traffic*, *High Fidelity*, and *Fearless*.] What's under your bed? Dust bunnies, cat fur, and dried puke, I would think—isn't that a turn-on? Know any great single men? Oh, and a volleyball. [What is your favorite number? Changes all the time. I'm kind of partial to prime numbers.] Favorite sport to watch? Bas-ketball and not on TV, only live. Say one nice thing about the person who sent this to you. Steve has one of the most loving, giving, and caring hearts of anyone I know. Person you sent this to who is *most* likely to respond? I don't know, life is so full of surprises… Person you sent this to who is *least* likely to respond? I don't know, life is so full of surprises.

ACTRESS 1: Number 29—"Person you sent this to who is *least* likely to respond." Normally that would be me. See, to *me*, this kind of thing is *incredibly* annoying and despite my love for Laura and all my other friends about whom I stood to learn "a lot of little-known facts," I would be inclined to respond with a swift delete.

(ACTRESS 1 grandly hits her delete key and swings around in her chair with glee. AC-TRESS 2 is visibly pissed.)

ACTRESS 2: Life is so full of surprises.

ACTRESS 1: But for some reason—maybe because I now lived three thou-sand miles away from Laura and every-one else back home in New York—I took the bait.

(ACTRESS 2 perks up and, still from her side of the stage and not relating directly to

*Throughout this play, bracketed text in-dicates cuts made for production at Yaffa's.

ACTRESS 1, poses the questions as AC-TRESS 1, also not relating directly to AC-TRESS 2, answers them as if she's filling out the questionnaire, albeit reluctantly.)

ACTRESS 2: Living arrangement?

ACTRESS 1: I live with the man who is the father of my child, and, of course, I also live with said child.

ACTRESS 2: What book are you reading now?

ACTRESS 1: Something called *Trans-Sister Radio* which my erotica editor gave me after telling me she thought I should write a "real" novel and a bunch of other flattering things, which made me want to see what kind of novels she has *already* published, so I'm reading it, but it's not very good.

ACTRESS 2: What's on your mouse pad?

ACTRESS 1: No mouse pad—I have a touch pad on a laptop.

ACTRESS 2: Favorite board game?

ACTRESS 1: Scrabble. Unless you count Password, which isn't a board game but my all-time favorite game. Are you getting the feeling I'm a bit verbose?

ACTRESS 2: Favorite magazine?

ACTRESS 1: The *New Yorker*.

ACTRESS 2: Favorite smells?

ACTRESS 1: Bread baking, my daughter, night-blooming jasmine.

ACTRESS 2: Least favorite smell?

ACTRESS 1: Rotting flesh.

ACTRESS 2: Favorite sound?

ACTRESS 1: Children laughing is good, so is the sound of my daughter sleeping soundly. Also, fabulous music. And the sound a man makes when he has an orgasm.

ACTRESS 2: Least favorite sound?

ACTRESS 1: My daughter shrieking, whining, or crying hysterically.

ACTRESS 2: Worst feeling in the world?

ACTRESS 1: Shame.

ACTRESS 2: What is the first thing you think of when you wake up in the morning?

ACTRESS 1: "Mommy! Mommy! Mommy-mommy-mommy!" [Who has time to think?]

ACTRESS 2: How many rings before you answer the phone?

ACTRESS 1: One. Or seven—let the goddam machine pick it up!

ACTRESS 2: Future child's name?

ACTRESS 1: Girl: Carlotta, boy: Lazlo.

ACTRESS 2: What is the most important thing in life?

ACTRESS 1: My kid. Serenity. Creativity. How the hell should I know? As you can see, I'm terrible at making choices.

ACTRESS 2: Favorite foods?

ACTRESS 1: Rare steak or prime rib, great pasta, watermelon, [French toast with real maple syrup, barbecue spareribs, seven-layer cake with buttercream mocha in the layers, good red wine, good red wine, good red wine—] oh, I could go on and on. And on.

ACTRESS 2: Chocolate or vanilla?

ACTRESS 1: Chocolate. But I wouldn't kick vanilla out of bed.

[ACTRESS 2: Do you like to drive fast?

ACTRESS 1: Yeah. "Fast-ish."]

ACTRESS 2: Do you sleep with a stuffed animal?

ACTRESS 1: No. Unless you count the man that I live with.

ACTRESS 2: If you could meet one person dead or alive?

ACTRESS 1: Oy vey, how can I choose this one?! Okay, I guess Jesus, just to find out what all the fuss is about.

ACTRESS 2: Favorite alcoholic drink?

ACTRESS 1: Good red wine. The "gooder" the better.

ACTRESS 2: Do you eat the stems of broccoli?

ACTRESS 1: Absolutely, why not? I eat everything.

ACTRESS 2: If you could have any job you wanted, what would it be?

ACTRESS 1: Ballerina. Or doctor. Or [award-winning] playwright.

ACTRESS 2: Ever been in love?

ACTRESS 1: Yes. Oh yes.

ACTRESS 2: Is the glass half full or half empty?

ACTRESS 1: Half empty, of course. Everyone knows that, don't they? Unless it's filled with good red wine.

ACTRESS 2: Favorite movies?

ACTRESS 1: Now you're killing me. There's just no way to choose, and so many years of movies!!! But okay, the obvious ones, like *Casablanca* and *The Wizard of Oz* and *The Seven Samurai*. But I also have a thing for [*Z*, *The Taking of Pelham 1, 2, 3*, *Annie Hall*, *Cousin Cousine*,] *The Tall Blond Man With One Black Shoe*—the original French one—almost all the Marx

Brothers' movies... God, this is almost as hard as the food question!

ACTRESS 2: What's under your bed?

ACTRESS 1: Don't know. I'm too old to get down there and check it out.

ACTRESS 2: What is your favorite number?

ACTRESS 1: Three.

ACTRESS 2: Favorite sport to watch?

ACTRESS 1: Ha! [Oh please.]

ACTRESS 2: Say one nice thing about the person who sent this to you.

ACTRESS 1: Laura is a beautiful, wonderful friend whom I love and who also eats the stems on broccoli so how bad could she be?

ACTRESS 2: Person you sent this to who is most likely to respond?

ACTRESS 1: I have no idea.

ACTRESS 2: Person you sent this to who is least likely to respond?

ACTRESS 1: Again, no idea. I don't even know yet who I'm sending it to... we'll see.

ACTRESS 1: *(Addresses audience.)* Silly. Embarrassing, for Christ's sake. Just a stupid Internet game—twenty-nine meaningless questions and flip answers.

ACTRESS 2: Say one nice thing about the person who sent this to you.

ACTRESS 1: "Laura is a beautiful, wonderful friend whom I love and who also eats the stems on broccoli so how bad could she be?" And on September eleventh, she got up early and went to work at the World Trade Center. What is the first thing you think of when you wake up in the morning?

ACTRESS 2: Something different every day. Usually I try to remember to be grateful for the day and what's ahead.

ACTRESS 1: It was essentially a temp job.

ACTRESS 2: If you could have any job you wanted, what would it be?

ACTRESS 1: She sometimes worked signing people in at business conferences for a company called Risk. It was a survival job she did now and then to pay the rent. She hated it—the people, the hours, the world of high finance in which moony, penniless Laura was lost like a jewel in a junkyard.

ACTRESS 2: If you could have any job you wanted, what would it be?

ACTRESS 1: Usually these conferences were held at ballrooms in various Midtown hotels. But on September eleventh, Risk was holding a seminar at Windows on the World, on the one hundred and sixth floor of the Trade Center. For all I know, it was the first time Laura had ever been in that building.

(ACTRESS 1 and ACTRESS 2 now relate to each other, interacting and playing the following as a playful, challenging, varied dialogue between friends who are "hanging out" together [except where indicated] but they don't yet touch each other.)

ACTRESS 1: If you could have any job you wanted, what would it be?

ACTRESS 2: I'd like to revitalize the summer theatre that my parents worked at in the 1950s in the White Mountains of New Hampshire. I'd be the artistic director.

(ACTRESS 1 looks dubious, as if to say "get real.")

ACTRESS 2: Okay, okay, okay! Maybe Julia, maybe John Kenneth or Jake.

ACTRESS 1: *(To audience.)* Children. More than anyone I know—including myself, the mother of a two-year-old—Laura was meant to have a child. For most of us, it's a desire or a duty or an accident or a choice. For Laura it was a calling. Unfortunately, at forty-one, she was single with no prospects. Does anyone still remember that Harvard-Yale study from the 1980s? It concluded that if you were a single woman over the age of thirty-five you had more chance of being killed by terrorists than of finding a husband. *(Back to ACTRESS 2.)* Favorite sound?

ACTRESS 2: Children laughing!

ACTRESS 1: Children laughing is good. So is the sound of my daughter sleeping soundly.

ACTRESS 2: Children laughing.

ACTRESS 1: Least favorite sound? My daughter shrieking, whining, or crying hysterically.

ACTRESS 2: Children. Laughing.

ACTRESS 1: What is the first thing you think of when you wake up in the morning? "Mommy! Mommy! Mommy-mommy-mommy!" Who has time to think?!

ACTRESS 2: What is the most important thing in life?

ACTRESS 1: *(To audience.)* One thing about having a single, childless girlfriend who desperately wants a baby: She makes a great sitter! Laura was practically godmother to my child.

(ACTRESS 2 crosses to ACTRESS 1.)

ACTRESS 2: What is the most important thing in life?

ACTRESS 1: How the hell should I know? Creativity.

(ACTRESS 2 looks dubious.)

ACTRESS 1: Serenity?

(ACTRESS 2 isn't buying it.)

ACTRESS 1: My kid!

(ACTRESS 2 is slightly happier with this answer, but still waiting for more.)

ACTRESS 1: How the hell should *I* know?! As you can see, I'm terrible at making choices. What *is* the most important thing in life?

ACTRESS 2: Love.

ACTRESS 1: *(To audience.)* Lest you think she was some kind of saint, let me assure you, she frustrated the hell out of me, out of all her friends. Why couldn't she get it *together*? She needed to lose weight. She needed to find a career, other than being a never-made-it actor and part-time temp worker. And she needed to stop *talking* about it and *have* that baby—even if it meant doing it alone. We first met in a twelve-step program...

ACTRESS 2: *(Calling from her side of stage.)* Favorite alcoholic drink?

ACTRESS 1: *(Calling back.)* Good red wine. The "gooder" the better.

ACTRESS 2: *(To ACTRESS 1.)* Definitely Veuve Clicquot champagne!

ACTRESS 1: *(To audience.)* ...It's a *spiritual* program...

ACTRESS 2: *(Addresses audience directly, "performing.")* The glass is twice as big as it needs to be... isn't that great?! No, it's half full. I *know* that's the truth. I just can't always get there.

ACTRESS 1: So she wasn't a saint. Just an angel. *(To ACTRESS 2.)* Is the glass half full or half empty? Half empty, of course. Everyone knows that, don't they?

ACTRESS 2: Unless it's filled with good red wine! No, it's half full. I *know* that's the truth.

ACTRESS 1: *(To audience.)* I just can't always get there.

(ACTRESSES now come together in some shared activity—something girlfriend-ish and fun, like hairbrushing or braiding, massage, etc.)

ACTRESS 1: *(To ACTRESS 2.)* Favorite movies?

ACTRESS 2: Hmm, so many... *Casablanca, Breakfast at Tiffany's, The Sound of Music*, a great Irene Dunne-Cary Grant movie called *The Awful Truth*, and *What's Up, Doc?* More recently, *Traffic, High Fidelity*, and... *Fearless*...

(Activity gets more intimate, with arms around each other, or hanging onto each other in a cozy, easy way.)

ACTRESS 2: Favorite foods?

ACTRESS 1: Rare steak or prime rib—

ACTRESS 2: Lasagna—

ACTRESS 1: Great pasta—

ACTRESS 2: Great salads with blue cheese, pears, and walnuts in them—

ACTRESS 1: Watermelon—

ACTRESS 2: Good breads, cheeses, and fruits—

ACTRESS 1: French toast with real maple syrup, barbecue spareribs, seven-layer cake with buttercream mocha in the layers, good red wine, good red wine, good red wine— oh, I could go on and on.

ACTRESS 2: And on!

ACTRESS 1: Favorite board game?

ACTRESS 2: Scrabble.

ACTRESS 1: Unless you count Password, which isn't a board game but my all-time favorite game. Are you getting the feeling I'm a bit—?

(ACTRESS 2 playfully claps her hand over ACTRESS 1's mouth to cut her off.)

ACTRESS 2: What is the most important thing in life?

(ACTRESS 2 releases ACTRESS 1 so she can answer.)

ACTRESS 1: The *New Yorker*.

(ACTRESS 2 clasps her hand over ACTRESS 1's mouth again.)

ACTRESS 2: What is the most important thing in life?

(Again she releases.)

ACTRESS 1: Don't know. I'm too old to get down there and check it—

(Again, hand over mouth.)

ACTRESS 2: What is the most important *thing* in life?

(Again, she releases.)

ACTRESS 1: The stems of broccoli, if they're tender or peeled?

(ACTRESS 2 waits.)

ACTRESS 1: Love.

(Pause. ACTRESS 2 slips out from their intimate pose and exits, leaving ACTRESS 1 alone onstage.)

ACTRESS 1: It's like she simply evaporated. Except for these twenty-nine questions stored on my hard drive. *(ACTRESS 1 reads or types a new version of the questionnaire.)* 1: Living arrangement—I live with it, like we all do. And I also live with my sensitive, anxious, needy two-year-old

for whom I must be dependable, ever-steady Mommy—protector, source, authority, haven, —"Mommy happy?" she asks me in a tiny, pathetic voice. "Mommy no sad?" Preternaturally brilliant as she *is*, of course, she couldn't have understood what happened. Yet in the days following the attacks she began demanding that we turn off the television when the news was on—"No like it! No like it!"—and started mumbling things like, "I'm safe. I'm safe with Mommy, I'm safe with Daddy…" So part of my new "living arrangement" is to go outside to the car to cry. 2: What book are you reading now? Forget it. When the cute little dictator doesn't force me to turn it off, I'm glued to the TV news like everybody else. [Who was it who said when the revolution comes it will not be televised?] 3: What's on your mouse pad? No mouse pad—I have a touch pad on a laptop and I continue to try and write. 4: Future child's name? Laura. 5: Chocolate or vanilla? Both! And as often as possible. Maybe I'll just never diet again, you know? And while we're at it, 6a: Favorite smells? All of them, everything my greedy little nostrils can inhale, I can't get enough. 6b: Least favorite smell? Rotting flesh. 7: Favorite sound? Children laughing is good, so is the sound of my daughter sleeping soundly. Also, fabulous music. Laura had a strikingly beautiful singing voice. We sang together a lot—Sondheim and Gershwin, [and Rodgers and Hart,] James Taylor and Laura Nero, and she knew a terrific harmony to "Amazing Grace." [8: Least favorite sound? "Amazing Grace" played on the bagpipes. 9.] What is the first thing you think of when you wake up in the morning? Usually I try to remember to be grateful for the day and what's ahead. [10: If you could have any job you wanted what would it be? Flag salesman. 11.] How many rings before you answer the phone?... You know, a few days later I called her house—I don't know why. Of course the machine picked up with Laura's voice on it. I don't know what I was thinking. It was a stupid thing to do. [12: Do you like to drive fast? *No.* 13: What is your favorite number? Two thousand nine hundred and thirty six. Or one. 14:] Favorite alcoholic drink? A half-empty half-full glass of good red wine and I wouldn't mind one right about now. 15: What's under your bed? Boogymen. 16, 17, 18, 19: Say one nice thing about the person who sent this to you. If you could meet one person dead or alive? Worst feeling in the world? What is the most important thing in life?

(Pause.)

ACTRESS 1: That's nineteen out of twenty-nine. I can come up with at least ten more questions, can't you? And since September eleventh, I'm often asked them in strident, enraged, political emails. But I've gone back to responding with a swift delete. I just need to get to that quiet place.

(ACTRESS 1 again hits the delete key, and then returns to audience.)

ACTRESS 1: I know it's silly, but I haven't yet been able to delete Laura's screen name from my AOL address book... 29: Person you sent this to who is least likely to respond? I don't know, life is so full of surprises.

(ACTRESS 1 sits in her chair, rocking gently, eyes closed, humming just a few bars of "Amazing Grace.")

ARM

Katie Bull

Transition in: VOCALIST, overlapping "Amazing Grace," sings from James Taylor's "Fire and Rain"—"Just yesterday morning, they let me know you were gone." There is an overlapping rhythmic build of a protest march drumbeat produced by the OUD PLAYER who is also a percussionist. Simultaneously, YOUNG COLLEGE ACTIVIST appears, chanting at the edge of the play space; her voice is also in a gradual build from a lower register to a higher, more urgent shout... "HELL NO WE WON'T GO! WE WON'T KILL FOR TEXACO! HELL NO..." etc.

This is all simultaneous with DOORMAN entering to change the sign to INDEPENDENCE AVE, and tear away the calendar to reveal a new date, JANUARY 2003.

YOUNG COLLEGE ACTIVIST stands on the edge of the march, and, by her physical actions throughout this entire piece, it should be clear that she is talking, reacting, and responding to her FRIENDS who are standing beside her or shouting to the MARCHERS as they pass by. The actor must keep track of where the imaginary FRIENDS have moved as the action progresses; are they behind her, in front of her, beside her? She holds her arms straight over her head and grasps a big sign that says: HEY GEORGE, SEND THE TWINS.

She is moving and chanting in rhythm with the drums. She is wearing colorful hip-hugging jeans, a big patterned Guatemalan sweater, and a hat and gloves. She's very cold, so she is jumping vigorously to the drum-

beat. All her movements and the vibrancy of her articulation contain hip-hop energy and gesture; she has been so immersed in that concert culture that it permeates her whole lively being.

Setting: January 15 anti-war protest march in Washington, D.C.

COLLEGE ACTIVIST: *Hell no we won't go we won't kill for Texaco! Hell no we won't go we won't kill for Texaco!* That's right, shit. Man. *(Turning to her FRIENDS.)* Does anybody have a throat lozenge? No? Shit. *Hell no we won't go we won't kill for Texaco!* Huh? I can't hear you! They went to the greenhouse, to get warm, it's freakin' freezing. It's freezing here, freezing as hell. *Hell no we won't go we won't kill for Texaco!* It's moving again… did they, excuse me miss, mih…mah…ma'am, did they… umm, sir, sih— did they find that boy? That little boy who got separated from his parents back there? Is that why we're moving aga… *is that why?* Nobody knows. Shit. Well. Don't they have a communications system or something? *(Looks around to see if there is some other way of knowing…)* Gotta just get into the beat, right? *Hell no…* I need to sit down for a minute and warm up, you guys, let's go into the Botanical Gardens, that greenhouse over on the other side of Independence Ave man, let's go! *(Listening to their response, which is clearly "No," she gets pissed and points to her cell phone.)* Then tell me where you're gonna be, where you're gonna *be,* I mean, in other words, like, *(Mimes talking into her cell.)* "Hello, I'm in front of the fucking Pentagon *o-fucking-kay?"* or like, "Hello, I'm in front of the fucking White House"—alright? Ugh, no human being can stand out here in a sweater. I should have worn. What?! Then, come with me, come with…come with me… *Let's not get separated!*

(She enters the Botanical Gardens greenhouse as VOCALIST and OUD PLAYER create fun "tropical" sounds that invoke exotic flora and bird life with live vocal interaction and percussion.)

COLLEGE ACTIVIST: *(Her eyes are down as she whips off her hat, scarf, and backpack, and sticks her sign between her legs. Her eyes move up toward the ceiling as she unzips her coat—lights bathe her in a warm glow. She is suddenly struck by the view, in total awe of the beauty which is new to her.)* You know, they've got like, plants and flowers from like…all over the world.

(She begins a circle with her hips that gently swirls in a funky rhythm. This lower body circle moves her upper body so that her eyes can take in the full circumference of the whole exotic ceiling—images of lush plants, vines, and giant flowers—images the actor must paint for the audience's imagination, and which the INSTRUMENTALISTS can paint with trills, birdcalls, and whistles.)

COLLEGE ACTIVIST: Wow, man…it's like, nothing you've ever… *(Her eyes follow the lines of vines down toward a tree.)* These are the largest lemons I've ever seen, they're like the size of grapefruits. Look at this lemon tree, *(Laughing.)* look at this *tree* man! *(Reacting to something her FRIEND says about hurrying up to get back into the march.)* I just need to go to the bathroom and then we can join back in, I was freezin' my cojones off… *(Looking around to see if she can see her other FRIENDS, the ones that came into the greenhouse earlier in the march.)* Do you see them? They went down closer to the stage at the rally, the other end— *(Her FRIEND doesn't get it.)* —no, no, not the monument end, the Capitol end, that stage. *(Suddenly totally psyched!)* That was the happening stage! *(Referring to Jesse Jackson.)* We missed Jesse. They wanted to get closer to that speaker on the plaza end. Ron, that guy from Vietnam, that Tom Cruise played in, umm, in umm… *Born on the Fourth of… (Sees another tree.) July* —holy shit, look at these limes! Have you ever? Dude. Well, look at the map, here, *(She shifts to the center of the play space where she mimes looking at a large map like the ones you see in museums next to exhibits.)* Oh look, there's a desert wing.

(Sound of the oud gently returns in a languid Middle Eastern tonality simultaneous with the slow entrance of a YOUNG AMERICAN GI, late teens, early twenties— a gangly kid in full desert fatigues and hat, holding a lizard on his arm with an ammo pack wrapped around its belly. He walks in a slow pedestrian pace and, as ACTIVIST is finishing in the Botanical Garden, the GI is changing the sign to read BAGHDAD, with an arrow pointing in one direction.)

COLLEGE ACTIVIST: I bet they're in that tropical part. It's right next to the bathrooms. Call them again, I don't know why they aren't picking up their cells. It's really kind of selfish of them. Let's check there before we go out again…

(She bounces off as GI tears the page from the calendar to reveal MARCH 2003. Setting: American military camp on the Kuwaiti border of Iraq.)

(Standing in a bright spotlight is PRIVATE JIMBO SHANK, the American GI. He's a very young soldier, fresh from high school, an all-American blond, very sweet-faced and boyish-looking. He unflinchingly balances the lizard on his arm. The light of the desert is intense. He stares squintingly into an imaginary television camera with a focal point fixed straight ahead, directly in front of him.

He is being interviewed on a morning show from America, live, and we can hear the voice of the INTERVIEWER as a live feed into his ear. The role of NEWSCASTER should be read by DOORMAN from an area of the playing space that is visually concealed but where his voice is clearly audible. NEWSCASTER voice should have that TV news faux sincerity. NEWSCASTER overlaps many of the ends of JIMBO's lines, cutting him off, obviously not really listening. JIMBO, however, finishes every line with a Southern gentleman's charm, smiling into the camera. We, however, becoming increasingly aware of the toll this is taking on JIMBO, who must appear more and more isolated, and finally, bewildered, in the arc of this short and difficult journey. JIMBO speaks a bit slowly; we might wonder if he's undereducated, or just a bit slow.)

JIMBO: *(With a big broad welcoming smile, answering a question he's just received.)* Yes sir, that is my battalion. Private Jimbo Shank. Seventh Division, sir. And, umm, Alabama, sir.

NEWSCASTER: So you're from Alabama… do we have anyone in our television audience from Alabama?! You can bet we do! Hello from home, Private Jimbo,

JIMBO: Hello.

NEWSCASTER: And where are you standing, Private Shank?

JIMBO: On the Kuwaiti border sir, with Iraq.

NEWSCASTER: There on the mission that many other brave young men and women your age are there to perform, and what does that entail today, Private Shank?

JIMBO: Our ground forces have been practicing ground maneuvers. Here. Right behind me.

NEWSCASTER: That's the desert in the background there. The light is very bright today. Tell us a little about yourself, Private Shank. Where's your hometown?

JIMBO: Birmingham, sir.

NEWSCASTER: Sweet Home Alabama!

JIMBO: *(Not laughing. Shifting his weight to accommodate the lizard.)* Ugh, that's correct sir, Alabama.

NEWSCASTER: I date myself. *(Awkward laugh.)* Well, the folks back home on the "Morning Show" want to know a bit about life over in the desert for our troops, can you share with us anything of your experience? How's the food?

JIIMBO: Food is, regular food, umm, limited menu. Keepin' us fit.

NEWSCASTER: Well, if we can get a closeup, folks, we've got a bit of a surprise for our viewing audience. Can you tell the viewers a bit about the private you've got there on your arm? Can we get a closeup?

JIMBO: *(Raises his arm for the lizard's closeup; trying to be serious despite the joke.)* The private here is a member of our battalion sir, and, agh, he is in training with us here to liberate Iraq.

NEWSCASTER: And what will his role be in this war?

JIMBO: He is serving as ammo transport for us sir. *(Cracking a smile.)*

NEWSCASTER: *(Cracking a false chuckle.)* What is that on his back, Private Shank?

JIMBO: That is an ammo pack sir, we tied it on around his little, his little belly here. Private Johnny will be transportin' ammo.

NEWSCASTER: Ammo? What kind of…

JIMBO: *(Proudly.)* Yes sir, that's a .226 ready-to-go round of machine gun ammo sir.

NEWSCASTER: I see. *(Laughing.)* For the viewers here, he is your company pet, correct?

JIMBO: *(The jig is up.)* Ah, yes sir, he's our battalion's mascot, we found him out here in the desert and adopted him. He eats with us, sleeps with us, he's one of us.

NEWSCASTER: And what does he eat, Jimbo?

JIMBO: Pasta mar-nar. *(Proudly.)* What we eat. He eats what we eat.

NEWSCASTER: He will be travelin' with you then?

JIMBO: Ah, yes sir, he will be travelin' with our division, and— *(Sudden pep-rally energy.)* Johnny will be with us when we take Baghdad sir! *(He shoots his arm up with the "V" sign.)*

NEWSCASTER: Can you hold up your arm—

(JIMBO holds his lizard arm closer to the camera.)

NEWSCASTER: —so we can get a better view… wow…there he is folks, Private First Class Johnny Lizard, on his way to Baghdad! Private Jimbo Shank, is there anyone back at home you'd like to say a special hey to?

JIMBO: Umm, my mom and pop, and my brother Mark— *(While talking, he mimes a cowboy quick-draw with an imaginary gun like he and Mark did when they were kids, and pretends to shoot at his brother in the camera.)* Hey, we're a hundred percent a-okay over here. We're ready.

NEWSCASTER: It does get a bit windy!

JIMBO: *(Suddenly bewildered.)* Ah— Yes sir, it does.

(A moment of silence and stillness as JIMBO squints into the camera and holds the lizard, adjusting his earpiece. He stares, somewhat stunned, into the camera. The sound of the oud returns. VOCALIST creates the effect of wind "Shhhhh" as lights fade.)

HAND

Katie Bull

Transition in: Lights shift their intensity toward the aisles of the venue where, amidst (or very close to the edge of) the audience, EMILY, a young college tourist, is wandering. She is no older than twenty-one, very fair-skinned, and blond, with long loose hair pulled away from her face by a blue headband. She wears a sleeveless blue 1950s-style antique dress that falls above her knees, exposing bare skin, à la college thrift store funk. She is sightseeing in brown Birkenstock sandals, and carries a worn leather or crocheted purse. The purse has a very long strap which is slung around her neck and across her torso. She is clinging to the strap with both hands, right at the point where it hugs her between her breasts, at the solar plexus. The cling, her wandering gait, and a stricken look tell us she is very lost. In the shadows at the edge of the playing space, TARIQ, a young Palestinian boy, stands watching her. He has a slight build, delicate bones, with closely cropped yet thick black hair. He wears a native white cotton tunic shirt, American-made jeans, and the leather sandals seen on nearly all men in the region.

JIMBO begins to exit, intersecting paths with EMILY, though they don't see each other. EMILY stands in the center of the playing space making a slow circle in place. She shifts forward several times as she circles, taking a step toward someplace, then retreats back to her fixed point, unsure of the right road to take.

Simultaneous with this action, DOORMAN enters to change sign to WAILING WALL (with an arrow pointing in a direction opposite the arrow for BAGHDAD). He then tears the page of the calendar to reveal AUGUST 1983.

Setting: Jerusalem, Old City, Muslim Quarter, Israel.

TARIQ: You are alone.

EMILY: *(Startled, moving away.)* Yes.

TARIQ: Don't be scared. You should not be here.

EMILY: I know. *(Looking around.)* I'm lost.

TARIQ: Where are you going?

EMILY: To the Wailing Wall, to meet my Israeli friend.

TARIQ: I see. Let me take you.

EMILY: *(Shaking her head, turning in a circle.)* —I—

TARIQ: You really have no choice, you are alone—

(TARIQ places his hand on her arm gently, stops her turning.)

TARIQ: —you should not be here. Can you see the men looking at you in danger? (He discreetly motions to the upstage corner of "shadows.")*

EMILY: No I didn't see that.

TARIQ: Well, they are looking at you—

EMILY: *(Seeing the MEN staring.)* Actually yes. *(She tries to move away but doesn't know which direction to go.)*

TARIQ: You show your legs, and your arms. This quarter is not for tourists. How did you get here? You have lost your way.

EMILY: I'm sorry. I was at the bazaar. I… it's like a maze.

TARIQ: Don't be scared. *(He circles around her, and she turns in place watching him from inside his circle.)* Look, my eyes, can you see? I will not hurt you. I take you to safety. Look. *(He smiles.)*

EMILY: *(Smiles.)* Thank you.

TARIQ: Take my hand. *(He presents his hand for her to hold.)*

EMILY: *(Blurting.)* Oh God.

TARIQ: Yes, "Oh God." Take my hand.

(She takes his hand. As he attempts to take the first steps to lead her, she does not move. Still holding his hand, she pulls back, frozen.)

TARIQ: You have to make a quick decision. Look, *(Smiles.)* see? *(Pointing down an alley that leads out of the intersection.)* Follow me.

(They move on a diagonal and freeze at the opposite end, as MUSICIANS fill the stopped motion with voluptuous sounds of spoken Hebrew and Arabic— "Tomatoes!" "Apples!"—in the lively cadences of the marketplace. TARIQ and EMILY move on another diagonal and freeze; again, MUSICIANS sing-talk the intermingled languages of the Old City. On the third diagonal, they speak as they walk; she is looking in all directions, unsure if this is the right thing to be doing.)

TARIQ: We must move quickly.

(TARIQ and EMILY freeze—MUSICIANS sing-talk—then back into motion. They walk side by side now.)

EMILY: Narrow streets.

TARIQ: Old, yes.

(They freeze—MUSICIANS sing-talk— then TARIQ takes a sudden sharp turn to lead EMILY on another diagonal, but she pulls away and their hands disengage.)

EMILY: It feels, it seems like we're going farther in.

TARIQ: This is the best way, it is faster. They know me. You are safe.

EMILY: I should really—go.

TARIQ: You can't go back. It's not safe. *(Holds out his hand for her.)*

EMILY: Oh God.

(She takes his hand. This diagonal brings them back to their starting point and then they retrace what is a figure eight, or the infinity pattern, like DNA.)

TARIQ: To cry to God only when we are lost or angry. This is the mistake. Do you understand?

EMILY: I think I know what you mean. Can we slow down?

TARIQ: No, it's for your safety.

EMILY: Where are we going? That's so… *(Stops.)* …dark in there… it's like a tunnel. *(Pulls her hand away from TARIQ forcefully. Steps back.)*

TARIQ: It's a passageway. Believe me, this is the way. Hold my hand, I tell you I will not hurt you.

(She smiles at him and takes his hand. They proceed through the tunnel; their bodies are

closer now, more as one, shoulder to shoulder. TARIQ is leading, and reassuringly uses both hands to hold EMILY's hand. They crouch because the passageway ceiling is lower, the walls more narrow, and it is very dark. MUSICIANS weave Middle Eastern tonalities on the oud with vocal scat that implies a racing heart, shallow gasps of breath, and rising tones like mounting fear. When they "emerge" from the tunnel, they stand to their full height. EMILY is visibly moved by what she sees.)

TARIQ: You see? These are the places where we live. Small homes, and over there, see, through these arches.

(They stop but do not let go of each other's hand.)

TARIQ: Those are many more homes.

(TARIQ stands in front of EMILY, leading her through more narrow streets. By having the actors switch hands behind TARIQ's back as they zigzag, the director can achieve the impression of weaving through the quarter.)

EMILY: I see, *all stone.* Beautiful.

TARIQ: Very beautiful. This is *our part* of the city.

(He begins moving again, looping upstage toward the same place where the first tunnel was.)

TARIQ: This will scare you, another passageway. It's very dark, but you will see, I will take you to the Wall.

(He senses her hesitation.)

TARIQ: I feel you pull away. You don't believe me.

EMILY: I am trying.

(They enter the second passageway. MUSICIANS are silent.)

TARIQ: I do not know you. I do not know your Israeli. They say we all hate, that is false. Let me show you something.

(He leads her in a strong line up onto the elevated stage. EMILY is immediately humbled and awed by what she sees. MUSICIANS sing and pray in both Hebrew and Arabic, the oud joins, and there is also the distant sound of a Christian church bell. The light bathes the actors in a golden glow.)

TARIQ: Overlooking the whole city. Beautiful.

(They absorb the sounds and the view. It is breathtaking.)

TARIQ: And there is the Wall. See, do you see?

EMILY: Oh yes, there it is!

(They stand, look, listen, still holding hands. The music subsides.)

EMILY: Oh, umm, how will we get there? We're up here.

TARIQ: You will go down these steps, they are steep, it is a short cut.

EMILY: Oh thank you. I. I'm sorry. I was afraid. I was… *(Searches for the word.)* I was… *doubting…you.*

TARIQ: *(Kidding her.)* You're traveling much?

EMILY: *(Laughing, embarrassed.)* This is my graduation trip; I took the Euro rail, stayed in youth hostels, I was going all through Europe, before I came to visit my Israeli… *(Suddenly reminded of the conflict.)* …Duvid. *(Pronounced Duh-VEED.)*

TARIQ: Listen, there is something I must show you.

EMILY: I am listening.

TARIQ: Over there.

(He releases her hand and points off in the far distance, beyond the Wall.)

TARIQ: Tell your Israeli.

EMILY: What?

TARIQ: The dome of that mosque.

EMILY: I see it, the dome.

TARIQ: It's called the Dome of the Rock.

EMILY: Oh, yes, yes. I read about it.

TARIQ: Tell him that a Palestinian boy's uncle and cousin were killed there. A boy, maybe his age, the same age. A boy's uncle and cousin. In a house of worship. You tell him they were killed there.

EMILY: Killed in the mosque?

TARIQ: The Dome of the Rock. A bomb. Didn't you hear? Read?

EMILY: I'm sorry. No.

TARIQ: *(Smiles, kidding her.)* Are you educated?

EMILY: *(Embarrassed.)* I just graduated…

TARIQ: From university?

EMILY: Yes.

TARIQ: I am going to university! Tell him, we don't want the killing. But now things get worse again. You should know these things. If you go to university.

EMILY: What else should I tell him?

TARIQ: Just to say, there can be no peace when a place of worship is no longer sacred. That killing begets killing. *(Smiles.)*

EMILY: Duvid is in the Israeli group Peace Now

TARIQ: Ah. *(Smiles.)* Alright. *(Gestures to the stairs.)* You can walk the rest of the way yourself, you can see the Wall now, right?

EMILY: *(Nodding.)* Yes.

(Pause.)

EMILY: Maybe, you want to come with me? I could introduce you?

TARIQ: See. I didn't hurt you.

EMILY: No, you didn't.

TARIQ: It was good you came with me. You were in a place of danger.

EMILY: *(Offers her hand.)* Will you come?

(TARIQ grasps her hand slowly and deliberately with both his hands. This is a more diplomatic and reserved fashion of hand holding; the cultural boundaries surrounding their personal space are returning. They are circling each other now, a more abstract stylistic reference to their first encounter. They continue to circle each other throughout the remaining dialogue.)

TARIQ: That… is not something I can do…

EMILY: Oh! What's your name?!

TARIQ: Ah, it's Tariq— what's yours?!

EMILY: Oh, it's Emily…

TARIQ: Goodbye Emily. Be careful. Be safe.

(They have turned by now to walk in opposite directions, but their hands trail behind them still touching. They freeze, the music rises. They are held in an image from Michelangelo's Creation, and we can see that their fingers are still touching. Loud drums signal—)

(The End.)

(Blackout.)

STAGING NOTES
Katie Bull

ORDER. *Message From the Driver must* be heard as the opening statement in an entire evening of works running with no intermission in the following order: *Message From the Driver, 29 Questions, Arm,* and *Hand.* Changing the sequence will take *Message* out of context; the "message" hidden in *Message From the Driver* will not be heard, and the piece could be taken as biased.

VENUE. Look outside of the traditional theater box—find an alternative venue that gets this project into the streets. The architectural shape and vibe of the venue chosen should be considered with these questions in mind: does the space have an intimate, welcoming, and festive feel? Does the space guide the audience into chance encounters that could lead to mingling and interactivity? Can the space support a comfortable experience of eating, drinking, and relaxing during the post-show Gathering?

PRE-SHOW "CIRCLE." Each night, before the audience arrives, a project director leads the "Circle." The actors are called together and place meditations on the themes they perceive within the plays into a basket. The cast and director stand in this circle, and a candle, which will later sit in the Welcome Area, is placed in the center of the Circle and lit in memory of those lost on 9/11 and those now suffering and dying due to terrorism and war. As the director lights the candle, she offers a "welcome to the benevolent forces that be" to guide the night's performance in honor of deeper human communication and peace. This can be done silently by the director as the flame is lit, or out loud; whatever the director feels will best support the strengthening of the "container" of the playing space. The Circle structure we used is drawn from both ancient Greek rituals for the honoring of the *teminos* and American Indian rituals for honoring the ever-present spirit world swirling around the act of storytelling. One meditation is drawn from the basket and read aloud. In this way, the decision of who is speaking is left to the forces of chance. The cast hold hands and close their eyes. The leader of the Circle initiates a hand squeeze which is passed hand to hand in a chain around the Circle, one hand squeeze at a time. When the director receives the last hand squeeze, she says, "I got it!" or something to that effect, to acknowledge the completion of the energy transfer, and the actors can let go of each other's hands and start acting.

THE "ENVIRONMENTAL IMPROV." When actors leave the Circle, they enter into character and move or sit about the space, and even outside the venue, in character, interacting with each other and with arriving audience members spontaneously; there are no planned improvisational "events"—improvisational interactions arise in different ways each night. What the audience must feel, either consciously or subliminally, is a presence of the cast in the environment as the audience enters.

THE WELCOME AREA. A very clearly defined Welcome Area must be identified for the audience so that as they enter, this is the first place they encounter in the space. The area should be festooned with fresh flowers, baskets of fresh fruit, and a large fragrant votive candle. A female production assistant dressed in colorful, festive attire welcomes the audience alongside the actor who plays the Doorman (from *Message From the Driver*). The Doorman ushers them to their seats. There should be a small fountain of water (can be electric) pouring over earth-stones, a dried sage (you may want to smudge the space beforehand), and the Circle basket of meditations.

THE MUSICIANS. Live musicians begin playing world music about ten minutes before the play is to start. There should be at least one oud player (or a guitarist) and one vocalist (a female jazz improviser is preferable). They should know Israeli, Palestinian, and American folk music, and they should both be able to improvise in compositional ways that support the themes, rhythms, and moods of the texts.

THE "GATHERING." When the plays are finished, we bring the audience into a Gathering. In setting up the space each night, we pay particular attention to creating a festive mood. We draw from elements of ritual which include fresh flowers, votive candles, live world music, and multicultural food platters. We did our 2004 performances at Yaffa's T Room, a Middle Eastern-themed restaurant in Tribeca. Yaffa's was decorated with murals of sand dunes and ancient imagery from the Middle East. There were red velvet curtains at the entrance doors, and the room was lit with beaded chandeliers and antique wall sconces on dimmers. We started the run in the spring with natural light flooding in from the Tribeca sky. As we came to the fall and the natural light waned, the presence of votive candles on all tables and illumination from existing antique light fixtures in the venue created an extraordinarily beautiful, elegant, intimate vigil. Our lighting designer created lighting fixtures to blend into the environment, and we increased their intensity to define the playing area, which was an elevated end of the restaurant and the aisles between the tables at the center of the cafe. At Yaffa's, restaurant waiters and Bull Family Orchestra production members originally brought food trays around to the tables, but we soon discovered that it was better to place the platters at stationed buffet tables so that audience members would migrate and mingle. Actors and directors assisted the room staff, and, in doing so, became hosts for the night's Gathering. As a result of breaking the fourth wall in this manner, we were really *there* when the audience wanted discussion—without forcing discussion. For the project to be complete in future productions, there must be a Gathering! We did not impose ourselves by soliciting feedback, but we were there as integral parts of a communion of which all could feel ownership. This Gathering is like a second act, a form of environmental theatre during which extraordinary conversations in response to the play can take place.

All of this was what we envisioned—a gathering place to have a healing, strengthening, and thought-provoking dialogue of reflection, affirmation, and the expression of questions so needed in our country right now. The night was a gentle yet festive grief ritual, a community gathering, a forum for conversation about 9/11 and our lives in this complex post-9/11 world.

NOTES TO THE *MESSAGE* ACTORS
Katie Bull

It should be noted that the actor playing the Driver must never appear "menacing"—but his statements and the effect of the statements should cause fear in the Woman. The question of whether he is a terrorist should be answered differently by different members of the audience, which means that the performance by the Driver must be underplayed and not obvious, so as to leave room for interpretation. His performance should show a man with a core of simple and direct faith. There must be ambiguity as to this man's actual involvement and intent with regard to the things he decides to discuss with the Woman in the taxi. This man simply believes what he believes, and he states things as fact with only a few moments of overt rage. Except for the moments that are identified in the script, which are very specific, he is calm and focused, even "light" in his delivery. In this manner, he will have all the more impact on the listeners. The Woman should never appear hysterical or terrified. She is a sleep-deprived mom; she is *not* made of steel—the conversation affects her. However, she doesn't let herself surrender to tears in the taxi, and while she may appear scattered at first with all her bags and it being the end of a long day and all—her genuine curiosity helps her to garner energy and focus, and have a conversation in the face of her fear. She maintains her wits and can ask real questions and offer real responses; the dialogue is not generated by the fear alone. The actor would be wise to note that the Woman is a teacher ("I was writing a syllabus"), a performer ("I'm just a singer"), and a mother of small children ("I've got small children on my mind"). The actor needs to get in touch with how these kinds of identities contribute to *a journalistic impulse* ("I need to know")—the impulse to sleuth out why, how, who, when, where. This is the impulse that impels the Woman to ask questions;

she is trying to piece together a puzzle. When she meets up with the Doorman of her apartment building after the taxi ride, the fact that she says—"he knew"—(referring to the Driver) implies that she may have also been asking questions out of a state of post-9/11 vigilance. In October 2001, Americans were directed on national television to embrace "vigilance" and keep their eyes open for "suspicious" activity. We were told by Colin Powell and George Bush "You are all soldiers" now, and they warned the terrorists that there were a million civilian eyes on the "front lines."

NOTE TO THE *29 QUESTIONS* ACTORS
Hillary Rollins

I trust the talent and insight of my fellow theatre artists and don't wish to interfere with their interpretation. But indulge me in just a few words of guidance: Resist the urge to sentimentalize. Resist the urge to begin in anger, pain, sadness, or despair. Despite the weight of the play's events, look unflinchingly for the humor (however dry or sarcastic), and don't be afraid to make the audience laugh. In fact, commit to making them laugh. Tears are their option.

NOTE ABOUT THE YAFFA'S CUTS FOR FUTURE STAGINGS
Hillary Rollins

The unusual form of this play means that the text is necessarily—and intentionally—repetitive. When I wrote it (one week after the events of 9/11), the challenge I set for myself was to use only what I "had left" of Laura and our friendship—an old email game with twenty-nine questions and answers which I still had stored on my hard drive. The reason was twofold: first, it was an acknowledgment of, and also a protest against, the fact that Laura had been suddenly silenced, save for this handful of seemingly meaningless sentences. Second, I felt that the inherent restrictions of this structure enabled me to approach subject matter that was so *un*restricted in scope and depth of feeling. So while Actress 1 (the writer) could speak freely when she directly addressed the audience, it was vital that she and Actress 2 (Laura) say everything they needed to say to each other using only the limited words from their remaining email "dialogue." These almost rhythmic repetitions, when interpreted and reinterpreted through the arc of personal and global change, take on new meaning and are the very essence of the play. But such a repetitive text presents a huge challenge for the actors and director. They have to create a more-than-usually colorful subtext and a deeply rich physical life onstage in order to paint with such a limited palette. Thus far, everyone has risen to that challenge spectacularly. I acknowledge the difficulties inherent in the form, and, in the New York production at Yaffa's T Room, the actors and directors ultimately found it necessary to make a few minor and judicious cuts, or "tweaks," to keep the through-line working and the audience engaged. I happily endorsed those cuts (and could agree to limited cuts in future productions as long as I am consulted). This published text is the original, uncut version with the Yaffa's cuts and changes bracketed, so that artists newly exploring the material can find their own solutions.

HONOR

TheDrillingCompaNY

THEDRILLINGCOMPANY is based on jazz—the collection of many voices around a common universal theme, or melody, as a springboard for the expression of the individual. Founded in 1999 by producing artistic director Hamilton Clancy, TheDrillingCompaNY initiates new theatre projects by commissioning writers to create new work around a common theme or idea. Its mission is to foster peace by promoting acceptance and awareness. Plays commissioned by TheDrillingCompaNY have been seen throughout New York City and in other theatres throughout America. Its short plays have been adapted into full-length plays and films, and the projects have connected artists throughout the country with one another. Besides short play projects, the company sponsors ongoing development of longer works with its Discovery Series of full-length staged readings, and free outdoor summer Shakespeare in the tradition of the Public Theater. It is in ongoing residence at 78th Street Theatre Lab, recognized around the world as a leader in new play development. Past projects include *In the Car*, *Neighbors*, *While You Wait…*, *Fathers*, *Connections*, *Service*, *Theft*, *Paper*, and *Both*. Full-length productions include *Don't Bring Me Down* by Brent Askari, *Big Apples* by Stephen Bittrich, *Windows on the World* by Peter Killy, *Dealers* by Neil Olsen, and Shakespeare's *Hamlet* and *Two Gentlemen of Verona*.

BRIAN DYKSTRA (*Mick Just Shrugs*) is the author of the plays *Brian Dykstra: Cornered & Alone, Hiding Behind Comets, That Damn Dykstra (the boxed set), Silence, STRANGERHORSE, Forsaking All Others, SexReligionPolitics, I Am/Lot's Wife, Lot's Wife, A Sane Policy* (commissioned by the Public Theater) and the screenplays *Double Down, Baggage Claim* (Fox2000), *Un-Screwed, AMAZOMBIES*, and *Another Bed* (short). He contributed short works to TheDrillingCompaNY's *Neighbors, While You Wait…, Connections, Service, Theft,* and *Paper.* Website: www.briandykstra.net.

ANDREA MOON (*A Friday Night Trans Am Ride*) is a native of Washington. She studied playwriting with Ruth Margraff, Sherry Kramer, and Susan Zeder, and performance with Pacific Performance Project in Seattle under co-artistic directors Robyn Hunt and Steve Pearson. Her short play *Swallow and Smile* was part of TheDrillingCompaNY's *Both* in 2003. Other works include *Draeptomania: Book One, Heat Lightning, Storm, Still Marie, Every Zipper Button Bow and Hook,* and *Boot Arias.* She is currently working on a PhD in theatre from the University of Colorado–Boulder.

SCOTT BAKER (*For the Benefit of Alfred Beamer*) attended the University of Tulsa and has studied theatre under Michael Moriarty and Wynn Handman. Among his diverse credits as an actor are stints in the Broadway production of *Oh! Calcutta!* and *Love Potion Number Ten* with the Coasters, the Drifters, and the Platters in Las Vegas. He is an original member of TheDrillingCompaNY and has appeared in many of its productions as actor and/or playwright. He is working on an evening of wild comedy sketches, vaudeville, sideshow stunts, and magic entitled "Elvis Is Alive and Well and Working at Starbucks."

STEPHEN BITTRICH (*Duty Honor Country*) has had plays produced around New York City by such companies as TheDrillingCompaNY, Vital Theatre, Pulse Ensemble Theatre, and 2nd Generation. His screenplay, *Desert Rites*, was a top thirty finalist in the first Project Greenlight contest. His ten-minute play *Brain Sucking* was produced at Actors Theatre of Louisville in 1993 and was subsequently published in *Dramatics* magazine, a publication for theatre educators. In 2002, his ten-minute play *Two Eggs* was a finalist in the Louisville Ten-Minute Play contest. Excerpts and whole plays can be read on his website: www.StephenBittrich.com.

JOANNA CHERENSKY (*'Til Death Do Us Part*) contributed the short play *Mrs. Schimowitz, 3B* to TheDrillingCompaNY's *Paper* and *The Regular* to TheDrillingCompaNY's *Service.* She is currently enrolled in USC's MFA writing for film and television program. She was a 2003 semifinalist for the Chesterfield Writer's Film Project, based at Paramount Pictures, for her first screenplay, *Man Trouble: The Search for Sperm*. From box office maven to writer, Joanna has been with TheDrillingCompaNY since its first production, *In the Car*.

ALLISON MOORE (*CUTRS!*) is a displaced Texan living in Minneapolis where she has been a McKnight Advancement Grant recipient and a two-time Playwrights' Center Jerome Fellow. Plays include *Eighteen*, *Hazard County*, *CowTown*, *The Strange Misadventures of Patty*, and *Urgent Fury* (2003 Cherry Lane Mentor Project, mentor: Marsha Norman). Her work has been produced by Actors Theatre of Louisville, Kitchen Dog Theatre, Centenary Stage Company, Meadows Basement, the Themantics Group, and the Playwrights' Center; and developed at Williamstown Theatre Festival, Madison Rep, Portland Center Stage, Alabama Shakespeare Festival, and the Jungle, among others.

DON CARTER (*Coming to the Table*) is the author of the short plays *Lost in the Garden* and *The Last Thing*, and of *Making Lunch* (co-written with David Marantz). Carter began writing solo work with the New York performance group Rumble in the Red Room in 1997. In 2001, he wrote, produced, and performed his solo show, *Finding Pieces* (also produced in the 2004 Midtown International Theatre Festival). As an actor, Carter performs on the New York stage and in regional theatre, independent film, and television. He holds an MFA in theatre/acting from Rutgers University and is a long-time student of Wynn Handman.

HAMILTON CLANCY (*founder/producing artistic director*) is originally from New Orleans, and trained at Catholic University and the Old Globe Theatre and in Manhattan with Wynn Handman. He has appeared as an actor off- and off-off-Broadway at the American Place Theatre, 78th Street Theatre Lab, and Shakespeare in the Park(ing) Lot, and regionally with the Vineyard Playhouse and Public Theatre in Maine, among others. With TheDrillingCompaNY, he has commissioned over two hundred short plays, produced *Windows on the World* by Peter Killy, *Dealers* by Neil Olson, and *Big Apples* by Stephen Bittrich, and has conceived and produced a dozen original short play projects. He lives in New York with his wife, actress Karen Kitz, and their son, Joe.

HONOR was first presented by TheDrillingCompaNY (Hamilton Clancy, Producing Artistic Director, and Karen Kitz-Clancy, Associate Artistic Director) on June 4, 2004, at 78th Street Theatre Lab, New York City, with the following cast and credits:

Mick Just Shrugs

D. Boone Kirks .... Tom Demenkoff
Mick .... Keith Fasciani
Directed by: Margarett Perry

A Friday Night Trans Am Ride

Caroline .... Karen Kitz
Theresa .... Nicole Longchamp
Evangeline .... Colleen Cosgrove
Directed by: Hamilton Clancy
Assistant Director/Brad's Voice: Dave Marantz

For the Benefit of Alfred Beamer

Beamer .... Don Carter
Laird .... Michael McMonagle
Directed by: Richard Harden

Duty Honor Country

Bobeck .... Kevin Draine
LaBonne .... Clinton Faulkner
Prisoner .... Moussa Kraish
Directed by: Edwin Owens
Assistant Director: Rebecca Allyn Jones
Original Music: Ofrit Shirna

'Til Death Do Us Part

Bill .... Dave Marantz
Sherry .... Natasha Hanina
Minister .... Bill Green
Directed by: Nancy S. Chu
Assistant Director: Lauren Felice Ayers

CUTRS!

Andrea .... Michelle Maxson
Directed by: Hamilton Clancy

Coming to the Table

Gail .... Colleen Cosgrove
Eric .... Moussa Kraish
Mat .... Dave Marantz

Heather .... Kate Kolenda
Jim .... Kevin Draine
Kathleen .... Michelle Maxson
Priest .... Bill Green
Mourner .... Tom Demenkoff
Soldier .... Clinton Faulkner
Runner .... Keith Fasciani
Girl .... Nicole Longchamp
Directed by: Hamilton Clancy

Scenic Design: Brian Ireland
Lighting Design: Jerry Browning
Sound Design: Michael Graetzer
Original Music: Thom Garvey
Stage Management: Laura Moss, Rosita Timm, and Billie Davis

INTRODUCING *HONOR*
Hamilton Clancy

In 1999, before embarking on a weekend trip with a new girlfriend, it occurred to me that it was our first trip in a car. I thought we would discover whether the relationship should continue if we could get along together in a car. During the trip, I mentioned this, and she concurred. We thought of all the magical things that happen to people in a car. She suggested I write a play about it. Later, it occurred to me that it would be faster and more interesting to suggest the idea to some quality playwrights I knew, and TheDrillingCompaNY began with *In the Car*. I lost the girlfriend. She's now my wife.

TheDrillingCompaNY is composed of all of the actors, writers, and directors who have worked in our projects. Perception determines reality. If you think you're a member of TheDrillingCompaNY, you are.

We have become part of the Short Play Revolution. Short plays have crept onto off-Broadway and are creeping onto Broadway. This is a new way to experience theatre. A composer remarked recently how it was not uncommon for an evening of music to offer several pieces of fifteen or twenty minutes in length, but that he had never considered experiencing theatre that way. It seems like the only way to fly for us now. *HONOR* is our tenth project around a common theme.

I choose themes by reflecting on current events. I try to distill some part of our collective conscience, not directly addressed. For each project, twenty-five writers are given the theme, an additional theatrical element, and approximately six weeks. For *HONOR*, I offered playwrights a flag. The goal is to initiate writing with an element of freedom and an element of the universal.

Why HONOR? In February, the decision to go to war in Iraq seemed dishonorable for many reasons, but soldiers were then and still are dying honorable deaths. I asked writers to reflect on how HONOR is used in our lives. When is it assigned, and, ultimately, what is its value? The revelation of events at Abu Ghraib made the timing of our inquiry even more pointed.

After six weeks, we gather members of the company to hear all of the plays on a single afternoon marathon reading, known to us as a Read Aloud. Actors are handed scripts cold. The goal is to hear the writer's words, hopefully read aloud by a sensitive actor, not necessarily some-one perfect for the role. After the Read Aloud, I choose plays for production. We assemble a variety of responses, and our hope is that the variety promotes a greater awareness. In the case of *HONOR*, there were actually two evenings produced. Published here is the first of those two.

HONOR is the culmination of many projects before it, none of which would be possible without the artistry, inspiration, integrity, and com-mitment to humanity within Bradford Olson, Dan Teachout, Karen Kitz, Rob A. Wilson, Eric Nightengale, and Gabriele Forster and the contributions of co-founders Lizabeth Allen, Ross Stoner, and Jenni-fer Shaw; board member Wendy Rothstein; supporters Jeffrey Grieb, Darren Seirer, Amor Towles, George S. Loening, Mary Ethel and Jerry Siefken, Margaret Booker, Tom and Libya Clancy, and Larry King; designer Tom Gleasson; playwrights C. Denby Swanson, Ed-ward Manning, P. Seth Bauer, Renee Flemings, and Neil Olson; and actors/directors Shelley Delaney, Carol Halstead, Peter Bretz, and Keno Rider.

In May, we HONORed the founders of 78th Street Theatre Lab, Mark Zeller and Dana Zeller-Alexis, for their commitment to new work in the theatre and for their contributions to the community as professional acting teachers. Without 78th Street Theatre Lab, we would have no home.

Mostly, I would hope to honor all those people who have perished in Iraq. The only honor left is to recognize the senselessness of their loss.

MICK JUST SHRUGS

by Brian Dykstra

MR. D. BOONE KIRKS, a high school principal, meets with MICK MARSHALL, a senior, one of his charges. KIRKS holds a crumpled paper bag. From out of the bag, he removes a small worn and faded American flag on a tired stick. He studies MICK, who might be a little nervous.

KIRKS: ...You want to explain this.

(MICK just shrugs.)

KIRKS: Mister Pelster tells me you were using this flag in his class for an art project. Is that true?

MICK: Mister Pelster is my teacher.

KIRKS: I'm aware of that.

MICK: So, would you believe me if I said it wasn't true?

KIRKS: Okay, how much trouble do you think you're in?

(MICK just shrugs.)

KIRKS: Then maybe the smart-mouth answers could be kept to a minimum. At least until you begin to ascertain just how much trouble you're in. That seems the much more intelligent choice, don't you think?

MICK: Okay. Yes. It's true.

KIRKS: What was the piece about?

MICK: Censorship of art in high schools.

KIRKS: ...Really?

(MICK just shrugs.)

KIRKS: Why was the flag suspended over a Bunsen burner?

(MICK just shrugs.)

KIRKS: Well, if you don't know, who does?

MICK: I was trying to show how dangerous and precarious it is to use the flag as the symbol to deny rights to the very citizens that flag is the symbol of protecting.

KIRKS: ...Could you say that again?

MICK: Yeah. But I really hate to have to explain my art.

KIRKS: ...The thing that troubles me most, and the thing that troubled Mister Pelster, was the half-full can of lighter fluid you'd hidden in the base of your project.

(KIRKS produces a can of lighter fluid from out of the paper bag. MICK eyes it.)

MICK: I could see where that would be a concern.

KIRKS: Thanks for being so understanding.

MICK: I cannot tell a lie. I was gonna soak the flag with lighter fluid, and then for the competition I was gonna fire up the Bunsen burner. So, can I go?

KIRKS: Why would you think you could go?

MICK: Because I told the truth. And we both know that after young George Washington copped to chopping down the cherry tree, he got away with it because he told the truth. So I expect the same treatment.

KIRKS: Except you told the truth in order to get out of trouble. Which is not the lesson of that story.

MICK: But then again, it never happened, did it? So, is the lesson that it's okay to lie to kids in order to get them not to lie?

KIRKS: Why do you want to burn the flag?

MICK: Bunch of reasons.

KIRKS: Name one.

MICK: All right. How about, because we live in a society where it's okay for educators to lie to kids in order to get them not to lie.

KIRKS: Okay. But if that's a failing, it's a failing of the educational system. Has little or nothing to do with the flag.

MICK: What?

KIRKS: Don't you think?

MICK: Are we really gonna— … Are you really gonna engage me in a debate? In, like, a real debate?

KIRKS: Why would that be so surprising?

MICK: First of all, I'm really, really smart.

KIRKS: Big deal.

MICK: I don't believe you.

KIRKS: Why not?

MICK: You're going to let it go for a while and when I start to make sense, you're going to apply some arbitrary power trip and I'm going to have to shut up and get sent into some kind of detention. And it'll be better for me if I don't piss you off. Because if I—

KIRKS: Language.

MICK: What, "piss you off?"

KIRKS: I'm not kidding.

MICK: See? Arbitrary.

KIRKS: It's school policy.

MICK: It's an arbitrary school policy.

KIRKS: You're right. I apologize.

MICK: I'm what? You do?

KIRKS: Yeah. Even though the courts decided that all constitutional guarantees are not necessarily afforded students in an educational setting, I agree with you that it is arbitrary. However, that's still not about the flag.

MICK: The flag is a symbol.

KIRKS: And you want to burn it. But my question remains. Why?

MICK: …Because it is too about the flag. You just said it: Constitutional guarantees are not always available to students in an educational setting.

KIRKS: That's my argument.

MICK: So.

KIRKS: Didn't you have one of your own?

MICK: What's wrong with yours?

KIRKS: We're discussing why you set up your art project. And, at the time you wanted to burn the flag, my reason didn't occur to you.

MICK: Maybe it was subconscious.

KIRKS: If you don't have any of your own reasons, just say so.

MICK: …I believe in a woman's right to choose.

KIRKS: You're kidding.

MICK: Why?

KIRKS: This is where you want to begin?

MICK: Why not?

KIRKS: She has that right.

MICK: For how much longer?

KIRKS: Do you know anybody who needed an abortion and couldn't get one?

(MICK just shrugs.)

KIRKS: What else?

MICK: You're really going to let me go here?

KIRKS: Why not? You haven't been all that impressive up to this point. And let me be up front. You've left me no choice but to punish you. Lighter fluid, in and of itself, is not allowed on school grounds. You can understand why, can't you? After all, you're "really, really smart."

(MICK just shrugs.)

KIRKS: So, what do you have to lose? Maybe there's some mitigating circumstance that will allow me to make the punishment more precisely fit the crime. Also, if you're going to burn the flag, you really should have an idea as to why.

MICK: The whole world hates our country.

KIRKS: That isn't true.

MICK: Well, the whole world hates our government.

KIRKS: So, you're going to pile on?

MICK: Some people are so afraid of us, they mail anthrax and hijack planes.

KIRKS: But the flag—

MICK: How bad did you guys have to screw up to make that happen?

KIRKS: "You guys"?

MICK: Yeah. You guys. Adults. Your generation. Or were you handed this mess? I mean, why does the NRA think making sure assault weapons are available is a good idea? How did you let it get to that? Why do they fight limitations and waiting periods? Why? I'm asking.

KIRKS: Well. Their argument is that it's a slippery slope.

MICK: I know. But the slope ain't that slippery. So, it really must be because they're crazy. Right?

KIRKS: They have a different point of view.

MICK: "A different point of view"?

KIRKS: Yes.

MICK: You mean like all crazy people?

KIRKS: That's not exactly—

MICK: And then after arming ourselves to the teeth, we're the only Western country who sentences its citizens to death. The only one.

KIRKS: Which point did you—?

MICK: Fifty-two percent of respondents in a recent poll would like to see the public execution of Osama bin Laden (if we catch him). And forty percent would be willing to purchase the right to see it on pay-per-view. Presumably with a bowl of popcorn in their laps. Forty percent. I would say that I don't know these people, but I must. I must know some of them.

KIRKS: That's a different issue. We'll need to take them—

MICK: Drug laws are stupid.

KIRKS: Do I even get to—

MICK: Pharmaceutical companies finance anti-drug campaigns in order to keep marijuana from cutting into market share by competing with their line of "mood enhancers." These anti-drug campaigns don't even bother telling the truth. It's just total scare tactics, trading on stereotypes that anybody who ever smoked a single bowl knows is total bullshit. Why should we believe you about other drugs? You lied to us about pot, half of you all are addicted to booze and pills, and way too many of my friends were medicated with Ritalin or whatever made raising them easier on their lazy parents. And, of course, Africans with AIDS won't get a second look because they can't pay for the pharmaceuticals. That's just tough, huh.

Sixty of the world's leading scientists (including twenty past Nobel winners) have accused the White House of knowingly and willfully lying about scientific realities in order to further pro-business and pro-military agendas. The administration's response up to present has been a big, fat "So?"

Companies get gift no-bid government contracts through political connections. Some states are considering not teaching evolution.

Laws are being bent and judicial appointments made in order to further a Christian right-wing agenda that's more interested in Armageddon than people.

Environmental laws are castrated in the name of progress, so rather than wasting profits on cleanup, corporations get to make more scratch, while the possibility of a clean environment becomes more and more remote.

Global warming is joked about. But the ozone is depleting and we've lost almost fifty percent of the world's coral reef in my lifetime. I'm seventeen years old. If that isn't a canary choking to death in Dick Cheney's coal mine, then what is it?

I can't remember the last time we were below something called Orange Alert.

Political debate has devolved into partisan rhetoric in almost every forum. So truth is held hostage while ultra-conservative, pill-popping, right-wing assholes like Rush Limbaugh spew hate all over the airwaves and complain about something they keep calling the Liberal Media. Which I don't even know what that is. Do they mean Hollywood? Because they can't possibly mean MSNBC, or Rupert Murdoch Fox. They can't mean talk radio. They can't possibly mean the news.

The Florida National Guard was mobilized to illegally turn away thousands of African American voters in the last presidential election. Nobody had to answer for that.

In the name of fighting terrorism, civil rights are being denied citizens of this country every single day. And most of the time, we don't even know it.

We eat shit.

Intelligent people are marginalized by being branded "the Cultural Elite" while the government is reacting to polling that gets taken in Darwin's waiting room.

I haven't even really gotten started on Iraq.

Half the people can't afford a hospital stay.

SUVs get shitty gas mileage. And nobody cares.

We have gay men and women unable to marry, because the majority says they can't. Never mind the majority is so fucking wrong on this issue it should be so collectively embarrassed that it shouldn't be able to utter the first syllable about it. In the fifties, interracial marriages were against the law. Well, outside of a few brainless white supremacist neo-nazi shitheads, we all agree that law was wrong, wasn't it? No matter what the majority said. Fuck the majority. And now they're squealing about a constitutional amendment that's the first one since Prohibition (later repealed, by the way) that's designed to limit rights.

We have people voting Republican who will never have even the hope of rising to the financial level where it might start to make sense to vote Republican. Habitually voting Republican, but who are, socially, actually pro choice and pro gun control, pro helping the poor, pro education, pro rights, but they vote Republican because they make more than a hundred grand a year and somehow the extra four thousand dollars they *might* have to pay to help fund a Democratic agenda is deemed too dangerous to the wellbeing of their bottom line.

Democrats are wishy-washy reactionary cowards who allow their political enemies to define them. Liberal is a dirty word because conservatives say it is.

Politicians from both parties are in the pockets of business because if you don't have a huge war chest there's no way you can win an election.

The Supreme Court just proved it's either a totally partisan body, or for the first time, it's become clear just how fallible it is. Neither option is particularly reassuring.

Our total dependence on oil has not only created the terrorists but it gives them the dollars and weapons they need to attack us. And, rather than address the reasons for their anger, we decide to fight fire with fire and burn everybody down.

Jesus is suddenly the star-slash-victim of a sadomasochist snuff film rather than a loving and forgiving anything. Now ready to fuel more religious tension in a country in need of a handful of dogmatic Valium.

Can't watch the local news or read a paper because it's all about who died in what fire, what cop got shot, what rapist is on the loose, what politician got caught fucking the intern, and (in a related story) who screwed who out of what.

In this environment, the idea that all I want to do is burn a flag because I can't find anything else lying around that represents all the evils in the world, rather than gather up my most disenfranchised classmates, raid our daddies' gun cabinets, and try to break the Columbine record, should have you all heaping praise on me about my remarkable restraint. But, instead, just me mentioning Columbine is going to land me in deeper shit, because isn't it so much better if we just don't talk about these things? I totally understand assassination, now. I totally understand feeling like whacking the president might be the very best thing for everybody. That asshole.

I'm scared. Okay? There's nothing to believe (or believe in). The flag gets wrapped around every nutcase with a position, and it's rotting from the inside. When all I can do is burn a flag, where do I go from there? I admit I'm too young to be this pissed off.

I want to burn the flag.

Which, last I checked (falling under the heading of free speech), is one of those constitutional guarantees I guess you're not compelled to grant me.

Fuck.

That's all I have. For now.

KIRKS: …It's not the flag's fault.

MICK: That's the best you got?

KIRKS: And it's lazy. It's the definition of lazy. Burning the flag. Whoopie. The last bastion of the disenfranchised quitter.

MICK: What do you suggest?

KIRKS: If it was me?

MICK: Yeah.

KIRKS: Make effigies.

MICK: What?

KIRKS: Effigies.

MICK: You mean those puppets?

KIRKS: But make them really, really well. The time and effort should show. They would be a little more expensive than you can afford. Well crafted. By themselves, they should be something like art. Burning them should be a sacrifice.

MICK: Who of?

KIRKS: Whoever you want.

MICK: Who would you do?

KIRKS: Usual suspects.

MICK: Who are who?

KIRKS: Bush. Cheney. Five Supreme Court justices. If you do the research, you'll figure out which five. Rumsfeld. Rice. Powell. Bush Senior. Jeb Bush. Hell, the whole Bush clan can go. Including Barbara. Corporate criminals. Enron. WorldCom. ImClone. Lay. Skinner. If you don't know who they are, look them up. Polluters. Find out who's getting away with the worst of it. Half the House and Sen-

ate. I'd lock them in a mini gas chamber and rig it to a fireball when the judges are nearby. But that's me. If I was going to do something like that.

MICK: There's no way you're this cool.

KIRKS: No, that's true. I'm not this cool. Sorry.

MICK: So, what is the catch?

KIRKS: The catch is I have a school to run. My only priority, here. So, no matter what I may think privately, I never said anything to you that might be construed as an endorsement of this kind of dissenting behavior.

MICK: I thought dissent was patriotic.

KIRKS: But not as much as patriotism. And patriots don't burn flags.

MICK: I'm just supposed to—

KIRKS: So, you're suspended from school for three days. You won't be allowed to enter anything in the art fair. You won't be allowed to attend the art fair.

MICK: What?

KIRKS: That'll go for next year, as well.

MICK: I'm a senior.

KIRKS: So, you're graduating. Better still.

MICK: But you get it.

KIRKS: There's nothing to get, we never had this conversation.

MICK: I heard you.

KIRKS: Prove it.

MICK: That sucks.

KIRKS: Welcome to America.

MICK: You suck.

KIRKS: And that's a tradeoff I gladly make in order to maintain order and discipline. Thank you for your honesty.

MICK: Wait a minute.

KIRKS: You can wait in the detention room until your parents arrive.

MICK: You agree with me.

KIRKS: Not relevant. Out of my office.

MICK: Should I be burning you in effigy?

KIRKS: Not on school grounds. Out.

MICK: I think we have to—

KIRKS: This is a public school, young man. Nobody cares what you think. Out.

MICK: But I—

KIRKS: Out.

(MICK gathers his bookbag and makes his way to the door. He wants to say something, but can't. He leaves. KIRKS picks up the flag. Defeated, he drops it in the trash can. He pours some lighter fluid on the flag. He lights a match and holds it over the trash can. As he drops the match into the trash can, the lights BLACKOUT.)

(Unless [as I MUCH prefer] you're going to let the actors burn the flag onstage. In which case, he holds the flag, touches the corner with the match, watches it burn for a moment, and drops the burning flag into the trash can. He watches it burn out. BLACKOUT.)

A FRIDAY NIGHT
TRANS AM RIDE

Andrea Moon

CHARACTERS

CAROLINE: A woman of the middle class (economically and morally speaking) turned artist and intellectual variety

EVANGELINE: A woman of the lower class (economically speaking) turned mystic variety

THERESA: A Latina

also

GUARD'S VOICE: The voice of a prison guard

BRAD'S VOICE: The voice of Evangeline's fiancé

SETTING

One and Three: In the waiting area between the elevator and the visiting room. No furniture, no decorations except a flag.

Two and Four: The visiting room of a county jail.

ONE

In a waiting area. No furniture. A door that enters from a hallway with an elevator. Another door on the other side, locked, with a buzzer attached. An American flag looks down on all who enter. The sound of the elevator dinging open. CAROLINE enters into the room from the hallway, a small slip of white paper in her hand. She walks to the other door and lifts her finger as if to ring a buzzer. She can't make herself do it. She decides to try a few opening lines.

CAROLINE: So, you're still breathing. …Too glib. *(Tries another.)* First I want to

say that no matter what happens, I'm here. *(No. Another.)* So, keeping your back to the wall? …Damnit. *(Another.)* I know you didn't mean to hurt anyone. Least of all me. *(Starts again.)* Hi. …Shit. *(And again.)* You look great in blue. Brings out your eyes. *(And finally.)* Listen I've been thinking of what I should say to you and so far I can't come up with—

(The ding of the elevator. CAROLINE quickly stops talking. THERESA enters, glances quickly at and away from CAROLINE. She goes over to the other door, pushes the button. The fuzzy voice of a GUARD comes out of the intercom.)

GUARD'S VOICE: Name?

THERESA: Ulloa. U-L-L-O-A. Two twenty-three B.

GUARD'S VOICE: Cell and pod.

THERESA: Two twenty-three B.

GUARD'S VOICE: Name again?

THERESA: Ulloa.

GUARD'S VOICE: Spell it.

THERESA: U-L-L-O-A.

GUARD'S VOICE: Uh. Not in our system. Take the elevator back—

THERESA: Yeah yeah.

(She walks away before GUARD can finish, and exits the way she came without even glancing at CAROLINE.)

GUARD'S VOICE: —downstairs and have them send him up again.

(CAROLINE walks over to the button nervously. Pauses. Turns around again.)

CAROLINE: Shit. Hi. Fancy meeting you here. I don't know what to say to you. *(She studies the flag for a moment, fingers the slip of paper nervously.)* Look, I can't help thinking about your aunt. Traveling across the countryside with her broken foot, her homeland falling all around her. I can see her in the heat, sweat dripping into her cast, toes throbbing, glancing at every face with suspicion, trying not to breathe in the panic for fear it will choke her. The image of your small body, of getting that body safely through the melee, safely out of that disintegrating country, the only thing spurring her on through her exhaustion. Your grandfather pulling on every connection he'd ever made, promises exchanged from the corners of tight smiles, bills pressed quickly into sweaty white palms, while the choppers whir up a maelstrom. To bring you to the one country in the world that has the pursuit of happiness written into its constitution as an indelible human right. Giving up their birthright to give you a chance. And this is how you honor their sacrifice? How you repay them? What were you thinking? You had everything and you pissed all over it. …Too righteous. No. No. Not too righteous. A person has to be accountable. You, even you have to be accountable. This is what you've done with all the freedom you won by escaping Vietnam, all the opportunity offered to you on a platter. Oh sure, you worked for it. I know, I can't possibly know how hard it was. Poverty prejudice etcetera etcetera, but you had the opportunity to…to work, the freedom to…the freedom to—

(The ding of the elevator. CAROLINE falls silent. EVANGELINE comes in talking.)

EVANGELINE: Stupid turd breath bacon-smelling doughnut-eating asshole. What did he think I was going to do, sanitize the guards into submission? Clean my way through the safety glass?

CAROLINE: I'm sorry?

EVANGELINE: Maybe, right? Grime and muck and…and germs are probably the only thing holding this hole together. He took my wipie.

CAROLINE: Your wipie?

(While she talks, EVANGELINE walks over to the button and pushes it.)

EVANGELINE: A wet wipe. He took my wet wipe. Like it's going to be some secret message or something. It was plainly sealed. Like vacuum sealed, you know?

GUARD'S VOICE: Just a minute.

EVANGELINE: Next time it's going in my cleavage. Though Porko was staring at that hard enough. Maybe down my pants. At least they haven't started searching there yet.

CAROLINE: A wet wipe?

EVANGELINE: For the phones. I always bring one.

CAROLINE: For the phones?

EVANGELINE: Yeah. You never know who was on it before you, you know? What foul disease they have. Sometimes they help just to kill the smell.

CAROLINE: Oh.

EVANGELINE: You've never thought about what's all over those phones, right?

CAROLINE: I've never…I've never done this. I mean. Been here.

EVANGELINE: Your boyfriend?

CAROLINE: I guess you could say that.

EVANGELINE: My fiancé. Well, I'd offer you a wipie for the phones but the Nazis took them. Big dangers, wet wipes.

CAROLINE: We don't…we don't get to see them?

EVANGELINE: Oh you'll get to see him. Sort of. Through like two-inch thick yellow glass slimed with sweat and snot and tears and grief and like pent-up anger and betrayal and disappointment (what are they doing in there, whacking off?) and shit like that. If you're sensitive at all to that kind of stuff, that energy, like I am, don't touch the glass. I never touch the glass.

CAROLINE: Touch the glass?

EVANGELINE: Oh, you'd be surprised. People, their hands, their foreheads, even their lips. Kissing on that glass like enough sexual frustration and it would somehow melt, you know, disappear or something right in front of them. Don't touch the glass.

CAROLINE: Don't touch the glass. Got it. We can't touch them. Hold their hands or… they're not in the same room.

EVANGELINE: Really haven't done this at all before, huh?

CAROLINE: No.

EVANGELINE: And he's never been down before?

CAROLINE: Down?

EVANGELINE: Inside.

CAROLINE: Inside? No.

EVANGELINE: Well. There's a first time for everything I guess.

CAROLINE: I guess so.

EVANGELINE: Are you going to cry?

CAROLINE: I don't know.

EVANGELINE: 'Cause you look like you're going to cry.

CAROLINE: Yeah, well. Lately. Sometimes. I just look like that.

EVANGELINE: You'll be fine. Just sort of hold the phone away from your ear, like this. A little bit. Other people might hear what he's saying, but at least you won't get cauliflower ear or something. Trust me. You'll thank me.

CAROLINE: Thanks.

EVANGELINE: Evangeline. *(To the intercom.)* Come on, Porkos.

CAROLINE: I'm sorry?

EVANGELINE: My name. Evangeline.

CAROLINE: That's pretty.

EVANGELINE: Thanks. My mother had an epidural. At least one, you know. And who knows what she was on before the labor.

CAROLINE: Caroline.

EVANGELINE: Do your friends call you Carol?

CAROLINE: No.

EVANGELINE: My friends call me Angel. You seem cool. You can call me Angel.

CAROLINE: Angel.

GUARD'S VOICE: Name?

EVANGELINE: Robinson. R-O-B-I-N-S-O-N. One sixteen A.

GUARD'S VOICE: Booth F as in fool.

(There is a buzzing sound, and, with a slight wave, EVANGELINE disappears through the door. CAROLINE watches her go, goes to push the button, but something else needs to be said.)

CAROLINE: What the hell am I doing here? You know what bothers me, is that I don't even know who you are anymore. This is a nightmare I can't wake up from. I don't belong here. Three days of trying to find you, find where they'd taken you and the shit they put me through, the way they look at me, like I'm not even there, like my fear and pain and confusion don't matter, like I don't have any right to know anything, I might as well have done the crime with the way they look at me and now I'm here and I don't even know who you are. The person I knew could never do this. How could you get involved with something like this? How could you do this to me? To us? How could you—

(Another elevator ding. THERESA comes breezing back in, shoots CAROLINE a slightly suspicious look, and pushes the buzzer.)

GUARD'S VOICE: Name?

THERESA: Ulloa. U-L-L-O-A. Two twenty-three B.

GUARD'S VOICE: Booth H as in help.

(The buzzing noise. THERESA exits.)

CAROLINE: Too self-centered. Stick with righteous. *(She finally pushes the button.)*

GUARD'S VOICE: Name.

CAROLINE: I'm sorry. Of the…of the person I'm visiting? I've never done this before.

GUARD'S VOICE: Prisoner's name, pod number, and cell number.

CAROLINE: Umm. Huu.

GUARD'S VOICE: Spell it.

CAROLINE: H-U-U.

GUARD'S VOICE: Pod and cell number.

CAROLINE: I don't know—

GUARD'S VOICE: Do you have a visitor's slip? It's on your visitor's slip. Beneath the inmate number.

CAROLINE: *(Looks down at the little piece of paper.)* Six-nine-seven-eight-three—

GUARD'S VOICE: Not the inmate number. Pod. And. Cell. Number.

CAROLINE: I'm sorry.

GUARD'S VOICE: Never mind, hold on a second. H-U-U. One thirteen A. Booth G as in genius.

(The buzzing noise. CAROLINE hesitates.)

GUARD'S VOICE: You have to push on the door to open it.

(She exits.)

TWO

The visiting room of a county jail. CAROLINE, EVANGELINE, and THERESA are sitting close to each other but slightly separated by some kind of structure or suggested by light. Each has the receiver of a phone to their left. EVANGELINE almost immediately picks up the phone, but doesn't hold it against her head. This allows us to hear BRAD'S VOICE tinny and far away. We should be able to understand some of what he says, but perhaps not all. CAROLINE and THERESA wait.

BRAD'S VOICE: You're a sight, baby.

EVANGELINE: It's good to see you, too. What happened to your eye?

BRAD'S VOICE: Aah, it's nothing. Stand up for me.

THERESA: *(To CAROLINE.)* Not here yet?

CAROLINE: No, not yet.

THERESA: They do this.

EVANGELINE: Why?

BRAD'S VOICE: Come on, baby. Stand up and turn around for me.

THERESA: Sometimes you wait and wait.

BRAD'S VOICE: Mmhmm. A sight.

THERESA: They come. They sit. They have to leave. Just like that. Visit is over.

BRAD'S VOICE: I swear you look better and better the longer I'm in here.

CAROLINE: They can do that?

EVANGELINE: Do you love me?

THERESA: They can do what they want.

BRAD'S VOICE: Of course I do.

EVANGELINE: Really, you love me?

BRAD'S VOICE: Yeah baby.

CAROLINE: I've never been here. Done this before.

EVANGELINE: Tell me.

THERESA: Some guards are good. You see him longer than the hour. Some are *cabrónes*. Five minutes and they scream "*Avalos*, time's up." One time one is good. One time one is *pandejo*. It works like that.

BRAD'S VOICE: Don't waste our time, baby. I just said I love you. Put the phone up to your ear and you'd hear it. What are you smoking? Put the phone up to your ear.

EVANGELINE: No. I don't know who's been on it. Do you love me more than your Trans Am?

BRAD'S VOICE: Baby, two totally different things—

EVANGELINE: I know. But do you?

CAROLINE: They can't do that. How can they get away with that?

THERESA: Who're we going to tell?

BRAD'S VOICE: You can't compare. Apples and oranges. Eminem and Peaches and Herb, baby.

EVANGELINE: But if you had to choose.

CAROLINE: The warden. Their lawyers.

BRAD'S VOICE: Between you and my Trans Am?

THERESA: Who're we going to tell that cares?

EVANGELINE: Like you couldn't have both. If you had to choose—

BRAD'S VOICE: Who would make me choose?

CAROLINE: That's not right. There are recourses. Built into the system, there have to be.

EVANGELINE: Say someone had a gun to your head.

BRAD'S VOICE: Who had a gun to my head?

THERESA: I don't understand. Recourses. *(She suddenly turns and picks up the phone.)*

EVANGELINE: Just someone—

THERESA: *Gracias al dios, no está como ayer. La espera y la espera.* [Thank God, it's not like yesterday. Wait and wait.]

BRAD'S VOICE: Like if you put a gun to my head and said me or your Trans Am?

EVANGELINE: Not me—

THERESA: *¿Pareces flaca, quitada la comida?* [You look thin, are you eating?]

BRAD'S VOICE: There'd be no choice. You freak on me like that, I'd drop you like a used hypo—

EVANGELINE: Not me.

BRAD'S VOICE: Then who?

EVANGELINE: Just someone. A stranger.

THERESA: *Ella no esta conmigo. Ella esta a la casa.* [She's not with me. She's at home.]

BRAD'S VOICE: Why would a stranger care about you and my Trans Am?

THERESA: *Con mi madre.* [With my mother.]

EVANGELINE: Just say they were messing with you and they put a gun to your head and you had to choose.

BRAD'S VOICE: I'd break their fingers and shove the gun down their throat 'cause that ain't right.

THERESA: *No me gritas.* [Don't yell at me.]

EVANGELINE: Just say, theoretically, say you had to choose. For me, okay? Just pretend for some reason you had to choose? Would you choose the car over me?

No me gritas.

BRAD'S VOICE: I don't know baby. It isn't just a car. It's a Trans Am. And not just any Trans Am but a 1973 SD-455 with rock crushers. We're talking tight. The symbol of distinction of an entire decade.

Pare gritar en mì. [Stop yelling at me.]

THERESA: *(Yells.) ¡Pare gritar!* [Stop yelling!]

EVANGELINE: It's a car.

BRAD'S VOICE: A 1973 Super Duty 455 Trans Am with a screaming chicken. In nearly mint condition.

THERESA: *Me vale. Ella es mi hija y ete lugar no es bueno para ella.* [I don't give a fuck. She's my daughter and this is not good for her.]

EVANGELINE: You said you loved me.

BRAD'S VOICE: Apples and oranges.

EVANGELINE: Jesus, you know, Brad. You know I'm out here. You know. Alone. It's lonely. And I get to see you once a week, twice if your mom's not in town or you two are pissed at each other. I'm loyal. As a dog.

THERESA: *¡Ocho ochenta! Usted grita. Yo no lo oigo.* [Blah! Blah! Blah! You're yelling. I don't hear you.]

THERESA: *Entonces acto como su padre.* [Then act like her father.]

EVANGELINE: I'm waiting, I'm not dicking around, I don't even touch myself without thinking about you and you can't just say, even if it's not true, that you'd choose me over a…a car.

BRAD'S VOICE: Trans Am. A 1973 SD—

EVANGELINE: Whatever! Some things are just wrong. There's something wrong with you, you know.

BRAD'S VOICE: Hold up. Why are you freaking? Did something happen to my car?

EVANGELINE: *(To CAROLINE.)* He's not here yet? Maybe you should go back out and buzz them. They'll leave you sitting like that… oh is that him? He's cute. Lucky girl. *(To BRAD.)* No.

BRAD'S VOICE: Angel, don't mess with my head. Did. Something. Happen. To. My. Car.?

(CAROLINE lights up. She puts her palm up against the glass as if to match TRANG's palm, then thinks better of it, removes it, and wipes it on her clothes.)

CAROLINE: Hi.

THERESA: *Ella lo pierde tambièn. ¿Sabe usted cuan duramente que esto es?* [She misses you too. Do you know how hard this is?]

BRAD'S VOICE: Look me in the eye and say that.

CAROLINE: Oh. *(She reaches down and picks up the phone.)*

THERESA: *Y no lo mantengo aparte.* [I'm not keeping you apart.]

CAROLINE: It's good to see you.

EVANGELINE: You're paranoid about your car?

THERESA: *Usted lo mantiene aparte.* [You're keeping you apart.]

CAROLINE: So, you're still breathing.

EVANGELINE: Now you're freaking and you can just step back, I'm out here making payments on your damn car.

BRAD'S VOICE: Put the phone up to your ear. Put the phone up to your ear. Put the phone up to your ear.

CAROLINE: We wouldn't want that. If you cry, you'll be branded as an easy mark.

EVANGELINE: No. Brad, I don't know who's been on this phone.

THERESA: *Me vale. Sea un hombre.* [I don't give a fuck. Be a man.]

EVANGELINE: You can't talk to me like that. You can't treat me like that. I'll walk out of here. Fine. *(She puts the phone up to her ear; we can no longer hear BRAD.)*

BRAD'S VOICE: Angel. Put. The. Phone. Up. To. Your. Ear.

CAROLINE: Then before you know it, you'll be somebody's bitch.

(EVANGELINE and THERESA both stop for an instant and glance at her before continuing.)

CAROLINE: God. I'm sorry. That's not funny.

EVANGELINE: Your car is fine.

THERESA: *No. Usted actúa como un cabrón.* [No, you're acting like an asshole.]

EVANGELINE: I am telling the truth. Do you think I would lie to you?

CAROLINE: More? Oh yeah, tons more. Like, so you keeping your back to the wall?

THERESA: *¿Cuándo largo esta vez?* [How long this time?]

EVANGELINE: If you don't trust me, that's your problem.

CAROLINE: You look great in blue, brings out your eyes. Better you than me, blue washes me out.

EVANGELINE: I'm not sending you a picture of your car.

THERESA: *Dígame.* [Tell me.]

CAROLINE: Don't drop the soap. That one's a classic, right?

EVANGELINE: Why don't you ever ask for a picture of me?

CAROLINE: None of this is actually funny, Trang. *(Starts laughing anyway.)*

THERESA: *¿Qué dice su abogado?* [What does your lawyer say?]

CAROLINE: I don't know what we're talking about.

THERESA: *Dígame.*

CAROLINE: I had this whole thing planned of what to say to you but now, but here—

THERESA: *Protéjame. Eso es chistoso. Mírelo.* [Protect me. That's funny. Look at you.]

EVANGELINE: Brad. Let's just. Let's just start again, okay? I'll admit that it wasn't fair, you know, booby trapping you like that about your car. Let's not fight, okay? There's so little time.

CAROLINE: Is that yours? A prison poet. That's a worthwhile skill. Maybe you could trade, you know, do birthday cards for mothers or girlfriends for extra slop.

EVANGELINE: Let's not dwell on the past, or try and see the future, let's just be here in this moment, you know, together, as together as we... Brad, I'm talking to you here.

(CAROLINE and EVANGELINE look over toward each other as if BRAD and TRANG have exchanged some kind of words.)

EVANGELINE: You think you're funny but you're not. Leave him alone and talk to me.

CAROLINE: You know him?

EVANGELINE: Forget it. Let's not talk about that.

CAROLINE: What did he do?

EVANGELINE:	CAROLINE:
Are we going to argue about this like the whole visit? Because if we are, why did I bother coming?	Right. Note to self. What else do you not talk about in there?

THERESA: *¡Caray! No eso largo. No eso largo. ¿Qué hare yo?* [Oh shit. Not that long. Not that long. What am I going to do?]

CAROLINE: No. I don't want to. It's not the same as touching you.

THERESA: *¿Cómo somos supuestos vivir?* [How are we supposed to live?]

CAROLINE: I don't have a lot of imagination right now.

EVANGELINE: Don't send her—

THERESA: *Yo no calmaré.* [I won't calm down.]

CAROLINE: I don't have a lot of anything right now.

EVANGELINE: —don't send her—

CAROLINE: And besides. I don't know who's touched that glass. Snot. Betrayal. Anger. Tears. I'm sensitive to that stuff.

THERESA: *¿Dónde obtendré ese tanto de dinero?* [Where am I going to get that kind of money?]

CAROLINE: That's beautiful too.

EVANGELINE: Don't you dare send her—

CAROLINE: I *know* who wrote that one. Don't educate me, okay. It's ridiculous. *(Starts to laugh again.)*

EVANGELINE: —to check on your car—

CAROLINE: Hilarious. How someone so smart can be such a dumbass.

EVANGELINE: Trans Am, whatever.

THERESA: *Nosotros lo necesitamos—* [We need you—]

CAROLINE: Well, I find Rilke hilarious. too. Here.

THERESA: *—fuera aquí.* [—out here.]

CAROLINE: In this particular situation. Incongruous.

EVANGELINE: Do you even care what's going on with me?

CAROLINE: Agree? Jesus. I can't breathe—

THERESA: *¿Por qué? ¿Por qué?*

CAROLINE: I don't care. I don't care if all good poetry is incongruous. I really couldn't give a flying fuck.

EVANGELINE: —for the last time, your fucking symbol of distinction is fine—

CAROLINE: Look. Look, your hand.

THERESA: *¿Por qué lo hizo usted?* [Why did you do it?]

EVANGELINE: It's fine. All right, Brad?

CAROLINE: The land of promise has turned you the exact shade of a dollar bill.

THERESA: *No. Yo no seré callado.* [No, I will not be quiet.]

EVANGELINE: Your fiancée's heart is broken.

CAROLINE: It's either this or cry. I'm sorry. I can't, I can't breathe—

THERESA: *Y no cuido quién escucha.* [I don't care who's listening.]

EVANGELINE: —but your stupid car is in one piece.

CAROLINE: I'm sorry, I'm sorry, I can't— *(Lets the phone drop and gets up to leave.)*

EVANGELINE: *(To CAROLINE.)* If you leave the stool, the visit's over.

(There is the muffled sound of TRANG banging on the glass trying to catch CAROLINE's attention.)

THERESA: *No. Yo no entiendo.* [No. I don't understand.]

EVANGELINE: *(To BRAD.)* Her first time.

THERESA: *Ella lo pide cada noche. Cada noche. Yo no sé lo que decirla. ¿Que su padre es un pendejo que no puede quedarse afuera del problema por seis meses?* [She asks for you every night. Every night. I don't know what to tell her. That her father is a dumbass who can't stay out of trouble for six months?]

EVANGELINE: Okay, Brad. Brad. It's none of our business. Okay, okay. Okay. Okay. Jesus, have him write her a letter. *(Hangs up the phone and follows CAROLINE.)*

THERESA: *No. No. Esté allí para su familia. Esté allí para su mujer y niño. Eso es es un hombre.* [No. No. Being there for your family, your woman, and your child, that's being a man.] *(Hangs up the phone, makes a gesture toward the glass and leaves.)*

THREE

CAROLINE comes hurrying into the waiting room. She visibly gets herself under control, looks up at the flag, and bursts out laughing. Gets it under control again. EVANGELINE enters behind her.

EVANGELINE: Hey, are you okay?

(As soon as she sees EVANGELINE, CAROLINE completely loses it and breaks out into uncontrollable hysterical laughter.)

EVANGELINE: Are you laughing or crying?

CAROLINE: I'm sorry. Oh God. I'm sorry.

(THERESA enters behind. Looks at CAROLINE, then at EVANGELINE, who shrugs her shoulders/shakes her head in bewilderment.)

THERESA: *Loco.*

CAROLINE: I'm sorry, it's just, oh God.

THERESA: Totally gone.

EVANGELINE: No. Just a little overwhelmed. Remember there was that woman, that Russian woman? Maybe you weren't there, she came in to see her son with his girlfriend I guess, the girlfriend was crying but she was real quiet, all hunched over herself saying a prayer or something. Then as soon as she saw him behind the glass, she totally flipped and launched herself at him, screaming in Russian and trying to claw through the glass. Now *she* was loco.

(CAROLINE, who just got herself kind of under control, completely loses it again.)

EVANGELINE: I'm not kidding. You know. It was real. It was scary. She was like eighty or something and I think she ended up having to go inside herself. I don't know what happened to her then. It's not a joke.

CAROLINE: I know. I know, I'm sorry. I just. It's just so, so monumentally wrong. It's ridiculous. It's like an episode of the *Twilight Zone* or something, *dee-doo dee-doo.* And this is people's lives. I mean people's whole lives. It's just so. So. *(She loses it again.)*

THERESA: So what?

CAROLINE: Wrong. Trang was two quarters shy of getting his master's in literature. His thesis was on Rumi. This place is a daytime television talk show. We drink wine and discuss freedom in abstract philosophy. We watch sunsets and sunrises instead of Jerry Springer and Ricki Lake.

EVANGELINE: I don't watch Jerry Springer.

THERESA: Who's Ricki Lake?

EVANGELINE: I have enough problems of my own. I don't need to watch Jerry Springer. All that negative energy, it just makes things worse.

CAROLINE: No, I mean. I mean. He's never even turned in a paper late. I don't know what he's doing here.

THERESA: Time. That's my guess.

CAROLINE: It's just, to go from standing in his kitchen in the dark looking at the moon through the window to standing in line down there, down there. It's… It's… There was a woman in front of me, and when I walked up behind her, she turned to me and smiled and… *(Waves her hand in front of her mouth.)* …empty, she had no teeth.

EVANGELINE: I watch sunsets.

CAROLINE: At least no readily apparent teeth. Just gums. I think they were gums, it's hard to tell, they were black. We're talking *Deliverance* mouth.

THERESA: No, yes, didn't you know? Only people who can afford dentists like sunsets.

CAROLINE: You see? This is wrong. And the babies, little babies all dressed up as if for church in taffeta dresses and tacky ribbons, all prettied up like dime store dolls going to see their daddies.

THERESA: Oh yeah, now that's funny. Babies who will never get to bounce on their *papa*'s knee. That's f-ing hilarious.

EVANGELINE: I'm sure she doesn't mean anything.

THERESA: Then maybe she better stop talking.

CAROLINE: *(Has mostly gotten herself under control again.)* I don't mean anything. I don't know what I mean. See, I'm sitting there and he has his palm up to the glass and it's almost green. Green. What is that glass made of? He's sitting there in that ridiculous—whatever that is—uniform. And that or the glass has turned his skin that color. I haven't seen him or heard his voice or touched him in three weeks and all I can think is how can someone's skin be that color?

THERESA: I'm telling you. The more you move your mouth the worse it gets.

CAROLINE: He's in there looking at me, he's reciting Rilke to me you know, and meanwhile there's guards and guns and the smell of the phones—

EVANGELINE: I did warn you about that—

CAROLINE: —and his palm is green and his skin is, and you're trying to…trying to get your man to tell you he loves you more than his car.

EVANGELINE: It's a Trans Am.

CAROLINE: *(Loses it again.)* I'm sorry. I don't mean anything. I'm sorry. It's so absurd and—

EVANGELINE: No, I mean. It's a really rare car. And it's not the car, it's what it symbolizes for him, you know? What it means for him to, you know, own it.

THERESA: Don't explain. She's a *chocha*.

CAROLINE: And...and...that— *(She points to the flag and breaks out in hysterical laughter again.)*

THERESA: Now that. That *is* funny. Liberty and justice for all. Yeah? You like that one. *(To EVANGELINE.)* That is funny. But it's the accent that makes it side-splitting, right *esse*? *(To CAROLINE.)* And how about this one: bring me your huddled masses. That *is* a good one.

CAROLINE: Huddled masses. That's what's going on downstairs. Herding the huddled masses.

THERESA: They're hilarious, aren't they? "Your tired, your poor, your huddled masses yearning to breathe free—"

(CAROLINE stops laughing suddenly.)

THERESA: "The wretched refuse of your teeming shore. Send these, the homeless, tempest-tossed to me. I lift my lamp beside the golden door." I memorized it when I became a citizen. All Americans have it memorized, right? Pretty fucking funny, right? Right, *chocha*? Why aren't you laughing now?

CAROLINE: I didn't mean. I only meant— *(The pendulum swings the other way, and she breaks into sobs as quickly as she broke into laughter.)* I'm so sorry. I'm sorry. I'm not handling the stress very well. I'm so sorry.

EVANGELINE: It's okay.

CAROLINE: It's just, one minute he's there and the next. Gone. On a different planet where there's no oxygen and people are all looking at you like you're the alien because no one breathes oxygen anymore—

THERESA: Jesus.

CAROLINE: —and I couldn't find him and I can't touch him and I can't talk to him and this place, this place is. So. So. Dehumanizing and he's such a good human, he's so good, and so smart, and beautiful, and he doesn't belong here—

EVANGELINE: No one belongs here.

CAROLINE: —and I can't do anything to help him and I don't know how long he has to be here and I'm so, I'm so, I'm so. It's such a waste. Oh God. I don't cry in front of people.

THERESA: Mingling with the wretched refuse now, huh?

EVANGELINE: Leave her alone. She said she was sorry. God. It's bad karma to kick someone when they're down. Everyone knows that.

THERESA: People who quote Rilke are never down.

CAROLINE: I am sorry. I didn't mean to offend you. Really. I'm just upset. I've never had to go through this before.

THERESA: Poor you. I'm going to see what they're breathing at the elevators.

(THERESA exits to the hallway. CAROLINE continues babbling.)

CAROLINE: I didn't mean anything. I just meant... he's never been in trouble before. This is supposed to be the land of opportunity for him. I mean, his family brought him here for a chance and I wanted to be mad, but it's just a stupid stupid mistake. This is not who he is, at the core. Not saying that this *is* what your your—

EVANGELINE: —fiancé.

CAROLINE: —Right, fiancé is at the core. That's not what I'm saying. Please don't think that's what I'm saying.

EVANGELINE: Nobody is this, you know whatever this is, at the core.

CAROLINE: Right. I'm not saying that. I'm just digging a hole here.

EVANGELINE: It's your first time. I cut people slack, you know, that's just the way I am. Nobody reacts well the first time.

CAROLINE: She must think I'm a complete patronizing bitch.

EVANGELINE: No. Well, yeah probably. You can't worry about what other people think of you, you know. She's just…mad. At everything. I heard, I heard her husband's a border brother.

CAROLINE: A what?

EVANGELINE: He's not legal. Not a citizen. It goes bad for them.

CAROLINE: It goes good for everyone else?

EVANGELINE: Well. Relatively, you know. Lawyers, due process, blah blah blah. The appearance at least is there. I mean not *in* here. In here, bacon rules the roost but, you know, there's that hope. But he doesn't even have that. Brad told me that no lawyer is assigned to the borders unless they can afford one themselves. So they just sit there, just waiting to be deported. And who knows when that will be, they've committed a crime so Mexico is in no hurry to get them back. I heard that he's in for something ridiculous too. Beating on some white guy who was hitting on her. Protecting his family's honor or some such negative machismo bullshit. Real big in *that* culture, you know. Now he's fucked. Brad also told me that guy was like inches away from getting his green card too. Now he'll never get it.

CAROLINE: That can't be right. How can that be right? We can't just lock people up indefinitely.

EVANGELINE: It happens. Don't worry, after a while, you learn to just accept it, go with the flow. All the waiting, the ups and downs, the lawyer drama. You have to let go or you'll end up with an ulcer. That's what I was saying about what people are at the core. You see, that's the thing, whatever is happening in your life, you know, that becomes normal.

CAROLINE: I don't want this to become normal.

EVANGELINE: Yeah well. Don't cry. Maybe you'll be lucky. If he's a college boy, his family must have money. He has a green card, right?

CAROLINE: He's a citizen.

EVANGELINE: Well, there you are. Could be worse. You know, it was probably the comment about the babies that put her over the edge. I know, I know, you didn't mean anything. It's just that she has a little one. That's what I hear anyway. She never brings her, thinks it's bad for her or something. I wouldn't mention babies around her. And don't mention the assault or his legality either. A total no-no to talk about it. She doesn't even know I know.

CAROLINE: Making friends and influencing people. That's my specialty.

EVANGELINE: We don't have any, thank God. I can't. Brad doesn't know that, but by the time he gets out of here it probably won't matter anyway. He does love me, you know.

CAROLINE: What?

EVANGELINE: It wasn't fair for me to try and make him choose. He really does love me. He does.

CAROLINE: I believe you.

EVANGELINE: It doesn't really matter, if you believe me. I just let it roll off me, what other people think, pebbles in a pond of calm. I mean, he didn't go to college. He didn't have the chance to go. He wanted to go to mechanic school, but he couldn't afford it. I guess I'm saying he can't tell me the way maybe I'd like him to, the way your poet can tell you. But he does love me.

CAROLINE: I…I'm sure. I mean. I'm sure he does.

EVANGELINE: You'd have to know him. To know what cars mean to him. This car is everything to him. You probably think that's stupid, but you see, when he was growing up, it was the car everyone wanted. Boys had pictures of it on their walls, you know. And now he owns it. He found it in a junkyard, rebuilt it himself, painted it. It's perfect. It's his. You get it?

CAROLINE: I. I guess.

EVANGELINE: I can't explain it very well. I bet your boyfriend could. He's very cute. Really. I don't normally go for Asian guys, but he looks…kind.

CAROLINE: That woman's husband can't really just sit there indefinitely, I mean, there has to be some recourse for him, right?

EVANGELINE: It's a Friday night. That's what it is. Cruising with the windows down and the stereo's up real loud, with the bass pumping so it's like replacing your heartbeat or something. You know that feeling?

CAROLINE: No.

EVANGELINE: Maybe you had a bad week, if you're lucky enough to have a job your boss yelled at you all week or the guys laughed and ribbed you rough for a stupid mistake, but it's a Friday night and the sun is down and the windows are open and maybe there's a girl beside you. You're cruising and all these people on the sidewalk are looking at you, they're all dressed up in their weekend finest, and you're just passing them by, leaving them behind, and maybe you can just see the moon, but it's outshined by the lights of the bars and streetlights and convenience stores and the women in their sequined dresses. They're all looking at you too, you know, in your car that's yours, that you built, with your own hands, it's you. They're looking at you. With. Desire. Like you're magic, you pulled this car off an old poster of their childhood walls and you made it real, made it run. They're looking at you like you're a magician. With respect. It's his respect. His freedom. That they can't take away. Even in here. You know? It means that he's somebody. Even in here. It's not fair to ask him to choose between his respect and me. That's all.

(The ding of the elevator. THERESA pops back in or just her voice is heard off.)

THERESA: Hey elevator. That is, if the princess can stand rubbing elbows with the teeming refuse.

(EVANGELINE starts moving toward the door; CAROLINE follows.)

EVANGELINE: I can't explain it very well.

CAROLINE: You explained it beautifully. If I had a pen, I would have written it down.

EVANGELINE: The thing is, he's got to have that thing. I know it. It's easy to get lonely and forget that it's not all about me. This place is designed to make you forget it, but we've all got to have that thing. You remember that.

CAROLINE: Her husband, he's—

EVANGELINE: Another thing, do your own time. You know? Really. You can't be worrying about someone else's time. Hang onto your Trans Am and do your own time. Remember that. You'll thank me.

(They exit.)

FOUR

CAROLINE sitting in Booth H. She waits. She glances around quickly, then reaches down into her pants, removes a wet wipe, and starts cleaning the phone. She looks up and smiles. She puts the phone to her ear and holds up the wet wipe.

CAROLINE: A friend gave it to me. So. Hi. It's much quieter this time of day. Though I still was in line for like an hour. I swear the porkos downstairs just pretend to be busy, just to keep you waiting. Some kind of power trip. The way it's all set up, it would make an interesting psychological study. Them in their own little plexiglass prisons, only elevated above you, of course. So they can look down their noses at you. I wouldn't think I'd be susceptible but I am. I threw up a couple of fifty-cent words when talking to the guard, trying to prove, I don't even know what. Why are you letting me ramble on like this? None of this is what I want to say to you. I'm sorry about last time. I lost it. I'm not as strong as, as I'd like to be. Or as I've witnessed people being. It was too much, the incongruity of this...this...

situation, you in this hole and reciting poetry to me. I. Angry. I wanted to be. I don't know. It could be worse. It could be worse for you. Listen, I remember when my mother died. And Susan called you. You drove twelve hundred miles and showed up on my doorstep at eleven o'clock at night. I was awake, sitting in that black leather rocker. I'd been awake and rocking for like two days. You came in with a bouquet of daisies that you'd obviously picked from the side of the road somewhere and by the look of them at least twelve hours previous, and you said, "Did somebody order flowers?" and I said, "If I see one more flower I'm going to puke," and you threw them over your shoulder and said, "Good, because there's not a single flower shop between here and Chicago." And you said, you said, "This will have to do," and you pulled out that Rumi book and you rubbed my feet, you rubbed my feet and read me Rumi for somewhere around twelve hours until I fell asleep. That was my first Rumi experience. I'm not torturing myself. It's the opposite. It's my Friday night Trans Am ride. Nothing. A poem. You wouldn't know her. She's not famous. Angel. No last name, just Angel. I don't have it memorized. It's just something I'm holding onto. To keep me human. You? What are you holding onto? *(She listens. She smiles. She puts her hand up on the glass and holds it there.)*

(End.)

FOR THE BENEFIT OF ALFRED BEAMER

Scott Baker

Setting: We see a small lectern placed on top of a table. The table is covered by a cloth that reaches all the way to the floor.

At rise: ALFRED BEAMER, a man who appears to be in his late fifties or early sixties, stands above the table, shuffling some papers. He takes a deep breath and begins to speak.

BEAMER: Excuse me! Excuse me! If I may take just a moment to interrupt you from your dinners, please allow me to thank you for coming here tonight to honor your friend, your mentor, your role model…me! The one, the only Alfred Beamer, and to celebrate all that I mean to you! I was thrilled by the way some of you responded immediately to the little engraved invitation I sent you. And I might add that the beautiful floral displays that some of you sent are simply breath-taking, although I would have thought that the six-hundred-dollar-a-plate dinner to honor me would have been quite enough. Let me remind you that the proceeds of this dinner, after I've given an altogether much-too-generous tip to the catering staff just to hear them stand around and say nice things about me… Let me remind you that all remaining money will go to create a life-size statue in my honor. I had toyed with the idea of selling commemorative dinner plates with my face on them, but plates do get broken, don't they? And the plans to make my birthday a national holiday are still pending. Write your congressman! Let him know you want Alfred Beamer Day! I won't take up anymore of your time, since I know that each of you is anxious to come up here and say wonderful things about me. The fact that tears will be welling up in my eyes as I listen to each of you tell how much I mean to you must not in any way prevent you from going as far as possible in your adulation of me. Let me know how I've enriched your life! How I've given meaning to your petty existence! Let Alfred Beamer know how great he is!! At a time like this, I am reminded of the words of Walt Whitman, who once wrote, "I celebrate myself, and sing myself!" While I might disagree with the grammar, the sentiment certainly seems appropriate. And let's face it, "I myself celebrate and sing me, myself" would have been the way I might have corrected his paper had he been in my freshman composition class; we must allow him some artistic license. He is, after all, Walt Whitman, and I guess it's alright to throw the old queen a bone. And don't worry! None of my detestable former wives have been invited here tonight. This occasion is to honor me, not to scream about late alimony checks. That's what I get for playing into the hands of lust-driven Lolitas who will do anything to get a better grade from Teacher. Call him "Daddy!" Even marry him! But, I digress. I know so many of you have so much to say, so, without any further adieu… Um… Without any further…Uh…

(BEAMER takes a large spiral notebook and pen from the lectern, produces a cellular phone from his pocket, looks at the top page of the spiral notebook to procure a phone number, and dials the phone. After a few moments of waiting, BEAMER speaks into the phone.)

BEAMER: Professor Bosley? Hello, Steven! It's Alfred Beamer! Alfred Beamer. We worked together at the university! Oh, a couple of years ago! Beamer! B-E-A-M-E-R! You don't? I taught Introduction to Theatre Appreciation. You're sure you don't remember? Our offices were right next to each other! I gave you a fruitcake one Christmas. You don't? Then I don't suppose you got the invitation to the… Oh! You did! No! It wasn't a mistake, not a mistake at all. I genuinely wanted you there. After all, we did work together and I had hoped… Oh! Oh! I see. So, I guess you won't be attending. Please! No! Don't apologize! Don't. There's no need. Seriously. You can't be expected to remember everybody, now can you? Well, I wish *you* the best, too! Please! No need to explain. "Life goes on," as Robert Frost once said. Thanks. Sure. *You* have a great day, too.

(BEAMER switches off the phone and puts it on the table. He makes a checkmark in the notebook with his pen at the bottom of the page. He picks up the page, studies the contents, and very slowly turns the page. We see, as he interrupts the turning of the page to study the contents of the next page, that the first page has a long list of names, followed by a YES and NO category. The YES column is blank, the NO column filled with checkmarks. He flips the page and studies the top of the next page. He dials a number. He waits. He speaks.)

BEAMER: Hello, Mother? It's Alfred. Alfred! Can you hear me? Good! Just calling to see how you are! Yeah? Well, that arthritis is a family thing! Our "curse" as I like to put it. I just wondered if you got the little invitation I sent you? Well, look for it. In the mail. I addressed it to you, care of the home. One of the nurses could escort you. *An invitation! Invitation…* To a special dinner that all of my friends are throwing in my honor… *my friends, Mother! Friends! My friends!*

(Suddenly, sparks fly from the phone, and BEAMER yells out in agony. He falls upstage of the table. We can't see him, since the table's covered. Lights flash! Thunder rolls! We hear heavenly choirs, followed by a grand chorus of bagpipes. We hear the singing of a SCOTSMAN amid the chaos.)

THE VOICE: "By yon bonny banks
            And by yon bonny braes
            The sun shines bright
            On Loch Lomin'…"

(THE VOICE speaks as smoke pours onstage.)

THE VOICE: Hello? Are y'here, meht? Meht?

(Enter ANGUS LAIRD, wearing kilts and Scottish regalia. BEAMER slowly rises from behind the table.)

LAIRD: Ah, there y'are, meht. C'mon, now! It's yer time to go! Time fer passing!

BEAMER: Passing?

LAIRD: Aye, passing!

BEAMER: What? A kidney stone?

LAIRD: Passing…

BEAMER: Gas?

LAIRD: Oh, the certificate will read "Official cause: Death by electrocution," due to the faulty wiring in that newfangular cellular phone you got. But nothing's wasted. Thanks to you and six others who haven't yet discovered the problem, those phones'll be recalled. And you thought cell phones only caused brain cancer! Well, only the ones that go off during theatrical performances!

BEAMER: Are you...Are you trying to tell me... That I'm...I'm...

LAIRD: Look behind the table, meht!

(BEAMER does so and gasps in disbelief.)

BEAMER: Oh, no! No! It looks like me, but much smaller. Wait! I can't be dead! I've never felt more alive!

LAIRD: So alive in fact, that your arthritis has magically disappeared!

(BEAMER discovers that his hands and legs move easily.)

BEAMER: Yes! It's a miracle!

LAIRD: That's on account of the fact that the arthritis was reserved for that shell behind the table. You're spirit now, man!

BEAMER: Who...or what are you? The Grim Reaper?

LAIRD: Do I look or sound "grim"? Do you see me carrying any farm implements?

BEAMER: Then who are you?

LAIRD: I don't suppose you ever heard of Angus Laird, King of the Scottish Music Hall? "Songs, dances, and snappy stories, with the kind assistance of a full-size talking figure made of wood with eyes and lips that move?"

BEAMER: No.

LAIRD: It was me that did the talkin' though.

BEAMER: Well, if you enjoy that sort of thing!

LAIRD: "Enjoy that sort of thing? *Enjoy that sort of thing!*" I'll have you know I gave a command performance for Queen Victoria!

(LAIRD uses BEAMER as a ventriloquist's dummy.)

BEAMER: *(As dummy, in a high, nasal voice.)* Hey, mate! What did the sea monster say to the portrait artist?

LAIRD: Dunno! What *did* the sea monster say to the portrait artist?

BEAMER: "My! Wot a remarkable 'Loch Ness!'"

(LAIRD lets BEAMER drop.)

LAIRD: Good, eh meht?

BEAMER: *(Not meaning a word of it.)* I'm very impressed.

LAIRD: Well, you should be. And I don't suppose you remember the Edinburgh Music Hall Fire of... Of course not, how could you? You never heard how Angus Laird, King of the Scottish Music Hall, raced back into the burning theatre to rescue the full-size talking figure with eyes and lips that move, only to be consumed by smoke and flame? There's a plaque in my honor, I'll have you know, on Adams Street in Edinburgh. Just look next time you're there! But I guess that won't be happening anytime soon now, will it? So you might as well enjoy having theatrical royalty serve as your guide to the next life.

BEAMER: Great! Some get angels, I get a vaudeville act!

LAIRD: The headline act of the Scottish Music Hall, who gave a command performance for Queen Victoria! Who has a plaque in his honor on Adams Street in Edinburgh! But, on account of my "fetching" personality, I spend eternity fetching the likes of you! Do you deserve theatrical royalty, Beamer? After the life you've led?

BEAMER: What if I tell you I'm not going?! In fact, I refuse to go!

LAIRD: "Refuse to go?! *Refuse to go*!!!!!!" Alright. Alright! I might understand you wanting to hang back under other circumstances! I can understand wanting to haunt a castle or a theatre, but this hovel?

BEAMER: This is a penthouse.

LAIRD: On the first floor! You must be joking!

BEAMER: But I'm not ready yet! I don't want to go!

LAIRD: You didn't want to be born, either, now did you? What a struggle you put up to stay with that which you knew, that which was comfortin' to ya! Seventy-eight hours you made your mother struggle!

BEAMER: A fact she never let me forget! But what about that list? The people I invited to that little party I was throwing? If somebody finds that list, I would just die. I mean, I would be so humiliated.

LAIRD: Some people go holding dirty pictures, you go holding a list of names. Don't worry, Beamer. Nobody paid attention to those invitations you sent. But now that you're gone, people will be crawling all over each other to say things in your honor! Things they never said when you were living!

BEAMER: Really? Why did they wait until I was dead?

LAIRD: And your former wife, Cathie, she'll even throw a cocktail party in memory of you!

BEAMER: A cocktail party? But Cathie's in Alcoholics Anonymous. She's been sober for six years!

LAIRD: When she hears of your passing, she'll have a relapse!

BEAMER: Good! And did I, you know, make it?

LAIRD: Make it?

BEAMER: You know!

(BEAMER points skyward.)

LAIRD: Oh, that! Sorry to say, meht, you're damned to hell for all eternity. You'll be burnin' right next to Hitler!

BEAMER: *What?!*

LAIRD: *(Breaks out in howls of laughter.)* I gotcha! You're such an easy crowd, Beamer! You? Of course you made it! Alright, meht! Time to cross over.

BEAMER: Wait! There are two things I have to ask you… things I've always wanted to know!

LAIRD: "Ask, and it shall be given ya! For now, we see through a glass, darkly, but then, face to face."

BEAMER: I have to know. What about reincarnation?

LAIRD: Do you want to take algebra again?

BEAMER: No way!

LAIRD: Then you'll be glad to know you'll never have to make this journey again! It's so much better where we're going!

BEAMER: My other question isn't spiritual.

LAIRD: Go on, meht, ask it!

BEAMER: It's embarrassing!

LAIRD: You'll never know until you ask. Ye can nay lick your lack till ya lick your own lackey!

BEAMER: What does that mean?

LAIRD: Don't know, I'm from the North. Out with it, man!

BEAMER: Well, I've always wanted to know...

LAIRD: All spiritual matters are just waitin' to be revealed to ya!

BEAMER: What's the truth...the real truth...about... What's underneath a Scotsman's kilts?

LAIRD: *(Takes a long pause, stares at BEAMER, looks in both directions and then slowly speaks.)* Let me put it this way! A woman visits Scotland and asks that very question of a Scotsman. The lass demands to know, "What's underneath a Scotsman's kilts?" The Scotsman says to the lass, "Put your hand inside my kilt and find out for yourself." The lass puts her hand inside the kilt and removes it. The Scotsman asks her, "What do ya think?" And the lass replies, "Gruesome!" Scotsman says to her, "Do that again and it'll 'grow some' more!"

BEAMER: A dirty joke? Seems like a cheap way to end a life!

LAIRD: And an even cheaper way to end a play!

BEAMER: What?

LAIRD: Never mind! Some'll get it, some won't! All the world's a stage and all that! One big vaudeville act, including jugglers.

BEAMER: Even mimes?

LAIRD: No. Come on now, Beamer! All sorts of loving souls are waitin' to see ya. Folks you haven't seen for years, all waitin' to celebrate your arrival!

BEAMER: You make it sound like it's going to be wonderful!

LAIRD: As we used to say in the Music Hall, "Friend, you ain't seen nothing yet."

(LAIRD offers his arm to BEAMER. BEAMER reluctantly touches LAIRD's arm as heavenly music plays. The MEN lock arms as bagpipe music plays. They dance off toward bright lights while singing "By yon bonny banks, and by yon bonny braes...")

DUTY HONOR COUNTRY

Stephen Bittrich

Setting: A trench in Iraq, somewhere on Route 1 between Kuwait and Nasiriyah in the early days of Operation Iraqi Freedom.

At rise: LaBONNE, an African American soldier—patriotic, even-headed, duty-bound—is standing in the trench to look at ground level with night vision binoculars. BOBECK, a white soldier—Southern, cynical, loud, and self-preserving—keeps his gun trained on an IRAQI PRISONER OF WAR. There is no love lost between the two Americans, but they are bound together in a test of survival. The Iraqi PRISONER is gaunt and exhausted and holds a tattered white kerchief in his hand.

BOBECK: Have you got 'em?

LaBONNE: *(Talking without looking at BOBECK.)* I can't see shit.

BOBECK: Motherfucker!

(Beat.)

BOBECK: They're probably kickin' ass in Nasiriyah by now.

LaBONNE: No. They'll find us. They'll find us…

BOBECK: Yeah, right. Would you like some hand cream while you jerk yourself off?

LaBONNE: You got any?

BOBECK: I ain't got shit. *(Looks in his pack.)* Damn. I really ain't got shit.

LaBONNE: *(Sits.)* I think it's a new moon or somethin'… cannot see a damn thing.

BOBECK: Yeah, it's black as a nigger's ass.

(LaBONNE gives him a shut-the-fuck-up look.)

BOBECK: Sorry. *(Beat.)* Black as a sand nigger's ass.

LaBONNE: You know, Bobeck, if I didn't know you had shit for brains—

BOBECK: Hey, let me ask you somethin'. How come all you blacks get to call each other…the "N" word…but the minute a guy as pale as me does it, he's a racist asshole?

LaBONNE: 'Cuz you ain't part of the club, son. It's like when you call your sister a "ho." You can do that because she's part of your redneck, inbred family, but if somebody else tries to call her a "ho"—

BOBECK: —I fuckin' slap 'em upside the head.

LaBONNE: Damn straight.

BOBECK: Thanks for clearing that up for me, bro'. *(Back to looking through his pack.)* Look at this, a couple of MREs, five rounds of ammo, a smashed fucking radio…

LaBONNE: How many MREs?

BOBECK: Six.

LaBONNE: What kind? Don't say scalloped potatoes.

BOBECK: At least two of them are scalloped potatoes.

LaBONNE: Make me wanna puke. We'll make Saddam's man eat 'em.

BOBECK: Fuck no! He ain't gettin' shit.

LaBONNE: Don't be a dick. We all need to eat.

BOBECK: Well, then he shouldn'ta signed up to be all he could be.

LaBONNE: Look at him, Bobeck. Man just wants to go home. He's no soldier.

BOBECK: Tough shit. I don't care how many pictures of his wife and kids he pulls out; this is Survival Iraq, and he's getting voted off the island. *(Smiles at PRISONER and wags his gun.)* Right? You hear me, don't cha, you fuckin' camel jacker. Saddam is a faggot. Right?

LaBONNE: Bobeck!

BOBECK: Yeah?

LaBONNE: Cut it the fuck out! Don't taunt the man.

BOBECK: This ain't no man. Look at him. Look in those two brown spots passing for eyes. Does he look like he has a soul?

(BOBECK wags the gun again. PRISONER holds up his white kerchief.)

LaBONNE: Bobeck!

(LaBONNE pulls BOBECK up sharply by his flak jacket.)

BOBECK: You ain't in charge of me, LaBonne.

LaBONNE: Come on! Let's stick together, brother, or we fuckin' dead meat out here. Enough fuckin' around. Let's follow procedure.

(BOBECK shakes loose, pauses, turns the gun on PRISONER again, though more calmly.)

BOBECK: That's right, that's right. I'm watching you. Ready for your seventy-two virgins yet? I didn't think so. *(Sits.)* Look at this grinnin' Jihad monkey-mother-fucker. Wavin' his little white flag. Thinks he's going home. This carpet pilot thinks he's going home before me. Gonna be bowin' down before Allah in his church—

LaBONNE: —mosque—

BOBECK: —smokin' his Arabian tobacky, stickin' it to his veil-wearin' ugly-ass old lady before me… and he will be…and he would be…

(PRISONER waves the flag.)

BOBECK: That's right, wave your little snot rag. Don't mean shit to me.

LaBONNE: *(Quietly.)* Keep it together, Bobeck.

(Long pause.)

BOBECK: So what's the plan, genius?

LaBONNE: There's no plan. Just stay here until first light. Maybe they'll find us by then.

BOBECK: Or maybe a horde of Republican Guard will be raining down on our ass by then.

LaBONNE: Well, there's a crispy fried Humvee three klicks from here that might give our guys a clue come morning. *(Beat.)* I'm open for suggestions. But I'm tellin' you nobody can see anything on a night like this.

BOBECK: *(After a beat.)* Wait for mornin'.

(A camel moans in the night, sending the American SOLDIERS into high alert rolling on the ground. PRISONER remains calm and smiles slightly.)

PRISONER: *(After a beat, looking for the English word.)* Camel…camel.

BOBECK: I didn't sign up for this shit, that's for sure.

LaBONNE: Yeah, I guess none of us did, but we're honor bound to answer.

BOBECK: Yeah right.

(Long pause.)

BOBECK: When did you sign up for the Guard, LaBonne?

LaBONNE: 'Bout week before Tropical Storm Allison.

BOBECK: No shit? I was deployed for that storm.

LaBONNE: Yeah?

BOBECK: Yeah.

LaBONNE: In Texas?

BOBECK: Houston. You're from Louisiana, right?

LaBONNE: Yeah, I was in Baton Rouge. They had it bad down there.

BOBECK: No shit. We did some real good for those people, hauling sandbags, helping evac flooded neighborhoods. There was this crazy old lady with this little rat pooch, Shiatsu or somethin', and she got caught in her pickup truck in high water. She was all panicky and wanted us to save her dog. Save her dog!

LaBONNE: Did you save the dog?

BOBECK: Damn straight! We knew what the hell we were doing, ya know, on home turf. Floods we could handle. We didn't train so much for desert warfare.

LaBONNE: No. *(Beat.)* Well, you're helping that old lady again, Bobeck, just in a different shit storm.

BOBECK: Oh yeah, she and her pooch are in real immediate danger of gettin' ravaged by Saddam. You're a regular Dudley Do-Right motherfucker, aren'cha?

LaBONNE: You think I'm messin' with you, man? What if one of these Saddam loyalists sets off a WMD in Houston? Or San Antonio? You've got about five air force bases in that area.

BOBECK: You gotta be kiddin' me, LaBonne.

LaBONNE: No.

BOBECK: Damn, I thought you were smart. There ain't no WMDs out there.

LaBONNE: Man, where have you been? President Bush—

BOBECK: Look at this tattered motherfucker sittin' here. This is the big Iraqi threat to the American way of life. Uniform in rags, hasn't eaten a good meal in like a month 'cept rats, probably inherited his boots off a dead soldier. Operation Iraqi Freedom is unfinished family business, that's all it is. And George Bush can kiss my lilywhite redneck ass.

LaBONNE: *(In his face.)* Soldier! Our commander in chief has called us to sacred duty. To quell the terrorist threat and keep America safe. To liberate the people of Iraq. Where's your—?

BOBECK: *Where's—my—what?*

(Beat; they stare each other down.)

BOBECK: Oh, I can't wait to go hold hands with liberated little Iraqi children. Dancing in the street. Don't you get it, LaBonne? This is all for nothin'. They don't want us here. They fuckin' hate us. Because one, we support the religious zealots that aren't them, the Israelis, and two, they realize this double-talk of freedom is all about Operation Iraqi Oil Freedom. And our being here will only inflame terrorism. It'll be like a goddamn hydra monster. Two heads growing for every one we cut off. And even after we kick Saddam's ass—which we will—some fuckin' Shi'ite motherfucker will step up to take his place. Damn, man! Wake up! *(Beat.)* The one salvation I got is that if I don't die tonight, in a hundred and fifty days my tour of duty will be over, and I'll be sippin' a Lone Star at Gilly's.

LaBONNE: Fuck you.

BOBECK: Hey LaBonne, you know your man Bush—

LaBONNE: He's not my man. But he's my commander.

BOBECK: Okay, okay, your man is Colin Powell. He gave a real perty speech at the UN, by the way. He's really lookin' after the brothers. But you know your Commander Bush in his first eight months in office was on the longest vacation in the last thirty-two years of the presidency. No shit. When Al Qaeda was putting the finishing touches on 9/11, GW was playing fetch with Spot, God rest his little soul. There were fuckin' memos circulating in the FBI and CIA about Arabs that were taking flying lessons with no interest in learning how to take off or land. Memos about terrorists planning to fly planes into buildings—

LaBONNE: Bush couldn't have stopped 9/11!

BOBECK: Right. Because he was on *vacation*!

LaBONNE: So why the hell you sign up, Bobeck?

BOBECK: Damned if I know. Seemed like a good idea at the time. Actually, as I recall, it was to avoid jail.

LaBONNE: You're a real patriot.

BOBECK: Yeah, that's me.

LaBONNE: I refuse to believe that this is for nothing. We're gonna free these poor people and bring a democratic way of life to them.

BOBECK: Oh yeah, we're here to free the people all right. Hey, how come we never give a shit about freein' people in places like Haiti?

LaBONNE: Can't help everybody, Bobeck. But if Haiti needs our help, I'm sure we will—

(Mortar fire explodes in the distance.)

BOBECK: Holy fuck! What the hell was that?

LaBONNE: I don't know. *(Rises to look with his binoculars.)* I still can't see a damn thing. I can see some flames—about twenty klicks off.

BOBECK: Do you think they're coming for us?

LaBONNE: No.

BOBECK: Sounded close.

LaBONNE: No. They don't know we're here.

BOBECK: Unless Dusty Nuts is leading them to us.

LaBONNE: I don't see how that's possible.

BOBECK: Come here, you!

(BOBECK searches PRISONER.)

LaBONNE: Leave him alone. What are you doing? He's clean.

BOBECK: He's got a bug or something. I know it. What are you hiding, Muhammad?

(LaBONNE stops looking over the top of the trench and squats down to grab BOBECK.)

LaBONNE: They're not coming for us! That fight is twenty klicks from here.

BOBECK: LaBonne, this prisoner is a liability.

LaBONNE: Be that as it may—

BOBECK: We need to travel light.

LaBONNE: Don't fuck around, man.

BOBECK: You know I'm not fucking around. We killed about a hundred of these Hucka-Luckas in the past twenty-four hours. What makes this one so special? His little white hanky? He's dead fuckin' weight.

LaBONNE: Soldier, it is your duty— "You are forbidden to kill or wound an enemy who, having laid down his arms, or having no longer means of defense, has surrendered."

BOBECK: You're a joke, LaBonne. We're also forbidden from attacking undefended targets. How many undefended targets do you think we've bombed the shit out of in the course of finding some defended targets? Let's off this dead weight and hump it back to Kuwait.

LaBONNE: That's not happening.

(BOBECK takes his gun off PRISONER and waves it casually in LaBONNE's direction.)

BOBECK: Who's gonna stop me?

LaBONNE: Holster your weapon.

BOBECK: I'm on prisoner watch.

LaBONNE: Don't wave that fuckin' thing at me, you Muppetfucker.

BOBECK: I thought you had more class than that, LaBonne.

(LaBONNE takes out his pistol.)

LaBONNE: I'm prepared to go all the way—all—the—way—for what I believe. How far are you prepared to go?

(Long pause as they stare each other down.)

BOBECK: I want to live! I just want to live!

(Softly, softly, the Iraqi PRISONER starts to sing. A plaintive song, native to his culture, cuts through the haze of violence. He does not look at the two American SOLDIERS or even seem to acknowledge the volatile situation unfolding; he just chants with quiet conviction his humble song. BOBECK holsters his gun first and slumps down, defeated, to the ground. LaBONNE lowers his gun to his side and watches PRISONER for a moment, then holsters his gun as well and sits beside BOBECK. PRISONER's song fills the still dark night. Lights fade slowly to black.)

(END OF PLAY.)

'TIL DEATH DO US PART

Joanne Charansky

Setting: Chapel, daytime.

SHERRY, a perky, petite woman (twenties) in a frilly white wedding dress, walks down the aisle toward BILL, her tall, greasy-haired intended. The "Wedding March" plays. SHERRY smiles at the guests, mouthing "I love you" and "Thanks for coming" to some. As she reaches the altar, MINISTER speaks.

MINISTER: Welcome to the joining of two souls, two lives into one joyous union.

(SHERRY beams. BILL looks frozen.)

MINISTER: As you know, marriage is a sacred contract, which should not be entered into lightly.

(SHERRY smiles adoringly. BILL doesn't crack.)

MINISTER: Sherry, am I correct that you and Bill have written your own vows?

SHERRY: Yes.

(There is a long pause. SHERRY looks at BILL, too happy for words. MINISTER smiles, fatigued.)

MINISTER: Would either of you like to read those vows?

SHERRY: Oops! Sorry. Nervous. Bill, would you like to start?

(BILL shakes his head nervously "no.")

SHERRY: Are you sure?

MINISTER: I do have another wedding in... *(Checks his watch.)* ...three hours.

SHERRY: Oops. Okay. I'll start. *(Turns slightly to face BILL.)* Bill...we've lived together for the past three years.

(A gasp is heard in the audience. SHERRY turns.)

SHERRY: *(To a WOMAN in the audience.)* I'm sorry Mom, but we had to. *(Whispers.)* Bill lost his job. Twice. *(Turns back to BILL.)* And in those three years, you've always been there for me. In good times, and in bad. You celebrated with me when I passed my secretarial exam— Friday's margaritas, good choice. And you held my hand when Whiskers died. *(SHERRY is tearing up.)* Thank you for taking him to the animal hospital and paying for the remembrance ceremony.

(BILL furrows his brow, trying to remember if he did this, or if the cat's still in the car. SHERRY turns to her MOTHER.)

SHERRY: *(To her MOM.)* He'll be so great with children. *(To BILL.)* And I know we've had our struggles. You've been out of work for two, almost three years. And you've tried. I swear there isn't a job in town that hasn't turned you down.

(SHERRY takes BILL's hand. He looks shaken, slightly wounded.)

SHERRY: I don't care that you didn't go to college, or even finish high school. None of that matters. Just you and me. Together. I love you, Bill, and I want to be your wife.

(SHERRY's face widens in a fit of joy. BILL looks like he just got fined by the DMV.)

MINISTER: Well, that was…honest. Bill?

(BILL stares at SHERRY.)

MINISTER: Bill, your vows?

BILL: Oh…right. *(Shuffles in his pocket for a wrinkled piece of paper. He opens the paper and scans it, trying to remember what he wrote. Finally, it looks familiar.)* Oh yeah, I remember. *(Turns to GUESTS to make an announcement. To GUESTS.)* I'm sorry if my words aren't as…sweet as Sherry's. I wrote these last night after a few of those margaritas. Two-for-one Tuesdays. Good deal. *(Turns back to SHERRY, alternately speaking and reading from his paper. Clears his throat.)* Sherry…all my life I've dreamed of being with a super-model. Someone tall and thin with unnaturally big boobs.

(SHERRY, who's short and a bit squat, looks confused. BILL makes gestures, outlining his ideal woman.)

BILL: I wanted legs, and arms, and tits for days.

(MINISTER looks offended.)

BILL: Breasts. I mean, breasts. *(Beat.)* And I had that. Boy, I had a lot of that.

MINISTER: Bill…

BILL: But back to us. You—Sherry, are better than all the tits and ass in the world.

(MINISTER coughs, clearing his throat.)

BILL: I'm sorry—I just. This is about Sherry and me. Us. *(To SHERRY.)* And I love us.

(SHERRY brightens.)

BILL: I love how you do my laundry even when you say it's for the very last time. And I love how you tease me when I check out other women and try to get their phone numbers while we're out. And I love how soft and sexy you are, even though you don't look good in a pair of jeans. *(Slowly.)* I don't mind. *(Beat.)* I love you, Sherry, and I'm ready to shack up. Or get married. Whatever.

MINISTER: *(Can hardly speak.)* Well, that was quite…heartfelt. So…refreshing to see a man and woman express such deep and true feelings about each other. It's obvious you spoke from the heart. So, Sherry, do you take this man…

SHERRY: Wait.

MINISTER: Wait?

SHERRY: Can we go back? Back to the vows?

MINISTER: We don't usually go back.

SHERRY: I forgot something. I have something to say.

MINISTER: If you feel you must.

SHERRY: I do. *(To BILL.)* Bill, I just bought a pair of jeans last Saturday. Do you know what size they were?

(BILL shakes his head "no.")

SHERRY: They were a size seven. A seven. Do you know what that means?

BILL: *(To MINISTER.)* Should I answer?

MINISTER: I think you should.

BILL: *(To SHERRY.)* What does that mean?

SHERRY: That means that Jenny Craig works. That all my hard work, my salads, my elliptical trainers, that was for you. For you and a pair of size seven jeans. And for you to say, at our wedding, that I don't look good in jeans…

BILL: I said you were sexy. *(To MINISTER.)* Didn't I say she was sexy?

MINISTER: You also mentioned tits and ass.

BILL: Right.

SHERRY: After all this. After I told my mother that I didn't mind that you were unemployed and unemployable with your bad wardrobe and greasy hair and stupid vocab. That's right. Egregious is not a word.

MINISTER: *(Interrupting.)* I'm sorry.

SHERRY: *(To MINISTER.)* Excuse me, these are our vows. This is between him and me.

MINISTER: Yes, I know. But as a minister of the cloth, and an avid reader, I must say that egregious is indeed a word.

BILL: See?

MINISTER: *(To BILL.)* I wouldn't get too cocky right now, alright?

(MINISTER shakes his head in disbelief. BILL and SHERRY are staring at each other.)

MINISTER: *(Clears his throat.)* Well, usually, after the vows, you, um, commit to each other. Are we still, um, on that page?

(MINISTER looks at SHERRY and then at BILL. He's not sure, and neither are they.)

SHERRY: *(To BILL.)* I can't marry someone who insults me at our own wedding.

BILL: *(To SHERRY.)* Well I can't marry someone who insults me. Says I don't have a job. *(To MINISTER.)* Unemployment is a job.

MINISTER: Okay, why don't we all cool off? Take a break. Bill, Sherry, need a breather?

BILL: Can we do that?

SHERRY: This is our wedding.

MINISTER: I know. And I want us all to remember it in the best light possible. So why don't we just sit down and relax?

(BILL and SHERRY look at each other, stunned, each afraid to sit down.)

MINISTER: Really. *(Takes a quick look at his watch.)* We have time.

(MINISTER takes a seat on the pulpit. SHERRY and BILL look at each other, then at their GUESTS, shrug, and sit down.)

MINISTER: Good. Now, follow me. Each of you take a deep breath in… *(He breathes in.)* And exhale.

SHERRY: Really, I don't kno—

MINISTER: Deep breath in…and exhale.

(Afraid to disobey, SHERRY and BILL inhale and exhale a few times together with MINISTER.)

MINISTER: Good. Now, why don't each of you tell me what first attracted you to the other person.

SHERRY: While we're sitting down?

MINISTER: While we're sitting down. Bill, you spoke before about your affection for women.

BILL: Tits and ass.

MINISTER: Yes. What about Sherry's tits and ass?

SHERRY: Hey.

MINISTER: I mean, what about her? What attracted you to Sherry?

BILL: *(Thinks about it, takes a minute.)* Her sister was taken. *(Laughs, pleased with himself.)*

MINISTER: Alright. Let's try this. What do you like about Sherry, Bill?

BILL: Like about her?

MINISTER: Like about her.

BILL: *(Thinks about it. Takes his time. As memories come, his face brightens.)* Sherry was the first girl who liked my car.

MINISTER: Okay. That's one.

BILL: Every other chick hated it. It has vinyl seats and no radio. I really had to charm 'em to score in that car. But Sherry...

MINISTER: Let's keep it PG, shall we?

BILL: Sherry said it wasn't my car she was dating. It was me.

(SHERRY looks touched.)

BILL: *(Looking at SHERRY.)* Sherry stood by me, after my first boss said he had never seen a guy who couldn't type or add or drive a stick shift. And after my next boss said he couldn't believe he forgot to call my first boss and ask for a reference.

MINISTER: She's understanding, then?

BILL: Yeah, that's it. Understanding. Any other guy would'a killed himself after that. Or run his dog over or something. But I couldn't. Not when I had Sherry to live for.

SHERRY: Oh Billy.

BILL: Sherry.

(The TWO embrace and start making out on the floor. MINISTER has to pull them apart.)

MINISTER: Okay. Break it up. Break it up. Geez, animals. *(Fiddles with his sleeves, straightening them out again.)* Now, Sherry. What is it that you love about Bill?

SHERRY: Billy.

MINISTER: Right. Let's say some good words about Billy.

SHERRY: *(Takes a minute to compose herself, her heart is bursting. To BILL.)* Billy was the first guy to take me to the drive-thru and not criticize when I ordered the double shake and fries.

BILL: That's my girl.

SHERRY: And Billy stood by me when I got in trouble for forgetting to file my taxes.

(SHERRY'S MOM gasps in the crowd.)

SHERRY: *(To her MOTHER.)* They were right on the bureau. *(To BILL.)* And he knew I meant to file them. He knew I just left them there, on the bureau...for six months.

MINISTER: So, you could say that Bill is understanding too.

SHERRY: *(Just realizing.)* You could say so.

MINISTER: And you could say, that the two of you, are meant for each other.

(SHERRY is smiling, about to burst, at BILL. BILL is smiling, about to burst, back.)

SHERRY: Bill.

BILL: Sherry.

SHERRY: Bill.

(The TWO are making out again. MINISTER can't take it.)

MINISTER: Enough enough. Let's get through the ceremony, shall we?

SHERRY: Are we still going?

BILL: I thought we were on a break.

MINISTER: No, sillies. There is no break in marriage. That's the point. Now stand up.

(MINISTER stands up. Then BILL gets up, holds out his hand, and helps SHERRY to her feet.)

MINISTER: That's better. *(To BILL.)* Billy L. Squire, do you take this woman as your lawfully wedded wife, to have and to hold, from this day forward, 'til death do you part?

BILL: Um, yes. Isn't there more to…?

MINISTER: And Sherry, do you take this man as your lawfully wedded husband, from this day forward, to have and to hold, in good times and the rough, 'til death do you part?

SHERRY: Sure, I, I…do.

MINISTER: *(At the audience.)* Rings, rings, rings.

(BILL fishes through his pockets and produces two rings. MINISTER takes them from his hand and offers one to BILL and one to SHERRY.)

MINISTER: Let these rings be a symbol, that the two of you belong with no one else.

(BILL and SHERRY look at their rings, realize that BILL has SHERRY's and SHERRY has BILL's, and switch.)

MINISTER: No one's gonna put up with your laziness and your unemployment and your overeating. You two are stuck with each other. For now and forever.

(SHERRY and BILL face each other, put the rings on each other's hand and smile.)

MINISTER: I now pronounce you husband and wife. *(Beat.)* Go ahead. Make out.

(Surprisingly, SHERRY and BILL take a moment and lovingly give each other a wedding-appropriate kiss. They turn to face a round of applause.)

BILL: *(Pleased.)* We did it! *(Beams.)*

SHERRY: *(Itchy.)* We're married.

(SHERRY is freaking out. Still beaming, BILL grabs her arm, and walks a stone-faced SHERRY back down the aisle, thanking GUESTS along the way. Without BILL dragging her, we don't think SHERRY would make it. His job finally over, MINISTER looks out into the crowd to pronounce…)

MINISTER: Hallelujah!

(THE END.)

CUTRS!
(JOIN US)

Allison Moore

PRODUCTION NOTE

The stage directions contain suggestions of some actions that may
occur at various times throughout Andrea's speech. The specific actions written will not work in every performance space. Directors are
encouraged to find their own solutions, but any action should be
stylized, as it is intended as a counterpoint to Andrea's ideas, not a
direct cause-effect. The play also can be produced as a monologue
only.

CAST OF CHARACTERS

ANDREA, thirties, well-dressed.

THE TIME

Now.

THE PLACE

The theatre, which is hosting a recruiting session for CUTRS!.

A tight light comes up on ANDREA, down-stage. She is in her thirties, casual-hip but not over the top. She is well-educated, mani-cured. She speaks with seriousness, directly to the audience. She sips from a bottle of Vita Water occasionally. Upstage, there is a piece of fabric about six feet wide that is stretched all the way across the stage. There is a gap between the bottom of the scrim and the floor, and an-other gap above the top of the scrim. The feet and calves of anyone passing behind the scrim are visible. Objects tossed into the air behind the scrim are visible above the top edge.

ANDREA: What are you doing?

That's my question. What are *you* doing for your country?

This is a difficult time, there is no doubt. And we all want to help. Don't we? Don't you want to do something to help?

I can see the answer in your eyes. Do you know what your eyes are saying? They're saying, "Yes." "Yes, we want to help, An-drea. But how can we make a difference?'

Let me tell you: *I was just like you.*

I was asking myself that same question when the answer was, quite literally, presented to me, in the form of an award. An award that myself and nine other amazing women in my beautiful home state of Minnesota received in January. When we were honored, the ten of us realized very quickly that we were finally being recognized for what may very well be the most important work of all in our country right now. And so I am here tonight to tell you about the Committee. And to ask you to join us in our work.

(Below the scrim, a WOMAN with shapely legs steps into view. She wears fashionable high heels. She strikes a pose.)

ANDREA: And let me be clear about this. This is about all the families who are struggling just to get by, and we must act. We do not do this work for ourselves. Oh no. We do it for America.

(A red two-square ball bounces once at the opposite end of the stage, and WOMAN in high heels runs off.)

ANDREA: Before the award and the trip, I was doing this on my own. And I'll be honest, I felt isolated, sometimes even hopeless. Because how can one person make a difference?

But when the ten of us came together in the airport that day, I felt such a sense of commonality. Because while we are not all cut from the same cloth—we live in different places, have different lives, and we certainly have very different tastes in fashion— *(She laughs, then returns to her serious tone.)* We found that we share the same philosophy. We share the deep conviction that this work needs doing. And thus, C, U, T, R, S—cutters—was born. I think the name says it all.

We want to CUT joblessness. We want to CUT despair.

(A woman's single BARE FOOT appears from behind the scrim. FOOT reaches down toward the floor, as though the woman stands unseen on a ledge and is searching out solid ground for her next step.)

ANDREA: You know everyone wants to talk about "the government," "the government." And fine: the government has a job to do. But the truth of the matter is that there are things the government cannot control. And the government cannot control the numbers.

New housing starts are up. Durable goods: down. Did the government do that? No.

Life as we know it is predicated on numbers that the government cannot control.

(BARE FOOT disappears.)

ANDREA: Now, certain people want you to think that because they roll Alan Greenspan out of his cryogenic chamber four times a year that the government has the *power* to make the economy better. And what? Like they're *choosing not to*? Like they're choosing to let three million Americans lose their jobs? I mean, say what you will about the president, but he *wants* to be reelected.

So who's responsible? We are.

Let me say that again: *We are responsible.*

You're thinking: "Um, excuse me, Andrea? You're a very persuasive speaker, so articulate and charismatic. But the last time I checked I was *not* the CEO of a Fortune 500 company, I didn't fire anyone!" But let me ask you: did you buy a new house this year?

(Above the scrim, a shiny colander is tossed into the air.)

ANDREA: Did you buy a car? A scooter? Some patio furniture?

(In quick succession, a fancy throw pillow and a tennis racquet are tossed into the air, visible for a moment above the top of the scrim.)

ANDREA: *(In a whiny voice.)* "But money's kind of tight, Andrea, and I don't *need* those things."

(More stern than ever.)

These shoes? I didn't *need* these shoes.

But the salesperson was this sweet older woman, and while she wasn't pretty and never had been, her clothes were freshly dry-cleaned, her hair was done, and she had walked into that store that morning as a *professional*.

And as she slid the shoe on my foot and looked up at me, eyes full of the hope of making her sales goal for the day and keeping her job, I had a vision.

I saw her, cashing her paycheck before dropping her clothes off at the dry cleaners.

I saw the dry cleaner balance his books and pay the press operator in the back.

And the press operator, he stopped at the bar on his way home, the smell of the chemical solvents blending with the cigarette smoke and cheap beer, and he tipped the waitress a little extra because he got paid that day. And the waitress with her aching feet took her crumpled dollars home at three a.m. and paid the babysitter for watching her kids *while she was at work and not on welfare!*

And I looked at that saleswoman kneeling on the floor in front of me, in supplication for the whole country, and I said *"I'll take them! What else can you show me?"*

*(WOMAN with the shapely legs and fashionable high heels steps into view again be-*hind the scrim. Throughout this next, bright new objects are tossed into the air and visible for a moment above the top of the scrim. With each object that is tossed, WOMAN takes a step toward the spot where the object appeared, until she makes it almost all the way across the stage.)*

ANDREA: Most of the jobs created in the past year are service jobs, and I, for one, intend to do *everything* I can to make sure that *those* jobs don't go anywhere!

When they ran the article in the *Pioneer Press* about the awards and the trip, some people wrote in, you know, to the editorial page? They said they thought it was "vulgar" that we were being honored with an all-expense-paid trip to Las Vegas. They "objected" to our getting hot stone massages and seaweed wraps and tipping the doorman at the Bellagio very, very well because we hadn't *done anything*.

What, like I do this for *fun*?

(A pair of cute shoes is tossed into the air above the scrim on the opposite side of the stage. WOMAN in high heels turns and runs across the stage toward the spot where the shoes appeared until she is all the way off-stage.)

ANDREA: Like I don't have anything better to do with my time?

Well let me remind you that no one *objected* after the World Trade Center attack when Mayor Giuliani asked people to come to New York and I maxed out my MasterCard and *got on a plane*. No one *objected* when the president got on TV the next summer and told people to *use* their tax rebate and I bought a *flat screen television*.

But apparently, some people think that the time for patriotism is over. Some people think it's not *appropriate* for a newspaper to be "glamorizing" such a "wasteful" life-style when so many people are going without the basics because they are unemployed. *(Beat.)* "Wasteful." *(Beat.)* This attitude, my friends, is the real enemy.

(The red two-square ball bounces once on the floor below the scrim.)

ANDREA: We all feel badly for the people who have been laid off. Let's agree on that. People like my friend, "Ted."

(The single BARE FOOT again dips into view below the scrim, searching out the floor. Throughout this next, as FOOT searches for the floor, the red ball bounces at times, as if punctuating what ANDREA is saying.)

ANDREA: "Ted," who is a hard worker and loving family man who can't find a job. His wife is working overtime, his daughter's mouth is a train wreck, but they can't afford their mortgage let alone braces. And it's *hard.* But do you really think you're going to *help* Ted by *not buying* a new beach tote?

By clutching your money in a tight, guilty fist instead of opening a charge account at IKEA? Do you?

(BARE FOOT disappears from view, the ball is no longer seen.)

ANDREA: Well then, let me tell you about another number. It's the most important number of all. It's called the Consumer Confidence Index.

(WOMAN in fashionable high heels steps into view behind the scrim, stands at a kind of military attention.)

ANDREA: It tells businesses and manufacturers if we are ready to get out there and BUY what they are SELLING.

(A SECOND WOMAN in high heels appears behind the scrim next to the FIRST.)

ANDREA: If we are going to *spend—*

(The two WOMEN begin to march in place.)

ANDREA: Or if we are going to *sit,* in our houses, in the dark, while overstock gets dusty on the shelves and distributors and manufacturers go *out of business,* taking *thousands* of jobs with them, *all because we FEEL BADLY for people like "TED"!* Let me tell you something: if everyone refinanced their houses and went to the *mall, we wouldn't need charity! They'd all have jobs!*

(The two WOMEN perform a series of choreographed military-style steps and turns, building to a crescendo with ANDREA.)

ANDREA: CUTRS is issuing a call! A call to *revolution!* A call to banish unemployment by banishing this debilitating guilt! Take every credit card they offer you! Fuck the voting booth and get your ass to the ATM! This is war! Your country needs you! *Spend! Spend!! Spend!!!*

(ANDREA stands, her fist raised in a power gesture. The two WOMEN have stopped and stand at attention. Silence, except the sound of breathing.)

ANDREA: My name is Andrea Anderson, and I am the founder of CUTRS: the Committee United to Radicalize Shopping. I was honored as a megastar by the Mall of America for spending more than a hundred thousand dollars there in 2003.

Your country needs you. Join us.

(End of play.)

COMING TO THE TABLE

Don Carter

As lights come up, the space is empty except for a rectangular table with two chairs. ERIC enters from right. He carries a bag to the table, puts it down, and pulls out a large golden seal—ornate and regal. He gently attaches the seal to the front of the table and sits down, pulling other supplies from the bag and putting them on the table (clipboards, sign-in sheets, pens, stacks of papers, etc.). GAIL enters from left. In one hand, she carries strips of white vinyl (two feet long by two inches wide) in a stack. In her other hand, she carries a writing tablet. She puts supplies on the table.

GAIL: Good morning.

ERIC: Good morning.

(GAIL crosses to table and sits, organizing the supplies.)

ERIC: So…do you think anyone will show up today?

GAIL: Eric, you know they will. They always do.

ERIC: Well you never know, Gail… today could be the exception.

GAIL: They won't let us down.

(From the corner of the stage, a SHY MAN enters. He looks lost, wandering and looking around the space.)

GAIL: *(Seeing MAN.)* You see? Good morning.

MAT: Oh, good morning.

GAIL: How are you today?

MAT: *(He does not look well.)* Good. Very good… thank you. *(He continues to look around the space.)*

(From the opposite side, a WOMAN bursts onstage. She carries a music libretto under her arm. She is quite nervous.)

ERIC: Hi.

HEATHER: Hello. Have you…? Did you…?

ERIC: Excuse me?

HEATHER: Nothing. *(She walks away, studying the libretto.)*

(A MIDDLE-AGED MAN enters and comes right up to the registration table. He looks at ERIC and GAIL and then at the supplies on the table.)

GAIL: Can we help you?

JIM: No. I'm waiting…I'm waiting for someone. *(He starts away from the table and then turns back.)* My wife.

ERIC: Oh.

JIM: Have you seen her?

(ERIC gestures toward HEATHER questioningly.)

JIM: No, that's not her… *(Under his breath.)* late.

ERIC: Hmm?

JIM: Nothing. *(Crosses to opposite side of the stage and waits. To himself.)* Late.

(Pause. A WOMAN enters, sees JIM, and crosses to him.)

JIM: You're late.

KATHLEEN: I'm *here.*

(They look at each other and begin a very soft conversation/argument that they repeat again and again.)

JIM: I can't believe you...

KATHLEEN: ...always...

JIM: ...never...

KATHLEEN: ...always can't believe...

JIM: ...you never...

KATHLEEN: ...never...

JIM: ...always can't believe you never...

KATHLEEN: ...never, always can't believe...

JIM: You're wrong.

KATHLEEN: Wro...

JIM: Wrong.

KATHLEEN: Right, right—I can't believe...

(Two MEN enter together. One is a PRIEST, the other a MOURNER. PRIEST has his arm around MOURNER and escorts him to the table.)

GAIL: *(Greeting them.)* Yes, right here.

(A SOLDIER enters from center stage—he is dressed in army fatigues. He surveys the space as if looking for intruders and approaches the table.)

SOLDIER: So what do I...?

ERIC: In just a minute sir. We're still waiting for...

(A young GIRL enters. She is carrying a report card with the word "HONORS" stamped on it. She has a ribbon in her hair. GIRL goes to the table.)

GAIL: Well now...

GIRL: I know, I know. *(She grabs one of the white vinyl strips from the table, hops to a specific place on the stage, drops the strip on the floor, and starts reading to herself from the report card.)* "Above average social skills, and an exceptional comprehension of world history and facts." *(She looks away from the card.)* Exceptional... *(Spells.)* E-X-C-E-P-T-I-O-N-A-L.

(A woman enters—she is a RUNNER. She also walks to the table, grabs a white vinyl strip, carries it to her specific spot, and places it on the floor. She starts to warm up for a race, touching and naming her leg muscles as she stretches them.)

RUNNER: *(Repeating throughout.)* Piriformis, superior gemellus, gluteus maximus, obturator internus, quadratus femoris, semitendinosus...

GIRL: *(To RUNNER.)* There are six hundred and thirty-nine muscles in the human body!

RUNNER: ...Semimembranosus, biceps femoris, adductor longus, adductor magnus, psoas major...

ERIC: Okay, that's everyone right?

GAIL: *(Nods.)* Um-hmm.

ERIC: Okay everyone, can I have your...

(They ALL turn.)

ERIC: ...thank you. *(Grabs a white vinyl strip from the table.)* Now let me explain how it all works. We're going to need you all to come up here to the table. We'll check you in, you'll pick up your lines,

(He holds up the white vinyl strip.) and we'll show you where to place them. Okay? Are there any questions?

MAT: *(From edge of stage.)* Yes. Excuse me. *(Approaching table.)* I don't think I'm supposed to be…

GAIL: Sir…

MAT: I was just walking…

GAIL: Sir…

MAT: …and somehow I just ended up… *(Points to where he entered from.)*

GAIL: Sir, I'm sure that there has been no mistake.

(GAIL walks him to the table to check him in.)

GAIL: Why don't we just get you checked in?

MAT: Do you really think…?

GAIL: Yes, look. *(She picks up her clipboard to show him.)* Here you are.

MAT: *(Looking at clipboard.)* Oh.

(The group lines up behind MAT to check in: HEATHER, PRIEST, MOURNER, KATHLEEN, JIM, GIRL, RUNNER, SOLDIER. GAIL has checked MAT in and brings him to his corner of the stage to get him situated. ERIC has checked in GIRL and takes her back to her line.)

ERIC: *(Pointing to GIRL's report card.)* Start here.

GIRL: *(Reads.)* "The quality of mercy is not strain'd,
It droppeth as the gentle rain from heaven
Upon the place beneath: it is twice blest."

(MAT looks over his shoulder at GIRL.)

GAIL: *(Putting MAT's line on the floor.)* Could you sit here? *(She points to the upstage side of the line.)*

MAT: Yes.

GAIL: And this is for you. *(She holds out a writing tablet.)*

MAT: Thank you.

(MAT reaches for the tablet, but GAIL puts it on the other—the downstage—side of his line, just out of his reach.)

GAIL: You can just grab that whenever you're ready.

MAT: Hmm.

GAIL: Good luck.

MAT: Thanks.

GAIL: *(Starts to go and then turns back.)* Oh. I'm sorry, I forgot.

(She hands him a pen.)

MAT: Yes. Thanks.

GIRL: "It blesseth him that gives and him that takes:
'Tis mightiest in the mightiest: it becomes
The throned monarch better than his crown…"

(MAT looks again at GIRL. ERIC is with RUNNER at her line and is showing her the route of her race. He points out the route through the audience as RUNNER listens. ERIC leaves her and she continues to warm up.)

RUNNER: Flexor digitorum longus, flexor hallucis longus, peroneus longus, peroneus brevis, tibialis anterior, extensor hallucis longus…

(GAIL is now with PRIEST and MOURNER. She puts their line between them on the floor.)

GAIL: *(To MOURNER.)* Could you kneel here?

MOURNER: *(He is very upset.)* Yes.

GAIL: And these are for you.

(GAIL hands pages to PRIEST.)

GAIL: Okay?

PRIEST: Yes.

(GAIL leaves them.)

PRIEST: *(Reading from the sheets.)* "We are gathered here today to celebrate the life of our dearly departed Jane…"

(MOURNER wails.)

PRIEST: "…who gave such sweet joy while she was with us and who continues to bring us joy now that she has passed…"

(MOURNER wails. ERIC is with HEATHER. He takes her music libretto and replaces it with the libretto for Mozart's The Magic Flute. *He opens it and points to a specific aria.)*

HEATHER: No, I can't do…

ERIC: Here. It's right here. *(He points to his clipboard.)*

HEATHER: But you don't understand. That's the most…

ERIC: *(Looking again at clipboard.)* Yeah, it's right here: "Queen of the Night."

(HEATHER looks at the clipboard. ERIC puts HEATHER's line on the floor and invites her to join him there.)

GIRL: *(To HEATHER.)* Wolfgang Amadeus Mozart was born in 1756!

ERIC: You should probably warm up, right?

HEATHER: *(Looking at libretto and back to ERIC.)* Yeah.

(She approaches the line. ERIC nods to her and walks away. HEATHER starts to warm up her voice. MAT is trying to reach the

writing tablet without crossing his line on the floor. During the next few minutes, he lays on the floor, reaching. He kneels, leans forward, he stands—bending at the waist… any number of variations to reach the notebook without crossing the line. PRIEST comforts MOURNER.)*

GAIL: *(Approaching KATHERINE and JIM.)* Hello.

JIM: Hello.

KATHLEEN: Hello.

GAIL: *(Looks at her clipboard and then puts their line between them so they are facing each other.)* Okay. Let's start. *(She waits.)*

JIM: Start what?

GAIL: Oh. *(She goes to the table, picks up sheets for each of them.)* Here we go.

(GAIL hands the sheets to them.)

KATHLEEN: *(Looking at her sheet.)* You're kidding, right?

GAIL: *(Shakes her head.)* Nope. Let's start here. *(Points to a line on JIM's sheet.)* "I, Jim…"

JIM: Is this really nec…?

GAIL: Jim…

JIM: "I, Jim, take you Kathleen…"

GAIL: Now Kathleen.

KATHLEEN: Oh God… "I Kathleen take you Jim…"

GAIL: Go ahead.

JIM: "To be my wedded wife."

KATHLEEN: "To be my wedded husband." Oh come on…

JIM: "To have and to hold…"

KATHLEEN: "From this day forward."

GIRL: *(To JIM and KATHLEEN.)* Fifty percent of marriages end in divorce!

(JIM and KATHLEEN look at GIRL.)

JIM: "To honor, to love, to cherish…"

GAIL: Good. Now Kathleen…

KATHLEEN: "To honor, to love, to cherish…"

GAIL: Um-hmm. Keep going. *(She crosses to join ERIC with SOLDIER.)*

JIM: "For better, for worse…"

KATHLEEN: "For richer, for poorer…"

JIM: "In sickness and in health…"

KATHLEEN: "Till death do us part."

(MOURNER wails. JIM and KATHLEEN repeat the vows softly as PRIEST speaks.)

PRIEST: *(Still with MOURNER, but noticing JIM and KATHLEEN's vows.)* "Dearly beloved, we are gathered together here in the sight of God and in the face of this company to join together this man and this woman in holy matrimony…"

JIM: "To honor…"

KATHLEEN: "To love…"

JIM: "To cherish…"

(As JIM and KATHLEEN repeat their vows, they degrade into their earlier argument. ERIC and GAIL are with SOLDIER)

SOLDIER: Where do I go?

ERIC: Here.

(He hands pages to SOLDIER. GAIL puts the line on the floor so SOLDIER is in the center of the space facing forward.)

GAIL: And here you are.

(SOLDIER steps up to the line.)

ERIC: Okay. You can go ahead.

SOLDIER: *(Looks at the pages and reads.)* "Normandy, Saigon, Snyder's Bluff, Artois, Prairie…" wait, these are all…

ERIC: Yup. Go on.

SOLDIER: "Prairie Grove, Plymouth, Lexington-Concord, Vittorio Veneto, Glasgow…"

GIRL: *(From her report card.)* "The capital of New Jersey is…"

SOLDIER: "…Yorktown…"

GIRL: *(To SOLDIER.)* No, Trenton.

SOLDIER: *(Looks at GIRL and continues.)* "My Lai, D-Day, Meuse-Argonne, Flodden, Stalingrad, Gettysburg…"

PRIEST: "We cannot dedicate, we cannot consecrate, we cannot hallow this ground."

(MOURNER wails.)

SOLDIER: "Marks Mills, Little Big Horn, Dien Bien Phu, Wyse Fork…" *(He looks to ERIC and GAIL.)* Is this all I'm supposed to do?

ERIC: No.

GAIL: *(Looks at her clipboard and goes to SOLDIER.)* No. You have to die.

(ALL onstage go silent)

SOLDIER: Oh.

ERIC: *(Approaches SOLDIER and points to the page he is reading.)* Let's go from here.

(JIM and KATHLEEN silently begin their wedding vows again. ERIC brings SOLDIER right up to his line. ERIC and GAIL back away.)

SOLDIER: *(Reading again.)* "Brietenfeltd, Guadalcanal, Vicksburg…"

(HEATHER decisively crosses her line and starts to sing the "Queen of the Night" aria. MAT is at his line, pen poised over the notebook on the other side. RUNNER has taken her mark for the race and is very focused.)

JIM: "To honor…"

SOLDIER: "Saratoga."

KATHLEEN: "To love…"

SOLDIER: "Selma."

JIM: "To cherish…"

SOLDIER: "Buck Head Creek."

(GIRL has removed the ribbon from her hair. She crosses her line—it's as if she has "grown up.")

GIRL: There were six hundred and eighteen thousand casualties in the Civil War.

KATHLEEN: "To honor…"

SOLDIER: "Mountain Meadows."

JIM: "To love…"

SOLDIER: "El Alamein."

KATHLEEN: "To cherish…"

GIRL: There were fifty million casualties in World War II.

SOLDIER: "Gaza."

KATHLEEN: "For richer, for poorer…"   RUNNER: On your mark…

SOLDIER: "Midway."   RUNNER: Get set…

JIM: "In sickness and in health…"

(JIM and KATHLEEN reach for each other's hand as they speak, and each then crosses the line to the other's side.)

SOLDIER: "Antietam."

KATHLEEN and JIM: "Till death do us part…"

RUNNER: Go!

(Gunshot. SOLDIER falls immediately to the ground. RUNNER takes off through the audience, beginning her race. Silence. MAT, standing at his line, finally steps over it, picks up notebook, and begins writing on the page. He speaks as he writes.)

MAT: "Eric enters. He carries a bag to a table and pulls out a golden seal—ornate and regal. He gently attaches the seal to the front of the table and then sits." *(MAT exits through the audience, writing/speaking as he goes.)* "He starts to pull items from the bag and place them on the table—clipboards, sign-in sheets…"

(PRIEST, MOURNER, JIM, KATHLEEN, HEATHER, GIRL, ERIC, and GAIL all surround SOLDIER on the floor.)

PRIEST: "We cannot dedicate—we cannot consecrate—we cannot hallow this ground." *(Pause.)* "The brave men, living and dead, who struggled here, have consecrated it far above our poor power to add or detract."

(PRIEST goes to lift SOLDIER. MOURNER dries his tears and crosses his line to help PRIEST. They carry SOLDIER off. KATHLEEN, JIM, HEATHER, and GIRL follow.)

ERIC and GAIL: *(As they all leave.)* Thank you. Thank you.

GIRL: *(To herself.)* "The quality of mercy is not strain'd,
It droppeth as the gentle rain from heaven
Upon the place beneath: it is twice blest."

(ERIC and GAIL go around and collect the lines and supplies, and bring them to the table. They put them in the bag. Then they both sit. Pause.)

GAIL: Well, do you think anyone will come tomorrow?

ERIC: Gail, you know they will. They always do.

(GAIL grabs one of the white lines and places it center stage so she is in profile. She waits for ERIC to join her. ERIC gets up and approaches line, facing GAIL.)

GAIL: See you then.

(She extends her hand across the line. ERIC shakes her hand.)

ERIC: Yes, I'll see you then.

(GAIL and ERIC cross the line to each other's side. They go to the table, collect the supplies, and wave to each other before they exit on opposite sides of the stage. All lights fade except a special light on the line at center stage. Fade to black.)

(END OF PLAY.)

KALIGHAT

Paul Knox

PAUL KNOX's plays have been seen at the Circle Repertory Company Lab, Circle East, the Neighborhood Playhouse, the 42nd Street Workshop, Harvard University, New York State Summer School for the Arts, SALAAM, with Desipina at the New York Tenement Museum, Columbia University Dramatists, the South Asian-American Theater of Boston at Wellesley College, and other locales as far as Cape Town. Paul has directed numerous other works, including William M. Hoffman's *Cornbury, the Queen's Governor* and *Gilles de Rais*. He is the executive director of Circle East, which he founded in 2000 with artistic director Michael Warren Powell, the former artistic director of the Circle Rep Lab. With Circle East, Paul has produced more than thirty short plays in festivals, three full-length plays including Craig Lucas's *Mother Bird*, and dozens of readings and workshops of plays in development. Paul is a co-recipient of the United Nations Society of Writers' Award for his exchange work with the Russian Academy of Theater Arts in Moscow.

Kalighat was first presented by the Indo-American Arts Council (Aroon Shivdasani, Executive Director) and the Baruch Performing Arts Center (Kathleen Eads, Managing Director; Ariadne Condos, Producing Director), in association with Circle East, on January 22, 2004, at the Nagelberg Theatre, New York City, with the following cast and credits:

Sister Mark .... Susham Bedi
Margaret .... Naheed Khan
Sister Alphonse .... Geeta Citygirl
Klaus .... Tyler Pierce
Brigid .... Grainne De Buitlear
Peter .... G.R. Johnson
Philip .... David Mason
Sydney .... Giuliana Santini
Salim (Bed 35) .... Rizwan Manji
Marina .... Anna Ewing Bull
Sister Jane .... Poorna Jagannathan, Nandita Shenoy (January 24)
Ram (Bed 22) .... Eliyas Qureshi
Sister Maria .... Reena Shah
Sister Christine .... Mami Kimura
Sister Francis .... Nitika Nadgar
Hari Lal (Bed 23) .... Prashant Kumar Gupta
Ahmed Rashad (Bed 26) .... Mina Botross
Rakesh (Bed 27) .... Mukesh Sethi
Fatim (Bed 28) .... Suneel(a) Mubayi
Akash (Bed 29) .... Kamal Sethi
Shiv (Bed 33) .... Shawn Rajguru
Ali (the New Patient) .... Simon Deonarian
Noor (Bed 36)/Dr. Jack's Patient .... Karam Puri
Asif Khan (Bed 37) .... Ranjit Gupte
Luke Gomez (Bed 38) .... Chandon Sethi
Raju (Bed 39) .... Ravi Kumar
Kali, Chinamasta, Sodasi ... Reena Shah, Mami Kimura, Nitika Nadgar

Director: Paul Knox
Associate Director: Susan Kellermann
Choreography: Myna Mukherjee
Scenic Designer: Mikiko Suzuki
Costume Designer: Reshma Patel
Lighting Design: Brian Aldous
Sound Design: Bart Fasbender
Props: Sangeeta Sibal and Anuvab Pal with the support of Soma Saha and Devendra Parekh in Kolkata and Nitin Puri in Mumbai
Production Stage Manager: Diane Healy
Stage Manager: Priyanka Mathew

The development of *Kalighat* was supported by the Joyful Noise Fund, Nancy Miller, and Jens Wennberg. Elise Thoron and William M. Hoffman provided dramaturgical support.

*NO MAN IS AN ILAND
INTIRE OF IT SELFE;
every man is a peece of the
CONTINENT, a part of the
MAINE; if a CLOD bee washed
away by the SEA, EUROPE is
the lesse, as well as if a Promonorie
were, as well as if a MANNOR
of thy FRIENDS or of THINE
OWNE were; any man's DEATH
diminishes ME, because I am
involved in Mankinde, And
therefore never send to know for
whom the BELL tolls; it tolls
for THEE*

*John Donne
1573–1631
Poet, Clergyman & Religious Writer
Dean of St. Paul's - 1621–1631.*

—As seen on the wall of St. Paul's Church (1857) in Calcutta

For Mary Lee Taylor Knox
and Marie McGuire Taylor and Margaret Plut Knox
and theirs and all mothers.

CHARACTERS

SISTER MARK: Forties-plus, South Asian. Superior at Kalighat.

MARGARET: Forties-plus, Bengali. Works and lives at Kalighat.

SISTER ALPHONSE: Forties-plus, South Asian. Directly under Sister Mark at Kalighat.

KLAUS: Forties, German.

BRIGID: Twenty-five, Irish.

PETER: Twenty-five, New Yorker.

PHILIP: Twenty-five, British.

SYDNEY: Twenty-five, Canadian.

SALIM (Bed 35): Twenty to twenty-five, Punjabi.

MARINA: Forties, British.

SISTER JANE: Twenty, Malayali.

RAM (Bed 22): Fifty to seventy, Bengali Hindu.

LUKE (Bed 38): Seventeen, Bengali Catholic.

NOOR (Bed 36): Thirty-five to forty-five, Bengali Muslim.

THREE NOVICES: Under twenty, South Asian. They also appear as dancers in the final scene.

SEVERAL OTHER MALE PATIENTS

ACT I
SCENE I

Covering the stage is a scrim on which is painted a mural of the sights of Calcutta, and framed with the words "Namashkara, Calcutta – The City of Joy." Sounds of the streets of Calcutta are heard: horns blaring, trolley bells ringing, calls to Muslim prayer, Hindu chanting, cows mooing, movie music, hawkers, nuns singing, bus conductors calling out destinations, etc., as well as songs of Rabindranath Takhore. A red sunrise appears behind the scrim as the lights fade to black.

The scrim disappears and three levels are seen. The highest is the chapel of the Mother House of the Missionaries of Charity in Calcutta. There is a simple altar with a tabernacle and crucifix behind it. The room is painted brown and beige, and has a few single light bulbs hanging from the ceiling. There is no decoration except for the shadows playing on the walls and floor as the lights from the street below filter through the gated windows. The middle level is the social room and bedroom area at the Modern Lodge. The rooms are dark and dingy green. The lowest level, across the stage floor, is the male ward at Kalighat, Mother Teresa's

Home for Dying Destitutes in Calcutta. There is a line of flat iron beds across the floor. Each one is home to a MAN. Through an archway the first bed of the female ward can be seen. There are metal cabinets which are the dispensary, and a wooden desk. There are doors stage left and stage center that both lead to the kitchen area and morgue. Above the bed farthest stage right is a shelf with a statue of the Virgin Mary surrounded by plastic red roses. There are birdcages built into the wall behind the beds, a picture of Mother Teresa and one of the Pope, and a blackboard on which is written, "Let every action of mine be something beautiful for God. Mother."

The MEN and BOYS in the beds are all sick. Some have skin diseases like leprosy and elephantiasis, some have TB, cholera, malaria, and other sicknesses related to malnutrition and exposure. Several Western volunteers (PETER, PHILIP, KLAUS, BRIGID) tend to the PATIENTS. It is late summer. The days are hot. The air is heavy with dust and humidity. The chaos of the place grows even greater as three NOVICES enter with SISTER MARK, SISTER ALPHONSE, SISTER JANE, and MARGARET.

SISTER MARK: How many dead today?

MARGARET: This man, and one woman, I think.

SISTER MARK: You think?

MARGARET: You go check. Bloody murder you screamed last time I wrapped someone up without asking. So she was still breathing, that's my fault?

(SISTER MARK starts to exit toward women's ward.)

SISTER ALPHONSE: Sister, there are some girls outside who want to admit a man. They say he has no family. He doesn't

look that sick to me. Shall I tell them to take him to Prim Dan?

SISTER MARK: What's the matter? No, no, bring him in. Put him there.

SISTER ALPHONSE: But so few free beds we are having today.

SISTER MARK: Margaret, what bed is that dead woman in?

MARGARET: Forty-two, unless she moved to one with a better view.

SISTER MARK: *(To KLAUS and PHILIP.)* You. You. Go outside and bring that man in.

(She exits. KLAUS and PHILIP drop what they are doing and step out.)

BRIGID: *(To PETER.)* That there is Sister Mark. It's her you'll be wantin' to talk to.

KLAUS: Which man?

SISTER ALPHONSE: Must I do everything myself?

(SISTER ALPHONSE exits as SISTER MARK re-enters.)

SISTER MARK: *(To KLAUS.)* You, there is a dead women in Bed 42. Get two novices to help you wrap her up.

KLAUS: But I must help…

SISTER MARK: She's not going to wait forever.

KLAUS: But, Sister Alphonse is wanting…

SISTER MARK: *(To PETER.)* You, brother, go with Sister Alphonse. *(To KLAUS.)* Now go. And put her on the Hindu side. Anyone seen Marina?

BRIGID: Oh, slipped me mind. Told me to tell ya she'd be a bit late. Had to cash a check, you know the Brits and their money. 'Course Indian banks bein' what they are may be better part of a week 'fore she gets here. Wants you to have a look at the man in Bed 16. Now, I don't know any better myself but I think the bloke's…

SISTER MARK: Brigid, go help Klaus.

BRIGID: Yes, Sister. Oh, Sister, that boy you sent outside was wantin' to talk to you. Quite a handsome one, don't you …? Oh, well it's his first day here, ya know, American, an actor he says, and…

SISTER MARK: Brigid—Klaus.

(PETER and PHILIP enter carrying a man. SISTER ALPHONSE is close on their heels.)

PETER: Jesus, he's heavy.

PHILIP: Just a bit awkward, really.

SISTER ALPHONSE: He's filthy, Sister. Shouldn't they give him a bath first?

SISTER MARK: No, too feverish. Maybe in the morning. Sister Jane, get started on the dressings. Bed 29.

SISTER ALPHONSE: He's not that sick. *(Screams at MAN.)* You don't belong here!

PHILIP: Just slide him in there. I'm Philip, by the way…

PETER: Hey. Peter. You a doctor?

PHILIP: No.

PETER: Looks like you know the ropes pretty well. How long you been here?

PHILIP: 'Bout a month. You learn fast. Start getting those clothes off him.

(PHILIP goes to get clean clothes. SISTER JANE and a NOVICE begin changing dressings.)

SISTER MARK: You're new. Sister Priscilla sent you?

PETER: Yes. I mean, no. Sister Priscilla? No, I just came.

SISTER MARK: You must register with Sister Priscilla at the Mother House.

PETER: Oh, I didn't know.

SISTER MARK: Name?

PETER: Peter.

SISTER MARK: Ah, very nice name. You're from America.

PETER: Yes, from New York.

SISTER MARK: New York? Do you know our sisters there?

PETER: Ah…no, but I'd sure like to meet 'em sometime.

SISTER MARK: Hmm. Sister Alphonse! Come and fill out a card on the new patient here. *(To PETER.)* What do you do in New York?

PETER: Ah, …I'm…an actor.

SISTER ALPHONSE: *(Shouting.) Tomar nam ki?*

SISTER MARK: I mean for a living?

PETER: Well, I've got a national for McDonald's running, and I just signed with a new agent for legit…

SISTER ALPHONSE: *(Still shouting.)* Hindu *ba* Muslim?

SISTER MARK: Well, I suppose we're all actors of one kind or other, no? Help your brother into his new clothes. Try to make him comfortable. Sister, come help the novices with the women's medicine. *(She hands a book to KLAUS.)* You take care of the men today. You have enough helpers, no?

KLAUS: Oh, but Sister…

(She leaves. KLAUS looks through the book with each patient's chart.)

KLAUS: It is all in English...bad English, too. *(He goes to medicine cabinet, carries a tray of tablets and liquids to a vacant bed and begins figuring dosages according to the book.)*

PHILIP: So, an actor, huh? What brings you here?

PETER: Looking for something more glamorous. I dunno. Guess I wanted to do something a little more fulfilling for a while. Or maybe I'm just running away.

PHILIP: Suppose everyone's running from or to something.

PETER: What about you? What brings you here?

PHILIP: I came to touch the bleeding heart of Jesus.

PETER: Yeah, right. Oh, sorry, you're serious. Well, gee, that's great. So, what else do we do?

PHILIP: Plenty. After the medicine we feed them, wash blankets, do bedpans, whatever we can by five forty-five.

PETER: What happens at five forty-five?

PHILIP: Closing time, we all go home.

PETER: Home? You mean, everyone?

KLAUS: Excuse me, you will help me with medicine? Bed number 38.

PHILIP: Grab a cup of water there and bring it to Bed 38.

KLAUS: Bed 37.

PHILIP: Thank you. We go home, the sisters go to pray.

PETER: *(To PATIENT 38.)* Namaste, take medicine? *(To PHILIP.)* Is there a doctor or nurse or something?

PHILIP: *(To PATIENT 37.)* Here you go, my man. *(To PETER.)* A doctor shows up every now and then. Marina's a midwife, which is close, I guess, and Sister Mark knows her stuff pretty well.

PETER: But, no one is here with them at night?

PHILIP: Well, Margaret.

PETER: Margaret? She's a doctor?

PHILIP: No. I think she used to be a patient. Just sort of stayed on. And Thursday's the day off. Nobody here at all on Thursday.

PETER: They're all just left here—alone? Unbelievable. So much for idyllic... I mean, Mother Teresa and everything. Maybe I could stay... if I talk to Sister...

PHILIP: It's the rule. You can't change it. None of us can.

PETER: Jesus.

PHILIP: Well, maybe.

KLAUS: This for Number 35.

(SYDNEY enters from the women's ward.)

SYDNEY: The women have a whole slew of fresh novices over there, you guys need help here?

PHILIP: This is Peter. Just arrived. America.

PETER: Hi.

SYDNEY: Oh, hello... there. Um. Sydney.

PETER: Really, wow. So beautiful.

SYDNEY: Excuse me?

PETER: Australia.

SYDNEY: Australia? Oh, no. Canada. I mean, my name is Sydney. I'm... ah... Canada. Not... Oh, God.

KLAUS: Bed 26.

SYDNEY: All these?

KLAUS: Yes, see?!!

(KLAUS shows her the book.)

SYDNEY: Okay, okay! *(To PATIENT.)* Hi there, time for your tablets.

PETER: Hi there, time for your tablets.

SALIM: May I have cough syrup also?

PETER: You speak English.

SALIM: Yes, thank you. From which place you are coming?

PETER: From New York, United States... America?

SALIM: Really?! Oh, I know New York. Big beautiful city. Like Calcutta?

PETER: Well, it's big.

SYDNEY: Here's your cough syrup, Salim.

SALIM: Thank you, madam.

PETER: Salim, huh? So, Salim, you grow up in Calcutta?

SALIM: No, no. I growing in Punjab, small village.

PHILIP: Sorry, Salim, duty calls. *(To PETER.)* Got to watch that one, and the gold in your teeth, too.

SALIM: Brother! Brother! You get me good blanket?

PETER: Huh? Oh, yeah, sure, I'll try.

KLAUS: Number 27. Wait, what is your name?

PETER: Peter.

KLAUS: Number 27, Peter. Wait! I am Klaus. Take this, too.

(MARINA enters, damp from the heat, and surveys the situation.)

MARGARET: *(To SYDNEY.)* Sister, did you remember about my niece?

SYDNEY: I hope we're not going to make a habit of this, Margaret.

(SYDNEY hands MARGARET a ten-rupee note.)

MARGARET: Oh, no. She is just so sick now. No money for medicine. You won't be telling Sister Mark, eh?

SYDNEY: No, I won't tell Sister Mark.

MARGARET: Ah, Marina, Sister has been asking for you.

MARINA: Didn't Brigid tell her I'd be late? Can't depend on her for the smallest...

MARGARET: Go see the new patient. Bed 34. I'll tell Sister you are here.

KLAUS: *(Holds up a bottle of Rolaids.)* Number 29, Peter.

PETER: Rolaids? That's it? Well, why not. "Spell relief R-O-L-A-I-D-S."

MARGARET: Ah, brother, welcome. Peter, yes? They tell me you are an actor. Myself am Margaret.

PETER: That's my grandmother's name—Margaret. Doesn't sound very Indian.

MARGARET: It's a Christian name. You think the sisters would let me live here if I weren't a Christian? I tell you what, if you like you call me Rekha.

PETER: *(To PATIENT.)* Here you go, time for your medicine.

MARGARET: So, brother. You act in movies, huh? On TV? Tell me, you know Pamela Anderson Lee?

PETER: No, I'm not a big *Baywatch* fan.

MARGARET: No? What about *The Bold and the Beautiful*? I love *The Bold and the Beautiful*.

PETER: 'Fraid not.

MARGARET: You married?

PETER: Ah, no.

MARGARET: No? Why no? You're very old.

MARINA: Margaret!

MARGARET: Oh, Sister will scream. You will be here tomorrow, no?

PETER: I don't know… I guess.

MARGARET: We will talk more then. I want to tell you about my niece. Very pretty girl!

(She scurries off. SISTER JANE and a NOVICE begin removing old bandages from the wounds of LUKE GOMEZ. He screams from the pain.)

SISTER JANE: Sister, sit down here and hold his hand.

(NOVICE nervously sits down.)

MARINA: Oh, that poor boy. How are you feeling today? You still look a little pale.

PHILIP: I'm much better. Went to Shishu Bhavan this morning. Love those kids.

MARINA: *(To MAN in Bed 34.)* Hello, you speak English? No? Oh, he doesn't look good, does he? What did Sister say about him?

PHILIP: Nothing I heard. This is Peter.

MARINA: Pleasure. You think he has TB?

PETER: You're asking me?

MARINA: Don't think he'll be able to eat. Let's try to get a drip into him. Philip, be a dear and get an IV bottle and try to find a new needle. Lord, is there a vein left in this arm?

PETER: Excuse me. Hello. *Namaste.*

RAM: *Mangi poot.*

PETER: Here's tablets for you.

RAM: Always more tablets. For what?

PETER: Um, to make you feel better?

RAM: Make me feel better. My bones feel as though they will push through my skin. I cannot hold cup to drink, cannot eat. Every day I am praying God to take me soon. There is no more time for this body on earth. You want to give me tablets to make you feel better? Give me a tablet to die.

PETER: I'm afraid they're just for indigestion.

RAM: Indigestion? No, no tablets today. Maybe a little water.

PETER: Oh, okay. Ah, *tomar nam ki?*

RAM: *Apnar nam ki.*

PETER: Huh?

RAM: *Apnar! Apnar!* You say "*apnar*" to your elders.

PETER: Oh, sorry.

RAM: *Amar nam* Ram. And yours?

PETER: *Amar nam* Peter. So, yo Ram, where did you learn such good English?

RAM: From the conquistadors. From school, of course.

PETER: Oh, sorry, I guess I just thought…

RAM: This is not America, young sahib, it takes more than speaking English not to end up in a place like this. And I speak Bengali, Hindi, Urdu, Oria, and a little French and Spanish, too.

KLAUS: Peter!

PETER: I have to get back to the medicine. I'll come check on you later, if that's okay?

RAM: *Hasta luego.*

SYDNEY: Philip's over there playing doctor with Marina. That just leaves us to finish pushing the drugs.

SALIM: Brother, brother, blanket! Remember, good blanket!

PETER: Yeah, yeah, soon as I can.

(SISTER ALPHONSE sees NOVICE holding LUKE's hand.)

SISTER ALPHONSE: What are you doing there? Holding his hand? What is the matter with you, Sister Jane?

SISTER JANE: But, Sister, the bandage is hurting him so. She was only trying to calm him.

SISTER ALPHONSE: Too young for that kind of work. Now it is his hand, who knows what she will be holding tomorrow?

(She sits down next to LUKE and takes his hand. At SISTER JANE's next move, he screams. MARINA and PHILIP try to give an IV to NEW PATIENT.)

MARINA: Oh, it just won't go in, dammit. You see a vein in the other arm?

SISTER ALPHONSE: Don't use that tape on him. Too expensive. Just use the regular tape.

SISTER JANE: But Sister, the wound. That tape will…

SISTER ALPHONSE: Do as I say!

SISTER JANE: Yes, Sister.

KLAUS: *(To PETER.)* Number 36. *(To SYDNEY.)* And this for 23. Wait, there is more. *(He splashes a used cup in some water, then fills it again.)* This, too.

(PATIENT in Bed 36 refuses his tablets and is trying to tell PETER something in sign language.)

PETER: What does that mean?

SYDNEY: Oh, Noor. He won't take them unless you crush them up. In the kitchen, find a couple spoons.

(PETER exits.)

MARINA: There… no… there, I think I've got one.

KLAUS: *(To SYDNEY.)* Number 24.

MARINA: Yes, there we go, now reach up there and flip that little switch. Philip, are you all right?

PHILIP: Yes, yes, I'm fine, just… woe. It's about time I got used to this sort of thing, isn't it.

MARINA: Sit down and put your head between your knees. I'll go get a cold cloth.

PETER: *(Entering with spoons.)* Hey, Phil, you lose a lens, or is that the way to Mecca?

PHILIP: Afraid this human pincushion here got the better of me.

PETER: You look terrible. Bet I could crush something up to make you feel better in no time.

MARINA: *(To PHILIP.)* Here we go, lean up a little bit. Feeling any better?

PHILIP: Yes, mother.

MARINA: Have you eaten anything today?

PHILIP: Tea and *chapatis* from a vendor in the Maiden, and for lunch I had banana porridge at Blue Sky.

MARINA: Good Lord, what do you expect, eating off the streets and in those ratholes.

PHILIP: I rather like that rathole.

MARINA: You want to stay here so badly, stop living on the cheap. This is not a contest.

PHILIP: Fine Marxist you are. I can't afford your upscale restaurants. I eat with the people.

MARINA: You'll be eating in hospital you're not careful. Oh, Noor, are you making trouble?

PETER: I crushed them up— he still won't take them.

MARINA: C'mon Noor, how 'bout if I give you my prettiest smile?

(NOOR continues making faces and waving his hands "no.")

MARINA: No? All right, we can't force him. Philip! Sit down and put that cloth back on your head! All your weaving about, you'll keel over and hurt someone.

(She hands spoons back to PETER.)

PETER: But doesn't he need them?

MARINA: A couple of crushed up TB tablets won't do much good for the little bit of lung he has left. Tell you what, in the back is some lotion. Go get it and give him a little massage. At least try to make him comfortable, hmm? Oh, I'll take those. Spoons aren't easy to find around here.

PETER: You're telling me.

SYDNEY: That's it for the medicine. You wouldn't happen to have a lighter, would you?

PETER: Sure, here.

SYDNEY: You, ah, want to join me?

PETER: No thanks, I'm trying to quit.

SYDNEY: *(Exiting left.)* Hmm. Hard pressed for torture, eh?

(NOVICES bring in pails of food, tea, and a stack of tin plates. SISTER MARK enters right.)

SISTER MARK: Ah, Marina, I am glad you are here. So, what is the matter with this man?

MARINA: Hello, Sister. Sorry I was late. Well, he looks and sounds like TB, but, Lord, such a fever.

(KLAUS, PHILIP, and NOVICES begin passing out food.)

SISTER MARK: TB and malaria. Bravo. You are getting very good at this. You will be here tomorrow, won't you? I have to be at the Mother House all day.

MARINA: Yes, Sister. Both shifts.

SISTER MARK: Good. Sister Alphonse will be in charge, but I need you to keep an eye on things. You understand? Did you cash your check?

MARINA: They had me running from clerk to clerk for two and a half hours and never would cash it.

SISTER MARK: How much is it for?

MARINA: Four hundred pounds.

SISTER MARK: Here, I'll give it to Mother. She'll see it gets cashed. How would you like it?

MARINA: Mostly hundreds. I believe the rate was sixty-four today.

SISTER MARK: Sixty-four? That's all? I'm sure we can do better.

MARINA: But how could you possibly...

SISTER MARK: Marina, we bank with the best. Come now, I want you to examine one of the women.

(They exit to women's ward, right. SISTER JANE speaks to PETER, who is still massaging NOOR's feet.)

SISTER JANE: Enough of that. It is time to eat now. Here, he can feed himself. Wash your hands and help this one. See if you can get him to sit up.

(SYDNEY enters left.)

SYDNEY: Oh, the looks I get out there. You'd think they'd never seen a white woman smoke a cigarette before. Any more spoons?

PETER: In that barrel.

SYDNEY: So, what's on the menu tonight? Ooh, rice and *dal*, and—fish heads. Sister Jane, the culinary wonder, strikes again, eh?

SISTER JANE: Oh, stop now. That's a delicacy in Bengal. Besides, it looks better than what I had last night.

SYDNEY: Yeah, come to think of it, looks better than what I had, too. *(To PATIENT.)* C'mon man, let's get you off your back for a while.

PETER: I'm making a bigger mess here than I started with.

SYDNEY: You'll get used to it.

BRIGID: Sydney, Rena won't eat. Maybe if you go...

SYDNEY: Oh, Lord, maybe she'd be better off if we just left her alone.

(BRIGID takes SYDNEY's plate and spoon and continues feeding PATIENT. SYDNEY exits to women's ward.)

BRIGID: Ah, Indian food, can't stand the sight of it. *(To PETER.)* So, how goes the first day?

PETER: Okay, I guess. *(To PATIENT.)* What? More fish? *(To BRIGID.)* Who's Rena?

BRIGID: TB patient. Bad shape, poor thing. About seventeen she is. Doctor says she's hardly any lung left at all. Eyes started going couple weeks ago. She'll only eat for Syd. Don't know what we'll do when she leaves.

PETER: Sydney's leaving?

BRIGID: In a week and a half, or two, we're not really sure. Don't imagine Rena'll last that long anyway. Sure it'd be a blessing. Beautiful girl, too, long black hair to here. Syd'll sit and comb it for an hour sometimes. The sisters'll try to cut it, but every time they do, poor girl hollers...!

PETER: Why cut it?

BRIGID: Lice.

PETER: Oh. Say, where are the good blankets?

BRIGID: Good blankets? There's some new ones the kids from Malta brought on their last day. Sister locked them up in the cupboard on the women's side.

PATIENT 23: *(To PETER.)* Brother, *pani.*

BRIGID: That's water. See if he has a cup under his bed.

(PETER fills his cup just as two OTHERS ask for water.)

PETER: Here you go. *Pani*, huh? I'll be speaking Bengali in no time.

(Several other PATIENTS ask for pani.*)*

PETER: Okay, okay, brother *pani*, brother *pani*!

PATIENT 37: Brother, *jhol*.

BRIGID: That's water too. He's a Hindu.

PETER: Different water?

BRIGID: Same water, different word.

PATIENT 23: Brother, biscuit?

PETER: Brother biscuit? Where am I supposed to find a biscuit?

BRIGID: In those big white tubs in back. Don't let Sister see you, though.

(PETER exits.)

BRIGID: *(To PATIENT.)* No more? I don't blame you at all. Don't think I'd be able to clean my plate neither. *(Goes to dump the leftovers in the garbage pail.)*

KLAUS: No, stop, don't throw that away!

BRIGID: Klaus, it's garbage, nothing more.

KLAUS: No, no, here, I will give it to someone outside.

SISTER JANE: Klaus, no! We cannot do that! *(Takes the plate and finishes dumping the remains.)*

KLAUS: Sister Jane, it is a terrible waste! People outside would…

SISTER JANE: Fine to give them food that has not been touched, but he has already eaten from this plate. We must not spread his diseases through them like they were charity.

KLAUS: I think already they have disease, and still they are hungry. We should not, Sister, waste what they could use.

SISTER JANE: Would we take that risk if it were our own brother, our own house? I think no. So we must not take that risk with our brother in the street.

KLAUS: *(Returning to feed PATIENT.)* A terrible waste.

PETER: *(Returning with biscuits.)* Okay, here you go.

PATIENTS 24 and 37: Brother, biscuit?

PETER: My God, I've created a monster.

LUKE: Brother, two biscuit?

(PETER exits.)

KLAUS: Philip, help me change this man?

PHILIP: Just a second.

(He brings dish over to barrel with the rest of the dishes. NOVICES begin cleaning up and take the dirty dishes to the kitchen.)

KLAUS: You are going to Adoration tonight?

PHILIP: No. I'll just get some dinner and turn in early. I'm not feeling too spry.

KLAUS: Ah, Calcutta crud.

PHILIP: Really, Klaus. I realize it's difficult, being German and all, but do you think you might make an effort to dignify your language somewhat?

(PETER enters with a fistful of biscuits, and a good blanket under his arm.)

PETER: Biscuits, biscuits! And here's your blanket, Salim. *(Cuddling it as if it were a new puppy.)*

SALIM: Oh ho! Thank you, brother!

PETER: Who else wants a biscuit? Here you go. How 'bout you, Ram? You want a biscuit?

RAM: No, thank you, brother.

(PETER sits down next to RAM and pops the last biscuit into his mouth.)

PETER: I don't know what they're all screaming about, they don't taste that great to me.

RAM: You will probably never have the same taste for food an Indian has.

PETER: Oh, I don't know, I've been doing all right with the food.

RAM: You be careful what you eat. Many of the Westerners come and get very sick here.

PETER: Yeah? Well, I think your buses are going to do my stomach a lot more damage than the food.

RAM: Oh, you have ridden on our buses?

PETER: Not by choice. When I was a kid, an Indian friend of my father's told me his brother'd been crushed to death when the bus he was hanging onto tipped over. Had nightmares for months.

RAM: Fine story for a child. Is that all he told you about our country?

PETER: Oh, I'd see pictures of cows all over the place, lots of people, colorful clothes, poverty.

RAM: There's more to Calcutta than what you see here. There's more than disease and poverty. Look around. Listen. Bengal has a very rich culture.

PETER: You always live here?

RAM: No. I am from Dacca. Bangladesh now. My wife and I came here after my son was killed in the war. After they killed our daughter. I was a teacher there, but here I could get work only in the jute factories.

PETER: And your wife?

RAM: Gone too. More than ten years ago. Couldn't adjust to life here. Too hard for her to live with no Alok, no Sunita.

SISTER ALPHONSE: *(To KLAUS and PHILIP.)* Don't let the novices see you changing that man. *(Seeing SALIM's blanket.)* Where did that come from? That is one of the new blankets!

KLAUS: Oh, oh, there she goes!

SISTER ALPHONSE: *(Pulls blanket off SALIM.)* Not to be used, these blankets. Who gave this to you? Huh?

PETER: I gave it to him.

SISTER ALPHONSE: Who is telling you to do this, huh? Him? You are listening to him?

PETER: Ah…yeah. So, what's the big deal?

SISTER ALPHONSE: Oh, you are very smart, aren't you. Sister Mark said they are not to be used.

PETER: He was cold, I gave him a blanket.

SISTER ALPHONSE: No! No no no. They are not to be used! And you are not to be in that cupboard, you understand? Now put it back where you found it. *(She throws the blanket at PETER.)*

PETER: How can I put it back where I found it if I can't go in the cupboard?

(SISTER MARK enters with MARINA.)

SISTER MARK: What is going on? My goodness, is there a fire in here?

SISTER ALPHONSE: *(Nearly hysterical.)* He stole that blanket! A new blanket from the cupboard in the women's ward.

PETER: Steal it? The door was open and I took it to give to a patient. He was cold.

How was I supposed to know they were sacred? What are they, cowhide or something?

SISTER MARK: Sister, go and get washed, it is almost time to go. *(To PETER.)* These are not to be used. There is still a lot of use in our old blankets. They should be dry by now. Bring them down from the roof and give them to whoever wants one.

(PETER leaves.)

SISTER MARK: Ah, I see you put a drip in him.

MARINA: Oh, please tell the sisters not to take the needle out, to just change the bottle. I don't think I could find another vein.

SISTER MARK: Whatever happens tomorrow, don't let Sister Alphonse get too upset.

MARINA: Don't worry, Sister, we'll manage.

SISTER MARK: *(Seeing LUKE's bandages.)* Oh, no no. Sister Jane, you changed this boy's dressings? You mustn't use this tape on him. Use the Menolin instead. He will never heal otherwise.

(SISTER JANE goes to change the dressing.)

SISTER MARK: No, no. Not now. There is not time. It will have to wait until tomorrow.

(PETER enters carrying a pile of old blankets.)

PETER: Philip, give me a hand with these.

PHILIP: Is this all of them?

PETER: I couldn't carry any more.

KLAUS: I will get what is left.

SISTER MARK: *(To KLAUS.)* Wait, brother, did you have any trouble with the medicine today? You're on your own tomorrow.

KLAUS: Ah, no, I don't think we have trouble, but your book, it is very difficult to read, in some places I must make guess.

SISTER MARK: You'll be fine. Don't get the morning dosage confused with the afternoon, and don't move any pages around. I have them all in order. If you have any questions, ask Marina.

KLAUS: Yes, Sister. *(He goes up to get the remaining blankets.)*

SISTER MARK: Sisters, come say your prayers, I don't want to be late tonight.

(SISTER MARK, SISTER ALPHONSE, SISTER JANE, and NOVICES gather beneath the statue of the Virgin Mary for prayers.)

SISTERS: Hail Mary, Full of Grace, the Lord is with you. Blessed are you among women and blessed is the fruit of your womb, Jesus. Holy Mary, Mother of God, Pray for us sinners now and at the hour of our death. Amen.

Dear Lord, the great healer, I kneel before You. Since every good and perfect gift must come from You, I pray, give clear vi-

(BRIGID enters from kitchen with SYDNEY.)

BRIGID: You know, I get washed up and I feel dirtier than when I started.

SYDNEY: Yeah, I know. What are you doing for dinner?

BRIGID: Well, I was going to go to Adoration first, and then, I don't know, maybe the fish at Kwality, seems the only thing I can keep down lately. What about you,

sion to my eyes, kindness and sympathy to my heart, and strength to lift at least a part of the burden of my suffering fellow man.

SISTER MARK: St. Joseph—

SISTERS: Pray for us.

SISTER MARK: Mary, Queen of Peace—

SISTERS: Cause of our joy, pray for us.

SISTER MARK: In the name of the Father,

SISTERS: And of the Son, and of the Holy Spirit. Amen.

KLAUS: Yes, I think I need to go after today, if just for some quiet time.

PHILIP: I'll find my quiet somewhere else, thank you.

BRIGID: What about you, Peter, will ya join Klaus and I for Adoration at the Mother House?

SISTER ALPHONSE: We can only take two to Adoration tonight. That's all there is room for in the ambulance.

PETER: No, guess not… Maybe some other time.

(MARINA enters with SYDNEY.)

MARINA: Where are you staying, Peter?

are you coming to Adoration?

SYDNEY: No, I'm not feeling too well either. I'll just grab something at Flurries, write some letters and turn in early.

(KLAUS enters.)

KLAUS: Only three blankets left, where should they go?

PHILIP: One more here, everyone else is taken care of.

SYDNEY: Here, give them to me, there's still a couple women who need one. *(Exits.)*

BRIGID: So, are ya comin' to Adoration with me?

PETER: Sudder Street. Modern Lodge.

MARINA: Oh good, you can ride back with us in the bus.

PETER: How 'bout we share a taxi?

PHILIP: Do you have any idea what a taxi would cost?

PETER: A dollar, maybe a dollar and a half.

PHILIP: That's fifty rupees, compared to eighty paise.

PETER: Well, gee, if you put it that way…

MARINA: We'll wait for you out front.

PETER: Great.

SISTER MARK: Come now. It's getting late. Sister Jane, turn out those lights. Margaret, do you have your keys?

MARGARET: Yes, Sister.

PETER: You need anything, Ram?

RAM: No, thank you, unless you can get the sisters to give us some hot water for a change. Brother, will you be riding the bus home?

PETER: Looks that way.

RAM: Hang on tight.

PETER: Thanks.

SALIM: Brother, brother! *Beede.*

PETER: Beede?

SALIM: Cigarette!

PETER: Salim! No! No cigarette!

SISTER MARK: Don't forget, Sister Alphonse will be in charge tomorrow.

MARGARET: I'll start praying now.

SISTER MARK: Don't be smart with me, Margaret. Come, brother, or I will lock you in for the night!

SALIM: Brother, biscuit?

SISTER MARK: Brother!

PETER: Goodnight, Salim!

(The lights dim. MARINA, SYDNEY, PHILIP, and PETER exit left. SISTER ALPHONSE leads the rosary as SISTERS, NOVICES, BRIGID, and KLAUS leave Kalighat and cross downstage to the stairs that lead to the chapel. They kneel in front of the altar as SISTER MARK brings forth the exposed sacrament. They bow, then rise and begin singing.)

SISTERS: *(Singing.)* All the earth proclaim the Lord, sing your praise to God.
Serve you the Lord, heart filled with gladness.
Come into His presence singing for joy.
All the earth proclaim the Lord, sing your praise to God.

SCENE II

SISTERS conduct Benediction in the chapel. In the shadows, life continues at Kalighat. As the lights come up at the Modern Lodge, SYDNEY writes a letter. PETER and PHILIP enter in fits of laughter.

PETER: He just sat there with this incredible look on his face.

SYDNEY: What's going on?

PETER: You were too much.

PHILIP: Me? You.

SYDNEY: Guys?

PETER: If I had to go home tomorrow, it'd be fine as long as I had that story to tell.

SYDNEY: Hello? What story?

PHILIP: And those taxi drivers?

PETER: Like out of some movie.

PHILIP: Can't believe we got out of there.

PETER: The faces on them.

SYDNEY: What faces, what taxi, what story!

PETER: We got off the bus and...

PHILIP: There were these two... you tell her.

PETER: We were just walking down the street...

PHILIP: Freeschool Street.

PETER: Yeah, and these two...

PHILIP: ...rickshaw drivers start ringing their bells...

PETER: ..."rickshaw, rickshaw"...

PHILIP: ...and I said, "No no, no rickshaw." And he said, "To Modern Lodge, how much you give?"

PETER: Like, how do they know where we're staying?

PHILIP: And he says, "Twenty rupees," and I...

PETER: And he says "Twenty rupees! For four blocks? I may be British but I'm not bloody stupid."

PHILIP: I did not say "bloody."

PETER: Whatever. And the driver says, "Okay, boss, how much you give?"

PHILIP: And I said, "How much would you give me to pull you?"

PETER: "Forty rupees!" And like that we've each got a rickshaw running up the street.

SYDNEY: Yeah, so you're each in your rickshaw and...

PHILIP: No!

PETER: No! We're pulling the rickshaws...

PHILIP: The drivers are in back...

PETER: ...and the people in the streets are...

PHILIP: ...laughing and running alongside us.

PETER: They actually handle pretty well, you know? Balance, good balance.

PHILIP: So we're about a block and a half down the road...

PETER: ...when this taxi driver cuts us off at an intersection...

PHILIP: ...jumps out of his car...

PETER: ...screaming this Bengali nonsense...

PHILIP: ...and the rickshaw drivers are screaming at him...

PETER: ...and the crowd is yelling and...

PHILIP: ...finally this shopkeeper starts yelling at us in English...

PETER: ...thank God...

PHILIP: ...that he's going to have us arrested for operating a rickshaw without a license.

PETER: And I say, "What's to operate, asshole?"

PHILIP: Idiot...

PETER: ...it was not smart. And since India's prisons are not tops on my sightseeing agenda...

PHILIP: ...nor mine...

PETER: ...we made a hasty getaway through the poultry section of New-market.

SYDNEY: Five months I've been here and the most excitement I've had was bargaining five paisa off a Campa-Cola.

PHILIP: Oh, you are a bright light, Peter. I haven't laughed like that in I don't know how long. Listen, there's a little church a few blocks away, Anglican. You're Catholic, I suppose?

PETER: Well, raised, yes. I'm in recovery now.

PHILIP: I beg your pardon?

PETER: That's code for "I have to sleep late on Sundays."

PHILIP: No matter. I thought I'd go tonight, to sit and pray, spend a little time with the Lord. Join me?

PETER: Gee, that does sounds like a lot of fun, but I'm kinda tired and I have to unpack and stuff.

PHILIP: Oh, yes of course. Well, I'm going to shower and shave. Just give a holler if you change your mind. *(Exits.)*

PETER: Oh, I'll holler. Man, he sure is into the church thing, isn't he?

SYDNEY: Boy, did you lighten him up, eh? Rarely see a smile on him, but laughing?

PETER: Actually, I was trying to lose him. All I could think about was this city and Kalighat today, and how they're all alone there tonight, and he was just going on and on that the Bible says this and the Bible says that...

SYDNEY: Well, now, we all need our diversions.

PETER: Diversion? Try denial.

SYDNEY: Oh, c'mon, so he believes in something. That's bad? He's committed, he works hard, cares a lot...

PETER: And I don't care!?

SYDNEY: I didn't say... hey, take it easy. I mean, I don't even know you, really. You're here aren't you?

PETER: Yeah, talking to you. Says a lot doesn't it. Forget it. Enough diversions. I'm going back. *(Goes to his room and grabs a few things.)*

SYDNEY: Back... New York?

PETER: No, Kalighat. No doctor, no nurse. I'm going back.

SYDNEY: You can't.

PETER: Come with me?

SYDNEY: No, I'm not... The doors are locked. What are you, gonna break in?

PETER: If I have to.

SYDNEY: Oh, please.

PETER: Fine. Goodbye. How do I get there?

SYDNEY: Hah! Take the bus, oh brave one.

PETER: I will! Where do I get it?

SYDNEY: Corner of Park and Chowringhee.

PETER: Park and what?

SYDNEY: Get off at Hazra and follow the smell of burning goat flesh to the temple.

PETER: How much is a taxi from here?

SYDNEY: Aren't you overreacting a bit?

PETER: *(Pulls out a map and guidebook.)* Great. Just sit there then and write your

little love notes. And Mother and her little helpers are off praying for redemption while all those men and woman are there alone, dying...

SYDNEY: They'll manage that just fine without your help.

PETER: That is the most callous... and I'm the one who doesn't care?

SYDNEY: Oh, I get it, we're playing "who's the biggest carer" now. Give it a rest. You were not the only one who was raised a Catholic.

PETER: Listen, sweetheart, I'm not interested in how you rationalize your faith.

SYDNEY: Forget the faith, *hon*, let's just talk rational. Hey, come back here, what is in your back pocket?

PETER: My wallet and passport...

SYDNEY: Give me that. Do you have any idea what that's worth on the black market?

PETER: A passport?

SYDNEY: I mean, mine's only Canadian, but I don't go running around with it hanging out of my pocket.

PETER: Gimme those!

SYDNEY: Get your head together first.

PETER: Sydney!

(She puts them down her shirt.)

PETER: Oh, Christ.

SYDNEY: How bad do you want 'em, eh?

PETER: You wanna put me to the test?

SYDNEY: You don't have a clue where you are, do you? Ten thousand dollars, American, for one of those little U.S. of

A. passports. You think you won't get your throat cut for that?

PETER: Give me my wallet.

SYDNEY: We all come here, stars in our eyes, bottled water, and all our shots. "I'm going to work with Mother Teresa." Most walk in the door, take one look, and run for the airport or spend the rest of their spring break in Goa smoking hash or at some yoga ashram experiencing the "real" India. Well, this is real too, it's not all of it, but it's a part unfortunately. And maybe I don't do as much as I should, but I'm doing as much as I can. And it's wrong, but I am proud that I manage to stick it out for a few hours each day...

PETER: ...and while you do it you watch the suffering and incompetence go on and on...

SYDNEY: Well, what are you gonna do, eh? Mr. Peter the Great? I mean, what's a four-foot-eight, seventy-something nun from Albania got that you haven't got? You're a big white man from America, with a big white mouth to match. I'm sure you could wipe out poverty and disease in Calcutta before the end of the fiscal year. Maybe you could get your visa extended and save the whole subcontinent.

PETER: You are like, really hostile, aren't you?

SYDNEY: *(Returns his passport.)* Do what you want, but there's people to wash tomorrow, medicine to give, and mouths to feed. We could use a hand.

PETER: So, Philip's diversion is religion, huh? What's yours?

SYDNEY: Cigarettes. And my letters, I guess. I try to write one a day.

PETER: Somebody's a lucky guy. Is he as faithful?

SYDNEY: Are you really that presumptuous or is this just you being not-so-subtly flirtatious?

PETER: Well, who's it to?

SYDNEY: My mother. Helps me keep some kind of perspective around here. She used to be a nun.

PETER: Your mother was a nun? I don't suppose that could be genetic, could it?

SYDNEY: That's an intriguing question. So, why didn't you go to Adoration tonight, it's pretty interesting.

PETER: Given the choice of riding across Calcutta at rush hour in an overcrowded Indian bus or in a Missionaries of Charity ambulance with Sister Alphonse glaring at me, I'll take the bus.

SYDNEY: She's not so bad once you learn to ignore her.

PETER: I haven't had a confrontation like that since Sister Mary Anton slapped me in the face when I walked into her seventh grade biology class wearing a yarmulke. Probably blew my chance of meeting Mother Teresa, didn't I?

SYDNEY: Go another night, or to mass in the morning. She'll be there if she's not out of town or too sick.

PETER: Really? You've met her? Far out! Did the earth shake? Tunnel of light? What?

SYDNEY: Oh, stop. She's just a human being.

PETER: Yeah, right.

SYDNEY: Thought you weren't a fan, eh? Oh, God, I was such a jerk—my first day. I went to Adoration with this big group from Malta. It was their last night and the sisters had tea and biscuits for them and Mother came and gave each of them a little plastic rosary. Here, I've got mine in here with the sapphires I bought in Bangkok, see?

(She brings a small jewelry box from her room. PHILIP enters and stands in the doorway listening.)

PETER: Lovely. *("Not.")*

SYDNEY: Well, what do you want. So, she's going down the line handing out rosaries and when she gets to the end of the line there I am, staring at her like a vision, and she puts this in my hands, looks me in the eye, and says, "Pray the rosary." And I think, "Oh, my God, she thinks I'm one of them." And I shout, "No, Mother, no! I can't. I'm not from Malta." And I flung the thing back and it smacked her right in the face and fell on the floor. I thought I was gonna have a seizure. She's so cool though, she just reached down, picked it up, closed it in my hands, and said, "That's all right, dear, you don't have to be from Malta to pray the rosary."

PHILIP: When Jesus taught us to pray, He said nothing about mindless repetition to His earthly mother.

SYDNEY: Don't start with me, Philip.

PETER: You got a problem with praying the rosary?

SYDNEY: Oh, you know, graven images, papists, that whole bit.

PETER: All those hours on your knees, Philip? You fingering some other kinds of beads?

SYDNEY: Now, that's not nice.

PHILIP: I'm just saying there are different ways of looking at things.

SYDNEY: Your way and the wrong way?

PHILIP: The Bible shows us how.

PETER: And the Talmud and the Koran and the Gita…

PHILIP: We all have choices to make.

SYDNEY: Not everyone is that privileged.

PHILIP: Which just means we have a lot of work to do. *(To PETER.)* You are a Christian, aren't you?

SYDNEY: Oh, Lord.

PETER: Well, I guess. Why?

PHILIP: You guess? There are Christians and there are Christians.

PETER: Oh. So you mean am I a Christian as opposed to a Christian, rather than am I a Christian as opposed to a Hindu or a Jew.

PHILIP: Yes.

PETER: And that makes a difference?

SYDNEY: Peter…

PHILIP: You wouldn't have come here if you were a Hindu or a Jew.

SYDNEY: Philip!

PETER: Really?

PHILIP: How could it not make a difference?

PETER: So, I can't be your friend if I'm not the right kind of Christian?

SYDNEY: Guys…

PHILIP: What kind of friends can two people be with such a fundamental difference…

PETER: I see, friendship based on the degree of my faith in what you believe.

SYDNEY: You know, I was always taught that these sorts of things really shouldn't be talked about at social sorts of gatherings and I just think that that is just very good advice. Don't you think? Friendship based on avoidance. Eh!

(MARINA enters wearing a red dress.)

MARINA: Sydney, have you any earrings I might borrow?

SYDNEY: Sure, take a look. *(Hands her the jewelry box.)* You're welcome to whatever you find.

MARINA: Thank you darling.

PHILIP: My my, look at you. So where is your young man taking you tonight?

MARINA: Dinner at the Blue Fox…

SYDNEY: How posh!

MARINA: …speaking of which, I hope you got a decent meal tonight. Then dancing at the Oberoi, or maybe the Park, or the Taj, or who knows, maybe all three! *(Holds up the ugly plastic rosary.)* Ooo, isn't that lovely.

PETER: Careful, Marina. Aren't you a Christian?

MARINA: Heavens no! Baptized agnostic and I've not strayed once. Oh, these are nice.

SYDNEY: Burma.

MARINA: Yes, oh perfect. At twelve, I joined the Communist Party and I've been praying to Karl Marx ever since. How do I look?

PETER: Red is definitely your color.

MARINA: Very good. You're really quite clever for an American.

PETER: Who's the lucky sahib?

MARINA: No sahib. A twenty-year-old computer student from Yemen, which would be an ideal little socialist country if they weren't so insistent on the Muslim thing too. He manages to make up for it though, in other ways. They keep them so pent up, those Muslim boys. Wouldn't know a girl from a Toyota if they saw one. But once freed from their culture's shackles, they know just how to release that clutch and shift into drive!

PHILIP: Honestly Marina, you are a wonder. How do you manage to spend all day caring for these people, holding their hands and looking into their dying eyes, and then pretty yourself up to go dancing and drinking and…all night long as if it were just a bad dream?

MARINA: Listen, you little prig, it is a bad dream, and when I wake up, I'm going to live my life the way I please with no interference from you or anyone else.

PHILIP: You're afraid I'm right, aren't you? That's what's under it, isn't it?

MARINA: Oh, really? And what's under your bullshit, Philip? As if we didn't know.

PHILIP: It's futile, your work. All the nursing in the world could never stop them flowing in, more and more and always worse. Admit it.

MARINA: Oh, do shut up.

PHILIP: The only hope is with God.

MARINA: Well then you'd better get on the line to that God you love so much and tell Him to get to work, 'cause He's made Himself an awful mess down here, and I'm not grateful for it.

(BRIGID enters carrying a package.)

BRIGID: Pastries!

MARINA: Now, if you'll excuse me I believe there's a good-looking young man waiting downstairs, and I'm going dancing. *(Exits.)*

PHILIP: She doesn't mean that.

BRIGID: So what crawled up her bum 'n died?

SYDNEY: Ah! Just in the nick of time, let's see what you've got.

BRIGID: Pastry, Philip?

PHILIP: *(Shouting after MARINA.)* Heretic! God's work is the only way!

PETER: Will you chill…? You can't beat her over the head with it. Here, have a pastry.

PHILIP: No, there must be an answer. If I can just open my heart enough to hear it. *(To PETER.)* Come with me? Come pray with me. You can help me, Peter.

PETER: I can't… No, Philip.

PHILIP: Fine, I understand. Goodnight then. *(Exits.)*

BRIGID: Well, if I thought it was going to upset him so, I never would have brought the darn things in.

SYDNEY: Oh Bridge, it wasn't you.

BRIGID: I say the word "pastries," they all fly off the handle like bats out of Hades!

SYDNEY: It wasn't… Oh forget it. Here, give me one of those. Another distraction, eh Peter? The best thing about India, you know? I can eat all I want and still lose weight. I swear, people find out, Jenny Craig'll go broke and Calcutta'll have another refugee crisis on its hands, eh?

PETER: I can just see it. The cover of the *Enquirer*, thousands of fat Westerners on a pilgrimage to learn the ancient slimming secrets of the impoverished.

SYDNEY: "Cut Calories the Cal-cutta Way."

PETER: "Dial 1-800-Diarrhea."

BRIGID: Oh, aren't you funny now, the both of you, with your fancy Western ways and your bottles of Lomotil. Just the salt of the earth, aren't you?

SYDNEY: Oh, lighten up. First Philip and now you.

PETER: It was a joke!

BRIGID: Ah, sure now, joke joke joke. You wait 'til diarrhea puts you in an Indian hospital. You won't be laughin' then.

PETER: You were in an Indian hospital?

SYDNEY: You don't want to hear this.

PETER: I do.

BRIGID: Well I was on a third class train out 'a Mughalsaree headed to Patna. It was a long, hot trip and I hadn't had any water, 'cause of course you're not supposed to drink the water. Well let me tell you, better to drink the water and have diarrhea than not drink the water, have diarrhea and get dehydrated too! So, my stomach starts to go on me and I dragged myself to the loo, which on an Indian train is a view of the tracks if you know what I mean. And I pulled out this load of cheesecloth I'd been savin' to try and stop the flow, but it didn't hold for long, so I just laid there on the floor 'a the toilet 'til I passed out from the dehydration. The next thing I knew, I was in hospital with a goat under my bed.

PETER: There was a goat under your bed?

BRIGID: He lived there. So they kept me for nearly a week, and my stomach hasn't been the same since. So, if it's sound advice you're wantin', forget what the guidebooks say, drink the water.

SYDNEY: Well, one diarrhea epic a night is my limit.

(KLAUS enters.)

SYDNEY: Klaus! Hang on a minute. *(Runs to her room.)* It finally came.

BRIGID: What took you so long?

KLAUS: Ah, I get lost. These streets, you know, such madness.

SYDNEY: *Webster's New World*, from Mom in today's mail.

KLAUS: Ah, so much help this will be.

PETER: Boning up on your vocabulary?

KLAUS: It is for my writing, my thesis, so to finish my Ph.D.

PETER: You're writing it in English?

KLAUS: No, German. Because, you see, what I hear is in English always, or Bengali or Hindi. I have the dictionary for Bengali-Hindi, and the English-Hindi, and the English-German, Deutsch-English, and they are all good to tell me which word should mean what in each of the languages, but this is no good if I cannot have the understanding of what the word is meaning in the first place. You understand?

BRIGID: Not a word.

PETER: What are you writing about?

SYDNEY: About us. Angelina Jolie is gonna play me in the film. *(To PETER.)* Why is that funny?

KLAUS: No, it is not like film, it is…a study, more…of my work, here. About my progress as in relationship to my work under analysis, and doing service.

BRIGID: Service for whom, one might ask?

PETER: You're an analyst?

KLAUS: No. I am, how do you say it? Coming through analysis?

PETER: Going through analysis.

SYDNEY: I think I like his way better.

KLAUS: I am therapist, but still I study to do the analysis, you see? My study makes me think, though, that I, ah, must make the progress more for myself, you know, before I can hope to do…to help other people do the work. That is why I come here. I hope, ah, to clear away the blocks, you see? To clear away the guilt I, ah…gather up as a child.

PETER: There's that Catholic guilt again.

KLAUS: Huh? Ah, no, I think, perhaps, Jewish.

PETER: Same thing.

SYDNEY: You're Jewish?

KLAUS: No, Catholic.

PETER: Then where do you get Jewish guilt?

KLAUS: From my father and my mother.

PETER: They're Jewish?

KLAUS: No. Catholic.

PETER: I don't get it.

SYDNEY: You've lost me, Klaus.

BRIGID: Oh Lord. The man has Jewish guilt for the same reason I can't eat a potato without blinking me eyes three times. Do they teach you anything in those schools over there? Perhaps a little something about world history, or are ya just too busy speedin' down your freeways with your guns and your drugs to pay any attention?

PETER: Now, c'mon, that's not fair. We have a lot of very serious Madonna fans too.

BRIGID: I rest my case. Leaders of the free world. Heaven help us all.

KLAUS: Shhh, Brigid. My brother, he was very much older than me, he was a small child at the War time. Dark, you know, was always sad. Because he feel angry, you know, at our parents, to stand by with so much evil around. When he was twenty-two, and I must be five, on his birthday, my mother make party with big cake. At the middle of the dinner, though, he stand up, shout, "I cannot forgive you," and cut his arm open with the hunting knife my father give to him as gift.

SYDNEY: Lord.

KLAUS: It was kind of punishment, I think, to my parents. I do not want to punish them, but I feel the guilt, you know, from just being. But, it is not something can be cut out, like a ah, cancer. No, it is not so simple. But maybe this helps it, this work here. It does not change history, I know, but…the air gets more clear and the guilt is maybe little more lighter to carry. Ah, listen to me, so much I talk. Well, good practice, I need. But I must, ah… Oh, the dictionary. Thank you again. You are going to Howrah tomorrow?

SYDNEY: Yeah.

BRIGID: Wouldn't miss it.

KLAUS: Until the morning then, when I see you. Ah, goodnight. *(Exits.)*

PETER: That was not the bedtime story I needed to hear tonight.

SYDNEY: You know, I watch him working, and he is just so… well, these horrible things will happen and he just walks right up and deals with it. Like Brigid here. No fear, totally calm.

BRIGID: Me? Oh, what rubbish.

SYDNEY: It's true. I don't know how you do the things you do. Like that woman they brought in from the tracks, 'bout a week ago, eh? They said she'd been hit by a train, but it really looked like someone had just taken an ax to her head and left her for dead. She wasn't though. Unconscious, but she was still breathing. And her body was just rigid, like from rigor mortis, but I think it was just from the pain. And this endless, paralyzed look of horror on her face. Her clothes were so… and the smell, well, she must have been laying in the mud there for days. I don't know how she wasn't dead. I mean, her head was one-third gone. And Klaus just pulled her into his lap and rocked her, and Bridge here just started cleaning her up, caressing her hands.

BRIGID: What else was I to do?

SYDNEY: I don't know, but I couldn't move. And oh the places my mind went. And, oh Lord, I couldn't figure out why there wasn't any blood, you know? I mean, her skull was gone from here to here. *(Points to just above her right eye with her left index and middle finger, and to behind and below her right ear with her right hand.)* But, no blood, just this white, I thought it was bone, I guess, but it was pulsing. And Sister Mark came and poured some kind of disinfectant on her head, and this white mass just started teeming, until it broke off in clumps and slithered away from this open crater that was her head, maggots, thousands. I suppose they were keeping it clean, the wound, but ech, there they were, just writhing and crawling everywhere, and these two just kept right on with it, didn't even flinch.

BRIGID: Well, I think I flinched a bit.

SYDNEY: No. Really, she didn't. And Klaus just kept holding her while Bridge and Sister Mark cut away the dead flesh, bandaged her up. And they just sat with her, rocking, caressing, and the horror slowly faded from her face, and her breathing relaxed, and her body slowly lost that terrible stiffness, and she just kind of melted into them and died. It was so beautiful and so terrifying. It was hard to imagine how one could exist without the other. And you were able to stay there with it. Oh, Lord, will I ever be able to face my fear like that?

BRIGID: Oh, well done, Sydney. He's sure to sleep soundly now. Will ya wake me for Howrah in the morning?

SYDNEY: Sure. Goodnight.

(BRIGID exits.)

PETER: Goodnight. Ah, listen, I'm sorry about before. I'm just a little, I don't know, confused.

SYDNEY: Don't worry about it. Sometimes it's hard to remember why we're here. When I first came I actually believed I was here to help somebody besides myself. What about you, eh? Why are you here?

PETER: Well, to face my fears, I guess. Not sure, really. Just sort of ended up here. See, I had a…friend. We lived…shared an apartment together. And he, my friend, always wanted to go to India. Especially after…he got sick. He was sort of spiritual, I guess. You know, always talking about the Buddha, karma, nirvana, you know, that kinda shit. I didn't even know where India was, but he was like obsessed.

SYDNEY: Was?

PETER: He died. April seventh. "If I can just swim in the Ganges," he'd say. He'd find his cure, his salvation. Well, there wasn't any medicine doing him any good. The sicker he got, the more we'd plan this trip. Johnny. Every day he'd waste away a little more. I tried to take care of him. But, it was hard, I mean, I'd come home and he'd be… Well, I sent him to the hospital on St. Patrick's Day. He didn't want to go, but I couldn't do it anymore. But I, ah…I didn't go see him. Didn't return his calls. I thought he'd get better… but I couldn't watch any more. Only strangers around when he died—or maybe no one at all. His family didn't want him, so I brought his ashes to Benares, gave him to his mother Ganges.

SYDNEY: He was your…lover?

PETER: Lover? The man I abandoned, sent away to die alone?

SYDNEY: You were afraid.

PETER: Yeah? So? Well, thank you very much but I'm not here looking for excuses from some stranger.

SYDNEY: Sorry, I didn't mean to…

PETER: No. I'm just a little touchy, I guess, guilty.

SYDNEY: Listen, in the morning some of us go work at Howrah, across the river. Mother has a children's home there. You're welcome to come.

PETER: No, I'm gonna go back to Kalighat.

SYDNEY: We'll go to Kalighat in the afternoon, but the brothers are there in the morning, so they don't need so many volunteers, and besides, it's good to be with children after Kalighat. Sort of balances things out, you know? You walk in the

door and they jump in your arms shouting "auntie, auntie, uncle, uncle…"

PETER: I don't really… I don't like children.

SYDNEY: You don't…? Well, come and
meet these kids. Totally unspoiled. I'll
wake you at six.

PETER: No, no, I'm gonna pass. I'm feeling a little…, you know, like I need to
shake off the day. Where did Marina say
she was going dancing?

SYDNEY: One of the hotels. Are you serious?

PETER: You wanna come?

SYDNEY: No, God!

PETER: It'll be fun. You look like you
could use a night out.

*(He steps close to her and takes her hand.
She recoils.)*

SYDNEY: No!

PETER: Ooops. Sorry. Not ready to face
your fear, eh?

SYDNEY: Leave your passport with me.

*(He holds his passport to her chest. She takes
it. He backs out of the room slowly and exits. She looks at the passport.)*

SYDNEY: Goodnight.

*(SISTERS begin singing as the lights fade
at the Modern Lodge.)*

SISTERS: Where streams of living water
    flow,
  My ransomed soul He leadeth,
  And where the verdant pastures grow,
  With food celestial feedeth.

*(Loud bhangra music covers their song. The
scrim is closed and behind it are shadows of
DANCERS reveling.)*

SCENE III

*The next day. The scrim opens revealing
Kalighat. LUKE is singing a Bengali song.
KLAUS dispenses medicine with SYDNEY
and BRIGID. PETER, wearing a red kerchief around his neck, is massaging RAM's
back. SISTER JANE and a NOVICE
change dressings. On the blackboard is written "Let My Hands Heal Thy Broken Body."
MARGARET sneaks a hand of gin with a
PATIENT. SISTER ALPHONSE chases
two frightened NOVICES across the room.*

SISTER ALPHONSE: You stupid, stupid girls. I can't trust you to do anything
right.

(MARINA enters up left.)

MARINA: Good Lord, Sister, what's the
matter now?

SISTER ALPHONSE: I told them, I told
them, "Put her on the Muslim side…"

MARINA: Calm down!

SISTER ALPHONSE: If I hadn't gone
in, her body would be on its way to the
Burning Ghats now.

MARINA: It's all right now, Sister!

SISTER ALPHONSE: *(To NOVICES.)*
…I don't want to see you. Go now, get
out!

MARINA: Sister, please…

SISTER ALPHONSE: Burn a Muslim
like a Hindu? I won't be responsible for
that!

MARINA: Sshh. It's fine now. You took
care of it. Listen, don't you have some
bookwork needs doing?

SISTER ALPHONSE: I pray and pray,
but I'll never be able to do the work Sister
Mark does.

(She goes and sits at the desk. At a level above, NOVICES appear with tubs of laundry which they wash with their hands and feet. Their washing becomes a kind of rhythmic dance.)

MARINA: How are you doing on the medicine, Klaus?

KLAUS: I think all right. We are out of this one. I give this instead. It's all right?

MARINA: Let's see, yes, they're both for malaria, I think. Why don't you make a list of what they're for?

KLAUS: Yes, is a good idea.

MARINA: Sister Mark will help you, or ask the doctor next time he's here. How were the children this morning?

KLAUS: Oh, good, but I cannot keep up to them.

MARINA: Yes, they keep you hopping.

RAM: *(To PETER.)* Last night, Yama came to me.

PETER: Yama?

RAM: God of truth and king of the dead. But his visit was only a dream and today I must pray once again for his return.

MARINA: How are you doing this afternoon, Ram? Been able to eat anything?

RAM: No, a little water, nothing else.

MARINA: Maybe I should put you on an IV.

RAM: No! Just let me be.

(MARINA waits a moment, then exits to the women's ward.)

PETER: Little tense around here today, huh?

RAM: The days are only as tense as you allow them to be.

PETER: You sound like some kind of guru.

RAM: You would sound like a guru too, Peter, if you had an accent like mine.

PETER: Hey, last night I went to a couple of clubs. You're right, it's not such a bad place after all.

RAM: I was hoping more for museums, temples, bookstores, but I'm glad you enjoyed yourself.

PETER: And today I got here a little early, so I went into Kali Temple. Wow, like some horror movie. They were sacrificing a goat. Really strange. Blood everywhere.

RAM: The blood of Mother Kali is as much about birth as it is about death.

SISTER ALPHONSE: *(Yelling to PETER.)* That's enough, brother. Time to move on to someone else now.

PETER: That woman so needs to be smacked.

RAM: Eh! You must practice tolerance for those you have no patience for. That is why you are blessed to know them.

SISTER ALPHONSE: Do Noor next, brother.

PETER: Coming, Sister—dear.

PATIENT 37: Brother, brother!

PETER: Yeah, yeah, you're next, I promise. Okay Noor, where do you wanna start, shoulders, back? The feet? Okay, leaves us nowhere to go but up, huh? God, so swollen. I hope they don't explode.

(BRIGID and SYDNEY come with meds. SYDNEY tries to give them to NOOR.)

BRIGID: Ach, you'll never get him to take them. Here ya go, tablet time!

PETER: Here, give them to me.

(NOOR makes massaging gesture.)

PETER: Not until you take your medicine.

(NOOR gestures "no.")

PETER: Look, you're going to take them and I'm not going to wait all day. Here, water.

(NOOR gestures "no"; gestures for massage.)

PETER: Yes, yes, yes! Forget it then, no massage.

(NOOR holds his hand out and with great histrionics, takes the tablets.)

SYDNEY: I don't believe it.

BRIGID: Did he take them?

SYDNEY: Yup.

BRIGID: And they say miracles only happen in the penny arcade.

(BRIGID and SYDNEY move on. PETER continues NOOR's massage. PHILIP enters.)

PETER: Where've you been?

PHILIP: I had to walk. Gave all my money to a family on Camac Street.

PETER: You what!?

PHILIP: I thought it would be good for me to sacrifice a little of my comfort for the Lord.

PETER: Philip, you're either very brave or very stupid.

PHILIP: I know the Lord will provide.

PETER: Yeah? Well, who knows. Listen, I passed a restaurant called the Moghal Darbar. Food's cheap and the rats are too small to climb on the tables. So let's stop by after this, on me.

PHILIP: No, I don't think so.

PETER: You gotta eat. 'Sides, you don't wanna take away my chance of doing a little charity do you?

PHILIP: Buying a meal for me is your idea of charity?

PETER: I just... well, I'm not really into the church thing, but I thought we could still hang out.

PHILIP: I won't be led astray.

PETER: Led astray...? What does that...?

(PHILIP places his hands on NOOR's head and closes his eyes.)

PHILIP: Just keep following the Lord, Peter. You are doing good work. Really, very good work.

(PHILIP leaves PETER and lays his hands on another PATIENT.)

PETER: Gee, thanks. And for my next scene I'll turn water into wine.

(NOVICES begin hanging the laundry up to dry.)

SISTER JANE: Klaus, I want you to know something. I feel... I am sorry for the way I spoke to you yesterday...about the food. You were trying to do good and I...

KLAUS: Oh no, Sister, please. It is me. I am so impatient, and so much I do not understand...

SISTER JANE: No, you are very patient, very generous with your...love. You know, Klaus, there are four vows in our order, poverty, chastity, service to the poorest of the poor, and the fourth, obedience, oh, always so difficult for me. But now, when I am looking at you I am trying to see you as my brother, but I am not feeling the love I have for Jesus, Klaus. I am feeling another kind of love.

KLAUS: Sister Jane, I...

SISTER JANE: I'm sorry Klaus. Please, don't talk. I—I have to go cry now.

SYDNEY: Is she all right?

KLAUS: No. But I think she must be alone.

SYDNEY: Hard life, eh?

KLAUS: Yes, hard life. And she make it hard for me too! *(He goes back to medicine.)*

PETER: Why do they do it?

SYDNEY: What?

PETER: Why do nuns become nuns? Why'd they want to cut themselves off from so much of life?

SYDNEY: Taking a vow of celibacy is not cutting yourself off.

PETER: Easy for you to say.

SYDNEY: Excuse me? As a matter of fact, Romeo, it is not so easy for me to say. As a matter of fact, I have been thinking very seriously about taking that vow myself.

PETER: You? Are you kidding? But you're such a… well, you're so sort of… normal.

SYDNEY: Normal? Oh, you are the biggest… well, you're the best argument for celibacy I've come across.

(She yanks PETER's kerchief off, revealing a huge hickey on his neck.)

SYDNEY: Oh, my God. What happened?

PETER: Sydney, give me the handkerchief.

BRIGID: Oh my word, it's bigger than the map of Africa!

SYDNEY: Did you get in a fight?

BRIGID: Oh, grow up Sydney. What, punched in the neck?

MARINA: Well, went a bit farther than dancing, I see. And very handsome he was.

BRIGID: Aaahhhh!

PETER: Marina!

MARINA: Oh really, Peter. Yes, you and your young man were doing an admirable job of pretending not to be dancing together, but I am a mother after all.

(MARINA leaves. BRIGID grabs the kerchief and hands it back to PETER.)

BRIGID: So, you like it rough, huh? Must be some Irish in ya. Still, I'd tell your Bengali boy to try a bit more "love" and a little less "bite" next time.

(BRIGID leaves. SYDNEY ties the kerchief around PETER's neck.)

PETER: Well, I guess I've been outed.

SYDNEY: I guess you have.

PETER: Ouch! Not so tight.

SYDNEY: So, I guess you're pretty much over, what was his name? Johnny?

PETER: What do you mean by that?

SYDNEY: Oh, c'mon. Picking up strangers in clubs?

PETER: Oh, now I'm supposed to live like a nun the rest of my life?

SYDNEY: What did he die from, Peter? Was it AIDS?

PETER: What difference does it make?

SYDNEY: Don't you think there's enough problems around here without you giving them any more?

PETER: I was a hell of a lot safer last night than these nuns are, going down the line giving shots with their used needles.

SYDNEY: I'm going to smoke. *(Exits.)*

SALIM: Brother! Brother, come here! I want to tell you a secret.

PETER: What, what is it, Salim?

SALIM: Promise me you will tell no one else of this secret. Then there is a favor I will be asking.

PETER: Ah, I don't know, Salim…

SALIM: No no, brother. No *baksheesh* for the secret. It is a gift. Then we discuss the favor.

PETER: All right, I promise.

SALIM: Brother, …I am an actor too.

PETER: And you want to meet my agent.

SALIM: Brother. I know who you are. I hear you talking now, and I know who you are. But I recognize even yesterday, when first I am seeing you. See? I am like you, brother. Even when I was little, my father, he beat me, say he will send me to the *hijras*, make me a real woman if I no change. I try to change. I pretend to be someone else, but I cannot. One day, I was maybe ten, I put red on my face, I was very pretty, and I put many bangles on feet and hands and I danced. I love to dance. But father come and find me. He get very angry, he wrap me in my ma's sari and tie me outside to a tree for whole village to see. They laugh and throw… When finally it come dark, my mother cut me free. But I no go inside. After everyone asleep, I take my father's gold and run away to Bombay.

PETER: Ten? Alone in Bombay?

SALIM: *Ha. ("Yes.")* But I make friends with boys more young than me. For some time I just steal food. Then I learn to do sex. I make good money. But I don't like. The police would come, take money, beat me, do sex on me. And when I older, I no

get so much money. Then I get sick. So I go back to village. But mother is dead, I don't know why. Only father is left. Too bad. I come to Calcutta and try to do some work. But I cannot, and I get more sick here. Sometimes in Bombay, Western man come and pay for me. Sometimes from America, very generous always. One man from Texas give me two hundred rupees! It's a lot, no! And kind too, so many like to beat me. Saudi mans, they like to beat me, but American mans never beat me, and pay good like they say. So I always dream of America, U.S.A. This is my favor, brother. I recognize you. You understand? I call you brother because I know who you are. Take me to America…

PETER: Oh, Salim. I…I can't…

SALIM: Brother, I can be houseboy for you. Americans like this. I can clean, I can cook, brother…

PETER: Salim, Salim, Salim, you don't understand, it's impossible…

SALIM: Impossible? It's America!

PETER: No, you don't know, Salim. You don't know me, Salim. I'm not rich. I'm nobody. Nobody.

SALIM: It is my dream, brother. It is my dream.

PETER: I…I…

SALIM: No, no. Don't answer. Wait. Please. You think. Maybe, brother, you will think of a way.

(LUKE begins singing a Bengali song. PETER leaves SALIM. BRIGID enters.)

BRIGID: You look awful. Why don't you get yourself a cup of chai and go sit up on the roof for a while.

PETER: No, I'm okay.

BRIGID: *(Pointing to PHILIP.)* What's got into him? Hasn't done a lick 'a work all day and now he's sittin' there with his hands on that man's head… Is he not feelin' well?

PETER: He's healing him.

BRIGID: With all the bedpans needin' changin'? Honestly, they're all a bit off kilter since they lost the empire. *(To SISTER ALPHONSE.)* Ah, Sister, I nearly forgot. You remember Vahjit? The little boy who left a couple weeks ago?

SISTER ALPHONSE: Ah! Yes.

(BRIGID hands her a crayon drawing.)

BRIGID: He's at Howrah now. Asked me to give this to ya.

SISTER ALPHONSE: To me? You are sure it is for me?

BRIGID: "For the round Sister with the big smile," he said.

SISTER ALPHONSE: What is it?

BRIGID: Well, it's the two of you. This is him lying down, and that's you up there.

SISTER ALPHONSE: What is that coming out of my back? It looks like he's hanging me.

BRIGID: Let me see. No, those are wings, Sister. An angel's wings.

SISTER ALPHONSE: Oh, how sweet. Well, I must make one picture for little Vahjit. You will deliver it for me?

BRIGID: Happy to.

(BRIGID exits. SYDNEY enters carrying a long black braid.)

SYDNEY: Sister, Rena, I… her hair, you said you wouldn't cut…

SISTER ALPHONSE: She had lice.

SYDNEY: You promised you wouldn't.

SISTER ALPHONSE: I promise Jesus, no one else.

SYDNEY: I just think… you said…

SISTER ALPHONSE: I said nothing.

SYDNEY: But…

SISTER ALPHONSE: What's done is done.

SYDNEY: It was all she had!

SISTER ALPHONSE: Enough now. What's done is done, I said. *(Exits.)*

PETER: Hey, you okay?

SYDNEY: I don't know, Peter. It makes me want to run away, and makes me want to stay forever.

(SYDNEY exits back to women's ward. NOVICES enter carrying pails of food. SISTER ALPHONSE is close on their heels.)

SISTER ALPHONSE: Bring that to the kitchen. Then go take the drip out of that man. Hurry or it will kill him.

(One NOVICE dumps a bucket, and rice spills out onto the floor.)

SISTER ALPHONSE: Oh, you clumsy fool!

(She tries to slap her.)

PETER: Hey!

SISTER ALPHONSE: Keep quiet you. Now get the drip out of him.

(NOVICE goes to PATIENT 37 and starts to remove the drip.)

SISTER ALPHONSE: If he dies, it will be on your head. *(She starts cleaning up rice.)*

PETER: I'll clean it up, Sister.

SISTER ALPHONSE: No, no, I…

PETER: I will clean it up—Sister!

(MARINA enters up left.)

MARINA: My God, Peter, can't I leave for a moment? *(To NOVICE.)* What are you doing? Oh Lord no… Sister Alphonse, have you any idea what I went through to get that needle into him?

SISTER ALPHONSE: The bottle was empty…

MARINA: The bottle could have been changed!

SISTER ALPHONSE: The air would have dripped down and killed him. I won't be responsible for that.

MARINA: Well, you just may be if I can't get another drip into him. Sister Jane?

SISTER ALPHONSE: I can only do what I know to do, Marina.

SISTER JANE: Yes, what is it?

MARINA: Help me get another drip into this man. Any new needles?

SISTER JANE: I will try to find one.

MARINA: Hurry. *(To SISTER ALPHONSE.)* Sister, it is not necessary to remove the needle when the bottle is empty. A new bottle can be attached without disturbing the flow.

SISTER ALPHONSE: You, brother.

PHILIP: Me?

SISTER ALPHONSE: Yes, come help me rearrange some of these patients.

MARINA: Is that really necessary?

SISTER JANE: Here, I found a needle, Marina, it is almost new.

SISTER ALPHONSE: You do your work, I'll do mine. *(To PETER.)* You, you can help us too. *(Pointing to LUKE.)* I want him nearer the front.

PETER: What for?

SISTER ALPHONSE: Don't ask questions, just do as I say. Put him on the floor for now until we make an open bed. Take that blanket off him… It's filthy.

KLAUS: Sister, please, I must change the pages in the book if you…

SISTER ALPHONSE: Noor, you are nice and quiet, you come up front.

PETER: What are you talking… he shouldn't be moved.

SISTER ALPHONSE: Put him there next to the boy.

PETER: Sorry, Noor.

SISTER ALPHONSE: Brother, I said get rid of that filthy blanket.

LUKE: Na, so cold!

SISTER ALPHONSE: Let go!

(PHILIP nearly falls over as LUKE loses his grip on the blanket.)

SISTER ALPHONSE: You'll get another one, don't worry. Change these two around.

KLAUS: Sister, wait. I must change the pages so the right name goes to the right number.

SISTER ALPHONSE: Don't worry, brother, everyone will be taken care of. Now come up here, we'll make some room.

(NOOR gives his blanket to LUKE and curls up on the floor.)

SISTER ALPHONSE: Ah, this man needs new clothes.

PETER: Go get some clean ones, Philip. I'll get started on him.

(PHILIP doesn't move.)

PETER: Philip? Forget it, I'll go. *(Goes off to get clean clothes.)*

SISTER ALPHONSE: Don't let the novices see you doing that. Noor can stay here. Brother, take the man in Bed 27 and put him down in, what is it, 36.

KLAUS: Yes, Sister, but tomorrow when I give medicine, how will I know who to give to?

SISTER ALPHONSE: Give me the book, I'll put them in order. Have you gotten the needle in him yet?

MARINA: No, I'm afraid it's hopeless.

SISTER ALPHONSE: Well, he had one bottle, that should be enough.

SISTER JANE: You've done all you can, Marina, we must put him in the Lord's hands now.

MARINA: I'm afraid that's exactly what we've done.

(PETER returns with the clothes and throws them into PHILIP's arms.)

PETER: You gonna help me or not?

PHILIP: I know you think I'm crazy or…

PETER: Yes, I do.

PHILIP: But it's too much. I can't help them like this. I've got to find the better way.

PETER: Playing faith-healer is the better way?

PHILIP: My faith is not play, Peter. It's a need, just as important as this one.

PETER: Your faith is a fucking luxury that nobody here needs!

MARINA: Peter! That's enough.

PETER: Yeah, fine, enough. Listen, I have great faith too, Philip, that you and your healing are a lot of shit. It's not about them, it's all for you, and it makes me sick.

PHILIP: Perhaps you shouldn't be here if you're not feeling well.

PETER: Oh Christ, we don't even speak the same language. Go ahead, do your thing. Just leave me alone, will you? Just…

(As he leaves, he trips over NOOR's body.)

PETER: God! Noor? Noor, I'm sorry, did I… Noor…Noor…Noor?

(SISTER JANE feels for NOOR's pulse, puts his arms across his chest and crosses herself.)

SISTER ALPHONSE: *(To PETER.)* Put him on the Muslim side. Come Sisters, come say your prayers before we leave.

(MARGARET brings a white cotton shroud and helps PETER wrap NOOR in it as SISTERS all gather by the door beneath a statue of the Virgin Mary. They begin their prayers as LUKE sings the following song in Bengali.)

LUKE: Early in the day it was whispered that we should sail in a boat, only thou and I, and never a soul in the world would know of this our pilgrimage to no country, and to no end.

In that shoreless ocean, at thy silently listening smile my songs would swell

SISTERS: Hail Mary full of grace, the Lord is with you. Blessed are you among women, and blessed is the fruit of your womb, Jesus. Holy Mary, Mother of God, pray for us sinners, now and at the hour of our death. Amen.

(Singing.) 'Tis the gift to be simple,

in melodies, free as waves, free from all bondage of words.

Who knows when the chains will be off, and the boat, like the last glimmer of sunset, vanish into the night.

'tis the gift to be free, 'tis the gift to come down to where you ought to be. And when we find ourselves in the place just right, 'twill be in the valley of love and delight.

(The following action and dialogue are simultaneous with LUKE's and SISTERS' singing.)

PETER: How could he be so cold, Margaret? How could he be so cold? Just a few minutes ago, his body was so warm.

MARGARET: Take him, brother. Put him on the Muslim side.

(KLAUS helps PETER carry NOOR's body off toward the morgue.)

PETER: Goodbye, Noor. Goodbye.

(Lights fade and the scrim is closed revealing a sunset across the image of Calcutta.)

ACT II
SCENE I

Behind the scrim, KALI dances in shadow, first wildly then ever more calm. As the scrim is opened, it is revealed to be MARGARET dancing for the MEN. She finishes as SISTER JANE sings alone in the chapel above.

SISTER JANE: *(Singing.)* Hear, oh Lord, the sound of my call.
Hear, oh Lord, and have mercy.
My soul is longing for the glory of You.
Hear, oh Lord, and answer me.

(KLAUS dispenses medicine with BRIGID's help, but cannot figure out which patient's chart goes with who. NOVICES change dressings and mop the floor. SISTER MARK

and MARINA examine PATIENTS. PHILIP prays over them. SISTER JANE leaves the chapel and makes her way to Kalighat. SISTER ALPHONSE feeds MAN whose IV had been removed.)

SISTER ALPHONSE: Two weeks ago he was so sick and now look, he is eating so well.

SISTER MARK: How is his fever today? *Kaemon acho?*

PATIENT: *Bhalo. Amake arekta mas dao.*

SISTER ALPHONSE: More fish? Already you have had two pieces.

SISTER MARK: Give him the fish, Sister. A small miracle perhaps, huh Marina?

MARINA: Beyond me.

(SYDNEY enters from the women's ward.)

SISTER MARK: Sydney? Come dear. Are you all right?

SYDNEY: Yes, I'm okay, Sister.

SISTER MARK: Really? I don't usually do this, but since she had no family— here, Rena was wearing this when she came to us. It's very small, but I think she'd want you to have it. I know you loved her very much.

(SISTER MARK gives SYDNEY a bangle.)

SYDNEY: Thank you, Sister.

(SISTER MARK touches SYDNEY's head and cheek, then exits.)

SYDNEY: It just never occurred to me that she might die when I wasn't there.

KLAUS: Who?

BRIGID: Rena.

SYDNEY: I just wanted to…be there… to hold her hand, that's all.

KLAUS: You give her your love. It goes with her still.

SYDNEY: Yeah. Okay, tablet time. What's next?

KLAUS: Oh, I don't know, I think maybe 36? Where is Peter today?

SYDNEY: Who knows. Probably out "dancing" all night.

BRIGID: No, he had a fever last night. Went to bed early. Should have checked on him this morning.

KLAUS: Number 28?

(SISTER MARK enters.)

SYDNEY: No, I think he's number 26.

KLAUS: *(To SISTER MARK.)* Sister, Sister! It is impossible. I don't know who is who, I don't know which medicine to give. It's terrible. I make so many mistakes…

SISTER MARK: What is the problem, brother?

KLAUS: This book. Sister Alphonse move all the patients again, now I don't know who is who!

SISTER MARK: Brother, relax, huh? Give me the book.

(She takes the pages out of the book, tosses them on the floor, and spreads them out with her foot while she looks around the room taking note of which PATIENT is where. She pulls a pencil from her sari, hands it to KLAUS and begins pointing to the various pieces of paper.)

SISTER MARK: Write. This is seven, ten, twelve, three, fourteen, one, six, two, no, this is two, this is where? Yes, eight. *Char, panch*—four and five. Thirteen, here. Nine and eleven. Other problems?

KLAUS: No, Sister. Thank you, Sister.

(SISTER JANE enters.)

SISTER JANE: Sister! Sister Mark! Quickly. Peter, with a man. So much blood he is coughing!

(PETER enters carrying a MAN who is covered in blood.)

SISTER MARK: Sister, go. Wet some rags to clean him up. Margaret!? *(To MAN.)* Oh, stop putting on such a show now. Look at the mess you are making.

MARGARET: Yes, Sister?

SISTER MARK: Run down the street and buy some ice. Quickly! Get money from Sister Alphonse.

(KLAUS brings a basin. BRIGID helps him clean the blood from MAN, then carries the soiled rags away. SISTER JANE takes KLAUS's place with the medicine. PHILIP goes to PATIENT and places his hands on his head. Covered in blood, PETER stands watching as the OTHERS care for him.)

SISTER JANE: Number 24. Number 23.

MARGARET: Twenty rupees! Twenty rupees! Twenty rupees!

SISTER ALPHONSE: I will not give you twenty rupees. You take five.

SISTER MARK: Give her the money, Sister. No time for bargaining. Hurry, Margaret. *(To MARINA.)* The ice will ease the coughing.

SISTER ALPHONSE: You are a thief, Margaret.

MARGARET: Pray for me, Sister. *(Exits.)*

SISTER ALPHONSE: Thief! I will not pray for you! Yes, yes, I will. Forgive me, dear Lord. I will pray for Margaret.

SYDNEY: *(To PETER.)* Come in back and I'll help you get cleaned up.

PETER: No.

SYDNEY: Peter, you're covered in blood!

PETER: No!

KLAUS: *(To SISTER MARK.)* There is nothing more we can do?

SISTER MARK: No. Just what you are doing, brother. That's all that can be done.

SISTER JANE: Number 26.

BRIGID: Number 26.

SYDNEY: Oh God, Brigid, how can it be so hot.

SISTER JANE: Number 27.

SISTER MARK: So much suffering. So close to Jesus he is.

SISTER JANE: And this.

(SISTER MARK holds MAN's eyes open as he continues coughing.)

SISTER MARK: I envy him that. Hindu or Muslim? Hindu or Muslim?

PHILIP: What about Christian, Sister? Couldn't he be a Christian?

SISTER MARK: Not by the looks of him. Hindu or Muslim?

PHILIP: Well then, perhaps it's not too late?

SISTER MARK: I'm afraid it is very late, brother.

SISTER MARK: Hindu or Muslim? *(To PATIENTS.)* Any of you know this man? Have you seen him before?

(No response. She looks in his pants.)

SISTER MARK: Ah, Hindu.

MARGARET: Ice, Sister. Here is your ice.

SISTER JANE: Number 28.

SISTER MARK: Spread it out on his chest.

(KLAUS spreads the ice on MAN's chest. The coughing begins to subside, and MAN relaxes a bit.)

SISTER ALPHONSE: Margaret! That little bit of ice couldn't have cost more than five rupees. Give me the change.

MARGARET: No change.

SISTER ALPHONSE: Give me the change.

MARGARET: You are calling me a liar?

SISTER ALPHONSE: God will get even with you, Margaret, you wait.

MARGARET: And maybe someday I will get even too, Sister, huh? *(Exits.)*

SISTER MARK: Give me those rags, I will burn them. No telling what his blood is infected with. *(Exits.)*

SISTER JANE: Number 33.

PHILIP: Oh Lord, if I can't save his soul, then You must let me heal his body.

(PETER faints. Everyone rushes to him.)

SYDNEY: Peter!

SISTER JANE: Oh my word. He's fainted, he's fainted! Go, get some water! Sister! Sister Mark!

BRIGID: Just can't give up the limelight for a minute, can you.

(PETER starts to come to. SYDNEY gives him some water.)

SYDNEY: Hey, you okay?

PETER: Huh, who...

MARINA: Oh, he's ice cold.

PETER: Where's... No, no. I'm fine. Don't. I'm fine.

BRIGID: Well, he's gettin' a little color back. Paler than death you were. I thought'cha was a gonner.

(SISTER JANE and BRIGID return to the medicine. MARINA joins KLAUS and PHILIP with the sick MAN. SYDNEY stays with PETER. SISTER MARK returns, feels PETER's forehead.)

SISTER MARK: You've had a fever, haven't you?

PETER: Yeah, I guess.

SISTER MARK: You know you shouldn't be here if you're sick.

PETER: Dr. Jack told me about this man and asked if I'd bring him in.

SISTER MARK: Dr. Jack? We don't usually accept Dr. Jack's patients. You shouldn't come if you are sick.

(She sits next to NEW PATIENT and takes his pulse.)

SISTER MARK: *(To PHILIP.)* Put him on the Hindu side.

PHILIP: But, but I feel a pulse…here.

SISTER MARK: It's your own pulse, brother. He is at peace. Now, I want you to take Peter home.

PHILIP: Just a little more time?

SISTER MARK: Klaus, go back to the medicine now. *(Exits.)*

KLAUS: You must let go, Philip. *(To SISTER JANE.)* I will finish the medicine, Sister.

SISTER JANE: No, it's all right, Klaus.

KLAUS: Sister Mark says I should finish the medicine.

(She gets up; KLAUS takes her place. SISTER MARK enters with a blanket and a

white shroud. She wraps the blanket around PETER, then with PHILIP still praying at his head, she kneels next to PATIENT, puts her head to his chest and listens.)*

SISTER MARK: Philip…Philip. There is no heartbeat. We must leave him to his rest. Please, come now.

PHILIP: No, just a little longer, just a… please.

SISTER MARK: Philip, our hearts break for the loss of our brothers, yes. But if we cannot accept their pain we stay separate from them, and separate from Jesus.

KLAUS: Number 33.

SISTER MARK: You cannot judge the will of God if you wish to grow in love for Him. Go now, see that Peter gets home safely.

(PHILIP lets go of MAN, stands and looks at PETER.)

PETER: We're taking a taxi.

(PHILIP turns and leaves as PETER follows. SISTERS begin singing.)

SYDNEY: You'll be okay? Should I come? You want me to bring you anything?

PETER: No, I'll be fine.

(PETER looks back at MAN, then leaves. NOVICES wrap his body in its shroud.)

SISTER MARK: Put him on the Hindu side.

KLAUS: Number 24.

SISTERS: *(Singing.)* Make me a channel of Your peace. Where there is hatred let me bring Your love. Where there is injury, Your pardon, Lord, and where there's doubt true faith in You. Make me a channel of Your peace. It is in pardoning that we are pardoned, in giving to all men that we receive, and in dying that we're born to eternal life.

(Lights fade.)

SCENE II

In the shadows, work continues at Kalighat. PETER enters his room at the Modern Lodge. PHILIP stands silently at PETER's door.

PETER: Oh, God, I'm dying. Someone's doing a voodoo dance on my stomach. Turn the fan on, huh?

(PETER undresses. PHILIP turns on the light. PETER shields his eyes.)

PETER: Oh, no, mother, make it stop!

(PHILIP turns off the light and turns on the ceiling fan.)

PETER: Open the shutter. Give me that water bottle...

PHILIP: Empty.

(PHILIP opens the blind, letting the moonlight in. PETER, dressed only in his shorts, stands woozily next to the bed.)

PETER: Shit. Hand me that *lunghi*, will ya?

PHILIP: I don't... what's happening?

PETER: Hey, the *lunghi*! What's the matter?

PHILIP: I'm...I don't understand.

PETER: *Lunghi, lunghi*! That piece of cloth on the chair!

PHILIP: No! I mean...

(PHILIP holds the lunghi *tightly in his hands and stands close to PETER.)*

PHILIP: Do you pray, Peter?

PETER: Um. Not intentionally.

PHILIP: I study the Bible, and sometimes I pray so hard my hands go numb. But, I

watch you, at Kalighat or with the children. You touch them, and they are full of life. That doesn't happen to me.

PETER: Well, you're so, sort of, rigid, Philip. You just gotta lighten up, you know, be yourself.

PHILIP: I made a promise, to the Lord. And I kept it. But He didn't... I don't understand.

PETER: I think I'd better sit down for this.

PHILIP: He tests me, you see? All my life, again and again. They come to me, demons. Men. You understand? I think you do. I try to turn away, to follow Him. I promised Him...

PETER: Promised what?

PHILIP: ...listened for His word and followed it. But evil speaks louder. I failed Him somehow, or He'd take it away.

PETER: Take what away?

(PHILIP reaches out and caresses PETER's face.)

PETER: Oh, I see. I'm not evil, Philip.

PHILIP: I see men, in my mind. I try to push them away so Jesus can come to me. I pray, I promise Him I'll resist, and if I overcome, I will be a healer like Him.

PETER: You are who you are, Philip. You can't change it.

PHILIP: He puts temptation in my path again and again. I thought I'd learned to hate their images, but then... how can I hate you, when all I want is to love you. And so I'm left with just me to hate.

PETER: Don't do that to yourself...

PHILIP: It's true. You're right. I am... and I can't fight anymore.

PETER: Finding the truth is not losing the battle.

PHILIP: Between eternal life and damnation? If I give in to desire, I lose the love of Christ.

PETER: If you believe you are from Him, of Him, how can you question His love for you? Shhh. Listen, "Simon Peter, turning about, seeth the disciple whom Jesus loved following: which also leaned on his breast at supper." John 21. Twelve years of Catholic school, that's what I remember. Tell me, Philip, what was different about Jesus' love for John than His love for His other disciples?

(PHILIP kisses PETER. At Kalighat, LUKE begins singing a Bengali song as the NUNS and other VOLUNTEERS close up and exit.)

PETER: Gee, I've never been kissed by anyone while suffering from dysentery before.

(PHILIP turns and hides his head.)

PETER: Don't run, Philip. Have you studied the Old Testament too?

(As PETER recites, he removes PHILIP's clothes. PHILIP reciprocates.)

PETER: First Samuel 18: "The soul of Jonathan was knit with the soul of David, and Jonathan loved him as his own soul. And Jonathan stripped himself of the robe that was upon him, and gave it to David, and his garments, even to his sword, and to his bow, and to his belt..." 20:41 "...and they kissed one another, and wept one with another, until David exceeded."

PHILIP: ...42, "And Jonathan said to David, the Lord be between me and thee, and between my seed and thy seed forever."

(Naked, they kiss again and lie down together. As the NUNS leave Kalighat and cross toward the Mother House, they sing.)

SISTERS: *(Singing.)* One bread, one body, one Lord of all,
One cup of blessing which we bless.
And we, though many throughout the earth,
We are one body in this one Lord.

(SYDNEY calls from offstage, then comes charging into PETER's room.)

SYDNEY: Peter, you here? Are you all right? You make it back okay? I brought some...oh, oh my God...

(PHILIP falls out of PETER's bed and starts grabbing for his clothes.)

SYDNEY: I...I...I'm sorry, no, don't stop, I mean, I really am. I didn't think... I didn't know...

(Hiding his face, PHILIP runs out of the room. PETER wraps the lunghi around himself and starts after him.)

PETER: Philip...Philip? *(To SYDNEY.)* Knocking is usually in order.

SYDNEY: Yes, but I never...well, obviously I shouldn't have worried. Bastard!

PETER: What?

SYDNEY: Pretending to be sick so you can...

PETER: I am sick...

SYDNEY: ...seduce the confused little Brit...

PETER: ...me? What do you know about...

SYDNEY: I have eyes.

(She shakes out the blanket on the bed and throws it on the floor.)

SYDNEY: I don't see any condoms either. Regular poster boy for responsible behavior, aren't you?

PETER: Like we could get that far before you blew in doing your little dance of repression...

SYDNEY: And what about your little dance, huh?...

PETER: ...so afraid of sex...

SYDNEY: ...obsession, that's your dance...

PETER: ...you're going to run away and be a nun.

SYDNEY: It is not running away. It is a choice I am making, trying to make... and I am not afraid of sex.

PETER: Yeah? So why does it upset you when I have it?

SYDNEY: Ah, your health for one.

PETER: I have done nothing to compromise anyone's health. So, cut the crap...

SYDNEY: It is not...

PETER: ...you don't like it because...

SYDNEY: ...why do I even bother?

PETER: ...when I have sex with another man it isn't in marriage.

SYDNEY: Well, it is about procreation...

PETER: Yup, there it is!

SYDNEY: ...that is what it's for.

PETER: So don't give me this crock about caring about my health...

SYDNEY: It's not just your...

PETER: ...and hide behind your pseudo-liberal attitudes.

SYDNEY: I'm a Catholic! Why does it surprise you that I believe things Catholics believe?

PETER: Hypocrite.

SYDNEY: I am not... How dare you?

PETER: No? Well tell me then, how is it that you Catholics see it as just fine to teach natural family planning, huh?

SYDNEY: What are you...?

PETER: Sex without procreation, isn't that what that is?

SYDNEY: It's... forget it. I don't owe you any explanations. Here. *(She throws a small box at him.)* I brought you some Bengali sweets. Bengalis are famous for their sweets.

(She heads toward the door just as MARINA enters.)

MARINA: Sydney, get some water. *(She feels his forehead.)* You look like you'll drop dead any moment. Sydney, turn on the light. Your stomach?

PETER: Yes.

SYDNEY: My ass.

MARINA: Eyes? Not yellow. Bit of a fever though. What have you been eating?

SYDNEY: More like "who."

PETER: I don't remember. Whatever it was is long gone now.

(The lights go out. SYDNEY and PETER speak simultaneously.)

SYDNEY: Loadshedding.

PETER: Damn! Oh no, the fan's stopping too.

MARINA: Sydney, get some candles.

SYDNEY: Yes, yes. God forbid he should have to sit in the dark. *(Exits.)*

MARINA: What's upset her?

PETER: India, I guess. Just a little too hot for her.

MARINA: Getting to all of us, isn't it? You taking chloroquine or fanzidar for malaria? You have to take fanzidar in Bengal.

PETER: Whatever's there.

MARINA: Chloroquine. We'll get you some fanzidar tomorrow.

(BRIGID and KLAUS enter. SISTERS light candles in the chapel, and MARGARET lights a few at Kalighat.)

BRIGID: Marina?

MARINA: In here! *(To PETER.)* I sent them out for water. You don't want to get dehydrated, you know.

PETER: I know.

BRIGID: What's with Philip? He nearly knocked me down going out the door with his suitcase in tow.

PETER: Suitcase? Shit. I gotta go after him.

MARINA: You'll stay right where you are.

BRIGID: Next time will ya have the decency to tell us you're sick so we don't worry ourselves to death? You might've been hit by a bus, for all we knew.

KLAUS: Here is water, and, yes, also some bread and peanut butter. You like peanut butter, yes?

PETER: Well, usually, but… *(Indicates his stomach.)*

KLAUS: Oh, of course.

BRIGID: Few pastries, too. Made a detour to Flurries. Let's see, there's banana

and honey, ooh nice and runny, that one. Here's one with this gooey mango stuff, or would you rather have the melty chocolate?

PETER: No, really, I couldn't.

BRIGID: Oh, go ahead. It's no trouble.

PETER: No, really! I couldn't.

(SYDNEY enters.)

SYDNEY: Candles.

MARINA: Wonderful. Let me see that mango one. Oh, that looks nice.

BRIGID: Help yourself. Klaus?

KLAUS: Ah, the chocolate, maybe.

BRIGID: Pastry, Syd?

SYDNEY: No, thanks. Hey, is that peanut butter? I haven't had peanut butter in, I don't know how long.

KLAUS: I will make for you. Knife?

PETER: Top drawer.

(MARINA hands PETER a glass.)

MARINA: Here, I mixed some of this powder stuff in your water. It replaces the electrolytes…

PETER: Yuch!

MARINA: …when you have excessive diarrhea. Bad?

PETER: You trying to kill me?

KLAUS: It make me sick too, when I tried.

PETER: Horrible! Quick, gimme the bottle to wash it down. Ah, Boy, yich. So, you guys go to the children's home this morning?

KLAUS: Yaa.

SYDNEY: Pity you were too ill to make it.

PETER: How were they?

SYDNEY: Neerman asked for you.

BRIGID: Ricoh threw up a tapeworm the size of a king cobra at least. There it was, swimmin' around in a puddle of vomit.

PETER: Thanks, Bridge. I was nearly feeling better there for a moment.

MARINA: Sydney, remind me to stop at the chemist's tomorrow. He's been taking the wrong malaria pills. I'm afraid what he may have picked up.

SYDNEY: Oh, he'll pick up anything.

PETER: Sydney!

BRIGID: I know someone who got hepatitis from fanzidar.

MARINA: Oh, that's ridiculous.

BRIGID: I should say it is.

KLAUS: Peanut butter.

SYDNEY: Thanks. You think he has malaria? I mean, what if it is something else?

PETER: I don't have malaria, and…

MARINA: Probably just an amoeba. If the fever gets worse, we'll take him to the hospital.

PETER: Hospital? Don't I have anything to say about this?

MARINA: No, dear. Is there another mango one?

BRIGID: Sure, here. *Ras gula*, Syd?

SYDNEY: Is that the fried syrupy one or the sticky balls soaked in honey?

PETER: Oh, enough with the food, already!

KLAUS: Oh, I am not thinking…

BRIGID: Sorry.

PETER: Christ! I feel like I'm in some bizarre Pasolini version of the Last Supper.

SYDNEY: Can I be Judas?

MARINA: …We'll go.

PETER: No, no. Stay, it's just the food, my stomach.

KLAUS: You're sure?

PETER: Yeah, I'm enjoying it. Kind of romantic, candles and everything. But what happens tomorrow?

BRIGID: I was at the Last Supper.

MARINA: Brigid, you've been hanging around with too many Hindus.

BRIGID: I don't mean the first Last Supper, I mean a re-creation of it.

KLAUS: A mass?

BRIGID: No, no. There was no hoopla at all.

KLAUS: Then what was it?

BRIGID: Well, it was up north of Patna. You know, where I was in hospital?

SYDNEY: With the goat under your bed.

MARINA: There was a goat under your bed?

PETER: Don't ask, please!

BRIGID: I was going to work in a leprosy village run by some boys who used to be in Mother Teresa's order. Left and went out on their own. I remember the first day, walking into that courtyard. Filled with roses, it was. Every color and such a sweet smell. White mud houses, with thatched roofs just like at home. Out of every door came these smiling faces, running to me, laughing. Some had no arms or were missing fingers or were using crutches. Their skin was scarred and their faces deformed. 'Course, they spoke hardly a word of English, you know, being from the villages. But that didn't stop me, no. I managed to carry on quite a conversation. Took me to see the fields and workshops. All self-sufficient. Beautiful weavings they sell. Very proud of that, they are. Finally we make it to the center building of the village. Inside, a meal is being prepared. The oldest brother reads from the Gita, then the Koran. Then he asked me to read from the Bible. We sat quietly for a bit, and then we ate together, a fine meal. And I thought to myself, this is the Last Supper. People from all over, coming together, trying to help each other through another day, not knowin' what tomorrow will bring. My very first Last Supper.

KLAUS: It's a beautiful story.

MARINA: It is? Why did the brothers leave Mother Teresa, Brigid?

BRIGID: Frustrated, I suppose… Guess they wanted to make things better for people, 'stead of just makin' 'em comfortable in their suffering. They weren't so concerned about getting to heaven themselves as they were in takin' away a little bit of the hell on earth.

MARINA: Well, I understand their frustration. Here we are, reusing needles. No pain meds. Is there really no money? I don't believe it. It's wrong, that's all. It's terribly terribly wrong.

SYDNEY: C'mon Marina, you can't impose your experience. It's a poor country. It's different here.

MARINA: That's no excuse. You suppose they act differently in Rome or New York, these nuns?

BRIGID: Well what business is it of yours if they don't? Least they're doing something.

MARINA: Perpetuating poverty and…

BRIGID: Perpetuating what you and your British lot left half the world to.

MARINA: Oh, visiting the sins of the father now, are we? I had nothing to do with colonialism. I loathe everything about it.

BRIGID: So you thought you'd introduce a little divide and conquer into a convent this time around?

MARINA: Just what is it you're holding me responsible for? You and your religious superstitions do more to divide than colonialism could ever hope to.

BRIGID: Oh, sure, religion gave you all a nice little guide to draw your lines.

BRIGID: Protestants to the north, Catholics to the south. Muslims to the east, Hindus to the west. And all the riches for the crown! Oh, you'll be living off your thieving for a thousand years.

MARINA: Oh, what in the hell nonsense are you talking now? Riches? Britain's a mess! You're all alike, you Irish…

KLAUS: Stop now. I don't want to hear anymore. Fighting? Go back to where you come from to do that. Go drag yourself to the middle age, I don't care. But don't do it here, don't make me listen.

MARINA: Sorry, Klaus.

BRIGID: Oh, fine thing for the German to tell us not to fight…

SYDNEY: Brigid!

KLAUS: Yes, yes. It is a fine thing for the German to tell you. I want we should go on, Brigid. I want we should change. No? You see every day, hungry people, no medicine, children. If once we were apes, now we are worse animal. The same hates for hundreds of years? The same blame? For what? Huh? For what? Useless.

SYDNEY: You're right.

KLAUS: They teach to me evolution, you know? And I believe it to be true. But now maybe no. There is no logic to explain that we cannot evolve beyond an animal that destroys itself. Is this why you come here?

BRIGID: No.

MARINA: No.

SYDNEY: I thought I knew exactly why I was coming here. Now, I'm just confused.

KLAUS: Ah, we none of us know. Really. I come. I expect to find ideal poverty, ideal suffering. Very silly, but true, no? Needy people waiting for me and I will give them comfort. Such arrogance, huh? I never knew I had.

BRIGID: But you do give them comfort. That's something, isn't it? Doing your bit. At least you're not making things worse.

MARINA: What makes you so sure? We don't even speak their language.

KLAUS: Maybe we do our bit, maybe not. I don't know. But I know when I go home I must remember that it is a real human being, real hunger, real pain I have seen. And I think I must do something every day, there at home. Instead to make the myth of the suffering, this is terrible. And when we make the saints out of human beings, we give ourselves just an excuse to stand away from what is our responsibility.

MARINA: Well, I promised Sister Mark I'd stick it out at Kalighat for another few weeks. But there must be something better. I might spend some time at the Rama Krishna Mission. I've heard they do good work. Or there's a Jain nun who runs some houses up in Bihar. Meanwhile, to bed. Ah, shall I wake you for Howrah in the morning, Bridge?

BRIGID: Well, now, that would be nice for a change. You shower first and I'll have a cup of tea waiting for you.

MARINA: Goodnight.

SYDNEY: Bridge, can I leave some stuff with you? I've decided I need to go away for a while. Maybe spend some time up north, out of the heat. I wanna travel light.

BRIGID: Sure, just drop it off in the morning.

(KLAUS, BRIGID, and MARINA exit. PETER starts to get dressed.)

SYDNEY: Where are you going?

PETER: Philip. I'm going to look for him.

SYDNEY: Where?

PETER: I never should have let him go.

SYDNEY: Peter, it's late. You can't...

PETER: I can.

SYDNEY: He doesn't need you.

PETER: What?

SYDNEY: I just think he'll be better off without you chasing after him.

PETER: You'd think it'd be a blessing if he threw himself in the river.

SYDNEY: That's not true.

PETER: No? Well, what is then, huh, Sydney? What is true?

(He exits. SYDNEY blows out the candles as NUNS begin singing.)

SISTERS: *(Singing.)* You satisfy the hungry heart with gift of finest wheat;
    Come, give to us, O saving Lord, the
    bread of life to eat.
    You give Yourself to us, O Lord, then
    selfless let us be,
    To serve each other in Your name, in
    truth and charity.

*("I Wish That It Would Rain," by the Temp-
tations, plays.)*

SCENE III

*Two weeks later at Kalighat. We hear the voice
of Lata Mangeshkar. Outside, it is pouring rain.
There is thunder and lightning. On the blackboard is written "The fruit of silence is prayer,
the fruit of prayer is faith, the fruit of faith is
love, the fruit of love is service, the fruit of service is peace. M. Teresa." KLAUS is working
on the medicine. PETER sits with RAM. LUKE
is teaching SISTER ALPHONSE a Takhore
song about* borsha, *the rainy season.*

SISTER ALPHONSE: Ha! You see, he is
the best Bengali teacher I have ever had.

*(She gives LUKE a hug and goes off singing
and laughing.)*

RAM: Finally the rains have come. They
bring change, new life.

PETER: They bring floods and pestilence.

RAM: So, we take the good with the bad.

PETER: I had to wade through water
waist deep to get home last night.

RAM: Sometimes it is better to take shelter and wait for the dangers of the storm
to pass.

PETER: You're a regular talking self-help
book, aren't you?

RAM: Ah, you are a young cynic, Peter,
like my son. Yet, he gave his life trying to
make our home free. A safe place for his
sister, for his mother. A place he imag-
ined. A place I will never see.

PETER: Don't you feel angry, Ram? Knowing you'll never see the ones you love again?

RAM: Sometimes. Sometimes just alone.
But life gives us a continuous lesson. And
so I learn.

PETER: I seem to keep walking away
from those lessons.

RAM: You can't walk that far. They'll keep
coming back until you're ready to meet
them. Think, Peter. Where has your life
led you? You are here, in the place of Kali.

*(There is thunder. The lights go out. Behind
RAM appears the goddess KALI. She stamps
out a slow rhythm in time to RAM's speech.)*

RAM: What does she offer you? See her,
clothed only in the darkness of night.
Mother Kali, making her home in the cremation grounds. Her hair, disheveled and
free, her necklace of ten skulls carries all
the sounds of the universe. Her right hand
makes the sign, "fear not," as her horrible
image forces our fear, strips us of pretense,
opens our way to cosmic truth. She dances
as Chinnamasta.

*(CHINNAMASTA appears from behind
KALI and takes up her dance.)*

RAM: She drinks of the river of blood
flowing from her own body. Her three-
eyed head she carries in her hand, she steps
forward to battle seeking to quench her
lust. She dances as Sodasi.

*(SODASI appears from behind KALI and
takes up her dance.)*

RAM: Red-faced, a mere youth of sixteen,
yet she is the seductress of God. Taking
him, loving him.

(The rhythm of the dance begins to speed up.)

RAM: United, three sides of the *yoni*, they make; the *desamahavidyas* with their seven sisters. Together as Kali Ma, her dance is unrestrained, fed by the vapors of the dead, the cremation ground her stage, she is growth, decay, death, and rebirth. Mother who destroys as she is mother who nurtures. Untameable, unpurifiable, unpredictable. She is the power of time which devours all. Overcoming the universe as she copulates with divinity. Beyond good and evil, she beckons to us, oh daughter of Himalaya. Listen to the songs of Kali as she dances her terrible dance.

(The dance becomes ever wilder.)

RAM: "When worlds collide
explode and shatter
Like bolts of thunder their clamor
provides the beat for your dance.
When in that awesome void
blood-oozing demons
sport and sing aloud
the gleeful refrain of their song
the unceasing beat of their verses
echo the thud of your footsteps.
O Sodasi, Chinnamasta, Kali Ma,
your dance is a dance of ecstasy.
Mother, O Mother,
lured helplessly
I watch your rapturous dance.
 When time and the immemorial worlds
    have been laid to waste,
In that lone silence there arises a brilliance,
    the brilliance of Shiva.
Your smouldering anger fades—In fond
    caress his hand you hold
and you begin again to dance your dance
    of bliss.
Mother, O Mother, indeed you have lured
    me to watch your rapturous dance."

Jai Ma, Jai Ma! Jai Kali, Jai Ma Bhavatarini!
    Ma! Ma! Kali Ma!

"Oh, One who helps the soul cross over,
forgiving One, end our fear!
Pick me up like a baby in Your arms.
Come shining like a star,
with a smiling face
and in fair dress, like the dawn
after a pitch-black night!
All these days, O Terrible Kali,
I've worshiped only you.
My puja is done, Mother.
Won't you put down your sword?"

(KALI, CHINNAMASTA, and SODASI disappear, and the lights return.)

RAM: Beauty, horror. Love, hate. Birth, death. Life is a cycle of contradictions, truths spoken, questions unanswered. From the moment we enter into this life, there is but one thing that is certain, Peter. And that is Mother. You understand? Follow her lead. Go now. I must take rest.

(PETER wraps RAM's blanket around him, fixes his pillow, and leaves.)

SYDNEY: Peter?

PETER: Sydney. You're back.

SYDNEY: Actually, I've been back a couple of days. I've been staying at the Mother House.

PETER: Oh?

SYDNEY: Tell me, did you find Philip?

PETER: No. I was out all night and the whole next day. Went to both train stations. I even went to churches. No sign of him.

SYDNEY: Did you go to the police?

PETER: Yeah, I did. They took a report, said they'd call if they found anything. I'm not expecting much.

SYDNEY: Look, about what I said that night... I know you care about him. I'm worried too. I'm worried about the both of you.

PETER: Yeah, well, I said some things too. I'm sorry. I didn't know Rena had died that morning.

SYDNEY: I miss her. It doesn't seem the same, coming here and not seeing her.

PETER: Is that why you went away?

SYDNEY: Maybe. Partially.

PETER: It scares me. Getting close to people, thinking of losing them. So where have you been for the past couple of weeks? I missed you.

SYDNEY: Really? I took a train up to Darjeeling, where Mother got her calling. Guess I thought if it could happen to her, it could happen to me.

PETER: Yikes!

SYDNEY: You should go. So beautiful. Surrounded by the white cliffs of the Himalayas. Watch the sunrise over Mount Everest. I'd go for walks through the hillside tea plantations. All by myself, so quiet, for hours each day just walking, praying, listening. Trying to hear something, you know? Some answer. Can I do this work forever? Do I have the strength? But I didn't hear anything. No mystical voice. One day I just sat down on a rock, looked down the mountain into the river running through the valley and cried. I don't know how long I was there, just lost track. Suddenly it got very dark and began to pour down, sheets. So much rain I couldn't see in front of me. I tried to run, but the mud started washing away from under my feet, so I grabbed onto a tree. I was drenched and so scared I'd fall down. It only lasted a few minutes, then it turned into a very gentle rain. I looked out across the mountains, the clouds separated and

the sun began to shine through, and a rainbow appeared across the entire valley. My heart was beating and I stared out over that loveliness and that question was just spinning around in my head. And it dawned on me, suddenly it made so much sense. The voice I was trying to hear was the question itself. It had been there all the time. And I knew the only way to answer it was to try.

PETER: So, you're going to…?

SYDNEY: Six months as an aspirant, a year as a postulate, then I enter the novitiate. It'll be seven years before I take my final vows.

PETER: Why, Sydney? Why the Missionaries of Charity? You could be anything. A doctor, a social worker.

SYDNEY: I know, I know.

PETER: They don't even let you read books.

SYDNEY: I can't really explain. It isn't like a choice I'm making, Peter. It's just a path I'm following. It's in my heart.

PETER: But…

SYDNEY: All right, so I've got a million anxieties about it. I'm terrified but I'm full of joy too. I know it's right. It's who I am, Peter. I can't be anything else. And now that I understand that, maybe I understand you a little bit better too. And I ask for your blessing.

PETER: I'll miss you.

(SYDNEY takes PETER's hand and they kiss. MARGARET enters. BRIGID, MARINA, and SISTER JANE follow.)

MARGARET: Oh, my God! Stop now! Sister Mark! If she sees, so much trouble you don't know.

BRIGID: My, my, you do like your life on the edge, don't you.

(SISTER MARK enters.)

SISTER MARK: Come now. Say your goodbyes. The ambulance will be here soon. You too, Sister Jane. *(She exits.)*

SYDNEY: Klaus? Here, I want you to have my *Lonely Planet* guide. It's pretty beat up, but it's still the best. Marina? These earrings looked better on you anyway.

MARINA: *(To SYDNEY.)* You know you don't have to stay. You can leave anytime you want.

SYDNEY: Bridge, my camera.

BRIGID: Oh, no. I couldn't.

SYDNEY: No. I want you to have it. Peter? You know, that was the first time I ever kissed a boy. I think I can live without that. Here. I don't suppose it'll mean anything to you, but this is the rosary I got from Mother Teresa. It means something to me.

PETER: I'll keep it always.

SYDNEY: Margaret? Here, go get your hair done.

(She hands MARGARET fifty rupees.)

MARGARET: Oh, thank you, sister. You have true charity in your heart.

BRIGID: Okay, everybody push together.

(BRIGID has handed the camera to a PATIENT, who takes a picture of SYDNEY, MARINA, PETER, KLAUS, BRIGID, and MARGARET.)

BRIGID: I'll send you all a copy. Now come, say goodbye to the women.

(BRIGID, MARINA, MARGARET, and SYDNEY exit to the women's ward. PETER stands between KLAUS and SISTER JANE.)

KLAUS: Ah, Peter. Shouldn't you go upstairs and get some blankets?

PETER: Huh? Oh, yeah. Sorry. *(Exits.)*

SISTER JANE: Oh, I am so glad. I need... want to talk to you.

KLAUS: What is it, Sister?

SISTER JANE: Last night Mother told me that I am to go away from here. Tonight I will leave for Africa, to work in one of our houses there.

KLAUS: Oh, well, that's wonderful, Sister. You must be very excited.

SISTER JANE: Yes, very excited. No. Last night I could not sleep. I cried all night long because I know I will not be seeing you anymore.

KLAUS: Oh, don't say this, Sister. This is...

SISTER JANE: Yes, I know. It is shameful. But these are my feelings. And I think Mother must have known. That is why it is for the best that I go now. I am sorry, brother. I wanted you to remember me. I wanted to give you something, but I have nothing. So this morning before mass, I went to the kitchen and I made these for you. It is not so special like Sydney's gift.

(She takes some small paper cutouts from the folds of her sari. They are of a sheep and a bird.)

SISTER JANE: This is the lamb of God, and this is the Holy Spirit. I have written my name on the back in English and in Malayalam, my native language. Please, remember me, brother. Please, remember me, Klaus.

KLAUS: I will, Sister Jane. I will remember you always.

(She touches her forehead to KLAUS's hand and exits. PETER enters with an armload of blankets.)

PETER: Here, Klaus. Give me a hand with these. Hey, you okay?

KLAUS: Yah, yah. I am okay.

(He takes the blankets and gives them out to the MEN. A huge black umbrella appears at the door. PHILIP peeks out over it.)

PHILIP: Pssst! Peter!

PETER: Who…? Philip? Where the hell…? I've been worried sick about you.

PHILIP: Sorry. I didn't mean to worry you. I'm fine though. Really, never better. *(He closes the umbrella, revealing himself dressed in a saffron-colored dhoti and kurta with a turban on his head.)*

PETER: Philip, why are you dressed like that?

PHILIP: Oh, I threw my suitcase in the river that night I ran off. Wanted to throw myself in too. I had nothing but the clothes on my back. I've been staying with a family of *hijras* in Park Circus. They gave me these.

PETER: *Hijras?*

PHILIP: Eunuchs. Well, most of them anyway. They dress as women, and, well, they can be a little crude, but they've been very kind to me. They found me curled up under a tree in the park, took me back to their home, fed me, gave me a place to sleep. Made me feel like a real human being. They're such outcasts, but they take such good care of each other. And they took me in just like I was one of their family. Never believed I'd be accepted anywhere before, being who I am. Anyway, there's this man who comes to the *hijra's* house every couple of days. I'm not sure, but I think he comes for sex. Well, he's taking me to Kerala tonight for the Pilgrimage of Sabarimalai to the shrine of

the boy god Ayyappa, born from the liaison of two male gods. Get it? The shrine is up in the mountains and the whole thing lasts a month. Women aren't allowed—it's all men. I'm told it's a very hot time.

PETER: Philip! Don't you think you might be going a bit overboard? I mean, eunuchs, mountain-top orgies? You are kind of new to all of this, you know.

(SISTER ALPHONSE enters and lurks, unseen, in the corner.)

PHILIP: Oh, no. No no no. No sex for me. I'm saving myself for the right man. However, I am praying that he comes soon. I'm sorry I ran off on you like that. Wasn't very nice of me, I know. But I was afraid, and I… well, I needed to find my own way. But you helped me admit, see things the way they really are. How can I thank you for that? Here, this is my parents' address. I'll be headed back there after the pilgrimage. And I want you to have my tape player—my very last possession. Think of me when you listen to it. And, oh, here, this is some *prasad* from the Hare Krishna bakery. Karma-free baking for a conscious life.

(He gives PETER a kiss on the lips, then exits.)

SISTER ALPHONSE: Brother.

PETER: Huh?

SISTER ALPHONSE: Who was that man?

PETER: Oh, that was…

SISTER ALPHONSE: …And why was he kissing you?

PETER: Well, that was Philip, Sister.

SISTER ALPHONSE: Yes?

PETER: You remember Philip, don't you?

SISTER ALPHONSE: Yes. I remember Philip. Why was he dressed like that?

PETER: Well, see, he's been living with some... oh boy. He's going away...he's going on a pilgrimage.

SISTER ALPHONSE: A pilgrimage?

PETER: Yes. Somewhere in Kerala, I think he said.

SISTER ALPHONSE: Why was he kissing you?

PETER: Well, he was trying to... he was saying goodbye.

SISTER ALPHONSE: Goodbye?

PETER: Yeah, goodbye. And that's his way, I guess, 'cause, well, because...he's gay, Sister.

SISTER ALPHONSE: Gay?

PETER: Yeah.

SISTER ALPHONSE: What is this?

PETER: What is...?

SISTER ALPHONSE: What is this "gay"?

PETER: You don't...

SISTER ALPHONSE: No. I don't know this...gay.

PETER: Oh, well, you see, he ah, he likes boys.

SISTER ALPHONSE: Likes boys?

PETER: Yeah. He, ah, he doesn't want to get married...

SISTER: Married?

PETER: ...to a girl. He wants to be with a man.

SISTER ALPHONSE: A man?

PETER: Yes.

SISTER ALPHONSE: You mean—he's a homo?

PETER: That's it.

SISTER ALPHONSE: Aahh! I knew there was something peculiar about him.

PETER: Peculiar?

SISTER ALPHONSE: Yes. I could see it in his eyes.

PETER: Could you?

SISTER ALPHONSE: Oh, Yes. So strange. I don't understand this at all. Why does this happen in the West?

PETER: The West?

SISTER ALPHONSE: Yes.

PETER: You mean, you think it doesn't happen here?

SISTER ALPHONSE: In India? Don't be daft.

(*She exits. MARGARET points to the tape player.*)

MARGARET: Ah, brother. It's a very nice machine.

PETER: Hmm? Oh, yeah.

MARGARET: Listen, brother. My niece, you know, my niece?

PETER: What about her?

MARGARET: She is very sick now, brother. I need to buy her medicine. I need money. You will give me twenty rupees?

PETER: Margaret, I've seen Sydney give you money, and Brigid. I thought that was for medicine?

MARGARET: It is very expensive, this medicine. She needs more.

PETER: How do I know you're not lying?

MARGARET: Why? Would it make it a smaller gift if I were lying?

PETER: Sorry, Margaret. I don't believe you.

MARGARET: You are standing there and I am standing here, and you don't believe me. Then you keep your twenty rupees, brother, it is so dear to you. And I will keep my prayer that I never be given so much responsibility that I can sit in judgment of other people's needs.

PETER: C'mon, Margaret, gimme a break. Do you have any idea how many times each day I am hounded by beggars?

MARGARET: I am not a beggar, brother. Not until you make me one just now. *(Exits.)*

PETER: Margaret! I didn't…oh, Jesus.

(PETER turns on the tape player. It plays Marvin Gaye's "I Heard It Through the Grapevine.")

PETER: All right. Go Philip. Okay, who needs a blanket?

(He begins passing out blankets while dancing a bit. The MEN respond happily to the music. BRIGID enters.)

BRIGID: Hey, I need two of those for the women's side.

(She takes blankets and dances off toward the women's ward.)

BRIGID: *(Singing.)* "Took me by surprise, I must say, when I found out yesterday…"

(PETER jumps up onto the beds and dances there while singing along with the tape. His moves are reminiscent of the dance of KALI. SISTER MARK enters and turns the music off.)

SISTER MARK: We can't have that here, brother.

(She puts the tape player in PETER's hands and crosses to the desk. PETER looks at all the MEN, then climbs down off the beds and follows her.)

PETER: Excuse me, I ah…Sister? I'm sorry, I didn't know you didn't allow music.

SISTER MARK: Oh, brother. Your music is not so bad, but if I let you play that, other volunteers will bring all that rock and roll in here. Then what will I do, huh?

PETER: But the men were really enjoying it. What if you were to…you know… just at certain times?

SISTER MARK: No.

PETER: But maybe if you were to, I don't know…regulate…

SISTER MARK: This machine is for the rich, brother. We must not impose it on our poor or they will lose faith that we are for them. Besides, we have work to do. You play your music and the sisters will forget their work and dance.

PETER: The work was being done. No one was dancing.

SISTER MARK: No? And just what were you doing then?

PETER: Um…performance art…?

SISTER MARK: Peter. I know you want to make things better for your brothers. I see your love for them. I watch you work. You pray very well. You see, Mother teaches us that we must "pray the work." Every action an act of love for Jesus. It is this balance of work for Jesus—prayer for Jesus that sustains us, feeds us. Sometimes this work is very hard. Sometimes it is very hard to pray. But if I stop, the work will take me over and leave me weak. And I will have nothing left for those I serve. If I am to be strong, I cannot let anything distract me from my work, I cannot let anything distract me from my prayer. You understand?

PETER: I don't know.

SISTER MARK: Maybe in time, Peter. Listen, I have a special job for you. How much longer will you be here?

PETER: 'Bout another month or so, I guess.

SISTER MARK: Good. In one month's time we will be having a visitor from Rome. A very special visitor. I'm going to have the ceilings and walls repaired and whitewashed. And I want you to repaint all the beds for me. A nice brown, I think. I will send Sister Alphonse with you to bargain for the paint. What do you say, huh?

PETER: Isn't that a lot of trouble to go to for some visitor from Rome? Wouldn't the money be better spent taking care of their needs?

SISTER MARK: What we do for our brothers in Rome we will also be doing for our brothers at home.

PETER: Okay, I'll do it. But there's something else...something else I'd like to do.

SISTER MARK: And what is that?

PETER: Thursdays. The day off. I'd like to come here on Thursdays when no one else is here...

SISTER MARK: ...No...

PETER: ...When the sisters don't come.

SISTER MARK: It is our day off...

PETER: ...I want to come...

SISTER MARK: ...our day of reflection...

PETER: ...they shouldn't be alone...

SISTER MARK: ...and it is impossible.

PETER: But the medicine.

SISTER MARK: Did you hear me?

PETER: I could come just long enough to give out the medicine.

SISTER MARK: It is forbidden.

PETER: But that's important. The antibiotics...

SISTER MARK: ...we do the best we can...

PETER: ...and the TB meds...?

SISTER MARK: ...you must understand...

PETER: ...They need them every day, don't they...?

SISTER MARK: ...why are you doing this...?

PETER: ...it's no good otherwise...

SISTER MARK: That's not the point!

PETER: Then what the fuck is the point!

(She slaps him.)

SISTER MARK: I don't know. Ten years I have been here at Kalighat. Day after day. And when you leave in a month, I will continue. Day after day. I am a simple human being, Lord forgive me. Just an instrument, Peter.

(She touches his cheek.)

SISTER MARK: How sorry I am. I struggle to show love, but in my weakness, I strike out—and at you, simply because you want to do good. *(She tugs at her sari.)* Look, look here, Peter. What do you see, huh? If you take a moment to look closely, you will see it is nothing but spun cotton wrapped around a frail fearful body. Dust. Something must be left to faith. One day. One day, I must take

time for rest, to be one with my community in silence to hear the voice of God, if
I am to see His face in the face of my
brother and sister, if I am to live in this
world with some hope of redemption. I
must trust that He will guide me, care for
them when I cannot. That His will be
done. How can I describe to you the need
I have for this intimacy with my Lord,
the joy I taste when I surrender to Him,
the love I feel in serving Him in the poorest of the poor? No, Peter. Thursday is
our day of prayer, of rest and reflection. It
is the one thing I must keep for myself.
And I ask that you keep it too.

(She exits to the women's ward. MARGA-RET enters.)

PETER: Margaret? Here, Margaret. I'm
sorry about before. Take this for your
niece. *(He holds out twenty rupees to her.)*

MARGARET: No, brother. I will get
medicine some other way.

PETER: Please, Margaret. Please take it.
Don't make a beggar of me.

MARGARET: No, I won't make a beggar
of you. Thank you, brother.

PETER: And here, take this too. Maybe your
niece will enjoy listening to some music.

(He hands her the tape player.)

MARGARET: Oh, brother! So happy this
will make her, you don't know. Oh, but
brother, what happens when the batteries
die? What will she do then?

*(PETER laughs and hands her another ten
rupees.)*

MARGARET: Ah ha, brother. Now you
are giving with a smile. Thank you, brother.

PETER: Thank you, Margaret.

*(MARGARET exits. MARINA crosses to
PETER.)*

MARINA: Peter. It's Salim. He's quite ill.
He's asking for you.

*(PETER crosses to SALIM and sits down
beside him on his bed. His breathing is very
labored. MARINA, KLAUS, and BRIGID
sit nearby.)*

PETER: Salim?

SALIM: Peter? Is it you, brother?

PETER: Yes, Salim. It's me. Man, you are
so hot. You are burning up with fever.

SALIM: But I feel so cold. Strange, no?
And my breathing, it is so difficult. I don't
know why. And it hurts so much in my
chest.

PETER: Isn't there something we can give
him?

(MARINA buries her head. KLAUS shrugs.)

SALIM: I'm afraid, brother.

PETER: It's okay, Salim.

SALIM: Hold me, brother.

PETER: I've got you. I've got you, Salim.

SALIM: I never went to Mecca, brother.
I wanted to, but I never went to Mecca.
Allah led me here instead, brother. To this
place. Maybe to find you, brother.

PETER: Maybe, Salim. Maybe.

SALIM: But my eyes, brother. Everything
is so dark. Why, brother?

PETER: I don't know.

SALIM: Since morning I cannot see.
What will I do, brother, if I cannot see?
How will I recognize America? How will
I see my dream?

PETER: Oh, Salim.

SALIM: Tell me, brother. Tell me about
your home.

PETER: Well, I live on an island, Salim. A beautiful island, with buildings that touch the sky and sparkle like diamonds at night. Can you see it?

SALIM: A beautiful island.

PETER: Rivers flow all around the island. And people come there from all over the world, over the bridges, speaking every language, carrying customs from every corner of the earth. And they all live there together, in peace. Mothers and fathers love all the children there, no matter who they grow to be. And all the children return their parents' love, and care for them till their dying day. And in the center is a huge park where people go to sing or play together or just to sit in the shadows by the lake and hold the one they love. And in the streets, people walk hand in hand there, without fear, without embarrassment. Because love there is honored and cherished for all people. There's no hunger, no homelessness, no crime or punishment, and no one is abandoned there. There is always medicine for the sick and there's never any loneliness. Because people are courageous there, you see? They lift up their neighbors, treat them as their own. And no one ever, ever has to run away, because everything they need, everyone they need, is right there. Can you see it, Salim? It's a city of joy, but it's far, far away. It's far, far away.

(SISTER MARK comes and feels for SALIM's pulse.)

SISTER MARK: Put him on the Muslim side, brother.

(She exits. SISTERS start singing "Alleluia," continuing through the end of the play. PETER holds SALIM's body to him, rocking him. SYDNEY appears in a light in the

chapel. NOVICES are wrapping her in a white sari.)

SYDNEY: Dear Peter, so often I think of you and wish I could share with you all I've come to know, facing every day the things that I've always feared. Struggling to serve and live in my new home. Finding joy in surrendering to the love of Christ.

(SISTER ALPHONSE cuts SYDNEY's hair.)

SYDNEY: May you find the love you search for too, Peter. And blessings. Always... Sydney.

(The light fades on SYDNEY. MARGARET brings a white shroud, and PETER begins wrapping SALIM's body in it. PHILIP appears in a light up left. He is shirtless.)

PHILIP: Dear Peter, I cannot tell you of the beauty of the mountains of Kerala, covered with mango and cashew trees. What a glorious world. Thank you, Peter. I'd never have seen it if you hadn't helped me to open my eyes. Soon, I'll return home, and begin my studies to be a preacher, and my ministry will be to the children of God who are like me. The love of Christ sings in my heart now. I pray that I may let others hear it. And I pray for you too. With all my love, Philip.

(The light fades on PHILIP.)

MARGARET: Go, brother.

(PETER lifts SALIM's body and kisses him.)

PETER: Come, Salim. Come, brother. I'll take you home.

(PETER carries SALIM across the stage and exits. Work continues at Kalighat as the scrim closes revealing a sunset across the image of Calcutta.)

(End of play.)

AUTHOR'S NOTE

As we moved toward production of *Kalighat* in 2004, I kept saying how eager I was for the play to finally be in my past and no longer in my future. It had been more than fifteen years since my first experience working at Kalighat, Mother Teresa's first home for the dying and destitute in Calcutta. Many readings and workshops at places like Circle Rep, La MaMa, and HERE, as well as living rooms of friends had ensued since. And there were years that a draft sat in a drawer until I decided to revisit it, and India. Endless helpful feedback had been processed: "It's not a play"; "Too many people"; "Who wants to hear about poverty?"; "Are you criticizing Mother Teresa?"; "You should be more critical of Mother Teresa"; "Too much about the Indians"; "Not enough about Indians"; "Not enough sex"; "Too much sex"; "So what if it's the truth, it would never happen that way." Even: "Can't there be more singing and dancing?"—the typical development process a playwright endures.

I soon learned that my impulse to please everyone led only to frustration and writer's block. I was lucky enough to be able to turn to Lanford Wilson at Circle, who gave me about the best piece of dramaturgical advice a playwright, young or old, could get. He told me that my job was definitely not to please everyone. Instead, I must know exactly what I was trying to achieve, trying to say, with my play. I must realize that more often than not, anyone giving me feedback on some level wants me to write the play they would write if they only had the guts and the patience to do it themselves. Listen to what they say, much will be useless, but try to translate the response into an answer to the question: "Have I communicated to them, given them the experience that I meant to?"

Well, it probably would have been easier to please everyone. What Lanford's generous advice forced me to do was to confront the truth of my experience and commit to sharing my perspective of that truth. I feel only marginally successful in accomplishing that, but then it is a pretty big task. Kalighat, the star of this play, is a special place, an important place. Words alone are not adept at conveying its spirit. But as the brilliant group of actors and designers breathed the life of Kalighat into the Nagelberg Theater for twenty performances in January of 2004, they carried people to a place they would likely never have the inclination, or privilege, to experience themselves. Even people from Calcutta told me they felt they had been home, and that told me that at least some small thing of that truth had been conveyed to at least a few.

Not everyone is able to enter *Kalighat*. Like Kali herself, it is forbidding as it is inviting. It is relentless in its demands for submission.

One long-time New York critic could not get past the fact that she didn't have a reserved seat waiting for her (do any off-off Broadway theatres have reserved seats?), so it should come as no surprise that the truth of her privileged life experience had left her unable to enter deeply into an experience that begins with a vision of the truth of poverty and suffering that a few privileged folks in the world will never have to face, but that many more live with day in and day out. But while some critics' work may let us know more about their biases than about the theatre, some are able to enter the experience with an open mind and heart. Martin Denton, the editor of this anthology, was able to enter *Kalighat* with that kind of openness. Because of that lack of guile, he was able to teach me things about *Kalighat* that I did not know, and I thank him for that.

Although plays are meant to be alive on a stage, my hope is that you, the reader, will find a way to let the experience of Kalighat wash over you with that same openness. And that the time you spend there reaps for you some of the same rewards that she has bestowed on me.

—Paul Knox

NOTE

In Act II, Scene III, Ram quotes from Subrahmania Bharati, Tamil (b. 1882), and Dvijendralas Ray, Bengali (1867–1913).

GLOSSARY

KALIGHAT: "Steps of Kali," this is what Mother Teresa's first home for dying destitutes is called since it is located in the Kalighat neighborhood of Calcutta in a part of Kali Temple, an important Hindu temple to the Goddess of Destruction.

PRIM DAN: Medical facility in Calcutta run by the Missionaries of Charity.

TOMAR NAM QUI?: Bengali, "What is your name?" (Your name what?)

NOVICES: Nuns who have committed to the order, but have not taken their final vows. The process is as follows: aspirancy, six months; postulancy, one year; novitiate, two years, ending in first vows; juniorate, five years, renewal of vows each year; tertianship, one year, ending in final vows; professed sister.

NAMASTE/NOMUSHKAR: Hindi/Bengali greeting; literally, "God be with you."

SAHIB: Term of respect.

HOWRAH: Section of Calcutta, actually another city across the Hooghly River.

CHAPATIS: Kind of fried Indian bread.

SARI: Native dress of Indian women. The sisters of the Missionaries of Charity wear a white sari with blue stripes.

BEEDE: Indian cigarette.

PANI: Muslim Bengali word for water.

JHAL: Hindu Bengali word for water.

DAL: Gravy or sauce made from lentils, peas, or beans.

LUNGHI: Native dress of Indian men.

RICKSHAW: A two- (or more) passenger carriage drawn by one man. Calcutta is the only city in the world that still has manually pulled rickshaws.

RUPEE: Indian currency.

PAISE: Penny. One hundred paise to the rupee.

LOADSHEDDING: A brownout or blackout.

PLATONOV! PLATONOV! PLATONOV!

OR THE CASE OF A VERY ANGRY DUCK

Based on Anton Tchekhov's Three-Act Drama *Platonov*

Eric Michael Kochmer

ERIC MICHAEL KOCHMER is an actor and playwright. He grew up on a farm in the country town of Tunkhannock, Pennsylvania. At Marymount Manhattan College in New York City, he was introduced to playwriting while working and training with Elizabeth Swados's ensemble, Company Mud, at La MaMa E.T.C. After graduating in 2002, Kochmer began working with Brian Snapp of Feed the Herd Theatre Company on Fugue theatre company's production of *Waiting for Godot*. Following this, he performed in his first original work, produced by Feed the Herd and directed by Ross Peabody, a one-man show entitled *I Dreamed of Dogs*. Subsequent work with the Herd includes: *HitMan*, *A Coyote Wearin Blue Suede Shoes* (inspired by a story by Ian Tabatchnick and directed by Snapp), and *Blackstocking Jenkins* (directed by Emanuel Bocchieri as part of *Blurring the Lines*). Kochmer directed Snapp's short piece, *this is not a knot*, at the Herd's 2004 Stampede Festival. In June 2004, his *Fragments of Ricky the Superhero: a Story about Love* played in the punk bar Siberia in Hell's Kitchen, directed by Peabody. Other works as an actor with Feed the Herd include: *The Foundation, ZooHuman, Gilgamesh*, and *The Madhouse of Mantua*. Other New York theatre productions as an actor include Swados's *Missionaries and Sublimnible Stratigery* (La MaMa), *Richard II* (Brooklyn Lyceum), *A Country Doctor* (Theresa Lang Theatre), and *Harms Way* (Trilogy Theatre). Kochmer starred in Anthony Ferraro's feature *Everything Unspoken* and can be seen in the features *Medium Hot* and *The Hangman's Noose*. His new play, *Robert and the Dawn*, premieres in the 2005 Stampede Festival (directed by Bocchieri).

Platonov! Platonov! Platonov! Or the case of a very Angry Duck was first presented by Feed the Herd Theatre Company (Brian Snapp, Artistic Director), as part of its annual Stampede Theatre Festival, on January 8, 2004, at the Trilogy Theatre, New York City, with the following cast and credits:

Platonov .... Eric Michael Kochmer
Sofya .... Natalie McLennan
Mary .... Metha Brown
Nicoli .... Ian Tabatchnick
Osip .... Kevin Kaine
Anna .... Kate Serpa
Ivan .... Joe Serpa
Sergy .... Jason Munt
Petrin .... Darrin Browne
Sasha .... Heather Carmichael
Understudy for Sergy .... Stefano V. Brancato

Director: Ross Peabody
Additional Text: Ross Peabody
Technical Director: Emanuel Bocchieri
Associate Director and Vocal Coach: Rachel Macklin
Stage Manager: Kelly Stark
Set and Lighting Design: Emanuel Bocchieri, Brian Snapp, and Stefano
  Brancato
Video Design: Ross Peabody and Ensemble
Costume Design: Rachel Macklin, Ross Peabody, and Ensemble

Visit www.feedtheherd.org.

Dedications

This play is for drunken nights with Ross Peabody and the year 1978.

AUTHOR'S NOTE

This is an early Chekhov story—his first full-length play actually—that I've turned into a one-act. All time and place are gone…only the words…only the circumstances…the lust…the soul…the hate…the silliness.

I have no issues with Chekhov's body of work. I think he is probably one of the most important authors in the world in the past two hundred years and will be for the next two hundred years. I really just wanted to get *Platonov* produced. When I kept on presenting the idea to my friends, they kept on asking—Why the hell do you want to do a Chekhov play…who's going to direct it? I liked the character of Osip, so I would have preferred acting in it rather than directing it…plus I had never directed at that time. So for about a year, the play kept on showing up in my pile of plays that I liked and I couldn't get it out of my mind.

During this time, I was writing and acting quite a bit with Feed the Herd and working with director Ross Peabody. One night, we were very drunk and decided that I would adapt *Platonov* into my style of writing and piss off all of the Chekhovian purists. In essence, we decided to create the stupidest Chekhov interpretation possible. I wanted to not only annoy the obnoxious know-it-alls (which I did by the way by making it work) but also give something to my video-game-playing brothers and sisters. I figured that by making the play as jumpy as a cat getting poked by a stick, I would always be giving them something to look at. The fact is, we got a group of brilliant actors who weren't afraid to take risks and really helped to make the story grow and become clearer to the audience each night.

NOTES ON STAGING

What I say about the show doesn't particularly matter. Whoever is going to do this play is going to do it any way they choose. The best way for me to describe this play is as a rhythm performance or a musical without music. My objective with this play was to try to take the inner subtleties of this Chekhovian story and make them obvious while having the actor present his own opinion at the same time. In short I, with the incredible help of Ross Peabody and Rachel Macklin, wanted to be able to give the inner beauty and concealed emotions to the audience on a plate with a satirical and Darwinist sheen…making it a social and dramatic comment…we constantly scrutinize the hardships of our privileged lives while we completely overlook the actual tragedies of life happening right in front of us.

There are no stage directions indicating entrances, exits, or any other movements. The reason for this is that I imagine all of the characters on stage together, each contemplating the inner motivations of the others. I'm not sure if it worked in our production, but we certainly tried to do it…and tried not to make it a distraction. Our production had two television sets facing the audience from the center of the stage. The actor playing Platonov was placed in a chair facing the televisions, with his back to the audience and the televisions placed on a specially designed cabinet tall enough for the audience to see. A spy camera was used by other characters, primarily Nicoli; or it would rest directly in front of Platonov, filming his reactions; or it would be turned off. This allowed Platonov's back to be to the audience for much of the show. We tried to make the camerawork as specific as possible and not make it a distraction or a gimmicky device.

The original prologue written for the play (which here appears as an appendix) was taken out and replaced by a new one written by Ross Peabody. Both prologues have the same objective: to introduce the attitudes of the characters to the audience. The one that I wrote is in the form of a frantic repetitive banter, whereas Peabody's is a straightforward outward rant by each character. For the purposes of our production we only used the latter, but, if desired, the original prologue could easily be placed in front of the prologue we used, or in back of it—whatever you like.

Change…add…adjust: do what you will with the script.

—E.M.K.

CHARACTERS

ANNA: a widow

SERGY: her stepson

SOFYA: his wife

GERASIM KUZMICH PETRIN: an entrepreneur and a landowner

MARY: a young chemistry student

TRILETSKY (also called IVAN): a retired colonel

NICOLI (also called TRILETSKY): his son, a young doctor

PLATONOV: a duck who is the village schoolmaster

ALEKSANDRA IVANOVNA (SASHA): his wife, daughter of Colonel Triletsky

OSIP: a horse thief

THIS IS A ONE-ACT PLAY IT DOES NOT STOP EVER

PROLOGUE

PLATONOV: I have come to the conclusion that I, Platonov, have been transformed into a duck. How do I know this, you ask? How do I know? I ask myself, yes, how do I know? Quack. Let me tell you the bit I've come to know. "Male ducks...can be veritable sex maniacs in the spring. Though some males and females 'marry' and remain monogamous, other males remain bachelors and rape other males' 'wives.' Married females will go to great lengths to hide from marauding bachelors, concealing themselves for an entire day in high grass. Bands of three or four bachelors will seek out a hiding female and take turns raping her." A cruising duck... "If they can't find a female, the more aggressive males will mount the least aggressive male of the group. It is not uncommon for two bachelors to hold down a third while he's mounted by another male. Homosexuality is not at all uncommon among ducks—or geese, for that matter." In effect, the duck has no taboos, no laws, no judgments. They are low low low low beasts. There is no moral backbone. No...imperative. Given the picture of these nasty habits, you would think the world would be appalled. Taken aback. Disgusted. But no. They take this in stride as they do all other social slights, peculiarities, and titters. Which brings me to my next point. As a man, no matter how you ruin yourself, you are still loved. Unconditionally. There is no judgment, no moral compass, no backbone. Ducks are still cute. But if you point these vile actions out, you are harangued, judged, shunned. You are a duck! But you are cute!! So I love you!!!! But that duck is violating his fellows! So long as he is cute, I will love him!! And on and on and on. You, sir, are a liar and a lout! And possibly a pervert. SEEEE?!?!? Whether these things are true or no, I have offended. I am the villain. And this is how my story goes. But wait. My question. How do I know? Because I know that mallards and moralists are made up of much the same stuff. And that they are the most notorious rapists of their natures. The first of his fellows, the second of the mind. I have been the second, so I therefore, I must know the first. Well, then...Platonov! Platonov! Platonov! I suppose, now, a very. Angry. Duck.

SERGY: This destruction extends a black wing on all the work of Platonov. The topic is omnipresent in the accessories of its fantastic: the construction of the large house of the proletariat, in the Excavation is a vast hole whose dimensions do not cease increasing. Nastja, the child of socialism, dies without ever to have been able to pronounce a human word. In the Fourteen, red, mothers are delirious by rocking their dead child, one eats soup of human bones, one manufactures coffins to take refuge there. As it is seen, the macabre images do not miss. They are supported by a semantics of wear (temporal sounds, colors, decelerations), physical and psychic dilapidation. The devastation of the world, in this exhausting search of the Utopia that are a number of accounts of Platonov, is completed on the madness, the loss of the identity, and sometimes the literal setting in parts of certain characters, like the hero of a Wind of rubbish and those of a happy Moscow.

IVAN: The readers of Platonov unanimously smelled the satirical intention of its writings, and contemporary criticism did not fail besides to be indignant some. In addition, the homogeneous word characteristic of the writing of Platonov conveys the doubt and translates the anguish. However Realism socialist suffers not absence from point of view "vivifying" and sententious—in the absence of being clear—, so that Platonov is author unacceptable, even if "…to deal with questions which already received answer is the privilege of the brains formed according to the principle of the internal organs of cow which are made, as each one knows, to digest a ruminated grazing ground."

PETRIN: Platonov is publisher of the encyclopedia of the Russian culture. He is presented erroneously erroneously erroneously as a historian.

ANNA: Like each summer, all a small company of neighbors and friends are found in holiday at the fine bottom of the Russian province, at the young widow Anna Petrovna. Platonov in fact part. Young ruined aristocrat, he became teacher, by spite and to mark his revolt with respect to his late father and of the company's contemptible judge. Hablor, shining and seducer, it is admired ones and is jealousy of the others. This year, the reunion with Sofia, woman he liked formerly and who was pilot ambitions of her twenty years, its desperate ardor and its mortuary multiply by ten. Explanations, adulteries, treasons, alcohol: the festival turns to the drama.

PETRIN: This part of youth, unfinished, that Tchekhov would have undertaken to write in 1881, to twenty and one years, at the same time as of the humorous tales he sold with the newspapers to make live its family, reveals an at the same time cruel and strange author, who delivers a criticism of all the levels of the company which

tours: owners cultivated, new rich person, soldiers, doctors, teachers, mujiks, or rigands. One also finds there germinates of them the broad topics which will be developed in *The Cherry Orchard, Uncle Vanya,* and *The Gull.*

MARY: As provided by the memorandum of agreement between the University and the Faculty Association, dean of the Faculty of Mathematics, is now looking into the matter of Professor Platonov, who was recently convicted of assaulting his wife. Her inquiry will be as broad as she judges necessary to enable a determination of whether action is required under the Memorandum of Agreement, and will be completed as quickly as circumstances allow. Since November, when Professor Platonov was charged with a number of serious criminal offenses, he has been on an extended research term at the University.

OSIP: Platonov, the man who gives his name at piece-rates, has the very whole life which is profiled in front of him. It springs with the ardor of somebody who wants nothing to refuse.

SOFYA: Intended for children from eleven to one hundred and eleven years. From notes: "This is not a textbook of psychology, nor even merely a popular exposition of old truths. The author, a well-known psychologist, has collected a large number of questions of interest to young people and has answered them briefly, popularly, entertainingly and in keeping with modern knowledge…the text includes some of the simplest psychological experiments which any reader can perform and which are conducive to a better understanding of the laws governing mental and social activity and manifesting themselves in work and everyday life."

SASHA: In response to the *Imprint's* article "Mixed Reactions to Professor's Return," January 26, I was amazed by Imran Aleem's point of view. Aleem says "What he does at home is different than what he does at work. It's two different things." Pardon me, but does Platonov have a split personality where he is one person in the confines of his residence and then another when he enters a different environment? I think not. Aleem would do well to read Jon Kabat-Zinn's *Wherever You Go, There You Are*. Platonov may be capable of putting on a professional face when he is in the academic world, but his emotions, values, and beliefs are still exactly the same as when he is at home. Platonov has shown, beyond a shadow of a doubt, that he has little to no respect for his wife, and quite possibly women in general. What would stop him from "losing it" with a student or co-worker and smashing them over the head? The most disturbing sentence in that entire article is that "others merely dismissed it." Dismissed it? It has been bystanders and those who do nothing that have traditionally frightened me, but now there is a new kind of evil showing its ugly head. Apathetics who are truly, in my eyes, confused in the realm of reality. This man beat his wife about the head with a rock. I ask you, how can that be merely dismissed?

NICOLI: "Platonov is simply the kind of malcontent who annoys people by pointing out their inadequacies to them, preferably in public. He is unkempt, proudly unconventional, a near-alcoholic. He is fatally attractive to women, and he more or less knows it, but not enough to stop and think about it. A dangerous urchin, a scruffy Adonis, a debonair tramp, an out-of-work apostle, a venomous buffoon. That is quite a respectable list, I think." And now I ask of you:

START OF THE PLAY

NICOLI: Where could the widow be?

SERGY: Here we are my beautiful wife, Sofya Yagorovnachorgaforgagorgaforgaborgachobia, here to see your old friend Platonov! Platonov! Platonov!

SOFYA: Yes…my kind kind kind kind wealthy husband. AND IT'S THE SUMMER SOLSTICE!

MARY: I'm afraid to see you, Platonov! Platonov! Platonov! I have my studies and my career to think about… not a silly duck that only thinks of his own feathers… Oh Anna! I can't see him! I hate him! I hate him! I have to work on my experiments! Hide my shame! Hide my shame! Ahhhhh!

ANNA: Oh don't worry Mary, ruin him if he screws you over. I am the WIDOW. My rich old limp husband is dead. But of course being a woman I don't get any of his money! But I'm sure someone will oblige an attractive, innocent widow—hello Nicoli!

NICOLI: Hi Anna, the widow! You are a beautiful widow. Oh hello my drunken father who did nothing with your life!

IVAN: Hello son who is a doctor that has never cured a soul and is letting the shopkeeper's wife die at this very moment! Where's your sister Sasha? Probably humping a duck! Ha! Ha! Ha! I'm old and drunk! I don't want to be here at all! Ha! Ha! Ha! Who are you?

PETRIN: MY NAME IS PETRIN AND NOT ONLY DO I NOT WANT TO BE HERE BUT THERE IS NO REASON FOR ME TO BE HERE AT ALL EXCEPT THAT I'M RICH RICH RICH! I OWN EVERYTHING! EVERYTHING! EVERYTHING!

SASHA: I love you so my trusting husband Platonov! Platonov! Platonov!

PLATONOV: Oh, and I love you my little baby machine!

ANNA: *(Playing chess.)* Your move good doctor…

NICOLI: Aha! I got your queen and your pawn… when is lunch? When is everyone getting here?

ANNA: They're already here my dear good doctor… they're probably about somewhere drinking and hee! Hee! Hee! …and whatever else they could be doing by themselves in some dark corner…

PLATONOV: Ha! Ha! Ha! Life has made me a sweet fool…sweet fool… Trickery, I married a dumb sweet country girl! Ahhh! Ha! Ha! Ha! I used to see myself as the next great emperor of the land, the next Columbus, even…even…even…even… even…even… I am a schoolteacher, Sofya Yagorovnachorgaforgagorgaforgaborgachobia. That is all.

SOFYA: You? A schoolteacher?

PLATONOV: Yes. Strange, isn't it…

SOFYA: Incredible! But…why not something more?

PLATONOV: It's a very long story, Sofya Yagorovnachorgaforgagorgaforgaborgachobia, Ha! Ha! Ha!

ALL: Ha! Ha! Ha!

SOFYA: But, of course, you did graduate from university?

PLATONOV: No, dropped out.

SOFYA: Dropped out?

PLATONOV: Dropped out.

SOFYA: Dropped out?

PLATONOV: Dropped out.

SOFYA: Dropped out?

PLATONOV: I don't understand your question, Sofya Yagorovnachorgaforgagorgaforgaborgachobia…

SOFYA: I mean, does that prevent you from serving a cause, or creating a great work of art—does it?

PLATONOV: No…no, no, no, no, no, no… AHHHHH!!!!!! Ha! Ha! Ha! Ha! Ha! Ha! Ha! Ha! Ha! Ha! Ha! I'm a pushpin—I'm surrounded by pushpins and I married a dumb wife!!!! I don't care about anything except for my own mediocre satisfaction!!!!!!! Ha! Ha! Ha! Ha! Ha!!!!!!

ALL: Ha! Ha! Ha!

SOFYA: What about doing good for the people of your country: for example, what about equal rights for women and all that? What about reformation of the peasants of our wonderful country?

PLATONOV: Surely not Sofya Yagorovnachorgaforgagorgaforgaborgachobia!!!! Ha! Ha! Ha! Ha! The equality of woman and all that??? Ha! Ha! Ha!

ALL: *(Except OSIP.)* Ha! Ha! Ha! Ha! Ha!

MARY: Platonov! Platonov! Platonov! I try not to laugh! But I have a weak heart!!!!!!!! All because of men!

PLATONOV: My Mary! How have you been?

MARY: I hate you! I hate you! I hate you! Platonov! Platonov! Platonov!

NICOLI: Allow me to brush up your memory, Platonov! Platonov! Platonov!, I went to your house FIVE TIMES…five times and all that you ever gave to me was a little little little ruble…and it was torn at that…so repressible and despicable that when I tried giving it to a miserly pathetic beggar he wouldn't even have it… "It's all ripped up," the beggar screamed. "But I'll take your chicken…your rubber chicken." Then he laughed at me…AT ME! Are we ready to eat yet?

PLATONOV: Save anyone lately, good doctor?—I hear the shopkeeper's wife is dying! Ha! Ha! Ha! Ha! Ha! Ha!

NICOLI: Yes, well, she's always dying, isn't she! I'd rather have something to eat than heal that old bag! Ha! Ha! Ha! Ha! Ha! Ha!

ALL: Ha! Ha! Ha!

PETRIN: It…It… HEY!!! It says here in this Russian paper that the Russian winter gets longer and gets longer and gets longer and gets longer… one day I will have a fine lady to call my own…call my own when it's cold outside… maybe a lady as honorable as Anna… until then I have to sit and suffer among you fine complacent people who sit idle and complain and do nothing nothing nothing… YOU'RE KEEPING ME FROM MAKING MORE MONEY YOU BORING BORING BORING PEOPLE!!!

PLATONOV: We're all deeply indebted to Petrin! Ha! Ha! Ha! Ha! Ha! Ha! Ha!

PETRIN: WHAT? WHAT? WHAT? Platonov! Platonov! Platonov! I have an admiration for women, beyond attraction! And I have an education, that's more than you can say! Ha! Ha! Ha! That's what? Huh? That's what? Say whatever you want about me! Whatever you want!

PLATONOV: And what has it taught you?

PETRIN: It says in the myth of life that man awakes with three paths to travel in his time in this world: If he walks down the road to the right, he will be eaten by

the jackals of the night… and if he travels down the road to the left, he will eat the jackals, and if he travels down the road before him, he will eat the flesh from his very bones. And now I ask you, Platonov! Platonov! Platonov! —what road will you choose?

NICOLI: What the hell does that mean?

PLATONOV: Oh Petrin! I'm so sorry! I'm so sorry! You're such a sweet and noble man who deserves all of the attention and praise possible… in fact why don't I let you have my dumb wife for a day? How about that? You educated charitable well-respected lord of the land! TAKE MY DUMB WIFE! Ha! Ha! Ha!

SERGY: Platonov! Platonov! Platonov! Calm down!

PLATONOV: I'm not going to calm down! What makes you so much better than me…besides your money? You have nothing when it comes to wit… I'll tell you that my friend. Ha! Ha! Ha! You have your land, you have your money… but I have all of the charm, my friend! I HAVE ALL OF THE CHARM! Ha! Ha! Ha!

ANNA: Platonov! Platonov! Platonov! will you please!

PETRIN: What? What? What? I'm an upright citizen of this land, if truth were told… who are you? That's what I'd like to know.

PLATONOV: I'll tell you who I am: I AM IN THE MIDDLE! I'M NOT ON THE RIGHT AND I'M NOT ON THE LEFT! It all comes down to granola bars. My dumb wife and I are conservative liberals! In some respects, the life we live and the values we share have more in common with left-wing counterculturalists than with many garden-variety conservatives. All I can tell you is that the crunchy granola lefties are often right about little things that make life richer. Take food, for example. After we married, Sasha and I had to teach ourselves how to cook. We quickly discovered how much better food tastes if it hasn't been processed. We'd go to farmers' markets in the city to buy produce, and before we knew it, we were making and canning our own apple butter. Not only did the stuff taste dramatically better than what was on offer in the supermarket, but there was a real sense of pride in knowing how to do these things for ourselves, like our grandmothers did. We realized one day that pretty much the only young to middle-aged people we knew who cared about these things were…lefties. Here's something else I've noticed: the Granola Conservatives I know tend not to be wealthy, but labor in the creative and intellectual vineyards as writers, professors, and artists. They also tend to be religious. It's foolish to go too far in metaphysicalizing questions of taste, but a big part of it, at least for those of us who are part of older Christian traditions, comes from learning to see the world sacramentally. In the sacramental vision, which is shared by Catholics and the orthodox, the spirit world is mediated through the material world, which is another way of saying we experience God in creation. To someone imbued with a sacramental vision, qualities inherent in things—from the food we eat to the buildings we live in—matter in profoundly spiritual ways.

SASHA: Platonov! Platonov! Platonov! it isn't nice!

NICOLI: Where could the widow be? I hope she isn't sick or hungry! I'm hungry!

MARY: Platonov! Platonov! Platonov! I try not to laugh! I have a weak heart! Hee! Hee! Hee! You better be in love with me!

(EVERYONE notices the lurking OSIP.)

ALL: (Except OSIP.) OHHHHHHHHH-HHHHHHHHHHHH!

OSIP: May I? (He removes his cap.)

ANNA: No you may not! How dare you! Why did you come here, you fool?

OSIP: To congratulate…

ANNA: You will do no congratulating here! Get him out of here, Platonov! Platonov! Platonov! Look at his eyes! Why! Look at his eyes! His eyes! The eyes of a wild wild wild beast!

ALL: (Except OSIP.) How many trees have you stolen from us this winter?

OSIP: Only three or four, your ladyship…

SERGY: Ha! Ha! Ha! I love everyone! EVERYONE I LOVE YOU! Even you strange creature from the darkness!

NICOLI: Look everyone, the strange creature from the darkness probably wants something to eat…wouldn't you? You strange abomination…wouldn't you like something to eat? Why…we could have dinner you and I right now…we could…

ALL: GO TEND TO THE SHOP-KEEPER'S WIFE! SHE'S DYING!

NICOLI: And she'll be dying tomorrow! AH! The wild beast is still here!

ANNA: You lie Osip, you lie!

OSIP: May I kiss your hand?

ANNA: Oh…go ahead…

OSIP: I'm much in debt to your ladyship for your kindness…

PLATONOV: Ladies and gentlemen, I have the pleasure of introducing one of the most fascinating anthropoids in the modern human zoo. One day he may kill me! Ha! Ha! Ha! Give a big happy hello to Osip, local horse and donkey thief, inspectoral parasite, and killer.

OSIP: I'm going to kill you, Platonov! Platonov! Platonov!

PLATONOV: Quack! Quack! Quack!

ANNA: Don't provoke him, Platonov! Platonov! Platonov! You don't know what he's capable of…

NICOLI: And what is it that you do, my good fellow, my good fellow, my good fellow?

OSIP: Theft, sir.

IVAN: An intriguing profession…

ALL: Where have you been skulking all winter? In prison?

OSIP: Maybe…it's cold in the wintertime!!!!

PLATONOV: Good Lord! He's grinning!

ALL: His eyes! His eyes! They come from the darkness!

PLATONOV: You reside high above all government and control! You are a low low low low low low thief! Quack! Quack! Quack!

OSIP: I have brought with me something for you, my precious love Anna. *(He takes out a rubber chicken.)*

ANNA: And what may that be?

PLATONOV: Thieving again, Osip? Yes?

OSIP: Oh, Yes sir…Thieving from nature sir.

ANNA: Good Lord! Now what!

PETRIN: What? What? What? He's crazy!

OSIP: He's soft and silky, like your ladyship. I thought that you'd want to hold him…

ANNA: Take it to the kitchen… No, never mind, Chef will want to serve him up.

IVAN: Rubber chicken à vin blanc… delicious!!!!! What time is it?

OSIP: I'll build a little home for him with twigs…

ANNA: All right! Enough! Get out!

SERGY: Platonov! Platonov! Platonov! Why are you hiding? Let's go inside and toast to my Sofya Yagorovnachorgaforgagorgaforgaborgachobia's health!

PLATONOV: I can't take my eyes off your wife.

SERGY: Yes. Well you should spend more time with her, make her feel welcome. I want you to be close, close, close friends. Yes. Yes. Yes.

NICOLI: Platonov! Platonov! Platonov! We're waiting! Where is the widow? I'm hungry!

PLATONOV: Ah! I would rather be feasting and drinking with you than these perilous bastards, Osip. You're so nice and sweet and comfortable. Your company is much more welcoming than the veracity of these bastards bastards bastards. You wouldn't hurt a duck…now would you?

OSIP: Oh, I can't say you're right with that comment sir, because I am going to kill you. But thank you anyway.

SASHA: Everyone's drunk!

IVAN: "I was just a silly boy with a bottle and my girl fell in love on a boat did I…"

SASHA: You shouldn't be allowed in a respectable household.

IVAN: Ahh! What was I saying…what was I saying… Another…Another couple of years of service and I would have been promoted… Then the next year, I would have been promoted again… again… again… and again. It was bound to happen… Yes…my dear Sasha… Used to think up strategies on how to ostracize the Turks… the Sandfaces…who are they now…WHO ARE THEY NOW!! But she's gone…gone… Ha! Ha! Didn't know how to use a rifle then and don't know how to shoot now… Ha! Ha! Ha!

SASHA: You're old—you ought to be setting an example…

IVAN: Blah, blah, blah…just like your mother…a dumb country girl… you have her eyes, her hair…and you walk like her, too, like a…funny funny funny funny funny little goose…just like your poor dead mother, dead, dead, dead, dead— I checked her she's dead… how I loved her! Your father is an honest man, children! Never ever have I robbed my fellow man or my country! And believe you me, all I ever had to do was to reach out my hand, and I'd have been rich and famous today!

NICOLI: That's admirable, Father, admirable indeed. Where are you going? Where's Platonov! Platonov! Platonov!

SASHA: Drunk, drunk, drunk. I don't know, he's probably drunk, that quacker! Nicoli, are you ever going to heal someone?

IVAN: You're a smart man, you…you… and you'll be a great doctor one day, too, you! I met the great Pirt…Pirt… skinisnian once, in Moscow…Marvelous brilliant physician…nice man, too. Though, never cured anybody, though.

NICOLI: I've never cured anyone either! I'm hungry!

SASHA: Come on Papa, it's time to go. Goodbye, Nicoli!

IVAN: Lord how we've sinned!!! My hands are dirty, filthy… Yes. Yes. Yes. How I loved your poor mother! Your poor dead, dead, dead, dead, dead, dead, dead, dead, dead, dead, dead, dead, dead, dead, dead, dead, dead, dead, dead MOTHER! Lord, how we've sinned! Never got down on my knees and prayed as a little boy! Never! Never! Now I serve no one! NO ONE! Terrible… Nicoli, my boy, why don't you get yourself a good widow? Ha! Ha! Ha! OR MAYBE A BIT OF CHICKEN! TERRIBLE!

(SASHA and IVAN exit.)

PETRIN: Let's play cards for the widow, fool!

NICOLI: (Dealing cards.) Un, deux, trois! Un, deux, trois! Un, deux, trois! Ready, gentlemen?

PETRIN: The ace of hearts…

SERGY: Never…mind…

NICOLI: Well?

SERGY: Queen of spades…

NICOLI: Well? Well? Well?

PETRIN: What? What? What?

ANNA: NICOLI! Why don't you cure someone?

NICOLI: It's the widow! It's the widow! I wonder if she's hungry! Ha! Ha! Ha!

ANNA: Nicoli…where are you? Why don't you come…come and dance with me? Come and dance with me in the moonlight. Dance, you marvel, dance! Platonov! Platonov! Platonov!

NICOLI: I'll dance…I'll dance…I like dancing and eating!

(All the MEN get up and run after ANNA.)

PETRIN: FOOLS! FOOLS! FOOLS! That's not how you woo a woman! You woo a woman with wine...with wine and love... FOOLS! FOOLS! FOOLS!

SERGY: Why are you so distant from me tonight, Sofya Yagorovnachorgaforgagorgaforgaborgachobia? What is wrong?

SOFYA: No worries, my love...

SERGY: You may not keep anything from me, Sofya Yagorovnachorgaforgagorgaforgaborgachobia! Wha! Wha! Wha!

SOFYA: We'll go away overseas, won't we? Maybe Canada? Yes?

SERGY: I don't see why you have to. I don't see why we have to. Why? Why? Why? I love you! I love you! I love you!

SOFYA: Uh...umm don't know... I want to, that's why! It's wonderful. Lovely. Alive and full of flowers. But we have to get out of here...now...alone...right away.

SERGY: We'll go away tomorrow...we'll leave here right away...

ALL: We'll go away tomorrow...we'll leave here right away! Don da da da da data da da da da da HEY!

SERGY: Anything...anything...anything...anything...for you my Sofya Yagorovnachorgaforgagorgaforgaborgachobia ... I love you! I love you! I love you!

MARY: I didn't want to be here because of you, Platonov! Platonov! Platonov! Why do you strut around like some kind of happy duck? Why don't you respect women, Platonov! Platonov! Platonov!

PLATONOV: Oh, I do! I do! Of course I do, my sweet chemistry student...but for now, why don't you go away for a while... maybe go in the kitchen where the rest of the women of your kind tend to go... we'll

talk later... Right now, I have to talk to my dear...my dear...my dear brother-in-law, Nicoli, here about the poor shopkeeper's wife that is dying... So, go away now!

NICOLI: Ha! Ha! Ha! And she'll be dying tomorrow... and I'll probably still be sitting around drunk rotting away with you! Ha! Ha! Ha! Where could the widow be?

PLATONOV: I have no idea, you complacent fool! Why don't you go tend to the shopkeeper's wife? She's dying! Now leave me alone! So you're here, Sofya Yagorovnachorgaforgagorgaforgaborgachobia? Are you alone?

SOFYA: Yes.

PLATONOV: Do you shun us, mere mortals that we are?

SOFYA: I'm not shunning you...

PLATONOV: Why do you hide from me, Sofya Yagorovnachorgaforgagorgaforgaborgachobia? Quack! Quack! Quack! Do I insult you?

SOFYA: No.

PLATONOV: Do you remember, Sofya Yagorovnachorgaforgagorgaforgaborgachobia? That spring by the pond?

SOFYA: I don't want to remember, Platonov! Platonov! Platonov!... Our past was wonderful, but try to reason with me you sweet duck... you're Platonov! Platonov! Platonov! you're the village schoolteacher... you're a quacker... you're married... so am I... and well, you're a duck... it's just wrong! Just plain wrong! Let's leave the past in the past... ohhhhh! But you were just a little boy...a little boy...and I was just a little girl...a little girl...

PLATONOV: And what do little boys and little girls do?

SASHA: I trust you! Platonov! Platonov! Platonov!

PLATONOV: Wait! Don't go, Sofya Yagorovnachorgaforgagorgaforgaborgachobia! Stay, please! Listen to me…I'm only just an ordinary schoolteacher… Quack! Quack! Quack! that's all I've done since we we we last saw each other…but that is not my passion. What have I done for Platonov! Platonov! Platonov! I've married a dumb sweet country girl… And now? I'm just a happy drunk duck mucking around in the same swamp I've already mucked around… Soon I will be old!… only then I'll be a fat old worthless duck. My God, it's shocking! I open my eyes up and all I see is mediocrity all around me, plaguing the earth, swallowing up my fellow man, and yet I sit here, arms and body in a limbo static state… I sit and watch in the dark of silence with the rest of my friends and say and do nothing… and one day I'll be forty…and nothing will change. I'll still walk around as the same fool I am today and with the same dumb wife and the same women will be falling at my feet… one day I'll be fifty… one day I'll be sixty… one day I'll be seventy… eighty… ninety…one hundred—dead on the ground, dust in the earth—and nothing will ever change for me… nothing will ever change… I will always be lusting around… no change in the horizon… and meanwhile I grow into a fat and dull and idle duck… my feathers are ruffled and one day I'll just be skin… My life is lost… All of my ambitions, all of my passions lost! The life of this duck wasted… I am impotent to intellect and substantial opinions… What is left? What is left? My feathers prick to the touch when I think of my death…My

feathers prick to the touch when I think of my death…My feathers prick to the touch when I think of my death… death…death… Oh Sofya, what have I done! What have I done!

SOFYA: I can't bear this any longer, take me now!

PLATONOV: Ha! Ha! Ha! I love women! Quack! Quack! Quack!

ANNA: What can I do for you, Petrin?

PETRIN: Well, you see, Anna… what I want to say is… listen, I'm rich…I need… I'm rich…you're a widow… I'm rich… and I am in need…

ANNA: Yes?

PETRIN: I am in need of a mistress… someone like you!

SOFYA: Oh Platonov! Platonov! Platonov! I'm a little schoolgirl all over again!

ANNA: So?

PETRIN: What I mean is, I don't expect you to love me… It's just that I do own a paradise…but there are no angels in it… God did not bestow upon me many attributes EXCEPT THAT I AM EXTREMELY RICH! HA! HA! HA! I was born to do great deeds and ended up doing lots and lots of little worthless ones… but to love—

ANNA: No. Maybe. You are rich, so maybe. Oh Platonov! Platonov! Platonov! You wild goose, there you are!

PLATONOV: What's the matter? You're a little more eager than usual…

SERGY: Sofya! Sofya! Sofya! I love you! I love you! I love you!

ANNA: Petrin just proposed to me. I could steal all his money and run away with you… pity that a lady can't sleep outdoors under this sky. When I was a girl, I always slept in the garden on the summer solstice…naked…naked… naked… naked on the wet summer grass. What about us, Platonov! Platonov! Platonov! We haven't seen each other in such a long long long time… We are friends, aren't we? Great good friends? Well, you know very well…don't you… that in between a boy and a girl there is only one step between acquaintances and lovers? Oh Platonov! Platonov! Platonov!

PLATONOV: Ha! Quack! Quack! Quack! Ha! I LOVE WOMEN!

SASHA: What's wrong, you poor fool… do you want some potatoes?

OSIP: What's wrong? What's wrong? I THOUGHT THAT ANNA THE WIDOW WOULD LOVE ME SOMEDAY, BUT NO, THAT DAY WILL NEVER COME FOR A POOR THIEF LIKE ME! Yes, potatoes would be wonderful!

SASHA: What happened? Tell me everything while I fix you some wonderful potatoes!

OSIP: How was this misery birthed in me? It happened with the simplicity of a fable. The vision…it comes to me… I'm walking down a trail in the woodland, not far from here… through the branches I spot the WIDOW standing upright in the cold spring water, her dress tucked up as to not get her dry clothes wet…and…and…and she's scooping up water with a leaf! Ha! Ha! Ha! Scoop it up…scoop it up…scoop it up and drink it down your throat! Ha! Ha! Ha! And then she drowns her whole head in it…die for me my love die for me… so I walk down to the waterside right up close to her and she doesn't look at me at all… as if saying "SCOUN-DREL! WHY SHOULD I EVEN LOOK AT YOU AT ALL?" "LADY," says I, "I just see you're having a fresh cold drink of clean water…" "What business is it of yours?" she says. "Get on out of here you dirty unworthy shameful unabashed swarthy peasant." Never even looked at me twice. Well, I must say I was frightened and hurt, and ashamed of being a peasant. "What are you staring at me for, fool? Never seen a woman before have you… or perhaps you've taken a liking to me?" "Oh yes!" says I, "Well…well…I like you! I like you a whole lot!" Says I, "You're a noble, sensitive, warmhearted individual, you're beautiful. Never in my life have I seen a more beautiful lady. Manka, our local beauty, the constable's daughter," says I, "Next to you?—why she's merely a donkey, a water snake, a chicken…a dead rotten chicken! You're so delicate! Why if I kissed you right now…" "Go ahead," she says. "Kiss me if you want to…" Since then, interestingly enough, I seem to have lost my mind AND HAVE BEEN BANISHED INTO THIS CRUEL WORLD OF MADNESS!… I'm going to shred the skin from this very flesh, my beloved Sasha… It's been such a long time since I've said grace… Her eyes are always there before me…when I sleep…when I eat these wonderful potatoes…when… when…when…AHHHHHHHHH!!! "Go ahead, scoundrel," she whispers, "Kiss me, you rank beast kiss me right on the lips with your power," and she giggles at me… Ahhhhhhhhhh! I feel like goring myself in the heart with a knife or ripping off my very head… I began doing anything she demanded. I killed a penguin for her, I captured a rooster, I refurnished her entire estate with stolen goods that took me many many many many many months to steal. I even brought her a live bear once. I tried to satisfy her every instance… everything she told me to do I did…I did…I DID!… Even if she told me to baste myself over a spit…I would have done it, Sasha…I WOULD HAVE DONE IT!!!… So Sasha, beautiful noble Sasha who is married to that bastard clown…I kept on going to her house, like a sick pedophile. Sometime ago I brought her a chicken, a rubber chicken, "Look at what I have brought to you, my worship…my only love…my only life," says I. "Look at this rubber chicken I brought you! Isn't it wonderful! Isn't it beautiful! WHY, ISN'T IT JUST A DREAM?" She just looked at me and stared with those sad wonderful eyes, "They say you're a villainous burglar, Osip, do they lie?" "They wouldn't lie to you my lovely…" says I. "We have to fix you," she said…"We have to fix you." Reform… but I'm a sick madman. "Off you go on a journey to Moscow. Go. And in a year you'll come home a different person." Once a rubber chicken, always a rubber chicken.

ALL: Once a rubber chicken, always a rubber chicken! HA! HA! HA!

SOFYA: Oh Platonov! Platonov! Platonov! I'm a little schoolgirl all over again!

PLATONOV: Hello my shy little friend…

MARY: NO! Get away from me, I don't want to love you…

PLATONOV: My little Mary… don't be so sad…

ANNA: Platonov! Platonov! Platonov! Run away with me!

PLATONOV: I can give you… your hair… I love your hair…

MARY: I hate you…I love you…I hate you… Hee! Hee! Hee! Oh you make me laugh, Platonov! Platonov! Platonov! I have a weak heart! Hee! Hee! Hee! If you screw me over, I'll ruin your life!

OSIP: I am not to worship in daylight, my lovely… I've caused a lot of worry, you know. ¡LE VOY A CHUPAR LA PIEL DE SU PROPIA CARNE! Ah, a very smart individual your husband is! Many fine qualities he possesses, except of course, HUMILITY! ¡LE VOY A CHUPAR LA PIEL DE SU PROPIA CARNE! AHHHH! To him, everyone's either a fool or a monkey. And that isn't ethical? I mean, if I were a good man, I wouldn't act like that at all… I would hold the thieves and murderers and lackeys and scoundrels and rascals and buffoons closest to my heart to hold. Why not? They are the most miserable souls on the face of the earth. If they are not ever to know comfort… they have mothers…someone loves them somewhere… Not a spark of equality in his heart…Spits on his whole soul I'm sure…That's why…that's why… ¡LE VOY A CHUPAR LA PIEL DE SU PROPIA CARNE! AHHHH! I could eat potatoes like these for a hundred years! Ha! Ha! Ha! Ha! Ha! Ha! Ha! Ha! Ha! Ha! Ha! Ha! Ha! Ha! Ha! Ha! Ha! Ha! Ha! Ha!

SASHA: I don't like what you're saying anymore, leave!

OSIP: I must leave. Going. Off. Why my dear pretty darling, you should have been to sleep hours ago… Ah, awaiting the arrival of said husband…yes?

SASHA: Yes.

OSIP: Well…as I said…I must leave. Going. Off. I'm off! Going home… I live where the dirt is my floor the dark night sky is my ceiling and no one knows of the roof and walls… Oh my lovely Sasha, he that has been cursed by God may make his home in this house…there's much room, though nowhere to lay head to pillow, Ha! Ha! Ha! Ha! Ha! Ha! Won't you see me sometime? Scream for Osip! Every chicken or donkey or snake knows where to find me...

NICOLI: Ha! Ha! Ha! It's all happening... I can feel it. I'll be a clown forever! Ha! Ha! Ha! I'll never cure the shopkeeper's wife again! Ha! Ha! Ha! Where could the widow be? Ha! Ha! Ha!

PETRIN: YES! YES! YES! What? What? What?

PLATONOV: Correction, my darling! A drunkard has neither left nor right! HE only has sideways, downwards, and backwards...

SOFYA: Oh Platonov! Platonov! Platonov! I'm a little schoolgirl all over again!

SASHA: Come, my drunken sweetheart, sit here! Please!

PLATONOV: Quack! Quack! Quack! Yes, let's sit...sit right here! Sit down right here on this fun little... Ha! Ha! Ha! Why aren't you asleep, my little idol of feline perfection? My dumb little wife? My little dumpling? My little rubber chicken... little rubber chicken.

SASHA: I was waiting for you. Quacker! They kept you out so late! I love you so, Platonov! Platonov! Platonov!

PLATONOV: Yes, late... Has the express come through yet?

SASHA: No, why?

PLATONOV: No reason, I just love the sound of it... uh let's love, should we my dumb dumb dumb wife? Quack! Quack! Quack!

SASHA: Oh, but you're so drunk...

PLATONOV: Why do you love me so much? Why do you trust me? Why don't you leave me? Why...

SASHA: Because you're my special one...my special one, Platonov! Platonov! Platonov! my special one!

PLATONOV: My goodness, Anna, why, what are you doing here? Are you lost?

SOFYA: Oh Platonov! Platonov! Platonov! I'm a little schoolgirl all over again!

PLATONOV: No... why is she a schoolgirl?

SASHA: Oh Anna, let me leave you alone with my trusting husband and get you some wine...

PLATONOV: Don't trust me...

MARY: Platonov! Platonov! Platonov! You make me laugh! I have a weak heart! Hee! Hee! Hee! You better love me!

SASHA: Why wouldn't I?

PLATONOV: Don't trust me...

SASHA: Oh! Don't be silly...of course I trust you...

NICOLI: Ha! Ha! Ha! Where could the widow be? Ha! Ha! Ha!

ANNA: You are so magnetic in this midnight light! Your...your eyes...when they gleam...

PLATONOV: I completely forgot she existed... quack...quack...quack...

ANNA: I completely forgot she existed too! Ha! Ha! Ha! Let's not get ahead of ourselves! Drive away those demons, my poor Don Juan...

ALL: Poor, poor, poor Don Juan!

IVAN: Yes, your mother was a nice one, she was...

ANNA: Shun out the devil, my poor poor poor Don Juan... don't let the devil unearth all of this happiness... Aren't you happy with where you are in life? With what you have become? With who you've seduced? I AM GIVING MYSELF TO YOU WILLINGLY! Aren't you happy about that, you worthless fellow?

PLATONOV: Of course I am! Oh. Yes… Yes. Yes of course. It's all trite! Trite! It's all a bunch of lousy tripe! I hate tripe!

ANNA: Platonov! Platonov! Platonov! Before you is a woman who is in love with you…and who you are in love with… The air is heavenly… CAN'T YOU FEEL IT! CAN'T YOU! Enough of this talking! Ah! I want to lose myself! You have no idea what my life is… I WANT TO BREATHE!

PLATONOV: Fine. Let's live. Meet me in the gazebo.

ANNA: See you in the gazebo, Platonov! Platonov! Platonov!

PLATONOV: Meet me in the gazebo, Sofya Yagorovnachorgaforgagorgaforgaborgachobia!

SOFYA: Yes, Platonov! Platonov! Platonov! Yes!

PLATONOV: Meet me in the gazebo, Mary!

MARY: Oh Platonov! Platonov! Platonov! You're making me laugh! I have a weak heart! Hee! Hee! Hee! I'm in love with you again! Hee! Hee! Hee!

PLATONOV: Yes, Hee! Hee! Hee! Now, just go go go get out of here and go to the gazebo!

PETRIN: What? What? What? SOMETHING HORRIBLE IS GOING TO HAPPEN SOON! I CAN FEEL IT IN MY BONES! Show me the way! The way to the widow! What's this? WHAT? WHAT? WHAT? Here, my dear Nicoli my dear Sergy my dear Ivan…here's where

the fools teach the other fools to forget God above and to cheat and to rob his fellow man! That's what we've come to… And here, my friend, is where that fellow… what the hell's his name?

ALL: PLATONOV! PLATONOV! PLATONOV!

PETRIN: Yes. And What? What? What? Where could Platonov! Platonov! Platonov! be?

NICOLI: I don't know… does anyone know where the widow is?

SOFYA: Platonov! Platonov! Platonov! I'm a schoolgirl all over again!

IVAN: I'm awfully tired! To hell with them all! Your mother was a nice one, she was. And if you were anything like her, you'd be a good doctor!

NICOLI: But… she used to beat me, Father!

IVAN: I TOLD HER TO! BECAUSE YOU'RE A LAZY NO-GOOD PEASANT!

SERGY: Wha!!! Wha!!! Wha!!! She doesn't love me anymore!

PETRIN: Ah!!!!! Ah!!!!!! Ah!!!!!!!! Who drank all of my champagne? WHO? WHO? WHO? I suppose you're drunk by now! DRUNK! DRUNK! DRUNK! I suppose all of you are drunk on my champagne by now! ALL OF YOU! Mine! Mine! Mine! It's all mine! All of it! The dress of the widow's is mine! I've given everyone everything! AND NOW I LOOK DOWN AT MY SWOLLEN FEET AND THE HEELS ON THE BOTTOM OF MY OWN SHOES ARE WORN OUT! MY FATHER! MY FATHER LIVED AND DIED A PEASANT! HE NEVER DARED COME WITHIN FIFTY METERS OF THIS

HOUSE! AND NOW I OWN EVERY-THING! EVERYTHING! EVERY-THING! I'M NOT GIVING ANYONE ANYTHING! ANYTHING AT ALL! EVERYTHING BELONGS TO ME!!!

SERGY: Wha!!! Wha!!! Wha!!! I want my Sofya!!!

NICOLI: Where could the widow be? SOMETHING HAS GONE TERRI-BLY WRONG! Maybe the shopkeeper's wife is dead! Ha! Ha! Ha!

IVAN: I'm awfully tired, the hell with all of you... that widow will drive you all mad...mad...

PETRIN: What? What? What? She's a countess a baroness...she's the devil... and I love her! I love the widow! I SWEAR TO YOU ALL! HA! HA! HA! HA! HA! HA!

ANNA: Hello Sasha!

SASHA: It's such a lovely night. The sum-mer solstice.

ANNA: I've had enough, Sasha, I'm go-ing home...

SASHA: I'll run down down to the cel-lar... oh Platonov! Platonov! Platonov! I love you so!!!

ANNA: Oh Platonov! Platonov! Platonov! We're alone again!

PETRIN: What? What? What? Where is the widow, you parasites?

PLATONOV: I've forgotten she even ex-isted. I'm a fool. Everything comes to this...

ANNA: Come quickly...

OSIP: Good evening, your ladyship. What brings you to our parts?

ANNA: What are you doing here?

OSIP: Taking in the wonders of the moon-lit night...

MARY: Oh Platonov! Platonov! Platonov! You're making me laugh! I have a weak heart! I WAITED AT THE GAZEBO, WHERE WERE YOU? Hee! Hee! Hee!

OSIP: My mother always said there's a sinner buried under every stump in the forest, and they shine so that people will pray for them... are you shining tonight, your ladyship?

ANNA: Enough, you fool! Go hunt some more rubber chickens and bring them to me... I'll take them... I'll take your rub-ber chickens as any good widow would... only promise me this: Don't touch Platonov! Platonov! Platonov! Do you hear me? Do you want to end up in prison? Or worse, in a monastery? There there don't cry. What are you, a child? Enough, I'm going home. Don't you dare touch him...

OSIP: I will kill him, your ladyship. Once a rubber chicken, always a rubber chicken.

ALL: ONCE A RUBBER CHICKEN! ALWAYS A RUBBER CHICKEN! HA! HA! HA!

NICOLI: Where could the widow be?

PLATONOV: I don't know... Ha! Ha! Ha! Why good doctor, I have no idea at all. Ha! Ha! Ha!

MARY: Oh Platonov! Platonov! Platonov! You're making me laugh, I have a weak heart! YOU LOVE ME, DON'T YOU? DON'T YOU? Hee! Hee! Hee!

PLATONOV: Yes. I love you! OF COURSE, I LOVE EVERYONE! NOW GO TO THE GAZEBO! HA! HA! HA!

SERGY: Wha!!! Wha!!! Wha!!!

SOFYA: Platonov! Platonov! Platonov! I'm a little schoolgirl all over again! Where are you? Don't you remember that summer by the lake?

PLATONOV: Yes. Summer again in the gazebo tonight! GO!

PETRIN: HA! HA! HA! It says in the myth of life that man awakes with three paths to travel in his life: If he walks down the road to the right, he will be eaten by the jackals of the night…and if he travels down the road to the left, he will eat the jackals, and if he travels down the road before him, he will eat the flesh from his very bones. And now I ask you, Platonov! Platonov! Platonov! —what road will you choose?

OSIP: Good evening, Platonov! Platonov! Platonov!

PLATONOV: What are you doing here, you menace?

OSIP: Taking in the night air… see how that stump is shining in the moonlight? Like a dead man rising up from his grave… there's another! Must be many sinners in this world, Platonov! Platonov! Platonov!

PLATONOV: Away with you, villain!

SOFYA: Platonov! Platonov! Platonov! I'm a little schoolgirl all over again. You could be my little schoolboy. Or the naughty teacher. Or the mysterious janitor who takes me in the closet at lunchtime…

NICOLI: Platonov! Platonov! Platonov! Finally here you are, now we can go hunting… oh, by the way, I was wondering, do you know where the widow could be?

PLATONOV: Leave me alone! QUACK! QUACK! QUACK!

SOFYA: What about that summer by the lake?

PLATONOV: GO TO THE GAZEBO!

NICOLI: What's wrong, my friend? I'm drunk! For the first time in my life, I'm drunk! God, how happy I am, my friend! You're so nice and faithful to my sister! If only I had wanted to be a doctor… BUT I DON'T WANT TO SAVE THE SHOPKEEPER'S WIFE! HA! HA! HA! LET'S GO HUNTING!

PLATONOV: I'm not going hunting. I'm an angry duck!! An angry angry angry duck.

SASHA: OSIP, YOU FOOL! You're lying!

OSIP: May the Lord above send down fire and flame to incinerate me if I'm lying! All of my relations shall be dammed in bitter eternal hell! May I never see heaven if I'm lying! He's gone to the widow's! Go after him, Sasha! Let him find her…let her find him…Let them meet! I shall murder him, Sasha! Never you fear, Sasha, never you fear, I'll dig out his heart with my bare hands… HE WILL KNOW HE HAS SINNED… don't you doubt me for an instant.

SASHA: No, sweet fool! Life will make him suffer. He has tricked us all! With this knife I end my life…with this knife I end my life…with this knife I end my life… Or…I'll end my life with this poison…this poison… NO! NO! I WILL JUMP IN FRONT OF A TRAIN! Goodbye Father, who I love so much and who is always so drunk… goodbye my brother, you'll be a great physician someday… Goodbye Osip my friend, I'm sorry the widow won't love you… REMEMBER ME, PLATONOV! PLATONOV! PLATONOV! REMEMBER ME!

OSIP: Oh Platonov! Platonov! Platonov! Oh!

ANNA: Platonov! Platonov! Platonov! Wake up! You happy duck!

PLATONOV: Go away…

ANNA: Sasha…she's gone…

PLATONOV: She's dead?

ANNA: Yes…

PLATONOV: GO AWAY!

MARY: Hee! Hee! Hee! Go away? I have nowhere to go. You sent for me. I am here. I am here because I fell in love with you after I graduated college with a degree in science that I worked very hard for. How am I supposed to return home with a straight guiltless face after I told them I would never return. How? How? How? My father has cursed my name… my mother will never forgive me! You told me you were in love with me! You son-of-a-bitch! You said that you were in love with me!

ANNA: Go away? What do you mean… "go away"?

PLATONOV: GO AWAY! GO AWAY! GO AWAY!

NICOLI: I'm not going anywhere! Ha! Ha! Ha! At least not until I've had my breakfast! Now where in the world could the widow be? I am feeling a bit light-headed. Has anyone seen my sister?

SASHA: I killed myself over an angry duck!

ALL: PLATONOV! PLATONOV! PLATONOV! THE VERY ANGRY DUCK! HA! HA! HA!

ANNA: Platonov! Platonov! Platonov! Come…this vodka's quite good actually… come on, let's have a little drink! Just one, and then after that we won't drink any more. Cheers! Now I'll have one, too… here's to all wicked men!

PLATONOV: Here! Here!

ANNA: Ha! Ha! Ha! Oh I am the widow! And I'm happy just where I am! Hmmm…this vodka's excellent! You have good taste…

PLATONOV: I'm not going away with you widow… not with anyone… I'm… I'm…finished…

ANNA: Platonov! Platonov! Platonov! Change your life! You're not distracted by anything, are you? You're not distracted by anyone… ARE YOU? STEAL THE MONEY AND GO AWAY WITH ME, YOU WORTHLESS FELLOW!

PLATONOV: I can't… I'm drunk… I have nothing left to give… I have no blood…no reflection…I can't love… I can't love widow… and without love… without love there is nothing but sad darkness…

ANNA: Oh Platonov! Platonov! Platonov! Don't be an indifferent fool… Nonsense! Of course you can love! I'll love you! I shall give you a lesson, my little bird!

PLATONOV: Too late too late…

OSIP: Good morning, Platonov! Platonov! Platonov!

PLATONOV: Oh not you again… Are you God? Will you help me? WHO ARE YOU? What do you want?

OSIP: I have come to bid you goodbye, dear sir.

PLATONOV: Why, are you leaving?

OSIP: Oh dear sir… I'm not leaving… YOU ARE!

PLATONOV: Really?

OSIP: I'll be taking you to hell! HA! HA! HA!

PLATONOV: Oh really? And you're taking me?

OSIP: Oh, yes yes yes, sir. Exactly. I have your horses prepared and hitched to the carriage. Exactly, sir.

PLATONOV: Well that's just marvelous! Just brilliant! You have come to kill me. That's just fine. Good good. Someone has to do the job. Quack! Quack! Quack!

OSIP: Do you know that I had a picture of you once, Platonov! Platonov! Platonov! I used to stare at it every day and every night for many years. I only knew you from a distance at this time. I didn't know you as the spiteful unregretting shameless duck that you are. I worshiped the floor you stood upon. I gave your dumb wife the highest respect only because of you. But then Platonov! Platonov! Platonov! I saw that you used your talents for wrong, your passion for substance and pleasure of the flesh! You are, sir, too bad of a man to live! Why was the lovely lovely lovely Widow Anna here just now? Why were you at the gazebo last night with Sofya Yagorovnachorgaforgagorgaforgaborgachobia? Why were you sniggering with Mary that hee hee hee girl? And where the hell is your wife? Which of these women do you love? And you think you're not a bad man, an evil man? YES! YES! YES! PLATONOV! PLATONOV! PLATONOV! Your day of tragedy unto hell is before us!

ALL: Oh please, you wild beast, you're terrifying us!

NICOLI: Platonov!...Platonov!... Platonov!...Platonov!...Platonov!... Platonov!... we all know now what you're doing...and I think it's kind of funny... I was wondering where the widow's been disappearing to all this time... why, I've been in love with her since I don't know when...and you've been ducking it out with her and those two others... I'm pretty impressed. You got away with it for a

while... I've being getting away with it my whole life...and no one will ever ever ever know my secret... Ha! Ha! Ha! Ha! Ha! Ha! But do you know where my sister is?

PLATONOV: Go away please!

PETRIN: What? What? What? What gives you and that plastic rubber chicken of yours the right to all of these orgies... ORGIES ARE IMMORAL! WHO DO YOU THINK YOU ARE?

PLATONOV: I don't know...

ALL: WHAT? WHAT? WHAT?

PLATONOV: Quack...quack...quack...

ALL: HA!

PLATONOV: I'm sick...

ALL: HA! HA!

PLATONOV: Help me...someone help me...

ALL: HA! HA! HA!

PLATONOV: I feel feverish... my arm hurts... I need to lie down...

ALL: HA! HA! HA! HA!

PLATONOV: It's true I don't want anything anymore, neither love, nor hate, the only thing I want is peace... I beg of you...

(EVERYONE laughs while PLATONOV talks.)

ALL: HA! HA! HA! AHHHHHHHH-HHHHHHHHHHHHHHHHHHHHHHH! HA! HA! HA! HA! HA! HA! HA! HA! HA! HA! HA!

PLATONOV: Our affair is over... that's what... no...I'm not going away with anyone... I'm sick... where shall I go? I'm burning with fever...I'm numb with cold... I wish it were over... what a situation... I was wrong...wrong... what can I do? I'm just a silly goose an angry duck a simple schoolmaster. Wrong. Wrong... my wife she's dead...dead... dead... she's committed murder to herself... I'm crushed like a dog... a wife that I've never brought anything but pains to her... pains...pains... AM I HAPPY, I ASK MYSELF! AM I HAPPY, I ASK MYSELF! Now, I really do have nothing. I'm burning with rage... I'm going to commit murder to myself... ¡HA TERMINADO EL ESPECTÁCULO! One angry duck less...duckless. SAVE MY SOUL! Replenish me save me, guide my steps... now I know: if you but once betray the one you love, you'll never escape the web of lies and deceit...

SOFYA: And to think I compared you to my favorite janitor!

PETRIN: Fool!

NICOLI: Ha! Ha! Ha! I'll never save the shopkeeper's wife! Ha! Ha! Ha!

ANNA: You're such a worthless duck!

SERGY: Sir...sir...sir!!! I...I...I was going to challenge you to a duel! But here I am in front of you instead crying as a baby would... Wha!!! Wha!!! Wha!!! I'm weak! ...I'm going... have I lost her for good? I'm going! I'm going! GOODBYE!!! There's nothing more to say... Give her back, Platonov! Platonov! Platonov! You're happy as it is! Save me my dear fellow... save me. I would have nothing... I had nothing and then she came bouncing into my life... and we had babies, we did we did...beautiful bouncing babies, Platonov! Platonov! Platonov! Don't tell me she's gone to you or I'll cry again... I'll cry now into the night and back into the day again and over and over and over and over again until I go crazy, Platonov! Platonov! Platonov! Don't take away my happi-

ness... Wha!!! Wha!!! Wha!!! Happiness is the point of life...at least that's what my father taught me...he did...he did I swear he did... and then he beat me... and then I had babies and I will beat them... yeah, one day he came home early and he said..."Guess what Sergy, my little whiney whiney boy?" And I said, "What Papa?" "I've taken the whole rest of the day off... and do you know why that I took the rest of the day off?" "NO, I don't Papa," I said. "To beat you yes...yes... I'm going to beat you like the little raggedy foxhound that you are." Wha!!! Wha!!! Wha!!!

PETRIN: What? What? What?

ANNA: You've been screwing everyone! You worthless duck! I WASN'T GOING TO LOVE YOU ANYWAY! HA! HA! HA!

SOFYA: Platonov! Platonov! Platonov! What are you doing? Where are you? I'm a little schoolgirl! That's what you wanted, wasn't it? A little little little schoolgirl!

MARY: Oh Platonov! Platonov! Platonov! I'll never forgive you! I have a weak heart! I'm going to die! Hee! Hee! Hee!

PETRIN: What? What? What?

IVAN: OH! OH! OH! That's my son-in-law...the foolzelbum! You took your pistol out of your pocket, you did you did! No more running around for you! And I know my Sasha was a dumb country girl just like my wife. But I accepted her, and I loved her and I respected her... AND GODDAMN RIGHT THE SEX WAS BORING BUT I LOVED HER! I loved my wife, I did I did...and I knew you were an unhappy duck when I first met you when you were a young duckling, a gorgeous young duckling but an unhappy young duckling nonetheless... SASHA IS

DEAD… and someday you're going to pay for what you did… I'm an old drunk but I'd say someday soon…maybe some force that we don't know will strike you down, you unrelenting duck, but you will die!

ALL: YOU WILL DIE, YOU WORTH-LESS DUCK!

PLATONOV: Yes. I shall shoot myself…I swear to you! A spell has been branded upon my forehead! Everything I touch I destroy. I bring misfortune to all! Misery to all! Pain…deceit…torture…eggs…lots of little eggs… Ha! Ha! Ha! Ha! Ha! Ha! What? What? What? Wha!!! Wha!!! Wha!!! Stop making me laugh, I have a weak heart! I'm a little schoolgirl, I am I am, a little sexy little schoolgirl, yes, Quack! Quack! Quack! Little a this little a that and where the hell is the widow? THE SHOPKEEPER WILL BE DYING TO-MORROW! I can't find my father… he's drunk…he's drunk…he's drunk… my wife she's dumb dumb dumb…babbling and babbling and babbling and Quack! Quack! Quacking! I repent…I repent all of it you high and mighty Lord you… Quack! Quack! Quack! I will live my life and be a good duck, sir. I will not have four-way orgies in the summer wind… nor will I, ever… and sir…oh sir… I will not get drunk anymore, sir, not on the holidays when a tempting young girl comes by my classroom with a bottle of good Russian vodka and she's not wearing anything but red socks and a bonnet… a blue bonnet…red socks and a blue bonnet… I love women… BUT I will not get drunk and fornicate with anyone any-more but my wife…my dead dead dead wife.

SASHA: I'm not dead anymore… Hee! Hee! Hee! The train broke down, the knife was dull, and the poison was wine! Hee!

Hee! Hee! I love you so, Platonov! Platonov! Platonov!

PLATONOV: I REPENT! I REPENT! I REPENT!

ALL: HE'S DONE IT AGAIN, THAT LUCKY LUCKY LUCKY DUCK! WE LOVE YOU!

PLATONOV: I'm a lucky duck…

ALL: HA! HA! HA! HA! HA! HA!

OSIP: PLATONOV! PLATONOV! PLATONOV! ONCE A RUBBER CHICKEN, ALWAYS A RUBBER CHICKEN!

(OSIP throws rubber chicken at PLAT-ONOV, which makes him fall…die—this action ends, lights go back up and returns as the beginning of the play—with possible ex-aggerated character adjustments.)

PLATONOV: I have come to the con-clusion that I, Platonov, have been trans-formed into a duck. How do I know this, you ask? How do I know? I ask myself, yes, how do I know? Quack. Let me tell you the bit I've come to know. "Male ducks…can be veritable sex maniacs in the spring. Though some males and fe-males 'marry' and remain monogamous, other males remain bachelors and rape other males' 'wives.' Married females will go to great lengths to hide from maraud-ing bachelors, concealing themselves for an entire day in high grass. Bands of three or four bachelors will seek out a hiding female and take turns raping her." A cruis-ing duck… "If they can't find a female, the more aggressive males will mount the least aggressive male of the group. It is not uncommon for two bachelors to hold down a third while he's mounted by an-other male. Homosexuality is not at all uncommon among ducks—or geese, for that matter." In effect, the duck has no taboos, no laws, no judgments. They are low low low low beasts. There is no moral backbone. No...imperative. Given the picture of these nasty habits, you would think the world would be appalled. Taken aback. Disgusted. But no. they take this in stride as they do all other social slights, peculiarities, and titters. Which brings me to my next point. As a man, no matter how you ruin yourself, you are still loved. Unconditionally. There is no judgment, no moral compass, no backbone. Ducks are still cute. But if you point these vile actions out, you are harangued, judged, shunned. You are a duck! But you are cute!! So I love you!!!! But that duck is violating his fellows! So long as he is cute, I will love him!! And on and on and on. You, sir, are a liar and a lout! And possibly a pervert. SEEEE?!?!? Whether these things are true or no, I have offended. I am the villain. And this is how my story goes. But wait. My question. How do I know? Because I know that mallards and moralists are made up of much the same stuff. And that they are the most notorious rapists of their natures. The first of his fellows, the second of the mind. I have been the second, so I therefore, I must know the first. Well, then...Platonov! Platonov! Platonov! I suppose, now, a very. Angry. Duck.

(Curtain.)

OPTIONAL ADDITIONAL PROLOGUE

ALL: Once upon a time lived a happy happy happy duck!

PLATONOV: I'm a happy duck! Ha! Ha! Ha! I'm a happy happy happy duck! Ha! Ha! Ha!

ALL: Ha! Ha! Ha!

PLATONOV: Horsewhipped and hogtied and bullshitted and horsewhipped and bullshitted and horsewhipped and hogtied and bullshitted and...and... and...and...

PETRIN: What? What? What?

ALL: Oh Platonov! Platonov! Platonov! You goosey!

IVAN: You're a silly, silly, silly goose.

NICOLI: Platonov! Platonov! Platonov! It's almost time to go hunting!

SASHA: I love you Platonov! Platonov! Platonov!

PLATONOV: Oh Sofya Yagorovnachorgaforgagorgaforgaborgachobia, I've loved you since I was a little boy and you were a little, little, little, little, little, little girl!

SOFYA: Oh Platonov! Platonov! Platonov! I've loved you since you were a little boy and I was just a little, little, little, little, little, little girl.

PETRIN: What? What? What?

SERGY: But I love you! I love you! I love you Sofya Yagorovnachorgaforgagorgaforgaborgachobia!

IVAN: That's my son-in-law!

OSIP: Your day of judgment has come Platonov! Platonov! Platonov! I'm going to kill you!

PLATONOV: Ha! Ha! Ha! Ha! Ha! Ha! Once a rubber chicken, always a rubber chicken! Ha! Ha! Ha! Ha! Ha! Ha!

ANNA: Take me now Platonov! Platonov! Platonov! Or I'll horsewhip you!

MARY: Platonov! Platonov! Platonov! I shouldn't laugh, I have a weak heart! I hate you, I love you!

SASHA: I love you Platonov! Platonov! Platonov!

ALL: Oh Platonov! Platonov! Platonov! You goosey!

PLATONOV: And again!

ALL: Once upon a time lived a happy happy happy duck!

PLATONOV: I'm a happy duck! Ha! Ha! Ha! A happy, happy, happy duck! Ha! Ha! Ha!

ALL: Ha! Ha! Ha!

PLATONOV: Horsewhipped and hogtied and bullshitted and horsewhipped and bullshitted and horsewhipped and hogtied and bullshitted and...and... and...and...

PETRIN: What? What? What?

ALL: Oh Platonov! Platonov! Platonov! You goosey!

IVAN: You're a silly, silly, silly goose.

NICOLI: Platonov! Platonov! Platonov! It's almost time to go hunting!

SASHA: I love you Platonov! Platonov! Platonov!

PLATONOV: Oh Sofya Yagorovnachorgaforgagorgaforgaborgachobia, I've loved you since I was a little boy and you were a little, little, little, little, little, little girl!

SOFYA: Oh Platonov! Platonov! Platonov! I've loved you since you were a little boy and I was just a little, little, little, little, little, little girl.

PETRIN: What? What? What?

SERGY: But I love you! I love you! I love you Sofya Yagorovnachorgaforgagorgaforgaborgachobia!

IVAN: That's my son-in-law!

OSIP: Your day of judgment has come Platonov! Platonov! Platonov! I'm going to kill you!

PLATONOV: Ha! Ha! Ha! Ha! Ha! Ha! Once a rubber chicken, always a rubber chicken! Ha! Ha! Ha! Ha! Ha! Ha!

ANNA: Take me now Platonov! Platonov! Platonov! Or I'll horsewhip you!

MARY: Platonov! Platonov! Platonov! I shouldn't laugh, I have a weak heart! I hate you, I love you!

SASHA: I love you Platonov! Platonov! Platonov!

ALL: Oh Platonov! Platonov! Platonov! You goosey!

PLATONOV: One more time!

ALL: Once upon a time lived a happy happy happy duck!

PLATONOV: I'm a happy duck! Ha! Ha! Ha! A happy happy happy duck! Ha! Ha! Ha!

ALL: Ha! Ha! Ha!

PLATONOV: Horsewhipped and hogtied and bullshitted and horsewhipped and bullshitted and horsewhipped and hogtied and bullshitted and...and... and...and...

PETRIN: What? What? What?

ALL: Oh Platonov! Platonov! Platonov! You goosey!

IVAN: You're a silly, silly, silly goose.

NICOLI: Platonov! Platonov! Platonov! It's almost time to go hunting!

SASHA: I love you Platonov! Platonov! Platonov!

PLATONOV: Oh Sofya Yagorovnachorgaforgagorgaforgaborgachobia, I've loved you since I was a little boy and you were a little, little, little, little, little, little girl!

SOFYA: Oh Platonov! Platonov! Platonov! I've loved you since you were a little boy and I was just a little, little, little, little, little, little girl.

PETRIN: What? What? What?

SERGY: But I love you! I love you! I love you Sofya Yagorovnachorgaforgagorgaforgaborgachobia!

IVAN: That's my son-in-law!

OSIP: Your day of judgment has come Platonov! Platonov! Platonov! I'm going to kill you!

PLATONOV: Ha! Ha! Ha! Ha! Ha! Ha! Once a rubber chicken, always a rubber chicken! Ha! Ha! Ha! Ha! Ha! Ha!

ANNA: Take me now Platonov! Platonov! Platonov! Or I'll horsewhip you!

MARY: Platonov! Platonov! Platonov! I shouldn't laugh, I have a weak heart! I hate you, I love you!

SASHA: I love you Platonov! Platonov! Platonov!

ALL: Oh Platonov! Platonov! Platonov! You goosey!

SOURCES

The entire text was inspired by Carol Rockamore's translation of *Platonov* by Anton Chekhov.

Sources for the monologues in the Prologue are as follows:

Platonov's monologue: Written by Ross Peabody with some text excerpted from Charles Panati's *Sexy Origins and Intimate Things* (New York: Penguin Books, 1998).

Sergy's and Ivan's monologues: Excerpted from the article "Andrei Platonov and Social Realism" by Celine Bricaire, *Vox Poetica* 11/15/02, as translated by Google.

Petrin's comment: From a biographical abstract of writer Andrei Platonov by Tatyana Tolstaya, www.logodrome.net/platonov.html.

Anna's and Petrin's monologues: Excerpted from a summary of Chekhov's *Platonov*, as used by La Comédie-Française for its production of the play, as translated by Google.

Mary's statement on Professor Platonov: From a University of Waterloo Media Relations news release, http://newsrelease.uwaterloo.ca/archive/news. php?id=2320.

Osip's first comment: From Eric Lacascade, director for Comédie-Française, as translated by Google.

Sofya's monologue: From Icehouse Books' description of K. Platonov's *Psychology As You May Like It* (Moscow: Progress,1963), www.icehousebooks.co.uk/book001005.htm.

Sasha's monologue: From the *Imprint Online, the University of Waterloo Student Newspaper*, 23:25 (2/2/01), Letter to the Editor by Patti Moses.

Nicoli's monologue: Excerpted from the October 2001 *UK Times* review of the Almeida Theatre's *Platonov*, adapted by David Hare.

Platonov's long speech beginning on p. 444: Excerpted and adapted from "Birkenstocked Burkeans" by Rod Dreher, *National Review* July 12, 2002.

PLAYS AND PLAYWRIGHTS 2001

Edited by Martin Denton
Preface by Robert Simonson

ISBN 09670234-2-4   Retail: $15.00

Washington Square Dreams by Gorilla Repertory Theatre

Fate by Elizabeth Horsburgh

Velvet Ropes by Joshua Scher

The Language of Kisses by Edmund De Santis

Word to Your Mama by Julia Lee Barclay

Cuban Operator Please... by Adrian Rodriguez

The Elephant Man—The Musical by Jeff Hylton & Tim Werenko

House of Trash by Trav S.D.

Straight-Jacket by Richard Day

PLAYS AND PLAYWRIGHTS 2002

Edited by Martin Denton
Foreword by Bill C. Davis

ISBN 09670234-3-2   Retail: $15.00

The Death of King Arthur by Matthew Freeman

Match by Marc Chun

Woman Killer by Chiori Miyagawa

The Wild Ass's Skin by J. Scott Reynolds

Halo by Ken Urban

Shyness Is Nice by Marc Spitz

Reality by Curtiss I' Cook

The Resurrectionist by Kate Chell

Bunny's Last Night In Limbo by Peter S. Petralia

Summerland by Brian Thorstenson

PLAYS AND PLAYWRIGHTS 2003

Edited by Martin Denton
Foreword by Mario Fratti

ISBN 09670234-4-0   Retail $15.00

A Queer Carol by Joe Godfrey

Pumpkins For Smallpox by Catherine Gillet

Looking For The Pony by Andrea Lepcio

Black Thang by Ato Essandoh

The Ninth Circle by Edward Musto

The Doctor of Rome by Nat Colley

Galaxy Video by Marc Morales

The Last Carburetor by Leon Chase

Out To Lunch by Joseph Langham

Ascending Bodily by Maggie Cino

Last Call by Kelly McAllister

PLAYS AND PLAYWRIGHTS 2004

Edited by Martin Denton
Foreword by Kirk Wood Bromley

ISBN 09670234-5-9   Retail $16.00

Sugarbaby by Frank Cwiklik

WTC View by Brian Sloan

United States: Work and Progress by Christy Meyer, Jon Schumacher and Ellen Shanman

The Shady Maids of Haiti by John Jahnke

Cats Can See The Devil by Tom X. Chao

Survivor: Vietnam! by Rob Reese

Feed the Hole by Michael Stock

Auntie Mayhem by David Pumo

The Monster Tales by Mary Jett Parsley

Sun, Stand Thou Still by Steven Gridley

ABOUT THE AUTHOR

MARTIN DENTON is executive director of The New York Theatre Experience, Inc. He is the founder, editor, and chief reviewer of nytheatre.com, one of the premier sources for theatre reviews and information on the Internet since 1996. He is the author of *The New York Theatre Experience Book of the Year 1998* and the editor of *Plays and Playwrights for the New Millennium*, and *Plays and Playwrights 2001, 2002, 2003*, and *2004*. He lives in New York City with two Siamese cats, Logan and Briscoe.

THE NEW YORK THEATRE EXPERIENCE

The New York Theatre Experience, Inc., is a nonprofit New York State corporation. Its mission is to use traditional and new media to foster interest, engagement, and participation in theatre and drama and to provide tangible support to theatre artists and dramatists, especially emerging artists and artists in the nonprofit sector. The principal activity of The New York Theatre Experience is the operation of a free website (www.nytheatre.com) that comprehensively covers the New York theatre scene—on, off-, and off-off-Broadway. The New York Theatre Experience also publishes yearly anthologies of new plays by emerging playwrights.

Additional information about the *Plays and Playwrights* series (ISSN 1546-1319) can be found at www.newyorktheatreexperience.org/publicationsnyte.htm.

Plays and Playwrights books are available in bookstores and online, or order directly from the publisher. Send a check or money order for the retail price listed above (plus $4.00 shipping) to:

The New York Theatre Experience, Inc.
P.O. Box 1606, Murray Hill Station
New York, NY 10156